Exploring PHP 8

Small Steps to Giant Leaps

Paul Tregoing

Exploring PHP 8: Small Steps to Giant Leaps

Paul Tregoing
Waterbeach, UK

ISBN-13 (pbk): 979-8-8688-2135-6
https://doi.org/10.1007/979-8-8688-2136-3

ISBN-13 (electronic): 979-8-8688-2136-3

Copyright © 2025 by Paul Tregoing

This work is subject to copyright. All rights are reserved by the Publisher, whether the whole or part of the material is concerned, specifically the rights of translation, reprinting, reuse of illustrations, recitation, broadcasting, reproduction on microfilms or in any other physical way, and transmission or information storage and retrieval, electronic adaptation, computer software, or by similar or dissimilar methodology now known or hereafter developed.

Trademarked names, logos, and images may appear in this book. Rather than use a trademark symbol with every occurrence of a trademarked name, logo, or image we use the names, logos, and images only in an editorial fashion and to the benefit of the trademark owner, with no intention of infringement of the trademark.

The use in this publication of trade names, trademarks, service marks, and similar terms, even if they are not identified as such, is not to be taken as an expression of opinion as to whether or not they are subject to proprietary rights.

While the advice and information in this book are believed to be true and accurate at the date of publication, neither the authors nor the editors nor the publisher can accept any legal responsibility for any errors or omissions that may be made. The publisher makes no warranty, express or implied, with respect to the material contained herein.

>Managing Director, Apress Media LLC: Welmoed Spahr
>Acquisitions Editor: Melissa Duffy
>Development Editor: Jim Markham
>Coordinating Editor: Gryffin Winkler

Cover Photo by Michael Eggerl on Unsplash

Distributed to the book trade worldwide by Springer Science+Business Media New York, 1 New York Plaza, New York, NY 10004. Phone 1-800-SPRINGER, fax (201) 348-4505, e-mail orders-ny@springer-sbm.com, or visit www.springeronline.com. Apress Media, LLC is a Delaware LLC and the sole member (owner) is Springer Science + Business Media Finance Inc (SSBM Finance Inc). SSBM Finance Inc is a **Delaware** corporation.

For information on translations, please e-mail booktranslations@springernature.com; for reprint, paperback, or audio rights, please e-mail bookpermissions@springernature.com.

Apress titles may be purchased in bulk for academic, corporate, or promotional use. eBook versions and licenses are also available for most titles. For more information, reference our Print and eBook Bulk Sales web page at http://www.apress.com/bulk-sales.

Any source code or other supplementary material referenced by the author in this book is available to readers on GitHub. For more detailed information, please visit https://www.apress.com/gp/services/source-code.

If disposing of this product, please recycle the paper

For Ben, my brother and friend.

Table of Contents

About the Author xxiii

About the Technical Reviewer xxv

Acknowledgments xxvii

Introduction xxix

Chapter 1: Getting Started 1

    Installing PHP 3

        With Apt 3

        With DNF 5

        With Homebrew 8

        Windows 10

        PHP Extensions 11

    Docker 12

        CLI Installation 13

        Debian/Apt 13

        Fedora/DNF 13

        MacOS/Homebrew 14

        Windows 14

        Verify Docker Server 14

        MacOS 15

        Images and Containers 15

        PHP on Docker 18

        Cleaning Up 21

        Multiple Versions 22

TABLE OF CONTENTS

- Web Server Integration 22
  - Nginx (via Docker Orchestration) 23
  - Built-in Web Server 27
  - Apache Module 30
- Configuring PHP 30
  - Directive Syntax 31
  - System Search Paths 32
  - Overriding `.ini` Settings 33
  - Module (Extension) Configuration 34
- Structure and Syntax 35
  - Source Code Files 35
  - PHP Embedded in HTML 36
  - Pure PHP Files 38
  - Introduction to PHP Syntax 39
  - PHP Coding Standards 43
  - PSR-1 44
  - PSR-12 45
  - Enforcing Standards 45
- Input (and Output) 45
  - The Server APIs 46
  - Outputting Data 47
  - The Output Buffer 48
  - Command Line Input 49
  - Accessing Environment Data 52
  - Accessing Files 53
  - Remote Files and Streams 56
  - Stream Functions 61
- Databases 62
  - Launching the DB 63
  - Connecting with PDO 64
  - Executing Statements 66

Selecting Results 67
Prepared Statements 68
Summary 69

Chapter 2: Data, Types, and Variables 71

PHP 8 Data Types 73
    Operations and Calls.. 75
Converting Data Types 76
    Different Types, Different Data.. 77
    Pitfalls of Automatic Conversion.. 79
Variables 82
    Legal Variable Names 83
Assigning Values and Types 84
    Scalar Types 84
    Compound Types 85
    The Special (Resource) Type... 86
    Forcing Type Changes.. 86
Constants 88
    Defining a Constant 88
    Predefined Constants 90
    Magic Constants 91
Superglobals 91
Referencing.. 93
Variable Variables.. 95
    Summary 96

Chapter 3: Functions 99

Declaring and Calling a Named Function 100
Function Arguments and Returning Data 102
    Arguments and Parameters... 102
    Returning 103
    Scalar Type Coercion 104
    Strict Types 106

TABLE OF CONTENTS

- Reference vs. Value ... 107
- Declaring Types ... 109
  - Type System vs. Type Declaration ... 110
  - Base Types ... 110
  - How to Declare Types ... 111
  - Composite Types ... 113
  - Nullable Types ... 113
  - Union Types ... 114
  - Intersection Types ... 116
  - Disjunctive Normal Form Types ... 117
  - Standalone Pseudo-types ... 118
  - Literal Types ... 118
  - The mixed (Super) Type ... 119
  - Return-Only Types ... 120
  - References and Return Types ... 123
- Advanced Arguments ... 124
  - Default Arguments ... 125
  - Variadic Arguments ... 125
  - Named Parameters ... 129
  - Mixing Call Styles ... 132
- Functions and Scope ... 134
  - Global vs. Local Scope ... 135
  - Named Functions Are Always Global ... 138
  - Function Arguments Are Always Local ... 138
  - Local Scope and Static Variables ... 139
  - Scope Persists Across Files ... 141
  - New Function, New (Local) Scope ... 142
  - Scoping Rules ... 143
- Variable Functions ... 144
- Anonymous Functions ... 146
  - Passing Functions As Data ... 147
  - Anonymous Functions and Scope ... 149

| Arrow Functions | 150 |
| Testing for Existing Functions | 152 |

Namespaced Functions 154
Calling Functions from Namespaces	155
Qualified Namespace Function Calls	156
Using Namespaces	157
Namespaces Are Not Scope	158

Functional Programming 159
First-Class and Higher-Order Functions	160
Pure Functions	160
Summary	161

Chapter 4: Logic and Control 163

What Is Truth? 164
Control Structures 164
Decision-Making	165
Repetition	169
Nesting, break, continue	172
Miscellaneous	174

Functions 176
| empty( ) Is a Problem | 177 |

Logical Expressions 178
Comparison Operators	178
Logical Operators	179
Short-Circuiting	180
Precedence and Associativity	181
Ternary Expressions	183
Null-Coalesce	184
Null-Safe	185
Bitwise Operations	186

Errors and Exceptions 187
| Error Levels | 188 |

TABLE OF CONTENTS

    Error Control 189

    Error Handling 191

    Exceptions 193

    Throwing Exceptions 193

    Catching Exceptions 194

    PHP 7 Errors 195

    Catching Different (Error) Exceptions 196

    DIY Exceptions 198

    Finally… 198

    Exception Handling 199

    Stack Traces 201

    Summary 206

Chapter 5: Arrays 207

    Creating and Accessing Arrays 208

        Accessing Elements 209

        Associative Arrays 211

        Multidimensional Arrays 212

    Manipulating Arrays 215

        Changing Element Values 215

        Appending New Elements 216

        Prepending New Elements 216

        Inserting into Arbitrary Positions 217

        Removing Elements 218

        Reindexing Elements 219

        Splitting Arrays 220

    Iterating Arrays 221

        With foreach 222

        Counting Elements 223

        With for 224

        Loop Expressions 225

        Skipping Iterations 226

Terminating Early.. 227
　　Traversing Multidimensional Arrays 227
　　Assignment During Iteration... 228
Extracting Array Data 231
　　With list( ) 231
　　list( ) with Keys 231
　　With extract( ) 232
　　Fetching a Subset of Elements with array_slice( ) 236
Combining Arrays 237
　　With ... (Splat Operator) 238
　　With array_merge( ).. 239
　　Splicing into Other Arrays 240
　　Combining into Associative Arrays 242
　　Replacing Elements with array_replace( ).. 243
Comparing Arrays 244
　　Comparison Operators.. 245
　　Finding Uncommon Elements... 246
　　Finding Common Elements... 247
　　Comparing Keys 248
　　Comparing Keys and Values 249
　　Normalizing Keys... 250
　　Comparing with Callbacks.. 251
Searching Arrays 258
　　Test Value Exists 258
　　Test Key Exists... 258
　　Find Key of Value 260
　　Minimum and Maximum Values 260
　　Searching by Callback 261
Sorting Arrays 263
　　By Value 263
　　By Key.. 264

xi

Preserving Keys... 265
Modifying sort( ) Behavior 266
By Size 267
Sorting by Callback 269
Natural Sorting 271
Randomizing Arrays 272

Functional Array Processing 274
Transforming with array_walk( ) 274
Creating New Arrays with array_map( ) 277
Creating New Values With array_reduce( ) 279
Multi-dimensional Arrays and Recursive Functions 280
Very Large Arrays and Generators 283
Summary 284

Chapter 6: Object Fundamentals **285**

Why OOP? 286

Making Objects 286
New Objects 287
Cloned Objects 289

Classes 290
Defining a Class 291
Property Getters and Setters 294
Property Hooks 296
Constructors 297
Destructors 299
Magic Methods 300
Anonymous Classes 302

Class (Not Object) Context 303
Static Members 303
Static Members in Class Context 306
Class Constants 307
Private Constructors 308

Interfaces	311
Declaring Interfaces	312
Multiple Interfaces	314
Extending Interfaces	316
Interface Constants	317
Property Hooks	317
Inheritance and Abstraction	**318**
Parent and Child Classes	319
Abstract Classes	321
Accessing Parent Members	323
Late Static Binding	325
Readonly	326
Final Classes	328
Traits	**329**
Extension and Constants	332
Enums	**334**
Basic Enums	336
Backed Enums	337
Enums as Classes	338
Namespacing	**341**
Finding and Loading Classes	**344**
Autoloading	345
Object Utilities	**349**
Magic Constants	349
Object Functions	352
Does It Exist?	352
What Is It?	354
What Does It Do?	357
Reflection	360
Attributes	364
Making Attributes	366
Summary	369

xiii

TABLE OF CONTENTS

Chapter 7: Numbers 371

Number Systems 372
Non-decimal Integer Literals 372
Scientific Notation 374
Converting Bases 374
Formatting 375

Operators, Constants, and Built-In Functions 376
Arithmetic Operators 377
Comparison Operators 379
Bitwise Operators 379
Constants 383
Built-In Functions 384
Limits and Precision 387
Integers 387
Floats 390
Floating-Point Precision 393

Random Numbers 398

Extensions 401
BCMath 401
GMP 404

Type Coercion 405
Explicitly Casting Strings to Numbers 405
Comparison Coercion 408
Summary 409

Chapter 8: Strings 411

Making and Manipulating Strings 412
Quoted Strings 412
Variable Interpolation (Substitution) 412
Special Character Escapes 414
Numeric Escape Sequences 416
Unicode Escape Sequences 417

Heredoc and Nowdoc	417
"Binary" Strings	420
Encoding (a Short History)	422
ASCII	422
"Extended ASCII"	423
Unicode	424
Transformation Formats	426
How About We… Don't Break ASCII, Maybe?	428
UTF-1 (Partial)	428
ASCII (Extremely Partial!)	429
FSS-UTF (Partial)	429
UTF-8 (Full)	430
PHP and UTF-8	430
The string Data Type	434
Operations, Type Coercion, and Safety	439
Operators and Type Coercion	439
Safety	440
Binary Safety	440
Multi-byte Safety	441
Core String Functions	444
Comparison and Analysis	446
Equal, Greater, or Less Than?	447
Collation	455
Similarity	457
Testing for Sub-strings	461
Counting	466
Conversion and Extraction	475
Creating Arrays or Variables	475
Extracting Sub-strings	484
Transformation and Formatting	494
Insertion	495

TABLE OF CONTENTS

    Substitution 499

    Edge... 508

    Whole String 514

    Encoding and Escaping 515

    Special Interpolation... 517

    Just for Fun 519

    Hashing and Error Checking 519

    Well Done! 522

The mbstring Extension 522

    Configuration 523

    (More) mbstring Functions 525

    Info and Settings 525

    Inspection 533

    Conversion 536

Cryptography.. 539

    The Password Problem.. 540

    The Password (Storage) Solution 542

    Password Hashing Algorithms... 545

    Verifying Integrity 547

    Encryption 548

    Shared Secret (Symmetric) 549

    Public Key 550

Regular Expressions 552

    Basic Syntax... 552

    Delimiters 553

    Modifiers 554

    Escape Sequences 557

    "Non-printing" Characters.. 557

    Unicode Properties 559

    Character Types 561

    Assertions 561

    Metacharacters 564

TABLE OF CONTENTS

    Quantifiers 565

    Character Classes 566

    Alternates 567

    Sub-patterns 568

    Back-References 572

    Once-Only 574

    Lookahead, Lookbehind 575

    Conditional 577

    Recursive 579

    PRCE Functions 580

    Multi-byte Regex Functions 590

    Find Longest 599

    Ignore Empty 599

  Other Language Extensions 600

    Summary 604

Chapter 9: Dates and Times 605

  The Unix Epoch 606

  Keeping Time 607

  Network Time Protocol (NTP/ntpd) 607

  The tz Database 608

  OOP Interface 609

    Building DateTime Objects 611

    Formatting Output 613

    Modifying `DateTime` 617

  Functional Interface 623

    Summary 635

Chapter 10: Programming with Objects 639

  Analysis and Design 640

    Problems and Solutions 641

    Modeling 641

    The UML 643

TABLE OF CONTENTS

    Classes and Interfaces 643

    Inheritance and Interface Implementation 644

    Traits 646

    Association 646

    Aggregation 648

    Composition 648

    Using Classes 649

The SOLID Principles 650

    Single Responsibility Principle (SRP) 650

    Open-Closed Principle (OCP) 652

    Liskov Substitution Principle (LSP) 655

    Interface Segregation Principle (ISP) 658

    Dependency Inversion Principle (DIP) 660

    In Conclusion 663

Design Patterns 663

    Creational Patterns 664

    Structural Patterns 667

    Behavioral Patterns 671

    Summary 674

Chapter 11: Programming for the Internet 677

Hypertext Transfer Protocol (HTTP) 678

    URLs 680

    HTTP(S) Requests 681

    Request Methods 683

    Idempotence 687

    Resource Paths and Routing 688

    Request Headers 693

    Cookies 696

    Query String Data 700

    Request (Body) Data 702

    Uploading Complex (and Binary) Data 707

Building and Parsing URLs	715
HTTP(S) Responses	721
Response Status	722
Response Headers	724
Output Buffering	725
Using a Library	727
Sessions	**729**
A Basic PHP Session	730
Session Cookie Management	733
Session Data	734
OOP API	736
Security Considerations	738
Session Fixation	738
Disable Transparent SID Support	739
Session ID (Re-) Creation	740
Careful with That Cookie	741
Tidying Up	742
Functions	743
Modifying HTML (and XML)	**744**
What Is HTML?	745
HTML Standards	747
Some History…	748
HTML Document Metadata	749
HTML Body Content	750
The Document Object Model	753
PHP dom Module	754
Elements and Nodes	755
Attributes	758
XPath	760
Axes (Not the Chopping Kind)	762
Abbreviations	762

TABLE OF CONTENTS

- Node Tests 763
- Predicates 767
- Predicate Operators and Functions 770
- But I'm Not Running PHP 8.4 :(.... 776
- Namespaces (Again!) 779
- One More Thing... 782
- querySelector( ) (Because XPath Looks Hard) 785
- Selector Syntax 788
- Selector Structure 788
- DOM Modification and Output 792
- Moving Elements 793
- Manipulating class 796
- Manipulating Other Attributes 797
- Removing Elements 799
- Creating and Adding New Elements 799
- Time for Coffee 801

Generating HTML 802
- Printing a String 802
- The Old-Fashioned Way 804
- The Problem 805
- A Solution 806
- The Philosophy of Twig (and MVC) 806
- Getting Started with Twig 807
- Template Syntax 809
- Twig Variables 811
- Twig Escaping 813
- Controlling Escaping 817
- Twig Filtering 819
- Twig Control Structures 821
- Twig Operators and Expressions 822
- Literals 822

Mathematics	823
Logical	823
Comparison	824
Tests	825
String Tests	825
Iterable Tests	826
Miscellaneous Operators	826
Twig Functions	827
Calling Functions	828
Defining Functions	829
Twig include( )	830
Twig Macros	832
Importing Macros	833
Twig Inheritance	834
Extending a Template	834
Using Other Templates	835
Extending Twig in PHP	837
Adding a Filter	838
Controlling Behavior	839
Adding a Function	840
Making Safe HTML (Native PHP)	842
String Manipulation	842
Encoding Meta-Characters	843
Removing Tags	843
But Couldn't I Just Use a Regular Expression?	845
Filter Functions	845
Summary	851
Appendix A	**853**
Bibliography	**859**
Index	**863**

About the Author

Paul Tregoing has worked with PHP for twenty years, beginning with five years as a senior software engineer in the frontpage team at Yahoo! He has worked in a variety of industries for organizations such as Bloomberg, the British Antarctic Survey, and AWIN. Paul was also the technical reviewer for *PHP 8 Objects, Patterns, and Practice* (5th, 6th, and 7th editions).

About the Technical Reviewer

Matt Zandstra has worked as a web programmer, consultant, and writer for over two decades. He is the author of SAMS *Teach Yourself PHP in 24 Hours* (three editions) and is a contributor to *DHTML Unleashed*. He has written articles for *Linux Magazine, Zend, IBM DeveloperWorks*, and *php|architect Magazine*, among others. Matt is also the author of the Apress book *PHP 8 Objects, Patterns, and Practice*, Volumes 1 and 2.

Matt was a senior developer/tech lead at Yahoo and an API tech lead at LoveCrafts. He now runs an agency that advises companies on their architectures and system management and also develops systems primarily with PHP, Python, and Java. Matt also writes fiction.

Acknowledgments

This book has been the labor of many years (on and off) and started life with a very different title and scope. My friend, fellow author (and the technical reviewer for this book) Matt Zandstra, told me that the best part about writing a book is you get to write a book, and the worst part is you have to write a book. Matt, you weren't wrong! My deepest thanks to you for all your help and advice.

I am fortunate that my editor at Apress, Mark Powers, liked what I was doing even if it wasn't what was planned, and with his support Apress agreed to a title change and a radical shift in the scope of the work. A huge thank-you therefore to Mark (who was so supportive in those vital initial years) and to the others at Apress: Melissa Duffy and Gryffin Winkler.

Along the way there were some drastic changes in my life. In 2024 my younger brother, Ben (to whom this book is dedicated), took his own life, right as I was coming to terms with the end of my marriage. During those dark, utterly bleak days I was blessed with the love and support of many friends. I would not be here – and this book would not exist – if it had not been for my children, Ingrid, my sister Julia, mum, Ben's friend (and now mine) Kate, Craig, Brother Dave, Demelza…. Thank you all for looking out for me when I was losing my mind with grief. Sincere thanks also to my team at Awin, who rallied around me when the going got tough. Nico, thank you for all your kindness, especially on the days where I just couldn't function. My gratitude also goes to Survivors of Bereavement by Suicide (`https://uksobs.com`).

Finally, special thanks to my partner, Anna: the final piece of the puzzle. Your honest and patient love continues to amaze me; I will endeavor to be worthy of it. I would not have finished this book without you (or Jess).

Introduction

When Apress approached me, several years ago, with the idea of writing my own book, I really did not know what I was letting myself in for. At that point I had been the technical reviewer for two editions of Matt Zandstra's *PHP 8 Objects, Patterns, and Practice* but had little experience of writing otherwise. For unfathomable reasons, Apress floated the idea of becoming an author and pitched a title to me, which I fleshed out to a full proposal. I settled in and began to write. That book failed utterly to spring forth from my mind, and instead something else began to emerge: the book you are reading now.

I realized quite early on in the writing process that what I wanted to do more than anything was to teach the *why* as well as the *how*. My reasoning was that the best thing I can do for you, the reader, is to show what is happening behind the curtain. This book therefore contains many gory details on how the machines work and how they talk to each other, because this is what informs the design choices of everything else that is layered on top – including PHP.

This book makes no assumptions about your level of understanding of computing in general, other than that you know how to operate one to a certain degree. We start with the basics of setting yourself up with an environment you can use to follow the myriad of examples contained within, as well as the fundamentals of programming and PHP syntax – the more experienced reader can, of course, skim over these parts. Once these foundational topics are covered, the book goes on to dive quite deeply into how things *really* work behind the scenes, especially text data (which is arguably the chief concern of web development).

Therefore, I think that even seasoned developers will find a lot of value within these pages, especially if (like me) you are self-taught – as so many of us jobbing web devs are. Over the years (decades!) I found that I was often descending down rabbit holes of computer science and web standards to fill in the gaps in my knowledge, and the fruit of those late-night reading and hacking sessions is presented here. May it serve you well.

Things change all the time in web development: frameworks, tools, even languages… they come and go like the seasons. Other things, however, stand the test of time. The protocols underpinning the web, and the machines doing the work, haven't changed all that much in the decades since a smart chap at CERN thought it would be great if

INTRODUCTION

electronic documents could somehow link to each other. Years from now you might no longer be working with PHP (perish the thought, of course!), but it is my intention that much of the information in this book will readily transfer to whatever language you find yourself writing.

One final thought from me: we live in interesting times. There is much hype and noise surrounding generative AI and large language models, and particularly their apparent ability to "create" software. Time will tell if that becomes a real prospect, but my intuition tells me that even if this technology lives up to the hype, the world will still need human engineers. It is important, perhaps never more so than now, that people continue to learn how to code. It is my fervent hope that this book can make a useful contribution on your journey toward mastering the art.

CHAPTER 1

Getting Started

We shall start at the very beginning. PHP is an interpreted language, which means that every time the source code of a PHP program runs, it is parsed (broken into pieces and analyzed) and executed by another program called the interpreter. The PHP interpreter is normally either a standalone binary executable or shared library embedded into a web server (Apache), and before we can run any PHP code, we need to make sure the interpreter is available on the system.

The standalone PHP binary is designed to be invoked like any command-line binaries on a system; you can type its name into a command shell (such as the popular Bash: https://www.gnu.org/software/bash/). It can be given a filename argument when invoked ("arguments" are the characters written after the command) and that file will then be interpreted and executed. It can also run interactively (individual statements are typed in and executed as they are entered), or even run in a special "cli-server" mode where the interpreter binds to a network port and offers basic HTTP functionality.

When running via a "full-fat" web server the PHP interpreter can either be a compiled module linked directly to the web server binary (e.g., a Windows .dll or Linux .so library file) or a CGI processor (which is a separate executable binary that the web server calls via the Common Gateway Interface). Don't panic if any of this is unfamiliar; all will be explained.

Many operating systems come with PHP preinstalled or at least have it as an optional package during the installation process. You can check if PHP is available on a Linux-based machine (or BSD-based, or actual Unix... these types of operating system are often referred to as *nix) with a simple shell command:

```
$ which php
```

```
Output:
/usr/local/bin/php
```

The `which` command searches the various file system paths stored in the shell's environment and reports back with the absolute path if the php binary is found. Another option would be to simply invoke PHP, like this:

```
$ php -v
```

```
Output:
PHP 8.4.5 (cli) (built: Mar 12 2025 01:55:56) (NTS)
Copyright (c) The PHP Group
Built by Homebrew
Zend Engine v4.4.5, Copyright (c) Zend Technologies
    with Zend OPcache v8.4.5, Copyright (c), by Zend Technologies
```

The precise output will vary but should give you the PHP version (8.4.5 in the example output above) and the *Server API* (SAPI) in parentheses. SAPI is shorthand for the various mechanisms that enable interaction between PHP and the rest of the system which is running it, such as file or network data streams, environment variables, HTTP data structures, and so on. The SAPI here is "cli" which means it is the standalone system binary that is being invoked. The CGI binary equivalent to php is usually named `php-cgi` and is also invokable from a shell.

```
$ php-cgi -v
```

```
Output:
PHP 8.4.5 (cgi-fcgi) (built: Mar 12 2025 01:55:56) (NTS)
Copyright (c) The PHP Group
Built by Homebrew
Zend Engine v4.4.5, Copyright (c) Zend Technologies
    with Zend OPcache v8.4.5, Copyright (c), by Zend Technologies
```

Notice that the SAPI part of the output is now "cgi-fcgi", indicating the server API is now PHP's "FastCGI" interface. If `php-cgi` isn't available on your system, try `$ php-fpm -v`. If neither is installed, then don't worry; I cover installation next. There's a little bit more work to do to get PHP running via a web-server, and we'll get to that too. First let's deal with what happens if PHP isn't installed on your system.

Installing PHP

There are several options available to you when installing PHP, from compiling PHP's C source code to downloading an archive file containing a ready-made installation. Another (excellent) option is to run PHP via a Docker container.

Most Linux distributions have a package management system, the two most common are Apt (e.g., Debian, Ubuntu - https://debian-handbook.info/browse/stable/sect.apt-get.html) and DNF (e.g., CentOS, Fedora, Redhat - https://docs.fedoraproject.org/en-US/quick-docs/dnf/). macOS lacks a default package manager, but there is the popular Homebrew installer available here: https://brew.sh. This section will not be an exhaustive guide to using OS package management tools, but is simply designed to get you up and running as quickly as possible.

With Apt

Debian's default Apt repositories tend to offer only the latest stable release of PHP, but there is a repository maintained by Ondřej Surý, which will enable installation of most minor versions of PHP. To prepare a Debian-based system to use this repository, use the following commands:

```
$ sudo apt-get update
$ sudo apt-get -y install lsb-release ca-certificates curl
$ curl -sSLo /tmp/debsuryorg-archive-keyring.deb https://packages.sury.org/debsuryorg-archive-keyring.deb
$ dpkg -i /tmp/debsuryorg-archive-keyring.deb
$ sh -c 'echo "deb [signed-by=/usr/share/keyrings/debsuryorg-archive-keyring.gpg] https://packages.sury.org/php/ $(lsb_release -sc) main" > /etc/apt/sources.list.d/php.list'
$ apt-get update
```

At the time of writing, these commands are taken from the installation script available at https://packages.sury.org/php/README.txt. With that done it should now be possible to install many different versions of PHP:

```
$ apt-cache search "php7.4 "
php7.4-cli - command-line interpreter for the PHP scripting language
php7.4-dev - Files for PHP7.4 module development
```

CHAPTER 1   GETTING STARTED

```
php7.4-fpm - server-side, HTML-embedded scripting language (FPM-CGI binary)

$ apt-cache search "php7.3 "
php7.3-cli - command-line interpreter for the PHP scripting language
php7.3-dev - Files for PHP7.3 module development
php7.3-fpm - server-side, HTML-embedded scripting language (FPM-CGI binary)

$ apt-cache search "php8.4 "
php8.4-cli - command-line interpreter for the PHP scripting language
php8.4-dev - Files for PHP8.1 module development
php8.4-fpm - server-side, HTML-embedded scripting language (FPM-CGI binary)
```

Debian users can switch between different versions of PHP if there are multiple installed. Let's first install PHP 7.4 and PHP 8.4:

```
$ sudo apt-get install -y php7.4
Reading package lists... Done
Building dependency tree... Done
...
$ sudo apt-get install -y php8.4
Reading package lists... Done
Building dependency tree... Done
...
```

Now let's see which version we'll get by default:

```
$ php -v
PHP 8.4.11 (cli) (built: Aug  3 2025 08:48:18) (NTS)
```

This should make sense: it's (at time of writing) the latest version and the last thing we installed. What if we want to run PHP 7.4, though? If you've followed the instructions so far, there should be two binaries on your system in addition to php: php7.4 and php8.4.

```
$ which php
/usr/bin/php

$ which php7.4
/usr/bin/php7.4
```

```
$ which php8.4
/usr/bin/php8.4
```

In fact /usr/bin/php isn't a binary at all but a Linux filesystem symbolic link (symlink):

```
$ ls -la /usr/bin/ | grep php
lrwxrwxrwx  1 root root         21 Jul  3 17:39 php -> /etc/alternatives/php
-rwxr-xr-x  1 root root    4850696 Jul  3 17:39 php7.4
-rwxr-xr-x  1 root root    6070784 Aug  3 09:48 php8.4
```

Notice that /usr/bin/php links to /etc/alternatives/php. The Debian alternatives system allows for easy switching of default programs. Let's change the default from 8.4 to 7.4.

```
$ sudo update-alternatives --set php /usr/bin/php7.4
update-alternatives: using /usr/bin/php7.4 to provide /usr/bin/php (php) in manual mode
$ php -v
PHP 7.4.33 (cli) (built: Jul  3 2025 16:39:22) ( NTS )
```

When it comes to juggling versions Debian's alternatives is pretty good, but there are other ways to achieve the same end. We will be exploring the use of Docker shortly.

With DNF

DNF (Dandified YUM) is an evolution of Yum, which has been the main package management utility of Redhat-based systems for many years. Using dnf at the command line is much like using yum, and indeed some distributions (usually truncated to *distro*) simply symlink yum to the dnf binary. We'll use the Fedora distro for the following DNF examples.

Like other package managers, dnf install php will give you the latest stable release for the version of the OS you are using, if you want to use earlier versions then it is necessary to add a repository. In the case of Redhat based systems this will be Remi's repository – https://rpms.remirepo.net/ – which contains vast amounts of installable resources for the PHP stack on these platforms. The repository is added with a

CHAPTER 1   GETTING STARTED

manual install of a .rpm file (RPM – Redhat package manager – is the tech underpinning DNF and Yum). In the following example I use Fedora 42 (installed as VM from the ISO installation file at https://download.fedoraproject.org/pub/fedora/linux/releases/42/Server/x86_64/iso/Fedora-Server-dvd-x86_64-42-1.1.iso). Find your release version number – $ cat /etc/redhat-release – and then use that to install the RPM file with from url https://rpms.remirepo.net/fedora/remi-release-XX.rpm

```
$ cat /etc/redhat-release
Fedora release 42 (Adams)

$ sudo dnf -y install https://rpms.remirepo.net/fedora/remi-release-42.rpm
Updating and loading repositories:
 Fedora 42 - x86_64 - Updates
 Fedora 42 openh264 (From Cisco) - x86_64
 ...

$ sudo dnf update -y
Updating and loading repositories:
 Remi's Modular repository - Fedora 42 - x86_64
 Remi's RPM repository - Fedora 42 - x86_64
 ...
```

Note that the name of the .rpm will vary with the version of Fedora, our examples here use release 42 so the file installed is remi-release-42.rpm. Now we can search the output of dnf search --showduplicates for the expanded list of PHP versions:

```
$ dnf search --showduplicates php | grep 'php74-php-0\|php84-php-0'
Updating and loading repositories:
Repositories loaded.
 php74-php-0:7.4.33-23.fc42.remi.x86_64 PHP scripting language for creating
 dynamic web sites
 php74-php-0:7.4.33-24.fc42.remi.x86_64 PHP scripting language for creating
 dynamic web sites
 php84-php-0:8.4.11-1.fc42.remi.x86_64  PHP scripting language for creating
 dynamic web sites
 php84-php-0:8.4.12-1.fc42.remi.x86_64  PHP scripting language for creating
 dynamic web sites
```

Older versions of the Remi repository use a slightly different naming convention for the top-level PHP packages, such as `php74-php-7.4.*.remi.x86_64` so you might need to adjust your `grep` pattern accordingly. The pattern `php74` would return dozens of matching packages because PHP is a fairly modular language: most of it is implemented as extensions (or modules) which can be installed independently. Let's go ahead and install PHP versions 7.4 and 8.4 onto our system.

```
$ sudo dnf install -y php74-php-0:7.4.33-24.fc42.remi.x86_64
$ sudo dnf install -y php84-php-0:8.4.12-1.fc42.remi.x86_64
```

There's a slight difference from Debian here...

```
$ which php
which: no php ...
```

... although the packages end up on the system, there's still some legwork to do. The PHP binaries are accessible after installation, just under slightly different names:

```
$ ls -l /usr/bin | grep php
lrwxrwxrwx 1 root root  32 Aug  1 00:00 php74 -> /opt/remi/php74/root/
                                                 usr/bin/php
lrwxrwxrwx 1 root root  36 Aug  1 00:00 php74-cgi -> /opt/remi/php74/root/
                                                 usr/bin/php-cgi
lrwxrwxrwx 1 root root  38 Aug  1 00:00 php74-phar -> /opt/remi/php74/root/
                                                 usr/bin/phar.phar
lrwxrwxrwx 1 root root  32 Aug 29 00:00 php84 -> /opt/remi/php84/root/
                                                 usr/bin/php
lrwxrwxrwx 1 root root  36 Aug 29 00:00 php84-cgi -> /opt/remi/php84/root/
                                                 usr/bin/php-cgi
lrwxrwxrwx 1 root root  38 Aug 29 00:00 php84-phar -> /opt/remi/php84/root/
                                                 usr/bin/phar.phar

$ which php84
/usr/bin/php84
```

We have php74 and php84 available from the command line, but not php. A simple symlink will suffice if that's a necessity for you:

```
$ sudo ln -s /usr/bin/php84 /usr/bin/php
$ php -v
PHP 8.4.12 (cli) (built: Aug 26 2025 13:36:28) (NTS gcc x86_64)
Copyright (c) The PHP Group
Built by Remi's RPM repository <https://rpms.remirepo.net/>
#StandWithUkraine
Zend Engine v4.4.12, Copyright (c) Zend Technologies
    with Zend OPcache v8.4.12, Copyright (c), by Zend Technologies
```

With Homebrew

As previously mentioned, macOS does not have a native CLI package manager, but the excellent Homebrew system fills the gap. To install Homebrew on your macOS simply run the following command:

```
/bin/bash -c "$(curl -fsSL https://raw.githubusercontent.com/Homebrew/install/HEAD/install.sh)"
```

Homebrew installation might also trigger an install of XCode Command Line Tools (XCode is Apple's native integrated development environment, and makes many standard development tools available on a macOS system), be sure to accept any extra XCode dependencies during this process. If you are installing onto a system that has Apple Silicon (rather than an Intel CPU) there might be additional steps to configure $PATH. The Homebrew installation process will prompt you if this is necessary.

Once installation is complete you can verify that everything works with this command:

```
$ brew doctor
Your system is ready to brew
```

Homebrew is generally a little easier to get along with if you require older versions of PHP, and will usually keep a few minor version releases actively installable. A package definitions for Homebrew is called a *formula*, and these are searchable as follows:

```
$ brew search php
==> Formulae
brew-php-switcher      php@8.1          phpmd
php                    php@8.2          phpmyadmin
php-code-sniffer       php@8.3          phpstan
php-cs-fixer           phpbrew          phpunit
php-cs-fixer@2         phpmd            ...
```

We can see there's php (latest version, 8.4 at the time of writing), then older versions with a @ symbol in their names: php@8.1, php@8.2 and so on. Let's install latest php:

```
$ brew install php
$ php -v
PHP 8.4.5 (cli) (built: Mar 12 2025 01:55:56) (NTS)
```

Just for fun, let's install PHP 8.1:

```
$ brew install php@8.1
$ php -v
PHP 8.2.10 (cli) (built: Aug 31 2023 19:16:09) (NTS)
```

As you can see, we still have the same version switching problem to overcome, which we'll get to shortly. Before that, here's what happens when we try to install PHP 7.4

```
$ brew install php@7.4
Error: php@7.4 has been disabled because it is a versioned formula!
```

Sooner or later, with Homebrew, you'll run into this problem. The package is still available, but the formula has an expiry date (feels appropriate for a beer-themed package manager). The solution, once again, is to add a third-party repository. In Homebrew parlance a repository is a *tap*, which maps a remote git repository to a local filesystem path. We'll use the shivammathur/php git repo.

```
$ brew tap shivammathur/php
==> Tapping shivammathur/php
Cloning into '/usr/local/Homebrew/Library/Taps/shivammathur/homebrew-php'...

$ brew install shivammathur/php/php@7.4
```

Switching between versions is a matter of controlling symlinks (note that the paths will vary depending on if macOS is running on Intel - /usr/local - or Apple Silicon - /opt/):

```
$ ls -la /usr/local/bin |grep php
lrwxr-xr-x   1 root    root         28 25 Sep 20:40 php -> ../Cellar/
php/8.2.10/bin/php

$ ls -l /usr/local/lib/php/
total 0
lrwxr-xr-x  1 pault   admin      40 25 Sep 20:47 20220829 -> ../../Cellar/
php/8.2.10/lib/php/20220829
lrwxr-xr-x  1 pault   admin      37 25 Sep 20:47 build -> ../../Cellar/
php/8.2.10/lib/php/build
```

Homebrew installs packages and their dependencies into /usr/local/Cellar/ and as we can see the conventional paths for PHP binaries and libraries are symlinked to the cellar where our various PHP version packages were installed. That's quite a few symlinks to control, fortunately it's also automated for you with brew link and brew unlink:

```
$ brew unlink php
Unlinking /usr/local/Cellar/php/8.2.10... 24 symlinks removed.

$ brew link php@7.4
Linking /usr/local/Cellar/php@7.4/7.4.33_4... 25 symlinks created.

$ php -v
PHP 7.4.33 (cli) (built: Sep  1 2023 04:09:59) ( NTS )
```

Simply brew unlink ... the existing linked package (you can always check the current mapping by seeing where the /usr/local/bin/php symlink is pointing to), then brew link ... the desired package.

Windows

The easiest way to install PHP onto a modern Windows system is to download the pre-built binaries from https://windows.php.net/download/. This page will offer a variety of versions, and both thread-safe and non-thread-safe variants (thread safety is required if running a web server that uses threads rather than processes for workers). The installation package is simply a `.zip` file containing the dozens of binaries (`.exe` and `.dll` files). Extract the contents to the directory of your choice (`C:\PHP` will be fine) and make sure that directory is part of your path, and you can simply invoke PHP from the command line like the examples above. The default default command-line environment for Windows (`cmd.exe`) is a little clunky, I highly recommend installing https://gitforwindows.org/ which bundles a nicer terminal GUI with a wide variety of GNU binaries that emulate most common *nix shell commands.

There is also the option of WSL (Windows Subsystem for Linux) which utilizes a virtual machine hypervisor to run a choice of Linux distributions, see https://learn.microsoft.com/en-us/windows/wsl/install to get started. There is of course the slightly more traditional option of running a VM via VirtualBox (or similar) https://www.virtualbox.org/wiki/Downloads but WSL is likely to be less hassle in the long run. Finally, there is Docker, which is the preferred method of running the code examples throughout this book. Read on for everything you'll need to get Docker up and running, giving you a powerful platform-agnostic execution environment.

PHP Extensions

PHP is modular: there is a core of functionality which is always available, and there are extensions which introduce new things into the language. For example, if your application will never interact with an LDAP server, there is no need for the LDAP functions (like `ldap_connect()`) or classes (in the `LDAP` namespace) to be installed. Every function, class, or constant defined in PHP takes system resources. In an environment where every millisecond counts (you might have a time budget measured in hundreds of milliseconds for a request to be fully processed) it makes sense to pare the interpreter down to the bare minimum.

To confirm that an extension (aka module) is enabled (or not) in your environment, simply run `php -m` to output the list:

```
$ php -m
[PHP Modules]
calendar
Core
ctype
date
...
```

Installing PHP extensions can be done via the package manager in exactly the same way that PHP itself was installed. Typically you can just combine the extension name with `php-` and search for that:

```
$ apt-cache search php-ldap
php-ldap - LDAP module for PHP [default]
php5.6-ldap - LDAP module for PHP
php7.0-ldap - LDAP module for PHP
...

$ dnf search php-ldap
Matched fields: name (exact)
 php-ldap.x86_64     A module for PHP applications that use LDAP
Matched fields: name
 php74-php-ldap.x86_64  A module for PHP applications that use LDAP
 php80-php-ldap.x86_64  A module for PHP applications that use LDAP
...
```

Once located, just use the package manager as normal.

Docker

An attractive alternative to trashing your filesystem or living in dependency hell is the hot new thing called Docker (well, maybe not that new anymore but it's still the hotness). Docker is a platform that enables software delivery using *containers*, which is fancy way of saying that software and all its dependencies (including OS and environment) are run in an isolated, virtualized space, a little bit like a *Virtual Machine* (aka a VM, which is a full-fat operating system running through a hypervisor such as VirtualBox or VMWare).

Unlike VMs, Docker containers on Linux are essentially running as just another service. They don't require the overhead of a hypervisor (unless running on a non-Linux system) and they have controlled access to the real hardware of the machine running the container, rather than the simulated hardware of a VM. For non-Linux systems, a single Linux VM is required because Docker depends heavily on Linux kernel features for resource isolation, but the details are abstracted away inside the Docker service so you don't have to think about them.

Multiple Docker containers are able to use just a single instance of the Linux kernel, and for this reason multiple containers are far more performant than multiple VMs. The isolation of containers from each other and the host operating system (via a Linux kernel feature called *namespacing*, a concept that also exists in PHP and we'll be learning about in great detail later) means that the container's view of the operating environment is restricted. Containers have their own process trees, users, filesystems, and network environment. Container access to host hardware devices (such as disk and network) is controlled by the docker server process `dockerd` (also known as the docker *daemon*, daemon processes in Unix and Linux operate in the background performing system level tasks). `dockerd` deals with grunt work of managing container life-cycles, mapping host filesystems into the container, creating virtual network interfaces so the container can access network services, and so on. Interaction with `dockerd` is usually through the docker CLI binary, or the Docker Desktop GUI.

CLI Installation

As with the PHP installations we saw in the previous section, your OS package manger should be capable of installing docker for you:

Debian/Apt

```
$ sudo apt-get update
$ sudo apt-get install -y docker.io docker-compose
$ sudo usermod -aG docker USER
```

Interacting with Docker on Fedora requires superuser privileges, the last command above adds USER to the docker group (change USER to whatever your user ID is) which gets around having to sudo every docker command. You might need to logout and back in again for it to take effect. See https://docs.docker.com/engine/install/debian/ for more details, or if you have any problems.

Fedora/DNF

```
$ sudo dnf -y install dnf-plugins-core
$ sudo dnf-3 config-manager --add-repo https://download.docker.com/linux/fedora/docker-ce.repo
```

CHAPTER 1   GETTING STARTED

```
$ sudo dnf install docker-ce docker-ce-cli containerd.io docker-buildx-plugin docker-compose-plugin
$ sudo usermod -aG docker USER
```

Again, we add USER to the docker group if we don't want to prepend every docker command with sudo. More details for Docker on Fedora can be found here: https://docs.docker.com/engine/install/fedora/

MacOS/Homebrew

```
$ brew install docker
```

More documentation at https://formulae.brew.sh/formula/docker

Windows

Docker is available for Windows via the Docker Desktop GUI software (which is also an option for Linux and Mac systems), and can be found at https://www.docker.com/products/docker-desktop/.

Verify Docker Server

The quickest way to test that docker is working after installation is to launch a container, there's even one specifically designed for this purpose.

```
$ docker run hello-world

Hello from Docker!
This message shows that your installation appears to be working correctly.

To generate this message, Docker took the following steps:
 1. The Docker client contacted the Docker daemon.
 2. The Docker daemon pulled the "hello-world" image from the Docker Hub.
    (amd64)
 3. The Docker daemon created a new container from that image which runs
    the executable that produces the output you are currently reading.
```

4. The Docker daemon streamed that output to the Docker client, which sent it to your terminal.

To try something more ambitious, you can run an Ubuntu container with:
$ docker run -it ubuntu bash

Share images, automate workflows, and more with a free Docker ID:
https://hub.docker.com/

For more examples and ideas, visit:
https://docs.docker.com/get-started/

If the docker server isn't running, you will see the following error:

docker: Cannot connect to the Docker daemon

This means that dockerd is not running which can be rectified by starting the Docker Desktop application, or using your system's service controls, for example:

Linux

$ sudo systemctl start docker

MacOS

$ open -a Docker

You can even start dockerd directly from the command line (which means it will run in the foreground and send all output to your shell):

$ sudo dockerd

More information can be found at https://docs.docker.com/config/daemon/start/

Images and Containers

The two fundamental building blocks of docker are *images* and *containers*. An image defines the filesystem contents and state of a container, and acts as a template for containers. The command docker run hello-world was an instruction to the Docker server to create a new container using the `hello-world` image, the output came from the container executing according to its configuration (and sending the output back to the parent shell). Although it is tempting to think of containers as being virtual machines they are not: containers should be conceptualized as single processes running in isolated environments, not general purpose machines.

Docker images are stored locally, if your `docker run` command specifies an image that can't be found locally Docker will attempt to download it from a repository. The default repository is `https://hub.docker.com` and the vast majority of official images for all kinds of software (including PHP) can be found there. When first running `hello-world` you might have noticed some informational output from Docker about locating and downloading the image:

```
Unable to find image 'hello-world:latest' locally
latest: Pulling from library/hello-world
719385e32844: Pull complete
Digest: sha256:4f53e2564790c8e7856ec08e384732aa38dc43c52f02952483e
3f003afbf23db
Status: Downloaded newer image for hello-world:latest
```

Images define a root filesystem for containers which consist of a series of read-only layers composed to form a single virtual filesystem (Docker uses OverlayFS for this). Multiple images can share the same set of layers, and multiple containers can read from the same layers when executing: this optimizes host disk usage compared to virtual machines. A new layer is only created when a change to the container filesystem occurs, and the new layer contains only the changes so it is usually very lightweight.

After successfully running the `hello-world` image, we can see that a copy of it stays on our machine:

```
$ docker image ls --filter="reference=hello*"
REPOSITORY          TAG              IMAGE ID        CREATED         SIZE
hello-world         latest           9c7a54a9a43c    4 months ago    13.3kB
```

The `--filter="reference=hello*"` filters the results based on repository name, just in case you're an old Docker hand and happen to have lots of other images already present on your system (in which case you probably skip the rest of this section). We can learn about the image by running `docker image inspect hello-world`, which dumps a lot of image metadata in a JSON format:

```
$ docker image inspect hello-world
[
    {
        "Id": "sha256:9c7a54a9a43cca047013b82af109fe963fde787f63f9e016f
        dc3384500c2823d",
        "RepoTags": [
            "hello-world:latest"
        ],
        ...
        "ContainerConfig": {
            "Cmd": [
                "/bin/sh",
                "-c",
                "#(nop) ",
                "CMD [\"/hello\"]"
            ],
        ...
        "RootFS": {
            "Type": "layers",
            "Layers": [
                "sha256:01bb4fce3eb1b56b05adf99504dafd31907a5aadac736e36
                b27595c8b92f07f1"
            ]
        },
        ...
```

I've truncated a lot of the JSON output, but there's two config nodes worth noting here. The RootFS node shows that hello-world has a single filesystem layer, which makes sense because it is a very simple image that does a simple job. The ContainerConfig.Cmd node shows what will happen when a hello-world container starts, in this case it is a shell command: /bin/sh -c "/hello". This is the heart of Docker (and containers in general): they run a process, not an entire (virtual) system.

CHAPTER 1   GETTING STARTED

PHP on Docker

There is a range of official PHP Docker images available at `https://hub.docker.com/_/php`, let's get one up and running. We'll use the `php:8.4-cli` image, which you can see has two parts compared to `hello-world`. The `php:8.4-cli` name is a combination of image and tag: `php` is the image, `8.4-cli` is the tag.

```
$ docker run php:8.4-cli
Interactive shell

php > $
```

That looked quite promising: we clearly had a PHP CLI binary running, albeit very briefly before exiting and returning us to our command prompt. Let's have a quick peek at the image metadata:

```
$ docker image inspect php:8.4-cli
...
        "Config": {
            "Hostname": "",
            "Domainname": "",
            "User": "",
            "AttachStdin": false,
            "AttachStdout": false,
            "AttachStderr": false,
            "Tty": false,
            ...
            "Cmd": [
                "php",
                "-a"
            ],
```

The default command for this image is `php -a` which puts PHP into interactive mode (we'll be looking at that in the next section) but we can also see that the Linux devices for handling input and output for command shells (`stdin` et al.) are not attached. To run a Docker container interactively, you can add a `-it` switch to the command.

```
$ docker run -it php:8.4-cli
Interactive shell

php > echo "hello world";
hello world
php >
```

By hooking our shell's I/O devices into the container, we can access the php binary that is running inside it and merrily hammer away to our heart's content. Another thing we can do with containers is override the default command, by specifying one of our own after the image name:

```
$ docker run -it php:8.4-cli php -m
[PHP Modules]
Core
ctype
curl
...
```

Here we're replacing php -a with php -m, the output of which is a list of all the available modules that PHP (inside the image) was built with. We can go even further and get our container to read in a file containing PHP code and execute it for us. This requires a little more CLI-fu, as we'll need to pass options to the docker command to tell it how to mount a host filesystem path into the container's RootFS. Let's create a simple PHP source code file, open up your preferred text editor and enter the following text:

```
<?php
echo "hello world" . PHP_EOL;
```

Note the <?php line at the very start of the file, this is a an *opening tag*, the PHP interpreter will treat everything after it as executable code until it reads either the end of the file or a closing ?> tag. From here on in all PHP code snippets assume you have an opening tag in your own code, and are omitted from the listing. Save this as hello.php and run it via the php:8.4-cli container:

```
$ docker run -v "$PWD":/usr/src/myapp php:8.4-cli php /usr/src/myapp/hello.php
hello world
```

The `-v "$PWD":/usr/src/myapp` switch tells the Docker server to mount our current working directory into the container using the path `/usr/src/myapp`. This means that if our current path contains the file `hello.php` then the container will be able to read it via `/usr/src/myapp/hello.php`.

To make this command even more useful, we can change the working directory of the PHP process inside the container, and add a network port mapping while we're at it. In fact let's cover all our bases and put it the container into interactive mode, and add a command alias for easy invocation.

```
$ alias docker-php='docker run -it --rm --net=host -p 8000:8000 -v "$PWD":/usr/src/myapp -w /usr/src/myapp php:8.4-cli php'
```

The bash command above creates an alias of `docker-php` which invokes `docker run` in interactive mode, with automatic removal of the container when it's done (more on this in a moment), mapping the host TCP 8000 port to the container's TCP 8000 port, with a volume mount of host current working directory to container `/usr/src/myapp`, and changes the working directory of the container's PHP process to `/usr/src/myapp`. It also specifies `--net=host` so the container is able to use the host's network directly, which will be useful in later examples when we launch other services in containers. On some image/system combinations you might see a warning like this in the first line of output...

```
WARNING: Published ports are discarded when using host network mode
```

... but it's nothing we need to worry about for the purposes of this book, this isn't a message from PHP. If you've chosen not to install PHP on your host system and prefer to keep everything containerized (which is exactly how I wrote this book), you can use an alias in lieu of an actual PHP binary. Wherever you see an example in this book like `php ...`, just substitute `docker-php ...` or any alias you like. To make an alias a permanent feature of your shell environment, add the alias command to the end of your shell configuration file in your home directory (`~/.bashrc` for bash, `~/.zshrc` for zsh and so on). Otherwise this alias is only available in the shell you ran the command in, and will vanish once that shell terminates.

Now that we have the `docker-php` alias in place we can do the following:

```
$ docker-php ./hello.php
hello world
```

```
$ docker-php -v
PHP 8.4.6 (cli) (built: Apr 11 2025 17:00:54) (NTS)
Copyright (c) The PHP Group
Built by https://github.com/docker-library/php
Zend Engine v4.4.6, Copyright (c) Zend Technologies

$ docker-php -a
Interactive shell

php > echo "hello world";
hello world
php >
```

Cleaning Up

If you've been following the text, you will have some stopped containers from earlier commands. Docker is conservative when it comes to garbage collection, and tends not to remove anything unless told to. Run docker ps -a (which is a shorthand form of the command docker container ls -a) to see all the containers Docker is aware of:

```
$ docker ps -a
CONTAINER ID    IMAGE           COMMAND                  CREATED
STATUS                     PORTS        NAMES
cd4276cc9300    hello-world     "/hello"                 3 minutes ago
Exited (0) 3 minutes ago                eager_haslett
d17bfc1196f3    php:8.4-cli     "docker-php-entrypoi…"   3 hours ago
Exited (0) 3 hours ago                  quizzical_sinoussi
d582caa6df2f    php:8.4-cli     "docker-php-entrypoi…"   3 hours ago
Exited (1) 3 hours ago                  vigorous_swanson
...
```

If Docker has seen prior use on your system for other things you'll possibly see those containers too. Containers can be removed by running the following command:

```
$ docker container prune
WARNING! This will remove all stopped containers.
Are you sure you want to continue? [y/N] y
```

```
Deleted Containers:
cd4276cc9300712fb1ec02045c5a89c5f0a60f7dd245009620273e87518762d4
d17bfc1196f3299232a51dfe212718abe65921229ff4913bccddf35ee3d87abc
d582caa6df2ffcb054e004c05730bdeba39771f97a384f6ea05789da8f1ccf12

Total reclaimed space: 0B
```

Multiple Versions

You can probably see that running arbitrary versions of containers is going to be a pretty straightforward affair; all you need is the correct version string and access to the image. No need to worry about managing dependencies because everything the container needs is packaged into the image already. Here's a quick demo:

```
$ docker run --rm php:7.4-cli php -v
PHP 7.4.33 (cli) (built: Nov 15 2022 06:01:17) ( NTS )
Copyright (c) The PHP Group
Zend Engine v3.4.0, Copyright (c) Zend Technologie

$ docker run --rm php:8.4-cli php -v
PHP 8.4.6 (cli) (built: Apr 11 2025 17:00:54) (NTS)
Copyright (c) The PHP Group
Built by https://github.com/docker-library/php
Zend Engine v4.4.6, Copyright (c) Zend Technologies
```

Docker makes managing multi-version environments a breeze. All of the code examples in this book were created using Docker, except where indicated. The official PHP images are lacking a couple of extensions that are required for some examples, so I have provided some image building resources at https://github.com/paultregoing/ExploringPHP8 (see the repo README.md for build instructions).

Web Server Integration

The core focus of this book is to explore PHP as a general purpose programming language, and is largely agnostic of which *Server API* (SAPI) you choose to run any of the code in (PHP Server APIs are coming up towards the end of this chapter). That said,

PHP was invented to handle HTTP and HTML and offers a lot of built-in functionality for running in a web server environment. Some of what we'll be looking at will require that the code is running within the context of an HTTP request, so let's have a quick look at how to get a web server up and running with PHP.

There are multiple web servers available, the two with the greatest market-share for PHP today are Apache and Nginx. We'll go with Nginx because it is relatively straightforward to install and configure compared to Apache. To install Nginx you have similar options to installing PHP (package manager, Docker, etc.) and for the sake of brevity – not to mention cross-platform compatibility – we shall use Docker containers. We'll also learn a little bit more about how to orchestrate containers so they can work together, so it's real value for money!

Nginx, unlike Apache, does not permit PHP to run as part of its process (via your system's linker). Instead it uses a standard for web-server interprocess communication called FastCGI, which is a binary protocol that permits long-running processes to service a series of requests. We will configure Nginx so that when it receives an HTTP request for a resource ending in .php the request is forwarded to a FastCGI compatible instance of PHP. We've already seen in the previous section how to get the official PHP CLI image running from the default Dockerhub repository, but this time we're going to need PHP's FPM (FastCGI Process Manager) image. Naturally there's an official image for Nginx too. Remember that Docker is about containing a process, not an entire system, so we'll need two containers: one for nginx and one for php-fpm.

Nginx (via Docker Orchestration)

Docker has a handy command for configuring multi-container projects: docker compose. Some systems also have a docker-compose (aka "compose v1") command available, but docker compose (aka "compose v2") is the shiny new way of doing things and should work everywhere. If you're working with an older version of Docker and docker compose isn't available, use the old docker-compose binary (you might need to install a separate package to get it). For our purposes the two are interchangeable.

We'll configure our two containers with a special config file – docker-compose.yaml – and we'll also need another special file – Dockerfile – for making changes to the base images before the containers are started. To enable nginx in one container to work correctly with php-fpm in another we'll need the following criteria met:

- Forward a TCP port on the Docker host system to TCP 80 in the `nginx` container.

- Configure `nginx` to function as a reverse proxy for `.php` resources.

- Shared network so that `php-fpm` container can receive the requests from `nginx`.

- Matching filesystem layouts between the two containers for the target PHP files.

To meet these criteria, our `docker-compose.yaml` looks like this:

```yaml
version: "3"
services:
  nginx:
    build:
      context: .
      dockerfile: ./Dockerfile
    ports:
      - "8080:80"
    networks:
      - internal
    volumes:
      - ./:/var/www/html
  php-fpm:
    image: php:8.4-fpm
    networks:
      - internal
    volumes:
      - ./:/var/www/html
networks:
  internal:
    driver: bridge
```

This yaml file defines a `services` node with two children, `nginx` (which uses the `nginx:1.25` image) and `php-fpm` (which uses the `php:8.4-fpm` image). The `networks.internal` node defines a shared network that both services can use, and is configured with the Docker's bridge network driver. `services.nginx` and `services.php-fpm` have matching `networks` and `volumes` nodes: both services will therefore be using the internal shared network so they can send network packets to each other, and both services will also mount the host path of `./` (the current directory) on the container path `/var/www/html`. In addition, `services.nginx` has a `ports` node which instructs `dockerd` to listen to TCP 8080 on the host and forward all traffic to the container on TCP 80 (we'll configure `nginx` to listen to that port in a moment).

`services.nginx` also has a `build` node. We need this because we're going to make a small but very important change to the `nginx:1.25` base image, we'll actually be building a new image (which is quite exciting if you're anything like me!) and running our nginx container from that. Notice that `services.nginx.build.dockerfile` has the value `./Dockerfile`, this tells `dockerd` to read `./Dockerfile` for the build instructions, let's create that next.

```
FROM nginx:1.25
ADD default.conf /etc/nginx/conf.d
```

This is very simple, it simply tells `dockerd` that our image is built on top of `nginx:1.25` and we'd like to put a file into the container's filesystem path of `/etc/nginx/conf.d` (we're overwriting the default container configuration with our own) and yes, you've guessed it, we now need to create the `default.conf` file...

```
server {
    listen 0.0.0.0:80;
    root /var/www/html;
    location / {
        index index.php index.html;
    }
    location ~ \.php$ {
        include fastcgi_params;
        fastcgi_pass php-fpm:9000;
        fastcgi_index index.php;
        fastcgi_param SCRIPT_FILENAME $document_root/$fastcgi_script_name;
    }
}
```

This Nginx configuration syntax defines a server that listens to traffic on TCP 80 from any external address and the server's filesystem root is /var/www/html (remember our volume mount in docker-compose.yaml). The default index file is index.php (i.e., a request to http://localhost/ will be mapped to /var/www/html/index.php), and any request URIs that end in .php will be proxied to TCP 9000 on the host php-fpm. Notice that this host has the same name as one of our services in docker-composer.yaml: when dockerd adds the containers to the shared network their names are resolvable to IP address (all handled magically for you by dockerd). The nginx container is able to resolve the hostname php-fpm to that container's IP address. TCP 9000 is the default port that the php:8.4-fpm container is configured to listen to, so there's no need for any extra config.

The only thing we need now is index.php, so let's create that next.

```
<?php
echo "<pre>Hello from php-fpm!</pre>";
echo "<pre>We are running under " . PHP_SAPI . " SAPI</pre>";
```

You should now have the following files in whichever directory you are working in:

```
$ tree --charset=asci
.
|-- Dockerfile
|-- default.conf
|-- docker-compose.yaml
`-- index.php

1 directory, 4 files
```

All that's left now is to tell Docker to bring up the containers:

```
$ docker compose up
[+] Running 2/2
 ✓ Container nginx-php-fpm-nginx-1    Created
 ✓ Container nginx-php-fpm-php-fpm-1  Created
Attaching to nginx-php-fpm-nginx-1, nginx-php-fpm-php-fpm-1
...
nginx-php-fpm-nginx-1  | 2023/10/14 17:37:52 [notice] 1#1: start worker process
```

And that's it. To stop the nginx container just hit ctrl+c in the terminal you started it from (where the log output is being sent), which will also stop the associated php-fpm container. Congratulations on building a multi-container Docker application! Now we can point a web browser at TCP 80 on the Docker host and the PHP we wrote (in index. php) will execute, with the results being sent back to our browser.

Figure 1-1. *FPM success response*

Built-in Web Server

PHP 5.4 added a new feature to the CLI binary: a built-in web-server. This is purely a development aid; it is definitely *not* intended for production use. With that said, it is a great way to test your code quickly in a web-server SAPI environment. Running the built-in web server is very simple: you run with PHP CLI binary with the -S switch, and a hostname/port combo (make sure to stop the nginx container from the previous example if it's still running):

```
$ php -S localhost:8080
[...] PHP 8.4.5 Development Server (http://localhost:8080) started
```

This starts the PHP CLI binary in cli-server SAPI mode: it will bind to TCP 8080 and listen for incoming traffic on the localhost IP address, and any log output will be sent to STDOUT. Open a new shell (the one we've just executed PHP with is currently occupied!) and run the following lsof command ("list open files"):

```
$ sudo lsof -nP -i TCP | grep 8080
```

CHAPTER 1 GETTING STARTED

The output will vary according to your preferred OS, user ID, phase of the moon, and so on. Here are some examples:

```
#Debian 13
php   54543   pault  4u   IPv6   81840                      0t0   TCP [::1]:8080 (LISTEN)

#Fedora 42
php   1794    pault  4u   IPv6   26225                      0t0   TCP [::1]:8080 (LISTEN)

#MacOS Sonoma
php   66720   pault  7u   IPv6   0xf5d86a0dc918232d   0t0   TCP [::1]:8080 (LISTEN)
```

In all cases we can see that php is listening on TCP 8080 to the local loop-back address (Debian using IPv4, the others IPv6). Only traffic originating from the local machine will get a response. If you want PHP to accept connections from any address, use this command: php -S 0.0.0.0:8080 (TCP 8080, any IPv4 address) or php -S [::]:8080 (TCP 8080, any IPv6 address). Be aware that this will expose port 8080 to all traffic, so be careful.

It is also possible to run a dockerized PHP binary in cli-server mode, but bear in mind the networking will be a little more complex. The container will need a port forward from the host, and will need to accept non-local traffic. The following docker command demonstrates how to do it:

```
$ docker run -it --rm \
  -p 8080:8080 \
  -v "$PWD":/usr/src/myapp \
  -w /usr/src/myapp \
  php:8.4-cli \
  php -S 0.0.0.0:8080
```

The -p 8080:8080 "switch" (specific options that control command behavior) maps host TCP 8080 to container TCP 8080, and the final php -S 0.0.0.0:8080 portion of the command is the invocation for the containerized PHP process. Make sure the port mapping with the -p switch aligns with the listening port inside the container.

When PHP is running in cli-server mode its default configuration is to use the current directory as the document root, and will use index.php as the default document. If you invoked php -S in the directory where we previously set up php-fpm and nginx containers then there's an index.php already available.

```
$ curl -v http://localhost:8080
*   Trying 127.0.0.1:8080...
* Connected to localhost (127.0.0.1) port 8080 (#0)
> GET / HTTP/1.1
> Host: localhost:8080
> User-Agent: curl/8.1.2
> Accept: */*
>
< HTTP/1.1 200 OK
< Host: localhost:8080
< Date: Sun, 22 Oct 2023 16:06:38 GMT
< Connection: close
< X-Powered-By: PHP/8.4.6
< Content-type: text/html; charset=UTF-8
<
* Closing connection 0
<pre>Hello from php-fpm!</pre><pre>We are running under cli-server
SAPI</pre>
```

As we can see from the end of the output, the SAPI reported by PHP has changed to cli-server. Using curl -v means we get verbose output and therefore we can see that in addition to the output of our simple program we also get some HTTP response headers (Host: localhost:8080, X-Powered-By: PHP/8.4.6, and so on). This is a function of the web-server SAPIs: they will automatically return certain headers in addition to the output of your program. Full details can be found in Chapter 11, "Programming for the Internet."

If you glance at the terminal in which the PHP server is running, there will be some output logged along the lines of the following...

```
PHP 8.2.10 Development Server (http://localhost:8080) started
[::1]:36978 Accepted
[::1]:36978 [200]: GET /
[::1]:36978 Closing
```

... which is of course very useful for debugging purposes.

Apache Module

Apache is a venerable web server that has been around for decades, and can integrate PHP in the same way as Nginx – as a CGI binary. PHP can also run as an Apache module, where the PHP binary is linked directly to the Apache process (as a `.so` or `.dll` library). The mode under which Apache is running PHP doesn't functionally impact the language: from PHP's perspective one web server is pretty much as good as another. Where this book touches on aspects of the language that need a web server environment we'll almost always use Nginx or PHP's `cli-server` SAPI, but I'll toss at least one Apache-driven example into the book somewhere to keep things (even more) interesting. If you're interested in learning about Apache, start here: `https://httpd.apache.org/`

Configuring PHP

PHP has many configurable options that control its behavior during execution. There are settings for logging errors (where to write, how much to write, and what types of errors), maximum memory use, controlling session data (for web-server SAPIs), and more. These options are collectively known as *directives* and are usually held in special files called *ini files* (named for their filename extension). Directives control both core PHP settings and those for extensions, and generally have default values when they are not explicitly set.

System-wide directives are typically located alongside other system-level configuration files such as the `/etc` path on Linux systems, or within the Apache config files (if running as an Apache module) such as `httpd.conf`. We'll look closely at this later on in this section.

Directives can also be set on a per-directory basis: every script in the same directory (or a descendant sub-directory) as the config is affected. This varies depending on the platform. For the CGI/FastCGI SAPI the files are named `.user.ini` – if running as an Apache module (`mod_php`) they are `.htaccess` files. If PHP is running on a Windows platform it also possible for some directives to be set via the system registry.

Finally, certain directives can be set during script execution using the built-in `ini_set()` function. It is also possible for PHP binaries (CLI, CGI/FastCGI SAPIs) to be invoked with directives as command line options.

It isn't necessary to reproduce the full list of directives here, the full list of configuration directives together with their default values and modes can be found at https://www.php.net/manual/en/ini.list.php and we will cover some of the commonly used ones in this section. It is important to know that every directive has a mode which sets where and how it can be defined. The four modes are:

Table 1-1. ini *directive modes (documentation only)*

Mode	Description
PHP_INI_USER	Can set with ini_set(), in .user.ini (CGI/FastCGI only), or the Windows registry
PHP_INI_PERDIR	php.ini, .htaccess, .httpd.conf, .user.ini
PHP_INI_SYSTEM	php.ini, httpd.conf
PHP_INI_ALL	Any of the above

The modes listed above are just labels within the documentation; they don't exist in the run-time language. The official PHP documentation, for example, gives the following information about the directive post_max_size (use to control how much data can be received from a client during an HTTP POST request): a default of 8M (eight megabytes) and a mode of PHP_INI_PERDIR. This means it is possible to set different value for post_max_size for PHP source code within different directories, you might need one particular URL to handle large file uploads but keep a tighter restriction for the rest, but there is no PHP_INI_PERDIR symbol in the language.

Directive Syntax

Directives have the syntax directive_name = Value and here's a short excerpt from the default php.ini installed onto most systems:

```
; Maximum amount of memory a script may consume
; https://php.net/memory-limit
memory_limit = 256M
```

The default file is actually a very good source of ready information and signposts detailed documentation, as you can see above. Comments are prepended with a semicolon, ;, the directive name and value are separated by =. The example above has two commented lines followed by a directive of memory_limit = 256M, which sets a maximum of 256 megabytes that can be allocated for a single running PHP process (any memory allocation above this limit will terminate the script immediately with an error message). Valid values for directives depend on the directive itself: for example memory_limit will accept an integer value for bytes or shorthand for large units (such 1G for 1 gigabyte), log_errors accepts either On or Off to enable or disable error logging.

It is permitted to use PHP constants (special symbols that are used in PHP programs, see Chapter 2, "Data, Types, and Variables," for more detail) in php.ini files, it is very common to see the error_reporting directive set to some combination of the error logging constants, for example, error_reporting = E_ALL, which translates as "show every type of error." See Chapter 4, "Logic and Control," for more details on PHP errors and how to handle them. Be aware that language constants aren't universally available (it's not possible to use them to set directives via the Windows registry, for example).

System Search Paths

When PHP starts up (either as a web-server module, via CGI, or the command line), it will search certain paths for these .ini files and read the contents looking for directives and their values. The filesystem path(s) that are searched will be configured during compilation of the PHP C source code and will vary by platform. We won't be covering compiling PHP from source in this book, but it is easy enough to determine which path your particular PHP binary will use.

```
$ php --ini
Configuration File (php.ini) Path: /etc/php/8.4/cli
Loaded Configuration File:         /etc/php/8.4/cli/php.ini
Scan for additional .ini files in: /etc/php/8.4/cli/conf.d
...
```

If the file php.ini exists, it will be read for config directives; in addition, if there is a SAPI-specific file such as php-cli.ini, then it will take precedence:

```
$ sudo cp /etc/php/8.4/cli/php.ini /etc/php/8.4/cli/php-cli.ini
$ php --ini
Configuration File (php.ini) Path: /etc/php/8.4/cli
Loaded Configuration File:         /etc/php/8.4/cli/php-cli.ini
...
```

The `--ini` switch isn't valid for all types of PHP binary (such as php-fpm), in which case we can run `php-fpm -i` for extremely detailed information dump:

```
$ php-fpm -i | grep "Configuration File"
Configuration File (php.ini) Path => /etc/php/8.4/fpm
Loaded Configuration File => /etc/php/8.4/fpm/php.ini
```

You might need to install it first, e.g., with `sudo apt-get install -y php8.4-fpm` or equivalent. Not all package managers bundle php-fpm with the rest of the core PHP packages, and not all php-fpm packages install a php-fpm CLI binary. If all else fails, use Docker:

```
$ docker run --rm php:8.4-fpm php-fpm -i | grep "Configuration File"
Configuration File (php.ini) Path => /usr/local/etc/php
...
```

Overriding `.ini` Settings

It is quite common for PHP to be used in multiple ways on the same system; the same codebase might target both web and CLI SAPIs. It is sometimes useful (or necessary) to adjust directives during execution or set (or override) values in the configuration file.

The `.ini` file syntax contains support for reading system environment variables, using the syntax `directive = ${ENV_VAR}`. Search your php.ini file with grep (the example below assumes a Debian-like config path; your system might differ):

```
$ grep 'memory_limit' /etc/php/8.4/cli/php.ini
memory_limit = ${PHP_MEMORY_LIMIT}

$ export PHP_MEMORY_LIMIT=128M
$ php -r "var_dump(ini_get('memory_limit'));"
string(4) "128M"
```

Here we have set the directive `memory_limit` to be `${PHP_MEMORY_LIMIT}`, then set the environment variable in bash with `export PHP_MEMORY_LIMIT=128M`. The final command is a single PHP statement `var_dump(ini_get('memory_limit'));` which returns the value. This way it is easy to configure PHP on a per-process basis, which is useful when you need to tune settings in the shell environment (every process in a Linux system has its own set of environment variables).

We've just seen `ini_set()` above and how it can be used to retrieve directive values during execution. This function has a counterpart: the built-in functions `ini_get()` and `ini_set()` respectively allow you to determine or define directive values during run-time:

```
$ php -a
Interactive shell

php > var_dump(ini_get('memory_limit'));
string(2) "-1"
php > ini_set('memory_limit', '128M');
php > var_dump(ini_get('memory_limit'));
string(4) "128M"
```

Finally, you can also pass directives and values when PHP is invoked by using the `-d` switch. This functions in much the same way as environment variable manipulation:

```
$ php -r "var_dump(ini_get('memory_limit'));"
string(2) "-1"
$ php -d memory_limit=512M -r "var_dump(ini_get('memory_limit'));"
string(4) "512M"
```

Here we're executing code immediately with the `-r` command line switch and using `-d memory_limit=128M` to change the maximum memory PHP is allowed to allocate (a handy trick if you have certain scripts that need extra memory and you might not have ownership of the overall system configuration).

Module (Extension) Configuration

A lot of "core" PHP is actually implemented as extensions (also known as modules). You might remember in the Docker section earlier we ran the command `php -m`, and the output was a list of installed modules. Modules often have their own configuration files, which are typically located in a sub-directory of wherever your main PHP config is found – e.g., `/etc/php/current/mods.available` for Debian-based systems. At the very least, these files contain a line such as `extension=module_name.so`, which is an instruction to link a shared object resource to the main PHP executable when it runs.

Often there are extension-specific config lines following this; let's take the ever-popular xdebug debugging extension as an example... It's quite common to see something like this in an `xdebug.ini` file:

```
extension=xdebug.so
xdebug.mode=develop,debug,trace
xdebug.discover_client_host=true
xdebug.discover_client_discovery_header=HTTP_X_FORWARDED_FOR
```

The first line has to be the instruction to link the `.so` file (otherwise none of the xdebug functionality will be available to the PHP binary); the remaining `xdebug.*` lines are various configuration options. In this case we're telling `xdebug` to support three different debugging modes, and it should attempt to connect back to the host initiating the connection to start a debugging session. Debugging PHP features to a small extent later in the book, but we'll just be using core PHP functions to do it. I highly recommend XDebug for large projects; you can get started by visiting `https://xdebug.org/`

Structure and Syntax

Now that we've covered how to install, configure, and run PHP, it's time to start looking at the language itself. You've already seen a few simple snippets of PHP code, which we've used to verify and test the various installation options. Now it's time to see how to build something more complex.

Source Code Files

Previous sections of this chapter have mostly relied on passing PHP code directly to the CLI interpreter, either using `php -r` (code is entered as part of command line invocation) or `php -a` (code can be entered via an interactive shell program). For anything more trivial than a few lines, you are best off storing the code in a file; the section on web-server SAPIs demonstrated this.

All PHP code in a file must follow an opening `<?php` tag, and there must be a closing `?>` tag if the file also contains non-PHP code. This has been the case since PHP's earliest versions, when its only purpose was to run as a web-server module. The use of opening tags is required even if the file contains nothing but PHP, although closing tags in this case are optional (and in fact there's an official coding standard that prohibits closing tags in pure PHP files; we'll explore coding standards in a bit). This will probably make more sense if we start writing some PHP, but before we do that, we'll launch another web server. In the interests of balance, we'll use an Apache environment; it's time for more Docker...

PHP Embedded in HTML

No matter which SAPI it's running, the PHP interpreter will emit any text in source code that is not contained in PHP tags directly as output. The idea is (or was) that you can mainly write declarative HTML, dipping into PHP code only when imperative programming is essential. The syntax of PHP tags deliberately resembles HTML tags for this reason, and there will be more said on this programming style in Chapter 11, "Programming for the Internet," where I will do my utmost to dissuade you from ever using it!

Anyway, back to the matter at hand, we're going to launch an old-school web server: Apache with PHP embedded inside (via `libphp.so`), for which there's an official Docker image:

```
$ docker run -p 8080:80 --rm --name apache_mod_php -v "$PWD":/var/www/html php:8.4-apache
...
[...] [mpm_prefork:notice] [pid 1:tid 1] AH00163: Apache/2.4.65 (Debian) PHP/8.4.11 configured -- resuming normal operations
[...] [core:notice] [pid 1:tid 1] AH00094: Command line: 'apache2 -D FOREGROUND'
...
```

This gets us an Apache2 server, running some flavor of the mod_php SAPI (for this particular PHP 8.4 image, the PHP_SAPI string is actually apache2handler, but it's the same thing). It is running in the foreground, so our shell is now busy receiving STDOUT and STDERR from the container (the php:8.4-apache image is configured to send Apache and PHP log output to /dev/stdout and /dev/stderr inside the container, and the container is configured to send those to the host's equivalent devices).

Open up a new shell, make sure the working directory is the same as the shell running the php:8.2-apache container from above, and create the following index. php file:

```
<!DOCTYPE html>
<html>
<head>
    <title>Old school PHP</title>
</head>
<body>
    <p>This paragraph is vanilla HTML</p>
    <?php
        print "<p>This paragraph was created with PHP SAPI: <pre>" . PHP_
        SAPI . "</pre></p>";
    ?>
</body>
</html>
```

We must give the file a .php extension even though it is actually HTML with embedded PHP; otherwise, the Apache server (as configured in the official image) will not send it to the PHP engine for processing. Finally, open up a web browser and send it to the following location: http://localhost:8080/index.php. You should get the following page:

This paragraph is vanilla HTML

This paragraph was created with PHP SAPI:

`apache2handler`

Figure 1-2. *Embedded PHP*

There we have it, pre-processed hypertext! The only PHP in the file above is contained between opening and closing tags:

```
<?php
    print "<p>This paragraph was created with PHP SAPI: <pre>" . PHP_SAPI .
    "</pre></p>";
?>
```

It's a simple `print` statement, much like those used earlier in the chapter. Let's create a similar file, but this time it'll be pure PHP, and we're going to use something called HEREDOC, which is a programmer-friendly way of creating multi-line chunks of text within code.

Pure PHP Files

Create a new file, `index2.php` in the same location as `index.php` with the following contents (remember to include an opening tag at the start):

```
$sapi = PHP_SAPI;

print <<<HTML
<!DOCTYPE html>
<html>
<head>
    <title>Old school PHP</title>
</head>
<body>
    <p>This entire document was created with PHP SAPI: <pre>{$sapi}
    </pre></p>
</body>
</html>
HTML;
```

This is a slightly more complex program; it has two statements. The first – `$sapi = PHP_SAPI;` – assigns the value of PHP_SAPI to a variable because we can't use constants in the next statement, which is use something called HEREDOC syntax – `print <<<HTML` .... This form of statement takes everything between the <<<HTML and HTML; lines and treats it as text. HEREDOC allows variables to be interpolated into the text, which is

accomplished with the {$sapi} portion. Don't worry if you're not sure about any of this just yet: we'll cover variables in Chapter 2, "Data, Types, and Variables," and the many ways to handle text in the appropriately named Chapter 8, "Strings."

If you request index2.php in the same way that index.php was, you should have the following in your web browser:

This entire document was created with PHP SAPI:

`apache2handler`

Figure 1-3. *Pure PHP*

Notice that in index2.php, we did not use a closing ?> tag. Closing tags should not be used in files that contain only PHP code, as they can trigger the sending of output to the browser: in a complex, multi-file PHP application, this might cause unwanted behavior if other PHP code has not had a chance to execute yet.

Introduction to PHP Syntax

Now we come to a very important topic: PHP's syntax. Your future as a PHP programmer (or indeed a programmer in general) depends largely on your grasp of language syntax: the rules by which the language is used. No pressure! The full syntax rules of PHP (or any general-purpose language) would cover dozens of pages, and attempting to reproduce them here would be a good way for me to ensure you don't finish this chapter. That said, we can tackle some fundamentals without overloading you too much at this point. For any readers that have experience with C or C++: you find PHP's syntax familiar, and that's not a coincidence. Like other languages implemented in C, PHP borrows a lot of syntax rules from it.

We can abstract PHP's syntax rules in a top-down way like this: valid PHP is composed of a sequence of *statements* (of various types) that are themselves composed from *expressions*. Expressions can be composed of *sub-expressions*, and both are composed from *operations*.

The following list summarizes this hierarchy:

- Header statements
- Declaration statements
- General statements
- Expressions
- Sub-expressions
- Operations

Header statements are found at the beginning of every PHP file, immediately after the opening tag. These are limited to `declare()` statements (which control execution directives for a code block), `namespace` declarations, and `use` statements (the latter two are used to partition code, which is covered in detail in Chapter 3, "Functions").

General statements are all other possible statements that are not specific to PHP file header sections. A statement can be considered as a "line" of code and separated from other statements by the semicolon `;` character (it is the semicolon that delimits statements; you are free to use as much spacing, indentation, and new lines as you wish). Function and class declarations are also considered to be (special) statements in PHP.

Expressions (and sub-expressions) are sequences of operations that are *evaluated*: this means they can be substituted for values in the statement. For example, the expression `2 * 2;` evaluates to `4`, `"a string" . " and another string";` evaluates to `"a string and another string";`.

Operations are composed of *operators* and *operands*. Operators determine the type of operation; there are mathematical operators (such as +, -, /), logical operators (such as AND &&, OR ||), and many others. Perhaps the most important is the assignment operator = that allows us to store and retrieve values. Operands are placed on either side of the operator; for example, `1 + 2` is a mathematical addition operation with operands 1 and 2. Some operations only require a single operand, such as auto-increment: `1++;` has a single operand 1 and a single operator ++. We will cover all of the operators in their relevant chapters.

We can further abstract operations in this way: operands can be *symbols* (also known as *labels*; these are the names of *variables*, *constants*, and *functions*) or *literal* values. Literal values are strings, numbers, and other raw values that do not require evaluation in order to have a value.

Now that is a lot to take in, so let's summarize with some code examples:

```
declare(strict_types=1); // Header statement

namespace Foo; // Header statement

class ClassDeclarationsAreStatements // General statement
{
}

function functionDeclarationsAreAlsoStatements () // General statement
{
}
```

The example above shows header statements (declare() and namespace) and the "special" general statements declaring a class and a function. Classes and functions are covered in detail in Chapter 3, "Functions," and Chapter 6, "Object Fundamentals," and the execution directive declare(string_types=1) in the next chapter. These are all special statements, and notice that the class and function declarations don't require semicolon terminators.

With the special cases out of the way, here are some examples of general statements that are composed of lower-order terms, such as expressions and operations. Remember that all symbols, operations, and expressions delimited by semicolons form the statement. The simplest possible statement in PHP, therefore, is a single literal value:

```
// A single literal is still a valid statement...
1;

// An operation containing literal values, this is also an expression that
evaluates to 2
1 + 1;

// We can assign an operation to a symbol.
$number = 1 + 1;
```

Above are three statements. The first is a single literal value, the second is an operation composed of a single operator and two literal operands, and the third is an assignment expression that takes the value of a sub-expression (which is a simple mathematical operation) and assigns it to a variable identified with the symbol (name) number. Note that the statement 1; is perfectly valid PHP code. The PHP interpreter has parsed it, found no problems, and allowed execution. It doesn't actually do anything, but neither does it emit any errors (there are various tools that will, however, warn about code such as this).

As a final exercise in this section, let's take a more complex statement and identify the syntax structures.

```
$number = 1 + 1;
var_dump(
    $number == 1 + 1
);
```

Output:
bool(true)

The code above contains two statements. The first assigns the result of an operation to the variable $number, as per the previous example. The second statement (which spans multiple lines) calls a built-in function var_dump(), and passes the result of a logical expression into that function. The syntax can be broken down into tokens (indivisible units) as follows:

Table 1-2. Syntax tokens

Token	Type
1	Literal value
+	Operator (addition)
=	Operator (assignment)
==	Operator (logical)
number	Symbol (variable)
var_dump	Symbol (function)
(	Beginning function invocation
)	End of function invocation
$	Variable reference

When statements are executed, the expressions they contain are evaluated right to left. Here are the equivalent expressions of each step as var_dump($number == 1 + 1) is evaluated, starting with 1 + 1 becoming 2:

```
var_dump($number == 1 + 1);
var_dump($number == 2);
var_dump(2 == 2);
var_dump(true);
```

For those of you who are feeling particularly curious (and/or brave) and would like to know the real syntax rules for PHP, the most authoritative place to go is the source code for PHP's parser: https://github.com/php/php-src/blob/master/Zend/zend_language_parser.y ... enjoy!

PHP Coding Standards

PHP does not have significant whitespace (any character sequence that represents horizontal or vertical spacing) as part of its syntax rules, and you are free to write all sorts of weird and wonderful things. For example:

```
var_dump(1+1);
var_dump(1     +1)      ;
var_dump     (
    1
    +
      1
)
  ;

Output:
int(2)
int(2)
int(2)
```

Each statement above gives the same result, but clearly not of all that code is particularly easy to read. Even diligent programmers with consistent styles will vary in their preferences, and large codebases often end up with a mashup of different approaches to laying out source code. For this reason we have coding standards.

Coding standards are simply a set of rules that dictate how source code should be written. These standards are only concerned with how source code is presented; they do not enforce *what* you write but simply *how* you write. Coding standards will not prevent the creation of bad code, but they do ensure that bad code is at least easy to read. The best place to start with PHP coding standards is the PHP Framework Interop Group (PHP-FIG); their homepage can be found at `https://php-fig.org/`.

The PHP-FIG maintains a set of PHP Standards Recommendations – PSRs – that are concerned with how to write PHP itself and how to design common components for tasks such as logging, caching, event handling, and so on. The aim of this work is to ensure interoperability between PHP code maintained by different teams. The idea is that libraries, components, or entire frameworks are more easily integrated into projects if everything follows the same standards.

There are, of course, many other coding standards for PHP, but typically most are supersets of the PHP-FIG standards, so the PSRs are well worth learning (and enforcing; we'll see how to do that in a moment). Let's start with the Basic Coding Standard, PSR-1 (`https://www.php-fig.org/psr/psr-1/`).

PSR-1

The PSR-1 coding standard sets out some important fundamentals that all source code files must follow. This includes the encoding scheme for the files (UTF-8 without a byte-order mark – see Chapter 8, "Strings," if you're not sure what this means), the open/close tag style, what files are allowed to do (either declare symbols or cause effects – change in program state – but not both), and the conventions for names (classes, functions, constants). Perhaps most importantly, PSR-1 also enforces something called *autoloading*, which is a technique for loading new source code at runtime to find undeclared classes. Autoloading is covered in Chapter 6, "Object Fundamentals." Most importantly, where PSR-1 doesn't enforce standards, it does strongly recommend consistency.

If you only follow the PSR-1 standard, you will have code that will easily integrate with other code written to the same standard. Moving beyond PSR-1, there is the Extended Coding Style, PSR-12 (`https://www.php-fig.org/psr/psr-12/`).

PSR-12

PSR-12 is built on PSR-1; in fact, the first rule of PSR-12 is that all code must follow PSR-1. It also adds to the standards for storing/transmitting source files by specifying the line termination character (Unix line-feed) and the removal of the closing tag sequence ?>. Perhaps controversially, PSR-12 also insists on four-space indentation (indent style is often the cause of many robust conversations among programmers).

PSR-12 contains a lot of fine detail on how to format things like class names, function names, and constants; it also enforces the layout of control structures, loops, spacing for operators and operands, and spacing for function parameter lists. There's a lot of detail that is unnecessary to reproduce here, but you are strongly encouraged to read the PSR documents; they will be referred to throughout this book (which will have all code examples conforming to the PSR-12 standard except where it is necessary to break those standards as part of an example).

Enforcing Standards

The PSR-12 standard contains a lot of information, and even seasoned veterans that have been using it for years will occasionally slip up and miss something (ahem…), so it's a good idea to use a scanning tool to make sure that standards are maintained on every change. For this we have PHP CodeSniffer (`phpcs`), which is fairly ubiquitous and the code scanning tool of choice for many high-profile projects. **Appendix A** contains everything you need to install and run both CodeSniffer and its related `phpcbf` fixer utility.

Input (and Output)

Any program you create will naturally need to access, transform, and output data in some form. Numbers, text, even images, and other more exotic forms of information are the lifeblood of software. PHP has several mechanisms available to make this task as painless as possible. The acronym *I/O* ("input/ouput") is quite common and will be used here. This section will discuss things like bytes and byte streams. If you're not certain what these terms mean, I recommend a quick peek at Chapter 2, "Data, Types, and Variables," which introduces the basic principles of data representation. Before we get started with PHP's I/O mechanisms, we need to look at the differences in *how* PHP executes, because this impacts what is available and what needs to happen.

CHAPTER 1   GETTING STARTED

The Server APIs

PHP was originally designed to run embedded in web pages, providing server-side processing before the server sent a response. PHP is now over two decades old and has long since grown into a richly featured general-purpose language that can be used for a wide variety of system-level tasks. An intrinsic aspect of PHP's execution is the Server API (SAPI). The SAPI governs the communication between your program running within the PHP engine and everything else happening outside your code, and there are different SAPIs tuned for the general requirements of the environment in which PHP is executing.

A PHP program that is called from a command shell has different needs to one that is servicing an HTTP request. A shell command almost never needs to worry about HTTP headers but might need to interact with a command shell's environment or obtain user input supplied when the program was invoked. Conversely, a web server might set a maximum execution time (there's no point in continuing to run code that has exceeded the timeout of the HTTP request) and restrict which parts of the filesystem PHP can access as a security precaution.

To determine at run-time which SAPI your code is working with, you can either call php_sapi_name() or find the value of the built-in PHP_SAPI constant:

```
$ php -a
Interactive shell

php > echo php_sapi_name();
cli
php > echo PHP_SAPI;
cli
php >
```

The major differences are between the cli SAPI and all the others. Every non-CLI SAPI will be running as some form of web-server (such as php-fpm, mod_apache) and needs to deal with the overheads of the HTTP protocol and standards for data transfer (such as email attachments): we'll cover these things in detail in Chapter 11, "Programming for the Internet." The cli SAPI differs from web SAPIs in the following .ini directives:

Table 1-3. cli SAPI directives – differences

implicit_flush	true	cli programs often need to display output immediately
max_execution_time	0 (unlimited)	cli programs might need to run for minutes or even hours
register_argc_argv	true	Needing to access to cli arguments is usually a given
output_buffering	false	A compliment to implicit_flush, buffering output is usually the exception not the rule
max_input_time	false	Not necessary because there is no client data pending when the program is first invoked

Outputting Data

In this section we're going to be looking in detail at the mechanisms that PHP has for obtaining data from external sources – i.e., data that isn't literally declared within the program code itself. Chapter 2, "Data, Types, and Variables," will break down exactly how data representation works in PHP, how the ones and zeroes of binary bits – packaged into 8-bit bytes – are used to represent numbers, text, and so on. That chapter will also show you how to store and manipulate data as your program executes. All of these parts of the book contain code examples that make extensive use of data output mechanisms (functions and language constructs) that will show the results of the code (usually as cli SAPI programs), so before we go any further, we should look at how these output mechanisms work. Here are the most common ways used to generate program output in this book:

Table 1-4. CLI output mechanisms

print, echo	Send data to the output buffer as a text "string"
print_r()	Converts data to a human readable string, can send to output or return for use as variable
var_dump()	Similar to print_r(), but gives more comprehensive information about data types

Note that `print` and `echo` have no parentheses (), because they are "language constructs," not functions. This distinction might be beyond you at the moment, but don't worry: Chapter 3, "Functions," contains everything you need to understand what PHP functions are and how they work. Skip ahead if you like!

The Output Buffer

I've mentioned output buffering twice so far in this section, but what is it? Well, it's quite simple: data output by your program can be sent immediately, or it can be accumulated in a temporary store for sending in one large chunk later on. This can be quite useful in the context of HTTP requests, where HTTP protocol header data has to be sent before the response body. A complex program might have already started to form the body before all the headers are calculated and sent. In particular, the `Content-Length:` header needs to know the full size (in bytes) of the response body, which you don't necessarily know until all your code is done. If your script has already started to spit out the response, then tries to send an HTTP header this would constitute a protocol error. PHP allows for "user-level" output buffers – that is, buffers that are under the control of your program. Here's a quick example:

```
ob_start();

print "What are we holding onto, Sam?";
print PHP_EOL;
print "That there's some good in this world, Mr. Frodo... and it's worth fighting for.";

$buffered = ob_get_clean();
print "Buffer contents:" . PHP_EOL;
print $buffered;

Output:
Buffer contents:
What are we holding onto, Sam?
That there's some good in this world, Mr. Frodo... and it's worth fighting for.
```

`ob_start()` creates an output buffer; from this point on everything, we output with `print`, etc., will end up stored in here. `ob_get_clean()` returns the contents of the buffer, which we store in the `$buffered` variable. From the output of the program, we can see that the first three `print` statements were buffered because they appear after the `Buffer contents:` line. There will be more to come on output buffering in Chapter 11, "Programming for the Internet."

Command Line Input

As stated above, the `register_argc_argv` directive controls whether or not command line arguments are made available to your PHP code. When enabled it provides a number of mechanisms you can use to access any data entered at the command line when the PHP binary is invoked. Here's a simple program – which we'll save in a file called `argv_argc.php` – that outputs the values of some special variables. PHP variables always start with the $ symbol followed by some kind of symbolic name; in this case, these are $argc, $argv, and $_SERVER. Each of these variables happens to be of a type called an *array*, which is a collection of scalar (single value) values (e.g., numbers, strings of characters, booleans). Each scalar value inside an array is an *element* of that array.

```
// argv_argc.php
var_dump($argc);
print_r($argv);
print_r($_SERVER['argv']);
```

The syntax `$_SERVER['argv']` is an example of *array access*: the square bracket notation tells PHP that you want to access one of the scalar values, and the bit inside the square bracket tells PHP which particular element you want to access. There is an entire chapter of this book devoted to arrays (called, in an act of stunning imagination on my part, Chapter 5, "Arrays"), and you are quite free to have a sneaky look at it right now if you like. Now let's run our code from the command line and supply some data for it to make use of:

```
$ php argv_argc.php some data
int(3)
```

```
Array
(
    [0] => argv_argc.php
    [1] => some
    [2] => data
)
Array
(
    [0] => argv_argc.php
    ...
```

A command-line shell will pass any text written after the command itself via a standard mechanism (STDIN); each item is delimited by some kind of space or tab character. Any program running in this way can access this data as *arguments* (a mechanism for passing data to functions, which we'll see in Chapter 3, "Functions," and Chapter 6, "Object Fundamentals"). In our case, the command is php, and the arguments are the filename argv_argc.php, some, and data. As you can hopefully see from the output of the program, we have two ways to access the argument values: either directly via $argv or as the argv element of the $_SERVER array. A count of the available arguments is provided via $argc. $argc and $argv are automatically created and made available everywhere in the program, and $_SERVER is a special type of array variable called a *superglobal*, which will have an argc and argv element populated with the same data. Superglobals are covered in Chapter 2, "Data, Types, and Variables".

In addition to arguments, CLI binaries can have options set using a mechanism known as *switches*. These take the form of -x (a "short" option) or --name_of_x (a "long" option) and can also be accessed in PHP using the core getopt() function. This function has a range of behaviors that might not be completely intuitive at first glance, so let's go step-by-step. First of all, here's a very simple form of the function that checks to see if a short -o has been supplied:

```
// getopt1.php
var_dump(getopt("o"));
```

Here's what happens when we call that code with and without the option:

```
$ php getopt1.php
array(0) {
}
```

```
$ php getopt1.php -o
array(1) {
  ["o"]=>
  bool(false)
}
```

It might seem a bit strange that getopt() confirms -o was supplied by assigning a false value to the "o" array key, but this just means that -o exists without any additional data. *nix programs often have other input associated with their switches, and in order to capture that extra data, we need to change the way we call getopt():

```
// getopt2.php
var_dump(getopt('o:'));
```

Notice the colon : after the o. This makes -o capture any text that immediately follows it (after zero or more space/tab characters):

```
$ php getopt2.php -o'some data'
array(1) {
  ["o"]=>
  string(9) "some data"
}
```

To specify long-form options, we add a second argument to getopt(), but this time it is an array of option names but still uses a colon for capturing values after the option. While we're at it, we'll add a second short option and make the capturing of -o optional (by specifying with a double colon ::) like this:

```
// getopt3.php
var_dump(getopt('xo::', ['bacon:']));
$ php getopt3.php -x -o=foo   --bacon 'is tasty'
array(3) {
  ["x"]=>
  bool(false)
  ["o"]=>
  string(3) "foo"
  ["bacon"]=>
  string(8) "is tasty"
}
```

CHAPTER 1   GETTING STARTED

Accessing Environment Data

Another conventional way of controlling program behavior is through a shell's *environment.* This is simply a table of key/value pairs; the key name is usually referred to as a *shell variable* (or *shell var* for short), and these can be viewed with on most *nix shells with the env command:

```
$ env
TERM_PROGRAM=Apple_Terminal
TERM=xterm-256color
SHELL=/bin/bash
...
```

Shells can make use of these using variable syntax, which is similar to PHP's: just put a $ character in front of the variable name:

```
$ echo $TERM
xterm-256color
```

All PHP SAPIs are able to access the environment of a process through the getenv() function. If the variables_order directive contains an E character, the $_ENV superglobal is also populated (the exact output will vary according to your system and settings):

```
var_dump(getenv());
var_dump(getenv('PHP_VERSION'));
```

Output:
```
array(15) {
  ["HOSTNAME"]=>
  string(12) "4d81e666b865"
  ["PHP_INI_DIR"]=>
  string(18) "/usr/local/etc/php"
  ...
string(6) "8.3.10"
```

Accessing Files

Command line arguments and environment variables are fine for passing small amounts of data into your program, but for larger amounts of data you are going to need to use something more robust, such as files. It's a little early in the book to get deep into what files really are: Chapter 8, "Strings," is where we'll look at what text data really is. However, this is a good point to look at how to read and write data to the filesystem. Additionally, it's important to realize that the filesystem of *nix-based system is also used to abstract network connections and data streams in general. Because of this, the PHP functions that interact with files can also be used to stream data from network connections (which we'll get to shortly), but first let's look at the basics. For this example, we have a simple text file on the path /data/sample.txt, the contents of which are designed to provoke meaningful conversations, and we're going to get PHP to create a string variable from the contents:

```
$fullText = file_get_contents(__DIR__ . '/data/sample.txt');
print $fullText;
Output:
Star Trek: Enterprise was underrated.
The Xindi were better antagonists than the Suliban.
```

Controversial, possibly, but it serves its purpose. This example uses features that are fully explained in Chapter 3, "Functions" and Chapter 8, "Strings." If this is the first programming language you've encountered, then feel free to take a look at those chapters to get more comfortable with those concepts before returning here. As an alternative to file_get_contents(), the file() function will create an array where each element is one line of the file:

```
$lines = file(__DIR__ . '/data/sample.txt');
print_r($lines);

Output:
Array
(
    [0] => Star Trek: Enterprise was underrated.
    [1] => The Xindi were better antagonists than the Suliban.
)
```

CHAPTER 1 GETTING STARTED

Reading an entire file in one go is fine, but might pose problems if the file concerned is particularly large. As we've seen already in the sections concerning configuration, PHP has a cap on how much memory it is allowed to allocate. Rather than dump the entire file into memory in one go, it is also possible to read and process a little at a time. Here's how to open a file and read a line at a time:

```
$handle = fopen(__DIR__ . '/data/sample.txt', 'r');
print fgets($handle);
print fgets($handle);
fclose($handle);
```

Output:
Star Trek: Enterprise was underrated.
The Xindi were better antagonists than the Suliban.

The function fopen() creates a file handle, a special type of resource variable that binds to the underlying data source (in this case the file) and is used by other functions to access that data. The first argument is the path to the file; the second is a mode parameter: 'r' for read-only (other modes include 'r+' for read/write, 'w' for write-only, and truncation to zero bytes). fgets() streams each byte of the file until it hits a newline and returns those bytes as a single PHP string. It is good practice to call fclose() on file handles that are no longer required because they consume operating system resources (file descriptors).

There's a variety of similar functions to fgets() that operate on a file handle resource, summarized below:

Table 1-5. Read functions

fgetss()	Get a line and strip HTML tags
fgetc()	Get a single character
fgetcsv()	Get a field from a delimited file format
fread()	Binary-safe file access (see Chapter 8, "Strings," for explanation of binary-safety)

There are, of course, corresponding write functions:

Table 1-6. *Write functions*

fflush()	Flushes buffered output to a file
file_put_contents()	Write data to file, either as an append or replacing entire file contents
fputs() fwrite()	Binary-safe write, appending data to the file
fputcsv()	Format an array of sub-strings to a single delimited format and append to file

In addition to reading and writing data, there are functions for performing other common filesystem operations:

Table 1-7. *Misc filesystem functions*

chmod()	Change file mode (permissions)
chown()	Change owning system account
copy()	Copy a file
delete() unlink()	Remove a file
file_exists()	Test that file or directory exists
filegroup()	Get group ownership
fileowner()	Get owning user account
fileperms()	Get permissions
filesize()	Get size in bytes
ftruncate()	Reduce file size to given length (loses data)
glob()	Find paths matching a pattern
is_readable()	Test file exists and is readable

(continued)

Table 1-7. (*continued*)

`is_writable` `is_writeable()`	Test file exists and is writ(e)able
`mkdir()`	Create a directory
`rename()`	Rename a file or directory
`rmdir()`	Delete an empty directory
`symlink()`	Create a symbolic link
`touch()`	Update access and modification times of a file will create an empty file if it doesn't exist already

If you have any familiarity at all with *nix filesystem commands, the functions above will look very familiar, which is to be expected because they are just wrappers around the system calls. Mileage may vary on Windows systems when it comes to symbolic links, which are handled very differently compared to Linux and Mac.

Remote Files and Streams

`fopen()` is not just limited to the local filesystem. By adding some more information to the path string, it is possible to access data from remote systems. Of course, it isn't possible to determine just how much data might be sent back by the other end, so I'll introduce another function: `feof()` tests a file handle to see if it is in an "EOF" (end of file) state. For local files this is simple: the file size is known, so when all bytes have been read, the handle can be set to the EOF state. For remote data, the underlying network socket has EOF set when the socket closes (remember, *nix systems abstract network data streams to the filesystem; this is what allows you to handle them like any other file):

```
$handle = fopen('https://github.com', 'r');

while (!feof($handle)) {
    print fgets($handle);
}

var_dump($handle);
fclose($handle);
var_dump($handle);
```

Output:
```
<!DOCTYPE html>
<html
  lang="en"
  data-color-mode="dark" data-dark-theme="dark"
  ...
```
```
resource(5) of type (stream)
resource(5) of type (Unknown)
```

The first argument to fopen() above is a URL (Uniform Resource Locator), as I'm sure you're aware. fopen() is able to parse this and work out a few important things: where to open the stream (by resolving the IP address of github.com), which TCP port to use (443 for https), and a few other things (the protocol handshaking required for HTTP). Be aware that this behavior is controlled by the allow_url_fopen directive in your .ini files, though it is usually enabled by default. Chapter 11, "Programming for the Internet," covers this in more detail.

Once the connection is established, the file handle is ready for use and assigned to the $handle variable. Then a simple while loop (see Chapter 4, "Logic and Control," for more info) reads from the handle a line at a time. In this case, we're simply printing out each line; a real-world program might be looking for patterns or modifying each line somehow… All of that kind of goodness is dealt with in Chapter 8, "Strings." After we're done with the handle (feof() tests the handle for EOF on every iteration of the loop), we call fclose() – you can see from the output that after this call $handle is no longer pointing to a stream.

One thing to note: handling input this way does not consume much memory, because we don't need to load the entire contents of https://github.com into memory before we start to print it out. Take a look at the following:

```
$handle = fopen('https://github.com', 'r');
while (!feof($handle)) {
    print fgets($handle);
}
var_dump(memory_get_usage());
```

Output:
```
...
int(407792)
```

Now compare it to this:

```
$handle = fopen('https://github.com', 'r');
$text = '';
while (!feof($handle)) {
    $text .= fgets($handle);
}
var_dump(memory_get_usage());
```

Output:
int(567592)

In the second example we're adding each line returned from fgets() to the $text variable, using string concatenation via the .= operator. $text accumulates (in memory) the bytes from the stream and significantly increases usage, as seen in the output.

Remote file interaction with fopen() is not limited to http. There are wrappers for many other protocols, which can be used as the scheme:// portion of a URL. They are as follows:

Table 1-8. URL schemes

file://	Explicitly access local filesystem
http:// https://	Web server access
ftp://	File Transfer Protocol
php://<stream>	Various I/O stream types (see below)
zlib://	zlib-based compression streams (requires PHP built with zlib support)
data://	RFC 2397 – data is included as part of the URL
glob://	Find paths matching a pattern
phar://	PHP Archive file format
ssh2://	Secure Shell v.2 (requires SSH2 extension)
rar://	RAR archive access (requires rar extension)
ogg://	Compressed audio (OGG/Vorbis codec, requires OGG/Vorbis extension)
expect://	Access other processes via STDIN/STDOUT/STDERR (requires Expect extension)

Which wrappers are supported on any particular PHP installation depends on a number of factors, such as installed extensions or compile-time options for PHP binaries. Full details can be found at `https://www.php.net/manual/en/wrappers.php`. The `php://` wrapper provides access to various I/O streams such as the Unix standard streams like STDOUT ("STandarD OUTput"), the 'body' data of HTTP requests, direct access to file descriptors (the operating system's way of representing files and network connections), and even memory/disk-backed temporary storage. Here's a summary of the `php://` wrappers.

Table 1-9. PHP wrapper I/O streams

`php://stdin`	Unix standard
`php://stdout`	streams `https://en.wikipedia.org/wiki/Standard_streams`
`php://stderr`	
`php://memory`	Temporary store either in memory or a temp file.
`php://temp`	
`php://input`	Read-only access to raw data for certain HTTP requests
`php://output`	Write-only access to the output buffer, similar to `print` or `echo` statements
`php://fd/n`	Direct access to file descriptor n (owned by the PHP process)
`php://filter`	Special wrapper allowing application of filters during stream access

```
$handle = fopen("php://stdout", 'w');
fwrite($handle, "Hi there!\n");
fclose($handle);
```

Output:
Hi there!

In truth we haven't accomplished anything that couldn't be done with a simple `print` statement. (`print` is a language construct that sends data to the output buffer; when PHP is running under the `cli` SAPI, the buffer is immediately flushed to the STDOUT standard stream. The code above is just skipping around the buffer.) Here's another example:

```
$handle = fopen('php://memory', 'r+');
fputs($handle, 'Live long and prosper.');
rewind($handle);
print stream_get_contents($handle);
fclose($handle);
```

Output:
Live long and prosper.

This time we're using the php://memory wrapper; bytes written to that handle (using the function fputs()) are stored in memory and are only accessible via the $handle stream resource. Part of the way a PHP stream handle works is that it maintains a pointer to a specific byte position in that stream, and after data is appended, the pointer is usually at the end of the stream. The call to fputs() has moved the pointer to the end, so we use rewind() to move the pointer back to the start, which then allows stream_get_contents() to consume all remaining bytes from the current pointer position. We'll have a look at some more stream_* functions in a moment, but first there's a special case I'd like to highlight.

The php://filter wrapper allows you to push stream data through various filters, which allows the data to be transformed before use in the program. For example, the data could be treated as text and converted to upper or lower case, or it could be handled as a zlib compressed stream and decompressed by the filter. To see a list of available filters for your installation, use the following function:

```
print_r(stream_get_filters());
```

Output:
```
Array
(
    [0] => zlib.*
    [1] => convert.iconv.*
    [2] => string.rot13
    [3] => string.toupper
    [4] => string.tolower
    ...
```

Using a filter requires the following syntax – `php://filter/read=<filter>/resource=<file_or_url>` – like so:

```
$text = file_get_contents(
    'php://filter/read=string.toupper/resource=./data/sample.txt'
);
print $text;
```

Output:
STAR TREK: ENTERPRISE WAS UNDERRATED.
THE XINDI WERE BETTER ANTAGONISTS THAN THE SULIBAN.

Stream Functions

The functions we've seen already in this section (such as `fopen()`, `fgets()`, `file_get_contents()`, and so on) all work on the principle of obtaining a special resource variable that represents a stream. If it hasn't become apparent by now, let's explicitly state what a stream actually is. At its most fundamental, a stream is simply a sequence of bytes. The bytes encode data, which becomes information when that data is handled in the correct context. Later chapters will expand on this idea; for now, just understand that streams are how programs send and receive data. The PHP stream resource, also known as "file handle" (even when that "file" is an abstraction of something else), has mechanisms built into it for operations such as consuming bytes, moving the pointer around, appending bytes, flushing, filtering, and so on. PHP has dozens of stream functions, which are intended to provide interfaces for controlling those stream operations.

I could at this point spend dozens of pages detailing all of the stream functions and no doubt put most readers to sleep or, worse, put them off the book entirely. So let's not do that – at this stage, there's more fundamental things to cover, like numbers, strings, arrays, functions, objects, and much more. However, once those fundamentals are in place, it might be a good idea to take a look at PHP's streams API. One day you might need to write PHP that can take dozens of gigabytes of data, transform it, and serve it to an HTTP client, and using streams becomes necessary to work around memory limitations. Here's a small selection of stream functions and a description of what they do, and you can learn more about them at `https://www.php.net/manual/en/ref.stream.php`

Table 1-10. Stream functions

stream_socket_client()	Connect to an Internet or Unix domain socket
stream_socket_server()	Create an Internet or Unix server socket – allows clients to connect to your program
stream_socket_recvfrom()	Receive data from a server socket
stream_socket_shutdown()	Close the server socket
stream_filter_register	Register a user-defined class as a stream filter (like php://filter)
stream_filter_prepend() stream_filter_append()	Attach a registered filter to a stream
stream_filter_remove()	Remove a filter

There is one more form of I/O, which you will see a great deal of when working on PHP web applications: databases. At heart these are just another form of stream (usually a network connection or via a Unix domain socket file if the database server is running on the same machine) but have their own sets of specialized modules in PHP, which we'll be looking at next.

Databases

Data persistence (making sure data hangs around after your program is done) generally boils down to two forms: filesystem and database. It's perfectly fine to store data in files, and in fact, PHP can do that automatically for some types of data associated with HTTP requests. For example, user session data, as we'll see in Chapter 11, "Programming for the Internet." However, managing complex data becomes challenging quite quickly if everything is backed by files. Chapter 10, "Programming with Objects," will introduce concepts such as *domain modeling*, where software components are created to model the reality of the problem that the software is designed to solve. Usually those components represent real things such as people, places, and actions, and require that data records for those entities be maintained. Imagine spreading thousands of files across a complex filesystem layout and having to manage it every time the application serviced a request... It would be quite a headache.

The definition of a database could also be applied to a filesystem: databases are simply a structured set of data held on a computer. In a way, filesystems are also databases. However, when we talk about databases in terms of applications, we normally mean an RDBMS (Relational Database Management System) such as `mysql` or `mariadb`, although there are other types such as "NoSQL" databases like `mongodb` (which are unstructured document collections). Such systems do actually store data to the filesystem, ultimately, though not in formats intended to be readable by other software. They also offer a great deal of other functionality for ensuring consistency, replication (where multiple databases can be used to serve the same data), indexing (specialized data structures to greatly speed up searching), and aggregation (functionality for grouping, counting, sorting, and so on).

This section is not going to be a comprehensive guide to DB programming. That's a topic for an entire book, and indeed there are plenty of them that focus on just that. What we will be doing here is setting up a simple RDBMS (using Docker, of course!) and showcasing some of the tools that PHP offers for interacting with it. Let's start by bringing up a containerized instance of `mariadb` (a popular fork of the well-known MySQL RDBMS). We'll be using a `docker-compose.yaml` approach just as we did for `nginx` earlier, which is overkill because there's only one container being "orchestrated." You can work out the command line equivalent as an exercise, if you prefer!

One final word of warning: this section is going to use some very basic object-oriented features of PHP. If you're not comfortable with the concepts of objects or classes, you could always return to this part of the book after reading Chapter 6, "Object Fundamentals."

Launching the DB

First of all, we need a simple `docker-compose.yaml` file:

```
version: "3"
services:
  db:
    image: mariadb:lts
    container_name: mariadb
    ports:
      - "3306:3306"
```

```
    environment:
      MYSQL_ROOT_PASSWORD: root123
      MYSQL_DATABASE: testdb
```

This contains enough information to launch a minimally configured `mariadb` server container, using the `lts` (Long Term Support) tagged image. The environment variables ensure it starts with an empty database called `testdb`, and the password for the `root` account is "`root123`". We'll need these for the connection information in a moment. To start the server, simply invoke `docker compose up` in the directory where the `.yaml` exists.

```
$ docker compose up
...
 ✓ Network mariadb_default   Created
 ✓ Container mariadb         Created
Attaching to mariadb
mariadb  | 2025-08-28 11:09:07+00:00 [Note] [Entrypoint]: Entrypoint script for MariaDB Server 1:11.4.3+maria~ubu2404 started.
...
```

There will be quite a few lines of output, plus the usual image-pull noise if this is the first time you've ever used the `mariadb:lts` image. This container is attached to the shell (`stdin`, etc.) you ran the docker command in, and it will continue to output its logs as it is used. That's fine for our purposes; just leave this running and open up a new command shell.

Connecting with PDO

The next thing we'll do is use PHP's PDO extension to connect to the server. You'll need to ensure that the necessary modules are installed:

```
$ php -m |grep -i 'pdo'
PDO
pdo_mysql
```

Both the `PDO` and `pdo_mysql` modules must be installed (grab them with your system package manager if not). If you are using the Docker images from this book's public Github repository, then these modules are already present in the image. To establish a connection to the server, we create a new instance of the PDO PHP class and pass it some arguments. The first is a connection DSN (Data Source Name), then the account name followed by the password. The DSN will vary depending on how you are running PHP.

If it is installed as a package on your system:

```
$pdo = new PDO(
    'mysql:host=127.0.0.1;port=3306;dbname=testdb',
    'root',
    'root123'
);
```

If you are running PHP inside a container, you'll need to make sure you can connect to the maridb container on the local loopback address 127.0.0.1 by ensuring the PHP container is using the host network. Here's a reminder of the Docker command alias from earlier in the chapter:

```
$ alias docker-php='docker run -it --rm --net=host -p 8000:8000 -v "$PWD":/usr/src/myapp -w /usr/src/myapp php:8.4-cli php'
```

In either case, the PHP code above is creating an instance of a PDO object; the strings in the parentheses are the constructor arguments (data that is used to build the object), and all of this is covered in Chapter 3, "Functions" (where function arguments and parameters are explained), and Chapter 6, "Object Fundamentals" (which explains how objects and classes work). For now, you just need to know that the first argument – 'mysql:host=127.0.0.1;port=3306;dbname=testdb' – is the connection DSN (Data Source Name), which breaks down into sections like so:

Table 1-11. DSN components

mysql:	The "driver" required – this tells PDO that we're communicating with a server that "speaks"MySQL
host=...	Where to contact the server, which can be an IP address, hostname, etc.
port=...	The TCP port on which the server is listening (MySQL defaults to TCP 3306)
dbname=...	The database we wish to use

CHAPTER 1   GETTING STARTED

The second and third arguments are credentials: username and password, respectively. One gotcha to watch out for is the `host=...` section: if this is set to `host=localhost` - and you have a *nix system - then PHP will try to connect to the database via a special file (called a Unix Domain Socket) and not a TCP port, the source of a number of questions on https://stackoverflow.com

Executing Statements

Now that we have a PDO connection to the DB, we can run some MySQL statements. Right now the `testdb` database is empty, so we're going to create a table, which is how MySQL stores data. Think of tables as being a bit like spreadsheets; they have columns and rows - the columns are the fields, and each row is a record:

```
$sql = <<< SQL
CREATE TABLE IF NOT EXISTS `test` (
    `id` int(10) NOT NULL AUTO_INCREMENT,
    `message` varchar(255) NOT NULL,
    PRIMARY KEY (`id`)
) ENGINE=InnoDB AUTO_INCREMENT=1
SQL;

$pdo->exec($sql);
```

This example uses a HEREDOC string (all explained in Chapter 8, "Strings") to build a MySQL statement using the `<<<` operator. The funny-looking `$pdo->exec()` is a bit like a function call, but the function belongs to an object. (We are jumping a little bit ahead of ourselves here; all these language features are explained in the relevant chapters, and I promise not to do this again! Probably.) The SQL itself is a `CREATE TABLE` statement, which defines the `test` table with two columns: `id` and `message`. We can check the result of this by accessing the running DB server (with, you guessed it, another docker command) and running an SQL query from the cli:

```
$ docker exec -it mariadb mariadb -uroot -proot123 testdb
...
MariaDB [testdb]> DESC test;
```

```
+---------+--------------+------+-----+---------+----------------+
| Field   | Type         | Null | Key | Default | Extra          |
+---------+--------------+------+-----+---------+----------------+
| id      | int(10)      | NO   | PRI | NULL    | auto_increment |
| message | varchar(255) | NO   |     | NULL    |                |
+---------+--------------+------+-----+---------+----------------+
2 rows in set (0.002 sec)
```

Next we can add some data to the table...

```
$pdo->exec("INSERT INTO test(`message`) VALUES('some text')");
$pdo->exec("INSERT INTO test(`message`) VALUES('some more text')");
$pdo->exec("INSERT INTO test(`message`) VALUES('even more text')");
```

... and confirm the results in the mariadb cli:

```
MariaDB [testdb]> SELECT * FROM test;
+----+----------------+
| id | message        |
+----+----------------+
|  1 | some text      |
|  2 | some more text |
|  3 | even more text |
+----+----------------+
3 rows in set (0.001 sec)
```

Selecting Results

SQL is a declarative language: rather than issue step-by-step instructions, instead the desired results are described, and the query engine makes the internal decisions about how to create the result set. When we want to retrieve a set of data from the DB, we need to use a SELECT statement; the method for doing this with PDO is a little different from what we've seen so far. $pdo->exec() simply runs the SQL in its argument and will only return a count of affected rows. To actually get data, we use $pdo->query():

```
$stmt = $pdo->query('SELECT * FROM test');
var_dump($stmt);

Output:
object(PDOStatement)#2 (1) {
  ["queryString"]=>
  string(18) "SELECT * FROM test"
}
```

The query() method returns an instance of PDOStatement, which we can use to iterate over the results. SELECT * FROM test simply means "return all fields for all rows in the test database." Here they are

```
foreach ($stmt as $item) {
    print "id: {$item['id']}, message: {$item['message']}" . PHP_EOL;
}
Output:
id: 1, message: some text
id: 2, message: some more text
id: 3, message: even more text
```

The foreach () language construct accesses the $stmt object, which supports array access and returns one row for every loop iteration. These concepts are explained in detail in Chapter 5, "Array," and Chapter 4, "Logic and Control."

Prepared Statements

For additional security, it is advisable to never put user input directly into database queries. A malicious user could write their own SQL code, knowing it will be inserted into one of your own queries: these are known as *injection attacks*, and we'll look at them in more detail in Chapter 11, "Programming for the Internet." The PDO API has the facility to automatically sanitize user input in the form of *prepared statements*, and it's generally a good idea to just use them everywhere:

```
$stmt = $pdo->prepare('SELECT message FROM test WHERE id = :id');
$id = 3;
$stmt->bindParam(':id', $id);
```

```
$stmt->execute();
var_dump($stmt->fetchAll(PDO::FETCH_ASSOC));

Output:
array(1) {
  [0]=>
  array(1) {
    ["message"]=>
    string(14) "even more text"
  }
}
```

The key to this is `$pdo->prepare()` which returns a `PDOStatement`, and `$stmt->bindParam()`. The initial query contains a token `:id`, and `->bindParam(':id', $id)` substitutes that token for the value of `$id` in a safe way: any malicious code would be wrapped in special quotes by the time it reaches the DB, rendering it non-functional (you'll likely get errors or just empty results back). `->execute()` does what it says and executes the query on the DB server, and `->fetchAll()` returns the entire set of results in one go (as an associative array thanks to the `PDO::FETCH_ASSOC` argument). We've jumped ahead of ourselves a little here in that there are concepts of object access and variable use that we've yet to cover; you can always revisit this section once you've read the relevant chapters.

These are the bare essentials for database interaction but should be enough to get you started at a basic level of safety and security. PDO is pretty much the standard interface that most PHP code uses for DB interaction; you can find the documentation for it at `https://www.php.net/manual/en/book.pdo.php`

Summary

Hopefully after reading this chapter and following the examples, you now have a fully working PHP environment! Whether you are using Linux, Mac, or Windows, you should be able to at least run PHP interactively with `php -a` and follow along with the examples. You also have the option of accessing this book's code examples at `https://github.com/paultregoing/ExploringPHP8`, and this repository also contains Dockerfiles, which you can use to build images based on the public `php-cli` images. These docker images are what I have used to write this book and should contain all the necessary modules and configuration for things to work seamlessly.

We also looked at the fundamentals of getting data into and out of your PHP programs and touched briefly (very briefly) on the concept of data streams, which will make a lot more sense once you've read Chapter 7, "Numbers," and Chapter 8, "Strings." We also had a brief introduction to databases and PHP's PDO extension. I hope you've enjoyed this first chapter!

CHAPTER 2

Data, Types, and Variables

When we write software, it is typically used for the transformation and transmission of data so that it can become information. The device that runs our programs (the hardware upon which our systems run) isn't aware of concepts such as human language or the protocols that drive the internet. Data is simply a sequence of bytes: a stream of ones and zeroes. Those byte values only become information when they are evaluated in their proper context. For example, consider the following sequence of bytes.

Binary:

01001000 01000101 01001100 01001100 01001111 00100000 01010111 01001111 01010010 01001100 01000100

Hex:

0x48 0x45 0x4C 0x4C 0x4F 0x20 0x57 0x4F 0x52 0x4C 0x44

This is raw data, and I bet you're having a hard time extracting information from it, right? Those 1's and 0's are relatively meaningless to humans, as are the corresponding hexadecimal values unless we know what they're for. (If you're unsure what a hexadecimal number is, Chapter 7, "Numbers," explains about different number bases.) If we decide to convert them to text using an encoding system called ASCII (American Standard Code for Information Interchange – which has been around even longer than I have) – then information emerges.

ASCII is a system for encoding characters into numbers; each numerical byte value corresponds to a character, and the table of byte value to character mappings is called a *codepage*. More modern codepages (such as Unicode) use longer byte sequences, but the most widely used (UTF-8) is a superset of ASCII (in order to preserve compatibility with older systems). We will examine the handling of text data in greater detail in a later chapter.

CHAPTER 2 DATA, TYPES, AND VARIABLES

For now, take a look at Table 2-1.

Table 2-1. *Character ordinal values*

Character	Hex	Binary
H	0x48	01001000
E	0x45	01000101
L	0x4C	01001100
L	0x4C	01001100
O	0x4F	01001111
<SPACE>	0x20	00100000
W	0x57	01010111
O	0x4F	01001111
R	0x52	01010010
L	0x4C	01001100
D	0x44	01000100

A few people might be able to read the raw binary data and convert it to text in their head (and those people exist; I've met a few over the years), but the rest of us need software to do the job. If your program reads those bytes as text (e.g., when outputting via a print statement), then you should see "HELLO WORLD" as the output. Applications designed for the display of text data handle the interpretation for us, and all we need to worry about is the actual reading and understanding part.

Likewise, programs that perform mathematics will usually treat their data as numerical. If we take the byte values from our example above and interpret the first four as an integer (a whole number), then we get the numerical value of 1280066888, or 1212501068, depending on which end of the byte sequence the CPU starts at (this is known as "big-endian" versus "little-endian"). Modern computers generally use at least four bytes to store an integer.

Binary:
01001000 01000101 01001100 01001100

Hex:
0x48 0x45 0x4c 0x4c

Integer:
1280066888 // on a little-endian CPU e.g. Intel
1212501068 // on a big-endian CPU

We can see that the same data – the same byte sequence – can represent different information depending on the context in which it is evaluated. Programming languages will generally store metadata (data about the data) about their data values. One of the most fundamentally important pieces of metadata is something called *data type*.

Data types are attributes that an interpreter (in our case, the PHP binary) or compiler uses to determine which operations can be safely performed on that data; "safe" in this case meaning "do what is expected." Numerical types can have mathematical operations performed on them, strings can be combined and searched, booleans are used in logical expressions, and so on.

The corollary to this is that non-compatible types and operations require that either the data type is changed to something compatible or the operation is prevented (usually causing termination of the program; in PHP's case, a "Fatal error" message is often the resulting output). How this comes about might depend on the language or the way the language is configured to behave when the program compiles or runs. There are usually also limitations on which type conversions are possible.

PHP 8 Data Types

Some languages, like C, are *strongly typed* (also known as *strictly* or *statically* typed). When variables are declared in C, they must always have a type declaration, and operations that are incompatible with the data type will cause errors. If you wish to treat a sequence of characters as a number, in C, it first has to be converted (or *cast*) to the required type.

PHP, however, is a *dynamically typed* (also known as *loosely* or *weakly* typed) language. It isn't necessary to declare type when creating a PHP variable; in fact, the language doesn't even have the syntax for doing this. PHP will automatically determine the data type for you from the values supplied when creating the variable, as we shall see later in the chapter.

PHP will also helpfully (or not so helpfully in some cases) *coerce* (automatically cast) data types for you when required. This can happen when certain operations require it; for example, a string might contain numerical characters, and if used in a mathematical operation (operations are discussed in the next section), it will be coerced to a numerical type (as we'll see in a later section of this chapter). PHP also has a type declaration system for functions. The inputs of functions can have their data types declared, and PHP will attempt to coerce incoming data at runtime if their types do not match. This is covered in depth in Chapter 3, "Functions."

The base data types used in PHP are as follows:

- `null`
- `bool` (boolean `true` or `false`)
- `integer` (a whole number, e.g., `123`)
- `float` (a number with a decimal point, e.g., `1.23`)
- `string` (a sequence of characters, e.g., `"Hello world"`)
- `array` (a collection of data)
- `object` (an instance of a class)
- `callable` (can be executed)
- `resource` (see below)

The first five types listed above are examples of *scalar* data. Scalars hold a single value: a boolean will be either true or false, an integer holds a single whole-number value, and so on. Strings, numbers, and booleans are commonly known as *primitive* types and are the building blocks of more complex data. Those of you with prior programming experience might be aware of IEEE (and other) standards concerning how computers store data, particularly numbers. PHP abstracts those types to the ones given above, but the underlying implementation does vary across different systems. This is covered in more detail in Chapter 7, "Numbers," and Chapter 8, "Strings."

Arrays and objects are *compound*, or *composite*, data types. They collect together multiple instances of other types – either scalars, other compound types, or a mixture of the two. (Unlike some strictly typed languages, PHP is quite happy to mix types in an array.)

callable data is *invokable*; it can be executed. Functions in PHP are *first class* (like in other languages such as JavaScript), which means they can be handled just like any other data, in that variables can reference them, and they can be passed into (and returned by) functions. Chapter 3, "Functions," and Chapter 6, "Object Fundamentals," explain these concepts in more detail.

Finally, the special case: a resource is an old concept in PHP that denotes a variable that refers to an external resource. A typical PHP application might read or write to files, send data to an FTP server, interact with databases, and so on. In previous versions of PHP file descriptors, network sockets, database handles, and so on were represented by variables with the data type of resource. Many resource types are now being phased out in PHP 8 and replaced by dedicated classes.

Although it isn't possible to declare a variable's type when creating it, it is possible to place restrictions on the types that a function (or object method) will accept as input and/or return as output. The type declaration system in PHP greatly expands on the base types presented here; full details are given in Chapter 3, "Functions."

Operations and Calls

Programs are written to manipulate data and transform it into information. The most fundamental form of data manipulation is an *operation*, that is, the use of *operators* to change, copy, or compare data values. An operation can look like this: x = 1 + 1 (which adds the values 1 and 1, then assigns the result to the symbol x), or this: x == y (compares the values of x and y and evaluates to a boolean true or false). There are many built-in operators in PHP; we'll examine them in their respective chapters (arithmetic operators are covered in Chapter 7, "Numbers," string operators in Chapter 8, "Strings," and so on).

A *call* occurs when control is passed to a subprogram within your main program, usually via a function or object method. Often this is done with data being sent to the subprogram from the calling code, and new data is usually returned when the function has completed its work. Calls look like this: someFunction($var); – the callable unit is someFunction, the parentheses indicate it should be executed, and the variable $var is being given to the call so it is available for use in the callable code. It is generally good practice to restrict the types of data the call will accept and declare the type of the return data. PHP's built-in functions and methods are normally type restricted for both incoming data (the arguments) and return data. It is also possible to define input and return types for user-defined calls too.

When a variable's type is incompatible with an operation or call, it is necessary to change it. For example, mathematical operations (such as + or *) work on numbers, and string concatenation (e.g., "hello" . " world") requires string data. This is either done explicitly by the programmer or implicitly by the PHP engine, as mentioned previously. Casting a scalar to another scalar is always possible, with some caveats on what the result might be. Casting compound types to scalar or other compound types isn't usually so straightforward, as we shall see.

PHP will attempt to change scalar data types to suit the call or operation, so the programmer generally does not need to worry about explicitly changing types. This can lead to problems if you are not aware of the rules that PHP will follow. It is also possible to prevent scalar type changes during calls; this is explained in Chapter 3, "Functions."

Converting Data Types

Let's have a quick demonstration of what we've covered so far and play around a bit with data types to see what's really happening.

We're going to use the largest unsigned 16-bit number, *65535*, and the numerical string "65535." If you're not sure what "unsigned" means in this context, the detailed explanation can be found early on in Chapter 7, "Numbers"; for now, just accept that it means we don't use up a bit to indicate if the number is positive or negative: unsigned integers are always positive.

PHP will happily switch back and forth between a number and a numerical string as required by the context in which the variable is used. This is known as *type juggling* or *type coercion*; here's a quick demonstration:

```
$str = '65535';
$int = 65535;

var_dump($str);
var_dump($int);

var_dump($int . ' is the largest 16-bit unsigned int.');
// . means 'concatenate these strings'.
var_dump($str + 1); // + means "add these two numbers together".
```

Output:
string(5) "65535"
int(65535)
string(41) "65535 is the largest 16-bit unsigned int."
int(65536)

When we perform a string operation (concatenation) using the integer $int, it is converted to an equivalent numeric string, and the expression evaluates to a string. Conversely, a mathematical operation (addition) using the string $str gives an integer value (and to achieve this, the integer equivalent of $str was used). PHP is quite happy to accept either type and convert as necessary. In this example, the integer *65535* was converted to the string '65535' during the expression $int . ' is the largest 16-bit unsigned int.', and vice versa when we added *1* to $str.

It is important to note that when a variable's type is converted (to suit the context it is used in), the original variable remains unchanged. PHP will substitute a type-converted value in the expression, then perform the operation:

var_dump($int . ' is the largest 16-bit unsigned int.');
var_dump($int);

Output:
string(41) "65535 is the largest 16-bit unsigned int."
int(65535)

In the example above, we can see that $int is still an integer after being used in a string context.

PHP's type coercion is a high-level abstraction of equivalence. In reality the data are quite different when the machine performing the operations is taken into consideration. Let's see how these two values are really represented.

Different Types, Different Data

To get the values of the bytes used to store our 16-bit number, we can use PHP's built-in dechex() function. This function takes integer input and returns a string containing the hexadecimal representation of that number.

CHAPTER 2 DATA, TYPES, AND VARIABLES

```
var_dump(dechex($int));
```

Output:
```
string(4) "ffff"
```

We can see that the decimal value *65535* is equivalent to the hexadecimal number *ffff*, which would be stored in memory as the bytes 0xff 0xff. The specific bytes stored for a single PHP integer would be at least 0x00 0x00 0xff 0xff (for a 32-bit system) – see Chapter 7, "Numbers," for more information.

We can do something similar to get the byte values for the string '65535', but first we need to use the built-in function ord(), which converts a character to its ordinal value in the ASCII codepage as a decimal. (Given that we've already seen how ASCII encodes characters to single bytes, it should already be apparent that the byte values for the numerical string are not going to be equivalent to the byte values of the integer, based on size alone!)

```
$byte1 = dechex(ord('6'));
$byte2 = dechex(ord('5'));
$byte3 = dechex(ord('5'));
$byte4 = dechex(ord('3'));
$byte5 = dechex(ord('5'));

var_dump($byte1 . $byte2 . $byte3 . $byte4 . $byte5);
```

Output:
```
string(10) "3635353335"
```

The code above might look a little intimidating to a novice programmer, but fear not, it's relatively straightforward. We're making five calls to ord(), one for each character in our string, because the ord() function only works with single characters. Each of those ord() calls is wrapped in a call to dechex() because ord() gives the decimal codepage value, and it's the hexadecimal value we need for comparison. As you can see, we're dealing with two very different pieces of data: *65535* is stored as 0x00 0x00 0xff 0xff (on a 32-bit system), and '65535' is stored as 0x36 0x35 0x35 0x33 0x35.

When we used an integer in a string operation (and a string in a mathematical operation), PHP transformed the data. This was necessary because 0xff 0xff expressed as a string is 'ÿÿ', and 0x36 0x35 0x35 0x33 0x35 expressed as an integer is *232820912949* (or something of similar magnitude depending on CPU architecture).

As PHP programmers, we don't need to worry too much about any of this low-level stuff (maybe buy a drink for the next assembly programmer you encounter), but it's good to know what's going on and why.

Pitfalls of Automatic Conversion

Hopefully the previous few examples have demonstrated how much is really happening when types are converted. PHP's automatic juggling of types is certainly convenient: we've just seen how we can treat numerical strings as numbers, or numbers as strings, and we didn't need to do anything special in our code to make that happen. There are also mechanisms for explicitly converting types (we'll see some in a bit), which trigger the same data changes.

This is great when it works, but there are times when it either doesn't work at all (usually emitting an error) or, worse, there are times when conversion is successful but with unintended results. Let's look at a few examples.

Casting composite types to scalar usually results in some form of error and possible termination of the program. Here's what happens when we try to use an array as a string or an integer:

```
var_dump("This is what happens when we stringify an array: " . ['an', 'array']);
var_dump(['an', 'array'] + 1);
```

Output:
```
Warning: Array to string conversion
string(54) "This is what happens when we stringify an array: Array"
Fatal error: Uncaught TypeError: Unsupported operand types: array + int
```

Using an array in a string context gives us a warning, but we at least get a usable (but not necessarily useful) string as the result, and our code continues to run. The mathematical operation that followed had an unhappier outcome: a fatal TypeError was emitted.

Using objects in a scalar context gives similarly poor results:

```
var_dump("This is what happens when we stringify an object: " . new stdClass());
```

Output:
```
Fatal error: Uncaught Error: Object of class stdClass could not be converted to string
```

In all of these composite-to-scalar examples we have legal PHP syntax. Linting this code with `php -l` would not indicate any issues, though other tools would highlight the problem (a good IDE would draw attention to the fact that an array is an illegal operand type in addition).

It isn't difficult to see why composite values are problematic in scalar contexts; they are fundamentally different types of, well, types. Casting scalars to other scalar types, on the other hand, is quite common (that's how I started this section off, after all). This is where PHP can get a little wonky, and in fact some effort has been made in PHP 8 to reduce the edge cases that have in the past led to bugs and security vulnerabilities.

We've already seen that strings can behave like number types. A string is considered to be numeric if it meets certain criteria. Namely, if it contains only digit characters (and a single decimal point for floats), with the exception that the number can have any amount of leading or trailing spaces, tabs, or newline characters (line feed, carriage return, etc.). So `"123"` is numeric (`"123"` and `"123"` would be equivalent), and `"100 Dalmatians"` is not, albeit with a rather hefty caveat. Here's a more fleshed-out demonstration, which we'll run twice, once for PHP 7.4 and again for PHP 8:

```
var_dump(is_numeric("123"));
var_dump(is_numeric("100 Dalmatians"));
var_dump("123" + 1);
var_dump("123" + 0.1);
var_dump("100 Dalmatians" + 1);
var_dump("Five-hundred" + 1);
```

Output: (PHP 7.4)
```
bool(true)
bool(false)
int(124)
float(123.1)
```

```
PHP Notice:  A non well formed numeric value encountered
int(101)
PHP Warning:  A non-numeric value encountered
int(1)

Output: (PHP 8.4)
bool(true)
bool(false)
int(124)
float(123.1)
Warning: A non-numeric value encountered
int(101)
Fatal error: Uncaught TypeError: Unsupported operand types: string + int
```

The first two lines demonstrate what PHP considers a numeric string to be, using its built-in is_numeric() function. We then use those strings in various operations: adding an integer to "123" means the string behaves like an integer, and adding a float coerces it to a float.

Things get more interesting when we use "100 Dalmatians": despite the fact that it is not strictly numeric, it does contain the number *100*, and, for better or worse, PHP allows that number to be extracted and used in numerical expressions, as we can see from the output. We're able to take the value *100* from the string and add a number to it, returning an integer value of 101. Granted, we get a notice message when that happens, but the code continues to execute.

We're also able, with PHP 7.4, to use a numberless string as a number in the expression "Five-hundred." In this case, the string is cast to the integer 0. This particular feature of PHP has led to issues in the past: in PHP 7.4 and earlier, the expression "a string" == 0 evaluates to true; combine this with the not-unusual practice of using integers 1 and 0 as substitutes for booleans, and we have a potential recipe for logical errors. PHP 8, however, has done away with this oddity; "a string" == 0 now evaluates to false, and the expression "Five-hundred" + 1 is illegal and emits a TypeError.

There's a lot more to say on the topic of type coercion in PHP, and in particular the edge cases and weird behavior to watch out for, which we'll review in this chapter and again where relevant.

CHAPTER 2   DATA, TYPES, AND VARIABLES

Variables

All programs, no matter how humble, need to manipulate data at some point in their lifecycle. Even the most universally simple program contains data. Here's a PHP version of the venerable "hello world."

```
echo "Hello World";
```

Output:
Hello World

The text between the double-quote characters is the data, a string literal, and the `echo` keyword is an instruction to output that data. Exactly where this data goes depends on how PHP is executing on your system. In a Unix/Linux shell context (where PHP is running in the `cli` or `cli-server` SAPI), the data will output to STDOUT (which is normally displayed in your console window).

"Hello world" is a nice way to confirm PHP is installed correctly, but not very useful beyond that. Real Programs™ will need to store, retrieve, and perform operations on their data. In the example above, after `echo` has done its work, the data is gone. If we needed to reuse that string of characters, we'd need to type it out again. What if you wanted to keep hold of it for future use or combine it with other data?

To persist data within your program, you'll need to create variables. These are used to store and retrieve data. In PHP, the `$` character prepended to a string forms the *symbolic name* used to read and write data to a memory address (don't worry, PHP manages memory assignment for you; no need to worry about things like stack and heap here).

```
$txt = "Hello World";

echo $txt;
```

Output:
Hello World

Let's break down what's happening. We define a *string literal* - `"Hello world"` - and assign this data to the variable `$txt`. Under the hood, PHP will deal with allocating memory and storing the data, determining its type, and keeping track of it via the `$txt` variable name. We then use this variable with the language construct `echo`. PHP retrieves the data from memory and uses it as per the normal behavior of `echo`, which sends the string of text for display somewhere.

Should you need to remove a variable so that it is no longer available in your program, use the built-in unset() function:

```
$txt = "Hello world";
unset($txt);
echo $txt;
```

```
Output:
Warning: Undefined variable $txt
```

Legal Variable Names

PHP only allows specific characters to be combined with the $ character to form variables. A legal variable name (the characters immediately after the $) starts with an underscore or ASCII letter, followed by any number of underscores, numbers, or ASCII letters. By "ASCII letter," I mean byte values 0x41 (A) to 0xff (ÿ) – be aware that not all of these are printable characters (e.g., 0x7f is a control character, and 0x80 does not have a symbol). And yes, you really can have any number of (legal) characters in a variable name; you'll commonly see these in generated code (e.g., the excellent Twig templating library).

The variable names you choose should be limited by good sense and the possible threat of violence from your team members. In addition to these rules, any good PHP project will be following some form of coding standard (e.g., PSR-12 – see https://www.php-fig.org/psr/psr-12/), which may further restrict your choices. The PSR standards (PSR-1 and PSR-12 to be precise) don't impose any particular limits on variable names, but the general convention is to use $camelCase.

Here are some examples of legal variables in PHP:

- $foo
- $_4
- $ÿ
- $__internal_0abebc74dd811fd7b4cfa4c6a2fdf870d7723c04e8d
  af6926b04914d6644935f;

CHAPTER 2 DATA, TYPES, AND VARIABLES

That last one should really only be created by another program. Here's an illegal variable declaration and the resulting error:

```
$4 = 4; // illegal, starts with a number
```

Output:
Parse error: syntax error, unexpected integer "4", expecting variable or "{" or "$"

Finally, variable names are case sensitive, as the following code demonstrates:

```
$variable = 'some text';
echo $vArIaBLe . PHP_EOL;
```

Output:
Warning: Undefined variable $vArIaBLe

Assigning Values and Types

Remember that earlier in the chapter, we examined the dynamic nature of PHP's data typing system? I mentioned that a variable's type is determined when its value is assigned, so let's look at that in more detail.

Scalar Types

```
$myString = "a string";
$myNumericString = "1";
$myInt = 1;
$myFloat = 1.1;
$myBool = true;
$myNull = null;

var_dump($myString);
var_dump($myNumericString);
var_dump($myInt);
var_dump($myFloat);
var_dump($myBool);
var_dump($myNull);
```

Output:
>string(8) "a string"
>string(1) "1"
>int(1)
>float(1.1)
>bool(true)
>NULL

When the PHP interpreter encounters a single-quote or double-quote character, it chooses the string data type for the variable $myString, even if the contents of the string are purely numerical, as in $myNumericalString. Similarly, the presence of a decimal point in the assignment of the literal number 1.1 to $myFloat means that the type has to be float; a non-decimal number will always be assigned as an int. Finally, true (or false) can only mean a boolean type, and null is null – this scalar type has only one possible value.

Compound Types

$myArray = [1, "two", true];
$myObj = new stdClass();

var_dump($myArray);
var_dump($myObj);

Output:
array(3) {
  [0]=>
  int(1)
  [1]=>
  string(3) "two"
  [2]=>
  bool(true)
}
object(stdClass)#1 (0) {
}

There's less guesswork here; the square bracket notation $myArray = [ ] always means an array, and the new keyword always denotes an instance of an object (in this case an instance of the PHP built-in stdClass). Arrays are covered in detail in Chapter 5, "Array," stdClass (and objects) are introduced in Chapter 6, "Object Fundamentals."

The Special (Resource) Type

```
$fh = fopen(__FILE__, "r");
var_dump($fh);
```

```
Output:
resource(5) of type (stream)
```

Here we're using the built-in fopen() function, which takes a filename (including path) and opens it (in this case for reading). The expression __FILE__ is a built-in constant, which evaluates to the current file that contains the source code being executed. We'll look at constants properly in a moment.

The variable $fh is reported by var_dump() as being a stream resource, a special type that can be used to access a continuous stream of bytes. Resource types are increasingly rare in PHP due to the drive to replace them with dedicated built-in classes. As of PHP 8.2 fopen() (which will open files or network sockets – Linux-based systems use the filesystem to abstract all sorts of data exchange mechanisms, including network sockets) still returns a stream resource, but this will likely change in a future release of the language.

Forcing Type Changes

We've already seen PHP's type coercion mechanism demonstrated, showing how types would be converted automatically depending on the operation or call being made. I also mentioned it was possible to explicitly control type conversion. Here's how to do it:

```
$num = '123';
var_dump($num);

$num = (int) $num;
var_dump($num);
```

Output:
string(3) "123"
int(123)

Just as we did in the previous section, we initialize a numeric string. PHP chooses the string type based on syntax, in this case the enclosing quote characters. Then we use the int data type in parentheses on the leftmost side of an assignment. Now we can see that $num is an integer. We can also do this on variable initialization:

```
$myNum = (string) 123;
$myNumStr = (int) "123";
$myFloatStr = (float) "1.23";
$myAlphaNumStr = (int) "123abc";

var_dump($myNum);
var_dump($myNumStr);
var_dump($myFloatStr);
var_dump($myAlphaNumStr);
```

Output:
string(3) "123"
int(123)
float(1.23)
int(123)

By putting the name of the desired type in parentheses before the literal value, we force the value to be cast to that type. $myNum would, without the (string), otherwise be an int, $myNumStr likewise would have been a string. Pay attention to $myAlphaNumStr, see how PHP has discarded the letters? All these type conversions have a set of rules that govern equivalence. This is particularly important when comparing values or testing for truthiness, which we explore in more detail in Chapter 4, "Logic and Control."

You are free to use type casting whenever a variable would be valid syntax in an expression. We've seen casting on initialization above; it can also be done during operations and function calls:

```
$expr = (string) 3 . ' is the magic number';
var_dump($expr);
var_dump((int) '123');
```

Output:
```
string(21) "3 is the magic number"
int(123)
```

It is also possible, with some caveats, to cast to and from compound types.

Constants

Some data doesn't need to change value or needs to be prevented from changing value. For these cases, we have constants. As the name suggests, these are fixed values and will retain the data they were initialized with for the lifecycle of your program. Constants can be declared anywhere in your source code and are available globally, which means they are accessible no matter where in your code you access them from.

Defining a Constant

Use the built-in function define() to create a new constant. define() expects two input values: a string, which will be the constant name, and then the value. The value can be any scalar, an array, null, or a resource. Objects (including iterables and callables, which are just special kinds of objects) are not permitted. Prior to PHP 7.3, it was possible to define a constant and make it case insensitive. This is now deprecated, and all constants are case sensitive. By convention, constant names are uppercase and words are separated by underscores:

```
define('MY_STR', "You can't change me");
define('MY_INT', 123);
define('MY_FLOAT', 1.23);
define('MY_ARRAY', []);
define('MY_RESOURCE', fopen(__FILE__, "r"));
define('MY_NULL', null);

var_dump(MY_STR);
var_dump(MY_INT);
var_dump(MY_FLOAT);
var_dump(MY_ARRAY);
var_dump(MY_RESOURCE);
```

```
var_dump(MY_NULL);
```

Output:
```
string(19) "You can't change me"
int(123)
float(1.23)
array(0) {
}
resource(5) of type (stream)
NULL
```

Once declared, a constant is accessed by using the name we gave it when we called define(). We can also use the const keyword to declare new constants:

```
const MY_STR = "You can't change me.";
```

If we try to re-declare a constant, we'll get an error:

```
define('MY_CONST', "You can't change me");
define('MY_CONST', "A new value");
```

Output:
```
PHP Warning:  Constant MY_CONST already defined
```

This is not necessarily fatal to your program; a warning is just a warning after all, but the constant value will (logically enough) be unchanged, which might impact code further in. We can avoid this altogether by using the built-in defined() function:

```
const SOME_CONSTANT = 'a string';

if (defined('SOME_CONSTANT')) {
    echo "SOME_CONSTANT is already defined" . PHP_EOL;
}

if (!defined('SOME_OTHER_CONSTANT')) {
    define('SOME_OTHER_CONSTANT', true);
}
```

Output:
```
SOME_CONSTANT is already defined
```

The `defined()` function will check if a constant already exists and return `true` if it does (and of course `false` if it doesn't). Two things to note here. The `const` keyword cannot be used unless it is in "top-level scope," which means it can't be used inside conditional blocks, functions, loops, or try/catch blocks (see Chapter 4, "Logic and Control," and Chapter 3, "Functions," for more info on what these are). In addition, `defined()` must be given the constant name as a string; otherwise, an error will be emitted if the constant being tested for doesn't exist:

```
var_dump(defined(I_AM_NOT_DEFINED));
```

Output:
Fatal error: Uncaught Error: Undefined constant "I_AM_NOT_DEFINED"

Predefined Constants

There are many predefined constants available from the moment your code starts to run, often of great use in obtaining information about the environment within which your code is executing. Here are a few examples:

```
var_dump(PHP_VERSION);
var_dump(PHP_SAPI);
var_dump(PHP_EOL);
var_dump(DIRECTORY_SEPARATOR);
```

Output:
string(5) "8.2.8"
string(3) "cli"
string(1) "
"
string(1) "/"

With so many constants already present globally, there's a chance you might accidentally attempt to redeclare one. The good news is that there are better ways to make constant data available throughout your application without polluting global data; take a look at Chapter 6, "Object Fundamentals," for ways in which classes and the new enum type can provide constants.

Magic Constants

PHP also provides a number of "magic constants," so-called because their values are determined when your code is evaluated, rather than when it is first compiled. All magic constants follow the naming convention of being wrapped in double underscores. They are as follows:

- `__LINE__` – line number of current file
- `__FILE__` – full path and filename of current file
- `__DIR__` – directory of current file
- `__FUNCTION__` – function name (will be empty if used outside a function)
- `__CLASS__` – will have a value if your code resides in a class method
- `__TRAIT__` – similar to __class__
- `__METHOD__` – another OOP feature, to be covered soon
- `__NAMESPACE__` – yet another OOP feature
- `ClassName::class` – and yet another OOP feature

As you can see, these magic constants follow a naming convention, and for this reason you should avoid declaring your own constants with double underscores. There's always the risk that one day your __CONSTANT__ is inadvertently added to the PHP magic constant list...

Superglobals

Similar to magic and predefined constants, there are some built-in globally available data structures called *superglobals* that you can make good use of throughout your code. These are not constants, and it is possible to modify them at runtime, though that is generally a Very Bad Idea. (Other code, not necessarily your own, may well be relying on this data. Better to copy the values somewhere and work with the copies instead.)

All the superglobals are themselves contained within a special (super?) superglobal called, rather intuitively, $GLOBALS. Below is a truncated view of that variable on my system, which in this example is running PHP 8.0 under the cli *SAPI* environment. This is a multi-dimensional array data structure; if it's the first time you've seen one, feel free to have a quick peek at Chapter 5, "Array":

var_dump($GLOBALS);

Output:
array(8) {
  ["_GET"]=> ...
  ["_POST"]=> ...
  ["_COOKIE"]=> ...
  ["_FILES"]=> ...
  ["argv"]=> ...
  ["argc"]=> ...
  ["_SERVER"]=>
  array(67) {
    ["HOSTNAME"]=>
    ...
  }
  ["GLOBALS"]=>
  RECURSION
}

Notice the *RECURSION* at the end of the structure; this means that $GLOBALS['GLOBALS'] is a reference back to $GLOBALS. If var_dump() continued to follow that reference, it would then hit another, then another, running in a loop until some part of the system gave up. We look at references in the next section, and recursion is also a topic in Chapter 5, "Array." Note that PHP 8.1 removed the $GLOBALS["GLOBALS"] reference.

Each of the top-level array elements (the keys with the leading underscore characters such as ["_SERVER"], and also ["argv"] and ["argc"]) are also superglobal variables. Simply prepend the key name (e.g., _GET, _POST, etc.) with a $ symbol to access it like this:

```
var_dump($_SERVER);
```

Output:
```
array(67) {
  ["HOSTNAME"]=>
  string(12) "e117b73245f4"
  ["PHP_INI_DIR"]=>
  string(18) "/usr/local/etc/php"
  ...
}
```

These data structures are extremely important. They contain vital information about the environment PHP is running in as it executes your code. I stress again: even though it is possible to do so, do NOT write to any part of the $GLOBALS array. Sooner or later some other component (e.g., a third-party library) is going to rely on the information in there. Wrap those values up in your own functions and classes.

If you have even a basic understanding of how web servers work, then $GLOBALS['_GET'], $GLOBALS['_POST'], $GLOBALS['_COOKIE'], and so on should be self-explanatory (they hold HTTP request parameters, cookie data, etc.). Those of you that have ever worked with a shell script or similar should be able to guess at what $GLOBALS['argv'] and $GLOBALS['argc'] are for (storing information about how PHP was invoked at the command line). We'll see these superglobals again in relevant chapters.

Referencing

Did you notice in the previous section that the $GLOBALS array contained an element named GLOBALS, and the value was given as *RECURSION*? The reason this is displayed is because the $GLOBALS array contains a *reference*: a special variable that acts as an alias for another variable. In this case, the value of $GLOBALS['GLOBALS'] is a reference for... $GLOBALS. In other words, it refers to itself, and var_dump() wisely decides not to output the same data again (and again, and again, and... you get the idea).

Think of references as one variable pointing to another. PHP will follow the chain until it gets to the "real" variable and work on that. This might sound complex but will probably make more sense if we see it in action:

CHAPTER 2   DATA, TYPES, AND VARIABLES

```
$a = 'some val';
$b = $a;
$b = 'new val';

var_dump($a);
var_dump($b);

$bref = &$a;
$bref = 'new val';

var_dump($a);

Output:
string(8) "some val"
string(7) "new val"
string(7) "new val"
```

We set $a to 'some val', and we assign the value of $a to $b. When we change $b, we can see that $a remains unchanged. However, when $bref is initialized and given its value, we use an additional modifier of &. This ampersand character modifies the behavior of assignment: it tells PHP that $bref is an alias for the same *zval* as $a. (Note that the & symbol is a bit of a special case in PHP; it isn't an operator as such but changes the behavior of variables in certain contexts.)

For those of you that have some exposure to C (the language PHP is implemented in), it might be tempting to think of PHP references as equivalent to C pointers, but they are not. In PHP, when a variable is assigned in your script, the PHP interpreter creates a data structure called a *zval*. A *zval* is not directly accessible in PHP code; they are internal to the PHP engine and defined in the C source code in which PHP is written. When a variable is initialized in PHP code, the engine creates a *zval*, and the variable name is used as an alias for it. When a reference is created in PHP, the two variables are now aliases for a single *zval*.

References used as above are rare and should probably be kept that way. Use them sparingly. You are far more likely to see variable references in the context of function parameters, and we'll revisit this particular feature of PHP variables in Chapter 3, "Functions."

Things get interesting when destroying variables that are referenced. Unsetting a reference itself does what you might expect: the reference variable is no longer available, but the referred variable continues to exist:

```
$a = 'a val';
$aRef = &$a;

unset($aRef);
var_dump($aRef);
var_dump($a);

Output:
Warning: Undefined variable $aRef
NULL
string(5) "a val"
```

However, unsetting a referred variable has a slightly less intuitive result:

```
$a = 'a val';
$aRef = &$a;

unset($a);
var_dump($aRef);
var_dump($a);

Output:
string(5) "a val"
Warning: Undefined variable $a
NULL
```

As you can see, even though $a no longer exists, its value (the underlying *zval*) still has a reference to it as far as PHP is concerned, so the data remains available to $aRef.

Variable Variables

Earlier in the chapter, we looked at the rules for variables. Remember that a variable is composed of a $ symbol and a name formed from (legal) characters? Well, here's a weird trick: the name can be a variable too! This form of variable is called (surprisingly) a *variable variable*, and they look like this:

```
$val = 'some value';
$name = 'val';
var_dump($$name);
```

Output:
```
string(10) "some value"
```

Notice the double dollar symbol $$name. When this code runs, PHP will evaluate $name, retrieve its value (the string `'val'`), and use it to form a new variable $val. $val already exists, and so its value (the string `some value`) is then used as the data for the call to var_dump. Pretty simple stuff.

Be warned: using variable variables can present problems for debugging. Normally a simple lint (from the command line run `$ php -l` followed by the filename) will warn you if you use an uninitialized variable in your code, which risks emitting a potentially fatal error. If you use an IDE (integrated development environment) to write code, it should highlight issues like this.

However, a variable variable can only be resolved at runtime. Unless the code in question is very simple, it can be difficult to spot broken variable variables.

```
$val = 'some value';
$name = 'wrongName';
var_dump($$name);
```

Output:
```
Warning: Undefined variable $wrongName
```

If we run the php cli binary in "lint" (syntax checking) mode against the above code, it won't find any issues.

```
$ php -l broken_variable_variable.php
```

Output:
```
No syntax errors detected in broken_variable_variable.php
```

Variable variables have their place, but, like references, you should use them sparingly.

Summary

Hopefully you now have an understanding of the difference between data and information and that the same data (the raw byte values) can represent very different information depending on context. The way that PHP uses any item of data is determined by metadata called *type*, and data types can be implicitly and explicitly controlled. The mechanism of type coercion (aka type juggling) was introduced, and we saw how this could lead to problems; we'll explore this in more detail in coming chapters. We also saw how to force PHP to execute code in a far more type-strict way, minimizing the potential for the type-coercion issues we'll see later.

From data representation, we then moved to the fundamental mechanism for storing and manipulating data: variables. Small but deeply important language features that they are. Obviously, you will see a great deal more use of them in the rest of the book, but it will be in the context of other features. They're everywhere, and you can't avoid them, which is the nature of fundamental things. We examined the ways that data types are controlled, both implicitly and explicitly. We also looked at creating and accessing global constants and the various predefined constant and variable data PHP provides for your convenience.

CHAPTER 3

Functions

The need for repeatable sets of instructions was recognized early in computing history. The 1950s onwards saw languages developed (such as FORTRAN or ALGOL) that supported *procedures*. Procedures (also known as *routines* or *sub-routines*) are reusable series of computational steps that have a mechanism for passing control to and from them. The formal mathematical basis for this kind of computation – *Lambda Calculus* – was developed in the 1930s by Alonzo Church. Church's work was based on the mathematical concept of *functions*, which are a way of conceptualizing dependencies between variables. In mathematics, functions take values (as input), perform operations, and return new values (as output).

Some languages (such as Visual Basic) distinguish between sub-routines (that don't return values) and functions (that do return values). PHP – like many others – simply uses the `function` keyword regardless of whether the routine accepts or returns values. In computing the words *routine*, *sub-routine*, and *function* are often generalized as *callable unit*. (Remember PHP's `callable` data type from Chapter 2, "Data, Types, and Variables.")

As programs grow in size and complexity, it is inevitable that repetition will creep in. Tasks often need to be performed multiple times, or the same complex logic needs to be applied in multiple places. There is a principle of software development called *DRY* (an acronym for "Don't Repeat Yourself") which, in *The Pragmatic Programmer: From Journeyman to Master* (Hunt & Thomas, 1999), stipulates that "Every piece of knowledge must have a single, unambiguous, authoritative representation within a system." This broad statement can apply to much more than just the code you write (e.g., documentation, build systems, or database schemas). It should naturally occur to most developers that it is sub-optimal to reproduce the same code in multiple places.

Imagine an application that, during its lifecycle, sends multiple emails. You could just write out (or copy/paste) all the code needed to interact with an SMTP server at every point that mail needs to be sent. Let's say that each time this happens you need fifteen lines of code. Now multiply that by the number of times mail is sent and then scatter it throughout your application. It's obvious that this scenario is creating a maintenance headache. One day you are asked to make a change that affects every email sent by the application. You have a pretty bad day. Then the bug reports start arriving.

Now imagine that, rather than repeating the mailing code every time the application needed it, you wrote it in one place and just called that code every time. Making a change affecting all emails now takes you half an hour, after which you can just get some coffee. You have a much better day, and there are (probably) no bug reports. This is why we should strive for DRY code. (In case you're wondering, the repeating email scenario isn't something I made up – it was a real problem I had to fix for a client.)

In this chapter, we will examine the following topics:

- Declaring Functions
- Calling Functions
- Named Functions
- Parameters and Arguments
- Data Types and Type Declarations
- Anonymous Functions
- Variable Functions
- Lexical Scope
- Namespacing
- Functional Programming

Declaring and Calling a Named Function

To declare a named function, use the `function` keyword, followed by the name of the function, then parentheses, then the function code enclosed in braces. Functions that have names (and not all functions do; more on this to come) must follow the same naming rules as variables: Start with a letter or underscore followed by any number of letters, underscores, or digits. Any alphabetic character of the extended ASCII character set is acceptable. The same guidance for variable naming is generally applicable to functions. To call the function, we simply write its name followed by parentheses. It is the presence of parentheses that tells the PHP engine it is dealing with a function:

```
helloWorld();
HELLOWORLD();

function helloWorld()
{
    print "Hello world!" . PHP_EOL;
}

Output:
Hello world!
Hello world!
```

The code above demonstrates a number of things. We create a function called `helloWorld()` using the `function` keyword and add a single statement inside the function braces: a simple `print` to show the program is working. The function is called by using its name followed by parentheses like so: `helloWorld()`. Functions defined in this way are sometimes called "user-land," a name that serves to differentiate them from PHP's many, many built-in functions.

Two important things to note here. Firstly, function names are not case sensitive (unlike variable names). `helloWorld` and `HELLOWORLD` in the context of a function are equivalent. Secondly, it is not necessary to define a function before using it. Before the code executes, the PHP engine has already parsed the text of the program and encountered the function declaration. At runtime the PHP engine already knows about `helloWorld()` and what it does. This is sometimes called "function hoisting," because semantically the function declaration behaves as if it had been placed at the top of the file (it has been hoisted to the top).

There is one caveat with function hoisting: if a function declaration is found inside a conditional statement or a conditionally included file, it cannot be used until PHP encounters it during execution.

```
goodMorning();
helloWorld();

if (true) {
    function helloWorld()
    {
        print "Hello world!" . PHP_EOL;
    }
}
```

```
function goodMorning()
{
    print "Good morning!" . PHP_EOL;
}

Output:
Good morning!
PHP Fatal error: Uncaught Error: Call to undefined function helloWorld()
```

Function Arguments and Returning Data

We've already examined the distinction between functions and sub-routines and the fact that PHP does not distinguish between them syntactically. The examples in the previous section were technically sub-routines; they did not accept input or return output. By adding a little more information to their declarations PHP functions can also accept data as input for use as named variables inside the function code block. Values are assigned when the function is called, and the calling code (usually) passes in the data.

Arguments and Parameters

To enable the passing of data into our functions we first add one or more variable names between the parentheses when the function is declared, separated by commas. Those variables can then be used inside the braces that define the function code block and the calling code will supply the data. The variables named in a function declaration in this way are called *parameters*.

Code that calls the function can then put expressions into the parentheses, the values of which are made available in the function body using the parameter names. The expressions inside the parentheses of the calling code are called *arguments*. It's quite common to see the words parameter and argument used interchangeably when discussing functions.

```
/*
 * $bar is a parameter, code inside the braces can use the
 * $bar variable to access the data sent by the caller
 */
```

```
function foo($bar) {}
/*
 * 'bar' is the argument. When the body of foo() executes
 * this value is assigned to the $bar parameter
 */
foo('bar');
```

Returning

Returning data from a function means that when control returns to the calling code the place where the function is called now has a value. This is achieved using the `return` keyword within the function body wherever you wish the function to finish execution, together with whatever expression is required to define the returned value. It is also possible for a `return` statement to return no value at all (more on this later).

```
$str = 'hello';

write('hello');
write($str);
print glue('hello', 'again');

function write($in)
{
    print "{$in}" . PHP_EOL;
}

function glue($start, $end)
{
    return "{$start} {$end}"  . PHP_EOL;
}

Output:
hello
hello
hello again
```

Here we have defined a function called `write()`, which works in much the same way as the previous example, but now we have added a parameter called `$in` to the function declaration. PHP will now expect that when `write` is called, either literal data, a variable, or any expression that evaluates to the expected type will be included as an argument. This is also known as "passing in" data. We call `write()` twice, once with a string literal and once with a variable holding string data.

We also have another function: `glue()`. Rather than printing within its block, it takes two inputs – `$start` and `$end` – and makes a single string from them. It then uses the `return` keyword to send this data back to the calling code. When `glue()` is called, the sequence of events happens like this:

- PHP stops executing the calling code
- Incoming data is assigned to the function parameter variables
- PHP executes the function block until it encounters the `return` statement
- Execution of the calling code resumes using the result of `glue()` in the remainder of the expression
- The `print` statement executes with the returned string data

It helps if you read `print glue('hello', 'again');` from right to left: first we encounter the `glue()` function call, then we encounter `print`. By the time `print` executes, `glue()` is done and we have our string, as if we'd actually written `print "hello again\n";`.

Scalar Type Coercion

In Chapter 2, "Data, Types, and Variables," we saw how PHP chooses data types for you when scalar variables are declared and assigned a value. In a similar spirit of convenience and helpfulness, PHP will attempt to manage type casting automatically when scalar types don't strictly match their operations. Type coercion also occurs in function calls.

To give a quick example, the built-in function `trim()` operates on strings by removing whitespace and returning the result. From the PHP documentation for the `trim` function, the function signature is `trim(string $string, string $characters = " \n\r\t\v\0"): string`. The main thing to note is `trim(string $string ...): string`, which means that the first argument passed to the function has to be a string, and that the value returned by trim() will also be a string. Here's what happens if we call the trim() function with a numerical argument:

```
$num = 123;
$res = trim($num);

var_dump($num);
var_dump($res);
```

Output:
```
int(123)
string(3) "123"
```

A stricter language would not allow numerical types to be used like this, but PHP simply converts $num to a string and trim() gets on with the job. Things aren't so magical for compound types, however. Let's try to call trim() with an array.

```
$myArr = ["string 1", "string 2"];
$res = trim($myArr);
```

Output:
```
Fatal error: Uncaught TypeError: trim(): Argument #1 ($string) must be of type string, array given
```

As we can see, even if we give trim() an array of strings, PHP still gives us a fatal error. As for the other compound types, it is possible to build objects that can become strings when used as such; these objects can also be callable or iterable, but you'll need to write code to make them behave like that. Compound types (arrays and objects) cannot be coerced or cast without some intervention first. The same is true of resource. We'll cover that later in the book when we look at objects in more detail.

And what about null? Well, null is simply a single byte with a value of 0x00. That's a valid ascii character (the "null byte") and therefore poses no problems to any code written to deal with string data. Passing null to the various string-handling functions in PHP will not cause any errors.

It's probably worth knowing that PHP used to have some serious vulnerabilities concerning null bytes in strings; most have been fixed since PHP 5.3, but be aware that if a null byte exists in the middle of string data, it will potentially be truncated beyond that byte. There are also techniques to bypass the protections that have been added to PHP. Penetration tests are recommended, as is input validation.

Strict Types

As mentioned in the previous chapter, it is possible to force the PHP engine to be strict about scalar types and prevent type coercion on calls. If a strict_types declaration is placed at the top of the source code file, the remaining code in that file will be subjected to stricter rules of scalar type checking when calls are made. One thing to note is that strict type checking is on a per-file basis; the declaration has to be added to all source code files where strictness is required:

```
declare(strict_types=1); // this MUST be the first statement in the
                          source file!

$num = 123;
$res = trim($num);

Output:
Fatal error: Uncaught TypeError: trim(): Argument #1 ($string) must be of
type string, int given...
```

The built-in function trim() is intended to only work with string data. When we pass an integer $num into the function, our program halts. When executing in this way, PHP will not intervene and change the type of $num – with predictably fatal results. Strict type checking only occurs on calls; operations are not affected:

```
declare(strict_types=1);

$str = "1";
var_dump($str * 2);

Output:
>int(2)
```

Reference vs. Value

There are two ways to pass data into a function, depending on whether or not you wish the incoming data to be altered. By default, PHP passes values into a function *by value* – this means that any changes made to the incoming argument data will not affect the value outside of the function scope. Consider the following code:

```php
function addCar ($inputArr) {
    $inputArr[] = 'Scirocco';
}

$cars = ['Golf', 'Polo'];
addCar($cars);

print_r($cars);
```

On first glance it looks as if this might put an additional element into the $cars array. In fact, this does happen in a way, just not to the original array. Instead, PHP will create a copy of the $cars array and add the new element there. PHP internally will use the same data (*zval*) for both variables unless addCar() makes any changes to it. If that happens, then PHP creates a copy, the function block works with the copy, and the original array declared outside the function remains unchanged. This behavior is an optimization feature known as *copy-on-write*. The output of the above code is as follows:

```
Array
(
    [0] => Golf
    [1] => Polo
)
```

To have the new element added to the global $cars array, we need to make it clear to the PHP interpreter that we don't want this copy-on-write behavior. To achieve this, we use a special reference operator & immediately before the $inputArr argument in the function declaration. Let's change our code accordingly:

```php
function addCar (&$inputArr) {
    $inputArr[] = 'Scirocco';
}
```

```
$cars = ['Golf', 'Polo'];
addCar($cars);
print_r($cars);
```

Output:
```
Array
(
    [0] => Golf
    [1] => Polo
    [2] => Scirocco
)
```

Notice that the $inputArr parameter now has the reference operator in front. This tells PHP that any changes should affect the original data that is passed in by the calling code. Now when we call addCar(), PHP does not create a copy of $cars, and the incoming data can be modified.

There also exists a mechanism for returning by reference, though it is a bit more cumbersome. Let's imagine that we want to keep count of something across the whole of our project, perhaps we want to tally every call to a database, something like that. We could, of course, use a global variable with all that entails (spoilers: global vars should be kept to an absolute minimum). There is a way, however, to achieve this using a function.

We can have our function return a reference to a static variable. A static variable will keep its value even when it goes out of scope at the end of function execution. We will examine the use of static variables in functions in much more detail later in this chapter when we explore the concept of *scope*. To get this working we first declare the function with an & character prepending the function name. Then we declare the locally scoped static variable, and finally we return it.

```
function &getCounter()
{
    static $i = 0;
    return $i;
}
```

Notice the static $i = 0; statement. Although it reads as if $i will be set to zero on every call, PHP will only execute this statement once (the first time the function is called). It's a little syntactic sugar to avoid any unwieldy if statements. Delicious!

Now let's make use of getCounter(). To assign the returned value by reference, we need another & (told you it was cumbersome), like so:

```
$countOne = &getCounter();
$countTwo = &getCounter();
$countOne++;
var_dump($countTwo);
$countTwo++;
var_dump($countOne);
```

Output:
int(1)
int(2)

$countOne and $countTwo are both referencing the locally scoped $i variable inside getCounter(). When we increment one, the new value is accessible from the other.

Declaring Types

It is good practice to define the data types that functions accept and return. This provides information to other programmers about how to use the function in an easily digested form (note that "other programmers" includes future you). A single statement (the beginning of the function declaration) can tell you at a glance how the function expects to be called and what it will evaluate to in expressions.

PHP 8 allows you to declare expected types for incoming arguments and returned data. Since PHP 7.0, every base data type is supported in function declarations with one exception: the resource type is not permitted (resource is a bit of a special case, as you might recall). Otherwise, you are free to use string, int, float, bool, array, and so on. Expanding beyond this, the type declaration system offers additional *pseudo-types*, such as constructs for declaring sets of types and types for defining function behavior. Pseudo-types only exist for use in declarations; you cannot cast data to these types.

Remember that types will be coerced unless PHP has been configured for strict behavior with a declare(strict_types=1) declaration, so a string that can be cast to an integer will be a legal value for a function that requires integer data (with all the caveats that entails).

Type System vs. Type Declaration

The type declaration system in PHP 8 is founded upon the built-in data types of the language, with extra features to make life easier (and code safer). PHP 8 offers us a range of base types: integers, floats, strings, null, booleans, arrays, and objects (together with the `callable` and `resource` special types).

Declarations will also accept the name of a `class`, `interface`, or `enum` (known as *class types* or *user-defined types*, although the latter is something of a misnomer because it includes built-in classes and interfaces). While it's true that a type declaration of `object` would suffice, often it's the class of the object that is of more interest. Allowing any old object into your function might be a recipe for disaster if your code is expecting the object to behave in specific ways. For example, a function might be coded to work with an instance of `DateTime`, which is passed in at call time. By declaring the argument type as `DateTime`, you can prevent an incompatible object from being passed in and generating errors.

PHP also offers a range of *standalone* pseudo-types, which combine with the primitives to form a set of *base types*. "Standalone" simply means "not part of a composite" (i.e., not part of a set of types; I promise this will make sense very shortly). A couple of the standalone pseudo-types are used exclusively for declaring how a function behaves when it completes execution, and these are known as *return-only types*.

Composite types are also supported. Composite types are pseudo-types too; they exist only to serve the needs of functions (and objects), and they define sets of types in declarations. A function might, say, return a string or null, or might expect an incoming object to implement multiple interfaces. Composite types are expressions that define sets of types in various logical combinations.

This is a lot to take in, but hopefully it will be clearer with some examples. Let's start with base types.

Base Types

Before we look at the mechanisms of declaration in detail, let's quickly look at the base types of the declaration system, starting with the built-in data types.

- `null` (only allowed as standalone with PHP >= 8.2)
- `bool`

- int
- float
- string
- array
- object

The following pseudo-types can be declared with functions.

- false
- true
- callable
- never (return-only)
- void (return-only)
- mixed
- callable

Finally, these are the supported class (user-defined) types.

- Class name
- Interface name
- Enum name

How to Declare Types

To define the data type of values returned by a function, put a colon after the closing parenthesis followed by the type keyword. For example, the `function getNumber(): integer`. Here are some examples of return type declarations; output is omitted, but see comments for detail:

```
function sayHi(): string
{
    return "Hi there!"; // valid return
}
```

```php
function getPi(): float
{
    return '3.14159265'; // can cast to a float so also valid
}

function getNow(): DateTime // function returns an instance of this class.
{
    return new DateTime('now');
}

function getMorePi(): float
{
    return 'Three point one four etc. etc.'; // Throws a TypeError
}
```

Be careful when using strict mode:

```php
declare(strict_types=1);

function getPi(): float
{
    return '3.14159265'; // is not a float, strict mode is on, TypeError
}
```

To define types for parameters, you place the type's keyword inside the parentheses just before the corresponding variable name like this: function mungeArray(array $array). The following code demonstrates type declarations for function arguments:

```php
function increment(int $num): int {
    var_dump($num);
    return $num + 1;
}
print increment('2') . PHP_EOL;
```

Output:
int(2)
3

Notice that we pass a string literal of '2' into the function increment(); we're not declaring strict_types=1, so PHP converts the incoming string to a number.

As we can see, declaring base types is straightforward. I've deliberately avoided the standalone pseudo-types, such as mixed, for now, but we will return to them later on. Things get a little more complex with composite types.

Composite Types

All composite types are combinations of base types, with rules for defining how you need the argument or return data to satisfy the declaration. You might require that a type matches one of a set, all of a set, or possibly one or the other (i.e., "either match this single type or this group of types"). Let's start with the simplest case.

Nullable Types

Added in PHP 7.1, by prefixing the type name with a question mark character (e.g., ?string, ?SomeClass), the declaration's meaning becomes "this type or null." To declare that a function returns a string or null, we can use function someFunction(): ?string like this:

```
declare(strict_types=1);

function doSomething(?string $in): ?string
{
    return ($in === null) ? null : 'Not null';
}

var_dump(doSomething('a string'));
var_dump(doSomething(null));

Output:
string(8) "Not null"
NULL
```

The code above should need little explanation if you've followed the rest of the chapter so far; it's running in strict mode to demonstrate that we're satisfying all of the type declarations for doSomething(). PHP has a weird quirk with nullable types, which we'll see in a moment.

Union Types

If a function accepts a range of types for a particular parameter or returns a range of types, it is possible to declare the set of valid types using each type keyword separated by the pipe symbol |.

Imagine we have a function that can work with either int or string data. To declare the union type, we'd use function someFunction(int|string $input). The order of types does not matter; string|int would also work, but repeating a type is fatal. int|string|int in our code would result in the following message in the error log: Duplicate type int is redundant. The following code demonstrates a union type in action.

```
function itsComplicated(int|string $in): string
{
    switch (gettype($in)) {
        case "string":
            return "You gave me a string";
            break;
        case "integer":
            return "You gave me an integer";
            break;
    }
}

print itsComplicated("string") . PHP_EOL;
print itsComplicated(1) . PHP_EOL;
```

Output:
You gave me a string
You gave me an integer

The function itsComplicated() has a single argument - $in. Its type is either string or int, so we declare a union type of string|int. The rest of the code is straightforward: we use the built-in gettype() to check the data type of the incoming data and go from there. Using a union in a return type declaration is no different:

```
function itsComplicated($in): int|string
{
    switch (gettype($in)) {
        case "string":
            return "You gave me a string";
            break;
        case "integer":
            return "You gave me an integer";
            break;
    }

    return 0;
}

if (itsComplicated(new stdClass()) === 0) {
    print "I'm not sure what you gave me, perhaps we'll cover it in a later
    chapter?" . PHP_EOL;
}
```

Output:
I'm not sure what you gave me, perhaps we'll cover it in a later chapter?

We've removed the parameter type declaration for $in, which means that we now need extra code to deal with the uncertainty of how our function might be called. Our function now returns either a string or int, and we must update the function declaration accordingly. To demonstrate, we pass an object (don't worry, we'll get to those) to itsComplicated() and test the output using a strict comparison of === 0.

The function returns 0 because the incoming data isn't string or integer; therefore, we execute the code in the if block. If we hadn't updated the return type of itsComplicated() and attempted to return anything other than a string, it would have resulted in another fatal TypeError.

If you're wondering if the shorthand nullable syntax exists for union types, the answer is a flat "no." Both nullable types and union types were debated at roughly the same time via PHP's RFC documents (the RFC for nullables pre-dates that for unions by about ten months), with nullables making it into the language first. When unions arrived, it was argued (successfully) that using the ? character in a union would introduce ambiguity. ?int|string could read as if only int was nullable. "But if the int is nullable then, logically, so is the string," you might argue, and you'd be entirely correct. But figuring that out is additional cognitive load, and our jobs are already difficult enough, so nullable union types are only achieved by adding |null to the declaration.

Intersection Types

The corollary to the union type is the intersection. With an intersection type declaration, we require that the data in question matches *all* the set of types (rather than just one). Logically, this restricts the valid members of an intersection to classes, interfaces, and enums because it's impossible for a data type to be both, say, a string and an integer at the same time. Even if PHP code often reads as if data somehow has multiple types, remember that internally the data type is being cast as required and can only be of one type at any particular time.

Imagine we have a function that needs to both iterate and count data. If we supply an object, it would be good to know it could be counted (e.g., with count()) and accessed like an array (e.g., with foreach). PHP 8.1 introduces the "intersection type," which is a special composite type, which defines a set of classes or interfaces, all of which the incoming (or outgoing) data must match. If union types are a logical OR, then intersections are a logical AND.

The code below illustrates this but makes use of concepts we haven't covered yet. For now, just accept that ArrayAccess and Countable are the names of two built-in interfaces in PHP, and interfaces can be explicitly implemented by classes. The type declaration ArrayAccess&Countable $data means "$data is an object that implements these two interfaces." ArrayObject is a built-in class that meets that requirement.

```
declare(strict_types=1);

function countAndIterate(ArrayAccess&Countable $data)
{
    print "Data contains " . count($data) . " things:" . PHP_EOL;
    foreach ($data as $datum) {
        var_dump($datum);
    }
}
```

```
$obj = new ArrayObject([
    'a car',
    'a guitar',
    'and a nice cold pint',
]);

countAndIterate($obj);

Output:
Data contains 3 things:
string(5) "a car"
string(8) "a guitar"
string(20) "and a nice cold pint"
```

When the new `ArrayObject` is created, we give it an array. Don't worry that it looks a bit like a function call (there is a function call involved, but we'll save those details for another time). For now, just understand it as "we made a new object and used some syntactic trickery to initialize it with data at the same time."

`ArrayObject` is essentially an object "wrapper" around the `array` data type, which provides certain required functionality. Our function `countAndIterate()` will only accept an object that has both `ArrayAccess` and `Countable` interfaces, which `ArrayObject` has, which makes `$obj` a valid value, so the call succeeds.

Disjunctive Normal Form Types

DNF types are a new feature in PHP 8.2; this rather intimidatingly named feature is simply a syntax that allows the mixing of union and intersection types. It's probably easiest to conceptualize DNF as an expression of a union type containing intersections, with the intersections enclosed in parentheses. Imagine we had three classes – named A, B, and C – and we wanted to declare that a type was allowed to be either the intersection A&B or A&C. The DNF would be (A&B)|(A&C). We could take things further and add some base types, e.g., (A&B)|(A&C)|array|null. Just remember that all intersections (anything requiring an &) must be enclosed in parentheses.

Let's demonstrate that by updating the previous example by making countAndIterate() also accept an array as a valid argument:

```
declare(strict_types=1);

function countAndIterate((ArrayAccess&Countable)|array $data)
{
    print "Data contains " . count($data) . " things:" . PHP_EOL;

    foreach ($data as $datum) {
        var_dump($datum);
    }
}
$niceThings = [
    'a car',
    'a guitar',
    'and a nice cold pint',
];

countAndIterate(new ArrayObject($niceThings));
countAndIterate($niceThings);
```

The output of each call to countAndIterate() is identical; notice the type definition for $data is now the DNF expression (ArrayAccess&Countable)|array.

Standalone Pseudo-types

As mentioned earlier in the section, there are standalone types that do not exist as primitive types but can be used in type declaration.

Literal Types

If a function returns (or accepts) boolean data, you can of course declare the type with the keyword bool. For example, allow me to present my patented decision-making algorithm:

```
function coinToss(): bool
{
    return (bool) rand(0, 1);
}

$msg = "Today I shall ";
$msg .= (coinToss()) ? "procrastinate." . PHP_EOL : "work on my book!" . PHP_EOL;

print $msg;
```

The function `coinToss()` returns `true` or `false` depending on the whim of the machine. It might explain why this book took me so long to write.

PHP 8.0 introduced a type declaration that also checked the data's value by allowing `false` as part of a union type. The argument for this was that historically many PHP functions return false on failure, so supporting user-defined functions with this type declaration made sense. For example, the built-in function for reading in an entire file has the following signature: `file_get_contents(): string|false`. There are many, many more built-in functions that follow this false-on-failure pattern.

PHP 8.2 added support for the complementary `true` type and did away with the need for unions; `false` and `true` can be used as standalone types. The benefits of allowing standalone `true` or `false` over `bool` aren't immediately apparent when examined from a purely functional perspective: why would we write a function that can only return `false`? In the context of objects (and especially class hierarchy), however, there are use cases that emerge. A parent class could provide a prototype method with a return type of `bool`; child classes can then overload this with `true` or `false` return types and provide more granular detail to your IDE or static analysis tools. If that last sentence was just so much gobbledegook, other chapters in this book have all the info you need.

A word of warning: don't try to use a `true|false` union. PHP will quite rightly tell you to use `bool` via a helpful fatal error message!

The mixed (Super) Type

PHP supports a type declaration of `mixed`, which is the top-level supertype (in that all other types are a sub-type of `mixed`, for the type theorists among you). The `mixed` type is (according to PHP official documentation) equivalent to the union `object|resource`

|array|string|float|int|bool|null. I'm hoping at least a few of you might have spotted an anomaly in that union declaration. `resource` has never been, and never will be, a standalone type.

Resources (which are variables containing references to operating system resources like file handles and network sockets) have always been a bit of a special case; they are also now phased out in favor of objects. Many resource-returning functions (from PHP 8.0 onwards) now return instances of resource classes, and the normal class type declarations should be used with these. For example, in PHP 8 `curl_init()` now returns an instance of the built-in class `CurlHandle`.

As you should expect, declaring a type of `mixed` means that *anything* (apart from `void` or `none`) is legal, even an old-style resource. In fact, it is the only way to get resources working with the PHP 8 type declaration system.

Return-Only Types

Finally, we come to the set of type declarations, which are only used for restricting what is returned from a function. These are as follows.

- `void`: the function returns control to the caller but no data.
- `never`: the function never returns control.

We'll look at the first two and save the final three for when we cover OOP. Firstly, `void` should be obvious. Use this when no data is returned (i.e., the final statement in the function block is `return;` – note the terminating semicolon). `never` should only be used for a function that never returns at all. Remember, a function without a `return` statement will still return control to the caller. The use case for `never` is a function that will terminate the script (e.g., with a `die()` or `exit()` statement). Here's an example of both in action:

```
// Only to be run in a CLI environment!
function shallWeContinue(): void
{
    $in = readline('Type something to continue, or press Enter on its own
    to abort' . PHP_EOL);
```

```
    if (empty($in)) {
        exit("And we're done!" . PHP_EOL);
    }
}

function mainLoop(): never
{
    while (true) {
        shallWeContinue();
        print 'Hey ho, on we go...' . PHP_EOL;
    }
}

mainLoop();
```

Output:
Type something to continue, or press Enter on its own to abort
go for it
Hey ho, on we go...
Type something to continue, or press Enter on its own to abort
And we're done!

shallWeContinue() does the job of asking for user input (from a command line prompt, via the readline() call), and handling the typed response. An empty user response results in a call to exit(), which immediately terminates the program – the end of the function scope (the closing brace, if you remember) is never reached. The use of the infinite looping while (true) { } construct means that mainLoop() can never return, and a good IDE should detect this infinite loop (or some other non-returnable context like a program-terminating statement) or otherwise highlight that the never return type is invalid. Let's tweak our code so that we break the while loop rather than exiting the program completely and see what happens:

```
function shallWeContinue(): bool
{
    $in = readline('Type something to continue, or press Enter on its own
    to abort' . PHP_EOL);

    return (!empty($in));
}
```

CHAPTER 3   FUNCTIONS

```
function mainLoop(): never
{
    while (shallWeContinue()) {
        print 'Hey ho, on we go...' . PHP_EOL;
    }
}

mainLoop();
```

Output:
Type something to continue, or press Enter on its own to abort
Uncaught TypeError: mainLoop(): never-returning function must not implicitly return

Now when we get an empty string from user input, the while loop is broken, the end of mainLoop() is reached, and havoc ensues with a suitably fatal error message. Happily, there is a simple fix:

```
function mainLoop(): never
{
    while (shallWeContinue()) {
        print 'Hey ho, on we go...' . PHP_EOL;
    }
    exit();
}
```

Instead of an implicit return, we have a nice explicit exit(), and the program functions as before. It should be obvious that having our mainLoop() behavior controlled by the side effect of another function is bad design; mainLoop() should have full control over its own behavior. exit() (and its alias function die()) are fully-fledged functions in PHP 8.4 – with a return type of never and accepting a single int or string parameter but prior to that existed as language constructs with special handling, although special handling still exists in PHP 8.4 to permit the continued use of exit/die without any parentheses.

By using the never return type, we have stated our intentions about how mainLoop() should behave. It only took some tiny changes to break our code in a very obvious way. Without the return type declaration, this code would have continued to function without error, which is fine, but who knows what damage further changes might have made? Better to fail early and either fix the code or change the design. (Hopefully I'm making a case for the use of type declarations here!)

Two things to note with the void return type. First, a void function will *always* return a value (and type) of null; be aware of this when using void returning functions in expressions. Second, void can never be a valid return type for functions that return by reference, even if the value of the reference is null.

References and Return Types

Functions that handle variable references (see earlier sections of this chapter) have some caveats when it comes to type declaration. First, let's look at pass-by-reference:

```
function breakMyArray(array &$things)
{
    $things = 'Oops!';
}

$arr = ['some', 'lovely', 'things'];
breakMyArray($arr);
print "Attempting second call to breakMyArray()" . PHP_EOL;
breakMyArray($arr);
```

Output:
Attempting second call to breakMyArray()
Uncaught TypeError: breakMyArray(): Argument #1 ($things) must be of type array, string given

Oh dear. It should be apparent why this happened, after all we changed our array into a string with the first call to breakMyArray() so of course it's not a valid type on the second. What's perhaps less obvious is that the type isn't enforced by the declaration of array on the &$things argument. The type checking is only done on function entry, not exit. Perhaps we can enforce it by specifying a return type for the function:

```
function breakMyArray(array &$things): array
{
    $things = 'Oops!';
}
```

Output:
Uncaught TypeError: breakMyArray(): Return value must be of type array, none returned

Ah, that's a hard no. Specifying a return type but not having a return statement in the function is not possible unless that type is void. Perhaps passing references around is something to be treated with caution? Something to think about!

Functions that return by reference also have a gotcha. Remember that void returning functions will always implicitly return null? What if we had a function that returns null by reference? (Note: if you're not sure what static means, we cover its behavior in more detail when discussing the concept of *scope* in a later section.)

```
function &getNull(): void
{
    static $val = null;
    return $val;
}

$ref = &getNull();
```

Output:
Deprecated: Returning by reference from a void function is deprecated
Fatal error: A void function must not return a value

Not one but two errors! Depending on which version of PHP 8 you are running you'll get the deprecation notice (returning by reference from a void function was deprecated in PHP 8.1) followed by a Fatal error. void functions will implicitly return null but an explicit return of a reference to null is not the same thing, so the void declaration is illegal. From PHP 8.2 onwards null is allowed as a standalone type, so the following declaration would be valid: function &getNull(): null (but would otherwise emit another fatal error for PHP <= 8.1).

Advanced Arguments

We've looked at the basics of passing data into functions, now let's build on that a little.

Default Arguments

PHP allows you to assign default values to function parameters when the function is declared. These are known as "default arguments." Using default values means that the calling code doesn't need to pass a value and will not generate an error if the parameter is missing. If calling code does pass a value, then the default is ignored and the passed-in value is used. Let's look at a simple example.

```
function addOneOrMore($a, $b = 1) {
    return $a + $b;
}
var_dump(addOneOrMore(2, 2));
var_dump(addOneOrMore(2));
```

Output:
int(4)
int(3)

We define a function addOneOrMore() with takes two parameters $a and $b and returns the sum of them. The second argument $b has a default value of 1. If addOneOrMore() is called without a second value, it uses the default, as we can see from the output. It is generally good practice to place arguments with default values at the end of the parameter list. Remember the "weird quirk" I mentioned, concerning nullable types? If a function parameter is declared with a default value of null then it is made implicitly nullable. function foo (string $foo = null) ... is implicitly function foo(?string $foo = null) ... and in version 8.4 this will emit a deprecation notice. It is scheduled for removal in version 9 and any parameter with a null default value must be explicitly made nullable.

Variadic Arguments

A function that supports variable numbers of arguments is called a *variadic* function. Some built-in PHP functions support variable numbers of arguments, a good example is sprintf(), which takes a formatting string as its first argument, and an arbitrary amount of strings after that with the caveat that the number of strings supplied must match the specified format:

```
echo sprintf('%s %s', 'hello', 'world') . PHP_EOL;
echo sprintf('%s %s %s', 'a', 'longer', 'string') . PHP_EOL;
```

Output:
```
hello world
a longer string
```

PHP provides a few useful built-in functions to help us handle variable numbers of arguments at run time: func_num_args(), func_get_arg(), and func_get_args(). Respectively, they will return a count of arguments used when the function is called, a specific argument, or an array of all arguments:

```
function testArgs(): void
{
    print "testArgs was called with " . func_num_args() . " arguments" . PHP_EOL;
    print "first argument value is " . func_get_arg(0) . PHP_EOL;
    print_r(func_get_args());
}

testArgs('I', 'hope', 'this', 'makes', 'sense');
```

Output:
```
testArgs was called with 5 arguments
first argument value is I
Array
(
    [0] => I
    [1] => hope
    [2] => this
    [3] => makes
    [4] => sense
)
```

We call testArgs() with five string arguments: testArgs('I', 'hope', 'this', 'makes', 'sense'). func_num_args() tells us we have five arguments and func_get_arg(0) returns the first (or zeroth, if you prefer) argument which is 'I'; func_get_args() returns an array containing every argument.

The built-in functions we've just looked at for interacting with function arguments are certainly very useful, but I'm hoping that you've noticed a problem: the lack of type safety. testArgs() has precisely no arguments in its declaration; therefore, we cannot enforce the data type at call time. If was testArgs() was implemented to handle only string data, and a somehow an object sneaked in during execution, we'd have problems:

```
function testArgs(): void
{
    foreach (func_get_args() as $str) {
        print $str . ' ';
    }
}

testArgs('I', 'hope', 'this', 'makes', 'sense', new stdClass());

Output:
I hope this makes sense
Fatal error: Uncaught Error: Object of class stdClass could not be
converted to string
```

Nasty. If only there was a way to enforce type... well there is!

PHP 5.6 introduced the "splat" operator ... which is demonstrated in Chapter 5, "Arrays". In that chapter, we use the ... operator to transform an array into individual variables (a process called array unpacking). The splat operator will (when used in a function declaration) also build an array from individual function arguments, with the added bonus that we can add a type declaration at the same time. Function parameters prefixed with the splat operator are called variadic parameters. Let's take the previous example and refactor it slightly to use splat:

```
function testArgs(string ...$in): void
{
    foreach ($in as $str) {
        print $str . ' ';
    }
}

testArgs('I', 'hope', 'this', 'makes', 'sense', new stdClass());
```

Output:
Fatal error: Uncaught TypeError: testArgs(): Argument #6 must be of type string, stdClass given

Now if we run this code, we still get an error, albeit a different one (a TypeError rather than a string conversion failure). PHP now fails to call `testArgs()` at all, rather than getting most of the way through the `foreach` loop before dying. The real benefit here is that the declaration is a statement of the function's behavior; it tells other programmers (including future you) how to use `testArgs()` correctly. In addition, a good IDE will highlight the type mismatch problem before the code ever runs.

It is also possible to mix conventional parameters with variadic (with the caveat that only the final one can be variadic):

```php
function testArgs(string $first, string ...$rest): void
{
    print $first . ' ';

    foreach ($rest as $str) {
        print $str . ' ';
    }
}

testArgs('I', 'hope', 'this', 'makes', 'sense', 'too');
```

Output:
I hope this makes sense too

It is also perfectly fine to unpack arrays when using them as function arguments. If our six strings were collected into an array, we would make the call like this:

```php
$strings = ['I', 'hope', 'this', 'makes', 'sense', 'too'];
testArgs(...$strings);
```

When the data arrives into the function, it will have been split into individual arguments. Prior to array unpacking being added to PHP (in version 5.6), there was another way to spread array elements when calling functions, using the built-in `call_user_func_array()`:

```php
$strings = ['I', 'hope', 'this', 'makes', 'sense', 'too'];
call_user_func_array('testArgs', $strings);
```

Both forms have identical output, but the preferred form today would be more concise ...$string. Indeed, the feature was added to the language for precisely this reason.

Incidentally, the change in behavior of the ... operator demonstrated above is an example of a general programming language feature called *operator overloading*. This is a feature that allows operators to do different things in different contexts. In our case ... is building an array when used in an argument declaration and decomposing an array into individual elements when used on arrays passed into a function at runtime. (For the curious: no, it isn't possible to change operator behavior like this in your own PHP code; it was discussed in an RFC for PHP 8, but the proposal was declined.)

Named Parameters

PHP 8 introduces a nifty way to pass data into functions using the parameter names. Up to now the order in which we passed variables into our functions has had to align with the order or arguments. Named arguments allows you to label each item of incoming data and PHP will assign the data to its corresponding function argument. Let's learn about classic albums, and also some PHP:

```
function knowYourClassicMetal(string $album, string $artist, string $year,
string $label): void
{
    print "{$album} by {$artist}, released in {$year} on {$label}" .
    PHP_EOL;
}

knowYourClassicMetal(album: 'Somewhere in Time', artist: 'Iron Maiden',
year: '1985', label: 'EMI');
knowYourClassicMetal(artist: 'Slayer', year: '1986', label: 'Def Jam',
album: 'Reign in Blood');
```

Output:
Somewhere in Time by Iron Maiden, released in 1985 on EMI
Reign in Blood by Slayer, released in 1986 on Def Jam

It's pretty straightforward. The syntax for named parameters is simply the variable name (without the dollar character) followed by a colon: someFunction(paramName: $someData). The order does not matter, because the data can be mapped to the parameter's variable name. Prior to this feature's addition, functions that needed lots of parameters tended to have associative arrays passed in. The example above could be written like this:

```
function knowYourClassicMetal(array $data): void
{
    print "{$data['album']} by {$data['artist']}, released in
    {$data['year']} on {$data['label']}" . PHP_EOL;
}

knowYourClassicMetal([
    'album' => 'Somewhere in Time',
    'artist' => 'Iron Maiden',
    'year' => '1985',
    'label' => 'EMI'
]);
```

Which is fine as far as it goes, but (as well as fiddly-looking syntax) it suffers from a problem. It's not possible to know if all the required data is present in the incoming $data array without some checks and balances, and a missing array element will result in an Undefined array key error.

Code like that above should include some tests on the existence of array keys. With named parameters any missing data will emit a different ArgumentCountError but these are more easily spotted before run time, especially by an IDE (which will typically prompt for required arguments and/or highlight any that are missing as code is written).

While we're on the topic of associative arrays and named arguments, here's a nice additional feature of named arguments. If an associative array is unpacked into a function, and the keys are strings that match the parameter names, then the array values will be mapped as if they were named arguments. (Note: unpacking arrays that have string keys is only supported from PHP 8.0 upwards.)

```
$data = [
    'year' => '1995',
    'label' => 'Earache',
```

```
    'album' => 'Slaughter of the Soul',
    'artist' => 'At the Gates',
];

knowYourClassicMetal(...$data);
```

Output:
```
Slaughter of the Soul by At the Gates, released in 1995 on Earache
```

In this example, PHP has helpful populated the function arguments that have variable names which correspond to the array keys.

Named parameters are also supported for built-in functions. The official PHP documentation will give the variable names used internally for function arguments. For example, the venerable built-in function `strpos()` has the declaration `strpos(string $haystack, string $needle, int $offset = 0): int|false`

We can call `strops` using named parameters like this:

```
print strpos(needle: 'Maiden', haystack: 'Iron Maiden Rules') . PHP_EOL;
```

Output:
```
5
```

Note that the `needle` and `haystack` arguments have had their orders reversed in the call, but because we've named them the call is still successful. Be aware, though, that there are a few rules to follow when using named parameters.

The argument names must be given as string literals, they cannot be dynamic. Which means it isn't possible to use a variable or some other expression. `someFunc($paramName: $value);` or `someFunc(getParamName(): $value)` will not work, both will result in a parse error (specifically `unexpected token ":"`) which is (happily) easily caught by a linter and should never make it to deployment. In addition, argument names can only be those found in the function signature. Any unrecognized names will generate an error.

Care must also be taken that arguments are only passed once. Duplication of named arguments isn't a syntax error, it won't be caught by a linter, and instead the code fails at run time with a fatal error. Here we duplicate the `artist` parameter:

```
knowYourClassicMetal(album: 'Somewhere in Time', artist: 'Iron Maiden',
year: '1985', label: 'EMI', artist: 'Iron Maiden');
```

Output:
```
Fatal error: Uncaught Error: Named parameter $artist overwrites previous
argument
```

Mixing Call Styles

Both named arguments and unpacked arrays can be combined with the traditional positional form, and if you're feeling particularly adventurous, it is even possible (since PHP 8.1) to put named parameters after an unpacked array. Some extra care needs to be taken, however. There are some gotchas.

First of all, positional parameters can only go before named. The following is absolutely fine:

```
knowYourClassicMetal('Painkiller', 'Judas Priest', year: '1990', label:
'Columbia Records');
```

Output:
```
Painkiller by Judas Priest, released in 1990 on Columbia Records
```

But this is not...

```
knowYourClassicMetal(album: 'Painkiller', 'Judas Priest', year: '1990',
label: 'Columbia Records');
```

Output:
```
Fatal error: Cannot use positional argument after named argument
```

Unpacked arguments have the same restriction. It's fine to use multiple unpacked arrays like this: testArgs(...$strings, ...$moreStrings). Otherwise, unpacked arguments must go after positional. Here's what happens if a positional argument is placed after unpacking:

```
$strings = ['I', 'hope', 'this', 'makes', 'sense'];
$moreStrings = 'too';
testArgs(...$strings, $moreStrings);
```

Output:
Fatal error: Cannot use positional argument after argument unpacking

However, named parameters can be used after unpacking (PHP 8.1 or later):

$albumAndArtist = ['Left Hand Path', 'Entombed'];

knowYourClassicMetal(...$albumAndArtist, year: '1990', label: 'Combat Records');

Output:
Left Hand Path by Entombed, released in 1990 on Combat Records

Care also needs to be taken over possible collisions between named and positional arguments. Remember earlier when we looked at how PHP will not allow duplicate named parameters in a call? When mixing named with positional or unpacked it is possible for this to happen in more subtle ways, which could result in code that only works sometimes – the hardest of all to debug!

The following code is legal syntax, it will not trigger any errors when linted, but the first argument corresponds to the $album parameter in the function declaration and the explicitly named album argument on the end triggers an error:

knowYourClassicMetal('Somewhere in Time', artist: 'Iron Maiden', year: '1985', label: 'EMI', album: 'Somewhere in Time');

Output:
Fatal error: Uncaught Error: Named parameter $album overwrites previous argument

Things can get even more obscure when utilizing an associative array with string keys as parameter names. Remember the rule about not putting positional arguments after named? That also applies to unpacked arrays. Observe:

knowYourClassicMetal(...['album' => 'Master of Puppets','artist' => 'Metallica',
    'year' => '1986', 'label'=> 'Elektra Records']);
knowYourClassicMetal(...['Master of Puppets', 'artist' => 'Metallica',
    'year' => '1986', 'label'=> 'Elektra Records']);

```
knowYourClassicMetal(...['album' => 'Master of Puppets', 'artist' =>
'Metallica',
    'year' => '1986', 'Elektra Records']);
Output:
Master of Puppets by Metallica, released in 1986 on Elektra Records
Master of Puppets by Metallica, released in 1986 on Elektra Records
Fatal error: Uncaught Error: Cannot use positional argument after named
argument during unpacking
```

The first two calls are fine. One has all named arguments and the other has the album title as the first array element (plus correct string keys for the rest). The third call omits the `'label'` key in the final array position and our program dies with an error.

And there we have it, all the weird and wonderful ways that functions can receive their arguments in PHP 8. Hopefully the lesson to take away here is that it's best to keep things simple. The more complexity in argument handling in your code, the more error prone it will be.

Functions and Scope

Now is an excellent time to introduce a very important concept in PHP (and programming in general), which is particularly important to functions, and that concept is *scope*. Scope (or more formally, *lexical scope*) can be generally defined as the part of a program where the association of identifiers with their data is valid. Throughout the code we've seen so far we have used variables, if you remember the chapter on data and variables, you'll know that the variables themselves are just references to data in memory. When PHP encounters a variable in an expression it will access the data and use it to evaluate the expression. Scope is essentially a set of simple rules that determine whether or not a particular variable can be used to access the intended data. (Note that although function names can be considered as identifiers, those are not subject to scoping rules.)

Global vs. Local Scope

Let's look at some code that breaks the rules.

```
$txt = "Let's break stuff" . PHP_EOL;

print $txt;
testScope();

function testScope(): void
{
    print $txt;
}

Output:
Let's break stuff
Warning: Undefined variable $txt
```

This code has a variable $txt, which is used in two places: on the first line (where it is initialized to a string), and then in the body of the testScope() function. On first glance this code might seem fine, but when we run it, we get a warning error that $txt is undefined on line 8. This happens because $txt isn't a valid identifier inside the body of testScope(). This is our first and most important rule: functions have their own scope. Variables declared outside a function are not automatically available inside a function.

When PHP executes a function, a new local scope is generated. Identifiers (and their data) created during the function's execution are isolated from the rest of the program. When execution exits a function, the scope is destroyed along with any identifiers (and data) that do not also exist outside of that scope. This is a necessary safety feature; otherwise, functions could inadvertently impact any other function that has the same identifiers. Imagine having to keep track of all that in your head *and* deliver features…

With this in mind, we can now see why testScope() is broken. As far as PHP is concerned, there is no $txt when it encounters it in the function body because it hasn't been defined there. Yet $txt does exist outside of the function, as we can see with our first call to print. Clearly there is another scope that exists outside of testScope(), and this is the *global scope*. Global scope exists for the lifetime of the program outside of any local scope. PHP differs from other languages in that global identifiers are not accessible in a local scope by default. Here's a JavaScript equivalent of the example above:

CHAPTER 3   FUNCTIONS

```
const txt = "Let's break stuff";

const testScope = function () {
    console.log(txt);
}

testScope();
```

The code above can be executed via Docker using the following bash command:

```
$ docker run -it --rm --name my-running-script -v "$PWD":/usr/src/app \
  -w /usr/src/app node:19-bullseye node js_scope.js
```

The above assumes the code is stored in the file js_scope.js and the output is simply "Let's break stuff" without any warnings. In JavaScript, local scope has access to parent scope. Not so with PHP.

There is in fact a way for testScope() to access $txt from global scope, by using the keyword global, or the superglobal variable $GLOBALS. Here are two ways to access global scope from a local scope in PHP:

```
$txt = 'Greetings from global scope' . PHP_EOL;
testScope1();
testScope2();

function testScope1(): void
{
    global $txt;
    print $txt;
}
function testScope2(): void
{
    print $GLOBALS['txt'];
}
```

Output:
Greetings from global scope
Greetings from global scope

Now that we've told PHP we want to use $txt from global scope, the code executes without any issues. All variables declared in global scope will have their names added as keys to the special $GLOBALS array and their data can be accessed accordingly. If the variable already exists, it will have its value replaced and herein lies one of the danger with global variables. Another thing to consider with using global inside a function is that the global variable will be created if it doesn't already exist:

```
function testGlobalVars(): void
{
    global $txt;
    $txt = 'Watch me stamp all over global data...';
}

var_dump($txt);
testGlobalVars();
var_dump($txt);
```

Output:
Warning: Undefined variable $txt in /usr/src/myapp/scope8.php on line 9
NULL
string(38) "Watch me stamp all over global data..."

As we can see, by declaring $txt as global in the local scope of testGlobalVars(), we have now added $txt to global scope. Exactly the same can be achieved by writing $GLOBALS['txt'] = ... in the body of testGlobalVars().

```
function testSuperglobal(): void
{
    $GLOBALS['foo'] = 'foo';
}

testSuperglobal();
var_dump($GLOBALS['foo']);
```

Output:
string(3) "foo"

Yet another danger of global. Hopefully you're beginning to see why global data should be treated with extreme caution.

Named Functions Are Always Global

As mentioned earlier, function identifiers are not subject to scoping rules. Here is a quick demonstration, notice that even though inner() is declared inside a local scope (that of the outer() function), it is still available globally.

```
outer();
inner();

function outer()
{
    function inner() {
        print "I am also global!". PHP_EOL;
    }
}
```

Output:
I am also global!

It is helpful to think of scope in terms of boundaries. The boundaries of local scope exist at the very beginning and end of the function block. All code that exists between the brace characters { } of the expression function foo() { } is locally scoped: the braces are the demarcations of the boundary. When the boundaries are crossed, scope changes. But in the case of function identifiers, as above, these are always put into global scope even if declared within another function's local scope. Only variables are scoped in PHP.

Some languages treat *all* blocks as having local scope – JavaScript generates a new local scope on every if block, for example – but this is not the case in PHP.

Function Arguments Are Always Local

The scope of variables defined as function parameters is always local:

```
$quote = "We've gone on holiday by mistake." . PHP_EOL;

function printQuote (string $quote): void {
    $quote = "We're bona fide, we're not from London" . PHP_EOL;
    print $quote;
}
```

```
printQuote($quote);
print $quote;
```

Output:
We're bona fide, we're not from London
We've gone on holiday by mistake.

This should look familiar, if not see the section "Reference vs. Value" above. Here we can see that the global $quote is not affected when we overwrite the data passed in during the call to printQuote() (the first line of the function body). This is because lexical scope changes to local when printQuote() is invoked, and this includes any variables used as function arguments. We have two variables called $quote in this code: one in global scope and one scoped locally to printQuote(). They share a name, but they are protected from each other. We've already seen earlier in the chapter how code like this works. We know that values are passed by-value by default during function calls. The change in lexical scope is the mechanism that facilitates this.

If we had defined $quote as a reference in the declaration – function printQuote (string &$quote): void { ... } – then we would still have a locally scoped $quote variable, but its value would not be a copy of the global string. A locally scoped &$quote would be a reference to the global $quote, and any changes to the local $quote would propagate to global $quote.

Local Scope and Static Variables

Earlier in this section, we established that any variables created within local scope are destroyed when the scope changes back to global (when the boundary between local and scope is crossed). The following code demonstrates this behavior:

```
function getCount(): int
{
    if (!isset($counter)) {
        $counter = 0;
    }

    return $counter++;
}
```

```
print getCount() . PHP_EOL;
print getCount() . PHP_EOL;
```

Output:
```
0
0
```

To the untrained eye, the function getCount() might look as if it should initialize an integer at value zero then count upwards in increments of one on each call but returns zero every time. We know better though: the scoping rules dictate that $counter is destroyed when execution leaves local scope, so every time getCount() is called $counter is initialized at zero.

We could get around this with a global variable of course, but there is a much tidier solution to the problem: the keyword static, which we have seen previously when we looked at return-by-reference.

A static variable (and therefore its value) will persist even when the scope boundary is crossed, which means it can be used to store data between calls. If we turn $counter from above into a static variable, we get a different result:

```
function getCount(): int
{
    static $counter = 0;

    return $counter++;
}
print getCount() . PHP_EOL;
print getCount() . PHP_EOL;
print $counter . PHP_EOL;
```

Output:
```
0
1
Warning: Undefined variable $counter
```

And now our getCount() function behaves correctly. When execution leaves the getCount() local scope the variable $counter and its value is retained. There are two things to notice here. Firstly, PHP does not reinitialize static $counter if it already exists – $counter only initializes the first time the function is called – so we don't need the isset() test. Secondly, $counter is still only available within the local scope of getCount(). This is why we are warned when we try to access it from global scope.

By using static in this way we have avoided a global $count variable. Imagine that we needed several different counting functions like this in our program, we'd soon end up with lots of ugly variable names like $count_1, $otherCount, $countThis, $countThat, and so on to avoid functions stepping on each other's data.

Scope Persists Across Files

Scope boundaries only exist when control passes into or out of a function. When code is spread across multiple files, scope is inherited from the calling code when a file is incorporated into the program via include, require, etc. Dividing a program into multiple source code files does not generate scope:

```
// include_scope0.php
$song = 'Run to the Hills';

include __DIR__ . "/include_scope1.php";

// include_scope1.php
print $song . PHP_EOL;

Output (include_scope0.php):
Run to the Hills
```

We have two source code files, include_scope0.php and include_scope1.php. We execute include_scope0.php, which defines a global variable $song and then tells PHP to read in the second file via an include statement. The second file inherits whatever scope is active when PHP reaches include __DIR__ . '/include_scope1.php' – in this case, global scope. This means that $song is available during execution of include_scope1.php and the print statement succeeds.

What if we include a file as part of a function definition? Well, instead of inheriting global scope, the included file inherits the scope of the function body at the point the PHP engine hits the include statement:

```
// include_scope2.php
$song = 'Hallowed Be Thy Name';
```

141

```
function printSong(): void {
    include __DIR__ . "/include_scope1.php";
};

printSong();

Output:
Warning: Undefined variable $song in /usr/src/myapp/include_scope1.php on line 3
```

This time we're including `include_scope1.php` during a function body. `$song` is still a global variable, so it isn't accessible from the scope of `printSong()` with predictable results. If we need this code to work, there is a mechanism for making out-of-scope variables available to a function, which we'll see in action when we look at anonymous functions later.

New Function, New (Local) Scope

So far we've looked at passing control to and from single functions, jumping between local and global scope. It's worth making the point that local scope is specific to each function, here's a quick demonstration:

```
function outer(): void
{
    $funcName = 'outer()';
    inner();
    print $funcName . PHP_EOL;
}
function inner(): void
{
    $funcName = 'inner()';
    print $funcName . PHP_EOL;
}
outer();
```

Output:
inner()
outer()

Hopefully this doesn't need too much explaining. We're generating - and destroying - two local scopes, one within the other. outer() is called from global scope, which generates a local scope. inner() is called from outer() which generates another, separate local scope. Both functions are free to create the same variable identifier; each is protected from the other by their own scope. When execution passes into inner() the scope for outer() is not affected, it still exists along with its variables.

Remember scope is only destroyed when the boundary is crossed, outer() scope persists until the end of the function body: we're free to call inner(), have it do its thing, and when control returns to outer() PHP just picks up where it left off.

Bear in mind that anonymous functions don't have identifiers like named functions, and that variables used as references to anonymous functions are of course subject to the same scoping rules as any other variable.

Scoping Rules

To conclude this section, let's summarize the scoping rules.

- Variables declared outside a function have global scope.
- Variables declared inside a function have local scope.
- Every function has its own local scope.
- Local scope is generated when execution passes into a function.
- Local scope is destroyed (along with all local variables and data) when exiting a function.
- Locally scoped variables can persist between function calls if they are declared as static.

We've spent a lot of time on discussing scope here, with good reason. The scoping rules are also applicable to objects as we shall see soon.

CHAPTER 3   FUNCTIONS

Variable Functions

So far we've called functions by using their names as symbols in our code, but in fact any expression, which evaluates to a string can also be used provided the string matches the function name. This is demonstrated below:

```
$funcName = 'myFunc';
$funcName();

function myFunc (): void
{
    print "Hello from myFunc" . PHP_EOL;
}
```

Output:
Hello from myFunc

Hopefully this should make immediate sense. Rather than write myFunc(); we have instead used an expression which will evaluate to the string literal value "myFunc". If parentheses are placed immediately after the expression, the corresponding function is called. The variable $funcNanme contains the string "myFunc", so when the PHP engine encounters the expression $funcName(); at run-time (reading from right to left), first the parentheses are recognized, then the variable name. The parentheses indicate a function call, but first the variable needs to be evaluated. PHP retrieves the string from memory, checks if myFunc() is declared, and calls it as normal. If the variable does not match a known function, then a fatal "Call to undefined function" error is the result.

Incidentally, I really do mean "any expression." Let's have a little fun:

```
'myFunc'();
('my' . 'Func')();

$my = 'my';
$func = 'Func';
($my . $func)();

function myFunc (): void
{
    print "Let's, ahem, get func-y" . PHP_EOL;
}
```

I'll spare you the output of terrible puns; take it on trust that all of the above code has legal syntax and is bug-free. If any of those expressions are confusing (perhaps you're wondering why I had to wrap the string concatenation of `'my'` . `'Func` in parentheses), see Chapter 8, "Strings."

Variable function calls are not without their problems though. Let's take a look at one of PHP's oddities: not everything that looks like a function is actually a function. For example, the language construct `print` is used extensively throughout this book. I have deliberately avoided using parentheses with `print` despite the fact that they are legal syntax. `print('hello world');` does exactly the same thing as `print 'hello world';`. Here's what happens if we try to "call" `print` as we called `myFunc` above:

```php
$msg = 'Important message' . PHP_EOL;
print($msg);

$funcName = 'print';
$funcName($msg);
```

Output:
```
Important message
Fatal error: Uncaught Error: Call to undefined function print()
```

The variable function call used on line 7 forces PHP to go and find a function called `print` and... there isn't one. As stated previously it is a language construct that happens to permit a function-like syntax. This problem exists for all other language constructs (`echo`, `require`, `list`, and so on). I recommend that you avoid using parentheses for language constructs in your code to avoid confusion.

Another issue with variable functions is one of debugging and analysis. Consider the following:

```php
$funcName = 'wrongFunc';
$funcName();

function myFunc (): void
{
    print "Hello from myFunc" . PHP_EOL;
}
```

Clearly, we'll get a fatal error if we try to run this. There is no function called `wrongFunc()` declared. However, there is nothing wrong with the syntax of this code. The error only emerges when it is executed. If we were to attempt to call the non-existent `wrongFunc()` by name it would be flagged by your IDE as you wrote it, and a static analysis tool like phpmd (PHP Mess Detector, a very useful tool for monitoring code quality available here: `https://phpmd.org/`) would also generate a warning. The variable call is far more likely to slip through whatever layers of analysis are in place to protect your codebase (in fact only a unit test would expose the issue). Use variable functions sparingly, they are best limited to call-backs handling where type declarations can enforce some checks and balances.

Anonymous Functions

There are occasions when functions don't need to be named, because of the way that they are called. Sometimes other functions require that they're given something callable as an argument, typically to be executed when the function is complete or needs to raise an error. These passed-in functions are known as *callbacks*. If you never need to call a function by its identifier (because another function will do the call for you), why bother naming it all?

When a function isn't given a name, it is an *anonymous function*. Another name for anonymous functions is *closure*, these are very commonly encountered in other languages (JavaScript, for example) and were added to PHP version 5.3. The name *Closure* is important in PHP because anonymous functions are implemented internally as objects of the built-in *Closure* class.

Here is how to declare an anonymous function:

```
function (string $txt): void {
    print $txt . PHP_EOL;
};
```

The above code is legal PHP syntax, but not particularly useful on its own. Most IDEs will likely highlight this code in some way because it is useless, there's no way to call this code.

Up to now we have been using function names explicitly to invoke them, but any expression that evaluates to a function or function name can also be used. The above code evaluates to a function, and we can call it using the standard calling mechanism of placing parentheses immediately after the expression (with the caveat that the entire declaration must also be wrapped by parentheses) like this: `(function () { // function body })();`. This technique of immediate execution is known as a *self-invoking* (or *self-calling*) function:

```
(function (string $txt): void {
    print $txt . PHP_EOL;
})("Go go go!");
```

Output:
Go go go!

Like any expression, anonymous function declarations can be assigned to variables, simply using standard variable assignment:

```
$anon = function (): void {
    print "Who am I?" . PHP_EOL;
};
$anon();
```

Output:
Who am I?

This looks very similar to the syntax for variable functions in the previous section, but there's a subtle difference. $anon is a direct reference to a function, rather than a string which evaluates to a function name. There's no need for PHP to evaluate a string then check it matches a known function name, and no danger of triggering a fatal error because the string doesn't match a declared identifier.

Passing Functions As Data

If you've been paying attention so far you have probably already figured out that the variable used to reference (and call) an anonymous function could also be the argument of *another* function declaration, like so:

```
handleCallback(function (): void {
    print "Who am I?" . PHP_EOL;
});
```

```
function handleCallback(callable $cb): void
{
    // do things then make the callback...
    $cb();
}
```

What we are seeing here is the beginnings of something quite powerful. Functions are sub-units of callable code, true, but here they are also being treated as data. They are values that can be treated like the result of any other expression. Just as an integer variable references an integer value, a function variable references a function.

Functions in PHP can be passed into – and returned by – other functions. This is a neat way of bouncing control around a complex program and treating functions as data opens the door to the "functional programming" paradigm, which we will look at toward the end of this chapter. For now, take a look at the following:

```
$cb = getCallback();
$cb();
getCallback()();

function getCallback(): callable
{
    return function (): void {
        print "Who am I?" . PHP_EOL;
    };
}
```

Output:
Who am I?
Who am I?

This time we're returning an anonymous function, which is perfectly reasonable given that we know functions can be treated like any other data. They even have their own dedicated data type of callable as we can see from the declaration function getCallback(): callable. We also know that any expression that evaluates to a function can be invoked. We do it by variable assignment: $cb is assigned the function reference as its value, then we invoke using $cb().

CHAPTER 3   FUNCTIONS

The second invocation – getCallback()() – might look a little funky. If this chapter has made sense so far (I really hope it has!), then it should be obvious that the expression getCallback() evaluates to an anonymous function, we can either invoke it immediately or store a reference to it in a variable for future use.

Anonymous Functions and Scope

Earlier we looked at the difference between local and global scope in PHP. If you're coming to PHP from a language that has different scoping rules (such as automatic inheritance of parent scope in JavaScript), then you might find yourself wondering why the following code isn't working:

```
function getCallbackWithArg(string $txt): callable
{
    return function (): void {
        print "You gave me the string '{$txt}'" . PHP_EOL;
    };
}

getCallbackWithArg('I hope this works')(); // spoilers, it doesn't
Output:
Warning: Undefined variable $txt in /usr/src/myapp/anon_func5.php on line 6
You gave me the string ''
```

Yep, definitely broken. Here's an equivalent in JavaScript:

```
function getCallbackWithArg(txt) {
    return function () {
        console.log("You gave me the string '" + txt + "'\n");
    };
}

getCallbackWithArg('I hope this works')();

Output:
You gave me the string 'I hope this works'
```

Why the difference? If you recall from earlier, with JavaScript there is automatic inheritance of parent scope. The inner and outer functions have their own scope, but in JavaScript the inner scope of the anonymous function has access to the outer scope of the parent function getCallbackWithArg(). Not so with PHP, however. For better or worse, PHP scoping rules are simpler. The good news is that there are two mechanisms for passing data from one local scope to another when a function definition contains another function definition.

First, there's the keyword use, which, in the context of anonymous function declarations, provides a way to make the variables of getCallbackWithArg() accessible in the anonymous function's scope when getCallbackWithArg() executes:

```
function getCallbackWithArg(string $txt): callable
{
    return function () use ($txt): void {
        print "You gave me the string '{$txt}'" . PHP_EOL;
    };
}

getCallbackWithArg('I hope this works')(); // spoilers, it does!
```

Output:
```
You gave me the string 'I hope this works'
```

That's the first way to pass parent scope into a nested function declaration. There is another mechanism for very simple cases...

Arrow Functions

Introduced in PHP 7.4, *arrow functions* are a special type of anonymous function that have automatic access to the parent scope and always return a single expression. They can be used anywhere a long-form anonymous function can be used. The syntax of an arrow function is fn () => EXPR, where EXPR is any single valid PHP expression (requiring exactly one closing semicolon). Return type declarations go after the closing parenthesis before the => arrow, and void isn't permitted because arrow functions *always* return.

Take a look at the following:

```
function getQuoteBot ()
{
    $quotes = [
        "We've gone on holiday by mistake.",
        "We're bona fide, we're not from London.",
        "We want the finest wines available to humanity.",
    ];

    $i = rand(0, 2);

    return function () use ($quotes, $i): string {
        return $quotes[$i] . PHP_EOL;
    };
}

$bot = getQuoteBot();
print $bot(); // Outputs one of the strings in the $quotes array
```

The parent function getQuoteBot() contains an array and generates a random number between 0 and 2. These are explicitly passed into the anonymous function, which is the return value. Obviously, this could be cleaner code; the thing to focus on is the anonymous function. It only contains a single expression, which is returned to the caller. An ideal candidate for conversion to an arrow function.

Here's what the anonymous function looks like when rewritten as an arrow function:

```
return fn (): string => $quotes[$i] . PHP_EOL;
```

The main thing to take away here is that we have access to the parent function's scope (no need to explicitly make them available with use) and we do not need to use a return keyword. The arrow function automatically returns the value of its single expression (in this case, one of the strings in $quotes concatenated with a PHP_EOL constant). An altogether cleaner and easier-to-read syntax.

Testing for Existing Functions

In the previous section, we saw how scoping provides a safety mechanism for data and that variables declared inside a function (local scope) do not impact data declared outside (global scope). We also saw that this does not extend to named functions: no matter what the scope is, when a named function is declared, it is available globally. As you might imagine, this can lead to problems when programs grow in complexity. Especially so when third-party library code is added into a project (which is inevitable unless one wishes to waste time reinventing various wheels).

As projects become more complex, the options for choosing names tend to shrink, and the likelihood of name collisions increases. Let's say you defined a function called `logMessage()`, then later added a library called `ShinyLogs`, which also defines a function `logMessage()`. Now every time you run your code, you get a fatal error.

This is what happens when a function declaration attempts to use an existing function name:

```
function collision(): void {}
function collision(): void {}
```

Output:
Fatal error: Cannot redeclare collision()

A function can only be declared once, and trying to do so again kills your program. A useful mitigation is the built-in function `function_exists()`; it is quite common to see code structured like this in large projects:

```
function collision(): void {
    print "Come at me bro!";
}

if (!function_exists('collision')) {
    function collision(): void {
        print "Critical dodge!";
    }
}

collision();
```

Output:
Come at me bro!

function_exists() accepts a single string argument and tests global scope for a function with the same name, returning boolean true if found (false if it isn't). By testing if collision() is already declared, we can skip declaring it again and killing our program. If collision() wasn't declared, the declaration inside the if block would have executed, and we'd have had the second version of the function in global scope. This particular trick is effective for avoiding runtime errors and historically was something of a necessity in PHP, when libraries installed with PEAR would commonly stomp all over your code (or each other's).

Another method of avoiding name collisions (prior to PHP 5.3) was to simply prefix the name you wanted to use with some other word, usually separated by an underscore or similar character. Thus, logMessage() might become MyProject_logMessage(), which is fine as far as it goes but does create issues of maintenance and readability (perhaps you already had several hundred calls to the original logMessage() before ShinyLogs became part of the project). The next section will show a more elegant way of mitigating name collision issues in global scope by using namespaces.

If for some reason you want to see *all* declared functions, there is the built-in get_defined_functions(), which will return an array of every single function registered when it is called. This can be rather large (a typical PHP installation will have thousands). Of more use might be get_extension_functions(), which will return every function for a named PHP extension:

```
print_r(get_extension_funcs('SPL'));
```

Output:
```
Array
(
    [0] => class_implements
    [1] => class_parents
    [2] => class_uses
    ...
```

A list of loaded extensions can be obtained via get_loaded_extension().

CHAPTER 3   FUNCTIONS

Namespaced Functions

Prior to PHP 5.3, all functions lived in global scope, and name collisions were common. The same was especially true of classes. To avoid the problem, unwieldy names were often used to prefix function and class names to make them specific to a library, filesystem path, or some other abstract method of organizing code. With namespaces, however, it is possible to group related functions together (along with classes, interfaces, and constants). If we take the example of colliding function names from the previous section, we can isolate the two functions in their own namespaces like so:

```
namespace {
    function collision(): void {
        print "Hello from root namespace." . PHP_EOL;
    }
}

namespace Other {
    function collision(): void {
        print "Hello from Other namespace." . PHP_EOL;
    }
}

namespace Other\SubOther {
    function collision(): void {
        print "Hello from Other\\Sub namespace." . PHP_EOL;
    }
}
```

In the first declaration – `namespace { ... }` – we are simply telling the PHP engine that the code doesn't use a namespace, so PHP uses root. We define a function `collision()`. Next, we enter a new namespace called `Other` and define another function called `collision()`. Finally, we enter a third namespace `Other\Sub`, and create another `collision()` function. We now have three namespaces in our code: root (or non-namespaced), `Other`, and `Other\Sub`. `Sub` is a sub-namespace of `Other`.

This example comes with a disclaimer. *It is NOT recommended to use multiple namespace blocks like this in a single file.* There are very few valid use cases for doing so and usually involve generated code (or writing books about the language). Best practice is to use a single namespace statement per file and organize namespaced source code files in a filesystem structure that maps to namespaces and sub-namespaces. Multiple namespace statements in a single file violates section 3 of the PHP-FIG PSR-12 coding standards. Don't get into the habit of using multiple namespaces like this!

With that said, let's examine the code. The keyword namespace followed (optionally) by a legal name (same rules as variable and function naming) denotes the following code is using that namespace. Using no name at all simply means the code is not in any particular namespace, so it uses the root namespace. The opening and closing braces that follow the declaration aren't necessary but are highly recommended for readability. Incidentally, the root namespace is often referred to as the "global" namespace, but this is inaccurate: things defined in root are not magically available globally, as we shall see. Also, using the word "global" might cause confusion with the concept of global scope. Scope and namespace are not the same thing, which we'll also be covering in a moment.

Now let's see how we use each namespaced version of collision(). We have a few options.

Calling Functions from Namespaces

```
namespace {
    collision();
}
namespace Other {
    collision();
}
namespace Other\Sub {
    collision();
}
```

Output:
```
Hello from root namespace.
Hello from Other namespace.
Hello from Other\\Sub namespace.
```

Here we are entering each namespace and calling collision(). The PHP engine will search whatever its current namespace is for the function. As we have defined collision() in each, we get the version specific to that namespace, which we can see in the output. If collision() wasn't defined in the namespace we were in, PHP would next check the root namespace, which we can see happening here:

```
namespace Other\New {
    collision();
}
```

Output:
Hello from root namespace.

There is no collision() defined in the sub-namespace Other\New so we get the root version, but what if we wanted to call the root version but we were currently in another namespace?

Qualified Namespace Function Calls

```
namespace Other {
    collision();
    \collision();
}
```

Output:
Hello from Other namespace.
Hello from root namespace.

This code is executing in the Other namespace. If we want to call the root version of collision(), we have to add some extra information in our expression. The backslash character turns our second call to collision() into a *qualified* function name. Rather than letting PHP follow its searching rules (check current namespace, then fall back to root), we have instead explicitly asked for the root namespaced function. If we want to call collision() from Other\Sub while not in the Other\Sub namespace, we can do it in two ways: qualified or fully qualified.

```
namespace Other {
    Sub\collision(); // qualified - namespace path is relative to current
    \Other\Sub\collision(); // fully qualified - namespace path starts
    from root
}
```

Output:
Hello from Other\\Sub namespace.
Hello from Other\\Sub namespace.

Notice the first call does not have a leading backslash, so PHP begins its search in current namespace. But the first call does include a sub-namespace name: Sub. Making a qualified call in this way means that PHP will append the sub-namespace name in the call to the current and search there. The current namespace is Other, the qualified call asks for the Sub sub-namespace, the result is PHP searches Other\Sub and calls the function from there.

The second call has a leading backslash, this is a fully qualified name starting from root space, and we get the same version of collision() as we can see from the output.

Using Namespaces

Using qualified names is a great way of being explicit about your intentions, but there is another way to achieve the same results and keep your code a little easier to read. Imagine that you were working in one namespace but needed to call a function defined in another. Even worse, the function in question does not collide with any defined where your code happens to be executing. Do you really need to litter your file with lots of calls to \Some\Deeply\Nested\Sub\Sub\Space\usefulFunction()? The good news is that you don't, because you can import symbols (functions, interfaces, classes, and constants) from other namespaces with the keyword use. To use a function from a specific namespace without qualifying on every call, add the statement use function.

```
namespace Some\Other\Space {
    use function \Other\collision;

    collision();
}
```

Output:
Hello from Other namespace.

Every call to collision() after PHP evaluates the use function statement will be made to \Other\collision(). If for some reason you need to use identically named functions from multiple namespaces, it is possible to create an *alias* using the keyword as.

CHAPTER 3 FUNCTIONS

```
namespace Some\Other\Sub\Space {
    use function \Other\Sub\collision as otherCollision;
    use function \collision as rootCollision;

    otherCollision();
    rootCollision();
}
```

Output:
Hello from Other\\Sub namespace.
Hello from root namespace.

Namespaces Are Not Scope

We explored the concept of scope earlier in the chapter and how it provided a mechanism for protecting variables and data inside a function from those outside: local vs. global scope. Namespaces are another way to prevent symbols in code from colliding with each other. Scope only concerns variables. A namespace concerns only functions, classes, interfaces, and constants. Changing namespaces does not change scope; only entering a function boundary can change scope. The following code should illustrate this:

```
namespace Other {
    $val = 'I am everywhere' . PHP_EOL;

    function greetings(): void
    {
        print "I am also everywhere, but did you get my name right?" .
        PHP_EOL;
    }
}
namespace {
    print $val;
    \Other\greetings();
    greetings();
}
```

Output:
I am everywhere
I am also everywhere, but did you get my name right?
Fatal error: Uncaught Error: Call to undefined function greetings()

First, we enter Other namespace and define a string variable $val, and a function greetings(). Next, we switch to root namespace and use $val in a print expression. The expression is valid because although $val was defined in a namespace, the scope was still global. After the print expression, we then call greetings(), fully qualified in the first instance and with no namespace qualification in the second. The second call fails because there's no greetings() defined in root namespace but here's the thing: when we defined greetings() in Other namespace it also went into global scope, but its true name became \Other\greetings(). Namespaced functions still have global scope, they just have more complex names.

All of the keywords we've used for interacting with namespaces are simply syntactic sugar (mmm, delicious) to avoid needing to pseudo-namespace our functions. Before PHP 5.3 our namespaced collision() functions would have been named collision() (root namespace), Other_collision() (Other namespace), Other_Sub_collision() and so on. The PSR-1 coding standard actually recommends using pseudo-namespaced function and class names for code targeting PHP 5.2 or earlier, as well as insisting on namespaced code for PHP 5.3 and later.

Functional Programming

It's quite likely that you will have at least heard the phrase "functional programming" (FP) at some point in your journey as a software engineer. It is often used in opposition to object-oriented programming (OOP), and I've endured many protracted arguments over the relative merits of these paradigms (and by extension which language is "the best") during my career. Which is exactly as much fun as it sounds. An advocate for the FP style would invariably point the finger at PHP and tut, for it was just another OOP language and filled with mutability and side effects. An OOP champion might then criticize FP for its tendency to allow programs to collapse into callback-hell singularities. Hilarity would often ensue shortly afterwards.

Here's the thing though: PHP has patterns from both functional and object-oriented paradigms. It has become increasingly more FP-like over time, even as it added more OOP features. I am advocating for neither over the other, but being aware of the features of these paradigms will, I believe, help you to get the best out of PHP.

Let's review some of the features of functional programming, given that we've just spent a fairly hefty chapter dissecting how functions work!

First-Class and Higher-Order Functions

Functions in a programming language are said to be "first-class citizens" if they can be treated like any other data. A language supports first-class functions if it allows them to be used as arguments to other functions, returned by other functions, or stored in variables. As we have seen earlier in the chapter, we can store anonymous functions in PHP with a variable, we can send functions to other functions as callbacks (hence the `callable` data type), and we can obtain one function from another. A "higher-order" function is one that takes one or more functions as an argument and/or returns a function.

This is a powerful feature, because it allows functions to be composed from other functions (and in due course we'll see how objects can be composed from other objects, an equally powerful tool). Examples of higher-order functions in PHP are `array_map()` and `array_reduce()`.

Pure Functions

A function is "pure" if it meets the following criteria: it has no side effects (no changes to local static variables, global variables, reference arguments, or I/O streams – so that's PHP buggered then), and it always returns the same output for the same input. In a truly FP language, no data is ever mutated (instead, new data is created, which is why FP languages are sometimes less memory efficient). Trying to adopt a pure functional approach for your code is going to pose serious challenges for a language invented to drive websites, and I don't suggest you try.

However, one great benefit of pure functions is that they are incredibly easy to test. The fewer side effects a function has, the easier it is to write tests for. Keeping side effects to a minimum *will* make your life easier, I promise.

Summary

Phew! That was quite a chapter; we covered a lot of ground and well done for making it this far. Believe me, writing it was no picnic either. I have some good news: the next giant chapter is actually going to be a lot less work because much of what we've learned in this one is transferable.

Let's recap quickly. We started with the basics: declaring functions with names, their parameters, and how to call them with or without arguments. We then looked at passing arguments by reference, how to define default arguments, and how to return data. Next came the type declaration system in all its glory and the more advanced parameter handling of PHP 8. Then came the really big stuff: lexical scope and namespacing (and learning those topics will serve us very well when we finally move onto objects in detail). As well as all of that, we also covered anonymous functions and variable functions and had a brief discussion on a rather large topic called functional programming (and trust me, we only skimmed the surface on that).

All of the rules and features concerning functions that we have studied in this chapter are (with the odd caveat here or there) also applicable to objects, because objects are at heart simply collections of functions. Scope, data types, namespacing… it's all going to look very familiar. In the meantime, feel free to have a short break. You've earned it.

CHAPTER 4

Logic and Control

Programs, even simple ones, will inevitably have to alter their behavior based on their inputs, or current state. Likewise, it's usually necessary to perform operations repeatedly: imperative languages (programming languages that are composed of step-by-step instructions) such as PHP have features that allow for the testing of data and the concise expression of repetitive sequences of code. This chapter explores logical operations and control structures. Logic operations generate boolean values (`true` or `false`), and the control structures of PHP often use these boolean values to determine their behavior. In this way we can build programs that make runtime decisions and achieve a great deal of work with minimal code.

PHP, like most languages based on C syntax, has the usual language constructs for controlling the flow of execution. Logic branches with `if` statements, compound variables can be iterated with `for` and `foreach`, and code blocks can be looped with `do` and `while`. More advanced forms of logic branching are available with `switch` and the recently introduced `match` construct.

In Chapter 1, "Getting Started," I introduced the concept of expressions. These are a high-level aspect of the syntax of PHP (indeed, of any programming language). Expressions consist of sequences of operations that are evaluated (generate data values), and they can be thought of as "code that reduces to a value." An expression, however complex, will always evaluate – or reduce – to a value. That value can then be tested – and the testing itself is an expression too. Chapter 1, "Getting Started," showed that expressions could be numeric. `1 + 1` reducing to `2` is a simple example. String operations are also expressions, like `'Hello' . ' world'` reduces to the single string `'Hello world'`. They can be more complex, of course, consisting of function calls, array access, or any other legal PHP operation.

A logical expression is one that ultimately evaluates to `true` or `false`. They usually contain comparison and/or logical operators, which are used to test operands, where the operands can be variables, literal values, or sub-expressions. Therefore, the key components of logical expressions are the *logical* operators, *comparison* operators, and *bitwise* operators. These are the units of code that determine the correct functioning of your program.

What Is Truth?

Program logic is driven by the idea of things being true or false. Code branches, and the flow of execution goes one way or another, based on decisions made on the basis of an expression being true or false. But here's the thing: how are these two absolute states represented? Well, we have the `bool` data type, which has two possible values of `true` or `false`. That's nice, but this is a loosely-typed language. Strings can become numbers, and objects can become strings, often without any intervention on the programmer's part. `bool` is no different: if an expression is evaluated in a boolean context, type coercion will happen. Like other loosely typed languages, there is a concept of "truthy" and "falsey": non-boolean values that are equivalent to `true` or `false`. Here's a synopsis:

```
var_dump((bool) null); // bool(false)
var_dump((bool) 0); // bool(false)
var_dump((bool) 0.0); // bool(false)
var_dump((bool) []); // bool(false)
var_dump((bool) ['foo']); // bool(true)
var_dump((bool) ''); // bool(false)
var_dump((bool) 'literally anything'); // bool(true)
var_dump((bool) '0'); // bool(false)!
```

As you can see, there's a gotcha: the string `'0'` is not empty; it contains a byte value of *0x30*, which has the binary value of 00110000, yet it's false. I highly recommend being as type-safe as possible when it comes to logical expressions (and, to be fair, all of your programming).

Control Structures

Control structures are simply a way to manage the order of execution of statements. By testing for a condition, it is possible to skip a set of statements or ensure statements that would otherwise be skipped are executed. They can be broadly grouped into two types: decision-making and repetition.

Decision-Making

The workhorse of logical decision in most code is the humble `if` statement. There have been numerous examples already throughout the book so far, but there's no harm in revisiting.

`if, else, elseif`

The complete structure consists of the keyword `if` followed by an expression contained in parentheses, which will be evaluated to `true` or `false`. If the result is `true`, execution will pass into a code block contained in braces:

```
if (true) {
    print "true" . PHP_EOL;
}
if (false) {
    print "false" . PHP_EOL;
}
```

Output:
true

Pretty straightforward stuff. It is possible to specify an alternative block should the `if` expression is `false`, using the `else` keyword…

```
if (false) {
    print "false" . PHP_EOL;
} else {
    print "else" . PHP_EOL;
}
```

Output:
else

…and even chain together multiple alternative branches with the `elseif` construct:

```
if (false) {
    print "false" . PHP_EOL;
} elseif (true) {
    print "elseif" . PHP_EOL;
```

```
} else {
    print "else" . PHP_EOL;
}
```

Output:
elseif

You can chain together as many elseif blocks as you like, but that code would grow untidy rather quickly. There is an alternative syntax for this control structure (and others) using colons...

```
if (EXPR):
    //one or more statements
elseif (EXPR):
    //one or more statements
else:
    //one or more statements
endif;
```

... but it is unusual to see it in modern PHP. The PSR-12 standard recommends that you use braces.

switch, match

An alternative to multiple if/elseif statements is the switch/case construct:

```
$var = 'foo';
switch ($var) {
    case 'bar':
        print 'bar' . PHP_EOL;
    case 'foo':
        print 'foo' . PHP_EOL;
}
```

Output:
foo

CHAPTER 4 LOGIC AND CONTROL

The code above is equivalent to the construct if ($var == 'bar') / elseif ($var == 'foo'), and note the weakly typed comparison: switch comparisons are always loosely typed. switch constructs provide a little more flexibility than just acting as syntactic sugar for if/elseif. Take a look at the following:

```php
function logicDemo(string $var): void
{
    switch ($var) {
        case 'bar':
            print 'bar ';
        case 'foo':
            print 'foo ';
        case 'qux':
            print 'qux ';
    }
    print PHP_EOL;
}
logicDemo('qux');
logicDemo('foo');
logicDemo('bar');
```

Output:
qux
foo qux
bar foo qux

This highlights an interesting feature of switch: once a case is matched, execution continues to "fall through" to the remaining cases, as we can see from the output. This behavior might be desired, but if not, then use the keyword break to prevent it:

```php
...
switch ($var) {
    case 'bar':
        print 'bar ';
        break;
    case 'foo':
        print 'foo ';
        break;
```

167

```
        case 'qux':
            print 'qux ';
            break;
    }
    ...
logicDemo('bar');
```

Output:
bar

Finally, just like a chain of if/elseif statements can have a final else block to execute if nothing else matches, switch has a default case. If we add one to the switch structure in logicDemo()...

```
        default:
            print 'default ';
            break;
    }
    ...
logicDemo('wibble');
```

Output:
default

... then we have a final alternative when all other cases fail to match.

Similar to switch is match, which allows a concise expression of multiple logical branches. There are, however, some important differences: match comparisons are strictly typed, they do not fall through, and they operate like functions in that they return values. However, don't be fooled into thinking match() is a function: it does not allow data typing of its single parameter, nor its "return" value. It also does not have a separate lexical scope; variables declared outside the match() block are accessible inside (indeed, they have to be). The following demonstrates the type strictness of match():

```
$var = 1;
print match ($var) {
    '1' => 'string',
    1 => 'integer',
};
```

Output:
integer

`match` "cases" can also be expressions, rather than values, which allow for more flexibility. Here's a form that uses logical comparison expressions:

```
$var = 42;
print match (true) {
    $var < 10 => 'low',
    $var === 42 => 'Life the universe and everything',
    $var < 100 => 'high',
};
```

Output:
Life the universe and everything

Notice how the expressions are tested in order, and the first true result is returned. In this case, $var is both equal to *42* and less than *100*, but it's the test for `$var === 42` that is executed first, and `match` does not fall through like a `switch` construct would.

Repetition

PHP offers the same structures for repeating code blocks as most other C-style languages.

for, foreach

Chapter 5, "Array" (in the section "Iteration"), has already explained these two constructs in detail, where it made the most contextual sense. After all, these are structures intended to iterate arrays or array-like data structures. Here's a quick recap of what they look like:

```
$rogueAgents = [
    'Aaron Keener',
    'Theo Parnell',
    'Alani Kelso',
];
```

```
$count = count($rogueAgents);
for ($i = 0; $i < $count; $i++) {
    print $rogueAgents[$i] . PHP_EOL;
}
foreach ($rogueAgents as $agent) {
    print $agent . PHP_EOL;
}
```

Output:
Aaron Keener
Theo Parnell
Alani Kelso

The output of both `for` and `foreach` loops is identical and given once above. Don't forget the `break` keyword (also shown in Chapter 5, "Array," in addition to the similar `continue` keyword) allows early loop termination:

```
foreach ($rogueAgents as $agent) {
    if ($agent === 'Alani Kelso') {
        break;
    }
    print $agent . PHP_EOL;
}
```

Output:
Aaron Keener
Theo Parnell

I guess Kelso might not be as rogue as the other agents... Anyway, for more detail you can always refer back to Chapter 5, "Array." Moving on from iterating structures, we have looping structures that are predicated on logical expressions.

while, do-while

The simplest looping construct is `while`. It takes an expression, which, if it evaluates to `true`, moves execution into a block of statements:

```
$i = 1;
while($i < 10) {
    if ($i % 2 == 0) {
        print "{$i} is even" . PHP_EOL;
    }
    $i++;
}
print "All done.";
```

Output:

```
2 is even
4 is even
6 is even
8 is even
All done.
```

This simple example initializes `$i = 1;` and increments it by *1* on each iteration of the loop. Before each iteration executes, the expression `$i < 10` is evaluated, so once the variable's value reaches *10*, the expression is `false`, and this causes the loop to terminate, and program control flows to the next statement. Of course, if the expression is always true, the loop will run forever (or at least until interrupted by some other means), for example:

```
$cliIn = fopen("php://stdin", "r");
while (true) {
    print "Enter 'stop' to terminate" . PHP_EOL;
    $input = fgets($cliIn);
    if (strpos($input, 'stop') !== false) {
        break;
    }
    print "You entered {$input}" . PHP_EOL;
}
fclose($cliIn);
print "Terminating.";
```

This simple "infinite" loop will continue to prompt for user input until a specific string is detected from STDIN. Here's what it looks like running:

```
$ php while2.php
Enter 'stop' to terminate
hello
You entered hello

Enter 'stop' to terminate
stop
Terminating.
```

The expression of a while loop is checked before any potential execution of the statements in the while block. If you need to run the block at least once, then do can be placed at the start of the block and while at the end – commonly known as a do-while structure:

```
do {
    print "I'm doing a thing." . PHP_EOL;
} while (false);
print "I've done a thing.";

Output:
I'm doing a thing.
I've done a thing.
```

Nesting, break, continue

We've seen how we can use break to exit a loop. Don't forget that break also stops execution inside a switch block (conceptually, a switch statement is like a loop that has an iteration for each case statement). It is possible to have loops within loops – an example of such a construct can be found in Chapter 5, "Arrays," for processing multi-dimensional arrays. break statements can have numeric values appended to them to indicate how many levels of nested looping should be terminated:

```
$multiArr = [
    ['duck', 'duck'],
    ['duck', 'goose', 'duck'],
```

```
        ['duck', 'nuke'],
        ['duck'],
];

foreach ($multiArr as $k => $arr) {
    foreach ($arr as $val) {
        switch ($val) {
            case 'duck':
                print "duck from subArr {$k}" . PHP_EOL;
                break;
            case 'goose':
                print "found a goose moving to subArr ". $k + 1 . PHP_EOL;
                break 2;
            case 'nuke':
                print "BOOM! No more game." . PHP_EOL;
                break 3;
        }
    }
}
Output:
duck from subArr 0
duck from subArr 0
duck from subArr 1
found a goose moving to subArr 2
duck from subArr 2
BOOM! No more game.
```

The key to this example is knowing that there are three levels of nesting. An outer foreach iterates $multiArr, an inner foreach iterates each sub-array of $multiArr, and the switch structure. Each case statement inside the switch block has a break statement. The elements of $subArr are strings: 'duck' triggers a single-level break (terminating the switch), 'goose' has a break 2, which terminates two levels of nesting (the switch and the inner foreach), and 'nuke' has break 3, which terminates everything. As we can see from the output, once 'nuke' is reached, it's game over, man.

There also exists the keyword `continue`, which is similar, though its effect is slightly different: it will stop the execution of the current iteration and begin a new one:

```
$arr = ['duck', 'duck', 'duck', 'goose', 'duck'];

$count = 0;
foreach ($arr as $val) {
    $count++;
    if ($val === 'duck') {
        continue;
    }
    print "Found a goose!" . PHP_EOL;
}
print "Visited {$count} elements.";

Output:
Found a goose!
Visited 5 elements.
```

Hopefully the above makes sense: the code in the `foreach` block terminates and begins a new iteration every time it hits `continue`, which is why we only see `'Found a goose!'` once. The point of `$count` is to simply prove that we iterated every element of `$arr`.

Miscellaneous

There are other language constructs that influence the flow of control but are specialized to certain tasks and not used to implement program logic as such (or at least they generally shouldn't, with a few exceptions). These are

Table 4-1. *Other control constructs*

declare	Sets directives, such as declare(strict_types=1)
return	Terminates a function, optionally passing back data
include	Read in a PHP source code file, the contents are executed immediately
require	Read and execute a PHP file, throws an error if the file isn't found
include_once	Like include but can only run once (repeats have no effect)
require_once	The require form of include_once
die exit	Terminate the program immediately
goto	No. Just don't. Not ever.

As noted in an earlier chapter, exit (aliased by die) are language constructs until PHP 8.4, where they became proper functions with special handling/parsing rules to support the construct-like syntax of calling them without parentheses.

It's possible to treat include and require as control structures (I've seen it done), but I strongly advise not to. Treat them simply as ways to organize your code and nothing more. goto is a way of having control jump around a program using labels. It's also another way to glimpse into the abyss of madness. Avoid it. I'm not even going to explain it to you.

Figure 4-1. *Do. Not. Use. Goto.*

CHAPTER 4 LOGIC AND CONTROL

Functions

There is a set of functions in PHP that see the most use in logical expressions. These functions typically test variables for their type or even if they exist at all. Knowing in advance that a variable exists, has a certain type, or contains non-null or non-false data means you can fine-tune the code that comes next. These functions are type-strict, in that the variable being tested must be of the type concerned and not coercible to that type or capable of behaving like that type (`is_array(new ArrayObject())` would return `false`, for example). The following functions all return a `bool` value:

Table 4-2. Control functions

`empty($var)`	Problematic, see explanation below
`is_array($var)`	`$var` is type `array` (not array-like)
`is_bool($var)`	`$var` is type `bool`
`is_callable($var)`	`$var` can be invoked
`is_countable($var)`	`$var` is an array or implements `Countable`

`is_double($var)`
`is_float($var)`
`is_real($var)`
	`$var` is type `float`

`is_int($var)`
`is_integer($var)`
`is_long($var)`
	`$var` is type `int`

`is_iterable($var)`	`$var` is array|Traversable or (PHP 8.2) `iterable` psuedo-type
`is_null($var)`	`$var` has the `null` value
`is_numeric($var)`	`$var` is either `int`, `float`, or numeric `string`
`is_object($var)`	`$var` is an object instance
`is_resource($var)`	`$var` is a special reference to external resource (e.g., file descriptor)
`is_scalar($var)`	`$var` is `int`, `float`, `string`, or `bool`
`is_string($var)`	`$var` is `string`
`isset($var)`	`$var` is declared, and has non-null value

Most of these functions should make sense just from reading their names and understanding PHP's data typing system. Let's have a couple of examples before I explain why empty() should be avoided:

```
var_dump(is_array([])); // bool(true)
var_dump(is_array(new ArrayObject())); // bool(false)
var_dump(is_iterable(new ArrayObject())); // bool(true)
var_dump(is_numeric(1)); // bool(true)
var_dump(is_numeric(1.1)); // bool(true)
var_dump(is_numeric('1')); // bool(true)
var_dump(isset($notDeclared)); // bool(false) - no error output
```

empty() Is a Problem

Most of these functions are quite specific in their requirements: the input needs to match strict type or value requirements, which makes them predictable and therefore safe. The function names themselves are self-explanatory: skimming through code that contains these functions should make sense without requiring too much thought. And then we have empty(). This function is a bit of a Swiss Army Knife: it is the equivalent of calling isset(), testing for values such as false, null, and empty [ ] – it does rather a lot of different things depending on context. The following demonstrates all the various ways that empty() can return true:

```
var_dump(empty($notDeclared)); // bool(true)
var_dump(empty(false)); // bool(true)
var_dump(empty(0)); // bool(true)
var_dump(empty(0.0)); // bool(true)
var_dump(empty('')); // bool(true)
var_dump(empty('0')); // bool(true)
var_dump(empty([])); // bool(true)
```

That's quite a variety of different states that empty() will happily report as true. You're probably better off using more specific tests such as isset() for non-declared variables, === 0 for integer zero, strlen() === 0 for empty string, and so on. empty() on an empty array makes the most sense semantically, so it's not without its uses, but tread carefully around code that contains empty() in logical expressions. Repeat after me: type-safe code is safer code.

CHAPTER 4 LOGIC AND CONTROL

Logical Expressions

We've now seen all of PHP's control structures, and to demonstrate them, some logical expressions were required. These expressions were necessarily simple to keep the examples clear. Typically, just simple comparison tests were used. If you've read Chapter 5, "Arrays," Chapter 7, "Numbers," and Chapter 8, "Strings," you'll be familiar with comparison operators. Let's just quickly summarize them again:

Comparison Operators

Table 4-3. Comparison operators

==	true if both operands are equal (types will be coerced)
===	true only if both operands are of the same type and equal
!=	true if both operands are not equal (types will be coerced)
!==	true if both operands are not equal or not the same type
<	true if the left-hand operand is less than the right-hand
>	true if the left-hand operand is greater than the right-hand
<=	true if the left-hand operand is less than or equal to the right-hand
>=	true if the left-hand operand is greater than or equal to the right-hand
<=>	Returns zero, less than zero, or greater than zero, depending on operand value

```
var_dump(1 == '1'); // true
var_dump(1 === '1'); // true
var_dump(1 != 1); // false
var_dump(1 !== '1'); // false
var_dump(1 <=> 0); // 1 - left-hand is greater
var_dump(1 <=> 1); // 0 - equal
var_dump(1 <=> 2); // -1 - left-hand is lesser
```

Now, comparison operations can drive logic, but they are the simplest kind of logical expression: a single predicate – a single property or relationship. $a > $b is a predicate that asserts that $a is greater than $b (and can be true or false). More complex logical expressions consist of multiple predicates and require that the predicates themselves are connected by special operators.

Logical Operators

If we have two predicates in an expression, then we need to reduce them to a single value to drive a control structure such as if or while. Let's call our predicates A and B. We could decide that the overall expression is true if both A and B are true, or either is true, or even if only one is true. Here are the logical operators that allow predicates to be joined together in these ways:

Table 4-4. Logical operators

&& and	Logical "AND", true if both operands are true
|| or	Logical "OR", true if either operand is true
xor	Logical "EXCLUSIVE OR", true if only one operand is true, but not both
!	Logical "NOT", true if the operand is false

Logical AND and OR have two representations in PHP because of something called operator precedence, which we'll get to in due course. Firstly, let's look at some simple examples:

```
var_dump(true and true); // true
var_dump(true && false); // false
var_dump(false or true); // true
var_dump(false xor true); // true
var_dump(true xor false); // true
var_dump(true xor true); // false
var_dump(!false); // true
```

CHAPTER 4   LOGIC AND CONTROL

Now we can combine comparison-based predicates with these operators to form more complex expressions such as

```
$a = 1;
$b = 2;
if ($a < $b && $b === 2) {
    print 'A < B AND B = 2' . PHP_EOL;
}
if ($a > $b || $b === 2) {
    print 'A > B OR B = 2' . PHP_EOL;
}
```

Output:
A < B AND B = 2
A > B OR B = 2

Hopefully you get the idea: the first expression has both predicates evaluate to true, and we've used logical && (AND); the second expression has only the right-hand side, which is true, but this time, we've used logical || (OR), which only requires one side to be true. It is perfectly fine to chain together many predicates, and parentheses can be included to improve readability:

```
if (
    (someFunction() === 'foo' && someOtherFunction() === 'bar')
    || fallbackFunction() === 'qux'
) {
    // whatever
}
```

Adding parentheses to a logical expression also impacts the precedence of operations – just like in mathematics – which we'll cover shortly.

Short-Circuiting

PHP will exit logical expressions early if the results are conclusive before the entire expression has been evaluated, as the following demonstrates:

```
function getTrue(): bool
{
    print __FUNCTION__ . PHP_EOL;
    return true;
}
function getFalse(): bool
{
    print __FUNCTION__ . PHP_EOL;
    return false;
}
if (getTrue() || getFalse()) {
    print "True!";
}
Output:
getTrue
True!
```

As we can see, getFalse() is never called because the left-hand predicate is true, so evaluating the next predicate is unnecessary. Something to bear in mind for performance.

Precedence and Associativity

Operator *precedence* is simply a set of rules that determine which operations occur first in expressions that contain multiples. For example, 1 + 2 * 3 would evaluate to 9 if we simply moved across the expression from left to right, applying each operator in turn: 1 + 2 * 3 becoming 3 * 3 before evaluating to 9. But the correct result (mathematically speaking and if executed in PHP) is 7; the * multiply operator has a higher precedence than + addition: 1 + 2 * 3 becomes 1 + 6, which evaluates to 7. Anyone with a passing interest in mathematics will see brainteasers like this in their social feeds all the time.

If two operators have identical precedence, then the next rule to apply is *associativity*, which is left- or right-handed. If we have an expression with adjacent operators of equal precedence, the associativity determines which operation happens first. The mathematical expression 10 / 5 / 2 evaluates to 1 because / is left-associative: 10 / 5 / 2 to 2 / 2 then 1. Comparison operators are non-associative (an expression with multiple comparison operators is not legal PHP syntax), but logical operators are, and this does have some interesting effects:

```
$bool = getTrue() and getFalse();
var_dump($bool);
```

Output:

```
getTrue
getFalse
bool(true)
```

The result of what is essentially `$bool = true and false;` is true, yet the expression `true and false` is logically false. Why is that? We can see that both functions were called; there was no short-circuiting here. The reason we get `true` assigned is because the assignment operator has higher precedence than `and`. PHP first evaluates `$bool = getTrue()`, assigns to `$bool`, and only then goes on to evaluate `getTrue() and getFalse()`. The `&&` operator has a higher precedence than `=`, and gives the more intuitive answer:

```
$bool = getTrue() && getFalse();
var_dump($bool);
```

Output:
```
getTrue
getFalse
bool(false)
```

Be aware that the operators **or**, **xor**, and **and** run at a very low precedence (in fact the lowest precedence of all of PHP's operators) and can give weird results if this isn't taken into account. You are, of course, free to enforce higher precedence of these operators by using parentheses, which should also have the happy side effect of improving readability. The full breakdown of PHP's operator precedence and associativity can be found at `https://www.php.net/manual/en/language.operators.precedence.php`

Ternary Expressions

Consider the following logic:

```
$test = false;
if ($test === false) {
    $val = 'default';
} else {
    $val = $test;
}
var_dump($val);
```

Output:
string(7) "default"

It's pretty straightforward; we want to assign the value of $test to $val, but only if it has a value to be used. Otherwise, we'll give $val the value of 'default'. It's a bit of a pain to write, though, and a fairly common construct, so PHP offers something called the *ternary* logical operator. So-called because it has three parts:

```
$val = ($test) ? $test : 'default';
```

The example above accomplishes the same thing as the example before it, but with far less code. The general form is (TEST_EXPR) ? EXPR_IF_TRUE : EXPR_IF_FALSE, any (legal) expression is acceptable in the three sections, and the entire ternary expression evaluates to EXPR_IF_TRUE or EXPR_IF_FALSE (depending on the outcome of the first TEST_EXPR):

```
$val = (false) ? 'whatever you like...' : 'this ' . 'could also be ' . 'anything.';
var_dump($val);
```

Output:
string(28) "this could also be anything."

Like control structures, ternary expressions can be nested, though it is generally recommended not to make a habit of it. Unreadable code will quickly follow. Where the result of TEST_EXPR is wanted as the result of the whole expression, you can use the short ternary expression form:

183

CHAPTER 4   LOGIC AND CONTROL

```
$test = 'something';
$val = ($test) ?: 'default';
var_dump($val);
```

Output:
```
string(9) "something"
```

The usual type coercion gotchas apply when $test is implicitly cast to a bool, as the following trick demonstrates:

```
var_dump(
    false ?: null ?: 0 ?: '0' ?: 'default'
);
```

Output:
```
string(7) "default"
```

This form is known as *ternary chaining* and will evaluate to the first (loosely typed) non-false value in the chain. A neat trick that will save a few lines of code.

Null-Coalesce

PHP 7.0 added a similar convenience feature that operates on null values (rather than falsy), which allows for the easy assignment of variables from others that might not exist or have null values. This is the *null coalescing* operator ??, it is an implicit logical test on the left-hand operand: and it works like this:

```
$val = $notDeclared ?? 'default';
var_dump($val);
```

Output:
```
string(7) "default"
```

It is possible to chain these operations together:

```
$val = $notDeclared ?? $stillNotDeclared ?? 'default';
var_dump($val);
```

Output:
```
string(7) "default"
```

CHAPTER 4 LOGIC AND CONTROL

Null coalesce works like isset() – $val = $notDelared ?? 'default' is logically equivalent to $val = (isset($notDeclared)) ?: 'default'; – which means that if $notDeclared is, well, not declared then no Warning error is emitted. Null coalesce is also very useful for array handling because it will check that keys exist; if the key doesn't exist, then a default value can be substituted:

```
$arr = ['foo' => 'bar'];
print $arr['qux'] ?? 'something else';
```

Output:
something else

Null coalesce can (since PHP 7.4) also be combined with assignment like this – ??=. This means that if the left-hand variable has a null value, then assignment takes place; otherwise, it doesn't:

```
$val1 = 'something';
$val2 = null;

$val1 ??= 'new val';
$val2 ??= 'new val';

var_dump($val1);
var_dump($val2);
```

Output:
string(9) "something"
string(7) "new val"

Null-Safe

When it comes to object access, there is an equivalent implicit logical test that has very similar syntax to the above. This is the *null safe* operator and is exclusively used with objects and their properties and methods. This allows for object calls, or property access, to safely fail and return null if the properties are null or the method returns null (the initial properties and methods need to exist, though):

CHAPTER 4   LOGIC AND CONTROL

```
class TheHellIsGoingOnRn
{
    public $solution = null;
    public function noClue(): void
    {}
}
$mystery = new TheHellIsGoingOnRn();
$prop = $mystery->solution?->answer();
$answer = $mystery->noClue()?->answer();
var_dump($prop);
var_dump($answer);
```

Output:
NULL
NULL

You can even use null safe on the object variable itself:

```
$noObject = null;
var_dump($noObject?->whatever());
```

Output:
NULL

Bitwise Operations

Just a quick word of caution concerning the bitwise operators in PHP – care should be taken because some of the logical and comparison operators in PHP are quite similar. These are the ones to watch out for:

Table 4-5. *Bitwise operators*

&	Bitwise AND – returns a value that has bits set (to *1*) where both operands have the same bits set
|	Bitwise OR – returns a value that has bits set where either operand also has a bit set
<<	Shift left all bits in the left-hand operand the number of places specified by the right-hand (each step multiplies by two)
>>	Shift right all bits in the left-hand operand the number of places specified by the right-hand (each step divides by two

You can probably work out the gotchas for yourself: bitwise & and logical &&, bitwise << and comparison <, and so on.

Errors and Exceptions

An important aspect of control in any code you write is dealing with any problems that might arise during execution. With a little forethought and care, any issue that might arise (perhaps even through no fault of your own) that might otherwise result in meaningless garbage can be transformed into useful information, or even something still useful to an end user. PHP has two principal mechanisms for when things go wrong: a set of internal error conditions, which if met will result in the emission of an error message, which has a variety of effects according to configuration, and an object-oriented exception model that can be used to gracefully communicate and handle runtime problems between components.

PHP errors can prevent the program from continuing (in the worst cases) or merely produce a message and carry on. Exceptions, on the other hand, are intended to interrupt the flow of the program and only prevent continuation if you choose to do so (or forget to write the code to deal with them). The language constructs for handling exceptions aren't strictly counted as control structures in other resources, but since they can impact the flow of logic, I've opted to include them in this chapter. PHP makes use of exceptions in all of its OOP APIs and in many other places too (there was a big push in version 7 to switch to exceptions over errors). The language also provides the function trigger_error(), which allows you to deliberately emit an error, though the exception model is generally preferred these days.

CHAPTER 4 LOGIC AND CONTROL

Error Levels

Not all errors are created equal. Some are more serious than others. An error might be truly unrecoverable ("fatal") and will kill your program instantly, or it could be a warning... or even just informational in nature. Some of these errors occur during script execution and are *runtime*, some occur during the initial parsing of code and are *compile-time*, and PHP will even complain (or explode) during *startup* before it has even had a chance to look at your code.

Runtime errors are going to be your biggest headache; anything that kills your program during startup or compile time should not make it onto a production system (because you'll be checking for those before deployment, right?) and tend to be obvious in their cause. PHP runtime errors fall roughly into four categories: fatal errors, warnings, notices, and deprecation warnings (which aren't strictly speaking errors, just the language giving you prior notice that the next version of PHP is going to break whatever you are doing).

PHP has the following predefined constants for runtime errors...

Table 4-6. Runtime error constants

Constant	Definition
E_ERROR	Unrecoverable, terminates execution
E_WARNING	Recoverable, execution continues
E_NOTICE	Recoverable, informational: can occur during normal operation
E_DEPRECATED	Recoverable, code flagged for removal in future version
E_USER_ERROR	E_ERROR emitted by `trigger_error()`
E_USER_WARNING	E_WARNING emitted by `trigger_error()`
E_USER_NOTICE	E_NOTICE emitted by `trigger_error()`
E_USER_DEPRECATED	E_DEPRECATED emitted by `trigger_error()`
E_RECOVERABLE_ERROR	Legacy can be recovered with custom handler
E_STRICT	Recoverable, informational: suggestions for forward compatibility
E_ALL	Equivalent to the set of all error constants (runtime or otherwise)

... and these for startup or compile-time:

Table 4-7. Startup/compile time error constants

Constant	Definition
E_CORE_ERROR	Unrecoverable, startup error
E_CORE_WARNING	Recoverable, startup error
E_COMPILE_ERROR	Unrecoverable, compile-time, script parsed as legal syntax
E_COMPILE_WARNING	Recoverable, compile-time, script parsed as legal syntax
E_PARSE	Unrecoverable, compile-time, syntax error in code

Each of these constants is an integer value, and these can be combined with bitwise operators to form logical expressions from multiple constants. For example, E_WARNING | E_NOTICE & ~E_DEPRECATED means "error level of warning or notice and not deprecated." These expressions are used either in configuration (as ini directives) or as arguments to runtime function calls.

Error Control

You can tell PHP which errors you want to see (or ignore) by setting the reporting level with either the error_reporting ini directive...

```
// php.ini
; use bitwise operators AND & and NOT ~ to enable all except E_DEPRECATED
error_reporting = E_ALL & ~E_DEPRECATED
```

... or at runtime with the error_reporting() function:

```
// deliberate Warning error
print $undefVar;
```

```
// report fatal Error runtime errors only
error_reporting(E_ERROR);
print $anotherUndefVar;
```

```
Output:
PHP Warning:  Undefined variable $undefVar...
```

With the error reporting level set to E_ERROR only, the warning that would have been emitted from `print $anotherUndefVar` is quietly ignored. You achieve the same effect with `ini_set('error_reporting', E_ERROR)`. PHP also offers an operator for controlling error reporting: the @ symbol. This can be prepended to any expression to suppress any errors that might be generated for that statement:

```
print @$undefVar;
print "All is well?!";
```

Output:
All is well?!

Obviously, you should tread very carefully around code that makes use of the @ error control operator and minimize its use in your own code. One potential (ab)use of this feature in older PHP code is `$val = @$arr['undef'];` (to suppress warnings if array keys are undefined), which is no longer necessary with the null coalesce operator. `$val = $arr['undef'] ?? null;` is a far cleaner piece of code.

In addition to displaying errors in program output (either in command line output for CLI SAPI programs or as part of the response body content for web server SAPIs), errors can be redirected to STDOUT or STDERR, logged to a file or the *nix syslog subsystem, or even wrapped in HTML tags to make them browser friendly. A common strategy for production PHP systems is to disable errors in program output with `display_errors = Off` and enable an error log file with something like `error_log = php_errors.log`. This makes sense because you almost never want to expose any information about your systems to your users. If `error_log` is not defined, then PHP will default to error logging according to the SAPI – STDERR for CLI, or the web server's error log (which means PHP's messages will be mingled with the server's own errors).

Some of the configuration directives are detailed below:

Table 4-8. ini config directives

ini directive	Purpose
error_reporting	Sets the reporting error level (typically using E_* constants)
display_errors	Enable/disable the sending of errors as program output
log_errors	Enable/disable error logging
error_log	File path of the error logging file, or syslog
html_errors	Wrap error messages in HTML tags for viewing in a browser

The full documentation for error-related configuration can be found at https://www.php.net/manual/en/errorfunc.configuration.php

Error Handling

If necessary, you can add to, or override, the default error handling behavior for a certain set of error levels. This can be useful for injecting your own logic into error-handling events. The built-in function set_error_handler() accepts a callable (e.g., an anonymous function, a string matching a declared function name, etc.), and an error level expression that matches the error levels you wish your callable to be invoked for. You cannot define a handler for E_ERROR (fatal) or any of the startup or compile-time error levels such as E_PARSE, E_COMPILE_ERROR, etc. If the handler callable returns false, then the default handler will be invoked immediately afterwards (return true to end error handling once yours is done).

```
// error_handler.php
error_reporting(E_ALL);
set_error_handler(function ($errno, $errstr, $file, $line) {
    switch ($errno) {
        case E_WARNING:
            print "WARNING!!! {$errstr}" . PHP_EOL;
            break;
        case E_USER_NOTICE:
            print "Just a notice... {$errstr}" . PHP_EOL;
            break;
    }
```

CHAPTER 4　LOGIC AND CONTROL

```
    print "{$file} : {$line}" . PHP_EOL;

    return true;
}, E_WARNING | E_USER_NOTICE);

print $undef;
trigger_error("TRIGGERED NOTICE", E_USER_NOTICE);
trigger_error("TRIGGERED WARNING", E_USER_WARNING);
```

Output:
WARNING!!! Undefined variable $undef
/usr/src/myapp/error_handler.php : 18
Just a notice... TRIGGERED NOTICE
/usr/src/myapp/error_handler.php : 19
PHP Warning: TRIGGERED WARNING in /usr/src/myapp/05.03_set_error_handler.php on line 20

Here we've used an anonymous function, which will be passed four arguments when an error is emitted. In order, these are the integer value of the error level, the error message itself, the full file path of the offending code, and the line number that triggered the error. We use the $errno argument with switch to determine which logic we want (just simple print statements in this case, but I'm sure you can imagine the possibilities), then the remaining message, file path, and line number arguments to form the rest of our message. After the callable, we then pass an error-level expression: we've set our handler to trigger on E_WARNING and E_USER_NOTICE.

Next, we cause some problems: an attempt to use an undefined variable (always an E_WARNING level error in PHP 8) and two calls to trigger_error() with levels of E_USER_NOTICE and E_USER_WARNING, respectively. You can see from the output that our handler is invoked for E_WARNING and E_USER_NOTICE, and the default handler is invoked for the E_USER_WARNING.

A user-defined error handler doesn't need to output any messages at all; the default handler can do that for you, and this is just an exercise. You could choose to do something more unusual, like, say, set a global flag to a new value, which would provide a mechanism for affecting the rest of the program's logic... but don't do that. Errors are a bit of a blunt instrument for controlling your program; there's a better way.

Exceptions

Writing your own error-handling code, triggering errors, and/or slavishly checking function return values everywhere – all of this gives you some ability to create logic in your code that is dedicated to managing problems. But it's a clunky approach and not what PHP errors are intended for: they're really just for reporting an issue and then either giving up or carrying on. A lot of the time you can deal with some part of your system going *poof* in a cloud of broken logic with some snazzy functions or a class (or two), but how best to reach that magic code? This is where exceptions come in.

Exceptions in PHP are objects, and this chapter appears before Chapter 6, "Object Fundamentals"; you might not yet be comfortable with concepts like classes, objects, methods, or properties. I'll give minimal explanations here concerning the object-oriented parts of the upcoming examples, and you can always refer back to this section once you've absorbed the fundamentals of object orientation in PHP. Or read ahead! It's up to you.

Throwing Exceptions

The mechanisms for using exceptions in PHP are pretty simple (phew!): you create an Exception object and throw it. Other code can catch that object, inspect it, and do whatever is necessary (including throwing it again). An object is just a data structure created from a template called a class, and in this case the class is Exception (it's built into PHP's core). You make one with the new keyword, then the class name followed by parentheses, and inside the parentheses we put some string data. It looks like a function call, and that's exactly what it is. The new keyword triggers a call to a special function called a *constructor*, which deals with the messy business of making a new object and returning a reference to it.

```
throw new Exception("Emergency... there's an emergency going on.");
```

```
Output:
PHP Fatal error:  Uncaught Exception: Emergency... there's an emergency
going on.
```

Now this is interesting because our newly thrown exception has in fact caused an E_ERROR to be emitted, which is why we see the PHP Fatal error. The error occurs because nothing caught the exception. This makes sense because exceptions are intended to change program flow, and if we don't have any alternative code for PHP to execute, then it rightly stops, which brings us to our next sub-topic...

Catching Exceptions

PHP's language construct for exception handling is the same as many others: try, catch, and finally. When you know that certain code is able to throw an exception, wrap it in a try { } block. A try block must then have at least one catch or finally block attached to it (to avoid a fatal E_ERROR). If a line of code inside the try block throws an exception (or calls something that causes an exception to be thrown), then execution immediately switches to the catch block, and the rest of the try block is abandoned:

```
function boom()
{
    throw new Exception("Emergency... there's an emergency going on.");
    print "I'll never be reached...";
}

try {
    boom();
} catch (Exception $e) {
    print $e->getMessage() . PHP_EOL;
}

print "It's still going on.";
```

Output:
Emergency... there's an emergency going on.
It's still going on.

The construct catch (Exception $e) tells PHP that if the thrown exception is an instance of Exception, then it should execute the code inside the braces. At this point, catch works a bit like a function call, with the thrown object passed as an argument $e, which the code inside the braces can then make use of. Our catch block code invokes a special function that "belongs" to the object – a *method* – using the -> operator.

$e->getMessage() simply means "call the getMessage() method of the $e object". getMessage() then accesses some internal string data of $e and returns it: you'll notice it's the same string we used to construct the Exception in the boom() function. Crucially, we don't trigger a fatal error, because this time we provided PHP with an alternative logical path in our code, and execution continues to the final line.

PHP 7 Errors

The core Exception class is not the only game in town. Version 7 upped its game with exceptions: many extensions switched from emitting errors to throwing exceptions, and many core error conditions were given their own exceptions to throw, all of which are of the Error class (or classes derived from Error, which we'll get to shortly). Here's an example:

```
try {
    notDefined();
} catch (Error $e) {
    print "Caught an Error" . PHP_EOL;
    print $e->getMessage() . PHP_EOL;
}
print "Carrying on..." . PHP_EOL;
notDefined();
```

Output:
```
Caught an Error
Call to undefined function notDefined()
Carrying on...
PHP Fatal error:  Uncaught Error: Call to undefined function notDefined()
```

Attempting to call an undefined function in PHP 7 onwards results in an instance of the Error class being thrown. Error objects behave just like Exception objects, and the throw language construct treats them identically, as does catch et al. Prior to version 7, calling an undefined function resulted in an E_ERROR emission. Here, in PHP 8, the second time we try to call notDefined(), we also end up with an E_ERROR emitted, but that's because the Error exception wasn't caught; the illegal operation itself did not emit the error. A subtle but important difference: The PHP Fatal error: Uncaught... message means you had a chance to handle the problem!

Catching Different (Error) Exceptions

We need to take a moment to discuss another object-oriented programming (OOP) fundamental: *inheritance*. Classes – as we've seen – serve as templates for objects; you make objects using the new keyword and a class name. It is also possible to define a class using another as a base. The keywords class and extends are used to tell PHP both that a new class exists and that it uses another class as its base (or parent). The statement class MyException extends Exception means that PHP creates a new class MyException, which has all the features of Exception. In OOP terms this is inheritance; MyException is a *subclass* (or *child*) of the parent Exception class; it will inherit all of the properties and methods of the parent and will behave exactly like it. Child classes can introduce new functionality or override parent functionality (to an extent), but this is beyond the scope of this chapter and will be covered in Chapter 6, "Object Fundamentals." Inheritance can be chained together: a base class A can have a child B, and B can have a child C, creating a (tree) hierarchy of relationships between them.

PHP's Error class is the parent of several child classes, such as ArithmeticError, TypeError, and ValueError. In turn, some of those have their own children: ArithmeticError has a child DivisionByZeroError, and TypeError has a child, ArgumentCountError. In this way, exceptions can be specialized, which is good because throwing and handling Exception objects everywhere is going to be tedious: you'd need to wade through all sorts of messages or other properties of each object to determine what the precise problem is. By introducing a hierarchy of exception classes, it becomes possible to elegantly switch paths in your code based on the exception's class, because you can attach as many catch blocks as you like to a try, using the type declaration of the object argument to filter the exceptions that are allowed into that block. Conceptually, the class used to create the exception object becomes part of the message, meaning you can handle DivisionByZeroError exceptions using a different code block to TypeError exceptions:

```
function surpriseBoom()
{
    if (rand(1, 10) % 2 === 0) {
        notDefined();
    } else {
        print 1 / 0;
    }
}
```

```
try {
    surpriseBoom();
} catch (DivisionByZeroError $e) {
    print "DIVIDE BY ZERO... OH SHI-" . PHP_EOL;
} catch (Error $e) {
    print "{$e->getMessage()} caught in generic Error handler" . PHP_EOL;
}
```

Output:
DIVIDE BY ZERO... OH SHI-
or...
Call to undefined function notDefined() caught in generic Error handler

The surpriseBoom() function is just a simple confection that effectively tosses a coin: 50/50 chance we'll end up either dividing by zero or calling an undefined function. Depending on the result of our logical expression, the function will accordingly throw either a DivisionByZeroError exception or a generic Error. The thing to notice here are the two catch blocks: both are defining a $e parameter but with different data types. When an exception is thrown in the try block, PHP will test the class of the thrown object against each catch block and execute the first matching type definition. This raises an important caveat: child classes count as their parents. If a type declaration says it will accept Error, then DivisionByZeroError will match it, because the child extends the parent (this is the *Liskov Substitution Principle* and is covered in precise detail in Chapter 10, "Programming with Objects"). What this means for us is that the most specialized class in the hierarchy must come first in the catch block order. If we'd put catch (Error $e) { ... first, then we'd never reach catch (DivisionByZeroError $e) because all DivisionByZeroError objects would satisfy the Error data type. Here's the proof:

```
try {
    throw new DivisionByZeroError("I divided by zero. :(");
} catch (Error $e) {
    print "{$e->getMessage()} caught in generic Error handler" . PHP_EOL;
} catch (DivisionByZeroError $e) {
    print "DIVIDE BY ZERO... OH SHI-" . PHP_EOL;
}
```

Output:
I divided by zero. :(caught in generic Error handler

DIY Exceptions

The technique of specifying multiple `catch` blocks with differing type declarations allows you to fine-tune your exception handling based purely on the class of exception being thrown. You can easily create specialized exceptions for any problem case arising in your code and use them to switch between `catch` blocks accordingly. To define your own class, just use the `class` and `extends` keywords as previously demonstrated:

```
class MyException extends Exception
{
    // extra functionality here if required
}
```

All class declarations have a block (delimited by { } braces) into which you can place additional code, but that's rarely required when making subclasses of `Exception` (which generally has enough functionality already). It's very common to see a slew of exception classes in third-party libraries that do nothing but extend another exception and define zero extra functionality: it's the class itself that's the important thing. One more thing to mention: classes can be namespaced just as you've seen in Chapter 3, "Functions," though I've not shown it here, and class namespacing is fully explained in Chapter 6, "Object Fundamentals." Namespacing gives you yet more options for specializing your exceptions (and avoiding name collisions, of course). If you are in a non-root namespace, don't forget to prefix `Exception` and `Error` with a backslash (the reasons why are explained in Chapter 3, "Functions") - for example, `catch (\Exception $e) { ... }` or `class SomeNamespacedClass extends \Exception`.

Finally...

There is an additional component to the `try/catch` construct, a way to define code that will always be executed in the event of an exception (irrespective of its type). The `finally { }` block must go at the end of any `catch` blocks, and it can even be used instead of `catch` blocks (a `try` must have at least one `catch` or `finally`). A `finally` block always executes, no matter if the exception is caught or not:

```
print "Doing something explode-y" . PHP_EOL;

try {
    throw new Exception('Boom!');
} catch (Exception $e) {
    print "Exception caught!" . PHP_EOL;
} finally {
    print "Sweeping up the mess..." . PHP_EOL;
}

print "... and carrying on.";

Output:
Doing something explode-y
Exception caught!
Sweeping up the mess...
... and carrying on.
```

One limitation of `finally` is that it cannot catch an exception for you, and although it will always execute if something throws one in your `try` block, an uncaught exception is still going to kill the script.

Exception Handling

Uncaught exceptions are handled by the (appropriately named) exception handler, which is some "magic" code that sits outside of your own program. Just as you can define your own custom error handler (albeit for limited error levels), so too can you define one for uncaught exceptions. As we've seen earlier in this section, an uncaught `Error` exception resulted in an `E_ERROR` being emitted; this would be the case for any throwable object of class `Exception` or `Error` – or a class that implements the `Throwable` interface. Interfaces are a definition of how a class behaves in terms of its public-facing properties and methods. When a class is declared as implementing an interface – `class Error implements Throwable`, for example – it must provide implementations of whatever `interface Throwable` defines. We'll go no further than that; just accept that PHP keeps track of all classes, their inheritance hierarchy, and the interfaces of both the class itself and the inheritance hierarchy, and interfaces can be used in type declarations.

PHP's default handler for uncaught Throwable objects will emit a fatal error detailing the class of the thrown object and any message it might contain. You can replace the default handler if you want to, using the built-in set_exception_handler() function:

```
// Error and Exception classes both implement a Throwable interface
set_exception_handler(function (Throwable $t) {
    print "Oh dear, you fumbled that." . PHP_EOL;
    print $t->getMessage() . PHP_EOL;
});

throw new Exception('ASPLODE');

print "Everyone ok?";
```

Output:
```
Oh dear, you fumbled that.
ASPLODE
```

Now, the main thing to notice here is that we didn't get an E_ERROR emitted. Which is nice? However, neither did our program continue; not so nice, maybe, but there is a good reason for it. Exceptions are designed to halt your program, unless they are properly caught, because something exceptional happened that makes it difficult/impossible/really inadvisable to continue. Catching an exception and handling the crisis correctly might leave your system in a state where continuing is possible; that's down to you. What has not happened above is a catch.

Exceptions "bubble" through a call chain: you can have functions calling other functions, calling other functions... many, many times. Each time this happens the calls "stack" up, and we're going to have a quick look at debugging these call stacks as the final part of this section. When exceptions are thrown, PHP walks back along this stack, or chain, of calls hunting for a try/catch construct – the function (or method) throwing an exception rarely deals with it itself. PHP will keep backtracking like this until the call stack is exhausted (at which point it's examining your entry-point script), and then if the exception is still uncaught, it will invoke the exception handler. And this is the problem: PHP now deems execution to be beyond the control of your code, and no matter what the handler does, control will not be returned. A custom exception handler gives you an opportunity to clean things up or (more usually) format a nice chunk of HTML for debugging purposes, but then it's game over.

Stack Traces

We've just learned about how function/method calls stack up: put simply, if we have three functions a(), b(), and c(), and each calls the next, this forms a call stack. In well-structured code you'll always have functions calling other functions, objects using other objects... the alternative is a heinous mess I don't want to even contemplate. This is relevant to exception handling because the catch block handling the exception does not necessarily exist in the function doing the throw(ing) – in fact it's rarely the case.

Call chains (aka the *call stack* or just *stack*) can be debugged with a technique called *bracktracing*: you trace your way backwards from the point of error to (hopefully) find the cause. There are also a couple of useful utility functions in PHP for generating traces manually, but first let's look at how to throw and catch in different places. We'll make three functions and set them up to call each other, and do a few other exception-related things while we're at it:

```php
function a()
{
    try {
        b();
    } finally {
        print "Uncaught in A..." . PHP_EOL;
    }
}
function b()
{
    try {
        c();
    } catch (Exception $e) {
        print "Caught in B..." . PHP_EOL;
        throw $e;
    }
}
function c()
{
    throw new Exception('Thrown in C...');
}
```

CHAPTER 4   LOGIC AND CONTROL

```
a();

print "never reached";
```

Output:
Caught in B...
Uncaught in A...
PHP Fatal error: Uncaught Exception: Thrown in C... in...

The call chain is a() calls b(), which calls c()... three calls deep. c() throws an exception but has a try block, but b() does so the exception is caught there. Remember that I said a catch block could also throw? That's exactly what's going on here. The same exception object is then thrown from b(), and this time is not caught in a(). Instead, we have a finally which executes its code, then the exception is handled: the default handler spits out an E_ERROR as usual and kills the script.

Now, if you've followed any of these code examples at home, you'll know that I've been omitting some of the default handler's output: the *Stack trace*. The E_ERROR message is actually:

```
PHP Fatal error:   Uncaught Exception: Thrown in C... in /usr/src/
myapp/05.11_call_chain.php:22
Stack trace:
#0 /usr/src/myapp/call_chains.php(14): c()
#1 /usr/src/myapp/call_chains.php(6): b()
#2 /usr/src/myapp/call_chains.php(25): a()
#3 {main}
  thrown in ...
```

You'll see these on all default E_ERROR messages from the default exception handler. It's standard fare in exception-based languages to dump a stack trace; go take a look at Java sometime (if you think PHP traces are a bit verbose, you're in for a shock). Each line of the trace output is numbered, with the call that produced the error at the top as the zeroth line. We threw the exception in c(), with the message 'Thrown in C...', and that's what the error message contains. The stack trace that follows is like a map that shows us how we got to the error state.

The first line of the trace is #0 /usr/src/myapp/call_chains.php(14): c() – this is an instruction to the programmer to look at line 14 of the call_chains.php file because that's where the call to c() is found. The next line shows us that c() was called because b() was executing at line 6 of call_chains.php... and so on. Read from top to bottom, we can decipher it like this:

- Exception thrown, line 22 of call_chain.php
- The reason for this is because c() was called at line 14...
- ... because b() was called at line 6...
- ... because b() was called at line 25, and...
- ... now we're at the main program (no more calls)

We didn't need a stack trace to understand why our code exploded; we literally have all three functions on screen at the same time (unless your terminal or IDE font size is unusually big, and even then all the calls are in the same file), but in the real world, you might struggle to juggle a stack that's a couple of dozen calls deep across as many files. Traces like this become invaluable debugging tools when projects are spread across hundreds of files, with hundreds of functions and/or objects.

debug_backtrace(), debug_print_backtrace()

You can also trigger your own stack traces if necessary; debugging doesn't have to be about fixing fatal errors. You might simply want to investigate the internals of a new library or framework. Want to know what happens before your brilliant new component's entry-point method is invoked by ShinyFramework? A trace can show you all the calls made from the framework booting up before the code that you wrote ever ran. They can be a great tool for learning. A few well-placed calls to PHP's debug_backtrace() or debug_print_backtrace() functions will generate a stack trace at the point where they are called. Calling either of these functions does not affect the flow of the program; it will resume immediately after the output.

debug_backtrace() will return a structured array with an element for each entry in the call stack; debug_print_backtrace() produces the same trace structure but then converts it into a formatted string (to save you having to write your own loops to render). Modify the previous example so that the implementation of function c() is as follows...

CHAPTER 4 LOGIC AND CONTROL

```
// ...
function c()
{
    print_r(debug_backtrace());
}
// ...
```

... running the program again first gives the following output for debug_backtrace()...

Output:
```
    [0] => Array
        (
            [file] => /usr/src/myapp/debug_backtrace.php
            [line] => 14
            [function] => c
            [args] => Array
                (
                )
        )
    [1] => Array ...
```

... which is an array structure, each element of which is a sub-array with elements corresponding to useful info about the call (file, line number, function name, and even arguments).

The output of debug_print_backtrace() is the same data but formatted into the same string you would see if the default exception handler had generated the trace. Modify c() again to the following implementation...

```
// ...
function c()
{
    print debug_print_backtrace();
}
// ...
```

... and run it as before. This time we get the following familiar output:

Output:
```
#0 /usr/src/myapp/debug_backtrace.php(14): c()
#1 /usr/src/myapp/debug_backtrace.php(6): b()
#2 /usr/src/myapp/debug_backtrace.php(27): a()
```

When objects are involved, there will be some additional indexes in the sub-arrays. I will need to jump ahead of the book again and put some object-oriented code here, but it's not much more challenging than when I showed how to make your Exception objects. The class keyword indicates a class definition, with public function foo() defining a method called foo(), which is just a function that belongs to the class.

```php
class A
{
    public function doA(B $b)
    {
        $b->doB();
    }
}
class B
{
    public function doB()
    {
        print_r(debug_backtrace());
    }
}
$a = new A();
$a->doA(new B());
```

Output:
```
    [0] => Array
        (
            [file] => /usr/src/myapp/05.14_object_backtrace.php
            [line] => 7
            [function] => doB
            [class] => B
            [object] => B Object ...
            [type] => ->
            [args] => Array ...
```

Now we can see some extra information: `class` and `object` give us information about the object the method *doB* was called on (although it retains the `function` key name); `type` concerns the context the call was made in. `->` means object context, and `::` would mean class (static) context. This might not mean much to you now; everything is explained in Chapter 6, "Object Fundamentals."

One final note to add: if the constant `DEBUG_BACKTRACE_IGNORE_ARGS` is passed as an argument to either of the backtrace functions, then the `args` index is omitted in the output; `DEBUG_BACKTRACE_PROVIDE_OBJECT` will omit the `object` index.

Summary

To misquote Douglas Adams: that about wraps it up for logic. The building blocks of control are easy enough to understand in isolation, but believe me, things can get very tortuous indeed. I recommend factoring out too many levels of nesting (either `if` statements, loops, or – horror of horrors – both embedded in each other). Beware of code that has closing braces like this:

```
                }
            }
        }
    }
}
```

Something I like to call "climbing mountains" (if you turn the code on its side it looks like a mountain range). There's nothing wrong with refactoring monster loops and logic into their own functions (and your static analysis tools will be happier too). Over the years PHP has introduced syntactic sugar like ternary statements and null-coalesce to make things less onerous – make good use of them. Live long and prosper. 🖖

CHAPTER 5

Arrays

Real-world problems usually require the storage, retrieval, and manipulation of related data. If data are related, then it makes sense to keep them collected together. A real data set could be, say, the names of people in a tutorial group. It would be possible to use scalar variables to represent each individual in the group, but this would mean maintaining many separate variables, an overly complex and definitely more error-prone approach. Grouping each value into a set makes more sense, and this is where the `array` data type comes in.

Two fundamental properties of arrays in PHP are that they are *countable* (they have cardinality; the number of elements in the array can be measured) and that they are *iterable* (capable of having an operation repeated on each element). A synonym of iterable is "traversable," and you will often see these terms used when discussing arrays. `Countable`, `Iterable`, and `Traversable` are reserved words in PHP 8: `Countable` and `Traversable` are interfaces for objects that can behave like arrays. `Iterable` is a pseudo-type that matches arrays and array-like objects.

Here we look at various techniques for manipulating arrays; PHP provides a plethora of built-in tools for working with arrays, as we shall see. These are the topics covered in this chapter:

- Indexed arrays
- Associative arrays
- Multidimensional arrays
- Accessing array elements
- ArrayObject
- Adding, removing, and changing array elements
- Iterating arrays
- Extracting data from arrays

- Combining arrays
- Comparing arrays
- Searching arrays
- Sorting arrays
- Calling functions on arrays
- PHP's built-in array functions

Creating and Accessing Arrays

There are two ways to create an array in PHP. The syntax is different, but the end result is the same: you can use either the language construct array() or the more recent (since PHP 5.4) short array syntax denoted by square brackets []:

```
$myArr1 = array();
$myArr2 = array('Bob', 'Alice');
$myArr3 = [];
$myArr4 = ['Bob', 'Alice'];

var_dump($myArr1);
var_dump($myArr2);
var_dump($myArr3);
var_dump($myArr4);
```

Output:
```
array(0) {
}
array(2) {
  [0]=>
  string(3) "Bob"
  [1]=>
  string(5) "Alice"
}
array(0) {
}
```

```
array(2) {
  [0]=>
  string(3) "Bob"
  [1]=>
  string(5) "Alice"
}
```

The `array()` language construct creates a new array, as does `[]`. The example above shows initialization with and without values, `[]` is an empty array, `['Bob', 'Alice']` is an array with two string elements.

The data values inside an array are usually referred to as *elements*. Array elements can be scalar or complex types. When an array is created in this way, PHP keeps track of the elements by indexing them. Each element is referenced by an integer value; the values are sequential and begin at zero.

Accessing Elements

To access the contents of an array, a special value called a *key* is required. An array key is a value that corresponds to the position of an element within the array. For the simple arrays we've seen so far, keys are simply sequential decimal integers corresponding to the position of the array element (starting at zero). Integer keys are also known as *indexes* (or *indices*). The key (or index) is then placed inside square brackets immediately following the array variable, for example, `$myArr[0]`. (Note that prior to PHP 8 it was also possible to access array elements with braces like this: `$myArr{0}`; this was deprecated in PHP 7.4 and is removed from the language from 8.0 onwards.)

Without diving too deep into zvals and gory PHP internals, the `$myArr` variable is a reference to an array, and we can think of the key notation (the bit inside the square brackets immediately following `$myArr`) as the reference to a specific element within that array.

In the output of the previous example, did you notice that Bob and Alice had numbers associated with them when the array was output with `var_dump`? Here's a reminder:

```
[0]=>
string(3) "Bob"
```

CHAPTER 5   ARRAYS

The 0 above means that Bob is the first (well, technically zeroth) element in the array. Continuing the example above, we can access the values of elements in $myArr3 individually:

```
$i = 1;

$output1 = $myArr3[0];
$output2 = $myArr3[$i];

print "Value of element 0 is {$output1}\n";
print "Value of element (\$i = 1) is {$output2}\n";
```
Output:
Value of element 0 is Bob
Value of element ($i = 1) is Alice

Here a literal integer value of 0 is used as the key to access the first element of $myArr3, and a variable (with an integer value of 1) is the key used to access the second element. PHP retrieves the values of the elements, which we then assign to other variables for use in subsequent statements (in this case, a print construct).

Array access sub-expressions will be coerced to integers if the array is numerically indexed. The example above demonstrates using variables as array indexes, but any expression that reduces to a value is legal syntax (provided it evaluates to an integer or a value that can be coerced). This includes values returned from function calls, as we can see in the following example:

```
$myArr = ['Alice', 'Bob'];

var_dump($myArr["0"]); // string is coerced to an int
var_dump($myArr["0" + "1"]); // operation can be coerced to an int
var_dump($myArr[2 - 1]); // expression evaluates to integer 1
var_dump($myArr[getArrayKey()]); // function returns integer 0

function getArrayKey(): int
{
    return 0;
}
```

Output:
```
string(5) "Alice"
string(3) "Bob"
string(3) "Bob"
string(5) "Alice"
```

While it's true that array access can be flexible, keeping syntax clean and simple is recommended. Common practice is to assign the result of an expression or function call to a variable first and then use that as the key.

Associative Arrays

When array elements are created, they are automatically given index values that can be used as keys to access them. It is also possible (and often desirable) to specify your own keys. Here's how it is done:

```
$myArr = [
    'lang' => 'PHP',
    'ver' => '8.4'
];

print_r($myArr);
print "Version of {$myArr['lang']} is {$myArr['ver']}\n";
```

Output:
```
Array
(
    [lang] => PHP
    [ver] => 8.4
)
Version of PHP is 8.4
```

Keys are associated with elements using the double-arrow operator =>. Legal values for keys are limited to decimal integers and strings (or expressions that evaluate to them). Type coercion rules apply to keys, so take care with types. (Don't try to use floats as keys, e.g., it will work with PHP 8, but it is deprecated due to precision loss). The array elements are accessed using the keys, which in this case are the strings "lang" and "ver".

It is worth noting that PHP doesn't distinguish between indexed and associative arrays internally. Indexed arrays are still associative arrays; they just have very strict rules about the keys of indexed arrays, namely, that they are sequential decimal integers. Also worth mentioning is the fact that it is not necessary to provide explicit keys for all elements. This is perfectly legal: $arr = ['foo' => 'bar', 'qux']. PHP will provide sequential decimal integer keys whenever it adds an element to an array.

Multidimensional Arrays

A multidimensional array is simply an array containing more arrays. As stated earlier, array elements can be compound types, and arrays are a compound data type:

```
$multiDArr = [
    [1, 2],
    [3, 4],
];

print "Value of second element of second array is {$multiDArr[1][1]}\n";
```

Output:
Value of second element of second array is 4

Here we've used an array declaration within another array declaration. The results are self-explanatory: the first and second elements of $multiDArr are arrays. A common concept when discussing multidimensional arrays is "inner" and "outer." In this example, the outer array is $multiDArr, which contains two inner arrays. Accessing inner array elements requires a slightly more complex bracket/key notation: a key followed by a sub-key: $multiDArr[1][1]. The first key corresponds to the outermost array, the next key (the first sub-key) to the first inner array, and so on. Be wary of code containing many array keys chained together; unless something deeply mathematical is going on, it's usually a sign that a refactor is needed (an example of traversing tree structures with recursive function calls can be found toward the end of this chapter).

It is possible to build very complex data structures using this technique, but care should be exercised: arrays of associative arrays might be better off being refactored to arrays of objects.

ArrayObject

It is possible for objects to behave like arrays. One advantage of using an object as an array is that PHP handles objects differently from other data types: objects are not copied on assignment (unlike arrays). As in earlier chapters, we're jumping ahead and doing some object-oriented programming. If the following examples are just completely baffling, you could always have a sneak preview of the first couple of sections in Chapter 6, "Object Fundamentals."

The main benefit of `ArrayObject` over arrays is that it's possible to modify an `ArrayObject` in different parts (scopes) of your application without having to keep track of references yourself (Chapter 3, "Functions," contains a full explanation of lexical scope). For example:

```
$guitarsObj = new ArrayObject([
    ['make' => 'Ibanez', 'model' => 'RG-8570z'],
]);

$guitarsArr = [
    ['make' => 'Ibanez', 'model' => 'RG-8570z'],
];

addGuitar($guitarsObj);
addGuitar($guitarsArr);

print_r($guitarsObj);
print_r($guitarsArr);

// type of $arr must be either array or ArrayObject
function addGuitar (array|ArrayObject $arr) {
    $arr[] = [
        'make' => 'Fender',
        'model' => 'American Ultra Stratocaster'
    ];
}

Output:
ArrayObject Object
(
    [storage:ArrayObject:private] => Array
        (
            [0] => Array
```

```
            (
                [make] => Ibanez
                [model] => RG-8570z
            )

        [1] => Array
            (
                [make] => Fender
                [model] => American Ultra Stratocaster
            )

    )
)
Array
(
    [0] => Array
        (
            [make] => Ibanez
            [model] => RG-8570z
        )

)
```

$guitarsObj is initialized as new ArrayObject and an array is given to the constructor. Whenever array operations are performed on $guitarsObj, the ArrayObject class manages the internal details. In our code we have an object that behaves like an array, and an actual array in the form of $guitarsArr. When we pass these two variables to the function addGuitar(), a new element is appended within the scope of the function. The function has a single parameter $arr, which can be either array or ArrayObject, declared using a union type declaration.

However, when we look at the results with var_dump() only $guitarsObj contains a new guitar. The reason for this is the change in scope when execution enters the addGuitar() function body. As soon as we make a change to the $guitarsArr array PHP creates a copy of it and that copy only exists within the addGuitar function. This new array (referenced by the $arr function variable) does not exist in global scope and is destroyed once addGuitar() completes and control returns to the main program.

Objects passed into functions are treated differently: they are not copied even if their state changes inside the function, so any changes made will persist once the function call is complete. If this bit of trickery is causing you some confusion, take another look at Chapter 3, "Functions."

There is a drawback to using `ArrayObject`: PHP array functions don't accept them as arguments. You can export their internal data using the `ArrayObject::getArrayCopy()` method and import new data with `ArrayObject::exchangeArray()`, so the option exists to shuffle data manually in and out of an array function call. Whether or not the trade-off in functionality is worth it will be up to you!

Manipulating Arrays

Arrays are mutable: they can have new elements added or the value of existing elements changed. Using the square bracket syntax from above, new values can be assigned.

Changing Element Values

```
$myArr1 = ["Bob", "Alice"];
$myArr1[1] = "Russell";
print_r($myArr1);
```

Output:
```
Array
(
    [0] => Bob
    [1] => Russell
)
```

Logically enough, if the combination of the array variable name and key is used as a reference to an array element for obtaining its value, then it follows that we should be able to use the same method to assign a new value to the element. Using this functionality, we replace Alice with Russell.

Appending New Elements

If we use the syntax from the previous example, but the brackets do not contain a key, PHP will create a new element in the array instead.

```
$myArr1 = ["Alice", "Bob"];
$myArr1[] = "Russell";
print_r($myArr1);
```

Output:
```
Array
(
    [0] => Alice
    [1] => Bob
    [2] => Russell
)
```

The keyless syntax simply tells PHP to add a new element to the end of the array and give it the next available key. We could have achieved the same results with the following code: `$myAddr[2] = "Russell";` provided we knew what the next index value of the key was going to be.

There is also a built-in array function `array_push()` that can be used to achieve the same result.

```
$myArr1 = ["Bob", "Alice"];
array_push($myArr1, "Russell");
```

Output is not given here, but it is identical to the previous example. It is worth noting that `array_push()` is not preferred for appending single values at a time because of the slight overhead of using a function call; it is really intended for appending multiple new elements in one statement. We'll see more of this function in the section "Combining Arrays" later in the chapter.

Prepending New Elements

It is also possible to put new values at the beginning of an array using another built-in function: `array_unshift()`:

```
$myArr = ["Bob", "Russell"];
array_unshift($myArr, "Alice");
print_r($myArr);
```

Output:
```
Array
(
    [0] => Alice
    [1] => Bob
    [2] => Russell
)
```

As promised, Alice has been added to $myArr as the first element. Notice that $myArr has also been reindexed, and the original elements now have new keys. `array_unshift()` has a counterpart – `array_shift()` – which is used for removing the first element, and we'll look at that shortly.

Inserting into Arbitrary Positions

Appending and prepending new elements is straightforward, as we have seen. What if we need to insert new elements in between existing ones? Fortunately, PHP's array toolbox has just the function we need: `array_splice()`. This function has a range of uses (the official PHP documentation states that it is used to "remove a portion of the array and replace it with something else"), but one of the parameters tells the function how many elements need to be removed, and that value can be zero.

This makes `array_splice()` useful for inserting new elements in arbitrary positions. The function signature is `array_splice(array &$original, int $offset, int $length, mixed $replacement)`. `$offset` is the starting position of the original array that we wish to change, `$length` means the number of elements to remove, `$replacement` is what, if anything, we'd like to insert (this can be a scalar or composite type):

```
$myArr = ["Rita", "Bob"];
array_splice($myArr, 1, 0, "Sue");
print_r($myArr);
```

Output:
```
Array
(
    [0] => Rita
    [1] => Sue
    [2] => Bob
)
```

Rita and Bob are going to be joined their friend, Sue. The order matters to us because of reasons, so we've told PHP to put the new element "Sue" into $myArr, starting at index 1, and to remove 0 other elements. The end result is that Sue is comfortably sat between Rita and Bob.

Removing Elements

Removing elements from arrays is a little trickier than adding or changing them. PHP has a built-in function for destroying variables – unset() – which can also be used to remove an array element either by index or (for associative arrays) by key:

```
$staff = ["Alice", "Bob", "Russell"];
$crew = [
    'captain' => 'Sisko',
    'medic' => 'Bashir',
    'engineer' => 'OBrian',
];
unset($staff[0]);
unset($crew['engineer']);
print_r($staff);
print_r($crew);
```

Output:
```
Array
(
    [1] => Bob
    [2] => Russell
)
```

```
Array
(
    [captain] => Sisko
    [medic] => Bashir
)
```

unset() does its job and destroys the value at index 0 in $staff. Note that the element has been completely removed from the array, and it now contains just two. You might also have noticed the keys have not been reindexed: Bob and Russell are still indexed with 1 and 2. The $crew array is associative, so we use one of the keys to unset $crew['engineer'] (poor Myles can't catch a break).

If the disruption of sequential indexing is for any reason problematic to your program, it is possible to remove array elements and update the indexes by using (you guessed it) more of PHP's convenient built-in array functions.

Reindexing Elements

When an indexed array is first created, the indexes are sequential, and the first index value is 0. If elements are removed, the sequence can be disrupted:

```
$myArr1 = ["Alice", "Bob", "Russell"];
$myArr2 = ["Alice", "Bob", "Russell"];

unset($myArr1[1]);
print_r($myArr1);

$myArr1 = array_values($myArr1);
print_r($myArr1);

array_splice($myArr2, 0, 1);
print_r($myArr2);

Output:
Array
(
    [0] => Alice
    [2] => Russell
)
```

```
Array
(
    [0] => Alice
    [1] => Russell
)
Array
(
    [0] => Bob
    [1] => Russell
)
```

When we remove an element from an array (in this case, using the `unset()` function), the indexes are not automatically updated, as we can see in the output of the first `print_r()`. After unsetting `$myArr[1]`, the second element in the array is now "Russell", but the index for that element is still 2. The index sequence is now 0, 2.

Two built-in functions, `array_splice()` and `array_values()`, are used here to force reindexing of arrays after an element is removed. In the case of `array_values()`, the elements of the input array are returned but with a new index; we then overwrite `$myArr1` with that returned array. We've already seen `array_splice()` in action; you might have noticed then that when we inserted new elements, the index values of all elements were updated. The outcome for each function in this example is identical; the only difference between using the two functions in this way is that `array_values()` will outperform `array_splice()` by about 10%.

Splitting Arrays

If for any reason you need to divide an array into equally sized sets, the built-in function `array_chunk()` will allow you to do just that:

```
$arr = [
    'a' => 'Alice',
    'b' => 'Bob',
    'r' => 'Russell',
];
```

```
$newArr = array_chunk($arr, 2, true);

print_r($newArr);

Output:
Array
(
    [0] => Array
        (
            [a] => Alice
            [b] => Bob
        )

    [1] => Array
        (
            [r] => Russell
        )

)
```

array_chunk() takes two required parameters, the array variable and the required size of each generated array, and an optional boolean flag that controls the preservation of keys. Unless told otherwise, array_chunk() will numerically re-index all elements in the returned arrays. array_chunk() returns an array containing the input data split according to the parameters.

Here we've asked for $arr to be split into arrays containing two elements and supplied an array of three. Note that the final array will not necessarily be the same size as the others, depending on the number of remaining elements in the original data.

Iterating Arrays

So far we've seen how to create arrays, access their elements, and make changes to their contents. Code designed to work with arrays will typically need to act upon the entire set of data that they contain. To do this, your program will need a way to access all array elements in an efficient way, and PHP provides various constructs to enable this.

With foreach

Probably the simplest way to execute a block of code for each element in an array is to use the language construct foreach. This construct requires an expression given in parentheses: foreach (Iterable as $val) or foreach (Iterable as $key => $val). The first form will set $val to each element in turn on each iteration; the second form also provides the element's key (useful for associative arrays). The names of these two variables follow the same naming rules as any other PHP variable:

```
$numbers = [1, 7, 6, 9];
$total = 0;

foreach ($numbers as $v) {
    $total += $v;
}

print "average of \$numbers is " . $total / count($numbers) . "\n";

$album = [
    'title'   => 'Number of the Beast',
    'artist'  => 'Iron Maiden',
    'details' => 'Work of genius',
];

foreach ($album as $k => $v) {
    print "'{$k}' has value: {$v}\n";
}

print "\$k = {$k} and \$v = {$v}\n";
```

Output:
average of $numbers is 5.75
'title' has value: Number of the Beast
'artist' has value: Iron Maiden
'details' has value: Work of genius
$k = details and $v = Work of genius

 foreach is intuitively named: it will execute the code between the braces for every element in the $album array, and a full explanation of this construct can be found in Chapter 4, "Logic and Control." When we process the $numbers indexed array, we simply need the value of each element, so we use as `$val`. On each iteration the current element value is made available within the loop (via the `$val` variable), which we then use to increment the value of `$total`.

In the case of the `$album` associative array, the keys are also useful metadata. We use the as `$key => $val` form. If we had used the as `$key => $val` form for the `$numbers` loop, then each iteration would have set `$key` to the current index value, 0, 1, 2, and so on. Notice that `$k` and `$v` retain the final values they were assigned by the foreach loop. Variables declared within foreach expressions persist within the scope that they're defined, even after the loop is complete, so be careful with their names!

Counting Elements

When traversing arrays, you might need to know how many elements an array contains. The built-in function count() will return an integer value count of the elements. For multidimensional arrays, count() can also make a count of sub-elements by passing the parameter COUNT_RECURSIVE:

```
$myArr = ['Alice', 'Bob', 'Russell'];
$i = count($myArr);

$multiDArr = [
    ['Alice', 'Rita'],
    ['Sue', 'Bob'],
];
$j = count($multiDArr, COUNT_RECURSIVE);

print "There are {$i} people in \$myArr\n";
print "There are {$j} people in \$multiDArr\n";
```

Output:
```
There are 3 people in $myArr
There are 6 people in $multiDArr
```

count() works with countable data types, and arrays are inherently countable, so the return value is as you'd expect: the number of elements in the array in `$myArr` is obviously three. The recursive count of elements in `$multiDArr` is six, which might seem incorrect, but don't forget that the sub-arrays are also elements: we have four strings distributed across two sub-arrays, so the total is six.

CHAPTER 5 ARRAYS

Other useful built-in functions that complement count() are is_array() (tests if a variable is an array), and is_countable() (tests if a variable can be counted, which includes arrays and ArrayObject).

With for

PHP, like many other languages, provides the construct for. This construct is designed to execute a block of code in a loop until something causes it to exit and return control to the main program. It is more complex than foreach in that it usually requires some foreknowledge about the array being processed. The for statement requires three expressions, which are placed in parentheses immediately following the keyword like this: for (expr_begin ; expr_before ; expr_after) { //DO SOMETHING }.

The three expressions are separated with semicolons; the first one is evaluated before the loop begins; the second one is evaluated at the beginning of each iteration, and if true, then the block executes; and the third one is evaluated after each iteration. Let's see it in action:

```
$myArr = ['Alice', 'Rita', 'Sue', 'Bob'];
$size = count($myArr);

for ($i = 0; $i < $size; $i++) {
    print "{$myArr[$i]} is here.\n";
}
print "\$i = {$i}\n";

Output:
Alice is here.
Rita is here.
Sue is here.
Bob is here.
$i = 4
```

This is a fairly typical pattern. The first expression – $i = 0; – initializes the variable $i to the integer zero, which is used as the key to access the elements of $myArr inside the loop's code block. The second checks that $i isn't larger than the maximum index of

$myArr; otherwise, we'd be using an invalid index value. The third increment increases $i by one after the iteration has completed (and all statements inside the block have executed).

Notice that $i retains its value after the loop has completed, for the same reasons as the previous example. All variables initialized in a `for` expression follow PHP's scoping rules and will have the same scope as $myArr and $count. It's quite common to reuse a counter like $i within the same block of code, so be aware that it persists after the loop is complete *and* now has an invalid value. If we tried to use $myArr[$i] after the loop was complete, we'd see an error like this: `PHP Warning: Undefined array key 4`. For more detail on how variable scope works, see Chapter 3, "Functions."

Loop Expressions

It is legal syntax for any (or even all) of the expressions of a `for` statement to be empty or contain multiple expressions separated by a comma. For example:

```
$myArr = ['Alice', 'Rita', 'Sue', 'Bob'];

for ($i = 0, $size = count($myArr); $i < $size; ) {
    print "{$myArr[$i]} is here.\n";
    $i++;
}
```

```
Output:
Alice is here.
Rita is here.
Sue is here.
Bob is here.
```

Here we've adapted the previous example, moving the initialization of $size into the first `for` expression and separating it from the initialization of $i with a comma. Notice that incrementing $i now occurs within the loop's code block rather than in the third `for` expression.

This isn't particularly useful and adds unnecessary clutter to the loop's code block; it's simply done here as a demonstration. Similarly, we could initialize $i and $size before the `for` statement, and our expressions could look like this:

CHAPTER 5   ARRAYS

```
$i = 0;
$size = count($myArr);

for ( ; $i < $size; ) {
    print "{$myArr[$i]} is here.\n";
    $i++;
}
```

Empty expressions might not appear to be useful with the trivial examples here, but there are use-cases for them. Imagine a scenario where complex logic might be required to determine if a loop should end; trying to fit complex tests into a `for` expression could well make for unreadable code.

Skipping Iterations

Sometimes it is useful to exclude certain elements from the loop operation. Perhaps the data type is incompatible with a certain function, or the value is of no interest. To force a loop to jump to the next iteration before the end of the block, you can use the construct continue:

```
$albums = [
    ['title' => 'Number of the Beast', 'artist' => 'Iron Maiden'],
    ['title' => 'Whatever', 'artist' => 'Some other band'],
    ['title' => 'Wasted Years', 'artist' => 'Iron Maiden'],
];

foreach ($albums as $album) {
    if ($album['artist'] !== 'Iron Maiden') {
        continue;
    }

    print "{$album['title']} is an Iron Maiden album.\n";
}
```

Output:
Number of the Beast is an Iron Maiden album.
Wasted Years is an Iron Maiden album.

The `continue` statement is executed when we don't find the band we're looking for. When a `continue` statement is evaluated, the rest of the block is skipped, and execution continues at the beginning of the block with the next element.

Terminating Early

As well as skipping array elements, it might also be necessary to end the loop entirely. For this we use the `break` construct in a similar manner to `continue`:

```
$myArr = ['Alice', 'Bob', 'Russell', 'Rita', 'Sue'];

foreach ($myArr as $name) {
    if ($name === 'Russell') {
        // Pretend something went horribly wrong with Russell
        print "{$name} went so wrong that we can't continue :(\n";
        break;
    }
    print "{$name} is fine.\n";
}
Output:
Alice is fine.
Bob is fine.
Russell went so wrong that we can't continue :(
```

Much like `continue`, `break` stops execution of the loop block. However, rather than carrying on to the next iteration, control is returned to the main program immediately.

Traversing Multidimensional Arrays

For more complex data structures, multiple loops can be nested within each other. The outer loop works on the parent array; the inner loop works on each child of the parent:

```
$guitars = [
    ['make' => 'Ibanez', 'model' => 'RG-8570z' , 'price' => '£2100'],
    ['make' => 'Fender', 'model' => 'American Ultra Stratocaster',
    'price' => '£1800'],
];
```

```
foreach ($guitars as $guitar) {
    foreach ($guitar as $prop => $str) {
        print "{$prop}: {$str}\n";
    }
    print "\n";
}
```

Output:
make: Ibanez
model: RG-8570z
price: £2100

make: Fender
model: American Ultra Stratocaster
price: £1800

The outer `foreach` sets `$guitar` to the first sub-array on iteration one; the inner `foreach` then iterates over each property and value within it. When the inner loop is complete, control is returned to the outer loop for a second iteration.

Of course, for arrays that are nested three-deep, three nested `for` or `foreach` loops could be used. This can quickly lead to unmanageable code, so exercise caution. Deeply nested arrays and/or loops should be regarded with equally deep suspicion! For more complex data structures, a recursive function call is probably more appropriate, which we'll look at later when we explore how to process arrays with our own functions.

Assignment During Iteration

During execution of a `for` loop, we work with an iterator variable (typically `$i`) to access each array element sequentially, and we can do whatever we like with that element (provided it's legal PHP syntax, of course). This includes changing values, for example:

```
$arr = [1, 2, 3];
for ($i = 0, $size = count($arr); $i < $size; $i++) {
    $arr[$i]++;
}
print_r($arr);
```

Output:
Array
(
    [0] => 2
    [1] => 3
    [2] => 4
)

This works because we're accessing $arr directly. The iterator variable $i changes on each loop, but we're using $arr (which exists outside the for code block) for access to the elements, so our changes will stick. Doing something similar with foreach requires a little more effort, as we'll see very shortly. But first, a warning: be careful with for loops when adding elements, as this classic bug demonstrates:

```
$arr = ["Alice", "Bob"];
for ($i = 0; $i < count($arr); $i++) {
    print "Adding a Russell!" . PHP_EOL;
    $arr[] = "Russell";
}
print_r($arr);
```

Output:
Adding a Russell!
Adding a Russell!
Adding a Russell!
Adding a Russell!
... several thousand iterations ...
PHP Fatal error: Allowed memory size of 134217728 bytes exhausted...

The problem here is we're testing the size of the array on each iteration – ($i = 0; $i < count($arr); $i++) – and the array is gaining an element on each loop. $i starts at 0, and the return from count($arr) will always exceed it, so logically the loop can never end (we run out of memory first). You should always be careful with count() and for loops. Notice the previous code example uses the expression for ($i = 0, $size = count($arr); $i < $size; ... to initialize $size as the count of array elements at the start of the loop and compare $i to $size on each iteration. This not only makes the loop safe; it is also more efficient (otherwise we're calling the count() function on every iteration).

When using foreach loops, making changes to elements requires a reference:

```
$arr = [1, 2, 3];
foreach ($arr as $ele) {
    $ele++;
}
print_r($arr);

foreach ($arr as &$ele) {
    $ele++;
}
print_r($arr);
```

Output:
```
Array
(
    [0] => 1
    [1] => 2
    [2] => 3
)
Array
(
    [0] => 2
    [1] => 3
    [2] => 4
)
```

In the first loop – foreach ($arr as $ele) – changing the iterator $ele had no effect on the original array. This is because $ele is treated as a new value if it is written to (PHP's copy-on-write behavior; see Chapter 3, "Functions," for a detailed explanation). If we want to make changes to the original elements, we have to add a reference operator & to the iterator variable when it is declared in the foreach expression foreach ($arr as &$ele). With the second loop, the values in the original array are changed.

Extracting Array Data

It is often useful to extract array elements into individual scalar variables, which can be done easily in a single statement with PHP's `list` language construct.

With list()

```
$myArr = ['Alice', 'Bob', 'Russell'];

list ($first, $second) = $myArr;

var_dump($first);
var_dump($second);

Output:
string(5) "Alice"
string(3) "Bob"
```

With the `list` construct, PHP traverses the $myArr array starting at the first element and assigns a copy of the value (modifying $first does not affect the value in $myArr and so on) to each variable contained inside the parentheses in turn, until all variables have a value. Notice that I only got the first two elements from a three-element array. `list` will stop once its variables have values.

In the case of there being more variables to assign than elements available, PHP will generate a warning error: `PHP Warning: Undefined array key ...` but otherwise will continue to execute (and any variables without an assigned value will get the default value of `null`).

list() with Keys

Since PHP 7.1, `list` can contain keys, or square bracket array notation can be used instead:

```
$myArr1 = ['Alice', 'Rita', 'Sue', 'Bob'];
$myArr2 = [
    'lang' => 'PHP',
    'ver'  => '8.4',
];
```

```
list (2 => $third, 3 => $fourth) = $myArr1;
[$first, $second] = $myArr1;
list ('lang' => $lang, 'ver' => $ver) = $myArr2;

var_dump($first);
var_dump($second);
var_dump($third);
var_dump($fourth);

print("{$lang}{$ver} FTW!\n");

Output:
string(5) "Alice"
string(4) "Rita"
string(3) "Sue"
string(3) "Bob"
PHP8.4 FTW!
```

In the first assignment (using `list`), we asked for explicit indexes (2 and 3), and the values of those third and fourth elements are assigned to the variables in the `list` parentheses. The second assignment statement uses square brackets and is syntactically equivalent to `list ($first, $second) = $myArr;`. It is, of course, also possible to use explicit indexes in the square bracket form: `[2 => $third, 3 => $fourth] = $myArr` is perfectly legal syntax. If using keys, all values must have them; it isn't possible to mix the two forms: `list($first, 1 => $second)` is illegal syntax.

With extract()

It is possible to save some effort when extracting scalars from arrays. Quite often the newly created variable names will align with the keys of the array providing the data, in which case the built-in function `extract()` will deal with creating the variables for you. If an array `['foo' => 'bar']` is passed to `extract()`, the variable `$foo` is created: it has a value of `"bar"` and exists only in the current scope (if `extract()` is called inside your function, the new variables exist only within that function). Bear in mind that $0, $1, etc., would be illegal variable names, so extracting from an indexed array requires a little extra work:

```
$arr1 = [
    'a' => 'Alice',
    'b' => 'bob',
];

$arr2 = ['Alice', 'Bob'];

extract($arr1);
extract($arr2, EXTR_PREFIX_ALL, 'student');

print "\$a: {$a}\n";
print "\$b: {$b}\n";
print "\$student_0: {$student_0}\n";
print "\$student_1: {$student_1}\n";
```

Output:
a: Alice
b: bob
$student_0: Alice
$student_1: Bob

extract($arr1) initializes two new variables using the keys of $arr1 as the variable names: $a has the same value as $arr1['a'], and so on. For the indexed array $arr2, we specify a prefix for the new variable names and pass the flag EXTR_PREFIX_ALL. This tells extract() that we wish each new variable name to begin with the string "student_", which has the happy effect of making our new names legal. Without EXTR_PREFIX_ALL, no variables would have been imported.

extract() has a return value: an integer value of the number of variables successfully imported and a variety of flags that can be passed as arguments to control its behavior. The default behavior is to overwrite any existing variables:

```
$name = 'Alice';
$arr = [
    'name' => 'Bob'
];
extract($arr); // $name will be overwritten
print "\$name: {$name}" . PHP_EOL;
```

CHAPTER 5   ARRAYS

```php
$name = 'Alice';
$arr = [
    'name' => 'Russell'
];
extract($arr, EXTR_PREFIX_IF_EXISTS, 'new');
print "\$name: {$name}" . PHP_EOL; // $name is untouched
print "\$new_name: {$new_name}" . PHP_EOL; // $new_name is created to avoid
                                           overwriting $name
```

Output:
$name: Bob
$name: Alice
$new_name: Russell

The code above demonstrates the default behavior of extract(). The extracted array contains a name key, which maps to an existing $name variable, so the variable is given a new values. When the EXTR_PREFIX_IF_EXISTS flag is set, the function will create a new variable using the given prefix; in this case, we specify a prefix new, so the new variable is $new_name. We can also get extract() to skip elements in the input array if they collide with existing variables:

```php
$name = 'Alice';
$arr = [
    'name' => 'Bob',
];
extract($arr, EXTR_SKIP, 'new');
print "\$name: {$name}" . PHP_EOL;
```

Output:
$name: Alice

Here's a summary of all the possible flags for extract():

Table 5-1. extract() flag constants

Flag	Effect
EXTR_OVERWRITE	Overwrite any existing vars (default)
EXTR_SKIP	Skip if var already exists
EXTR_PREFIX_SAME	Prefix vars on collision
EXTR_PREFIX_ALL	Prefix all vars
EXTR_PREFIX_INVALID	Prefix if var name would be invalid (e.g., numeric)
EXTR_IF_EXISTS	Only import var if existing
EXTR_PREFIX_IF_EXISTS	Prefix only if var already exists
EXTR_REFS	Create vars as refs to original array elements

In all cases except EXTR_REFS, only one flag is allowed, and if the flag would result in a prefixed variable being created, then the prefix argument must be given, we saw this earlier when we extracted from an indexed array – extract($arr2, EXTR_PREFIX_ALL, 'student');. EXTR_REFS is an interesting one because it can be combined with another flag and will result in the new variables being created as references to the original element; this is demonstrated below:

```
$arr = [
    'name' => 'Bob',
    'age' => 'Forty-seven',
    'favouriteToy' => 'Benelli M4 Tactical',
];
extract($arr, EXTR_REFS|EXTR_PREFIX_ALL, 'rusty');

$rustyName = 'Russell';
$rustyAge = 'Eleven';
$rustyFavouriteToy = 'Action Mans';

var_dump($arr);
```

Output:
```
array(3) {
  ["name"]=>
  &string(3) "Bob"
  ["age"]=>
  &string(11) "Forty-seven"
  ["favouriteToy"]=>
  &string(19) "Benelli M4 Tactical"
}
```

We can see that $arr has been updated by changing the values of the imported variables; note the output of var_dump() shows that each element now has a reference operator next to the type (&string(7) "Russell", etc.). The expression EXTR_REFS|EXTR_PREFIX_ALL is a *bitwise OR* operation, and you can find an explanation in Chapter 7, "Numbers": it's quite a common pattern seen in PHP functions.

Extreme caution is advised if using extract(), especially in global scope. One slip and critical data might be lost, or the global symbol table becomes polluted with unnecessary variables. It should also never be used on superglobal data ($_POST, $_GET, et al.) because the values in those special arrays can contain unfiltered user input, which should always be handled with care (and suspicion). Removal of this function from the language has been suggested on at least one occasion on the PHP *#internals* mailing list (https://externals.io/message/100637).

Fetching a Subset of Elements with array_slice()

To extract a sub-set of elements from an array, we can use the built-in array_slice(). This function will return sequential elements of an array starting at an offset parameter and ending once the required length parameter is satisfied.

```
$myArr1 = ["Alice", "Rita", "Sue", "Bob", "Russell"];

$myArr2 = array_slice($myArr1, 1, 3);

print_r($myArr2);
print_r($myArr1);
```

```
Output:
Array
(
    [0] => Rita
    [1] => Sue
    [2] => Bob
)
Array
(
    [0] => Alice
    [1] => Rita
    [2] => Sue
    [3] => Bob
    [4] => Russell
)
```

array_slice fetches the sequence of elements specified by its second (offset) and third (length) parameters and returns those elements as a new array. Here we've specified that we want a sequence of three elements starting at index 1. Note that the original array is not altered.

Combining Arrays

A very simple way to join two arrays together is to use the + operator like this: $array1 + $array2;. When called with two arrays as operands, this will append the right-hand array to the left and return a new array. If two keys are present in both operand arrays, then the left-hand elements are given priority.

```
$myArr1 = [1, 2];
$myArr2 = [3, 4, 5, 6];

$myAssocArr1 = ['lang' => 'PHP', 'ver' => '8.4'];
$myAssocArr2 = ['engine' => 'Zend', 'ver' => '4.4'];

print_r($myArr1 + $myArr2);
print_r($myAssocArr1 + $myAssocArr2);
```

Output:
```
Array
(
    [0] => 1
    [1] => 2
    [2] => 5
    [3] => 6
)
Array
(
    [lang] => PHP
    [ver] => 8.4
    [engine] => Zend
)
```

Looking at the union of the associated arrays, we can see that the ver key retains the value from $myAssocArr1 because it was the left-hand operand in the expression. The engine key/val pair is added to the union from the right-hand operand as a new element. The union of the indexed arrays is [1, 2, 5, 6]: remember that indexed arrays are just implemented as associative arrays with sequential integer keys; therefore, elements 0 and 1 from $myArr1 are chosen because it is the left-hand operand.

With ... (Splat Operator)

We have already seen array_push() in action (to append a new element to an existing array) with the caveat that it was (slightly) inefficient. A better use of array_push() is joining two arrays together but requires that we use the ... operator. Note that doing it this way modifies $myArr1 which might not be ideal depending on your use case.

```
$myArr1 = ["Alice", "Bob"];
$myArr2 = ["Rita", "Sue", "Russell"];

array_push($myArr1, ...$myArr2); // equivalent to array_push($myArr1,
                                 "Rita", "Sue", "Russell");

print_r($myArr1);
```

Output:
Array
(
    [0] => Alice
    [1] => Bob
    [2] => Rita
    [3] => Sue
    [4] => Russell
)

The splat operator ... transforms the elements of $myArr2 into individual values and supplies them to array_push, as if it had been called with four arguments (the target array and the three string elements of the second array). We must do this otherwise, the result will be that $myArr2 is inserted as a sub-array of $myArr1.

PHP 7.4 added support for using the splat operator within an array expression. For example, $myArr = ["Alice", "Bob", ...$myOtherArr]; would create an array with "Alice" and "Bob" as the first two elements, then every element of $myOtherArr following them (rather than $myOtherArr as a sub-array).

With array_merge()

Another useful function for combining arrays is array_merge(). For indexed arrays, this will return a new array with the elements of both arrays concatenated in the order in which they were combined, leaving the original arrays unmodified. The output of the following is identical to the previous example.

```
$myArr1 = ["Alice", "Bob"];
$myArr2 = ["Rita", "Sue", "Russell"];

$merge  = array_merge($myArr1, $myArr2);

print_r($merge);
```

Output:
Array
(
    [0] => Alice
    [1] => Bob

```
    [2] => Rita
    [3] => Sue
    [4] => Russell
)
```

array_merge() does exactly what it says and merges two arrays together and returns the result. If indexed arrays are input, then all of the values of both arrays are combined in the order they were supplied. The resulting array is then reindexed (in this case, element 0 of $myArr2 becomes element 2 of the new array, and so on).

A word of warning: array_merge() behaves differently with associative arrays. If the same keys exist in the input arrays, then they will overwrite each other. Only one value will be present in the output (which will be set to whatever array_merge() encountered last).

```
$assoc1 = [
    'a' => 'Alice',
    'b' => 'Rita',
];

$assoc2 = [
    'a' => 'Sue',
    'b' => 'Bob',
];

print_r(array_merge($assoc1, $assoc2));

Output:
Array
(
    [a] => Sue
    [b] => Bob
)
```

Splicing into Other Arrays

If we need to insert the elements of one into an arbitrary position of another, array_splice is our friend (again). The method is similar to that seen earlier on in the section on array manipulation, but instead of a scalar value, we pass an array.

```
$myArr1 = ["Alice", "Bob", "Russell"];
$myArr2 = ["Rita", "Sue"];

array_splice($myArr1, 1, 0, $myArr2); // offset = 2, length = 0
print_r($myArr1);
```

Output:
```
Array
(
    [0] => Alice
    [1] => Rita
    [2] => Sue
    [3] => Bob
    [4] => Russell
)
```

We've already seen array_splice in action but this time we pass another array to insert, rather than a scalar. array_splice will extract the elements of the array to be inserted and drop those into $myArr1 (starting here at offset 1) in the order they exist in $myArr2.

array_splice() can also replace elements when it splices in the new data, controlled by the second (offset) and third (length) function parameters. It is possible to replace all elements after the offset by passing null as the length:

```
$myArr1 = ["Alice", "Bob", "Russell"];
$myArr2 = ["Rita", "Sue"];

array_splice($myArr1, 2, null, $myArr2); // offset = 2, length = null
print_r($myArr1);
```

Output:
```
Array
(
    [0] => Alice
    [1] => Bob
    [2] => Rita
    [3] => Sue
)
```

We can remove a fixed number of elements starting at the offset by passing a positive integer:

```
$myArr1 = ["Alice", "Bob", "Russell"];
$myArr2 = ["Rita", "Sue"];

array_splice($myArr1, 1, 1, $myArr2); // offset = 1, length = 1
print_r($myArr1);
```

Output:
```
Array
(
    [0] => Alice
    [1] => Rita
    [2] => Sue
    [3] => Russell
)
```

There are more permutations of offset and length that can achieve other outcomes such as starting the offset from the end of the array, or removing elements from offset until a fixed number of positions from the end of the array. Full documentation for the function can be found at https://www.php.net/manual/en/function.array-splice.php.

Combining into Associative Arrays

PHP offers the capability to easily create associative arrays using two other arrays of equal length: one for keys and the other for values. The use cases might be marginal, but it will save time and effort if it ever becomes necessary.

```
$keys = [
    'title',
    'year',
];

$albums = [
    ['A Night at the Opera', '1975'],
    ['A Day at the Races', '1976'],
];
```

```
$assocArr = [];
foreach ($albums as $album) {
    if (count($keys) === count($album)) {
        $assocArr[] = array_combine($keys, $album);
    }
}

print_r($assocArr);

Output:
Array
(
    [0] => Array
        (
            [title] => A Night at the Opera
            [year] => 1975
        )

    [1] => Array
        (
            [title] => A Day at the Races
            [year] => 1976
        )

)
```

We loop over $albums and test that the number of elements is equal to the number of keys (if the two arrays provided to array_combine() are of different sizes, it will return false and emit an E_WARNING error). If the test passes, array_combine() generates a new associative array, which is then added to $assocArr.

Replacing Elements with array_replace()

It is possible to selectively overwrite elements of an array with elements of another, using the built-in array_replace().

```
$carData = ['make' => 'Audi', 'model' => 'Golf', 'variant' => 'VRs'];
$correctData = ['make' => 'VW', 'variant' => 'GTI'];

$carData = array_replace($carData, $correctData);

print_r($carData);

Output:
Array
(
    [make] => VW
    [model] => Golf
    [variant] => GTI
)
```

array_replace() takes two arrays as arguments and builds a new one from them. The input array keys are compared, and if the keys match, the element from the second array is used; otherwise, it will be the element from the first. As we can see from the example, $correctData contains two keys that are also present in $carData, so the values for make and variant are VW and GTI, respectively. As the model isn't present in $correctData, the value from $carData is used instead.

This function can take multiple replacement arrays (e.g., array_replace($array, $replace1, $replace2, $replace3);). It will perform the same key checking, the rule being that if multiple instances of a key are found in the replacement arrays, it is always the last one encountered that is used in output. If $replace2 and $replace3 both have a key called foo, it is $replace3['foo'] that will be used in output.

Comparing Arrays

We have seen multiple examples so far of accessing array elements for use in various statements. All the usual rules of variable comparison apply to those elements, be they numbers, strings, booleans, etc. It is also possible to compare entire arrays to each other in a single statement.

Comparison Operators

PHP has various comparison operators, as we have seen in previous chapters. Valid array comparison operators are given in the table below.

Table 5-2. *Array comparison operators*

==	Equality: `true` if values equal (types coerced)
===	Identity: `true` only if values equal *and* types match
!=	Inequality: `true` if values not equal (types coerced)
!==	Non-identity: `true` if values not equal, or types don't match
<>	Inequality (alternate form)

These operators should already be familiar to you, if not then feel free to take a quick look at Chapter 4, "Logic and Control." The following example summarizes their use, output is given in the code comments in-line with each var_dump():

```php
$indexed1 = [0, 1, 2];
$indexed2 = [0, 1, 2];
$indexed3 = ['0', 1, '2'];
$indexed4 = ['0' => '0', 1 => 1, '2' => '2'];

$assoc1 = ['make' => 'VW', 'model' => 'Golf', 'variant' => 'GTI'];
$assoc2 = ['variant' => 'GTI', 'make' => 'VW', 'model' => 'Golf'];

var_dump($indexed1 == $indexed2); // true
var_dump($indexed1 == $indexed3); // true
var_dump($indexed1 == $indexed4); // true

var_dump($indexed1 === $indexed2); // true
var_dump($indexed1 === $indexed3); // false
var_dump($indexed1 === $indexed4); // false

var_dump($assoc1 == $assoc2); // true
var_dump($assoc1 === $assoc2); // false
```

Arrays are considered to be equal if they contain the same key/value pairs. Types are coerced for both keys and values: we can see this when comparing the four indexed arrays ($indexed4 is technically an associative array because not all of its keys are integers). When using the weakly-typed == operator, all four are considered equal. Ditto for the associative $assoc1 and $assoc2.

However, using the strict === operator, type *and* element order are also taken into account. $indexed1 === $indexed3 evaluates to false because types do not match, $indexed1 === $indexed4 is false because of types and order, $assoc1 === $assoc2 is false because the order of elements is different.

Finding Uncommon Elements

PHP provides a built-in function, array_diff(), which will compare an array to one or more comparison arrays and return all values that are not found. Keys are not compared nor is order important. If an element occurs multiple times in the first array it only needs to match a single time with the second (or subsequent) arrays to be discarded from the returned set. However, the inverse is not true: all occurrences of an unmatched element will be included in the return:

```
$car1 = ['mark' => 1, 'Golf', 'VW', 'Golf', 'GTI', 'GTI'];
$car2 = ['GTI', 'VW', 'Scirocco', '1'];

print_r(array_diff($car1, $car2));
```

Output:
```
Array
(
    [0] => Golf
    [2] => Golf
)
```

$car1 and $car2 both contain the strings 'VW' and 'GTI', but 'Golf' is not found in $car2. This is therefore considered a difference and is added to the returned array twice because it is found twice in $car1. Type coercion is in force here and 'mark' => 1 is considered equal to '1'. Finally, 'GTI' occurs twice in $car1 but, because it is also found at least once in $car2, it is not considered a difference, and it is omitted from the returned set of elements. Notice that keys are preserved from the first array. 'Golf' occurs twice in $car1, with the (automatically generated) keys of 0 and 2, those keys are retained in the results array that is returned to var_dump().

Also worth bearing in mind: array_diff() will sort arrays before comparison, and type coercion is the norm:

```
var_dump(array_diff([1, 2, 3], [3, 2, 1]));
var_dump(array_diff(
    ['make' => 'VW', 'model' => 'Golf'],
    ['model' => 'Golf', 'make' => 'VW'],
));
var_dump(array_diff(['1', '2', '3'], [1, 2, 3])); // type juggling will
                                                  happen here
```

Output:
```
array(0) {
}
array(0) {
}
array(0) {
}
```

Finding Common Elements

The corollary to computing the difference between sets is computing the intersect. This time we're finding the elements of the first array that also occur in subsequent arrays. Just as before, keys will be preserved from $car1 and multiple occurrences of an element in the first array will mean multiple occurrences in the results array. This time elements are added to the results if they can be found in all comparison arrays.

Let's swap array_diff() for array_intersect() using the same data in the example above:

```
print_r(array_intersect($car1, $car2));
```

Output:
```
Array
(
```

CHAPTER 5　ARRAYS

```
    [mark] => 1
    [1] => VW
    [3] => GTI
    [4] => GTI
)
```

The value 1 is present in $car1 and $car2, so is added to the results. The key for 1 is 'mark' in $car1, 3 in $car2, and $car1 keys are preserved in the results. GTI is found in both arrays, occurs twice in $car1, so we get both elements in the results (with $car1 keys... apologies for car/key punning).

Just like array_diff(), array_intersect() will also perform type coercion, and sort the arrays, before comparison:

```
print_r(array_intersect([1, 2, 3], ['3', 2, '1']));
print_r(array_intersect(
    ['make' => 'VW', 'model' => 'Golf'],
    ['model' => 'Golf', 'make' => 'VW'],
));
```

Output:
```
Array
(
    [0] => 1
    [1] => 2
    [2] => 3
)
Array
(
    [make] => VW
    [model] => Golf
)
```

Comparing Keys

For associative arrays, it is possible to find elements with common keys between an array and one or more comparison arrays using the built-in array_intersect_key().

```php
$car1 = ['make' => 'VW', 'model' => 'Golf'];
$car2 = ['make' => 'VW'];

print_r(array_intersect_key($car1, $car2));
print_r(array_diff_key($car1, $car2));
```

Output:
```
Array
(
    [make] => VW
)
Array
(
    [model] => Golf
)
```

Much like `array_intersect()`, `array_intersect_key()` compares the first input array to the second (and any subsequent) array and returns common elements. However, this time it is the keys that are compared. $car1 and $car2 both have the common key make, but it is the corresponding element of $car1 that is placed in the returned array. `array_diff_key()` does the inverse, so it returns model and its value.

Comparing Keys and Values

If you wish to compare associative arrays based on keys *and* values, PHP offers the functions `array_diff_assoc()`, and `array_intersect_assoc()`. These three functions perform exactly as their non-associative counterparts, with the added condition that keys are also compared. Here are some examples:

```php
$car1 = [
    'make' => 'VW',
    'model' => 'Golf',
    'variant' => 'GTI 8v',
    'colour' => 'Oak Green', // car nerds: there was a limited run of 8v
                                GTIs in this colour ;)
];
```

```
$car2 = [
    'make' => 'VW',
    'model' => 'Golf',
    'variant' => 'GTI 16v',
    'COLOUR' => 'Oak Green',
];

print_r(array_diff_assoc($car1, $car2));
print_r(array_intersect_assoc($car1, $car2));

Output:
Array
(
    [variant] => GTI 8v
    [colour] => Oak Green
)
Array
(
    [make] => VW
    [model] => Golf
)
```

Hopefully the output makes sense given what you now know about array_diff() and array_intersect(). Note that one of the elements in the output of array_diff() was [colour] => Oak Green despite both cars being painted in this rather glorious shade. This happens because array keys are case sensitive. Fortunately, there are ways to normalize array keys before comparison.

Normalizing Keys

Should you find yourself with the task of comparing associative arrays with keys that differ in case but are otherwise equivalent (e.g., comparing colour to COLOUR) then array_change_key_case() is the solution. This function accepts an array as its first argument, then an optional flag (CASE_UPPER or CASE_LOWER), and returns an array with keys updated accordingly.

```
// ... $car1 as before

$car2 = array_change_key_case($car2, CASE_LOWER);

print_r($car2);
print_r(array_diff_assoc($car1, $car2));

Output:
Array
(
    [make] => VW
    [model] => Golf
    [variant] => GTI 16v
    [colour] => Oak Green
)
Array
(
    [variant] => GTI 8v
)
```

With the two arrays now agreeing on the key for color, we get a single key and element returned from array_diff_assoc(). If normalizing keys requires more than just changing case, there are also functions available in PHP to compare keys and/or values using callback functions.

Comparing with Callbacks

It might sometimes be the case that comparing array elements requires a little more work than just type coercion and direct value comparison. The logic for testing equality can be more complex when the elements being compared are not scalars. The array functions we've seen in this section (array_diff() and array_intersect()) have counterparts designed to handle callback functions. (A callback occurs when function A() is given function B() as an argument – A(B); – with the intention that A() will be responsible for calling B() in some way, see Chapter 3, "Functions," for a deeper explanation.)

These are all the array comparison functions that accept callbacks; most accept a single callback, but there are two exceptions:

CHAPTER 5   ARRAYS

Table 5-3. Array comparison functions

Function + params	Description
array_udiff(arr1, arr2, ..., func)	As array_diff(), compares elements using func
array_udiff_assoc(arr1, arr2, ..., func)	As array_diff_assoc(), compares elements using func
array_diff_uassoc(arr1, arr2, ..., func)	As array_diff_assoc(), compares keys using func
array_diff_ukey(arr1, arr2, ..., func)	As array_diff_key(), compares keys using func
array_udiff_uassoc(arr1, arr2, ..., func1, func2)	As array_diff_assoc(), compares elements using func1, keys using func2
array_uintersect(arr1, arr2, ..., func)	As array_intersect() compares elements using func
array_uintersect_assoc(arr1, ..., arr2, func)	As array_intersect_assoc() compares elements using func
array_intersect_uassoc(arr1, ..., arr2, func)	As array_intersect_assoc() compares keys using func
array_intersect_ukey(arr1, arr2, ..., func)	As array_intersect_key() compares keys using func
array_uintersect_uassoc(arr1, arr2, ..., func1, func2)	As array_intersect_assoc() compares elements using func1, keys using func2

As with the basic intersect and diff functions, there can be an arbitrary number of array arguments, the first one will be compared in turn to all the others (with the same precedence rules for duplicates). The final argument (or arguments where two callables are required) will be treated as the callback(s).

Now let's see a couple of them working to give you a feel for how to use them. And to indulge myself, I'm going to imagine a fantasy classic car garage. This garage uses a database to store cars that are advertised for sale, and a different database to keep track of cars that are out for repair. If a car is out for repair it can't be sold, so we have a little program that maintains the list of cars for sale based on current repair status data.

There's just one small problem: the data stored for sales has a different model to that for repairs. In fact, the only common property between the two is the car registration number (or index if you prefer). Let's further complicate matters by having our data sources as multidimensional arrays. The internal comparison function used by array_diff() and array_intersect() isn't going to work for us here, it's only intended for comparing scalars (and will emit various errors if used with composite type elements). Instead, we're going to write a small function that just tests a small part of each element's data and use it as a callback to array_uintersect():

```php
$advertised = [
    [
        'registration' => 'AAA 1A',
        'model' => 'Ford Prefect'
    ],
    [
        'registration' => 'BBB 1B',
        'model' => 'Vauxhall Viva'
    ],
];

$outForRepair = [
    [
        'registration' => 'AAA 1A',
        'fault' => 'Missing towel',
    ]
];

$deListUntilRepaired = array_uintersect($advertised, $outForRepair,
function ($ads, $reps) {
    return $ads['registration'] <=> $reps['registration'];
});

print_r($deListUntilRepaired);
```

CHAPTER 5   ARRAYS

Output:
```
Array
(
    [0] => Array
        (
            [registration] => AAA 1A
            [model] => Ford Prefect
        )

)
```

    $advertised and $outForRepair contain collections of data for each car (represented here as sub-arrays, they could just as easily have been objects). We have two cars advertised, one out for repair, and the one out for repair happens to also be currently on sale. Our code aims to discover which cars need to be removed from sale by finding the intersect (the idea being that we can then send the intersect results elsewhere to update the sales database).

    The only reliable way to compare the different array structures is via the common 'registration' key, so we have an anonymous function as the third argument to array_uintersect(), which performs a comparison between two elements' 'registration' value (see Chapter 3, "Functions," if you're not sure what an anonymous function is). The callback function is called every time array_uintersect compares elements between its own input arrays; each element being compared comprises the arguments to the callback. Elements from the first array $advertised will always passed to the callback as the first argument, $outForRepair as the second.

    An important point to note is the type of comparison we are performing. We're using the spaceship operator <=>, which compares two values and returns -1, 0, or 1 depending on whether the first operand is less than, equal to, or greater than the second. The callback function must return an integer less than, equal to, or greater than zero. The reason why the callback has to return in this way, and not just return a boolean to indicate a match, is because it isn't just used for computing the intersect. (Note that when the spaceship operator is used with string operands, it is alphabetical precedence that is tested.)

    Remember that array_diff() and array_intersect() will sort input arrays before comparison? With array_uintersect() *the callback is also used for sorting*. This is a subtle point and isn't made clear in the official PHP documentation. If we had simply returned something like $ads['registration'] === $reps['registration'] the callback would have been indicating that the second element was always greater than first (and the intersect would have been empty).

For checking keys, the callback works in much the same way: it must function correctly for sorting as well as comparison. Let's say that the two databases don't just have different data models, they also have different key values. This causes us a problem with array_uintersect because the callback for value comparison is also a callback for sorting, which means it doesn't just compare values between $advertised and $outForRepair it also compares values in each array against each other. Let's make a small change to $outForRepair and run it through array_uintersect() as before:

```
// ... $advertised as before

$outForRepair = [
    [
        'x_registration' => 'AAA 1A',
        'x_fault' => 'Missing towel',
    ]
];

$deListUntilRepaired = array_uintersect($advertised, $outForRepair,
function ($ads, $reps) {
    return $ads['registration'] <=> $reps['x_registration'];
});
print_r($deListUntilRepaired);

Output:
Warning: Undefined array key "x_registration"...
Array
(
)
```

There are two problems here. First, when the callback is used to sort $advertised we get a warning, because there is no x_registration key in the sub-arrays of $advertised. Second, and more subtle, is that the computed intersect is unreliable because internal sorting is broken. When $advertised is sorted we're testing a key string (which will always have a value) against an undefined value, and the result is always 1: PHP is being told that every element is greater than every other element, this has the effect of reducing

255

the sorted array to a single element (the last one tested). When it comes to the value comparison step, only the last element in the first array is compared to elements of the comparison array(s). In our case, the last element in $advertised had the registration value of 'BBB 1B', it is the only value tested against $outForRepair, and the intersect is empty.

To fix the sorting step, we need a little more logic in the value comparison callback function:

```php
$deListUntilRepaired = array_uintersect($advertised, $outForRepair,
function ($ads, $reps) {
    if (isset($reps['x_registration'])) {
        return $ads['registration'] <=> $reps['x_registration'];
    } else {
        return $ads['registration'] <=> $reps['registration'];
    }
});
print_r($deListUntilRepaired);
```

Output:
```
Array
(
    [0] => Array
        (
            [registration] => AAA 1A
            [model] => Ford Prefect
        )

)
```

By recognizing that the comparison callback is also a sorting callback (and compares values within arrays as well as between), we can write it in such a way that differences in sub-array keys can be managed however we wish (and if we'd used objects, we could account for different property names or method calls in the same way).

Remember when we looked at array_change_key_case(), I promised there was a way to handle keys that had a greater difference than just case? Let's revisit that example, but instead of changing the case of every key, we'll use a key comparison callback function:

```php
$car1 = [
    'make' => 'VW',
    'model' => 'Golf',
    'variant' => 'GTI',
    'colour' => 'Oak Green',
];
$car2 = [
    'X_MAKE' => 'VW',
    'X_MODEL' => 'Golf',
    'X_VARIANT' => 'GTI 16v',
    'X_COLOUR' => 'Oak Green',
];
print_r(array_diff_uassoc($car1, $car2, 'keyComparison'));
function keyComparison ($k1, $k2) {
    return strcasecmp($k1, ltrim($k2, 'X_'));
}
Output:
Array
(
    [variant] => GTI
)
```

In addition to a mismatch of case, we've also prepended each key in $car2 with 'X_': simply changing the case of the keys won't be enough here. By using our own key comparison function we can first clean up the keys of $car2 by stripping the leading 'X_' characters with PHP's built-in ltrim() function. We also make use of strcasecomp(), another built-in which allows case-insensitive string comparison, and returns 1-, 0, or 1 which is exactly what our callback needs to do as well. (For more details on those two string functions see Chapter 8, "Strings.") Note that the two arguments to keyComparison() are the keys (strings) of $car1 and $car2. Value comparison callbacks are given the elements being compared; key comparison callbacks are given the keys. One more point to make here: our callback is now a named function, so we pass its name as a string as the callable argument.

Searching Arrays

Earlier in the chapter, we look at ways to process all the elements of array by iterating them with loops. Sometimes your program might only need to work with a sub-set of elements, or maybe just one. You might not know in advance where in the array a particular element can be found, or you might only want to test if a particular value exists. PHP offers a range of functions to make these tasks simple.

Test Value Exists

Iterating through an array and testing each value until the required one is found isn't a particularly onerous task. If you've read through the entire chapter so far you have all the tools needed to achieve this. However, PHP provides a built-in function which gets the job done in one line:

```
$arr = ['Alice', 'Bob', 'Russell'];

if (in_array('Russell', $arr)) {
    print "I found a Russell!\n";
}
```

Output:
I found a Russell!

in_array() takes two arguments: the value you want to find and the array to be searched. It returns true if the value is found, false if not. Note that strings are case sensitive and types will be coerced. A stricter search (where value and type are tested) can be enabled by adding a third boolean parameter: in_array($val, $array, true). Note that in_array() does not search recursively, it will only search the first dimension of multidimensional array.

Test Key Exists

If you need to test for particular key rather than value then array_key_exists() works in much the same way as in_array():

```
$amps = [
    'Marshall' => 'EL34',
    'Fender' => '6V6'
];

if (array_key_exists('Marshall', $amps)) {
    print "Big bottle amps FTW!" . PHP_EOL;
}
```

Output:
Big bottle amps FTW!

array_key_exists() confirms that the key Marshall is present in $amps and returns true, if the key wasn't found it would return false.

Similar results can be obtained with the built-in isset() function, which will accept a wide variety of data types and return true if they exist and have a non-null value:

```
$amps = [
    'Marshall' => 'EL34',
    'Fender' => '',
    'Vox' => null,
];
print (isset($amps['Marshall'])) ? "Found a Marshall" . PHP_EOL : "";
print (isset($amps['Fender'])) ? "Found a Fender" . PHP_EOL : "";
print (isset($amps['Vox'])) ? "Found a Vox" . PHP_EOL : "";
print (isset($amps['Dumble'])) ? "Found a Dumble" . PHP_EOL : "";
```

Output:
Found a Marshall
Found a Fender

From the output we can see that isset() will return true if the array key is pointing to an empty string (it was also do this for bool false or int 0), but an explicit null returns false. A key that doesn't exist will of course also be false (who's even seen a Dumble amp anyway?!). Chapter 4, "Logic and Control," discusses which non-boolean values are usually considered true or false in more detail (and also explains the ternary logical operation – (CONDITION) ? VALUE_IF_TRUE : VALUE_IF_FALSE ; – used in this example.

Find Key of Value

in_array() simply tells you if a value exists in array. If you need to know *where* the value is (or at least the first occurrence), then array_search() is the tool for the job:

```
$arr = ['Alice', 'Bob', 'Russell'];

$artists = [
    'Jimi Hendrix' => 'Stratocaster',
    'Eric Clapton' => 'Les Paul',
    'Dave Gilmour' => 'Stratocaster',
];

print "Bob is element no. " . array_search('Bob', $arr) . "\n";
print array_search('Stratocaster', $artists) . " played a Stratocaster\n";

Output:
Bob is element no. 1
Jimi Hendrix played a Stratocaster
```

array_search($val, $array) returns the key for the first instance of $val it finds or false if the value isn't found. There are two Stratocaster playing genius guitarists in $artists but Jimi is the first one found. Pop quiz: how would you fetch all of the Stratocaster players? array_intersect($artists, ['Stratocaster']); will do the job!

Minimum and Maximum Values

PHP provides the functions min() and max(), which work in two ways: finding the largest and smallest values in an array (e.g., min($array)) or comparing two scalars (e.g., max($val1, $val3)). The results of calling this on an array of numbers should be obvious. For mixed data types, the standard comparison rules apply:

```
$arr = [1, 2, 3];

print "min val of \$arr: " . min($arr) . "\n";
print "max val of \$arr: " . max($arr) . "\n";

Output:
min val of $arr: 1
max val of $arr: 3
```

Searching by Callback

PHP 8.4 introduced four new array functions which work by iterating keys and values, and passing them to a callback function. The first two we'll look at are array_find() and array_find_key(). Both these functions will iterate over the searched array and pass the values (and keys, if required) to the callback function, which should return a bool value. On the first true callback return, array_find() returns the corresponding element value, and array_find_key() returns the corresponding key, like so:

```
$guitars = [
    'Suhr',
    'Stratocaster',
    'Stratocaster',
];

$axe = array_find(
    $guitars,
    fn ($val): bool => strlen($val) > 4
);

$index = array_find_key(
    $guitars,
    fn ($val): bool => strlen($val) > 4
);

print "Let's play the {$axe} today." . PHP_EOL;
print "It's the one in position {$index}";
```

Output:
Let's play the Stratocaster today.
It's the one in position 1

Here we've used array_find() and array_find_key() in conjunction with a simple arrow function, you can also use a standard anonymous function or a string containing the name of a declared function. The signature of the callback is (mixed $val, mixed $key): bool – in other words, it must accept mixed for element values as the first parameter and mixed for element keys as the second (optional) parameter. Our arrow function tests the length of the $val string with strlen() > 4 and returns the boolean

CHAPTER 5 ARRAYS

result. `$guitars[1]` has the value `'Stratocaster'`, so that's what the two functions return. (`$guitars[2]` would also return true but neither function gets that far.) Two Strats *and* a Suhr feels a little extra to me but who am I to judge?

The next two functions are slightly different. `array_any()` returns true if just one callback iteration returns true, and `array_all()` returns true if every callback iteration returns true. Here they are in action:

```
$artists = [
    'Jimi Hendrix' => 'Stratocaster',
    'Eric Clapton' => 'Les Paul',
    'Dave Gilmour' => 'Stratocaster',
];

$anyStrats = array_any(
    $artists,
    fn ($val): bool => $val === 'Stratocaster'
);
$allStrats = array_all(
    $artists,
    fn ($val): bool => $val === 'Stratocaster'
);

var_dump($anyStrats);
var_dump($allStrats);
```

Output:
```
bool(true)
bool(false)
```

The example above demonstrates some fairly clear logic: only some of the artists played Strats (OK, I know Clapton changed to Fenders, but he was always best with a Gibson in his hands). One tiny difference between `array_any()` and `array_all()` is that the former only iterates to the first true result, so the callback isn't firing unnecessarily, and `array_all()`, of course, has to iterate the entire array.

The two examples above are relatively trivial and simply demonstrate the use of these new functions. Remember that you can process keys and values together and implement any logic you like in the callbacks, which opens up a lot of possibilities.

Sorting Arrays

It is not uncommon to want to process arrays in value or key order: perhaps the data simply needs to be rendered in numerical or alphabetical order, or maybe you're implementing an algorithm that works best on sorted data. Whatever the reason, PHP has you covered.

By Value

To arrange elements in an array by ascending value order, we can use the built-in function sort(). sort() also has a counterpart, which will sort in descending order: rsort(). By default elements are compared using standard comparison, but this behavior can be modified. Let's take a look at a simple example:

```
$numbers = [1.2, 1, 10, 5];
$words = ['foo', 'Bar', 'BAR', 'Foo'];

sort($numbers);
sort($words);

print_r($numbers);
print_r($words);
```

Output:
```
Array
(
    [0] => 1
    [1] => 1.2
    [2] => 5
    [3] => 10
)
Array
(
    [0] => BAR
    [1] => Bar
    [2] => Foo
    [3] => foo
)
```

The default behavior of `sort()` is to modify the input array rearranging its elements according to the standard rules, then re-index them. Re-indexing is fine when you need it and overly aggressive when you don't. For example, if we sort an associative array:

```
$assoc = [
    'make' => 'VW',
    'model' => 'Golf',
];

sort($assoc);
print_r($assoc);
```

Output:
```
Array
(
    [0] => Golf
    [1] => VW
)
```

... we can see that the keys have been replaced by numeric indexes. There is a sorting function designed to handle associative arrays, which we will come to shortly.

By Key

If sorting by key order is needed, then `ksort()` (to sort in ascending order, or `krsort()` for descending) will rearrange an array into key order.

```
$arr = [
    'a' => 'Alice',
    'r' => 'Russell',
    'b' => 'Bob',
];

ksort($arr);
print_r($arr);
```

Output:
Array
(
    [a] => Alice
    [b] => Bob
    [r] => Russell
)

Preserving Keys

Remember that sort() reindexed the sorted array with numeric keys, even if the array was associative? If that causes problems for you, then asort() (and arsort()) will sort by value but preserve keys.

$words = ['foo', 'Bar', 'BAR', 'Foo'];
$assoc = ['foo' => 'foo', 'bar' => 'bar'];

asort($words);
asort($assoc);

print_r($words);
print_r($assoc);

Output:
Array
(
    [2] => BAR
    [1] => Bar
    [3] => Foo
    [0] => foo
)
Array
(
    [bar] => bar
    [foo] => foo
)

Modifying `sort()` Behavior

The built-in function `sort` accepts a variety of predefined constants (as a second argument) that will modify sorting behavior. We'll pick three: SORT_REGULAR (the default), SORT_NUMERIC, and SORT_STRING. While we're at it, let's bring together some of the techniques we've seen throughout the chapter.

```
$sortFlags = [
    'regular' => SORT_REGULAR,
    'numeric' => SORT_NUMERIC,
    'string'  => SORT_STRING,
];

$data =[
    'regular' => ['a', '-2', '-1', '-5.7', '-57', '0', '1'],
    'numeric' => ['a', '-2', '-1', '-5.7', '-57', '0', '1'],
    'string'  => ['a', '-2', '-1', '-5.7', '-57', '0', '1'],
];

foreach ($data as $flag => $arr) {
    sort($arr, $sortFlags[$flag]);

    print "{$flag}: \t";

    foreach ($arr as $ele) {
        print "{$ele}\t";
    }

    print "\n";
}
```

Output:
```
regular:    -57 -5.7    -2  -1  0   1   a
numeric:    -57 -5.7    -2  -1  a   0   1
string:     -1  -2  -5.7    -57 0   1   a
```

We're working with a set of negative and positive numbers, and a letter has also been thrown into the set to demonstrate how type coercion affects sorting and comparison. The keys of each sub-array of $data are used as a map to the sort flag we wish to use (defined in $sortFlags). When we iterate over $data we call sort() with the appropriate flag then print out the newly sorted elements. Here's what each flag means.

SORT_REGULAR is the default behavior of sort: PHP's standard comparison rules are used. In PHP 8 this means that the elements are compared as if they were operands in an expression using the <=> operator which we've already seen earlier in the chapter when we looked at comparison with callbacks. The numbers sort as you would expect (-57 as the lowest value), with the string "a" as the largest value. This is because '1' <=> 'a' evaluates to -1 (the right-hand operand is larger).

SORT_NUMERIC forces numeric comparison. Here "a" is placed alongside the number zero because PHP will coerce strings to 0. 1 <=> (int) 'a' evaluates to 1 (the left-hand operand is larger).

SORT_STRING forces string comparison in ASCII alphabetical order. '-57' is considered to have a larger value than '-5.7' because of the third character in each string: '.' <=> '7' evaluates to -1 because it comes first (and has a lower byte value) in the ascii code page.

There a few more flags available:

- SORT_LOCALE_STRING – string-based comparison, based on current locale (controlled by the built-in setlocale() function).

- SORT_NATURAL – string-based, using a "natural" ordering, see "Natural Sorting" later in this section.

- SORT_FLAG_CASE -combine with SORT_STRING or SORT_NATURAL (e.g., SORT_FLAG_CASE|SORT_NATURAL) using bitwise OR to compare strings case-insensitively.

By Size

sort and its companion functions (asort(), ksort(), rsort() et al.) are not limited to primitive types. They will also accept arrays containing composite types. A moderately useful application for this functionality could be to arrange a multi-dimensional array by the size of the sub-arrays:

```
$a = array_pad([0], rand(0, 10), 0);
$b = array_pad([0], rand(0, 10), 0);
$c = array_pad([0], rand(0, 10), 0);
```

CHAPTER 5 ARRAYS

```
$ordered = [
    'a' => $a,
    'b' => $b,
    'c' => $c,
];

asort($ordered);

foreach ($ordered as $k => $arr) {
    print "\${$k} size is " . sizeof($arr) . "\n"; // Output will vary
                                                   because of the
                                                   random sizes
}
Output:
$c size is 1
$b size is 4
$a size is 8
```

Here we first create three randomly sized arrays using the built-in `array_pad()` function. Next, we store them in a parent array $ordered. Finally, we pass this array of arrays to `asort()`. `array_pad()` is a built-in function that adds elements to the end (or beginning) of an array, the value of each added element is specified in the third argument. Thus, `array_pad([0], rand(0, 10), 0)` simply means "add a random amount (between zero and ten) of zeroes to the input array". The effect is that $a, $b, and $c are now of random lengths (this example only cares about array size, not the values of the elements). When PHP sorts arrays, it compares the number of elements, and our output will show us that the arrays in $ordered are now in ascending size order.

If the array contains objects, then it is sorted according to object properties. The sorting rules for object arrays are complex; in fact, they're downright arcane and take into account the number of public and private properties, then the values of those properties, then the class name of the object. The code examples to demonstrate `sort()` behavior would take up multiple pages and leave most readers (and probably the author) none the wiser; there's little value in doing so. When it comes to sorting arrays of objects, or arrays of mixed types, it's far better to define your own rules, which you can do as follows...

Sorting by Callback

To sort an array using your own callback function, you can use the built-in functions usort(), uasort(), and uksort(). If you remember from the section "Comparing Arrays" there were callback handling functions like array_uintersect(). These three sorting functions work in a very similar way. You should hopefully be comfortable by now with the idea of a callback being used to sort arrays because, as we learned, the callbacks for array_uintersect() et al. were used for both comparison *and* sorting. This is no different. Nevertheless, a quick example is called for, so here we go:

```php
$tele = new stdClass();
$tele->model = 'Fender Telecaster';
$tele->year = 1958;

$strat = new stdClass();
$strat->model = 'Fender Stratocaster';
$strat->year = 1962;

$jem = new stdClass();
$jem->model = 'Ibanez Jem 777';
$jem->year = 1988;

$guitArr = [$strat, $jem, $tele];

usort($guitArr, function ($a, $b) {
    return $a->year <=> $b->year;
});

print_r($guitArr);
```

Output:
```
Array
(
    [0] => stdClass Object
        (
            [model] => Fender Telecaster
            [year] => 1958
        )
```

```
    [1] => stdClass Object
        (
            [model] => Fender Stratocaster
            [year] => 1962
        )
    [2] => stdClass Object
        (
            [model] => Ibanez Jem 777
            [year] => 1988
        )
)
```

Here we build three objects that all created from PHP's built-in `stdClass`, and add year (of manufacture) and `model` properties to them, to create three distinct objects. The three objects are stored in the `$guitArr` (ahem, sorry) array, and our task is to sort them by the year of manufacture.

The anonymous function given to `usort()` is called repeatedly to compare two objects and determines the order based on comparison of the year property of each object. The final, sorted array has a `'Fender Telecaster'` at the start (1958 was a good year for them), `'Fender Stratocaster'` in the middle (made in 1962, also a great year), and an `'Ibanez Jem 777'` at the end (being a relative youngster, still awesome instruments though).

`usort()` iterates the array and calls the anonymous function repeatedly to compare two objects. The anonymous function simply compares the year property of each object, using a spaceship operator <=>. This way `usort` can figure out if `$a->year` is less-than, equal-to, or greater-than `$b->year`. By comparing different pairs of elements against each other, the array is eventually sorted (using the *Quicksort* algorithm, if you are wondering). The resulting sorted array has `'Fender Telecaster'` at the start (1958 was a good year for them), `'Fender Stratocaster'` in the middle (made in 1962, also a great year), with `'Ibanez Jem 777'` at the end (wonderful things, thanks, Uncle Steve).

Natural Sorting

We saw earlier that SORT_STRING caused elements to be arranged in alphabetical order. If those strings contain only alphabet letters, the results are generally intuitive. However, if strings contain digits, then the sorting sometimes looks a little off.

Imagine a driver traveling at 70 mph needing to read information quickly from some smart sign on the roadside. Let's say she's looking for a particular numbered road and only has a few seconds to do so. Take a look at the following:

```
$motorways = ['M1', 'M11', 'M6', 'M20', 'M4', 'M23'];

sort($motorways, SORT_STRING);
print getMotorways($motorways) . "\n";

natsort($motorways);
print getMotorways($motorways) . "\n";

function getMotorways (array $motorways): string {
    $str = '';

    foreach ($motorways as $m) {
        $str .= "$m, ";
    }

    return rtrim($str, ', ');
};
```

Output:
M1, M11, M20, M23, M4, M6
M1, M4, M6, M11, M20, M23

$motorways is an array of strings corresponding to some of the finest roads in the United Kingdom. Let's pretend that this data arrives into our system in some random order and our code is used to generate the list of roads on our hypothetical smart sign. Here we're comparing the results of sort($array, SORT_STRING), and natsort($array): the results are quite different.

The reason the two functions produce these results is because an alphabetical (SORT_STRING) comparison treats each digit of a number individually rather than atomically, whereas a natural sort treats consecutive digits as numbers. For example, 'A100' is

CHAPTER 5 ARRAYS

smaller than 'A20' when compared alphabetically because the character "1" occurs earlier in the ASCII codepage than the character "2". A human in a hurry, however, might prefer to see 'A20' in a list before 'A100.

For use cases like this, `natsort()` produces the needed result. Note that `sort()` accepts the modifier flag of SORT_NATURAL to produce the same behavior.

Randomizing Arrays

The opposite of `sort()` and its brethren is `shuffle()`:

```
$arr = [1, 2, 3, 4];
shuffle($arr);

print_r($arr); // $arr is randomised, output will vary
```

Output:
```
Array
(
    [0] => 3
    [1] => 1
    [2] => 4
    [3] => 2
)
```

`shuffle()` generates a new set of randomized index values for the elements, then puts the array into that order. For that reason, `shuffle()` is not safe to use on associative arrays unless you want to lose all the keys. However, there is a way to shuffle an associative array and preserve key association by using shuffle on the output of `array_keys()`:

```
$car = [
    'make' => 'VW',
    'model' => 'Golf',
    'variant' => 'GTI 8v',
    'colour' => 'Oak Green',
];
```

```
$newCars = [];
$newKeys = array_keys($car);
shuffle($newKeys);

foreach ($newKeys as $k) {
    $newCars[$k] = $car[$k];
}

print_r($newCars);

Output:
Array
(
    [variant] => GTI 8v
    [make] => VW
    [colour] => Oak Green
    [model] => Golf
)
```

The output will vary every time, of course, but that's the point! An astute person might perhaps wonder if there was a way to leverage uasort() for a similar purpose, perhaps something like this:

```
uasort($arr, function () {
    return rand(-1, 1); // returns a random int -1, 0, or 1
})
```

The answer is no. uasort() implements the Quicksort algorithm; you will find (especially with large arrays) that the "randomized" keys will tend to stick near to their original positions (because the algorithm partitions the original array into sub-arrays first).

A final word of warning about shuffle(): it is not cryptographically secure. If you need the new order to be unguessable, you will need to create your own function based on random_int(), random_bytes, or the Random\Randomizer API. See Chapter 7, "Numbers," for more detail.

CHAPTER 5 ARRAYS

Functional Array Processing

We've seen a lot of very useful built-in functionality for common array handling tasks so far but there will inevitably be times when you will have to roll-your-own. In this section we'll look at the tools PHP gives you for more complex processing requirements.

Transforming with `array_walk()`

Sometimes it is necessary to rewrite data structures. Perhaps your program fetches data from an API call, but the data isn't well formatted for your needs. PHP provides the built-in function array_walk(), which allows you to apply a callback function to every element in an array:

```
$cars = [
    [
        ['make', 'VW'], ['model', 'Golf GTI']
    ],
    [
        ['make', 'VW'], ['model', 'Corrado VR6']
    ],
];

array_walk($cars, 'applySanity');
print_r($cars);

function applySanity (&$val)
{
    $val = [
        $val[0][0] => $val[0][1],
        $val[1][0] => $val[1][1],
    ];
}
Output:
Array
(
    [0] => Array
```

```
    (
        [make] => VW
        [model] => Golf GTI
    )
    [1] => Array
    (
        [make] => VW
        [model] => Corrado VR6
    )
)
```

Our imaginary API call has returned a small data set of cars. Let's pretend that we're feeding this data into a template for rendering. Sadly, the template is expecting a different, associative structure, and we need to restructure the entire thing. Here, we have a function - applySanity() - which will do this for us. We use array_walk() to visit every element and transform it into a more sensible form.

The important thing to realize here is that the $cars array is changed in-place: array_walk() does not build a new array. We need to use the reference operator & in the signature of applySanity() otherwise we'll trigger PHP's copy on assignment.

If you're wondering if array_walk() can also manipulate keys, the answer is no. The callback function can have up to three arguments. array_walk() will first supply the iterated element (this argument is required), then two more optional parameters. The second callback argument is the key for the element, and the third callback argument is the third parameter passed to array_walk() (should you need to pass any other data into the callback function).

The full signature is array_walk(array $array, callable $callback, mixed $anything): bool and the signature of $callback will be function (mixed $value, int|string $key, mixed $anything): void. However, any attempt to access $key by reference will be ignored (and generate a warning error). Let's try to manipulate keys of the parent array as we re-structure:

```
$cars = [
    'car1' => [
        ['make', 'VW'], ['model', 'Golf GTI']
    ],
];
```

```
array_walk($cars, 'applySanity2', 'CHANGED_');
print "\n\nAfter applySanity2:\n";
print_r($cars);

function applySanity2 (&$val, &$key, $append)
{
    $key = $append . $key;
    $val = [
        $val[0][0] => $val[0][1],
        $val[1][0] => $val[1][1],
    ];
}
```

Output:
Warning: applySanity2(): Argument #2 ($key) must be passed by reference, value given in php shell code on line 7

After applySanity2:
Array
(
    [car1] => Array
        (
            [make] => VW
            [model] => Golf GTI
)

)

Although array_walk() does its intended job with respect to values, the keys remain unchanged; our assignment to $key had no effect because it is treated as if it was passed by value. PHP also warns us that we're being naughty. Note that the error message is somewhat counter-intuitive!

Finally, although it would seem that passing the third argument to applySanity() by reference would be useful for building new data structures (and leaving the originals intact) this doesn't work, neither does it cause any errors. For that functionality, see the next example – array_map().

Also note that like many other built-in PHP array functions, `array_walk()` comes in a multi-dimensional flavor. If you need to apply your callback to elements in sub-arrays use `array_walk_recursive()`.

Creating New Arrays with `array_map()`

An alternative to `array_walk()` is `array_map()`, which also applies a callback function to every element in the array. The difference is that `array_map()` does not make any changes to the input array. Instead, it returns a new array, leaving the original data untouched. This has drawbacks in memory usage, but also (arguably) provides a benefit.

Anything (that is legal PHP code) can happen within `array_walk()` (just as it can in a `for` or `foreach` loop), which can introduce cognitive load. There is no guarantee that `array_walk()` – or a regular loop construct – won't trash your data. If the callback function is complex or large, this gets harder to see at a glance. `array_map()` guarantees that only new data will be introduced and for that reason some programmers prefer it:

```
$cars = [
    [
        ['make', 'VW'], ['model', 'Golf GTI']
    ],
    [
        ['make', 'VW'], ['model', 'Corrado VR6']
    ]
];
$values = [
    20000,
    12000
];
```

```
$newCars = array_map(function (array $car, int $value): array {
    return [
        $car[0][0] => $car[0][1],
        $car[1][0] => $car[1][1],
        'value' => $value,
    ];
}, $cars, $values);

print_r($newCars);
```

Output:
```
Array
(
    [0] => Array
        (
            [make] => VW
            [model] => Golf GTI
            [value] => 20000
        )

    [1] => Array
        (
            [make] => VW
            [model] => Corrado VR6
            [value] => 12000
        )

)
```

array_map() takes a minimum of two arguments: the callback to be executed for each element and an array. It can optionally take further arrays: each iteration of the callback will be given the n-th value of each array, meaning you can work on multiple arrays in parallel – just make sure the number of elements in each is the same! Here we are combining the data from two arrays and condensing them into a single new array, and this time we're using an anonymous function rather than a named one. Although it is not shown here, examining the contents of the original arrays would show that they retain their original values.

Creating New Values With `array_reduce()`

Similar to `array_map()`, PHP's built-in `array_reduce()` allows you to define a callback function, which will execute for every element. Rather than producing a new array of equal size, `array_reduce()` instead accumulates data to be returned once processing is finished. The returned data can be a scalar or compound type. Like `array_map()`, the original array will remain unchanged:

```
$stock = [
    ['brand' => 'VW', 'model' => 'Golf GTI', 'value' => 20000],
    ['brand' => 'VW', 'model' => 'Scirocco GTI', 'value' => 16000],
    ['brand' => 'VW', 'model' => 'Corrado VR6', 'value' => 12000],
    ['brand' => 'Ford', 'model' => 'Escort RS2000', 'value' => 35000],
    ['brand' => 'Ford', 'model' => 'Sierra RS Cosworth', 'value' => 25000],
    ['brand' => 'Peugeot', 'model' => '205 GTI', 'value' => 10000],
];

$stockTally = array_reduce(
    $stock,
    function (array $accumulator, array $element): array {
        $accumulator[$element['brand']] += $element['value'];
        return $accumulator;
    },
    ['VW' => 0, 'Ford' => 0, 'Peugeot' => 0] // unset array keys
                                             now generate Warning
                                             errors in PHP8
);

print_r($stockTally);

Output:
Array
(
    [VW] => 48000
    [Ford] => 60000
    [Peugeot] => 10000
)
```

We have an initial array of classic cars and we're interested in the total value of cars broken down by brand. We want to take our initial array, which contains six different cars from three different brands, and produce a new array with a total value for each of the three brands. We call array_reduce() with three arguments: the array we want to reduce, a reducer function (we're using a closure, but named functions are also fine) that will be called for every element, and an initial value.

The first time the closure is called, it is passed the initial value as the first argument ($accumulator) and the value of the first element. The reducer function *must* return the accumulator when it is complete. As the function is called for each element, $accumulator is modified. When the final element is processed, array_reduce() returns the final state of $accumulator. If there were no values to process (e.g., an empty array was supplied), array_reduce() would simply return the initial value.

In our example, a six-element multi-dimensional array of arrays, each with a sub-array containing three key/value pairs, has become a flat associative array containing three elements. Imagine if all we cared about was the total value of all cars: we could take our multi-dimensional $stock array and (with an appropriate reducer function) calculate a single integer. This is why the verb "reduce" is used to name the function.

Multi-dimensional Arrays and Recursive Functions

We have already seen multi-dimensional arrays in action earlier in the chapter, although the examples have been quite simple. Imagine you had a problem that involved processing something more complex, with three, four, or even more dimensions. Let's say our solution required that we examine every element in every array. Even a relatively simple question like "how many distinct occurrences are there of each value?" becomes difficult to answer, despite the fact that PHP has (you guessed it) a built-in function for counting the number of times a distinct value is found in an array:

```
$arr = ['Alice', 'Bob', 'Bob'];

$struct = [
    ['Skoda', 'Fabia', 'VRs'],
    ['Skoda', 'Fabia', 'VRs'],
];

print_r(array_count_values($arr));
print_r(array_count_values($struct));
```

Output:
```
Array
(
    [Alice] => 1
    [Bob] => 2
)
PHP Warning:  array_count_values(): Can only count string and integer values, entry skipped...
```

$arr is a simple flat array. 'Alice' occurs once, and 'Bob' occurs twice. The output of array_count_values() is an associative array where each key is a distinct value of the input array, and each value is an integer count of the number of times that value is found. However, $struct – a multi-dimensional array – generates a "PHP Warning" message. array_count_values() only works if the value is an integer or a string (which makes sense because PHP arrays can only have integers or strings as keys).

What if we wanted to evaluate objects (that couldn't be coerced to string values), or floats? We've reached the limits of PHP's built-in array functions at this point. We need to write our own code and have it execute for all elements in the structure. There is a classic solution for a program that needs to traverse a multi-dimensional data structure, the recursive function call:

```php
$struct = [
    ['Alice', 'Bob', 'Bob'],
    ['Alice', 'Bob', 'Bob'],
    ['Alice', 'Russell', 'Bob'],
];

print_r(recursive_array_count($struct));

function recursive_array_count(array $array, array &$ret = []): array {
    foreach ($array as $ele) {
        if (is_array($ele)) {
            recursive_array_count($ele, $ret);
        } else{
            (isset($ret[$ele])) ? $ret[$ele]++ : $ret[$ele] = 1;
        }
    }
```

```
        return $ret;
}
```

Output:
```
Array
(
    [Alice] => 3
    [Bob] => 5
    [Russell] => 1
)
```

A recursive function is simply a function that calls itself. When traversing $struct with our user-defined function recursive_array_count(), we test if the current element in the foreach loop is an array. If it is, we call recursive_array_count() again and pass the current element (and a reference to $ret so we can keep a tally of the counts in the second call) so the loop can iterate for the sub-array before returning control to the first call of recursive_array_count(). This will happen every time our function encounters an array, so be aware of potential pitfalls such as circular references, very large arrays, and so on.

For example, calling a recursive function on the following has some nasty side-effects:

```
$struct =[
    ['Alice', 'Bob', 'Bob'],
    ['Alice', 'Bob', 'Bob'],
    ['Alice', 'Russell', 'Bob'],
    &$struct,
];
```

Here $struct contains a reference to itself. If recursive_array_count() was called on this structure, it would continue to call itself every time it hits the reference, which contains yet another reference, and so on. Execution can never return to the calling program and eventually Something Bad will happen. This could be stack overflow, exceeding memory_limit, or hitting a recursion limit if using a tool like xdebug. The ultimate outcome depends on your system configuration, but none are desirable.

Very Large Arrays and Generators

Imagine you have a use case involving arbitrarily large (or unknown) amounts of data and your system is constrained by memory. Let's say you attempted to iterate over a large array of integers like this:

```
$arr = range(0, 1000000);

foreach ($arr as $val) {
    // do something
}

print "Peak memory usage " . memory_get_peak_usage() . "\n";
```

Output:
Peak memory usage 17169304

Here we create an array of one million sequential integers and iterate over it. (It's not important what the foreach does here; we just want to consume memory.) Nearly 34 megabytes have been allocated during script execution. What if I told you there was a way to do this that only consumed around five-hundred kilobytes of peak memory?

To mitigate scenarios like this, PHP introduced a new language feature called generators in version 5.5. A generator is a special function that does not use the return keyword; instead, it uses yield and will generate a value each time it is iterated.

In our example above, we'll replace PHP's built-in range() - which is currently building an array of one million numbers - with a generator:

```
function gen_range(int $start, int $limit) {
    for ($i = $start; $i <= $limit; $i++) {
        yield $i;
    }
}

foreach (gen_range(0,1000000) as $val) {
    // do something
}

print "Peak memory usage " . memory_get_peak_usage() . "\n";
```

Output:
Peak memory usage 425776

If a function uses `yield` instead of `return`, PHP creates an object with type `Generator` and interface `Iterator`. These objects behave like arrays (because of the `Iterator` interface) but only require enough memory to track the state of the currently yielded variable. For this reason, our peak memory usage is now around 1.2% of the previous example. It's a good idea to consider using generators for tasks like fetching lines from large files or iterating remote data sets. Generators allow you to break up intensive workloads into smaller jobs by only having to work on the subset of data that they yield on each iteration.

Summary

In this chapter, we have seen the fundamentals of PHP arrays and looked at many useful array-handling functions. You now know what arrays are, how to build them, and how to use them. Starting with simple indexed arrays, we moved on to associative arrays, then multi-dimensional array structures. We also examined techniques for iterating, combining, comparing, sorting, and searching.

It should be noted that most of the PHP array functions have both an associative and a recursive form. In this chapter, we've mainly focused on the simpler cases, but it's safe to assume that if an array function exists, there will be an associative and a recursive form of it. A good place to start if you want to learn more is the official PHP documentation for array functions: https://www.php.net/manual/en/ref.array.php

We also looked at functional ways to process array data, the techniques of mapping and reducing. The use of map/reduce functions is contentious; some developers swear by it while others swear *at* it. There is obviously a performance hit when using `array_reduce()` or `array_map()` vs. traditional loops because `for` and `foreach` do not introduce the overhead of placing function calls on the stack or forcing new arrays to be allocated. The tradeoff with map/reduce is that we can see at a glance that the code inside the mapping or reducer function will not have any side effects on the original data.

CHAPTER 6

Object Fundamentals

Objects have been a feature of PHP since version 3, and a great deal of PHP's built-in functionality is provided by objects (even if at glance, it doesn't seem that way; for example, anonymous functions are implemented internally as `Closure` objects). In addition to core PHP, most of the popular frameworks and libraries are implemented in the OOP style. We've already had some exposure to objects in previous chapters, and now is a good point to get the fundamentals down.

This chapter will focus on the object-oriented programming (OOP) features that PHP offers and how to use them. There might well be some features that don't make much sense or seem pointless at first: don't worry. The purpose of this chapter is simply to demonstrate what PHP has in its object toolbox. Why certain OOP features exist, and the best ways to use them, will be covered in Chapter 10, "Programming with Objects," later. For now, we will focus on the *what* and leave the *why* for later.

Here's what we will be covering in this chapter:

- Object instantiation
- Accessing static and non-static members
- Object context vs. class context
- Classes, anonymous classes, and their members
- Inheritance, abstract classes, and final classes
- Overloading and late static binding
- Interfaces
- Traits
- Enums

- Namespacing

- Autoloading

- Magic constants and introspection

Why OOP?

We're about to dive into quite a large topic, and if you're completely new to OOP, it might seem a little daunting. Although the focus of this chapter is mainly on the mechanisms of OOP, let me at least give a brief overview of its advantages.

> *Encapsulation* – OOP allows data to be gathered together along with the functions that operate on them, and for those data and functions to be hidden from the rest of the program. By hiding data and code inside single units (objects) and controlling the flow of data between them, we can write safer and more robust software.
>
> *Modularity* – decomposing software into a set of modules reduces the complexity of individual units of code. A problem is easier to understand (and solve) if it is broken into smaller problems. Modularity and encapsulation are closely related: the mechanisms of encapsulation enable modular design.
>
> *Reusability* – OOP allows generalized, abstract units to define functionality that is then available to more specialized units through a mechanism called inheritance. When designed correctly, no repetition occurs.

Making Objects

What is an object? Simple, it's an instance of a class. And a class is a template for an object. (Don't you just love circular definitions?)

To be more specific, a class is the collection of related function definitions (called *methods* to distinguish them from non-object functions), property declarations, and initial state (state being the values of class and object properties at any given point during execution). The properties and methods of a class are collectively referred to as *members*. Member properties and functions typically require that an instance of the class (an object) are created before they can be accessed, so let's do that.

New Objects

```
$obj = new stdClass();
var_dump($obj);
```

Output:
```
object(stdClass)#1 (0) {
}
```

The keyword new combined with the classname stdClass and parentheses is an expression that tells PHP to make a new instance of stdClass, and we assign it to the variable $obj. PHP 8.4 allows you to omit the parentheses if they are empty, otherwise you can use them to pass argument data to the new object like a function call. The output of var_dump() isn't tremendously exciting because, well, stdClass is pretty boring.

stdClass is PHP's "generic, empty class" and intended to be a blank canvas. It is often seen when other data types are cast to objects, for example:

```
$beer = (object) ['Adnams', 'Bass'];
var_dump($beer);
```

Output:
```
object(stdClass)#1 (2) {
  ["0"]=>
  string(6) "Adnams"
  ["1"]=>
  string(4) "Bass"
}
```

stdClass also makes an appearance as the return of some PHP built-in functions:

```
var_dump(
    json_decode('{"beverage":"White Russian"}')
);
```

CHAPTER 6   OBJECT FUNDAMENTALS

Output:
```
object(stdClass)#1 (1) {
  ["beverage"]=>
  string(13) "White Russian"
}
```

stdClass is quite the workhorse. It is even possible to manipulate its properties at runtime. In the next example we use the object operator -> to add a property to a stdClass object, and again to access the property's value:

```
$lebowski = new stdClass();
$lebowski->hates = 'The Eagles';
print "I really fn hate " . $lebowski->hates . ", man." . PHP_EOL;
```

Output:
```
I really fn hate The Eagles man.
```

It should be noted that runtime dynamic property creation is deprecated in PHP 8.2, although permitted for objects of type stdClass. Your own classes can use a new mechanism in PHP 8 called attributes to declare that they allow dynamic properties; we will cover attributes further on in the chapter. It is not permitted to add methods to an object. If Chapter 3, "Functions," made sense, you might be wondering if we could just add an anonymous function like this:

```
$lebowski->getMusicTaste = function () {
    echo "I really hate {$this->hates}, man.";  // an object references
                                                //   itself via the reserved
                                                //   $this variable
};

var_dump($lebowski);
$lebowski->getMusicTaste();
```

Output:
```
object(stdClass)#1 (2) {
  ["hates"]=>
  string(10) "The Eagles"
  ["getMusicTaste"]=>
```

```
  object(Closure)#2 (0) {
  }
}
Fatal error: Uncaught Error: Call to undefined method
stdClass::getMusicTaste()
```

Adding the anonymous function is fine (notice that the object property getMusicTaste is an instance of the Closure class, which is how PHP stores anonymous function internally), and it becomes another property of the object. Calling a property in this way is not allowed, despite the fact that it is a callable type. Them's the rules I'm afraid. There are tricks that can be pulled to execute the closure we added to $lebowski, including one we've seen already in Chapter 3, "Functions": the self-invoking function:

```
($lebowski->getMusicTaste)();
```

Output:
```
Fatal error: Uncaught Error: Using $this when not in object context...
```

Now we've managed to call the "new method," but the result is still a fatal error. This is because getMusicTaste() is still not an object method; it is simply a Closure object that $lewbowski->getMusicTaste() is a reference to. The clue is in the error message: "not in object context." The $this magic variable only exists under some very exact circumstances; details are coming up.

Cloned Objects

Another way to make a new object is by cloning an existing one. Simply use the clone keyword:

```
$lebowski = new stdClass();
$lebowski->hates = 'The Eagles';

$theOtherLebowski = clone $lebowski;
var_dump($theOtherLebowski);
```

Output:
```
object(stdClass)#2 (1) {
  ["hates"]=>
  string(10) "The Eagles"
}
```

As you can see, the cloned object has received the original's hates property. All of the cloned objects' properties will be copied, but be aware that these are "shallow" copies. Any references to other objects will remain as references on the clone:

```
$obj = new stdClass();
$obj->childObj = new stdClass();
$obj->childObj->prop = 'Original property';

$cloned = clone $obj;
$obj->childObj->prop = 'New property';

var_dump($cloned->childObj);
```

Output:
```
object(stdClass)#2 (1) {
  ["prop"]=>
  string(12) "New property"
}
```

The examples above show the fundamentals of creating objects, but the stdClass object we've used so far is lacking in features, and our attempts to add functionality were met with mixed success. What we really need if we're going to build a useful object in PHP is our own class.

Classes

As stated earlier, a class is a blueprint for an object. It contains a set of methods, properties, and usually some initial state for the object when it is first instantiated.

Defining a Class

To define a class, we use the keyword `class`, followed by a legal class name, then followed by its definition contained in braces. Legal class names follow the same rules as variable and method names, and the PSR-1 coding standard states that class names MUST be declared in StudlyCaps (also called PascalCase – each sub-word in a compound name has a leading capital letter).

Within the braces we define all of the members that the class needs. Variables are the properties, and functions are the methods. It might not be desirable to expose every member to calling code (remember how we changed the properties on an instance of `stdClass` in the previous section). Access to members from outside the class is controlled by the keywords `public` and `private`, anything declared as `private` can only be accessed by code inside the class. There is a third level of access called `protected`, which is used to control how members are inherited (covered in the next section).

Data hiding (encapsulation) is a fundamental aspect of OOP. You should only expose the properties and methods that are essential for another part of your program to make the object function correctly. Hide everything else:

```php
$quoteBot = new QuoteBot();

print $quoteBot->getQuote();

class QuoteBot
{
    public array $quoteStash = [
        "Obviously, you're not a golfer." . PHP_EOL,
        "That's just, like, your opinion, man." . PHP_EOL,
        "Forget it, Donny You're out of your element." . PHP_EOL,
    ];

    public function getQuote(): string
    {
        return $this->quoteStash[rand(0,2)];
    }
}
```

Output:
That's just, like, your opinion, man.

We've defined a fun little class, `QuoteBot`, that provides inspirational quotes on demand. It has a public array property `quoteStash` and a public method `getQuote`. The use of an access level keyword is optional, and default access for all class methods and properties is `public` if it is omitted (but most PHP coding standards will demand that access level is explicitly set).

The implementation of `getQuote()` accesses the `quoteStash` array via the object operator like this: `$this->quoteStash[]`. `$this` is a special variable that can only be used inside the lexical scope (inside the function boundaries) of an object's methods, and it references the object instance executing the method.

Remember at the end of the previous section we had a problem when attempting to use `$this` in a function? The error message was `'Using $this when not in object context'`, and it happened because, despite being used in the lexical scope of *a* function, it was not a function that was defined as a class method. You can only use `$this` during execution of code that exists inside a class method and only when it is being called on an object instance of that class. First you define the method, then you instantiate the class with the new keyword. Only then does `$this` have an object context. (We'll look at this idea of *context* in the next section.)

The `QuoteBot` class on its own does nothing. In order to actually use any of the code in `QuoteBot` it is necessary to instantiate it first, which is what happens on the first line `$quoteBot = new QuoteBot()`. Notice that we can call it before its declaration: this is similar to the function hoisting we saw in Chapter 3, "Functions": PHP parses the entire code before running the first line, so it already knows all about `QuoteBot` and therefore is able to build it at the very beginning of the program. There is also a mechanism for finding undeclared classes (autoloading), which we will look at later in this chapter.

I'm hoping that the method declaration for `getQuote()` looks familiar from Chapter 3, "Functions." All of the rules concerning type declaration, scope, parameter handling, and so on that we encountered in that chapter apply to class methods too.

To demonstrate the relationship between class methods, properties, and state, consider the following:

```
$quoteBot1 = new QuoteBot();
$quoteBot2 = new QuoteBot();

$quoteBot2->quoteStash = [
    "Don't get uptight with me, man." . PHP_EOL,
    "I could take double anything you could." . PHP_EOL,
    "Very, very foolish words, man." . PHP_EOL,
];
```

```
print $quoteBot1->getQuote();
print $quoteBot2->getQuote();
```

Output:
Forget it, Donny You're out of your element.
Don't get uptight with me, man.

We've made two QuoteBot objects, but with the second one we've swapped out the array of quotes (which we can do because the access level to quoteStash is public), and now our two bots have diverged. One is clearly quoting a different film to the other. When the two objects were created they had identical state: methods and properties were the same. By changing the internal state of $quoteBot2 we change its output. If we were to introduce a third instance of QuoteBot into our code, it would behave like $quoteBot1 because it would have the initial state as per the class definition.

Let's say we want to restrict access to quoteStash, because we never intended the quotes to be changed. To hide that array data from code outside the class, we use the keyword private:

```
$quoteBot2 = new QuoteBot();

$quoteBot2->quoteStash = [
    "Don't get uptight with me, man." . PHP_EOL,
    "I could take double anything you could." . PHP_EOL,
    "Very, very foolish words, man." . PHP_EOL,
];

class QuoteBot
{
    private array $quoteStash = [
        "Obviously, you're not a golfer." . PHP_EOL,
        "That's just, like, your opinion, man." . PHP_EOL,
        "Forget it, Donny You're out of your element." . PHP_EOL,
    ];

    // we'll need some more code in a moment...
}
```

Output:
Fatal error: Uncaught Error: Cannot access private property
QuoteBot::$quoteStash

This is encapsulation: we've made our class safer by hiding $quoteStash. Now we know that the output of getQuote() is always going to be from the initial values in the array. When we attempt to change the array via $quoteBot2->quoteStash = ... it fails with an error.

Property Getters and Setters

It is generally a good idea to make class properties private and provide access methods if they need modification from outside the class. When done like this the class can exercise some control (either type checking, or additional logic) over the incoming data. Let's add a method to the class that allows access to the private property:

```php
public function setQuoteStash(array $stash): void
{
    $this->quoteStash = $stash;
}
```

Now we can use setQuoteStash to overwrite the private $quoteStash array:

```php
$quoteBot2 = new QuoteBot();

$quoteBot2->setQuoteStash([
    "Don't get uptight with me, man." . PHP_EOL,
    "I could take double anything you could." . PHP_EOL,
    "Very, very foolish words, man." . PHP_EOL,
]);

print $quoteBot2->getQuote();
```

Output:
Don't get uptight with me, man.

CHAPTER 6 OBJECT FUNDAMENTALS

This might seem like a lot of work for little benefit but remember that setQuoteStash gives us control over the incoming data. The declaration of public array $quoteStash means that the property can only be overwritten by other arrays, which gives a small degree of type safety. Even better, we can make use of PHP's "splat" operator ... to enforce the data type of array elements (for a detailed explanation of "splat" see the section "Advanced Arguments" in Chapter 3, "Functions"):

```
public function setQuoteStash(string ...$stash): void
{
    $this->quoteStash = $stash;
}
```

Now let's try to use some broken data with the setter:

```
$bot = new QuoteBot();
$bot->setQuoteStash(...[
    "Don't get uptight with me, man." . PHP_EOL,
    new stdClass(),
]);
```

Output:
```
Fatal error: Uncaught TypeError: QuoteBot::setQuoteStash(): Argument #2 must be of type string, stdClass given...
```

The declaration setQuoteStash(string ...$stash) means "take all incoming arguments and build the $stash array out of them, they must all be strings." What we've done is enforce an array with the class property declaration, and automatic array creation from all the data passed into setQuoteStash(), where we add another layer of type enforcement. As a result, our code is much safer than it was with just a public property!

This pattern of data hiding is central to OOP, and used correctly, it makes for safer and more robust code. setQuoteStash() provides limited safe write access to a hidden internal property, and the corollary getQuoteStash() (not shown here but easy enough to imagine) would provide read access. You will often hear functions like this referred to with the term "getters and setters."

CHAPTER 6 OBJECT FUNDAMENTALS

Property Hooks

A new (and fairly significant) feature for PHP 8.4 is the *property hook*. The getter/setter boilerplate is often criticized as a needless chore, but 8.4 brings a shiny new toy that allows you to define blocks of code in-line with the property. These blocks will execute on direct access (read or write) of a property:

```
class Lebowski
{
    public bool $isBowling = false;

    public string $status = 'is being very undude' {
        get {
            return ($this->isBowling) ? 'abides' : $this->status;
        }
        set (string $status) {
            $this->status = $status;
        }
    }

    public function printStatus(): void
    {
        print "The dude {$this->status}" . PHP_EOL;
    }
}

$lebowski = new Lebowski();
print "The dude {$lebowski->status}" . PHP_EOL;

$lebowski->status = 'is out of his element';
$lebowski->printStatus();

$lebowski->isBowling = true;
print "The dude {$lebowski->status}" . PHP_EOL;
```

Output:
The dude is being very undude
The dude is out of his element
The dude abides

The `Lebowski` class defines a get property hook on the `public string $status` property. Whenever this property is accessed, the hook block is called – which must return data of the same type as the property. To clients of the class, this looks like seamless property access, and the hook will also execute in `$this` context, as shown by the call to `::printStatus()`. The set property hook shown here is technically redundant and is included simply to show the full syntax of the feature.

Constructors

It's quite common for at least some of the initial state of an object to be controlled by client code, there is a method available for passing data at instantiation time: the *constructor*.

A constructor is a special method that is executed every time a new instance is created and is commonly used to set the initial state of the object (so common, in fact, that PHP 8 introduced a feature to promote constructor parameters to object properties, we'll see this in a moment). Here's a new `QuoteBot` with a constructor, you'll notice that it looks very much like a setter method. For extra safety there's a quick check of the `$quoteStash` array size when the constructor executes, used to store a new class property that ensures we'll never go out of bounds when making use of the array:

```
class QuoteBot
{
    private array $quoteStash;
    private int $numQuotes;

    public function __construct(array $stash)
    {
        $this->quoteStash = $stash;
        $this->numQuotes = count($stash) - 1; // used as array index
    }

    public function getQuote(): string
    {
        return $this->quoteStash[rand(0, $this->numQuotes)];
    }
}
```

Perhaps you've been wondering up until now why the syntax for instantiating classes included a function-call-like set of parentheses? Well, that's the mechanism for passing data into the constructor method: it's an automatic call to the object's __construct() method once the object has been created by the new keyword. Now we can initialize our QuoteBot with the desired state (the array of quotes) as we create it:

```
$quoteBot2 = new QuoteBot([
    "Don't get uptight with me, man." . PHP_EOL,
    "I could take double anything you could." . PHP_EOL,
    "Very, very foolish words, man." . PHP_EOL,
]);
```

PHP 8 introduces a convenience feature called *constructor property promotion*. This allows us to use a shorthand syntax on the constructor declaration to automatically (automagically?) have class properties defined. Let's use that feature for the $quoteStash property:

```
class QuoteBot
{
    private int $numQuotes;

    public function __construct(private array $quoteStash)
    {
        $this->numQuotes = count($this->quoteStash) - 1; // used as
                                                        array index
    }

    // ... rest of class code
}
```

We've removed the explicit declaration private array $quoteStash = [];, and added a visibility keyword to the parameter of __construct(). Any variable in the constructor parameters that is given a visibility keyword is automatically set as a property (of the same name) on the class. In this example we are creating the $this->quoteStash array when the constructor is called (and an array is passed in). We can, of course, also promote protected and public properties this way.

With constructor property promotion you are free to mix and match; not every variable has to be promoted. The following code is perfectly legal:

```
public function __construct(
    private $foo,
    $bar,
    private $qux
) {
    $this->doSomethingWith($bar);
}
```

Destructors

The inverse of __construct() is __destruct(), which is called when an object no longer has any references (which means there is no longer any way to access it and it becomes eligible for garbage collection) or when PHP shuts down at the end of the program lifecycle. Here's a simple demonstration:

```
class FinkBot
{
    public function __construct()
    {
        print "Let's spit on our hands and get to work." . PHP_EOL;
    }
    public function __destruct()
    {
        print "I tried to show you... something beautiful." . PHP_EOL;
    }
}

$bot = new FinkBot();
print "Welcome to Los Angeles, Mr. Fink." . PHP_EOL;

unset($bot);
print "That's all, folks." . PHP_EOL;
```

Output:
Let's spit on our hands and get to work.
Welcome to Los Angeles, Mr. Fink.
I tried to show you... something beautiful.
That's all, folks.

The order of events is as follows. `$bot = new FinkBot()` instantiates the object, which triggers the call to `__construct()` gives us our first line of output. `unset($bot)` (after the `print` statement) removes the only reference to the object, which triggers the `__destruct()` method immediately and generates the third line of output. There's a final `print` statement just to demonstrate that PHP is still running at this point. Had we not called `unset()`, the destructor method of $bot would be invoked after the final statement of our program. Bear in mind that destructors that are triggered by PHP shutdown can be called in any order.

Magic Methods

PHP classes can define specially named methods which will be called when certain operations are performed on objects of the class, these are known as *magic methods*. We've already seen two magic methods: `__construct()` and `__destruct()` and learned that they are always called when objects are created and destroyed. There are several other magic methods which can be implemented, which will then be called on an object during certain operations. For example, if an object is referenced in a string context PHP will check for a `__toString()` method (an emit an error if none is available):

```php
class Finkbot
{
    public function __toString(): string
    {
        return "I tried to show you... something beautiful." . PHP_EOL;
    }
}

$finkBot = new Finkbot();

print "What does Finkbot say? {$finkBot}";
```

Output:
What does Finkbot say? I tried to show you... something beautiful.

The full list of PHP's magic methods and their calling contexts is as follows:

Table 6-1. *Magic methods*

Method	Context
__construct()	Object instantiation - new SomeClass()
__destruct()	Object destruction - unset($obj)
__call()	If inaccessible method is invoked - $obj->inaccessible()
__callStatic()	If inaccessible static method is invoked - $obj::inaccessible()
__get()	If inaccessible is read - $obj->inaccessible
__set()	If inaccessible is written - $obj->inaccessible = 'val'
__isset()	If isset() or empty() called with inaccessible property - isset($obj->inaccessible)
__unset()	If unset() called with inaccessible property - unset($obj->inaccessible)
__sleep()	Execute before serialization - serialize($obj)
__wakeup()	Execute after serialization - unserialize($obj)
__serialize()	Return assoc. array representation - serialize($obj)
__unserialize()	Return value (usually object) from serialized - unserialize($str)
__toString()	Used as a string - print $obj etc.
__invoke()	Called as a function - $obj()
static __set_state()	When used with var_export($obj)
__debugInfo()	When used with var_dump($obj)
__clone()	When cloned - $new = clone $obj

All magic method names are prefixed with two underscore characters, and methods named in this way are reserved, so don't use __ to prefix your own method names.

Anonymous Classes

Since PHP 7, it has been possible to use *anonymous classes*. Like anonymous functions, these are runtime declarations that are immediately evaluated when PHP encounters them. And like anonymous functions (that evaluate to a `Closure` instance, which is then either passed to other code or assigned to a variable), anonymous classes are evaluated to an object with all the members defined in the class body, which is then either assigned to a variable or passed to other code for immediate use:

```
$bot = new class(['some', 'quotes'])
{
    public function __construct(private array $quoteStash)
    {
    }
};

var_dump($bot);

Output:
object(class@anonymous)#2 (1) {
  ["quoteStash":"class@anonymous":private]=>
  array(2) {
    [0]=>
    string(4) "some"
    [1]=>
    string(6) "quotes"
  }
}
```

An anonymous class is intended to be used when a one-off object instance is required and are usually quite simple in their construction. Here we're making use of the anonymous class constructor so we have to add parentheses after the keyword `class` (so that data can be passed into the `__construct()` method). If the constructor is not used, the statement could be simplified to `$bot = new class { ... };`. Note that a closing semicolon is necessary because this is a runtime statement.

Anonymous classes are still classes and support all the features of regular classes. Member declaration works the same way, accessing static and non-static members works the same way, and so on. We will look at inheritance, interfaces, and traits later in the chapter, and all of those features work with anonymous classes too.

Class (Not Object) Context

In the previous section, our QuoteBot class didn't actually do anything until we created an object. Before we could make calls to the class methods, we needed an instance to work with – created with the keyword new. There is a mechanism, however, to access class methods and properties without instantiation. To do this we use a keyword you might remember from Chapter 3, "Functions": static.

Static Members

Properties accessed (or methods executed) statically are said to be running in class context, rather than the context of an instantiated object.

The syntax and rules for class context code are slightly different from those for objects. Let's change our QuoteBot class a little and see how it all works:

```
class QuoteBot
{
    public static $quoteStash = [
        "I'm a writer, you monsters! I create!",
        "I'll show you the life of the mind!"
    ];
}
```

With the quoteStash publicly accessible again, let's try to access it from an object instance:

```
$quoteBot = new QuoteBot();
print $quoteBot->quoteStash[1];
```

Output:
Notice: Accessing static property QuoteBot::$quoteStash as non static
Warning: Undefined property: QuoteBot::$quoteStash
Warning: Trying to access array offset on value of type null

CHAPTER 6 OBJECT FUNDAMENTALS

Wow, three errors... a notice and two warnings. Nothing fatal, but our code doesn't do what we hoped for. This is because static properties cannot be accessed with the same syntax used to access non-static (the object operator ->). We have to access them using a different operator, and the syntax for doing so is given in the Notice error in the output:

print QuoteBot::$quoteStash[1];

Output:
I'll show you the life of the mind!

The double-colon operator between QuoteBot and $quoteStash is called the *scope resolution operator*, which isn't very intuitive (this has nothing to do with global vs. function lexical scope). A better name might be something like context resolution operator, or class context operator, because its purpose is to express that the target property or method does not exist in object context. (Still, it's more intuitive than its internal name of PAAMAYIM NEKUDOTAYIM, which is Hebrew for "double colon.")

As you can see, we don't need to instantiate a QuoteBot object to access a static member, but (unlike access via an object) we do need to use the dollar symbol with the property name.

Accessing static methods on objects works in the same way. Let's add one to QuoteBot:

```
public static function insight(): string
{
    return "I've always found that writing comes from a great inner
    pain." . PHP_EOL;
}
```

The syntax for calling the code is as you'd expect:

print QuoteBot::insight();

Output:
I've always found that writing comes from a great inner pain.

Although we haven't used an object instance, static members are also accessible from objects in the following way:

print $quoteBot::insight(); // not $quoteBot->insight()
print $quoteBot::$quoteStash[0]; // not $quoteBot->$quoteStash

304

Output:
I've always found that writing comes from a great inner pain.
I'm a writer, you monsters! I create!

Cast your mind back to the section "Local Scope and Static Variables" in Chapter 3, "Functions," where I demonstrated a trick for getting locally scoped variables to persist across multiple calls to a function. We saw a function getCount() that initialized a counter variable like this: static $counter = 0, which meant that $counter retained its value even though it went out of scope (so it could be used to store data between calls). Static properties behave in a similar way. Here's an OOP version of the getCount() function:

```php
class Counter
{
    private static int $count = 0;

    public function getCount(): int
    {
        return $this::$count++;
    }
}

$counter1 = new Counter();
$counter2 = new Counter();

print "counter1 has count: " . $counter1->getCount() . PHP_EOL;
print "counter2 has count: " . $counter2->getCount() . PHP_EOL;
print "counter1 has count: " . $counter1->getCount() . PHP_EOL;
```

Output:
counter1 has count: 0
counter2 has count: 1
counter1 has count: 2

We're calling a getCount() on different object instances of the same class, but because the internal $count property is static it exists in class context so all instances share the same data. Notice the use of $this:: in the implementation of getCount(), the scope resolution operator is required for accessing static class members during execution of object context methods. There is, however, a slight hitch if you need to access class members from a method that is also static...

Static Members in Class Context

The special variable $this is made available in an object's methods, and it's how we access the object's other members, using the object operator -> or scope resolution operator :: depending on the context of the target members. The problem with static methods is that there is nothing for $this to reference: no object has been instantiated, so there cannot be a $this when executing in class context. So, instead of $this, we use the self keyword. self provides access to the class context members:

```
public static function getQuote(): string
{
    return self::$quoteStash[rand(0,1)];
}
```

Here we have a static method getQuote(), it has to use self::$quoteStash to access the static $quoteStash class property.

Static methods are restricted to other static members: it isn't possible to call a non-static method or reference a non-static property, and doing so will cause a fatal error:

```
class QuoteBot
{
    private function getInsight(): string
    {
        return "I've always found that writing comes from a great inner
        pain." . PHP_EOL;
    }
    public static function insight(): void
    {
        print self::getInsight();
    }
}
QuoteBot::insight();

Output:
Fatal error: Uncaught Error: Non-static method QuoteBot::getInsight()
cannot be called statically
```

CHAPTER 6 OBJECT FUNDAMENTALS

There is no way to access non-static from static, because $this is not available (which is as it should be; object context code has state that class context does not, and such an operation would be unsafe). It's fine for a non-static method to call another static member; however,

```
class QuoteBot
{
    private static function getInsight(): string
    {
        return "I've always found that writing comes from a great inner
        pain." . PHP_EOL;
    }

    public function insight(): void
    {
        print self::getInsight();
    }
}

$bot = new QuoteBot();
$bot->insight();
```

Output:
I've always found that writing comes from a great inner pain.

The example above shows an alternative to using $this::. Previously, in the Counter class, we accessed a static property with $this::, in the QuoteBot example above, we use self:: to access the static member getInsight(). Both are perfectly valid, though conventionally it's a little more common to see self:: used in object context code (because less thought is required: self is always available and works identically).

Class Constants

We've seen how to define global constants in Chapter 2, "Data, Types, and Variables." Classes are also able to define constant properties, which are declared with the const keyword. Let's add one to QuoteBot:

```
public const FILM = "Barton Fink";
```

The visibility of class constants is controlled in the same way as other members, with `public`, `protected`, and so on. It is not possible to declare a type for a constant in PHP <= 8.2, but support for typed class constants was added in PHP 8.3. By convention (and many coding standards), class names are usually all uppercase with words separated by underscores; otherwise, they're subject to the usual variable naming rules.

Accessing a class constant also uses the scope resolution operator:

```
print QuoteBot::FILM;
print $quoteBot::FILM;
```

This is why we needed the dollar symbol for static property access: so that property access is syntactically distinct from accessing class constants.

Private Constructors

Here's an interesting technique that makes use of class context code to control how objects are created.

It is possible to declare a constructor as `private` in PHP. This has the obvious effect of hiding the `__construct()` method; it is no longer callable from outside the class. This is what happens when you try to instantiate a class with a `private` constructor:

```
class SingleQuoteBot
{
    protected array $quoteStash = [
        "Obviously, you're not a golfer." . PHP_EOL,
        "That's just, like, your opinion, man." . PHP_EOL,
        "Forget it, Donny You're out of your element." . PHP_EOL,
    ];

    private function __construct()
    {
    }

    public function getQuote(): string
    {
        return $this->quoteStash[rand(0,2)];
    }
}
```

```
$bot = new SingleQuoteBot();
```

Output:
```
Fatal error: Uncaught Error: Call to private QuoteBot::__construct() from global scope
```

We've successfully broken our class. It can't be instantiated at all!

By changing the access level to `private`, the automatic call to `__construct()` that occurs after the statement `new QuoteBot` is evaluated isn't possible. It can only happen within the scope of a class method. This means that we can still instantiate a new QuoteBot, but we'll need to do it via some method that executes in the class context (object context isn't possible because we can't make QuoteBot objects until they've executed their `__construct` method).

Here's a class context method (note the declaration is `public static function`) that works with the `self` keyword to instantiate a new instance:

```
public static function getInstance(): self
{
    return new self();
}
```

Now we can build new SingleQuoteBot objects like this:

```
$bot = SingleQuoteBot::getInstance();
print $bot->getQuote() . PHP_EOL;
```

Output:
```
Obviously, you're not a golfer.
```

So far, so useless. The real power of taking control of `__construct()` lies in the fact that we get to hide instance creation in the class itself. Which means we can do this:

```
class SingleQuoteBot
{
    protected static $instance = null;

    private function __construct(private string $quote)
    {
    }
```

309

```
    public static function getInstance($quote): self
    {
        if (self::$instance === null) {
            self::$instance = new self($quote);
        }

        return self::$instance;
    }

    public function getQuote(): string
    {
        return $this->quote;
    }
}

$bot1 = SingleQuoteBot::getInstance(
    "Of all the gin joints in all the towns in all the world, she walks
    into mine"
);
$bot2 = SingleQuoteBot::getInstance("any old nonsense.");

print $bot1->getQuote() . PHP_EOL;
print $bot2->getQuote() . PHP_EOL;
```

Output:
Of all the gin joints in all the towns in all the world, she walks
into mine
Of all the gin joints in all the towns in all the world, she walks
into mine

By storing the first `SingleQuoteBot` instance in a static class variable and only creating it once if it doesn't exist already, we've set up the `SingleQuoteBot` class to have a single instance. Even though we try to build a second bot with a different quote, the `getInstance()` method (in this example it is known by the name "factory method") when we call the second object's `getQuote()` we get the original text. Every "object" returned from the factory method is in fact a reference to the same object instance.

In this way a single object permeates throughout the entire system and can be used at any point with confidence that it's always the same object acted upon. This is a pattern known as the *Singleton*. It has obvious advantages for objects that are perhaps expensive to create, or hold a lot of data, or never need to be duplicated. It forms the basis of other patterns and we'll be looking at some of these neat tricks when we explore *design patterns* in Chapter 10, "Programming with Objects."

Interfaces

The public members of a class form its interface. These publicly accessible properties and methods are how an object of that class is intended to be used. When writing documentation for a class, it is normal convention to give only the names and types of public properties, public constants, and the signatures (names, parameters, return types) of public methods.

Here's a sample from the official PHP documentation for the `SimpleXMLElement` object interface:

```
class SimpleXMLElement implements Stringable, Countable,
RecursiveIterator {
/* Methods */
public __construct(
    string $data,
    int $options = 0,
    bool $dataIsURL = false,
    string $namespaceOrPrefix = "",
    bool $isPrefix = false
)
public addAttribute(string $qualifiedName, string $value, ?string
$namespace = null): void
public addChild(string $qualifiedName, ?string $value = null, ?string
$namespace = null): ?SimpleXMLElement
public asXML(?string $filename = null): string|bool
//and so on and so on
```

This tells us that a SimpleXMLElement object can be constructed with between one and five parameters (the first has no default value) to control initial state, it has public methods `addAttribute()`, `addChild()`, `asXML()`, and so on, and how to call those methods with the necessary parameters. The `implements Stringable, Countable, RecursiveIterator` portion of the declaration lists the interfaces provided by the class. This serves as a kind of contract to client code, interfaces guarantee that objects of this class will behave in certain ways.

It is also possible in PHP to formally declare interfaces in code, and to use them as type declarations.

Declaring Interfaces

An `interface` declaration in PHP is code that is very similar to a class declaration but serves to only define the methods a class must implement. Interfaces are defined in the same way as a class but with some caveats. An interface can only declare constants and method signatures (not implementation), they cannot declare properties. Additionally, only public methods and constants are declared. Any attempt to add properties or private members will result in fatal errors. Here's a working example of an interface:

```
interface QuoteBotInterface
{
    public function getQuote(): string;
}
```

This code does not produce any output; it simply exists to define how something that implements it will work. Here's how we can make use of it:

```
class QuoteBot implements QuoteBotInterface
{
    private array $quoteStash = [
        "Obviously, you're not a golfer." . PHP_EOL,
        "That's just, like, your opinion, man." . PHP_EOL,
        "Forget it, Donny You're out of your element." . PHP_EOL,
    ];

    public function getQuote(): string
    {
```

```
        return $this->quoteStash[rand(0,2)];
    }
}
```

Now we have a class that implements an interface and fulfils the requirement of implementing the interface's getQuote() method. The class implementation must be compatible with the interface declaration: no changing return types or parameters is allowed, and visibility must remain public.

So far this looks like a lot of hassle, but it is useful because interfaces can be used as type declarations:

```
function useQuoteBot(QuoteBotInterface $bot): void
{
    print $bot->getQuote();
}
```

Now we have a function that relies on the interface of the object passed into it: the class is irrelevant so long as it implements QuoteBotInterface. Let's build a couple of classes that make use of it:

```
class LebowskiBot implements QuoteBotInterface
{
    // quoteStash array and getQuote() implementation
}

class FinkBot implements QuoteBotInterface
{
    // quoteStash array and getQuote() implementation
}

function useQuoteBot(QuoteBotInterface $bot): void
{
    print $bot->getQuote();
}

$lebowski = new LebowskiBot();
$fink = new FinkBot();

useQuoteBot($lebowski);
useQuoteBot($fink);
```

Output:
Forget it, Donny You're out of your element.
I've always found that writing comes from a great inner pain.

We can see that our useQuoteBot() function is quite happy with either object type (LebowskiBot or FinkBot), only the interface matters. We could have declared useQuoteBot() to use the two different classes using a union type declaration (these are covered in great detail in Chapter 3, "Functions"):

function useQuoteBot(LebowskiBot|FinkBot $bot): void

However, this is not good design. By instead making useQuoteBot() dependent on the interface (rather than composite type declaration), we are adhering to an important design principle called *Dependency Inversion* which is one five important OOP design principles known by the acronym SOLID, which we will examine in Chapter 10, "Programming with Objects."

Multiple Interfaces

A class in PHP can only extend one parent (single inheritance), but it can implement multiple interfaces. In the section "Declaring Types" in Chapter 3, "Functions," I showed an argument intersect type declaration of ArrayAccess&Countable. ArrayAccess and Countable are built-in interfaces; if a class implements them, then they are guaranteed to have certain functionality (objects of that class can be counted to an integer, and they can be traversed like an array). Let's do something similar here, but in reverse. We'll create a function that has an object parameter with two interfaces as an intersect type, and a class that satisfies that type declaration.

The function below requires an object with both the Countable and JsonSerializable interfaces. Like Countable, JsonSerializable is a built-in interface and specifies a function jsonSerialize(): mixed where the return is a data structure that can be processed by PHP's json_encode() function:

```
function debugCrew(Countable&JsonSerializable $crew): void
{
    print "\$crew contains " . count($crew) . " officers." . PHP_EOL;
    print json_encode($crew, JSON_PRETTY_PRINT) . PHP_EOL;
}
```

Here's the class:

```
class CrewDataWrapper implements Countable, JsonSerializable
{
    public function __construct(private array $data)
    {
    }

    public function count(): int
    {
        return count($this->data);
    }

    public function jsonSerialize(): mixed
    {
        ksort($this->data);
        return $this->data;
    }
}
```

Countable objects must implement function count(): int, and JsonSerializable objects must implement jsonSerialise(): mixed. Both of these required methods are implemented.

Finally, we glue it all together with some procedural code:

```
$crew = new CrewDataWrapper([
    'major' => 'Kira',
    'general' => 'Martok',
    'captain' => 'Sisko',
    'doctor' => 'Bashir',
]);

debugCrew($crew);

Output:
$crew contains 4 officers.
{
    "captain": "Sisko",
    "doctor": "Bashir",
```

```
    "general": "Martok",
    "major": "Kira"
}
```

There's no functional limit to the number of interfaces a class can implement, obviously system resources are theoretically exhausted at some point, but I can only imagine how big the number is. Prepare for uncomfortable questions in code reviews if you have a double-digit number of them.

Extending Interfaces

Interfaces can be extended. This means that one interface can have all the members defined in another, then implement their own on top. This feature is called *inheritance* and classes can do it too; we'll be getting to that in a moment. Any class implementing an extended interface must also implement any methods inherited from parent interfaces or suffer the consequences:

```
interface Foo
{
    public function doFoo();
}

interface Bar extends Foo
{
    public function doBar();
}

class FooBar implements Bar
{
    public function doBar()
    {
        // bar things...
    }
}
```

Output:
```
PHP Fatal error:  Class FooBar contains 1 abstract method and must therefore be declared abstract or implement the remaining methods (Foo::doFoo) ...
```

Interface Constants

Interfaces are also permitted to declare constants. These will become class constants wherever the interface is implemented; here's a quick example:

```
interface QuoteBotInterface
{
    public const QUOTE = 'I am not a number! I am a free man!';
}
class GenericBot implements QuoteBotInterface
{
}
class LebowskiBot implements QuoteBotInterface
{
    public const QUOTE = "I'm a writer, you monsters! I create!";
    // only since PHP 8.1
}
print GenericBot::QUOTE . PHP_EOL;
print LebowskiBot::QUOTE . PHP_EOL;

Output:
I am not a number! I am a free man!
I'm a writer, you monsters! I create!
```

Note that overriding a `const` declared in an interface is only possible from PHP 8.1 onwards.

Property Hooks

The new hotness in PHP 8.4 is property hooks. We've seen how to implement them in class declarations, and they can also be defined in interfaces. Interfaces do not normally allow the definition of properties, but hooked properties are an exception to that rule. Where an implementing class is required to provide hooks, add braces containing the required hooks, each followed by a semicolon:

```
interface Lebowski
{
    public string $status { get; }
    public string $beverage  { get; set; }
}
```

Here we've defined `$status` with a get property hook and `$beverage` with both get and set. The implementing class would then have to supply some code for both of those, which fire every time the property is accessed, and I'll show you how to do this later. Note: it is not possible to define a default value for a hooked property in an interface; only the implementing class can do that.

Inheritance and Abstraction

Another fundamental feature of object orientation is *inheritance*. Inheritance is the mechanism by which a class may extend the functionality of another, which facilitates reusability. The inheriting class is known as the *parent* class or *superclass*, the derived class is the *child* or *subclass* (the parent/child relationship giving the mechanism its name).

Parent classes are usually more generalized versions of subclasses. Imagine we had to represent cars in our system, we might have to deal with many different brands and could have classes such as `Volkswagen`, `Ford`, `Audi`, and so on. There will likely be common properties and methods for all of them, and reproducing those common members violates the DRY principle (Don't Repeat Yourself).

If we put those shared members into a parent class of `Car`, then we can use inheritance to ensure that the child classes have the properties and methods they all need, and it only needs to be declared once. The keywords `public`, `protected`, and `private` have a role to play here. Subclasses will inherit `public` and `protected` members, but not `private`. Make sure to use `protected` if you intend for subclasses to inherit a hidden member. Subclasses are also allowed to change the visibility of members, but only to a less restricted level. Thus, `protected` members can become `public`, but not vice versa.

Duplicated code means extra maintenance effort and more chances for bugs to creep in, but by using a parent class (with `public` or `protected` members), we only need to write code once, and any inheriting class automatically has it too.

Parent and Child Classes

To create a parent/child inheritance relationship, we use the PHP keyword extends. Let's organize QuoteBot into a generalized parent and specialized child classes:

```
class QuoteBot
{
    protected array $quoteStash = ['', '', ''];

    public function getQuote(): string
    {
        return $this->quoteStash[rand(0,2)];
    }
}

class LebowskiBot extends QuoteBot
{
    protected array $quoteStash = [
        "Obviously, you're not a golfer." . PHP_EOL,
        "That's just, like, your opinion, man." . PHP_EOL,
        "Forget it, Donny You're out of your element." . PHP_EOL,
    ];
}

class FinkBot extends QuoteBot
{
    protected array $quoteStash = [
        "I'm a writer, you monsters! I create!" . PHP_EOL,
        "I'll show you the life of the mind!" . PHP_EOL,
        "I've always found that writing comes from a great inner pain." .
        PHP_EOL,
    ];
}
```

Here we have a parent class QuoteBot and two child classes of it called LebowskiBot and FinkBot. The keyword extends in the child class declaration tells PHP that LebowskiBot and FinkBot are children of QuoteBot. Note the access level of $quoteStash is set to protected. This hides the property from code outside the class but allows it to be inherited by subclasses.

The child classes automatically have $quoteStash and getQuote() members, but the children re-declare $quoteStash with their specialized data. This is another feature of inheritance: child classes can replace the parent implementation with their own; this is known as overriding. Note the use of the protected keyword here – protected members, like private, are not accessible outside the class but are made available for use or overloading in the child class. private members are not inherited by children.

If we instantiate one of the child classes from above, we can see that the inherited method is available for use:

```
$lebowski = new LebowskiBot();
print $lebowski->getQuote();
```

Output:
That's just, like, your opinion, man.

Parent and child classes also have a special relationship in the type declaration system. Any type declaration that is a class will also accept an instance of a subclass. For example:

```
function printQuote(QuoteBot $bot): void
{
    print $bot->getQuote();
}
```

We declare a simple function to make use of an instance of QuoteBot, passed in as its only argument. It's perfectly fine to pass in a child of QuoteBot:

```
$fink = new FinkBot();
printQuote($fink);
```

Output:
I'll show you the life of the mind!

As stated, a child class can override a parent member, but it cannot reduce visibility; therefore, all of the public methods and properties of a parent will be available for a child class too. This restriction on inheritance means that substituting a child for a parent will always be safe, another important OOP principle.

Abstract Classes

It is sometimes the case that the parent class is too generalized to be of practical use in a project. This is quite normal and is actually a driver of good object-oriented design (making modules dependent on abstractions of other modules). With PHP it is possible to declare a parent class as abstract, along with some (or all) of its methods:

```
abstract class Car
{
    abstract public function getBrand(): string;

    abstract public function getModel(): string;
}
class VwGolf extends Car
{
    public function getBrand(): string
    {
        return 'Volkswagen';
    }

    public function getModel(): string
    {
        return 'Golf GTI';
    }
}
```

Here we have a parent class Car and a child class VwGolf. Car has been declared using the abstract keyword and has two abstract methods. Methods declared this way do not have an implementation; instead, any class extending the abstract parent is responsible for providing it. We can now use Car as a type declaration, and any child of Car will fulfil the dependency:

```
function carInfo(Car $car) {
    print "{$car->getBrand()} {$car->getModel()}" . PHP_EOL;
}
carInfo(new VwGolf());
```

Output:
Volkswagen Golf GTI

Abstract method declarations behave in much the same way as method declarations in interfaces, as seen in the previous section. Just like interfaces, the child class must provide an implementation or trigger a fatal error. Another similarity to interfaces is that only methods can be abstract; there are no abstract properties in PHP.

The one advantage abstract classes have over interfaces is that they can also provide implementations for non-abstract methods. Abstract classes are non-instantiable, but otherwise they are classes in every other respect. Here's a demonstration:

```
abstract class Car
{
    protected static $noise = 'VRRRRM!';

    public function beepHorn(): void
    {
        print "Beep beep!" . PHP_EOL;
    }

    abstract public function makeNoise(): void;
}
class VwGolf extends Car{
    public function makeNoise(): void
    {
        print self::$noise . PHP_EOL;
    }
}

$car = new VwGolf();
$car->makeNoise();
$car->beepHorn();
```

Output:
VRRRRM!
Beep beep!

We can see that the child class VwGolf has inherited the static $noise property and public beepHorn() method from the parent Car class. VwGolf has also implemented the abstract makeNoise() method (as it must do).

Abstract classes enable the sharing of code between child classes, in addition to controlling the interfaces of children. There is also another PHP mechanism for reusing code in classes that sits outside the inheritance hierarchy: traits, which we will look at later in the chapter.

Accessing Parent Members

It is sometimes necessary to access the parent implementation of an overloaded method, often during the execution of __construct. PHP provides the parent keyword to enable this. Suppose we had a parent class that was a general representation of something. If our software needed to model cars and motorbikes, we might have a parent Vehicle class. In this scenario, let's say we set the number of passengers on instantiation using the constructor method. Now let's imagine that we need to model another type of vehicle, which needs a more complex operation for initializing its maxPassengers property:

```
class Vehicle
{
    public function __construct(
        protected int $maxPassengers
    ) {
    }
}
class Train extends Vehicle
{
    public function __construct(int $carriages)
    {
        parent::__construct($carriages * 30);
    }
```

```
    public function getMaxPassengers(): int
    {
        return $this->maxPassengers;
    }
}

$train = new Train(4);
print "This train can carry {$train->getMaxPassengers()} passengers.\n";
```

Output:
This train can carry 120 passengers.

The parent implementation of __construct() is a simple assignment via constructor property promotion. Train overloads __construct() and requires a calculation: the number of carriages in the train multiplied by the capacity of each carriage. By invoking parent::__construct() we're actually calling the Vehicle implementation __construct(), which sets the maxPassengers property for the instantiated object $train object. This example is a little contrived, but it serves to demonstrate how to access parent methods. Accessing parent properties works in a similar way:

```
class Vehicle
{
    protected static string $iAm = 'Vehicle';
}

class Car extends Vehicle
{
    protected static string $iAm = 'Car';

    public static function whatAmI(): void
    {
        print "I am a " . self::$iAm . PHP_EOL;
        print "I am also a " . parent::$iAm . PHP_EOL;
    }
}

Car::whatAmI();
```

Output:
I am a Car
I am also a Vehicle

If you remember when we looked at class context (static) methods, we used the keyword self in conjunction with the scope resolution operator :: to access other static members. parent looks similar, doesn't it? There is an important difference; however, you might have already spotted it: parent::__construct() is not a static method.

A child calling or referencing a parent member will always use the scope resolution operator, so it resembles a static call even when accessing non-static members. The same restrictions apply as they do for self: you cannot access object context code from class context. While we're on the subject of accessing parent members and static context, there's something to be aware of…

Late Static Binding

Take a look at the following code; we've redesigned our Vehicle/Car class hierarchy a little. We'd like to use the DRY principle and not declare whatAmI() in every child class:

```
class Vehicle
{
    protected static string $iAm = 'Vehicle';

    public static function whatAmI(): void
    {
        print "I am a " . self::$iAm . PHP_EOL;
    }
}

class Car extends Vehicle
{
    protected static string $iAm = 'Car';
}
```

This code might look OK on first glance: we overload $iAm in the child class as before, but now we've moved the whatAmI() method into the parent Vehicle class. If we invoke Car::whatAmI(), it should use Car::$iAm, right?

```
Car::whatAmI();
```

Output:
```
I am a Vehicle
```

Oops. Even though we're calling whatAmI() in the context of the Car class, the method is using the context of the class where it is declared: self will always resolve to the declaring class. What we need is a way to resolve $iAm to the called class (in this case, Car). Fortunately, PHP has a feature called *late static binding*, which provides exactly what we need. If we swap self for static in whatAmI():

```
public static function whatAmI(): void
{
    print "I am a " . static::$iAm . PHP_EOL;
}
```

Output:
```
I am a Car
```

Readonly

PHP 8.1 introduces a new keyword, readonly, which is used to indicate that class properties can only be initialized once. Once set, the value of a readonly property cannot be overwritten, not even by the class itself. PHP 8.2 also allows entire classes to be declared readonly, which has the effect of setting readonly on all class properties.

Some caveats with readonly properties: they cannot be initialized outside of the class, so they must be assigned a value either in a constructor or setter method. Using a setter is not preferred because they can be called multiple times, as the following example shows:

```
class DataObj
{
    public readonly string $nonConstructedProp;

    public function __construct(
        public readonly string $someProp,
    ) {
    }
```

```
    public function setNonConstructedProp(string $val): void
    {
        $this->nonConstructedProp = $val;
    }
}

$obj = new DataObj('prop1');
var_dump($obj);
$obj->setNonConstructedProp('prop3');
$obj->setNonConstructedProp('prop4');

Output:
object(DataObj)#3 (1) {
  ["nonConstructedProp"]=>
  uninitialized(string)
  ["someProp"]=>
  string(5) "prop1"
}
Fatal error: Uncaught Error: Cannot modify readonly property
DataObj::$nonConstructedProp in ...
```

This simple data wrapper class (which is a typical use case for readonly) uses readonly both in a promoted constructor property and a regular class property. Notice we've used a setter for $nonConstructedProp and called the setter twice, triggering an error.

The following shows an entire readonly class:

```
readonly class DataObj
{
    public function __construct(
        public string $prop
    ) {
    }

    public function setProp(string $val): void
    {
        $this->prop = $val;
    }
}
```

CHAPTER 6 OBJECT FUNDAMENTALS

```
$obj = new DataObj('prop1');
$obj->setProp('new val');
```

Output:
Fatal error: Uncaught Error: Cannot modify readonly property DataObj::$prop in ...

The error has been triggered again to demonstrate the DataObj::$prop has been made readonly via the class declaration. Both of these examples should serve to demonstrate that readonly properties are best set via a constructor (which is only ever called once).

Final Classes

It is sometimes desirable to prevent inheritance mechanisms. For this reason, we have the final keyword. Classes declared as final cannot be extended. Class constants and methods may also be declared as final, which prevents overloading in a subclass. The following examples demonstrate these restrictions.

Attempt to override a final class method:

```
class SuperClass
{
    final public function doThing(): void
    {
    }
}
class SubClass extends SuperClass
{
    public function doThing(): void
    {
    }
}
```

Output:
Fatal error: Cannot override final method SuperClass::doThing()

From the example above we can see that extending SuperClass is fine, but overloading the final method doThing() emits an error. Now we'll attempt to extend a final class...

```
final class SuperClass
{
}
class SubClass extends SuperClass
{
}
Output:
Fatal error: Class SubClass cannot extend final class SuperClass
```

... with predictable (fatal) results.

Declaring classes or methods final has its place, which is obviously when extension or overriding must be prevented. Doing so, however, might conflict with a fundamental principle of OOP, something called the "Open/Closed Principle," which mandates a module (or class, in this case) must be open for extension but closed for modification. We cover these principles in detail in Chapter 10, "Programming with Objects." If you're wondering, it is common to see final used for classes designed to test other classes.

Traits

Some object-oriented languages allow inheritance from multiple parent classes but PHP is not one of them. The object model of PHP is one of *single inheritance*. To mitigate this limitation (although it can be argued that single inheritance is a limitation that exists for good reasons), *traits* were added to the language.

A trait declaration looks a lot like a class declaration:

```
trait Engine
{
    protected int $fuelLevel = 0;

    public function printFuelLevel(): void
    {
        print "There are {$this->fuelLevel} litres remaining!" . PHP_EOL;
    }
```

```
    public function consumeFuel(int $amount): void
    {
        $this->fuelLevel -= $amount;
    }

    public function refuel(int $fuelAmount): void
    {
        $this->fuelLevel += $fuelAmount;
    }
}
```

Note that, unlike interfaces, we are free to use `protected` and `private` members. To use a trait within a class, the keyword `use` is placed inside the class declaration like so:

```
class Car
{
    use Engine;
}
class SpaceShuttle
{
    use Engine;
}
$golf = new Car();
$enterprise = new SpaceShuttle();

$golf->refuel(50);
$enterprise->refuel(18_000_000);

$golf->consumeFuel(10);
$enterprise->consumeFuel(500_000);

$golf->printFuelLevel();
$enterprise->printFuelLevel();

Output:
There are 40 litres remaining!
There are 17500000 litres remaining!
```

CHAPTER 6 OBJECT FUNDAMENTALS

Now we have two vehicle objects that are not particularly related to each other but share the common trait of possessing an engine. The use Engine; statement functions like a copy-and-paste when PHP parses the code: the trait code is placed inside the class as if it had been written there in the first place. This actually leads to some idiosyncratic behavior: a class that uses a trait cannot itself also declare any of the properties or methods of the trait:

```
class SaturnFive
{
    use Engine;

    protected int $fuelLevel = 500_000;
}
```

Output:
SaturnFive and Engine define the same property ($fuelLevel) in the composition of SaturnFive

The key point here is the word "composition." When a trait is used in a class PHP simply adds in the code, as far as it is concerned, the definition of SaturnFive is this:

```
class SaturnFive
{
    // use Engine trait code is embedded into SaturnFive class here...
    protected int $fuelLevel = 0;

    // the rest of the Engine trait members, followed by...

    protected int $fuelLevel = 500_000;
}
```

One workaround for this is to have the trait in a parent class, then the child is free to overload in the normal way. For example:

```
class Rocket
{
    use Engine;
}
```

```
class SaturnFive extends Rocket
{
    protected int $fuelLevel = 500_000;
}
```

Extension and Constants

Like interfaces traits can declare constants, if running PHP 8.2 or later:

```
trait DefaultQuote
{
    // requires PHP 8.2
    public const QUOTE = 'I am not a number! I am a free man!';
}

class GenericQuoteBot
{
    use DefaultQuote;
}

print GenericQuoteBot::QUOTE . PHP_EOL;
```

Output:
```
I am not a number! I am a free man!
```

Unlike interfaces, it is not possible to extend a trait: there is no inheritance hierarchy. Traits really are just a mechanism for expanding a short statement into a chunk of source code (a little like macros in C), they transform your code *before* it is interpreted. There is, however, a trick for "extending" a trait by pulling one trait's code into another:

```
trait DefaultQuote
{
    private const QUOTE = 'I am not a number! I am a free man!';
}

trait GetQuote
{
    use DefaultQuote;
```

```
    public static function getQuote(): string
    {
        return self::QUOTE;
    }
}
class GenericQuoteBot
{
    use GetQuote;
}

print GenericQuoteBot::getQuote() . PHP_EOL;
```

Output:
I am not a number! I am a free man!

Here we've chained our traits together: GetQuote defines a public static getQuote() method and also has a use DefaultQuote; statement. This means that the (now private) const in DefaultQuote is available in GetQuote. GenericQuoteBot uses the GetQuote trait, which in turn uses the DefaultQuote trait. The composed class declaration that is subsequently interpreted by PHP is essentially this:

```
class GenericQuoteBot
{
    //DefaultQuote trait expands to this:
    private const QUOTE = 'I am not a number! I am a free man!';

    // GetQuote trait expands to this:
    public static function getQuote(): string
    {
        return self::QUOTE;
    }

    use GetQuote;
}
```

Enums

The last class-like construct in PHP we're going to look at is the *enum*. The enum is PHP's implementation of an enumerated type, which in general terms is a data type consisting of a fixed set of values. These can be helpful when you want to restrict the values of things to valid states.

One of the classic examples of an enum type uses the suits of a deck of cards. We can represent the suit of a card with an enum consisting of four strings: "Clubs", "Diamonds", 'Hearts', and "Spades". If a Card class exists in your program, you can restrict its ::$suit property to one of the four enum values (and never have to worry about accidentally breaking code if someone tries to play the four of cabbages).

Prior to the introduction of the enum type in PHP 8.1, this was usually achieved with class constants and would probably look something like this:

```php
class Suit
{
    public const CLUBS = 'clubs';
    public const DIAMONDS = 'diamonds';
    public const HEARTS = 'hearts';
    public const SPADES = 'spades';
}

class Card
{
    public function __construct(
        private readonly string $suit,
        private readonly string $value
    ) {
    }

    public function getFullName(): string
    {
        return "{$this->value} of {$this->suit}";
    }
}

$card = new Card(Suit::SPADES, "ace");
print "The {$card->getFullName()}, the {$card->getFullName()} \m/" . PHP_EOL;
```

Output:
The ace of spades, the ace of spades \m/

This isn't a terrible approach; we can test and assign data against the constants Suit::CLUBS, Suit::HEARTS, etc. and make our code safer, but only up to a point. The type checking done in Card::__construct() is on the values of the Suit constants, not the class itself. If we add the following method to Card...

```
public function getSuit(): string
{
    return $this->suit;
}
```

... and do something silly like this ...

```
$card = new Card("cabbages", "four");

switch ($card->getSuit()) {
    case Suit::CLUBS:
    case Suit::DIAMONDS:
    case Suit::HEARTS:
    case Suit::SPADES:
        // carry on with the game
        break;
    default:
        throw new \Exception('Preposterous!');
}
```

Output:
Fatal error: Uncaught Exception: Preposterous!

... we break our code. We could add some more code to the Card constructor to check the incoming value is one of the four constants of Suit, but that's old PHP. Here's how to solve the problem with an enum.

Basic Enums

```
enum Suit
{
    case CLUBS;
    case DIAMONDS;
    case HEARTS;
    case SPADES;
}

class Card
{
    public function __construct(
        private readonly Suit $suit,
        // rest of class declaration
```

We've restricted `Card::$suit` by declaring the constructor property `$suit` with the enum type `Suit`. Now we're forced to use a `Suit` enumerated case when constructing a new `Card`, rather than any old string:

```
var_dump(new Card(Suit::SPADES, 'ace'));
$card = new Card('cabbages', 'four');
```

Output:
```
object(Card)#1 (2) {
  ["suit":"Card":private]=>
  enum(Suit::SPADES)
  ["value":"Card":private]=>
  string(3) "ace"
}
Fatal error: Uncaught TypeError: Card::__construct(): Argument #1 ($suit) must be of type Suit, string given...
```

This is safer code, and we're no longer allowed to play a four of cabbages (feel free to invent that game, it sounds like fun). There's a small drawback to enums in this form, let's see what happens when we try to use the `Card::getFullName()` method:

```
$card = new Card(Suit::SPADES, 'ace');
print "The {$card->getFullName()}, the {$card->getFullName()} \m/" . PHP_EOL;
```

Output:
Fatal error: Uncaught Error: Object of class Suit could not be converted to string...

In their basic (sometimes called "pure") form, enum cases don't actually have values, or rather they don't have scalar values. Pure enums cannot be cast to strings or any other scalar type, which breaks getFullName() and getSuit(), which have string type declarations and perform string operations. When we implemented Suit::SPADES as a string constant, we were able to freely use it in a string expression. That is not the case when we use a pure enum, but fortunately there's a solution.

Backed Enums

A backed enum gives each enumerated case a scalar value, with the following syntax:

```
enum Suit: string {
    case CLUBS = 'clubs';
    case DIAMONDS = 'diamonds';
    case HEARTS = 'hearts';
    case SPADES = 'spades';
}
```

By giving the enum a scalar type with enum Suit: string, we are declaring that the enum is backed by a scalar type of string. Naturally this means that all values for each case must be strings, and additionally all cases must have a value. A backed enum is not permitted to have any cases without values.

To access the enum value a little extra code is required due to internal implementation details. Each case is an object in its own right, and we have to access a read-only property to get to the value set in the declaration:

```
public function getFullName(): string
{
    return "{$this->value} of {$this->suit->value}";
}
```

Card::getFullName() is now accessing the value property of the Suit case, from which we obtain its scalar value:

```
$card = new Card(Suit::SPADES, 'ace');
print "The {$card->getFullName()}, the {$card->getFullName()} \m/" .
PHP_EOL;
```

Output:
```
The ace of spades, the ace of spades \m/
```

Backed enums are somewhat restricted. The entire enum must be declared either int or string (and it's not possible to use a union of int|string), and every case must have a unique value.

Enums as Classes

So far, enums look a bit like classes, and enum values look like static properties. We even get OOP-flavored errors when we misuse enums. In fact, enums *are* classes, or rather, they are built on classes. PHP implements enum cases as (single) object instances of the enum "class":

```
var_dump(Suit::class);
var_dump(gettype(Suit::CLUBS));
var_dump(get_class(Suit::CLUBS));
var_dump(Suit::CLUBS->value);
```

Output:
```
string(4) "Suit"
string(6) "object"
string(4) "Suit"
string(5) "clubs"
```

It is even possible to do class-like things with enums. For example, we can implement an interface, then use that interface in a type declaration:

```
interface CastSpell
{
    public function cast(): string;
}
```

```
enum WizardSpells: string implements CastSpell {
    case MagicMissile = 'Thunk! Thunk! Thunk!';
    case Thunderwave = 'KABOOM!';

    public function cast(): string
    {
        return $this->value . PHP_EOL;
    }
}
function doMagic(CastSpell $spell)
{
    print "You cast a spell, it goes " . $spell->cast();
}
doMagic(WizardSpells::MagicMissile);
doMagic(WizardSpells::Thunderwave);

Output:
You cast a spell, it goes Thunk! Thunk! Thunk!
You cast a spell, it goes KABOOM!
```

Here we have a `CastSpell` interface implemented by the `WizardSpells` enum. `WizardSpells`, just like a class, must provide the interface's `cast()` implementation. The function `doMagic()` accepts a single argument `$spell`, which must be an object that implements the `CastSpell` interface, and `WizardSpells` passes the type check.

What is important to note here is the call to the `cast()` method: it is called on the enum cases, not the enum itself. Remember, it is the cases that are the objects. Conceptually, you can think of `WizardSpells::MagicMissile` as being functionally equivalent to `abstract class WizardSpells` and `class MagicMissile extends WizardSpells`. Therefore, when we call `WizardSpells::MagicMissle->cast()` the value of `$this` in the `cast()` method is set to `WizardSpells::MagicMissile`.

Pure and backed enums can implement interfaces (the `implements` keyword goes after the type declaration for backed enums) and define methods (either their own or those specified by an interface). An enum may not have properties, however, nor can they be extended. Although protected methods are legal in an enum declaration, they can never be inherited, so stick to `public` and `private` visibility.

Enum cases behave like subclasses of an abstract parent, where the parent is the enum. Thus, all cases of WizardSpells have "inherited" the cast() method. Just like abstract classes, an enum cannot be instantiated...

```
$spells = new WizardSpells();
```

Output:
Fatal error: Uncaught Error: Cannot instantiate enum WizardSpells

... and of course we can't instantiate an enum case because it is already an object. It is possible to define an enum method that can be called on the enum itself provided we declare the method to be static. Let's add the following to WizardSpells:

```
public static function panic(): void
{
    print "You panic and fall over." . PHP_EOL;
}
```

Now we can call panic() from either a case or the enum:

```
WizardSpells::panic();
print "You recover and cast a noisy spell... "
    . WizardSpells::Thunderwave->value . PHP_EOL;
WizardSpells::Thunderwave->panic();
```

Output:
You panic and fall over.
You recover and cast a noisy spell... KABOOM!
You panic and fall over.

There's one more trick up the sleeve of enums: it is possible to define constants. These function in the same way as class constants.

```
enum BardInstrument
{
    case Bagpipes;
    case Harp;
    case Zither;

    public const DEFAULT = self::Harp;
}
```

```
class Bard
{
    public function __construct(
        public BardInstrument $instrument
    ) {
    }
}

var_dump(new Bard(BardInstrument::Bagpipes));
var_dump(new Bard(BardInstrument::DEFAULT));

Output:
object(Bard)#1 (1) {
  ["instrument"]=>
  enum(BardInstrument::Bagpipes)
}
object(Bard)#1 (1) {
  ["instrument"]=>
  enum(BardInstrument::Harp)
}
```

As we can see, it's perfectly fine for an enum constant to refer to one of the enum cases (and is a good use case for the feature).

Namespacing

Just as with functions and variables, classes can also be namespaced, and the syntax and rules are identical to those seen in Chapter 3, "Functions." Here's a quick recap:

```
namespace Fink {
    class QuoteBot
    {
        public static function insight(): void
        {
            print "I've always found that writing comes from a great inner
            pain." . PHP_EOL;
        }
```

CHAPTER 6   OBJECT FUNDAMENTALS

```php
        }
    }
}
namespace Lebowski {
    class QuoteBot
    {
        public static function insight(): void
        {
            print "...dude, let's go bowling." . PHP_EOL;
        }
    }
}
namespace {
    \Fink\QuoteBot::insight();
    \Lebowski\QuoteBot::insight();
}
```

Output:
I've always found that writing comes from a great inner pain.
...dude, let's go bowling.

Hopefully this should look familiar. The same caveat to multiple namespaces mentioned in Chapter 3, "Functions," applies here too. I've used multiple namespaces and placed their contents inside braces for the sake of brevity. PSR-12 coding standards dictate that only one namespace should be declared per file. The vast majority of namespaced class declarations that you encounter in the real world will look similar to the following (opening PHP tag included for reference):

```php
<?php

namespace Lebowski;

class QuoteBot
{
    // rest of file
```

If you are following a coding standard such as PSR-1, classes must be declared in a namespace of at least one level and, in addition, must follow the autoloading standard of PSR-4. This means that namespace hierarchy (top-level namespace, sub-namespace, sub-sub-namespace, etc.) can be mapped to the filesystem storing the source code. A typical PSR-4 compliant project might have an "entry" script named main.php and store its classes in a directory structure that maps to the namespace structure of the project:

```
$ ls -la
drwxrwxrwt  16 user    wheel    512 21 Aug 20:42 .
drwxr-xr-x   6 user    wheel    192  1 Aug  1970 ..
drwxr-xr-x   4 user    wheel    128 21 Aug 20:42 Application
-rwxr-xr-x   1 user    wheel     46  6 Aug 12:46 main.php

$ ls -la Application
drwxr-xr-x   4 user    wheel    128 21 Aug 20:42 .
drwxrwxrwt  16 user    wheel    512 21 Aug 20:42 ..
drwxr-xr-x   2 user    wheel     64 21 Aug 20:42 Email

$ ls -la Application/Email
drwxr-xr-x   3 user    wheel     96 21 Aug 20:46 .
drwxr-xr-x   4 user    wheel    128 21 Aug 20:42 ..
-rw-r--r--   1 user    wheel      0 21 Aug 20:46 Manager.php
```

The first few lines of Application/Email/Manager.php will therefore look like this:

```
<?php

namespace Application\Email;

class Manager
{
    // rest of declaration
```

By setting up namespaced classes in this way, it is possible for PHP to locate and load classes on demand using a mechanism called autoloading, which just so happens to be the very next section of this chapter...

CHAPTER 6   OBJECT FUNDAMENTALS

Finding and Loading Classes

A well-organized software project spreads its code across multiple files, and we've seen in previous chapters how to load source code from other files. Classes are no different. Just as a function cannot be called until the file containing its declaration has been parsed by PHP, a class cannot be used until PHP has loaded it. To demonstrate, we'll create three source code files...

```
//10.01.php
class SomeClass
{
}

//10.02.php
$someClass = new SomeClass();

//10.03.php
require __DIR__ . '/10.01_SomeClass.php';

$someClass = new SomeClass();
var_dump($someClass);
```

... and run the code in 10.02.php and 10.03.php:

```
Output: (10.02.php)
Fatal error: Uncaught Error: Class "SomeClass" not found...

Output: (10.03.php)
object(SomeClass)#1 (0) {
}
```

Here we've split our code across three files. The first (10.01.php) contains a simple class declaration; the other two instantiate the class (or try to). 10.02.php exits with a fatal error: Class "SomeClass" not found, but 10.03.php is successful because it loads the source code for SomeClass with a require statement. In order to use SomeClass, it is necessary to include or require the file containing the class declaration.

Of course, we could simply put every class declaration into a single file, but that would quickly become a maintenance headache of epic proportions as the number of classes in a project grows (say, beyond about three). In addition, multiple class declarations in a single file is specifically prohibited by the PSR-1 coding standard (section three, to be precise).

On the other hand, explicitly requiring every file containing a class declaration also becomes problematic, not to mention wasteful of system resources. If defining classes on a one-per-file basis is going to work in a frictionless way, we need to automate it somehow. This is where autoloading comes in.

Autoloading

In general programming terms, autoloading simply means that sections of a program can be fetched from storage when needed, rather than being explicitly imported. In PHP, autoloading is specific to classes and the other class-like constructs (`interface`, `trait`, and `enum`). To enable this mechanism, you must create a function that is able to `require` or `include` the file containing the missing declaration. This loading function must then be registered with PHP's `spl_autoload_register()` function. Here is a quick example:

```
spl_autoload_register(function ($className) {
    $fileName = '10.01_' . $className . '.php';
    print "{$className} is not declared, attempting to load from ./{$fileName}" . PHP_EOL;
    require __DIR__ . DIRECTORY_SEPARATOR . $fileName;
});

$someClass = new SomeClass();
var_dump($someClass);

Output:
SomeClass is not declared, attempting to load from ./10.01_SomeClass.php
object(SomeClass)#2 (0) {
}
```

This is autoloading in its simplest form. In reality, the mapping will be slightly more complex because classes that are distributed in a namespace hierarchy are also distributed across a filesystem. The good news is that thanks to PSR-4, all we need to do is transform PHP's namespace path into a filesystem path (directory separator characters vary across systems, but the namespace separator is always a backslash) and know where the top-level namespace exists on the filesystem.

CHAPTER 6 OBJECT FUNDAMENTALS

Given the following filesystem layout (using the linux `tree` command, macOS users might need to run `$ brew install tree` first):

```
$ tree --charset=ascii
.
|-- 10.05_main.php
`-- MyApplication
    |-- SomeClass.php
    `-- SubNamespace
        |-- SomeOtherClass.php
        `-- ThisClassOverHere.php
```

... then inside 10.05_main.php we can register an autoload function like this:

```
spl_autoload_register(function ($class) {
    print "LOADING : {$class} from namespace " . __NAMESPACE__ . PHP_EOL;
    $class = str_replace("\\", DIRECTORY_SEPARATOR, $class);
    require __DIR__ . DIRECTORY_SEPARATOR . $class . '.php';
});
```

The magic constant __NAMESPACE__ will evaluate to the current namespace (more on this very shortly). Our namespaced classes look like this:

```
// MyApplication/SomeClass.php
namespace MyApplication;

use MyApplication\SubNamespace\SomeOtherClass;
use MyApplication\SubNamespace\ThisClassOverHere;

class SomeClass
{
    private $otherClass;
    private $thisClassOverHere;

    public function __construct()
    {
        $this->otherClass = new SomeOtherClass();
        $this->thisClassOverHere = new ThisClassOverHere()
    }
}
```

```
// MyApplication/SubNamespace/SomeOtherClass.php
namespace MyApplication\SubNamespace;

class SomeOtherClass
{
}

// MyApplication/SubNamespace/ThisClassOverHere.php
namespace MyApplication\SubNamespace;

class ThisClassOverHere
{
}
```

Let's tie it all together, like a rug ties a room together:

```
//main.php
$class = new \MyApplication\SomeClass();
var_dump($class);

Output:
LOADING : MyApplication\SomeClass from namespace
LOADING : MyApplication\SubNamespace\SomeOtherClass from namespace
LOADING : MyApplication\SubNamespace\ThisClassOverHere from namespace
object(MyApplication\SomeClass)#2 (2) {
  ["otherClass":"MyApplication\SomeClass":private]=>
  object(MyApplication\SubNamespace\SomeOtherClass)#3 (0) {
  }
  ["thisClassOverHere":"MyApplication\SomeClass":private]=>
  object(MyApplication\SubNamespace\ThisClassOverHere)#4 (0) {
  }
}
```

And there we have it. Namespaced autoloading, PSR-4 style. Notice that when each class is loaded, the value of __NAMESPACE__ is empty, even when SomeOtherClass is instantiated inside the constructor of SomeClass. This is because even though we're using namespaced classes, the calling code never left the root namespace (aka "non-namespaced," often called "global" namespace, which is something of a misnomer in the author's humble opinion).

CHAPTER 6 ■ OBJECT FUNDAMENTALS

It is possible to queue up multiple autoloading functions with spl_autoload_register(), every time class autoloading is triggered, the registered functions will be called in order until the required class is loaded. The following will demonstrate.

Copy ./MyApplication/SubNamespace/ThisClassOverHere.php to a new file with a .inc extension:

```
$ cp ./MyApplication/SubNamespace/ThisClassOverHere.php ./MyApplication/SubNamespace/ThisClassOverHere.inc
```

Next, add the following code to a new file...

```
// multi_autoload.php
spl_autoload_register(function ($class) {
    $fullPath = __DIR__ . DIRECTORY_SEPARATOR
        . str_replace("\\", DIRECTORY_SEPARATOR, $class) . '.inc';

    if (file_exists($fullPath)) {
        print "Loading {$class} from {$fullPath}" . PHP_EOL;
        require $fullPath;
    }
});

spl_autoload_register(function ($class) {
    $fullPath = __DIR__ . DIRECTORY_SEPARATOR
        . str_replace("\\", DIRECTORY_SEPARATOR, $class) . '.php';

    if (file_exists($fullPath)) {
        print "Loading {$class} from {$fullPath}" . PHP_EOL;
        require $fullPath;
    }
});

$class = new \MyApplication\SomeClass();
```

... and run it:

```
$ php multi_autoload.php
Loading MyApplication\SomeClass from /usr/src/myapp/MyApplication/SomeClass.php
```

```
Loading MyApplication\SubNamespace\SomeOtherClass from /usr/src/myapp/
MyApplication/SubNamespace/SomeOtherClass.php
Loading MyApplication\SubNamespace\ThisClassOverHere from /usr/src/myapp/
MyApplication/SubNamespace/ThisClassOverHere.inc
```

Notice how `ThisClassOverHere` has been loaded by the first autoload function, which will search for files ending in `.inc`? Obviously, this is a contrived example (we could test for .inc and .php files in a single function) but serves to illustrate the principle. The popular Composer dependency manager uses multiple autoload functions internally to provide support not only for PSR-4 compliant projects but also for the older (now deprecated) PSR-0 standard and even support for loading classes that otherwise could not be autoloaded at all.

Object Utilities

We've covered a lot of material in this chapter, and hopefully you now have a thorough grounding in PHP's object model. Let's wrap things up with a look at the extra utility PHP provides beyond the object model itself. There are several built-in functions and other features in PHP to make working with objects and classes easier and code more concise.

Magic Constants

We've seen a useful magic constant already, `__NAMESPACE__`, it's called a magic constant because its value changes depending on where it is used. Here's all of the magic constants related to OOP.

Table 6-2. Magic constants

Constant	Value
__CLASS__	Class name including namespace
__METHOD__	Method name including class and namespace
__NAMESPACE__	Current namespace
__TRAIT__	Trait name including namespace

CHAPTER 6 OBJECT FUNDAMENTALS

Let's see them in action:

```
class Magician
{
    public function debug(): void
    {
        print __CLASS__ . PHP_EOL;
        print __METHOD__ . PHP_EOL;
    }
}

$magician = new Magician();
$magician->debug();
```

Output:
Magician
Magician::debug

The code above demonstrates __CLASS__ and __METHOD__ constants. Their values correspond to the declaration they are used in, not where they are used. For example:

```
class Quentin extends Magician
{
}

$magician = new Quentin();
$magician->debug();
```

Output:
Magician
Magician::debug

The values for __METHOD__ and __CLASS__ have not changed despite being called from an instance of a child class. Likewise, __NAMESPACE__ behaves in the same way:

```
namespace Brakebills {
    class Magician
    {
        public function debug(): void
```

```
        {
            print __NAMESPACE__ . PHP_EOL;
        }
    }
}

namespace Fillory {
    class Quentin extends \Brakebills\Magician
    {
    }

    $magician = new Quentin();
    $magician->debug();
}

Output:
Brakebills
```

Things get a little more complex when we use traits:

```
namespace Fillory {
    trait Niffin
    {
        public function debug(): void
        {
            print __TRAIT__ . PHP_EOL;
            print __CLASS__ . PHP_EOL;
            print __METHOD__ . PHP_EOL;
        }
    }
}

namespace TheRealWorld {
    class Alice
    {
        use \Fillory\Niffin;
    }
```

```
    $magician = new Alice();
    $magician->debug();
}
```

Output:
Fillory\Niffin
TheRealWorld\Alice
Fillory\Niffin::debug

__TRAIT__ behaves as we would expect; its value is set to the trait (and its namespace) where the declaration lives. So too is __METHOD__. __CLASS__, however, is set to where it is used (not declared), because traits are not classes. In addition to these magic constants, every class (and object) has a ::class constant available, which returns a string value of the fully qualified name.

Object Functions

There are built-in functions designed to work with classes and objects; we've seen spl_autoload_register() already. Some of these functions are used to find out what classes, traits, and interfaces are available. Others will return information about specific classes or objects, a technique known as introspection.

Broadly speaking, the object functions will either tell you an object or class exists at all, tell you what an object is, or tell you what you can do with it.

Does It Exist?

```
namespace Application {
    trait SomeTrait
    {
    }

    enum SomeEnum
    {
    }
}
```

```
namespace {
    print_r(get_declared_classes());
    print_r(get_declared_interfaces());
    print_r(get_declared_traits());
}
Output:
Array
(
    [0] => InternalIterator
    [1] => Exception
    [2] => ErrorException
    ...
    [238] => Application\SomeEnum
)
Array
(
    [0] => Traversable
    [1] => IteratorAggregate
    [2] => Iterator
    ...
)
Array
(
    [0] => Application\SomeTrait
)
```

The three functions demonstrated here – get_declared_classes(), get_declared_interfaces(), and get_declared_traits() – will return every class, interface, and trait currently declared. Notice that enum SomeEnum is in the declared classes array (there is no get_declared_enums() function), and the only declared trait is the one we explicitly declared in the Application namespace – there are no built-in traits in the core language.

These functions are useful, but if you know exactly which class (or trait, or interface) you need, then the following functions can be used:

```
namespace Application {
    class SomeClass
    {
    }

    trait SomeTrait
    {
    }

    interface SomeInterface
    {
    }

    enum SomeEnum
    {
    }
}
namespace {
    var_dump(class_exists('Application\SomeClass'));
    var_dump(trait_exists('Application\SomeTrait'));
    var_dump(interface_exists('Application\SomeInterface'));
    var_dump(enum_exists('Application\SomeEnum'));
}
Output:
bool(true)
bool(true)
bool(true)
bool(true)
```

Note that the fully qualified name is required in all cases.

What Is It?

The built-in functions get_class() and is_a() can be used to check the class name of an object instance:

```
$obj = new stdClass();

var_dump(get_class($obj));
var_dump(is_a($obj, 'stdClass'));
var_dump(is_a($obj, stdClass::class));

Output:
string(8) "stdClass"
bool(true)
bool(true)
```

There is also get_called_class(), which behaves in a similar way to late static binding to return the name of the class or object executing the function at run time:

```
class Magician
{
    public static function staticDebug(): void
    {
        var_dump(get_called_class());
    }

    public function debug(): void
    {
        var_dump(get_called_class());
    }
}

class Quentin extends Magician
{
}

$magician = new Magician();
$quentin = new Quentin();

$magician::staticDebug();
$magician->debug();
$quentin::staticDebug();
$quentin->debug();
```

CHAPTER 6 OBJECT FUNDAMENTALS

Output:
```
string(8) "Magician"
string(8) "Magician"
string(7) "Quentin"
string(7) "Quentin"
```

To complement get_class(), get_called_class(), and is_a() all functions that are concerned with an object's class, there are also functions concerned with class hierarchy. These are get_parent_class and is_subclass_of():

```
class Magician
{
}

class Alice extends Magician
{
}

class Niffin extends Alice
{
}

var_dump(get_parent_class(Niffin::class));
var_dump(get_parent_class(new Alice()));
var_dump(is_subclass_of(Niffin::class, Magician::class));
var_dump(is_subclass_of(new Alice, Magician::class));
```

Output:
```
string(5) "Alice"
string(8) "Magician"
bool(true)
bool(true)
```

get_parent_class() and is_subclass_of() both accept either objects or class name strings as the first argument, the second argument to is_subclass_of() must always be a class name string. Note that get_parent_class() returns the immediate parent class: Niffin is a subclass of Magician in the hierarchy, but get_parent_class() reports Alice because Niffin extends Alice.

What Does It Do?

Finally, there are functions for finding out about class and object members. get_class_methods() returns public methods, get_class_vars() returns public properties, they both accept either object instances or class names:

```
class Wizard
{
    public int $level = 1;
    private int $exp = 0;

    public function magicMissile(): void
    {
        // hurt stuff
    }

    protected function longRest(): void
    {
        // snooze
    }
}

$wiz = new Wizard();

print_r(get_class_methods($wiz));
print_r(get_object_vars($wiz));

print_r(get_class_methods(Wizard::class));
print_r(get_class_vars(Wizard::class));
```

The output of get_class_methods() and get_object_vars() is identical for $wiz and Wizard::class:

```
Output:
Array
(
    [0] => magicMissile
)
```

CHAPTER 6   OBJECT FUNDAMENTALS

```
Array
(
    [level] => 1
)
```

Note that get_class_methods(), get_class_vars(), and get_object_vars() only return information about public members when called from outside the class. Additionally, get_object_vars() and get_class_vars() are specific to objects and classes, respectively.

If called from inside the class, the protected and private members are also returned. If we add the following method to the Wizard class…

```
public function showMembers(): void
{
    print_r(get_class_vars(self::class));
    print_r(get_class_methods($this));
}
```

… we can see all properties and methods regardless of visibility.

```
(new Wizard())->showMembers();
```

Output:
```
Array
(
    [level] => 1
    [exp] => 0
)
Array
(
    [0] => magicMissile
    [1] => longRest
    [2] => showMembers
)
```

CHAPTER 6   OBJECT FUNDAMENTALS

It is also possible to test for specific members, both public and non-public:

```
var_dump(property_exists($wiz, 'level'));
var_dump(property_exists(Wizard::class, 'exp'));
var_dump(method_exists(Wizard::class, 'magicMissile'));
var_dump(method_exists($wiz, 'longRest'));
```

Output:
bool(true)
bool(true)
bool(true)
bool(true)

One more function exists that will report an object's properties: the interestingly named get_mangled_object_vars(). This function will return hidden object properties as well as public, albeit with some caveats:

```
class Cleric
{
    public int $level = 2;
    private int $exp = 0;
    protected int $gold = 1;

    public function prayerOfHealing(): void
    {
        // fix stuff
    }
}
var_dump(get_mangled_object_vars(new Cleric()));
```

Output
Array
(
    [level] => 2
    [Clericexp] => 0
    [*gold] => 1
)

359

Unlike get_object_vars() we can now see the protected and private properties, and their values, but they've had their names changed. Private properties are prefixed with the class name (exp becomes Clericexp) and protected properties are prefixed with a * character (gold becomes *gold).

Reflection

The functions we've just looked at are very useful for introspection in a pinch. If you want to quickly figure out if an object possesses specific capabilities, then a single call to, say, method_exists() can usually get the job done. For cases where a more in-depth analysis of an object, class – or even individual methods or properties – PHP offers the Reflection API. This API consists of a variety of classes in the root namespace, all with a name beginning with Reflection – there's ReflectionObject (for introspecting objects), ReflectionMethod (for methods), even ReflectionEnum and ReflectionFunction (for enums and functions). Reflection is not specific to PHP, the term *reflective programming* refers to code that is able to inspect and even modify its own structure and behavior. You can find reflection used extensively in testing frameworks such as PHPUnit.

This sub-section of the chapter will serve as a quick introduction to reflection in PHP, and I highly recommend *PHP 8 Objects, Patterns, and Practice* (Matt Zandstra) for further reading (for both reflection and OOP in general). As always, let's kick the tires, starting with a slightly modified version of the Cleric class from the previous example...

```
class Cleric
{
    // ... level, exp, and gold properties as before
    final public function prayerOfHealing(): void
    {
        // fix stuff
    }
}
```

... which has an additional final modifier added to the prayerOfHealing() method. To inspect an entire class, we have the choice of instantiating a new ReflectionClass object or a new ReflectionObject, which do not differ in their interfaces (ReflectionObject extends ReflectionClass, in fact). The general rule is to choose the (reflection) class that matches the information you have at the time. If we had a class name, we'd use new `ReflectionClass('SomeClass')`, if we have an object, we'd use new `ReflectionObject($object)`. Let's make an object and use `ReflectionObject`...

```
$obj = new Cleric();
$refObj = new ReflectionObject($obj);
```

... and take it for a spin. First up, we'll inspect the properties:

```
print "Class {$refObj->getShortName()} has the following properties..." .
PHP_EOL;
foreach ($refObj->getProperties() as $refProp) {
    $modifiers = Reflection::getModifierNames($refProp->getModifiers());
    $modifiers = implode(' ', $modifiers);
    print "   {$modifiers} {$refProp->getType()->getName()}: ";
    print $refProp->getName() . PHP_EOL;
}
```

Output:
```
Class Cleric has the following properties...
   public int: level
   private int: exp
   protected int: gold
```

As you can see, the `ReflectionObject` instance offers a variety of methods for discovering the public (and private) members, in addition to other information about the class. We've also used the `Reflection::getModifierNames()` static method to transform the bitmasked integer returned by `ReflectionObject::getModifiers()` into human-readable strings.

The following table lists a (non-exhaustive) selection of `ReflectionClass`/`ReflectionObject` methods:

Table 6-3. *Reflection methods*

getAttributes()	Class attributes as `ReflectionAttribute` instances
getConstants()	Class constants as `ReflectionConstant` instances
getInterfaces()	Implemented interfaces as `ReflectionInterface` instances
getMethods()	Class methods as `ReflectionMethod` instances
getModifiers()	Class modifiers (e.g., `final`, `abstract`) as integer
getName()	Class name (including namespaces) as `string`
getNamespaceName()	Namespace(s) as `string`
getShortName()	Class name without namespaces
getParentClass()	Get extends class (if any) as `ReflectionClass` instance
getProperties()	Class properties as `ReflectionProperty` instances
getTraits()	Get traits used (if any) as `ReflectionTrait` instances
hasConstant() hasMethod() hasProperty()	Test if member exists
isEnum()	true if object is an enum

The relevant constant/method/property reflection classes have similar methods available. For example, we've already seen `ReflectionProperty::getType()` used above to obtain a `ReflectionType` instance, on which we then called the `::getName()` method. This is the essence of the reflection API in PHP: language features have a corresponding reflection class, and those classes have logically named methods for inspecting the facets of those features. The `ReflectionMethod` class offers `::getReturnType()` and `::getParameters()`. `ReflectionEnum` class offers `::getCases()`, and so on... you get the idea. Add the following snippet to the previous code to see some of this in action:

```
print "... and methods" . PHP_EOL;
foreach ($refObj->getMethods() as $refMethod) {
    $modifiers = Reflection::getModifierNames($refMethod->getModifiers());
    $modifiers = implode(' ', $modifiers);
    print "   {$modifiers} {$refMethod->getName()}(): ";
```

```
        print $refMethod->getReturnType()->getName() . PHP_EOL;
}
```

Output:
```
... and methods
  final public prayerOfHealing(): void
```

In addition to the plethora of OOP tools, it is also possible to reflect functions...

```
class Treasure {}
class Party {}
class Dungeon {}

function delve(Party $party, Dungeon $dungeon): Treasure
{
    // adventures go here
    return new Treasure();
}

$refFunc = new ReflectionFunction('delve');

print "Function {$refFunc->getName()}() ".
    "should be called with parameters..." . PHP_EOL;

foreach ($refFunc->getParameters() as $param) {
    print $param->getType()->getName() . ': ';
    print '$'. $param->getName() . PHP_EOL;
}
```

Output:
```
Function delve() should be called with parameters...
Party: $party
Dungeon: $dungeon
```

... and even use ReflectionFunction::invoke() to call them:

```
var_dump($refFunc->invoke(new Party, new Dungeon));
```

Output:
```
object(Treasure)#5 (0) {
}
```

Naturally, this trick also works via `ReflectionMethod::invoke()`.

This has been just a brief taste of PHP's reflection API. You are most likely to encounter it buried inside frameworks and powering the kinds of libraries that focus on testing and code analysis, and that's a little beyond the scope of this book. If you're interested in learning more, you can start with the official documentation at https://www.php.net/manual/en/book.reflection.php. There is, however, a new (for PHP 8) feature that makes particular use of reflection, one that you might make good use of generally in your own code.

Attributes

PHP 8 introduces a new way to provide information about elements of your code (such as classes, methods, functions) without altering that code, in the form of *attributes*. You use classes and (especially) interfaces to define structure and implementation, and you can add information to them to control other aspects of your software, but this comes with a price: you can end up with interfaces bloated with public constants, properties, and/or methods. Attributes allow you to annotate your code with metadata, which is accessed via reflection, keeping your runtime interfaces trim and focused.

Attributes are – at heart – classes in their own right, which are attached to the constructs in your code using a special syntax `#[AttributeName(param: val, ...)]`, which goes immediately before the statement they are intended to mark. There are no PSR standards for attribute syntax (PSR-12 predates the addition of attributes) but the convention tends to be that an attribute statement starts on its own line, and follows the PSR-12 standards for class instantiation. PHP provides several predefined attributes and a mechanism for creating your own, and it's the reflection API that powers them at runtime. Here's an example of how to use attributes using the predefined `#[Deprecated]`:

```
#[Deprecated(message: 'Time to migrate!', since: '1.0')]
function oldFunc(): string {
    return 'Use something else' . PHP_EOL;
}

print oldFunc();
```

Output:
PHP Deprecated: Function oldFunc() is deprecated since 1.0, Time to migrate! ...
Use something else

The built-in attribute #[Deprecated()] is placed immediately before the declaration of oldFunc(), and when that function is called it emits an E_USER_DEPRECATED error. The attribute syntax looks suspiciously like an object instantiation, and that's exactly what it is: those named arguments are in fact constructor arguments. Behind the scenes, an instance of the Deprecated attribute class – which was given message and since constructor arguments – now lives in memory and PHP uses it whenever the attributed function is called. You can't make use of that Deprecated instance, it isn't "userland" code as such: think of attributes as a configuration meta-language that runs adjacent to the main program (because, well, that's exactly what they are). The full list of predefined attributes is as follows:

Table 6-4. Built-in attributes

#[Attribute]	Used to define your own attribute classes
#[AllowDynamicProperties]	Required in PHP >= 8.2 to mark classes allowing dynamic property (like stdClass does)
#[Deprecated]	Flag deprecated functionality
#[Override]	Mark a method as overriding the parent's, will emit error if no parent implementation
#[ReturnTypeWillChange]	Mark an overriding method to allow a different return type to parent
#[SensetiveParameter]	Mark method/function parameter data to be hidden in any stack trace

Prior to PHP 8 there were comment-based solutions (usually as *docblock* format comments /** */) which were not standardized or enforceable by the language and you'll see lots of things like this in older PHP...

```
/**
 * @SomeAnnotation
 */
```

```
class SomeClass
// ...
```

... where `SomeAnnotation` would be a class provided by the library supporting the annotation and propped up by code that will go and read your source code files. Most major frameworks and libraries (Symfony, Laravel, PHPUnit, etc.) used comment annotations and migrated to attributes on the release of PHP 8.

Making Attributes

To create your own attribute, you simply need to mark a class with `#[Attribute]`, which immediately makes it available for use within the rest of your code. (The attribute class still needs to follow the same rules as regular classes for autoloading and namespacing, so if your attribute is in a different namespace, then import it with use.) Let's try it out:

```
#[Attribute]
class Healer
{
}

#[Attribute]
class Fighter
{
}
```

The attribute classes `Fighter` and `Healer` don't actually do anything, but even empty classes can be useful in a system like this. In our case they're going to serve simply as meta-properties for other classes, which we can test when those marked classes are used at runtime. Let's mark some classes with these attributes:

```
#[Healer]
class Cleric
{
}

#[Fighter]
class Barbarian
{
}
```

```
#[Fighter]
#[Healer]
class Monk
{
}
```

Note that the Monk class has both attributes; it's possible (and very common) for multiple attributes to mark a statement. With all that done, we can now introspect Cleric|Fighter|Monk objects during the course of execution to access the metadata. What do we do with fighters and healers? Form a party, of course:

```
class Party
{
    private array $healers = [];
    private array $fighters = [];

    public function addMember(Cleric|Barbarian|Monk $member)
    {
        $refObject = new ReflectionObject($member);
        $refAttrs = $refObject->getAttributes();
        foreach ($refAttrs as $attr) {
            if ($attr->getName() === Healer::class) {
                $this->healers[] = $member;
            }
            if ($attr->getName() === Fighter::class) {
                $this->fighters[] = $member;
            }
        }
    }

    public function getHealers(): array
    {
        return $this->healers;
    }
```

```
        public function getFighters(): array
        {
            return $this->fighters;
        }
}
```

The ::addMember() method is where we inspect the incoming fighters or healers and place them in the correct private array as they join. Each $member object is used to create a new ReflectionObject, and from there we can access any attributes via ReflectionObject::getAttributes(), which will return an array of ReflectionAttribute objects (one per attribute). All we need to do is loop over each object's attributes looking for a match between the attribute class name and ReflectionAttribute::getName() (which will be the fully qualified name including any namespaces). By using attributes, we have kept our interfaces free of extra properties (or methods) for figuring out if they fight or heal. Since we've gone to all this trouble, let's make use of our attributes and classes:

```
$friartuck = new Monk();
$conan = new Barbarian();
$galadriel = new Cleric();

$genremuddle = new Party();

$genremuddle->addMember($friartuck);
$genremuddle->addMember($conan);
$genremuddle->addMember($galadriel);

var_dump($genremuddle->getHealers());
var_dump($genremuddle->getFighters());

Output:
array(2) {
  [0]=>
  object(Monk)#1 (0) {
  }
  [1]=>
  object(Cleric)#3 (0) {
  }
}
```

```
array(2) {
  [0]=>
  object(Monk)#1 (0) {
  }
  [1]=>
  object(Barbarian)#2 (0) {
  }
}
```

Hopefully you'll have also noticed how I chose to access the attributes: once on the way in, rather than every time `getHealers()` or `getFighters()` is called. Using attributes and reflection naturally comes with a small performance hit, so you might need to make decisions when using them in performance-sensitive areas of your code (keep them out of loops or heavily used functions).

Attributes can be passed data as we saw when using `#[Deprecated]`, and because they are fully formed PHP classes you can also implement methods and whatever logic you like inside them. `ReflectionAttribute::newInstance()` will return a new instance of the attribute class; from there you can use it like any other object. But don't. Attributes are about metadata, not logic; they should describe the code they mark, not serve as code themselves. I hope this quick introduction to reflection and attributes has been useful; there's more to be said on the topic, but there's only so much space in this book. *PHP 8 Objects, Patterns, and Practice* covers these aspects of object-oriented PHP in more detail!

Summary

This chapter contains enough information so that any OOP code encountered in the following chapters will make sense. We've covered the essentials of object creation and use, how to define classes, the difference between objects and classes, and how to access static and non-static members.

We've also touched upon some of the core concepts of OOP, such as inheritance, abstraction, and composing classes from traits, which I will be referring back to in Chapter 10, "Programming with Objects." These mechanisms might not appear to be particularly game-changing when viewed in isolation, but in the context of object-oriented analysis and design, their essential nature will emerge. I promise!

I also gave an introduction to introspection, the process of discovering the structure and capabilities of objects. We will return to this topic when we look at the reflection API.

Hopefully you are now nicely set up for the remaining content in this book and also primed for our imminent deep dive into object-oriented analysis and design.

CHAPTER 7

Numbers

What is a computer? The answer to that question today would be something along the lines of "an electronic device that stores, retrieves, and manipulates data." In the seventeenth century, the answer would have been "a person that computes" (said person would be engaged in performing calculations, usually with a mechanical aid such as an abacus). The original computers were humans that were good with numbers.

A computer programmer today, especially in the context of web development, is probably more concerned with processing text than crunching numbers (although text processing is an abstraction of mathematical operations). PHP is not a natural choice for "doing math" with a computer: other languages exist that are primarily designed for such tasks. A statistician would probably prefer to work in R, an engineer would build models in Matlab, and mathematicians might opt for Wolfram's Mathematica or the venerable (and highly performant) FORTRAN. Python is currently a popular choice for data scientists, and rumor has it that Perl is still out there in the wild and helping bioinformaticians on a daily basis…

Nevertheless, PHP is built with C, which is a general-purpose language with a rich set of mathematical features, and PHP exposes much of that functionality. Indeed, PHP's built-in mathematics functions are often wrappers around C's standard <math.h> and <stdlib.h> libraries. PHP was originally conceived as a pre-processor for HTML; today it is a general-purpose language in its own right, with a rich set of features and functions for processing numeric data.

In this chapter, we will be covering the following:

- Number systems and formatting
- Language operators
- Type casting and coercion
- Built-in mathematical functions
- Limits

- Precision
- Random numbers
- Language extensions

Number Systems

A number system is simply a set of symbols (digits) used to represent numbers. For example, the decimal system uses ten digits; they are 0, 1, 2, 3, 4, 5, 6, 7, 8, and 9. These should be instantly familiar; it's been quite a popular system for representing numbers from as far back as the 1st century. As we count our way through the cardinal numbers (positive integers, starting at one), we eventually run out of digits (in the decimal system this happens when we reach ten), at which point we begin to use two digits (when we reach one hundred), then three (when we reach one thousand), and so on.

The number of digits used in a number system is called the *base* (or more formally the *radix*). Decimal is Base 10, and feels natural to humans because, well, we (typically) have ten convenient counters on our hands. Binary is Base 2 (using the digits 0 and 1), which is more natural for electromechanical or electronic systems built from arrays of switches (also known as computers). Some cultures use other bases such as six (Southern New Guinea), twenty (Aztec), or even sixty (Sumerian, Babylonian - we still use Base 60 numbering today for measuring time, trigonometry and other things).

PHP provides built-in functionality for four common number systems for integer (whole number) operations: binary (Base 2), octal (Base 8), decimal (Base 10), and hexadecimal (Base 16). In case you haven't encountered a number system with a base larger than ten before, when we've exhausted the digits 1-9, we represent the remaining numbers with letters (A-F in hexadecimal). So ten in hex is A, fifteen is F, sixteen is 10, twenty-six is 1A and so on. There is also support in PHP for arbitrary number bases (up to Base 36), the notation for this base combines digits 0-9 and the letters A-Z.

Non-decimal Integer Literals

To demonstrate how to represent the same number using PHP's four different systems, let's first pick an interesting number: the Ramanujan-Hardy number *1729* will do nicely. (If you don't know the story, the mathematician Srinivasa Ramanujan realized some interesting properties of this number while seriously ill in hospital. His friend and

CHAPTER 7 NUMBERS

fellow mathematician G H Hardy came to visit and mentioned that he'd arrived in a taxi numbered 1729, and he thought the number was "dull". Ramanujan begged to differ!)

In mathematics, the binary, octal, and hex representations of *1729* are, respectively, *11011000001$_2$*, *3301$_8$*, and *6C1$_{16}$*. Here's the PHP syntax for them:

```
$binRamanujan = 0b11011000001;
$octRamanujan = 03301;
$octPHP8_1Ramanujan = 0o3301; // This notation was added in PHP 8.1
$hexRamanujan = 0x6c1;

var_dump($binRamanujan);
var_dump($octRamanujan);
var_dump($octPHP8_1Ramanujan);
var_dump($hexRamanujan);
```

Output:
```
int(1729)
int(1729)
int(1729)
int(1729)
```

Here we can see that binary numbers (Base 2) must be prefixed with 0b, octal (Base 8) with 0 (or 0o for PHP 8.1 or later), and hex (Base 16) with 0x. One interesting thing to note is that in all cases the output is a decimal integer. The same number is represented in different ways syntactically but does not differ internally: a (32-bit) four-byte integer or (64-bit) eight-byte integer (depending on processor architecture). When using non-decimal literals, take care to ensure valid digits are used. Here is what happens if we use digits that are out of bounds:

```
var_dump(0b01012); // Parse error: syntax error, unexpected integer "2" ...
var_dump(0o778); // Parse error: syntax error, unexpected integer "8" ...
var_dump(0xFFG); // Parse error: syntax error, unexpected
identifier "G" ...
```

The specific error emitted by each line is given in the code comments. In all cases it's a fatal syntax error but easily caught by a linter.

Scientific Notation

PHP also supports scientific notation (aka standard index form), where a number is expressed as $n \times 10^x$. This notation uses the letter 'e' bounded by numbers on either side. If we wanted to express Ramanujan's number in this form, we'd write 1.729×10^3, which looks like this in PHP:

```
var_dump(1.729E3);
```

Output:
```
float(1729)
```

Note that the value is a float, not an integer.

Converting Bases

In the previous section we saw how to represent numbers in the non-decimal base systems using appropriate prefixes in the literal values and that PHP will always use the decimal notation when casting numbers to strings. If we need to display the non-decimal notations, there are built-in functions for doing that:

```
var_dump(decbin(1729));
var_dump(decoct(1729));
var_dump(dechex(1729));
```

Output:
```
string(11) "11011000001"
string(4) "3301"
string(3) "6c1"
```

The three functions are decbin(), decoct(), and dechex(). Each accepts an integer - or a value that can be cast to an integer - and returns the string representing that integer in the required base.

Correspondingly, bindec(), octdec(), and hexdec() will respectively convert a valid binary, octal, or hex string to an integer:

```
var_dump(bindec('11011000001'));
var_dump(bindec('0b11011000001'));
var_dump(octdec('3301'));
```

```
var_dump(octdec('0o3301'));
var_dump(hexdec('6C1'));
var_dump(hexdec('0x6C1'));
```

In all cases the output will be int(1729). Using the PHP literal notation prefixes is fine, but optional. Be warned that these three functions will accept invalid characters, which will be ignored (and generate a deprecation notice in PHP 7.4 or later). Handling invalid characters in this way will be removed from a future version of PHP, so consider yourselves suitably warned:

```
var_dump(hexdec('Z6c1')); // deprecated in PHP >= 7.4
```

Output:
```
Deprecated: Invalid characters passed for attempted conversion, these have been ignored
int(1729)
```

As previously mentioned, arbitrary number bases up to Base 36 can also be handled. The built-in function base_convert() accepts a string representation of a number in any base and will return the representation in a chosen target base. For example, base_convert('z', 36, 10); would return string(2) "35":

```
var_dump(base_convert('11011000001', 2, 10));
var_dump(base_convert('0o3301', 8, 10));
var_dump(base_convert('6c1', 16, 10));
```

Output:
```
string(4) "1729"
```

Again, any invalid characters present in the source string are ignored with a deprecation notice.

Formatting

The representation of numbers is limited internally in PHP to integers and IEEE double-precision floating point (fully explained in the "Limits and Precision" section). However, there are many conventions when it comes to displaying numbers for human consumption, usually to make them easier to read or to meet certain conventions depending on locale or the problem domain (e.g., finance).

PHP provides a useful built-in function, number_format(), to make life easier. This function requires a minimum of one argument - the number (as a float) to be formatted - and up to three optional arguments to control the output: the number of decimal places, the character to use as the decimal separator, and the character to use as the thousands separator:

```
$number = 100000000000.01;

// number_format(
//     float $num,
//     int $decimals = 0,
//     ?string $decimal_separator = ".",
//     ?string $thousands_separator = ","
// ): string
print number_format($number, 0, '', '') . PHP_EOL;
print number_format($number, 2, '.', ',') . PHP_EOL;
print number_format($number, 2, ',', ' ') . PHP_EOL;
```

Output:
100000000000
100,000,000,000.01
100 000 000 000,01

Here the number *100000000000.01* is formatted to different locales (the French convention is to separate thousands with a space and use a comma as the decimal separator).

Operators, Constants, and Built-In Functions

We've already covered operators and their behavior in a previous chapter, but let's recap the ones that are used for numeric operations. The language operators of PHP that are relevant to mathematics are fairly intuitive. $a + $b will add two variables together either as integers (if both are integers) or floats (if either are floats), casting as necessary (if possible). $a * $b will multiply the operands, and so on.

CHAPTER 7 NUMBERS

Arithmetic Operators

```
var_dump(1 + 2);
var_dump(2.1 - 1); // will cast 1 to 1.0 and return a float
var_dump('2' * '4.5'); // will cast both strings to floats and
                      return a float
var_dump(1_000_000 / 2); // special decimal integer syntax for readability
```

Output:
int(3)
float(1.1)
float(9)
int(500000)

That covers the four basic (or *radical*) mathematical operations: addition, subtraction, multiplication, and division. The final line uses a new decimal integer syntax introduced in PHP 7.4, which allows underscores, which are typically used to partition the number into thousands, like commas might be used when writing *1,000,000*.

The + and - operators can also be used to make changes to variables in the following way:

```
$intString = '12345';
$fltString = '123.4';
$num = 1;

$intString = +$intString;
$fltString = +$fltString;
$num = -$num;

var_dump($intString);
var_dump($fltString);
var_dump($num);
```

Output:
int(12345)
float(123.4)
int(-1)

377

CHAPTER 7 NUMBERS

The expression +$a converts $a to a numeric type (if possible, the usual type conversion rules apply), and -$num will make a positive number negative. Moving beyond the basics, we can work with exponents (calculating x^n) and perform modular arithmetic (calculating the remainder after division):

```
var_dump(2 ** 16);
var_dump(10 % 3);
```

Output:
```
int(65536)
int(1)
```

2 ** 16 gives us the sixteenth power of 2, which is 65536, and 10 / 3 is 3 with a remainder of 1.

Finally, there are operators for C-style increment and decrement: ++ and -, respectively:

```
$a = 1;
var_dump($a++);
var_dump($a);
var_dump(++$a);
```

Output:
```
int(1)
int(2)
int(3)
```

From the above we can see that $a++ increments the value after it has been evaluated in the expression (called *post-increment*), then on the final line, we use ++$a to increment before evaluation (*pre-increment*). Exchanging ++ for -- in the code above would adjust values by -1 but otherwise work the same way.

Using just this handful of operators, it is possible to construct all sorts of wonderful equations, but for the sake of convenience and your sanity, PHP comes loaded with many built-in functions, which we will be reviewing shortly.

Comparison Operators

Naturally, there will be many times when values need to be compared in order for your program to function correctly. We've already seen these in action (e.g., Chapter 4, "Logic and Control"), but let's quickly review comparison operators in the context of numbers and other numerical data:

```
$a = 1;
$b = 2;
$strA = '1';
$strB = '2';

var_dump($a == $b); // True if values are equal
var_dump($a == $strA); // True (string is cast to int)
var_dump($a === $strA); // True if values AND types are equal
var_dump($a != $b); // True if values are not equal
var_dump($a <> $b); // Same as !=
var_dump($a !== $strA); // True if values are not equal OR types are
                           different
var_dump($a < $b); // True if $a is less than $b
var_dump($a > $b); // True if $a is more than $b
var_dump($a <= $b); // True if $a is less than or equal to $b
var_dump($a >= $b); // True if $a is more than or equal to $b
var_dump($a <=> $b); // Returns -1, 0, or 1 if $a is less than, equal to,
                        or greater than $b
```

There are some potential pitfalls to be aware of when comparing numbers, especially when PHP's type coercion is triggered (e.g., when comparing an integer to a numerical string). Don't worry; we'll get to them soon.

Bitwise Operators

Binary operations are supported by PHP: operators exist to evaluate and manipulate data at a binary level. It should be noted that PHP is not an optimal language for bitwise operation due to limitations on how data is stored. Your code might only care about a small integer that can be represented as a single byte value (*255* or smaller), but PHP uses an internal C data structure called a zend_long to store it, and those are fixed at four or eight bytes in length depending on the platform.

Nevertheless, here's how to perform bitwise operations in PHP:

```
$allOnes = 0xFF; // int(255) uses 8 bytes for storage on 64-bit systems
print decbin($allOnes) . PHP_EOL;
print decbin($allOnes << 1) . PHP_EOL;
print decbin($allOnes >> 1) . PHP_EOL;
```

Output:
11111111
111111110
1111111

Here we've allocated a byte value of *0xFF* to $allOnes. Hexadecimal digits require four bits because there are sixteen of them. *1111* in binary is *F* in hexadecimal; therefore, *11111111* is *0xFF*, a byte with all bits set to *1*. The << operator is a *left shift*; it shunts all the bits one place to the left and sets the rightmost to zero, resulting in *111111110* (or *00000001 11111110* if you prefer). The inverse is *right-shift* >> and pushes all bits to the right, so we get *1111111* (*01111111*).

Essentially, a single left shift is a binary multiplication by two, and a single right shift is a binary division by two:

```
var_dump($allOnes);
var_dump($allOnes << 1);
var_dump($allOnes >> 1);
```

Output:
int(255)
int(510)
int(127)

Remember, these are binary integers, not decimal, so the right-shift gives us decimal *127*, not *127.5* (binary division and decimal division are quite different things). We'll cover the gory details of decimal vs. binary and integer vs. floating point in the next section. Another thing to note is how the "sign" bit is preserved. PHP uses IEEE signed integers; the leftmost bit of the most significant byte is used to set a number to positive or negative (and we'll look at this in more detail later too). For now, take a look at the following:

```
$num = -9223372036854775745;

print decbin($num) . PHP_EOL;
print decbin($num << 1) . PHP_EOL;
print decbin($num >> 1) . PHP_EOL;
var_dump($num << 1);
var_dump($num >> 1);
```

Output:
1000000000000000000000000000000000000000000000000000000000111111
1111110
1100000000000000000000000000000000000000000000000000000000011111
int(126)
int(-4611686018427387873)

At first glance you might not fully understand what's happening here. Bit shifting to the left turned our huge negative integer into a much smaller positive one! If left-shift multiplies by two, what happened?

The answer lies in the leftmost bit. Notice when we left shift, the leftmost *1* is set to the value on the left, which is *0*. This transforms the integer into a positive value, and also greatly affects the magnitude. As for the change in magnitude (from 10^{18} to 10^{2}), once you've read the section on limits and precision later on, you'll understand.

There are also logical bitwise operators - AND &, OR |, and XOR ^ - that can also be used for manipulation:

```
$leastSignificant = bindec('00011111');
$mostSignificant = bindec('11111000');

var_dump(decbin($mostSignificant & $leastSignificant));
var_dump(decbin($mostSignificant | $leastSignificant));
var_dump(decbin($mostSignificant ^ $leastSignificant));
```

Output:
string(5) "11000"
string(8) "11111111"
string(8) "11100111"

Here we have two binary values with five contiguous bits set: one with the most significant digits and one with least, which means only bits four and five are set in both. Bitwise AND ($mostSignificant & $leastSignificant) positionally compares the bits in each operand and sets the return bits to *1* where both are the same, so we get *00011000*. Bitwise OR ($mostSignificant | $leastSignificant) will set the return bits to *1* in each position where either operand has a bit set, so we get *11111111*. Finally, bitwise XOR ($mostSignificant ^ $leastSignificant) sets return bits to *1* in the positions where either operand has *1* set, but not both, so we get *11100111*.

Table 7-1. Bitwise operator effects

Operator:	AND &	OR |	XOR ^
Input 1:	11111000	11111000	11111000
Input 2:	00011111	00011111	00011111
Result:	00011000	11111111	11100111

Caution needs to be taken when using bitwise operations in expressions that also contain comparisons:

```
$leastSignificant = bindec('00011111');

var_dump($leastSignificant); // int(31)
var_dump($leastSignificant == true); // returns bool(true) which casts
                                     to int(1)
var_dump($leastSignificant ^ $leastSignificant == true); // equivalent to
                                                  00011111
                                                ^ 00000001
var_dump(($leastSignificant ^ $leastSignificant) == true); // equivalent to
                                                  00000000 == true
```

Output:
int(31)
bool(true)
int(30)
bool(false)

If you remember from the chapter on logic, the == operator has a higher precedence than the bitwise operators, so it is evaluated first. On the final line of the example above, we're testing the result of $leastSignificant ^ $leastSignificant. Because of the parentheses, the line above evaluates $leastSignificant == true before using the result of that in the bitwise XOR operation.

Finally, here's one more logical bitwise operator, which will also serve to illustrate the memory inefficiency of PHP for handling integer data at the bit level:

```
$num = bindec('11111111');
var_dump(decbin(~ $num));
var_dump(~ $num);
```

Output:
```
string(64)
"1111111111111111111111111111111111111111111111111111111100000000"
int(-256)
```

Here the operator is ~, which is (logically enough… sorry) the NOT operator. This flips every bit to its opposite value, so *1001* would become *0110* and so on. Except that in this case, we've ended up with rather a lot of ones on the left-hand side and a decimal value of *-256* instead of *0*. Why?

Well, remember at the beginning of the section it was stated that all integers are a C data type called *zend_long*? When we specified that we wanted an integer with the first eight bits set to *1* (giving a value of *0xFF* or decimal *255*), what PHP actually assigned in memory was this: *00000000 00000000 00000000 00000000 00000000 00000000 00000000 11111111*. The bitwise NOT of that 64-bit value is, of course, *11111111 11111111 11111111 11111111 11111111 11111111 11111111 00000000*, which is *-256* (you'll see why below).

Constants

There are several built-in PHP constants that provide easy access to commonly used mathematical constants such as *Pi* or *e*:

```
$r = 10;

var_dump(M_PI * $r ** 2);
```

Output:
```
float(314.1592653589793)
```

The full list of constants is as follows.

Table 7-2. Mathematical constants

Constant	Approximate Value	Description
M_PI	3.14159265358979323846	*pi*
M_E	2.7182818284590452354	*e*
M_LOG2E	1.4426950408889634074	*$log_2(e)$*
M_LOG10E	0.43429448190325182765	*$log_{10}(e)$*
M_LN2	0.69314718055994530942	*$log_e(2)$*
M_LN10	2.30258509299404568402	*$log_e(10)$*
M_LNPI	1.14472988584940017414	*$log_e(pi)$*
M_PI_2	1.57079632679489661923	*pi/2*
M_PI_4	0.78539816339744830962	*pi/4*
M_1_PI	0.31830988618379067154	*1/pi*
M_2_PI	0.63661977236758134308	*2/pi*
M_SQRTPI	1.77245385090551602729	*pi^{-2}*
M_2_SQRTPI	1.12837916709551257390	*$2/pi^{-2}$*
M_SQRT2	1.41421356237309504880	*2^{-2}*
M_SQRT3	1.73205080756887729352	*3^{-2}*
M_SQRT1_2	0.70710678118654752440	*0.5^{-2}*
M_EULER	0.57721566490153286061	Euler's constant γ

Built-In Functions

Finally, to round out the base language mathematical toolkit, PHP has many built-in functions of the kind you should expect to see in any general-purpose programming language. In addition to functions for performing common computations such as square roots, logarithms, or exponents of *e*, there are also utility functions (such as number base conversion, testing for infinite values, and so on). Most of them are wrappers around the equivalent function in C.

Here's the full list of core mathematical functions in PHP 8.

Table 7-3. Mathematical functions

Function	Description
abs(n)	Absolute value
acos(n)	Arc cosine
acosh(n)	Inverse hyperbolic cosine
asin(n)	Arc sine
asinh(n)	Inverse hyperbolic sine
atan2(n1, n2)	Arc tangent of two variables
atan(n)	Arc tangent
atanh(n)	Inverse hyperbolic tangent
ceil(n)	Round fractions up
cos(n)	Cosine
cosh(n)	Hyperbolic cosine
deg2rad(n)	Returns radian equivalent of n degrees
exp(n)	Calculates e^n
expm1(n)	exp(n) - 1, accurate when n close to 0
fdiv(n1, n2)	IEEE float division by zero non-fatal
floor(n)	Round fractions down
fmod(n)	Returns remainder (modulo) as float
hypot(n)	Returns hypotenuse of a RA triangle
intdiv(n1, n2)	Integer division
log10(n)	Base-10 logarithm
log1p(n)	log(1 + n), accurate when n close to 0
log(n, b)	Natural logarithm or log base b if set
max(n1, ...nX)	Find the highest value in all n
max(arr)	Find the highest value in array

(*continued*)

Table 7-3. (*continued*)

Function	Description
min(n1, ...nX)	Find the lowest value in all n
min(arr)	Find the lowest value in array
pi()	Get value of pi (returns M_PI)
pow(n1, n2)	Returns n1 ** n2
rad2deg(n)	Returns the degree equivalent of n radians
round(n)	Rounds a float n
sin(n)	Sine
sinh(n)	Hyperbolic sine
sqrt(n)	Square root
tan(n)	Tangent
tanh(n)	Hyperbolic tangent

These are the utility functions.

Table 7-4. Numerical utility functions

Function + params	Description
base_convert(s, n1, n2)	Numerical string n from base n1 to n2
bindec(s)	Binary string s to decimal int
decbin(n)	Decimal int n to binary string
dechex(n)	Decimal int n to hexadecimal string
decoct(n)	Decimal int n to octal string
hexdec(s)	Hexadecimal string s to decimal int
is_finite(x)	True if x is a legal finite number
is_infinite(x)	True if x is infinite (out of bounds)
is_nan(x)	True if x is not a number
octdec(s)	Octal string s to decimal int

Limits and Precision

Real numbers go on forever. Think of a number, the biggest you can imagine, then add one. See? (No, infinity does not count.) Computers, the electronic kind we know and love, do not possess arbitrarily large amounts of storage. There are limits on how big numbers can get before the limits of system architecture are hit.

There are (courtesy of the IEEE) standards concerning the representation of numbers in computer memory. Different combinations of hardware and operating systems mean there are differences in system limitations. PHP provides tools for accessing information about those limits.

Integers

Depending on the platform and PHP version, a PHP integer will either be 32 or 64 bits long (or alternatively 4 or 8 bytes long) and always signed (which means one of those bits is used to indicate if an int is negative or not). This means the maximum range of a PHP integer is either *-2,147,483,647* to *2,147,483,647* or *-9,223,372,036,854,775,808* to *9,223,372,036,854,775,808*. We can find out at run time what the integer limits are by using some built-in constants:

```
print PHP_INT_SIZE . PHP_EOL;
print PHP_INT_MAX . PHP_EOL;
print PHP_INT_MIN . PHP_EOL;
```

Output:
```
8
9223372036854775807
-9223372036854775808
```

Most computers today have 64-bit processors, and if your PHP binary is also 64-bit, then the value of PHP_INT_MAX will be the maximum signed integer value, and PHP_INT_SIZE will be "8" (because an IEEE 64-bit integer uses 8 bytes of memory). A 32-bit PHP binary running on a 64-bit system will have PHP_INT_SIZE of "4" regardless of hardware.

This is what happens if we're running on a 64-bit platform and exceed the maximum integer size:

```
$largeNum = PHP_INT_MAX;

var_dump($largeNum);
var_dump(++$largeNum);
```

Output:
int(9223372036854775807)
float(9.223372036854776E+18)

PHP has converted the number to a `float` type because it isn't possible to represent *9223372036854775808* as an 8-byte integer. This allows us to count beyond the PHP_INT_MAX limit, but at the cost of precision. Notice that we have lost some significant digits after the conversion. `9.223372036854776E+18` in standard index notation is *9.223372036854776 x 10^{18}*, which is *9223372036854776000*.

Without this change in data type, however, we would have a problem. When computers run out of bits to store ever larger integers, it triggers something called *integer overflow*. Think of it like a mechanical odometer on a car (if you're old enough to remember such things). As each number on the dial reaches nine, it spins back to the zero position and increments the next dial along. Eventually you run out of dials, and the entire odometer resets to zero. Some very old cars only stored five digits on theirs; when the mileage went to the next dial position from 99,999, it reset to 00,000. Something similar is happening in your computer's memory.

The 64-bit binary representation of PHP_INT_MAX is *01111111 11111111 11111111 1111111 11111111 11111111 11111111 11111111*. Remember, it is a signed integer, so the first bit is used for indicating positive or negative; in this case, it's set to zero. With signed integers, the leftmost bit is always negative, and its magnitude is equal to the largest number that can be represented with all the remaining bits set to "1". Therefore, for a 64-bit integer, the leftmost bit is equal to -2^{63}, or -9,223,372,036,854,775,808.

If we count one more than *01111111 11111111 11111111 1111111 11111111 11111111 11111111 11111111* we reach *10000000 00000000 00000000 00000000 00000000 00000000 00000000 00000000*, which in 64-bit-signed-integer-ese is *-9,223,372,036,854,775,808 - 0* (the value of the left-most bit minus the values of the remaining 63 bits). Let's convert a few numbers beyond *PHP_INT_MIN* to binary to demonstrate how this wonky machine counting is working:

```
print decbin(PHP_INT_MIN) . PHP_EOL;
print decbin(PHP_INT_MIN + 1) . PHP_EOL;
print decbin(PHP_INT_MIN + 2) . PHP_EOL;
print decbin(PHP_INT_MIN + 3) . PHP_EOL;
```

Output:
1000000000000000000000000000000000000000000000000000000000000000
1000000000000000000000000000000000000000000000000000000000000001
1000000000000000000000000000000000000000000000000000000000000010
1000000000000000000000000000000000000000000000000000000000000011

Hopefully this shows clearly how, as we start counting back toward zero from -2^{63}, we accumulate bits on the least significant (rightmost) side. This is why PHP is casting integers to floats when they exceed PHP_INT_MAX. Loss of precision can be a pain if not properly understood and managed, but integer overflow is by comparison catastrophic to calculations. It is relatively easy to break calculations, like this, for example:

```
$largeNum = PHP_INT_MAX + 1;
dumpLargeNum((int) $largeNum);

function dumpLargeNum(int $num): void
{
    var_dump($num);
}
```

Output:
int(-9223372036854775808)

The corollary to counting beyond PHP_INT_MAX is, of course, counting in reverse beyond PHP_INT_MIN, and logically the same problem integer overflow problem exists:

```
$largeNum = PHP_INT_MIN - 2000; // because loss of precision with float
dumpLargeNum((int) $largeNum);

function dumpLargeNum(int $num): void
{
    var_dump($num);
}
```

Output:
int(9223372036854773760)

Floats

Floats exist to handle numbers that have fractional components, i.e., numbers with a decimal point such as *1.729*. In addition, if we need to deal with very big numbers, we need floats for those too, and we've just seen how numbers are automatically converted to floats when they exceed PHP_INT_MAX. Why would this be the case? What can a float do that an int can't?

Floating-point numbers (as defined by the IEEE-754 standard) have three components: a sign bit, bits to represent a *mantissa*, and bits for the *exponent*. If you remember the scientific notation from the "Number Systems" section of this chapter, it had two numeric portions separated by an "E" character, the rightmost digits being the power(s) of ten that the leftmost were multiplied by (thus `1.729E3` = *1.729 * 10³ = 1729*). The mantissa (or *magnitude*) is the left-hand number and the exponent is the right-hand. For a 64-bit floating-point number, 1 bit is used for the sign, 52 bits are used for the mantissa, and the remaining 11 for the exponent.

This means floats can store decimal numbers that have hundreds of powers of ten, far greater in magnitude than the 64-bit *PHP_INT_MAX* (which tops out at eighteen powers of ten), but at the cost of precision: the mantissa can only reliably store up to fifteen significant digits (some sixteen-digit decimal numbers can be represented in 52 bits, but not all of them). Just like integers, floating-point numbers come with their own caveats and limitations:

```
print PHP_FLOAT_MAX . PHP_EOL;
print PHP_FLOAT_MIN . PHP_EOL;
print PHP_FLOAT_DIG . PHP_EOL;
```

Output:
1.7976931348623E+308
2.2250738585072E-308
15

Logically, of course, there are upper and lower limits on float size, for exactly the same reasons as there are integer limits. The values of PHP_FLOAT_MAX and PHP_FLOAT_MIN depend on the platform running PHP (32-bit vs. 64-bit), just as before. The constant

PHP_FLOAT_DIG is the number of digits that can be rounded in a float without precision loss. In other words, the maximum number of digits allowed in the mantissa before we need to worry about rounding errors:

```
$num = 1234567890123456; // 1.234567890123456 x 10 ** 15 fifteen
                                        decimal digits
$floatNum = (float) $num;
var_dump($num); // int(1234567890123456)
var_dump($floatNum); // float(1234567890123456)
var_dump((int) $floatNum); // int(1234567890123456)

$num = 12345678901234567; // 1.2345678901234567 x 10 ** 15 sixteen
                                        decimal digits
$floatNum = (float) $num;
var_dump($num); // int(12345678901234567)
var_dump($floatNum); // float(12345678901234568)
var_dump((int) $floatNum); // int(12345678901234568) rounding error
                                        is present
```

Output:
```
int(1234567890123456)
float(1234567890123456)
int(1234567890123456)
int(12345678901234567)
float(12345678901234568)
int(12345678901234568)
```

Let's play a bit more and see what else we can break:

```
$largeFloat = PHP_FLOAT_MAX;

var_dump($largeFloat + 1);
var_dump($largeFloat + 1E291);
var_dump($largeFloat + 1E292);
```

Output:
```
float(1.7976931348623157E+308)
float(1.7976931348623157E+308)
float(INF)
```

The code above shows that (on a 64-bit platform) when managed to exceed PHP_FLOAT_MAX, the float $largeFloat has been given a special value of INF (INF is also a built-in constant). Think of this as meaning "too big" rather than true infinity: the number is now simply too big to represent using the IEEE float format. The floating-point specification IEEE-754 uses similar (but more complex) bit trickery to the signed integer: one bit for the sign, 11 bits for the exponent (the powers of ten in standard index), and the remaining bits for the mantissa (the significant digits of the number). Once we've run out of bits, all we can do is flag the value as exceeding limits.

Here are a few examples of how float(INF) behaves in code:

```
$largeFloat = PHP_FLOAT_MAX + 1E292;

var_dump($largeFloat);
var_dump(is_numeric($largeFloat));
var_dump(is_infinite($largeFloat));
var_dump($largeFloat - PHP_FLOAT_MAX);
var_dump($largeFloat / PHP_FLOAT_MAX);
var_dump($largeFloat / $largeFloat);
var_dump($largeFloat / (PHP_FLOAT_MAX + 1E292));
```

Output:
```
float(INF)
bool(true)
bool(true)
float(INF)
float(INF)
float(NAN)
float(NAN)
```

We can see that once a number hits float(INF), there's no coming back. Much like how infinity behaves in mathematics. The built-in functions is_numeric() and is_infinite() both return true: the data type is still float, and is_infinite() exists purely to test for floats that have exceeded their bounds.

The last two lines are interesting though: they have the value float(NAN), which stands for "not a number." Like the constant INF, PHP also provides a built-in constant of NAN. Strictly speaking, infinity is not a number either, and either INF or NAN values are an indicator that your code is off the rails. The presence of either in a calculation will result in INF, -INF, NAN, or occasionally zero as a result:

```
var_dump(1 / INF); // float(0)
var_dump(NAN * INF); // float(NAN)
var_dump(INF / NAN); // float(NAN)
```

Output:
float(0)
float(NAN)
float(NAN)

As well as numbers so big they are treated as infinite, it is possible to have numbers so infinitesimally small that they cannot be expressed as floats any more. When this happens, the value is simply changed to zero:

```
$tinyFloat = PHP_FLOAT_MIN;

var_dump($tinyFloat);
var_dump($tinyFloat / 10);
var_dump($tinyFloat / 1E3);
var_dump($tinyFloat / 1E15);
var_dump($tinyFloat / 1E16);
```

Output:
float(2.2250738585072014E-308)
float(2.225073858507203E-309)
float(2.225073858507E-311)
float(2.5E-323)
float(0)

Notice that as we accumulate values on the exponent (by dividing by powers of ten), we lose precision in the mantissa. This enables us to go beyond the limits of 10^{-308}, which might feel counter-intuitive: after all, 10^{-308} is larger than 10^{-323}. Think of PHP_INT_MIN as the smallest float available with maximum PHP_FLOAT_DIG precision.

Floating-Point Precision

Now for some fun. Take a look at this.

```
var_dump((0.1 + 0.7) * 10);
```

CHAPTER 7 NUMBERS

Looks pretty straightforward, right? The answer should be *8* in a sane world? Well on most systems the result of that calculation is actually something like float(7.999999999999999). Which is definitely very close to *8*, so we could give it a pass? How about this:

var_dump(floor((0.1 + 0.7) * 10));

Output:
float(7)

This error arises because certain rational decimal numbers (that have a finite number of decimal digits, unlike, say, *pi*) cannot be accurately represented with floats, because the binary equivalent is irrational. *0.1* and *0.7* are two of them. The binary representation of these numbers is only approximate. As more operations are performed with floats, the possibility grows of accumulated precision errors. These often become most apparent during comparison:

```
$bankBalance = 50.00;
$bankBalance -= 49.95;
$bankBalance -= 0.05;

if ($bankBalance < 0.0) {
    echo "Overdraft fees!" . PHP_EOL;
}
var_dump($bankBalance);
```

Output:
Overdraft fees!
float(-2.8449465006019636E-15)

In the imaginary scenario above, we have some code that uses floats to maintain a bank balance and a test to see if the balance drops below zero. Despite having enough funds to cover the two debits, we still fall into the overdraft fees trap. And this is why financial apps tend to work internally with integer values of the smallest currency units.

We can summarize the problems that IEEE floats have as follows:

- Significant digits are limited; therefore, all irrational numbers (like *1/3* or *pi*) are rounded to an approximation

- Some rational decimal numbers (like 0.1 in Base-10) cannot be represented precisely with the binary floating-point system (in Base-2)
- Comparison sometimes yields unexpected results, as do functions like floor() and ceil()

What can we do about it? Well, there's always rounding; that's pretty intuitive. Straight away, though, we run into problems with that. PHP supports four different rounding strategies with the built-in function round():

```
var_dump(round(1.55, 1, PHP_ROUND_HALF_UP)); // If omitted, third argument
                                             defaults to this
var_dump(round(1.55, 1, PHP_ROUND_HALF_DOWN));
var_dump(round(1.55, 1, PHP_ROUND_HALF_EVEN));
var_dump(round(1.55, 1, PHP_ROUND_HALF_ODD));
```

Output:
float(1.6)
float(1.5)
float(1.6)
float(1.5)

In addition to needing to manage rounding strategies across your code, there's also some juggling to do with the second parameter of round(), which is the required precision (the number of decimal digits to round to). If you're handling very small numbers, the required precision is correspondingly large:

```
var_dump(round(1.51E-10, 10));
var_dump(round(1.51E-10, 11));
var_dump(round(1.51E-100, 100));
var_dump(round(1.51E-100, 101));
```

Output:
float(2.0E-10)
float(1.5E-10)
float(2.0E-100)
float(1.5E-100)

CHAPTER 7   NUMBERS

A good alternative to rounding is instead to test the significance of the difference between two floats. To do this we first need a special number, which is the system *epsilon*. This is the smallest floating-point number that satisfies *x + 1.0 != 1.0*. In other words, the epsilon is the smallest float we can add to 1.0 so that it no longer equals 1.0. This number will of course vary between 32-bit and 64-bit systems and is accessible via the built-in constant PHP_FLOAT_EPSILON.

One way to compare floats for equivalence (not equality) is to take the absolute value of their difference and compare to epsilon:

```
$a = 0.8;
$b = 0.1 + 0.7;
$absoluteDiff = abs($a - $b);

if ($absoluteDiff < PHP_FLOAT_EPSILON) {
    print "Float values are equivalent..." . PHP_EOL;
    var_dump(PHP_FLOAT_EPSILON);
    var_dump($absoluteDiff);
}
```

Output:
```
Float values are equivalent...
float(2.220446049250313E-16)
float(1.1102230246251565E-16)
```

Which is fine for tiny numbers but does not work well for very large floats:

```
$a = PHP_FLOAT_MAX;
//    1.7976931348623157E+308 = PHP_FLOAT_MAX (64bit)
$b = 1.7976931348623156E+308;

var_dump(abs($b - $a)); // absolute
```

Output:
```
float(1.99584030953472E+292)
```

Even though our two numbers are equivalent to the 15th significant digit, the absolute difference is in the order of 10^{292}! What we really need to do is compare the *relative difference* to epsilon, which factors in the magnitude of the comparison:

```
$a = PHP_FLOAT_MAX;
//   1.7976931348623157E+308 = PHP_FLOAT_MAX (64bit)
$b = 1.7976931348623156E+308;

var_dump(abs(($a - $b) / $b)); // relative
var_dump(PHP_FLOAT_EPSILON);
```

Output:
float(1.1102230246251568E-16)
float(2.220446049250313E-16)

Now we're using a relative calculation, we can see that actually the two numbers are very close and within system epsilon.

There are other algorithms for float comparison, such as this one from the legendary Donald Knuth:

```
$a = PHP_FLOAT_MAX;
//   1.7976931348623157E+308 = PHP_FLOAT_MAX (64bit)
$b = 1.7976931348623156E+308;

if (
    abs($a - $b) <= PHP_FLOAT_EPSILON * $a  &&
    abs($a - $b) <= PHP_FLOAT_EPSILON * $b
) {
    print "Two largest floats are equivalent" . PHP_EOL;
}
```

Output:
Two largest floats are equivalent

There is far more to floating-point arithmetic than I have covered here, but hopefully I've given enough information to highlight the care and attention required when working with numbers like this. The next time you encounter someone tearing into PHP for its terrible bugs when working with floats, feel free to enlighten that person by laying the blame at the feet of the IEEE and hardware vendors! Every single issue with floats demonstrated here exists in C and all the languages implemented in it.

CHAPTER 7 NUMBERS

Random Numbers

Randomness is highly useful in applications, whether you're working with simulations or cryptography. PHP offers a range of functions to generate random data for multiple use cases.

Let's look at two of the earliest to be implemented in PHP (version 4!): rand() and mt_rand():

```
var_dump(rand()); // random int between 0 and a system-dependent maximum
var_dump(mt_rand(0, 6)); // random int, min 0 and max 6
var_dump(rand(-1, 1)); // random int min -1 and max 1
var_dump(getrandmax()); // varies with platform
var_dump(mt_getrandmax()); // varies with platform
```

Output:
```
int(549992859)
int(4)
int(-1)
int(2147483647)
int(2147483647)
```

The final two lines will output int(2147483647) on a non-Windows platform. mt_rand() uses a different, faster algorithm than rand(), and since PHP 7.1 mt_rand() has replaced rand(). (rand() is still a valid function name but is now an alias of mt_rand()).

If a random float between 0 and 1 is required, the function lcg_value() will provide it for you:

```
var_dump(lcg_value());
```

Output:
```
float(0.2606030773622016)
```

Note that when specifying min and max value arguments, they must lie between 0 and the value of getrandmax() or risk impacting the randomness of the result. Herein lies a problem with random numbers generated by machines. Generating a random number on a machine designed for calculating and ordering number sequences is not a simple task. In the case of rand(), mt_rand(), and lcg_value(), the values of the output are potentially predictable and therefore not suited for any kind of cryptographic use.

CHAPTER 7 NUMBERS

There are generally two approaches to random number generation (RNG): software-based and hardware-based. Software generation relies on deterministic algorithms (behavior is determined by input, passing through the same states) and is predictable. For this reason, software-based RNG is often called *pseudorandom*. In contrast, hardware-based RNG uses unpredictable (at least over the short term) physical processes such as isotope decay or radio static.

On Linux systems the special file /dev/urandom collects noise from hardware (via the device drivers) and is usually what is used by PHP's cryptographically secure random number functions. Let's take a look at random_bytes() and random_int():

```
var_dump(random_int(0, 100));
var_dump(random_int(0, getrandmax()));
var_dump(random_bytes(1));
var_dump(random_bytes(8));
```

Output:
```
int(89)
int(1212946012)
string(1) "?"
string(8) "y./vGp?"
```

Naturally, the output varies on each execution (with true randomness!), but you get the idea. random_int() always requires a min and max argument, and random_bytes() always requires a length argument. Now you can enjoy cryptographically secure random numbers whenever you need them.

In addition to the built-in functions, PHP 8.2 also introduced an OOP interface for random numbers as part of its core. The new API is available in the built-in \Random namespace (for more info on namespaces and objects, see Chapter 6, "Object Fundamentals"). Here are a few examples; feel free to read up on how classes and objects work if you need to and return to this section:

```
$randomizer = new \Random\Randomizer();

var_dump($randomizer->getInt(0, 100));
var_dump($randomizer->getBytes(8));
```

Output:
```
int(30)
string(8) "???W?9"
```

CHAPTER 7 NUMBERS

As you can see, the output looks very much like that from the previous example (random_bytes() and random_int()), and that's because those functions are wrappers around the Randomizer class. By default, the Randomizer uses a crypto-secure engine to generate numbers, but others can be specified during instantiation should you want or need to:

```
// Mersenne Twister engine - NOT crypto secure
$randomizer = new \Random\Randomizer(new \Random\Engine\Mt19937());
```

Using the Randomizer class like this provides additional functionality over the secure functions we've already looked at:

```
var_dump($randomizer->nextInt());
var_dump($randomizer->shuffleBytes('I love random numbers'));

$arr = ['I', 'love', 'random', 'numbers'];

var_dump($randomizer->shuffleArray($arr));
$keys = $randomizer->pickArrayKeys($arr, 2);
foreach ($keys as $k) {
    print $arr[$k] . ' ';
}
```

Output:
```
int(2990379820754061450)
string(21) "eb   vemosannrd olruIm"
array(4) {
  [0]=>
  string(1) "I"
  [1]=>
  string(6) "random"
  [2]=>
  string(4) "love"
  [3]=>
  string(7) "numbers"
}
```

Extensions

We've covered the bulk of PHP's core "Math" API, and that should be sufficient for any trivial use case and quite a few non-trivial ones too. If the time comes, however, when the core toolkit is proving to hinder rather than help your work, there are some PHP extensions available. The two extensions that we're going to look at here might not be installed on your system; you can check by running the following command:

```
$ php -m
Output:
[PHP Modules]
bcmath
Core
...
gmp
...
xmlwriter
zlib
```

For the examples in the section to work, the modules bcmath and gmp need to be listed in the output. See Chapter 1, "Getting Started," for information on installing language extensions if you don't see these modules listed.

BCMath

BCMath exists for when you simply need to deal with numbers that are too big even for a 64-bit system. It allows the manipulation of arbitrary precision numbers (integers and decimals) as numeric strings. Numerical strings will also work but emit a warning error.

CHAPTER 7 NUMBERS

Table 7-5. BCMath functions

Function + params	Description
bcadd(s1, s2, d)	Add strings s1 and s2, optional d decimal digits
bcsub(s1, s2, d)	Subtract s2 from s1, optional d
bcmul(s1, s2, d)	Multiply s1 and s2, optional d
bcdiv(s1, s2, d)	Divide s1 by s2, optional d
bcmod(s1, s2, d)	Modulus of s1/s2, optional d
bcpow(s1, s2, d)	s1 ** s2, optional d
bcpowmod(s1, s2, m, d)	bcmod(bcpow(s1, s2), m);, optional d
bcsqrt(s, d)	s $^{-2}$, optional d
bccomp(s1, s2)	-1 (s1 < s2,) or 0 (s1 == s1) or 1 (s1 > s2)
bcscale(n)	Set decimal digits for subsequent bc func calls

Let's take a look at some of those functions:

```
$largeNum = (string) PHP_INT_MAX;
$largeNum .= '00000000000000000000';
$largerNum = $largeNum . '0';

var_dump(bcadd($largeNum, $largeNum));
var_dump(bcdiv($largeNum, 11));
var_dump(bcdiv($largeNum, 11, 4));
var_dump(bcmod($largeNum, 11));
var_dump(bcpow($largeNum, 2));

var_dump(bccomp($largeNum, $largeNum));
var_dump(bccomp($largeNum, $largerNum));
var_dump(bccomp($largerNum, $largeNum));

// BC Math handles decimal point numbers
var_dump(bcadd('100.01', '100.02', 2));
```

```
bcscale(1); // we need everything to 1 d.p. for the next calls
// Remember 0.1 + 0.7 != 0.8 in floating point arithmetic?
$trickyFloat = bcadd('0.1', '0.7');
var_dump(bccomp($trickyFloat, '0.8')); // now it does!

Output:
string(40) "1844674407370955161400000000000000000000"
string(38) "83848836698679780063636363636363636363"
string(43) "83848836698679780063636363636363636363.6363"
string(1) "7"
string(78) "850705917302346158473969077842325012490000000000000000000000000000000000000000"
int(0)
int(-1)
int(1)
string(6) "200.03"
int(0)
```

Hopefully everything above is self-explanatory. Note that our gotcha from floating-point arithmetic (*0.1 + 0.7* giving a result of *0.7999999999999999*) is handled just fine by bcadd() and bccomp() on the final two lines. Now you can enjoy stupidly large numbers *and* rational numbers that break IEEE floating point. Remember that BCMath is intended to deal with string representations of numbers; mixing these functions with PHP's core mathematical functions and operators might yield unexpected results. At best the giant numbers output from BCMath will be cast to floats with all the caveats that come thereafter.

```
$largeNum = (string) PHP_INT_MAX;
$largeNum .= '0000000000000000000';
var_dump($largeNum - 1);

$veryLargeNum = $largeNum . str_repeat('0000000000', 30);
var_dump($veryLargeNum + 1);

Output:
float(9.223372036854776E+38)
float(INF)
```

CHAPTER 7 NUMBERS

GMP

Another arbitrary-length number library is GMP, which is focused purely on integer mathematics. GMP is based on the GNU Multiple Precision library and is more richly featured than BCMath. GMP offers dozens of functions; let's take a look at a selection:

```
$largeNum = (string) PHP_INT_MAX;

print gmp_add($largeNum, $largeNum) . PHP_EOL;
var_dump(gmp_binomial($largeNum, 2)); // Binomial coefficient C(n, k)
var_dump(gmp_nextprime(PHP_INT_MAX));

$bin1 = gmp_init('00011111', 2);
$bin2 = gmp_init('11111000', 2);

var_dump(gmp_hamdist($bin1, $bin2)); // The Hamming distance between two
                                     //                 binary numbers
```

```
Output:
18446744073709551614
object(GMP)#1 (1) {
  ["num"]=>
  string(38) "42535295865117307919086767873688862721"
}
object(GMP)#1 (1) {
  ["num"]=>
  string(19) "9223372036854775837"
}
int(6)
```

I've picked a few random and/or interesting functions to look at. gmp_add() does what it says and adds numbers. Just like BCMath, any number larger than PHP_INT_MAX needs to be a string or a GMP number class, which is returned by gmp_init() if you need to build one manually and generally returned by most GMP functions. GMP functions usually accept a range of types: GMP objects, strings, ints, etc. The GMP class itself is castable to a string: the return value of gmp_add() is a GMP object, but it will happily behave as a string or number in an expression.

We've only scratched the surface of GMP here; the official PHP documentation for this extension is a good place to start for further info.

https://www.php.net/manual/en/book.gmp.php

There are also extensions for statistics (based on DCDFLIB and RANDLIB) in case you're in need of a cheeky chi-square or t-test, and financial trading (based on TA-Lib) if phrases such as "three-line strike" or "time series forecast" tend to crop up at your day job. These are quite specialized, as you'd expect, and beyond the scope of this text. Again, your starting point is the official PHP documentation.

https://www.php.net/manual/en/book.stats.php
https://www.php.net/manual/en/book.trader.php

Type Coercion

In Chapter 2, "Data, Types, and Variables," we saw how strings could be converted to numbers and vice versa. Previous versions of PHP had some problems with numeric and numerical strings (numeric means "all characters are digits," numerical means "some characters are digits") that could lead to security problems.

Explicitly Casting Strings to Numbers

Casting a numeric string (containing only valid number digits) to a number is straightforward; just remember that the only base support is Base 10. Numerical strings (containing non-digits or partially invalid digits) are a little trickier:

```
var_dump((int) 'speed: 100.1 mph'); // alphabet characters
                                    encountered first
var_dump((int) '100.1 mph'); // decimal point ignored
var_dump((float) "\t 100.1 mph"); // decimal point included
var_dump((float) '1,000,000'); // decimal 1000000 in common format
var_dump((int) '1f'); // hexadecimal 31
var_dump((int) 'ff'); // hexadecimal 255
var_dump((int) '0xff'); // same but using common hex notation
var_dump((int) '1111'); // binary 16
var_dump((int) '012'); // octal 10
```

CHAPTER 7 NUMBERS

Output:
int(0)
int(100)
float(100.1)
float(1)
int(1)
int(0)
int(0)
int(1111)
int(12)

Here we are processing an assortment of numerical strings. We're explicitly casting most of them to integers (with one example casting to a float). In order for PHP to successfully convert a string to a number, the first character encountered must be a digit, with a few caveats. Leading spaces, tabs, and the various new-line characters are fine, as demonstrated on line three with the string "\t 100.1 mph" (a tab character and a space prepend the numeric portion of the string). PHP will continue to convert the string until it hits a non-digit character, the exception to this rule being the decimal point: if PHP is attempting to cast to a float, then a single decimal point is included along with all digits immediately following. If casting to an integer, a decimal point will end the conversion.

Thus, 'speed: 100.1 mph casts to *0* (the value for any non-numerical string), '100.1' casts to (integer) *100* or (float) *100.1*, and '1,000,000' casts to *1* (numeric type casting is not aware of number formatting). The remaining examples demonstrate attempts to cast numbers from different base systems (hexadecimal, binary, and octal). In all cases the conversion rules remain the same, and they are treated as Base 10 in PHP 8 (although PHP was actually capable of converting hexadecimal strings until version 7.0, this "feature" was removed).

At the beginning of the section I mentioned that numerical type juggling could lead to security problems; let's look at one. Imagine we have a secret stored somewhere, a hexadecimal string generated from a hashing algorithm like SHA256. We compare this to a user-supplied token, which is submitted to our application as a JSON data structure; if they match, then access is granted. What could possibly go wrong if that secret hash string began with a '0'? Quite a bit, as it turns out.

```
$secretHexValue = 'b94d27b9934d3e08a52e52d7da7dabfac484efe37a5380ee9088f7ace2efcde9';
$userInput = '{ "token": 0 }';
```

```
$userData = json_decode($userInput, true);

var_dump($userData);

if ($secretHexValue == $userData['token']) {
    print "I just got hacked :(" . PHP_EOL;
}
Output: (PHP 7.4)
array(1) {
  ["token"]=>
  int(0)
}
I just got hacked :(
```

In the code above, the built-in json_decode() function is used to transform the $userData JSON string to an associative array. JSON supports a limited set of data types, and in this case "token": 0 means the "token" property has an integer value *0* (which is confirmed in the var_dump() output).

Our hypothetical hacker is passing a malicious JSON payload, and the loosely typed comparison between $secretHexValue and $userData['token'] results in the secret string being cast to an integer. It's true that this vulnerability will only trigger under certain conditions (the secret hash string needs to have either leading '0' digits followed by a letter or the letters A-F as the first character, and it will cast to *0*), so it's only a vulnerability some of the time. But hackers are persistent, and eventually they'll get you...

This demonstration might look like a lot of the rest of the code in this book (contrived to demonstrate a single point), but it is actually a simplified version of a real-world exploit that existed in the Laravel framework some years ago (one that compromised cross-site request forgery protection).

The same code running under PHP 8 would not trigger the issue: the rules around type coercion and loosely typed comparison are different from previous versions (we'll take a closer look in a moment). Another fix is, of course, to use a strongly typed comparison between $secretHexValue and the malicious token value.

```
if ($secretHexValue === $userData['token']) {
```

This is a much safer check between the two variables; always use strict comparison when dealing with user input. Input validation is also essential: if we'd tested the user-supplied token's data type to make sure it was a string, we would have been alerted to problems before comparison. Input validation is something we will explore in Chapter 11, "Programming for the Internet."

Comparison Coercion

The security issue demonstrated above was triggered by a loosely typed comparison, and historically, this has been a source of bugs and confusion. PHP will coerce strings on both sides of a comparison to numbers if they are numeric:

```
var_dump('0e1' == '0e2');
var_dump('0e1' === '0e2');
var_dump('0e1' == '0');
var_dump('0e1' === '0');
```

```
Output:
bool(true)
bool(false)
bool(true)
bool(false)
```

We're comparing two scientific notation strings (which represent the floats *0.0* and *0.00*) and a scientific notation string to an integer string (*0.0* and *0*). You can see that in both cases a loosely typed comparison evaluates to true, but the strongly typed comparison is false.

Naturally, if one of the operands is a number type, the string will be coerced. However, a new feature of PHP 8 is that it will only coerce numeric strings in these cases; numerical strings (containing non-digit characters) are not due to the historic issues around numerical coercion. If you wish to loosely compare a numerical string to a number, it is now necessary to explicitly cast it first.

```
var_dump('100' == 100);
var_dump('100 monkeys' == 100);
var_dump((int) '100 monkeys' == 100);
```

```
Output: (PHP 7.4)
bool(true)
bool(true)
bool(true)

Output: (PHP 8.4)
bool(true)
bool(false)
bool(true)
```

It is best practice to use strongly typed comparison, especially in matters of security, and explicit type casting. Be cautious with type juggling! For more detail on comparison rules, see Chapter 4, "Logic and Control."

Summary

Hopefully you now have a strong grasp of how to make numbers work for you in PHP. We've covered the main pitfalls of numeric computation on silicon. The problems highlighted in this chapter are not PHP's "fault" as such; the limits are generally imposed lower down in the system.

We've seen what happens out there at the edges of 64-bit floating-point arithmetic, or when rational decimals don't have rational binary counterparts, and some strategies to mitigate those problems. The BCMath and GMP extensions can help out greatly when large numbers need precise calculations, and I've signposted other extensions to help any of you working with stats or trading data.

Finally, we looked at PHP's type coercion system in the context of numbers and the potential issues therein. I hope I've made a case for type safety in your future programming adventures.

The open source community is a great place to start if your use case isn't covered here. Linear algebra, complex numbers, matrices, and cryptography (especially) are all areas of interest in some sections of the PHP community. Go forth and enjoy yourselves! The sky's the limit (the sky is not represented by a 64-bit integer).

CHAPTER 8

Strings

Computers, as I'm sure you are aware, are designed to manipulate numbers – in fact, they're brilliant at it, and it's why we invented them. However, a jobbing programmer (like yours truly) making their living on the good old internet tends to spend most of their working day handling text. Unless you're working in some financial sector, you likely won't have to perform very many numerical tasks, and those that do crop up tend to require a level of math you likely acquired around the age of eleven. (On one occasion in my career, I needed to implement some linear algebra, but it was over twenty years ago, hasn't happened again, and I didn't use PHP for it.)

In Chapter 7, "Numbers," we saw a variety of PHP features (both core and extended) for crunching numbers in lots of fun ways, and the good news is there are plenty of tools in the box for crunching text with PHP as well. Personally, I prefer PHP over many other languages for manipulating text, especially if I need to do so in the context of web applications. PHP was invented to make backend (hyper) text processing easier. It's literally in the name: "PHP: Hypertext Preprocessor" (admittedly a retcon but a good one). PHP isn't necessarily the quickest tool for some forms of string processing, but it has many features to make back-end web development less of a headache.

This chapter is a deep dive into all things concerning the handling of the `string` data type, which was introduced in Chapter 2, "Data, Types, and Variables," and has been used throughout the book so far in many of the code examples. If you haven't read that chapter yet, then I strongly recommend that you do; this chapter builds on the concepts discussed there. In this chapter we will cover the following topics:

- Creating strings
- Manipulating strings
- Operations and built-in functions
- Encoding
- Multi-byte strings

- Binary safety
- Cryptography
- Regular expressions
- Language extensions

Making and Manipulating Strings

Strings are everywhere in this book; you'll have already seen many examples of their use, but let's get the formalities out of the way in one place. The basic syntax for creating string literals is straightforward. There are four ways to do it: single-quoted, double-quoted, *heredoc*, and *nowdoc*. Let's look at quoted strings first.

Quoted Strings

```
$str = 'I am a string';
$anotherStr = "So am I";
```

Both of the above forms do the same thing: create a string with the contents set to the text inside the quotes. The difference between these two forms is that double-quoted strings have some extra features.

Variable Interpolation (Substitution)

Double-quoted strings allow the interpolation of variables. A variable inside a double-quoted string will be substituted for its value (with the caveat that the variable must exist in the same lexical scope as the string, naturally). The example below also uses the string concatenation operator . with the PHP_EOL constant, which outputs the appropriate newline sequence for your system – there's a lot more to come on those in this chapter. Here's the most important difference between the two quote styles:

```
$str = 'world';
print 'Hello $str' . PHP_EOL; // $str isn't interpolated
print "Hello $str" . PHP_EOL; // Value of $str is inserted into the string
```

Output:
Hello $str
Hello world

It is also possible to use more complex variable expressions if they are wrapped in brace characters, such as array elements or object properties:

```
$array = [
    'interpolation',
    'a_key' => 'test',
];

$obj = new class
{
    public string $prop = 'String';
};

print "{$obj->prop} {$array[0]} {$array['a_key']}" . PHP_EOL;
```

Output:
String interpolation test

There are some slightly wonky rules around what you can get away with when using the complex interpolation syntax. Functions can be used, but only if they return the name of a variable (which is then interpolated); the return value itself can't be interpolated:

```
function strange(): string
{
    return 'wibble';
}

$wibble = 'an odd design choice';

print "This is {strange()}" . PHP_EOL;
print "This is {${strange()}}" . PHP_EOL;
```

Output:
This is {strange()}
This is an odd design choice

However, object method call return data *can* be used for interpolation:

```
$obj = new class
{
    public function fine(): string
    {
        return 'And this is just fine!';
    }
};
print "{$obj->fine()}" . PHP_EOL;
```

Output:
And this is just fine!

There used to be a noticeable performance penalty with double-quoted strings in older versions of PHP, but things have improved over the years. There is still a slight overhead in both processing and memory use, though, so it's considered better practice to use double quotes only when you need their additional utility.

Special Character Escapes

Another useful feature of double-quoted strings is that they allow escape sequences. Certain special characters can be represented by a combination of a backslash character followed by a particular letter...

Table 8-1. String letter escape sequences

Sequence	Character
\n	linefeed LF *0x0A*
\r	carriage return CR *0x0D*
\t	horizontal tab HT *0x09*
\v	vertical tab VT *0x0B*
\e	escape ESC *0x1B*
\f	form feed FF *0x0C*

... or symbol:

Table 8-2. String symbol escape sequences

Sequence	Character
\\	backslash
\$	dollar
\"	double-quote

Some of the non-printing control characters are rarely seen in the wild, but tabs and linefeeds are fairly ubiquitous. Here's a quick demo of how these escapes work:

```
$hello = "Hello world.";

print "\"Lorem ipsum\" is standard text for testing typographic
systems.\n";
print "The variable \$hello has a value of \"{$hello}\"" . PHP_EOL;
print "Vertical\vtabs\vdo\vthis. Here is a backslash: \\" . PHP_EOL;
```

Output:
```
"Lorem ipsum" is standard text for testing typographic systems.
The variable $hello has a value of "Hello world."
Vertical
        tabs
            do
                this. Here is a backslash: \
```

Note that the first line of output uses a single \n linefeed character; on Linux (or similar) systems and any web browser, this will move the cursor to the next line, but on Windows systems it does not: Windows has historically used \r\n characters to denote a line ending in text. (This is why I have used the built-in constant PHP_EOL throughout this book, because it will always produce the correct line endings for the platform the code runs on – more to come on string constants shortly.)

Numeric Escape Sequences

There are also escape sequences for setting character byte values directly, using octal or hexadecimal notation:

```
print "\110\145\154\154\157 " .
   "\x57\x6f\x72\x6c\x64" . PHP_EOL;
```

Output:
Hello World

Octal escapes take the form "\N" where N is a valid octal value for an 8-bit byte; hexadecimal escapes are similar: "\xN" where N is a valid 8-bit hexadecimal value. (If you're not sure how to use numbers in base 8 or 16, see Chapter 7, "Numbers," for a detailed explanation.) The "Hello" portion of the output was produced with escaped octal values. Octal *110* is *72* in decimal, and codepoint *72* in the ASCII codepage is the capital letter "H," octal *145* is lowercase "e," and so on. "World" was produced in a similar way: hexadecimal *0x57* is ASCII capital "W," etc.

Because these are 8-bit bytes, the legal range of values for these escape sequences is octal *0–377*, hexadecimal *0x00–0xFF*. It is possible for an octal escape to overflow the maximum value (because the highest three-digit octal number is *777*). If that happens, a warning error will be emitted, and the byte value will be set to *0x00*:

```
var_dump(bin2hex("\400")); // octal 377 + 1
```

Output:
Warning: Octal escape sequence overflow \400 is greater than \377
string(2) "00"

Overflow is not possible with hexadecimal escapes because the maximum number of digits after the \x sequence is two:

```
var_dump(bin2hex("\x100")); // hex FF + 1
```

Output:
string(4) "1030"

Here we can see that the string "\x100" has been parsed as byte value *0x10* and the ASCII character "0" (byte *0x30* in the codepage). This also serves to demonstrate that you can quite happily mix-and-match numeric escape sequences with regular text, just as we did with the special character escapes above.

Unicode Escape Sequences

The final type of escape sequence is the Unicode escape. This takes the form "\u{N}" where N is the hexadecimal Unicode code point of the desired character. This chapter has an entire section devoted to the fascinating (well, to some of us) history of character encoding in computing, a multi-decade journey that has led to the Unicode system, which is ubiquitous across the entire internet. For now, here's a very quick demonstration:

```
print "I hope this works... \u{1F4A5}" . PHP_EOL;
print "Unicode is a superset of ASCII.\u{0A}This proves it\u{21}" . PHP_EOL;
```

```
Output:
I hope this works... 💥
Unicode is a superset of ASCII.
This proves it!
```

Here we've used three Unicode code unit values: *0x1F4A5* ("Collision Symbol"), *0x0A* ("Line Feed"), and *0x21* ("Exclamation Mark"). Whether or not you see the collision symbol depends on your system's encoding settings and fonts, but the other two are identical to the ASCII code points (a deliberate design choice) and will not cause any issues (unless you're using something exotic from 1980s Japan). Lots more to come on this soon.

Heredoc and Nowdoc

For larger string literal character sequences that might become cumbersome to express with quotes, PHP supports the multi-line *heredoc* syntax:

```
$heredoc = <<<IDENTIFIER
Lorem ipsum dolor sit amet, consectetur adipiscing elit, sed
do eiusmod tempor incididunt ut labore et dolore magna aliqua.
IDENTIFIER;

print $heredoc . PHP_EOL;
```

Output:
Lorem ipsum dolor sit amet, consectetur adipiscing elit, sed
do eiusmod tempor incididunt ut labore et dolore magna aliqua.

The heredoc operator <<< is followed by an identifier symbol (which follows the same naming rules as variables and functions), which must then be immediately followed by a newline. By convention, heredoc identifiers are uppercase and contain only A-Z alphabet characters, but you are free to use digits (provided they are not the first character), underscores, and so on. Every character following the newline is then treated as string text until the identifier is repeated on a terminating line (and it must occur as the only text on that line), followed by a semicolon and then another newline.

PHP 7.3 or later allows the terminating identifier to be indented to the same minimum level as the text it contains (prior to that it had to begin on the first column of a newline), and indentation of the string output is relative to the indentation of the terminating identifier:

```
$heredoc = <<< TNG
    Captain's log, stardate 43930.7. The Enterprise has been in attendance
    at the biennial Trade Agreements Conference
        on Betazed. For the first time, the Ferengi are present...
  TNG;

print $heredoc . PHP_EOL;
```

Output:
```
  Captain's log, stardate 43930.7. The Enterprise has been in attendance at
  the biennial Trade Agreements Conference
      on Betazed. For the first time, the Ferengi are present...
```

If the terminating identifier is indented incorrectly, an error will be emitted:

```
$heredoc = <<< TNG
    Captain's log, supplemental. I have just been advised of a highly
    unusual project undertaken by Commander Data.
      TNG;
```

Output:
Parse error: Invalid body indentation level (expecting an indentation level of at least 6)

Heredoc also supports the same variable interpolation as double-quoted strings:

```
function getVarName ()
{
    return 'stardateStr';
}

$stardateStr = 'Stardate 43996.2';

$obj = new class
{
    public function getEnemy(): string
    {
        return "Borg";
    }
};

$str = <<<TNG
Captain's log, {${getVarName()}}. The Enterprise remains concealed in the
dust cloud. And, to my surprise, the {$obj->getEnemy()} have maintained
their position waiting for us to come out of hiding. I have no explanation
for their special interest in me or this ship.
TNG;

print $str . PHP_EOL;
```

Output:
```
Captain's log, Stardate 43996.2. The Enterprise remains concealed in the
dust cloud. And, to my surprise, the Borg have maintained their position
waiting for us to come out of hiding. I have no explanation for their
special interest in me or this ship.
```

There is also an equivalent to the single-quote string literal: *nowdoc*. Nowdoc syntax is identical to heredoc, but with the identifier symbol declaration enclosed in single quotes (but the terminating identifier must not be quoted). Just like single-quoted strings, nowdoc does not perform any variable interpolation.

```
$str = <<< 'TNG'
Captain's log, {${getVarName()}}. The Enterprise remains concealed in the
dust cloud. And, to my surprise, the {$obj->getEnemy()} have maintained
their position waiting for us to come out of hiding. I have no explanation
for their special interest in me or this ship.
TNG;
```

Output:
```
Captain's log, {${getVarName()}}. The Enterprise remains concealed in the
dust cloud. And, to my surprise, the {$obj->getEnemy()} have maintained
their position waiting for us to come out of hiding. I have no explanation
for their special interest in me or this ship.
```

"Binary" Strings

The final form of language construct for creating string data is something of an historical oddity. Throughout this book, we have seen older versions of PHP mentioned, versions 7, 5, and earlier. The astute amongst you might have noticed the lack of PHP 6: this is because PHP never had an official version 6 release, although one was certainly planned and worked on. The principle reason that version 6 was abandoned is directly related to the material in this chapter: the handling of text data. PHP 6 was intended to revolutionize how string data was treated internally by PHP: all strings were to be Unicode, and PHP 6 was going to have "native Unicode support." The precise nature of Unicode is explored in detail in the next section of this chapter, but in a nutshell, it meant a fundamental change in what strings were.

Up to PHP 5, strings were simply a sequence of bytes with no special meaning. PHP 6 was going to differentiate between a byte sequence and a string of characters because of the growing use of multi-byte characters in text data. PHP is a language invented for the web, and the web was adopting multi-byte character encoding at a rapid pace; the idea was that PHP should naturally support this with as little friction as possible. In anticipation of this differentiation between strings-as-byte-sequences and strings-as-character-sequences, PHP 5.2 introduced the binary string syntax `b'this is a binary string'`; that would indicate that the data was not to be treated as Unicode text and retain the default string handling features of PHP <= 5.x.

PHP 6 was abandoned not least because of the difficulties in implementing full support for Unicode, which is a vast collection of collation rules in addition to being a vast collection of characters (as we'll see in the next section). But the syntax for binary strings still exists and has not been deprecated (yet), and therefore, the following code is perfectly legal even in PHP 8.4:

```
var_dump("a string" === b'a string');

$str = <<<STR
a string
STR;

var_dump($str === b'a string');

Output:
bool(true)
bool(true)
```

Here we've used a type-strict === comparison, and in both cases the b''; form is identical to the other strings. All strings in PHP are "binary strings" – a sequence of bytes with no special significance to PHP relative to any particular character encoding – interpretation is left to the client. Note that the phrase "binary string" is sometimes encountered when describing a string composed only of the digit characters "1" and "0," used to represent a binary number, such as you might encounter with the function bindec() (see Chapter 7, "Numbers," for more detail), but generally "binary string" is usually synonymous with "byte stream" or "buffer," which we'll cover later.

The development effort around PHP 6 and full Unicode support began to outstrip the value it was adding to the language, and so PHP 6 was shelved, PHP 7 became the successor to PHP 5, and Unicode support was instead added to the language via functions and built-in classes. Here endeth the lesson. If phrases such as "Unicode" and "multi-byte characters" are unfamiliar to you, fear not: we'll see all of this in detail throughout the rest of the chapter.

(Footnote: it can be argued that PHP 5.3 represented the true release of PHP 6 because it added so many new things to the language, if you're the arguing type...)

Encoding (a Short History)

Chapter 2, "Data, Types, and Variables," began with an example of how string data is represented in memory by a sequence of bytes where each byte value was mapped to a particular character. This equivalence between value and character is called *encoding*. Encoding enables machines to transfer (and store) text characters, and Morse code is one of the earliest examples of such a system: four symbols (long and short dash, long and short space) were initially used to encode the English alphabet, digits *0* to *9*, some limited punctuation, and a handful of control sequences (called "prosigns"). Other examples of early encoding schemes include Braille, signal flags on ships, and so on. Encoding requires that the sender and receiver agree on what the signals mean, which of course requires standards that define them. The story of the evolution of character encoding standards on computer systems is a long one and only of interest to certain types of people (I am absolutely one of those types of people, but recognize I'm in the minority), so we'll skip towards the end...

ASCII

The basis for modern electronic character encoding began with the American National Standards Institute (ANSI) and their ASCII63 (American Standard Code for Information Interchange, 1963) standard, which eventually saw wide adoption (prior to ASCII63, encoding was highly vendor-specific, as indeed it continued to be for many years after 1963). The ASCII system uses seven bits to store the numerical value of the character, which means there are 128 available *codepoints*. Codepoints are numbers that are assigned to characters within a *code page* (sometimes called a *code space*), where the code page is the full set of characters. (Fun fact: we get the term "code page" from the days when system technical manuals would have the character mappings printed out for lookup – a literal page in a book.) These days other terms exist, such as *character set*, *charset*, or *charmap*; they all mean the same thing: a set of characters mapped to numeric values (either specific sequences of bits or ordinal numbers). Why seven bits? Well, this standard dates from a time when an extra bit would have represented significantly increased costs in data transfer and storage. An IBM Model 350 hard disk in 1956 stored 3.75 megabytes, weighed over a ton, and could only be leased – not bought – for around $3000 a *month*!

ASCII63, with its 7-bit *code unit* (the number of bits used to store a character value), meant that a whopping 128 codepoints were available in the code page. This was a previously unheard-of luxury; older systems might only have used six bits (looking at you, IBM of the 1950s), meaning only 64 possible codepoints. 7-bit ASCII meant both uppercase *and* lowercase Latin characters were possible (gasp!) with enough room left over for the Arabic digits, common punctuation, a smattering of currency symbols, and some control characters. Another aspect of seven-bit ASCII that ensured its success was the fact that the characters were *collatable*: rules existed within ASCII for comparing and sorting subsets of codepoints ("A" has a lower codepoint value than "B," both are lower than "a," and so on), and this was not always true of encoding systems, even those designed for computing, such as IBM's legendarily awful punchcard-derived *EBCDIC*. All of this is fantastic... right up until you need to use, say, Cyrillic characters.

"Extended ASCII"

To be fair, the ASCII committee likely didn't have the needs of Russian (or any other non-English) users uppermost in their minds in the 1960s. Other standards quickly emerged to meet the growing needs of the rest of the world, beginning with ISO/IEC 646 (ECMA-6), which was another 7-bit system closely related to ASCII but allowed variation of certain codepoints; multiple national standards were derived from it. Next came probably the most significant, ISO-8859 (offering 256 codepoints at eight bits per point), which consisted of a series of standards for encoding multiple languages. Examples include ISO-8859-1 (Latin-1) for Western Europe and ISO-8859-5 (Cyrillic) for Serbia, Ukraine et al.

These multiple 8-bit encoding schemes are usually collectively known as *extended ASCII*, but that is something of a misnomer: the ANSI had nothing to do with their creation. Nevertheless, a stop-gap solution had been found to cram a lot more characters into existing systems, and all of this too was fantastic... right up until you need to, say, open a text file from a Serbian ISO-8859-5 system on one using ISO-8859-1. Oh, and for extra giggles, toss in some proprietary "extended" sets such as those developed for DOS and Windows. Hopefully the inherent problems of multiple overlapping standards are obvious (assuming you didn't experience it firsthand like some of us had too): in an era when systems from very different countries and cultures were increasingly interacting with each other, this approach to character encoding was throwing up problems with information transfer.

CHAPTER 8 STRINGS

Unicode

In 1987 three engineers from Xerox (Joe Becker) and Apple (Lee Collins and Mark Davis) were tasked with answering a significant question: what if it was possible to produce a single encoding system that includes every character from every living language? (And later that would grow to include so-called "dead" languages, not to mention little pictures of smiling faces.) The answer was always "yes, provided you have enough bits"; the real challenge was finding a way to do it that didn't chew up vast amounts of disk and network unnecessarily. For example, if the sum total of characters across all languages is a big number like *250,000*, then we'd need a code unit minimum of 18 bits ($2^{18} = 262144$) in our code page to represent them all. Fine, but for English language text we already know we can get the job done with seven bits, so our hypothetical 18-bit encoding would have 11 zeroed bits on every Latin-1 character: around 63% of all Latin-1 files stored and transmitted in such a system would contain redundant zeroed bits. The bulk of text data for North American or Western European systems in such a system would therefore consist of redundant bits. Indeed, it was precisely this calculus that led to the original 7-bit design of ASCII63.

Growing beyond 8-bit codepoints was always going to be inevitable in such a system, but there already existed examples of 16-bit encoding solutions. Interoperability even between similar Western character sets was a growing challenge, but what about alphabets whose size exceeds a 256-point (8-bit) code page? Some of the oldest living languages in the world have alphabets measured in thousands of characters, after all. Various East Asian countries had rapidly growing computing needs in the latter half of the twentieth century, and with alphabets containing thousands of characters, they had little choice but to adopt a wider bit length long before it became a necessity in the Western Hemisphere. The GB 2312-1980 encoding standard covers the Simplified Chinese character set (it was originally a mere 6,763 Chinese characters, not including punctuation and other symbols), and the Japanese Industrial Standard (JIS) X 0208 specifies a double-byte encoding for Japanese characters (containing 6879 characters) and dates from 1978. There was also an international standard published in 1971 (ISO 2022) that set out ways in which computer systems could use double-byte or variable-width (variable numbers of bytes) in their character encoding.

Becker, Collins, and Davis conducted three main investigations: comparison between fixed and variable width encoding systems, impacts on storage requirements for 16-bit encoding, and estimates of character counts for all alphabets currently in use. From this the initial architecture of *Unicode* was derived. Unicode's name is derived from "universal," "uniform," and "unique": all of the world's language needs are *universally* met, characters are represented *uniquely*, and the code units are *uniform* (meaning the code units are a fixed size; this is now definitely NOT the case as Unicode and its related transformation formats have evolved with time, as we shall see).

A key innovation of Unicode was the (eventual) abstraction of the code page from its machine representation. Rather than specify byte values for characters, each point in the Unicode character set simply has an ordinal number, which allows for flexibility in implementation across various machine architectures. An implementing system just needs to find a way to represent the integer codepoints; how that happens is not the concern of Unicode (anymore, but the original specification had more to say about it). Although not intended in its initial fixed-width design, it is this abstraction that allowed for variation in the *transformation format* and led to the efficiency and backwards compatibility of the variable-width *UTF-8*. It has also allowed Unicode to grow far beyond its initial scope of 65,536 characters. Today, Unicode (version 17.0) contains over one million possible codepoints covering all languages, with rules for their collation, and even languages that haven't been spoken outside of an academic context for thousands of years (there are codepoints for Cuneiform, Ancient Egyptian, and Coptic scripts). Not all one million codepoints are assigned; there are large blocks of currently unused codepoints providing future-proofing.

PHP technically doesn't have "native" Unicode support because, well, full support for the Unicode specification would be incredibly complex. Unicode doesn't just offer millions of codepoints and the freedom to implement at the machine level; it also contains rules for combining characters (diacritical marks), bidirectional scripts (for when you'd like to mix left-to-right English with, say, right-to-left Hebrew... stay tuned for an example), truncating characters, and more. This complexity is necessary because human language is complex. However, PHP from version 7 onwards has offered expanded support for the use of Unicode in strings.

PHP 7.0 introduced the "Unicode codepoint escape syntax," which means you can use the following meta-character sequence inside double-quoted string literals:

```
print "\u{5408} \u{6c23} \u{9053}" . PHP_EOL;
```

Output:
合 氣 道

The syntax is \u{ORDINAL} where ORDINAL is the hexadecimal ordinal value of the character, which means the character 合 is codepoint *U+5408*, which is the 21512th character in the code page. More details available here: https://www.unicode.org/cgi-bin/GetUnihanData.pl?codepoint=5408.

There are also two mbstring extension functions that are useful for moving between Unicode codepoint values and the associated characters. mb_ord() will give the decimal ordinal value of a character, and mb_chr() accepts an integer decimal codepoint value and will return the character:

```
var_dump(mb_ord("\u{5408}"));
var_dump(mb_chr(21512));
```

Output:
```
int(21512)
string(3) "合"
```

There are many other mbstring extension functions for handling multi-byte strings (of a variety of encodings, not just UTF-8); this chapter will make extensive use of them.

Transformation Formats

The original specification for Unicode also encompassed the mechanism for transferring data between systems, in that all 65,536 codepoints in the original design were to be represented by two bytes (16-bit). While Unicode was being worked on by Apple and Xerox, the ISO was also independently developing the parallel standard of ISO-10646 (known as the Universal Coded Character Set, or UCS), and the two groups agreed to synchronize their efforts to ensure the two code pages would be compatible. Both used a fixed two-byte (16-bit) code unit, which came to be known as UCS-2.

Both the Unicode Consortium (a non-profit organization incorporated in 1991 by the teams that had been working on the Unicode specification) and the ISO quickly realized that even 16-bit code units were insufficient to achieve the goal of providing for all the characters and symbols of human language. A four-byte system (UCS-4) was proposed in one of the drafts of ISO-10646; the Unicode consortium resisted this fixed-width system on the grounds that even on comparatively modern systems this would result in wasted storage, memory, and network bandwidth. The character encoding form that came to be known as UTF-16 was created as an alternative.

UTF-16 retains the two-byte format for the first 65,536 codepoints of Unicode/UCS and a pair of two-byte units for the rest, making it a variable-width code unit. The proposed, fixed-width four-byte system UCS-4 (ISO-10646) is still kicking around today as UTF-32. The main argument for retaining a fixed-width encoding is that some algorithms for string processing are far faster for fixed-width data (there's no need to evaluate every code unit when finding the nth character, for example, making a UTF-32 implementation an $O(1)$ problem vs. $O(n)$ for variable-width).

UTF-32 does see some use for internal application storage on Unix and Linux systems but is rarely encountered in, say, the world of web development. The argument concerning fixed-size characters is also debatable when one considers the fact that some Unicode characters are composed of multiple codepoints. The diacritical marks mentioned earlier combine base letters with one (or more) accent characters (e.g., "a" + "`" to make "à"), and some of the recently added emoji alphabets use multi-codepoint characters: "Man: Bald" 👨‍🦲 is composed of "Man" 👨, "Zero Width Joiner", and "Emoji Component Bald" 🦲! Take a look at the following:

```
var_dump("\u{1F468}\u{200D}\u{1F9B2}");
```

Output:
string(11) "👨‍🦲"

Now, a word of warning. Not all systems perfectly implement the Unicode standard, and there are dozens of versions of the Unicode standard. Ideally when you run the code above, you'll get a bald chap appearing. My MacBook Pro running the latest MacOS renders correctly, but a 10-year-old unpatched Linux distro might well show the separate "Man" and "Emoji Component Bald" glyphs (and possibly a numeric value for the non-rendering joiner). That's one of the points this chapter tries to make: encoding is hard, maintaining software as encoding standards change is even harder. We'll have some more multi-codepoint fun (with flags) later. Anyway, back to our example.

The code above uses a special string syntax called a *Unicode escape sequence*. When the sequence \u{XXXX} is used in a double-quoted string, it will be substituted for the Unicode character at codepoint XXXX. \u{1F468} is the "Man" emoji character at codepoint *1F468*, *200D* is a special non-printing character used to join *1F468* and *1F9B2* ("Emoji Component Bald") to give us our follically challenged, male-identifying human. If your terminal software is Unicode-compliant (and your system has the necessary font installed), you should see the correct emoji.

UTF-16 sees more widespread use: Windows until very recently used UTF-16 internally, and the ECMAScript standard (from which all JavaScript engines are derived) specifies a UTF-16 compatible internal format for string data. UCS-2, UCS-4, UTF-16, and UTF-32 all shared a common problem: none of them can be compatible with ASCII, because the minimum size of their code units is two or four bytes.

How About We... Don't Break ASCII, Maybe?

In order for ASCII-encoded data to be readable by a system using variable-width encoding, logic dictates that the minimum code unit size has to be one byte. An attempt was made by the ISO, in a draft of ISO-10646, to make such a transformation format. UTF-1 proposed a minimum of a single byte and up to four bytes to provide the codepoints necessary to meet the Unicode specification. UTF-1 (which you've probably never heard of until now) is consigned to the dumpster of failed standards proposals because of one glaring flaw: it did not protect the existing and widely used ASCII standard.

UTF-1 describes special byte values called *continuation bytes*, which are the valid values for second and subsequent bytes of a multi-byte sequence (where the leading byte in the sequence also has a value from a certain range). For UTF-1, if a byte value of 0xA0 or greater is read, it means that the next two to four bytes are also part of the code unit. In this way it is possible to support millions of codepoints but keep the most commonly used characters within two or fewer bytes. The table below shows all of the UTF-1 valid byte values for single- and two-byte codepoints (sequences with three or more bytes have been omitted).

UTF-1 (Partial)

Table 8-3. UTF-1 codepoint ranges

First codepoint	Last codepoint	Byte 0	Byte 1
U+0000	U+009F	00–9F	
U+00A0	U+00FF	A0	A0–FF
U+0100	U+4015	A1–F5	21–7E, A0–FF

Now let's have a brief excerpt from a similar table for ASCII and play a game of "can you spot the problem"...

ASCII (Extremely Partial!)

Table 8-4. ASCII codepoint

Codepoint	Character	Byte value
47	/	0x2F

If you're struggling, have a look at the third row of the first table. Byte 0x2F lies within the range 0x21–0x7E; this means that UTF-1 continuation bytes collided with part of the 7-bit ASCII code page. In this case a UTF-1 encoded string could be misinterpreted as containing a forward slash character, which happens to be a special character for describing Unix file systems (it is the directory separator). UTF-1 went quickly and quietly to its grave and was replaced by the saner FSS-UTF (File System Safe UCS Transformation Format).

FSS-UTF specified that only values 0x00–0x7F (the 7-bit ASCII range) were valid for single-byte characters. Multi-byte characters could only be expressed by bytes 0x80 or greater; the valid encodings for one- to three-byte characters are given below.

FSS-UTF (Partial)

Table 8-5. FSS-UTF codepoint ranges

First codepoint	Last codepoint	Byte 0	Byte 1	Byte 3
U+0000	U+007F	00–7F		
U+0080	U+207F	80–BF	80–FF	
U+2080	U+8207F	C0–DF	80–FF	80–FF

The proposed FSS-UTF was modified further by Ken Thompson of Bell Labs (the story goes that Thompson's modifications were jotted down on a napkin over dinner in 1992) and, in 1993, became UTF-8. It was adopted by the Internet Engineering Task Force (IETF) in RFC 2277 (https://datatracker.ietf.org/doc/html/rfc2277).

CHAPTER 8 STRINGS

UTF-8 (Full)

Table 8-6. *UTF-8 codepoint ranges*

First codepoint	Last codepoint	Byte 0	Byte 1	Byte 3	Byte 4	Byte 5	Byte 6
U+0000	U+007F	00–7F					
U+0080	U+07FF	C0–DF	80–BF				
U+0800	U+FFFF	E0–EF	80–BF	80–BF			
U+10000	U+1FFFF	F0–F7	80–BF	80–BF	80–BF		
U+200000	U+3FFFFFF	F8–FB	80–BF	80–BF	80–BF	80–BF	
U+4000000	U+7FFFFFFF	FC–FD	80–BF	80–BF	80–BF	80–BF	80–BF

The main reason why UTF-8 differs from FSS-UTF something called "self-synchronization": this means that overlapping code units do not form valid code units themselves. This prevents errors in transmission: all that's needed to work out the code unit boundaries is the stream of bytes itself, and this allows a program reading a UTF-8 byte stream to start at an arbitrary point and detect character boundaries correctly.

PHP and UTF-8

As stated above, PHP does not have "native" support for Unicode (the definition of which is debatable anyway), but it *does* have full support for UTF-8, both as data and as the encoding of PHP programs themselves. If you remember from earlier chapters, legal symbols for variable and function names are defined as follows:

[a-zA-Z_\x7f-\xff][a-zA-Z0-9_\x7f-\xff]*

This regular expression (we'll be having lots of fun with those soon, I promise) describes the uppercase and lowercase ASCII Latin alphabet (codepoints *0x41-0x5A* a-z and *0x61-0x7A* A-Z), the Arabic digits (codepoints *0x30-0x39*), and underscores (codepoint *0x5F*). It also allows for the extended ASCII (ISO-8859-1 et al.) range of *0x80-0xFF* (plus the final ASCII codepoint *0x7F*, which happens to be the DELETE control character). Therefore, any multi-byte UTF-8 string will meet the criteria for a legal symbol name (the lead byte is in the range *0xC0–0xFD*, and continuation bytes are in the range *0x80–0xBF*), and any valid single-byte UTF-8 character simply needs to be in the range a–z, or A–Z, or 0–9, or an underscore _.

It's worth noting that although PHP's symbol naming rules allow for UTF-8 encoded text, UTF-8 is not enforced. It is possible to use a single byte in the *0x80–0xFF* range as a symbol, which we can demonstrate with a hex editor (which allows binary-level editing). Take the following text and save it to a file called foo.php (encoding doesn't matter; we're about to break it):

```
<?php

$x = 1;
var_dump($x);
```

Now, using a hex editor, edit the file. The example below uses a MacOS hex editor called Hex Fiend, which is available for free. Find both occurrences of the sequence 2478…

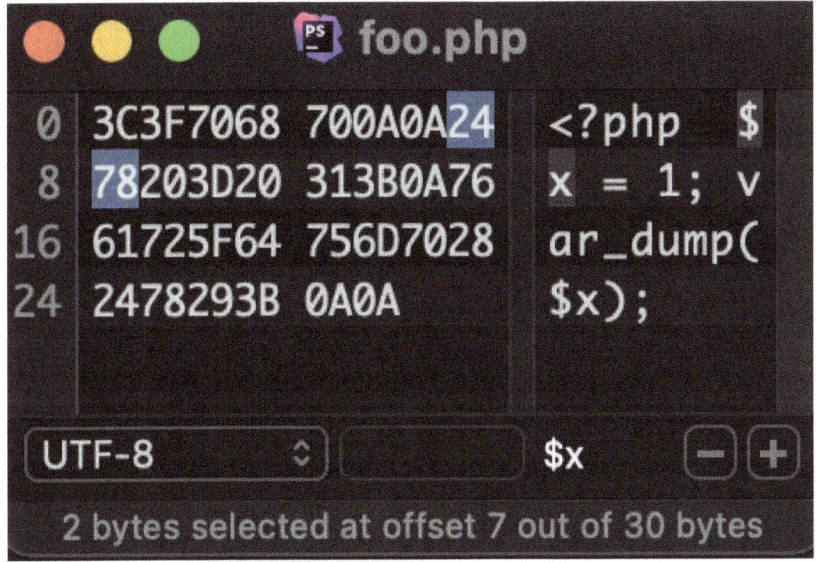

Figure 8-1. *hex edit of raw byte values before…*

… and change them to 2480 …

CHAPTER 8 STRINGS

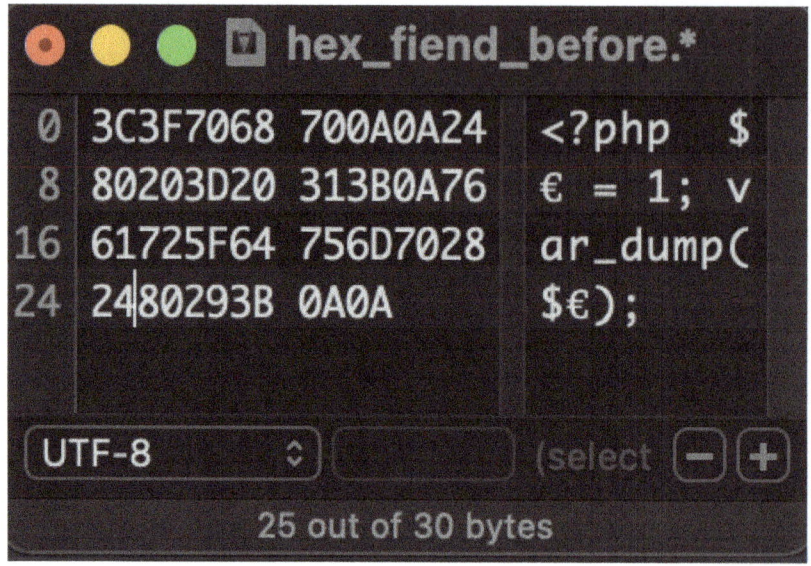

Figure 8-2. *hex edit raw byte values after...*

Make sure to save the changes. What we've done here is swap the x character of $x for a different byte value: *0x80*. This is an invalid sequence in UTF-8 (*0x80* is a continuation byte, and the *0x24* byte before it is not a valid leading byte), and extended ASCII encodings (ISO-8859-*) do not use the range *0x80–0x9F* for printable characters. The specification for UTF-8 states that invalid sequences should be handled gracefully by clients, so attempting to view foo.php in an editor or shell might generate warnings, but it should show a placeholder character where the x used to be.

```
$ cat foo.php
<?php

$? = 1;
var_dump($?);
```

My trusty Mac/PHPStorm combo renders a question mark placeholder, but yours will very likely be something different, perhaps a numeric placeholder. Those of you following along at home might get something like $<80> = 1; var_dump($<80>); – it will vary between systems and their age. The big question now is will it execute? It does, because we haven't broken any of PHP's rules on variable name symbols.

```
$ php foo.php
int(1)
```

What we have done, though, is created something that breaks a basic coding standard: PSR-1 stipulates (valid) UTF-8 encoding for all source code files. I chose a non-printing (extended control character) value of *0x80* to demonstrate that broken UTF-8 will still execute provided it satisfies the symbol naming rules; I could have chosen *0xBF*, which *is* a printable character in ISO-8859-1 – inverted question-mark ¿ – in fact, *0xA0* to *0xBF* are all printable in ISO-8859, so I highly recommend making sure any old PHP source code files you might inherit are correctly converted to UTF-8 (assuming you are working with PHP 7 or higher). I don't say this because PHP will have problems running the code; we've just demonstrated that PHP's only criterion for symbols is a valid sequence of bytes. Conversion is recommended because if everything is UTF-8 everywhere, you will ensure the entire toolchain (from IDEs and editors to continuous integration systems) will be frictionless, and any string literals that become output to other clients will be correctly rendered.

You are free to use UTF-8 liberally in your PHP programs; here are a couple of examples:

```
$∑ = 1 + 1; // ∑ (Greek sigma) denotes a summation operation
'הפה' = $'הפה'; // This snippet of Hebrew is a right-to-left string,
                directionality depends on your editor!
```

Note the example in Hebrew will very likely cause you some problems unless your system is correctly set up for the language and you type the characters in one at a time. PSR-1 specifies that all PHP source code files must be UTF-8 encoded, but that does not mean anyone is obliged to use a UTF-8-capable editor. The code above will execute just fine: as far as PHP is concerned, the variable $∑ is just a legal three-byte symbol (*0xE2 0x88 0x91*), but the file might not be readable to all users of your code. In the extended ASCII encoding of ISO-8859-1, the sequence *0xE2 0x88 0x91* maps to three codepoints: "â", plus two non-characters: a non-UTF-8 text editor is likely going to struggle with that.

In addition, the Hebrew characters used above are bidirectional: a fully Unicode-compliant editor will render them *before* the dollar symbol (even though they occur after the dollar symbol as the PHP parser reads it, which means they're legal). Not all editors, and especially not all command shells, are fully Unicode compliant – they might, say, accept the encoding and show the correct characters but render the text in the wrong direction, or just blow up completely (in my experience).

It is generally recommended that ASCII symbols be used to maximize portability, though this does constitute a modern variant of ASCII's intrinsic problem of trying to force the entire world to speak English. Feel free to go wild in your comments, though!

The `string` Data Type

It might have surprised you earlier in the chapter to learn that PHP, even in the third decade of the twenty-first century, does not have native Unicode support. Given the ubiquitous nature of Unicode on the web today, this might sound a little ridiculous, but this isn't the oversight it might appear to be. Strings in PHP are agnostic of encoding: there is no code page used by PHP internally when handling `string` data; the `string` data type is simply implemented as an array of bytes (known as a *buffer*) and an integer value indicating the length of the array. That's it. There is no metadata telling your code what language the string is meant to represent, and there are no limitations on the contents of the buffer: pick any byte value you like from *0x00* to *0xFF* and pile them up until you run out of memory.

If you remember from Chapter 2, "Data, Types, and Variables", I made the point that the machine doesn't have any concept of what the data represents in terms of information; it is up to our software to make sense of it. In a similar way, PHP string data does not evaluate to any sequence of characters until evaluated against an encoding, they really are just buffers full of bytes. This is why PHP does not have a byte data type (unlike C, Java, or C#) or a built-in buffer data structure (like JavaScript); PHP strings already perform that function.

With that said, you might be confused as to how any string-handling code you've seen up to now can actually work, and the answer is… it's complicated. String operations are just manipulations and comparisons at the byte level. Below is a string concatenation operation, widely used in PHP:

```
$hello = "Hello";
$space = "\x20";
$world = "World";
$exclamation = "\x21";
```

```
$concat = $hello . $space . $world . $exclamation ;
var_dump($concat);
var_dump(bin2hex($concat));
```

Output:
```
string(12) "Hello World!"
string(24) "48656c6c6f20576f726c6421"
```

The string concatenation operator – dot . – is just joining four buffers together. To drive the point home, the example above mixes string literal values with byte escapes, the syntax of which is \x followed by an 8-bit hexadecimal value and enclosed in double quotes. "\x20" is therefore a single byte with a decimal value of 32. The codepages for ASCII, ISO-8859-1, and Unicode/UTF-8 all agree that *0x20* is a space character, and *0x21* is the Latin exclamation punctuation mark. The output of bin2hex() shows us the values of each byte in the new $concat buffer: 48656c6c... is the first four bytes of the sequence: *0x48 0x65 0x6c 0x6c* or H e l l... you can work out the rest.

Here's a slightly tweaked version that uses Unicode escapes instead of UTF-8 bytes to demonstrate that Unicode is a true superset of ASCII:

```
$hello = "Hello";
$space = "\u{20}";
$world = "World";
$exclamation = "\u{21}";
// concatenate and var_dump() as before...
```

Output:
```
string(12) "Hello World!"
```

The use of Unicode codepoint escapes *does* require some encoding awareness on PHP's part, in that it will internally have to calculate the UTF-8 code unit bytes that correspond to the codepoints before assignment, but the resulting data is still a byte stream and nothing more. The previous section demonstrated that Bald Man was a multi-codepoint character in Unicode; let's take a look at the byte stream PHP generated when creating the Bald Man buffer:

```
$baldMan = "\u{1F468}\u{200D}\u{1F9B2}";

var_dump($baldMan);
var_dump(bin2hex($baldMan));
```

Output:
string(11) "👨"
string(22) "f09f91a8e2808df09fa6b2"

Again, there's a chance your system will produce different output when rendering a multi-codepoint character. Let's break down the output of `bin2hex()` and see how it maps to UTF-8.

Table 8-7. *UTF-8 code units for "Bald Man"*

UTF-8 code unit	Unicode codepoint	Character
F0 9F 91 A9	U+1F468	👨 (Man)
E2 80 8D	U+200D	ZERO_WIDTH_JOINER
F0 9F A6 B2	U+1F9B2	🦲 (Bald)

PHP Unicode escapes will always generate UTF-8 code units, but it's still just a byte stream, and you still need a UTF-8-compliant browser/editor/console to view the bald man. (If you have any particular interest in the recent emoji additions to Unicode 15.1, start here: https://unicode.org/emoji/charts/.)

Comparison operators ==, <, and > (more detail in Chapter 4, "Logic and Control") will also work with string buffers, as will built-in functions that use comparison internally, such as the array-sorting function `sort()`:

```
$things = ['Zebra', 'Apple', 'Orange', 'banana'];
sort($things);
print_r($things);
```

Output:
```
Array
(
    [0] => Apple
    [1] => Orange
    [2] => Zebra
    [3] => banana
)
```

CHAPTER 8 STRINGS

This is a lexicographical sort; the strings have been arranged in alphabetical order (A–Z first, then a–z second). If we were to use digits, they would be placed before alphabet characters, with punctuation placed before digits:

```
$things = ['Zebra', 'Apple', '.-Orange', '0-banana'];
// sort() and print_r() ...
```

Output:
```
Array
(
    [0] => .-Orange
    [1] => 0-banana
    [2] => Apple
    [3] => Zebra
)
```

This works because ASCII was designed with this kind of operation in mind: the ASCII code page is organized in (English) lexicographical order. At no point during execution of the above code has PHP become aware of the English language, and the internal logic of sort() is predicated purely on the byte values in the buffers. Let's write that code one more time, but using ASCII (and therefore UTF-8) byte values...

```
$things = [
    "\x5a\x65\x62\x72\x61", // Zebra
    "\x41\x70\x70\x6c\x65", // Apple
    "\x2e\x2d\x4f\x72\x61\x6e\x67\x65", // .-Orange
    "\x30\x2d\x62\x61\x6e\x61\x6e\x61" // 0-banana
];
sort($things);
print_r($things);
```

Output:
```
Array
(
    [0] => .-Orange
    [1] => 0-banana
    [2] => Apple
    [3] => Zebra
)
```

CHAPTER 8 STRINGS

Now we can clearly see how `sort()` is really functioning: by comparing byte values. `.-Orange` starts with the lowest value byte, *0x2e*, and is placed first in the array. Next comes `0-banana`, which begins with *0x30*, and so on.

So far, so good. Now let's see what happens when we throw some non-Latin, multi-byte strings into the mix...

```
$polishNames = [
    "Łukasz",
    "Marcin",
    "Tomasz",
];
sort($polishNames);
print_r($polishNames);
var_dump(bin2hex("Tomasz"));
var_dump(bin2hex("Łukasz"));

Output:
Array
(
    [0] => Marcin
    [1] => Tomasz
    [2] => Łukasz
)
string(12) "546f6d61737a"
string(14) "c581756b61737a"
```

For those of you not familiar with the Polish alphabet, the order of the sorted array is actually incorrect. The character Ł lies between L and M in the Polish alphabet but sits at Unicode codepoint U+0141 (Latin Capital Letter L with Stroke), which is quite a way beyond U+004C (L) and U+004D (M). Furthermore, the UTF-8 code unit for Ł is *0xC5 0x81*. PHP's `sort()` function knows nothing of Polish or Unicode and just blindly organizes the strings by byte value. *0x54* is a lower value than *0xC5*, so `Tomasz` is placed before `Łukasz` in the ordered array. There's no special treatment of strings here; in order for the byte values to have any meaning as a natural language, we would need to apply some regional collation rules. The good news is PHP has some useful features for doing exactly that (as you should expect from a language specializing in processing text for the world's websites), which we will examine in detail later on in the chapter.

Operations, Type Coercion, and Safety

PHP has a wealth of built-in features designed to make text processing a breeze, and this includes use cases spanning multiple geographical regions. Unicode and UTF-8 are the open standards that the internet uses to enable platforms and systems to interoperate with as little friction as possible. In addition, there are common data interchange formats such as JSON and XML, which are de facto standards on the web today; PHP offers deep support for both (and more). This chapter examines all of this in detail, but now we'll turn our attention to the low-level tools that exist for manipulating strings.

Operators and Type Coercion

The previous section demonstrated a common string operation: concatenation. That's pretty much the only string-specific operation in the language, but comparison operators will also work with strings.

```
var_dump("Stardate " . "43989.1");
var_dump("abc" > "xyz");
var_dump("123" == 123);
var_dump("123" === 123);
```

Output:
```
string(16) "Stardate 43989.1"
bool(false)
bool(true)
bool(false)
```

Bear in mind that when comparing two strings, all that counts are the byte values; the comparison `"abc" > "xyz"` simply compares three bytes to three bytes. The alphanumeric collation that we interpret (as humans that can read the Latin alphabet) is just how ASCII was designed. Remember, this all falls apart once we step outside of the ASCII range (as we saw with the Polish alphabet in the previous section).

The numerical comparisons in the final two lines are a little different. `"123" == 123` is not a type-strict comparison, so coercion will happen: casting either of those values so they match types results in either two identical strings or two identical integers.
The final comparison is type-strict, so it can never be true (a string is not an integer). Chapter 7, "Numbers," contains many examples of casting or coercing strings to numbers

and does not need to be repeated here. Objects can also be cast to strings provided they implement a magic __toString() method; see Chapter 6, "Object Fundamentals," for examples.

Concatenation itself will trigger type coercion (to a string)...

```
var_dump("122" . 1);
Output:
string(4) "1221"
```

... and mathematical operations will coerce to a number:

```
var_dump("122" + 1);
var_dump("124" - 0.6);

Output:
int(123)
float(123.4)
```

Safety

PHP offers many (oh so many) functions for string manipulation (or mangling, if you prefer). Before we get started, there are two very important concepts to be aware of: *binary safety* and *multi-byte safety*.

Binary Safety

As we now know, PHP strings aren't really text; they are buffers containing bytes and metadata indicating the length of the buffer. Some languages use a null byte – *0x00* – as a string terminator (e.g., the language that the PHP interpreter is written in: C); PHP generally does not (it uses the length metadata). Binary safety is a property of PHP functions: a binary unsafe function would treat a null byte as a terminator and potentially truncate the buffer once it encountered the first *0x00* byte value. For example, a buffer might contain the data for an image with potentially hundreds of null bytes and would not survive an encounter with a binary unsafe function: in such a scenario the resulting data output by the function would no longer be an intact image.

Therefore, a binary safe function is one that does not ascribe any special meaning to a null byte, and the function will act on the entire buffer. Most PHP string functions are binary safe; the few exceptions will be noted in this section. For now, here's a quick example:

```
var_dump(strlen("A\x00 null byte."));
var_dump(strcoll("abc", "abc\x00def"));
var_dump(strcmp("abc", "abc\x00def"));
```

Output:
int(13)
int(0)
int(-1)

The code above uses three different string functions. `strlen()` returns the length of the string (from the buffer length metadata); the native C equivalent would have returned 1 (terminating after the "A" byte), but PHP uses the buffer length metadata and returns 13. `strcoll()` compares strings by locale (the set of rules for formatting and comparing data by region, we'll get to this shortly) and returns 0 if they match, which is the case here despite the two strings being obviously different (but matching up to the null byte of the second string). Clearly, `strcoll()` is not binary safe because the second argument contains seven bytes, not three; what's happened here is that evaluation of the second string terminated early at the null byte. `strcmp()` is also a very similar string comparison function to `strcoll()`, but *is* binary safe, so it returns -1 (the left-hand argument is smallest, at three bytes).

Multi-byte Safety

In a similar vein to binary safety, multi-byte safety is a property of functions that are aware of multi-byte encoding systems and will differentiate between characters and bytes. PHP core offers many built-in functions for handling string data, but they do not differentiate between single-byte and multi-byte encodings and will give incorrect results when the text encoded in the string steps outside the ASCII range.

Here's a simple example: the function `strlen()` will return the length of a string. Let's look at a simple ASCII string vs. something outside the ASCII range... I'm choosing the Polish alphabet for this. Unless stated otherwise, all non-ASCII strings in this section are using PHP's default encoding of UTF-8.

CHAPTER 8   STRINGS

```
$lat = 'ABCDE';
$pol = 'AĄBCĆ';

var_dump(strlen($lat));
var_dump(strlen($pol));
```

Output:
```
int(5)
int(7)
```

$lat contains the first five letters of the English (Latin) alphabet, and $pol contains the first five letters of the Polish alphabet. When we pass those strings to strlen(), we get a count of five for $lat but seven for $pol. It shouldn't come as any surprise (if you've read the rest of the chapter so far) to learn that the Ą and Ć characters have been UTF-8 encoded with multiple bytes. strlen() is simply returning the number of bytes in the string; we can confirm this by looking at the byte values for $lat and $pol:

```
var_dump(bin2hex($lat));
var_dump(bin2hex($pol));
```

Output:
```
string(10) "4142434445"
string(14) "41c4844243c486"
```

As you'd expect, $str has five bytes of values *0x41–0x44* (the letters A–D in the ASCII range), $pol contains a seven-byte sequence *0x41 0xc4 0x84 0x42 0x43 0xc4 0x86*: Ą has been encoded as *0xc4 0x84* and Ć as *0xc4 0x86*. Remember that the string data type is just a buffer containing bytes, and non-ASCII characters will be UTF-8 encoded; the behavior of strlen() should not be at all surprising. This important differentiation between bytes and information isn't (in my experience) made explicit enough, and even today I still see (and fix) bugs in production systems that result from a lack of multi-byte safety.

The good news is there is a simple solution, which we'll get to in a moment, but first here's another example of multi-byte strings throwing up issues when they're not handled correctly. We'll use my friend Łukasz as the test subject. Sorry, Łukasz, let me buy you a beer to make amends! Just to drive the point home:

```
$me = strtolower('Paul');
$friend = strtolower('Łukasz');
```

```
print "{$me} and {$friend} are going for a pint." . PHP_EOL;
```

Output:
```
paul and Łukasz are going for a pint.
```

This time we're using the built-in function `strtolower()`, which will transform uppercase characters in a string to lowercase. Except that here it only worked on my name: Łukasz should have been transformed to łukasz, but we can see from the output that this has not happened. The reason for this is that `strtolower()` explicitly states (in the official documentation) that it will only work for a limited subset of ASCII characters (A–Z).

Clearly, neither of the two string functions above is capable of handling multi-byte text, but fortunately for us, PHP offers multi-byte versions of the vast majority via the `mbstring` module. Most PHP installations will have this module installed by default. You can verify its presence on your system with the following command:

```
$ php -m
[PHP Modules]
...
mbstring
```

This module offers versions of the core string functions that are aware of multiple Unicode-based encodings, not just UTF-8, and also utility functions for detecting and converting the encoding of string data. In the next section of this chapter, we'll be looking at the core string manipulation functions (and their multi-byte counterparts), and we'll cover the multi-byte utility functions in a following section. Let's take a quick look at the multi-byte safe versions of our last two examples; we'll swap `strlen()` and `strtolower()` for `mb_strlen()` and `mb_strtolower()`:

```
$lat = 'ABCDE';
$pol = 'AĄBCĆ';

var_dump(mb_strlen($lat));
var_dump(mb_strlen($pol));
```

Output:
```
int(5)
int(5)
```

Now, instead of counting bytes with `strlen()`, we are counting characters with `mb_strlen()`, and both strings are five characters long...

```
$me = mb_strtolower('Paul');
$friend = mb_strtolower('Łukasz');

print "{$me} and {$friend} are going for a pint." . PHP_EOL;
```

Output:
```
paul and łukasz are going for a pint.
```

... and we have the expected lowercase conversion for both names for our trip to the pub. Człowiek nie wielbłąd, pić musi!

In general, the multi-byte equivalent of a core string function is the name of the function prefixed with `mb_`, so it's easy enough to remember. If you are *absolutely* certain that the text to be processed is ASCII and can never be multi-byte data, then by all means stick with the non-multi-byte functions (they're faster). Otherwise, you are better off using the `mb_*` versions, and this is especially true if handling data from outside the program, such as user input (command line or HTTP requests), text retrieved from a database, and so on. Remember that in this glorious modern era, even a URL is permitted to contain UTF-8 characters!

Core String Functions

In the previous sections we've seen a few examples of the functions built into the PHP core for examining or manipulating string data. PHP – a language invented for building web pages – is designed for handling text in the context of web applications and offers a large number of ready-made functions for common tasks in such problem domains. The purpose of this section is to teach the principles of PHP's string functions, grouped by common use cases. It is not intended to act as a quick reference for the entire collection of core (and multi-byte) functions (though every function is at least mentioned here). For an exhaustive list of string functions (and their usage), start with the official PHP documentation, which can be found at https://www.php.net/manual/en/ref.strings.php and https://www.php.net/manual/en/ref.mbstring.php.

Now, before we continue a word of caution. PHP is not a new language and has (arguably) a somewhat chequered past. PHP 8 is far more carefully designed and curated than in previous decades, but it still contains the legacy of its earlier years.

This is perhaps nowhere more apparent than in the collection of core string functions. They vary in naming convention, parameter handling, and error emission. A lot of the function names are quite confusingly similar, and multiple similarly named functions exist where perhaps a better design might have been a single function with extra parameters. For example, `strpos()` is used to search strings for sub-strings, but there also exist `stripos()`, `strrpos()`, and `strripos()`, which are case-insensitive and reverse direction forms. An alternative design might be `strpos($direction, $case_sensitive, ...$args)` as a way to reduce cognitive load on the programmer, and some of the string functions do have these features. It is also the case that a small number of functions also have aliases (alternative names). I can only apologize.

I have (roughly) sorted the string handling functions into six categories, given in the table below with example use cases. Note that regular expression functions (which would neatly slot into the "Comparison" and "Extraction" categories) are omitted here and will have their own dedicated section following this one (something for you to look forward to). We'll also close out the chapter with a look at other string extensions in PHP (including those for cryptography).

- **Comparison and Analysis** – Collation, character/sub-string counts, phonetic analysis.

- **Conversion and Extraction** – Fetch sub-strings, create arrays of sub-strings or tokens, get/set byte values.

- **Encoding and Escaping** – Add/remove slashes, handle HTML, injection attack protection.

- **Formatting and Transformation** – Change case, add/remove spaces or newlines, interpolate values, substitute portions of strings, and more.

- **Hashing and Error Checking** – Compute hash value, e.g., CRC32, MD5.

The goal of this section (which, to be honest, could have been a chapter in its own right) is to present the core string functions of the language. There are also some very frequently used language extensions (such as `mbstring`, `iconv`, `intl`, and `hash`) that introduce their own functions to the global scope, and we'll certainly cover some of these in an upcoming section. That said, the aim of this chapter has been to impress on you, dear reader, the pitfalls of confusing PHP's string data type with human language, and the most common bugs I've found in production PHP code occur when multi-byte encoded text is passed through core string functions (which are not aware of encoding at all). To that end, this section will also present `mbstring` equivalent functions to core functions (where they exist), with comparisons between the core and `mbstring` forms and examples of how the core functions tend to fail when they're tasked with processing multi-byte data. One of my goals in life is to never again have to fix code that should have used, say, `mb_strlen()` instead of `strlen()`. It's important to have dreams.

Anyway, on with the show...

Comparison and Analysis

The simplest way to compare two strings for equivalence is, of course, to use the comparison operators == or ===. This will trigger a byte-by-byte comparison and return true if the two buffers are identical (the weakly-typed == will of course coerce data types when comparing a string to a non-string). This is useful for comparing strings that you might use, say, as internal values in a program, but not so useful when you introduce natural language or user input (with associated variance in typing ability or degrees of hostility and malicious intent). Furthermore, it might well be the case that it is only a portion of the string that is of interest, or the frequency with which certain characters or sub-strings occur.

Writing your own functions to iterate a (string) buffer looking for patterns of bytes is perfectly doable in PHP. To iterate over the bytes in a string buffer, you can simply treat the string as an array:

```
$str = 'PHP is a glorious language!';

$count = strlen($str);
for ($i = 0; $i < $count; $i++) {
    print $str[$i];
}

print PHP_EOL;
```

Output:
PHP is a glorious language!

Here we use a `for` loop to iterate over each byte in the `$str` buffer. `$str[0]` accesses the zeroth byte (P), `$str[1]` the next (H), and so on. The reason this works is because strings actually *are* arrays (in a sense). Strings in C (the language in which the PHP interpreter is written) are implemented as arrays of single bytes (the *char* C data type, which is something of a misnomer because it covers ASCII non-character byte values, as well as the 8-bit range *0x80–0xFF*), and PHP internally stores strings using a similar construct. Writing and maintaining code like this is perfectly fine but will quickly grow tiresome and is also very likely to be unnecessary because PHP has many (oh so many) use cases already covered.

Equal, Greater, or Less Than?

Table 8-8. String comparison functions

`strcmp()` `strnatcmp()`	Test if a string is less than, greater than, or equal to another
`strcasecmp()` `strnatcasecmp()`	Test if a string is less than, greater than, or equal to another, ignoring case for ASCII letters
`strncmp()` `strncasecmp()`	Binary-safe comparison of first N bytes
`substr_compare()`	Search sub-string for a matching string, restricted with offset and length
`strcoll()`	Locale-based comparison

Testing if one string equals another is a basic task, for which we can of course use logical == or ===. A closely related logical use case would be when sorting the order of strings, where it is necessary to test which value is greater (and the rules for establishing what counts as greater-than or lesser-than will vary; we will get to this a little later on in this section). You can use the spaceship operator for such a test: the expression "a" <=> "a" will return 0 (both are equal), "ab" <=> "ac returns -1 (the left-hand operand is less than), "a" <=> "B" returns 1 (the right-hand operand is less than). The core string functions listed in the table above can also be used for testing strings in this way.

strcmp(), strcasecmp(), strnatcmp(), strnatcasecmp()

We've already seen strcmp() in the previous section, when we looked at the concept of binary safety (and proved that strcmp() is binary safe). strcasecmp() is a case-insensitive form of strcmp(), strnatcmp(), and strnatcasecmp(), using natural sorting (also demonstrated in Chapter 5, "Arrays"). In all cases, the functions work by comparing two input strings, returning a negative integer if the first string is less than the second, 0 if both are equal, and a positive integer if the first string is greater than the second. The devil is in the detail, though. Here's an example, using good old British motorways, just like when we looked at array sorting.

```
var_dump(strcmp("M1", "M4"));
var_dump(strcmp("M4", "M11"));
var_dump(strcmp("M1", "M11"));
var_dump(strcmp("M1", "M18"));
var_dump(strcmp("M11", "M18"));
```

Output:
int(-3)
int(3)
int(-1)
int(-1)
int(-7)

The example above serves to illustrate a couple of things. First, notice that the comparison does not use natural sorting: the second line compares the strings "M4" and "M11" and returns 3, indicating that "M4" is "greater than." Comparison in this way orders the motorways like this: M1, M11, M18, M4... but *4* is less than *11* or *18*, right? The second thing to notice is the return values, which have a direction (positive, negative) and magnitude. "M1" and "M4" are three apart, and "M11" and "M18" are seven apart, but "M1" and "M18" are one apart! What gives?

The answer lies in how strcmp() works internally: it is performing a simple binary comparison. strcmp() traverses the byte arrays of both strings and compares values in each position and applies the following logic:

- If bytes don't match, compare byte values, return the difference (return *byte-1–byte-2*).

- If bytes match, continue to next position.

- If no bytes remain on either, the strings are the same (return 0).
- If bytes remain on one but not the other, the other is smaller (return -1 or 1).

This will hopefully make more sense if we switch to hex escapes in our strings. The letter M is (in UTF-8 and ASCII) a single-byte character *0x4d*; the digits *0–9* are also single bytes in the range *0x30–0x39*.

```
$m4  = "\x4d\x34";
$m1  = "\x4d\x31";
$m11 = "\x4d\x31\x31";
$m18 = "\x4d\x31\x38";

var_dump(strcmp($m4, $m11));
var_dump(strcmp($m4, $m18));
var_dump(strcmp($m11, $m18));
var_dump(strcmp($m1, $m11));
```

Output:
int(3)
int(3)
int(-7)
int(-1)

All strings begin with byte *0x4d* and will begin to vary on the second or third byte. Thus, $m4 is greater than $m1 by three because 0x34−0x31 = 3, and $m11 is seven less than $m18 because 0x31−0x38 = -7. The comparison of $m1 and $m11 returns -1 because of the difference in byte length. Once you understand that strings are just streams of bytes (that can also be treated as arrays), the binary comparison becomes obvious when looking at the results.

The strcasecmp(), strnatcmp, and strnatcasecmp() functions introduce a little more logic to the comparison algorithm. The functions with case in their names ignore case, which means that "A" and "a" are equivalent, as are "B" and "b", and so on; therefore, strcasecmp("AbC", "aBc"); would return 0. The nat functions also introduce natural sorting, in that numerical strings will have entire numbers considered, not just a digit-by-digit comparison:

```
var_dump(strnatcmp("M4", "M18"));
var_dump(strnatcmp("M40", "M18"));
```

Output:
int(-1)
int(1)

Here we can see that with a natural comparison, "M4" would be ordered before "M18" (because the entire numbers are compared). Note that the "M40" and "M18" comparison returns 1, and not 3. The nat functions only return -1, 0, or 1; they do not return the difference between non-matching bytes in equal-length strings.

A quick word on safety with these functions: All of the str*cmp() functions are binary safe, as the following demonstrates:

```
var_dump(strcmp("abc\x00a", "abc\x00z"));
var_dump(strnatcmp("abc\x00123", "abc\x00125"));
var_dump(strcasecmp("ABC\x00123", "abc\x00125"));
var_dump(strnatcasecmp("abc\x00M4", "abc\x00M11"));
```

Output:
int(-25)
int(-1)
int(-2)
int(-1)

Multi-byte safety is a trickier concept with these functions. Consider the following:

```
$mbStr1 = "\u{141}ukasz";
$mbStr2 = "Zebedee";

print "{$mbStr2} and {$mbStr1} are out of order." . PHP_EOL;
var_dump(strcmp($mbStr1, $mbStr2));
```

Output:
Zebedee and Łukasz are out of order.
int(107)

Now, the two strings aren't equal, clearly, but strcmp() is reporting that "\u{141}ukasz" is greater than "Zebedee" by a value of *107*. Well, this is true if we look at byte values:

```
print bin2hex($mbStr1) . PHP_EOL;
print bin2hex($mbStr2) . PHP_EOL;
```

Output:
c581756b61737a
5a656265646565

Remember the binary comparison rules: the two strings differ at the very first byte, and of course *0xc5* is greater than *0x5a* (by decimal *107*, in fact).

Technically strcmp() and strnatcmp() are multi-byte safe because they are not tools for comparing characters; they are designed only for the comparison of arrays of bytes. strcasecmp() and strnatcasecmp() will fail hard, however, once outside the ASCII range (A–Z, a–z), because they only contain logic for dealing with the basic Latin alphabet: All that's happening is bytes *0x41*–*0x5a* (A-Z) map to bytes *0x61*–*0x7a* (a-z). For example:

```
$A = "\u{41}"; // Unicode codepoint for A
$a = "\u{61}"; // a

$latinCapital_L_WithStroke = "\u{141}"; // Ł
$latinSmall_L_WithStroke = "\u{142}"; // ł

var_dump(strcasecmp($A, $a));
var_dump(strcasecmp(
    $latinCapital_L_WithStroke,
    $latinSmall_L_WithStroke
));
```

Output:
int(0)
int(-1)

Unicode codepoints *0x41* and *0x61* are ASCII characters; they're mapped to each other and so return 0 (no difference). The Polish character Ł and its lowercase form ł lie way outside the ASCII range, strcasecmp() has no knowledge of Unicode, and the result is -1.

There is no multi-byte safe form of strcasecmp() or strnatcasecmp(), but one way to get around this is to make use of mb_strtolower() before calling strcasecmp().

```
$polishChars1 = "\u{141}\u{143}\u{146}";
$polishChars2 = "\u{142}\u{144}\u{145}";
```

```
print "Comparing '{$polishChars1}' to '{$polishChars2}'" . PHP_EOL;

var_dump(strcmp(
    mb_strtolower($polishChars1),
    mb_strtolower($polishChars2)
));
```

Output:
Comparing 'ŁŃṇ' to 'łńṆ'
int(0)

The two strings contain the same characters, but in mixed case (as we can see in the first line of output). mb_strtolower() converts both to lowercase, and we use strcmp() for a straightforward binary comparison. The result is 0, and we know our strings contain the same characters. Be warned that this will be many times slower than strcasecmp(), but it will yield correct results!

strncmp(), strncasecmp()

Similar to strcmp(), strncmp() will do a byte-level comparison of two strings starting with the first byte. The function expects exactly three arguments: two strings and an integer value indicating how many bytes to compare. The function returns -1, 0, or 1 if the first string is, respectively, less than, equal to, or greater than the second. The input strings can be of arbitrary length but must have a minimum length matching the third argument. Otherwise, it works in the same way, returning integer -1, 0, or 1:

```
var_dump(strncmp("Fender Stratocaster", "Fender Telecaster", 5));
var_dump(strncmp("Fender Stratocaster", "Fender Telecaster", 8));
var_dump(strncmp("Fender\x00Stratocaster", "Fender\x00Telecaster", 8));
```

Output:
int(0)
int(-1)
int(-1)

The third example above demonstrates the binary safety of strncmp(), a return value of -1 showing that the function was able to compare the strings beyond the null byte. Multi-byte strings can be used with strncmp(), but the comparison is byte-level: the output of the function can be trusted for testing equality but should not be used to evaluate if one multi-byte string is ordered above or below another: `strncmp()` and `strncasecmp()` are not aware of encoding. Hopefully by now this warning will be redundant, but here it is anyway: remember that "case-insensitive" `strncasecmp()` only applies to ASCII range characters.

```
var_dump(strncasecmp("iBanEz JeM", "IbAnEZ rG", 6));
var_dump(strncasecmp("Zebedee", "\u{141}ukasz", 2));
```

Output:
int(0)
int(-75)

In the second line, the name 'Łukasz' should be ordered before 'Zebedee' (assuming we want the ordering to respect the Polish alphabet: more on this in just a moment), but the return value -75 places 'Zebedee' before 'Łukasz'. Note that `strncasecmp()` return values deviate slightly from `strncmp()` (which only returns -1, 0, or 1); this doesn't affect its use as a sorting function, but be aware you'll need to account for it if used in a logical expression. (Interestingly, the official PHP documentation states that `strncasecmp()` should only return -1, 0, or 1 since PHP 8.2, but this is not the case.)

substr_compare()

The `substr_compare()` function is very similar to `strncmp()` but allows you to specify an offset and an optional length and can be set to case-insensitive comparison (again, this only works properly for ASCII strings). It will compare a sub-string of bytes from the first argument (as per the offset and length) to the second (up to the specified length), returning a negative or positive number if the comparison is not equal, and zero if it is.

```
$mijRG = 'Ibanez RG 550 Genesis'; // seriously good VFM this one ;)

// signature is substr_compare($string1, $string2, $offset, $length = null,
$caseInsensitive = false);
// search 'Ibanez' for 'Ibanez'
var_dump(substr_compare($mijRG, 'Ibanez', 0, 6));
// search 'Ibanez' for 'RG 550'
var_dump(substr_compare($mijRG, 'RG 550', 0, 6));
// search 'RG 550' for 'RG 550'
var_dump(substr_compare($mijRG, 'RG 550', 7, 6));
```

```
// negative offset counts from end of string
var_dump(substr_compare($mijRG, 'O Genesis', -9, 9));
// turn off case sensitivity
var_dump(substr_compare($mijRG, 'O gEnEsIs', -9, 9, true));
```

Output:
int(0)
int(-9)
int(0)
int(0)
int(0)

I highly recommend that if you use this function, that length is *always* specified. It is possible to omit this argument (or pass null when also providing an explicit argument for case sensitivity), but the default value for length is not particularly intuitive. Rather than simply being the length of the second string parameter, it is in fact one of two values: either the length of the second parameter or the length of the first parameter minus the offset, whichever is larger.

```
var_dump(substr_compare($mijRG, 'Ibanez', 0));
```

Output:
int(1)

The example above might seem intuitive on first glance, but as we can see from the output, the result is that whatever substring of $mijRG we ended up with, it is not equal to the string literal 'Ibanez'. Without an explicit length argument, the default value is a choice of either 6 (the length of the string 'Ibanez') or 21 (the length of $mijRG minus an offset of 0); 21 is larger, so the function call ends up being the equivalent of substr_compare($mijRG, 'Ibanez', 0, 21); and the return is 1. $mijRG is greater than the string 'Ibanez' (of course it is; it has more bytes). In truth, I have rarely seen this function used in the wild, and any code that needs to search sub-strings for patterns usually ends up being a regular expression or multiple function calls (one to extract the necessary sub-string and another to do the comparison). Nevertheless, you might encounter it on your travels, so you need to know what it does. One more thing: if you're this far into the section and starting to wonder why substr_compare() uses a function parameter to control case-sensitivity, but other functions have named equivalents (e.g., why isn't there just another parameter for strcmp() to control that behavior, why do we need `strcasecmp()`?), then you're in good company. I've often wondered the same, and I suspect the answer is simply that this part of PHP is one of the oldest and therefore has had the most organic growth.

Well. So far, so good. We've seen functions that can be used to sort strings at a byte level, and if those strings happen to be ASCII (*not* extended ASCII!) encoded English, then we get the added bonus of those strings sorting alphabetically (which is a consequence of the design of ASCII, not any special effort on PHP's part). There is also a further refinement to the art of sorting strings in the Unicode era of programming: the application of geographically (or culturally) localized rules (rules of *collation*), which requires that we know something about the human language represented by the byte sequences in the string buffers (and more importantly, we can express that knowledge in our programs).

Collation

Collation is the comparison and organization of text, but (as I hope you are now painfully aware) strings only become human-readable text when interpreted as a certain set of characters. In order to correctly collate collections of strings as human language, we need to apply some encoding rules. As you now know, binary comparison will only correctly collate pure ASCII strings (remember the ASCII codepage was designed with collation in mind, but it was also only designed with the English language in mind); it clearly won't work for multi-byte characters. Binary comparison will also fail to correctly collate the various single-byte ISO-8859 encodings, which put the non-ASCII characters into the extended (8-bit) *0xC0–0xFF* range. For example, if we use the ISO-8859-9 Turkish language codepage, the character Ç (which lies between C and D in the Turkish alphabet) is encoded as byte *0xC7*. If sorting using a binary comparison (e.g., `strcmp()`), any words beginning with Ç would be placed after any starting with A–Z or a–z.

This isn't a problem specific to PHP; it's a problem that exists across the entire spectrum of human interaction with computer systems, it's been a problem for decades (the Encoding section of this chapter explains why), and it's the reason operating systems contain things like `libicu` (International Components for Unicode C++ library) and the `locale` utilities and libraries. For now, it's enough to know that there are system libraries for handling character sorting rules that PHP is able to hook into. Part of PHP's configuration is the ini setting `default_locale`, the value of which is the name of the particular system locale library required for any functions or classes that are able to make use of it. When your script calls a locale-aware function (e.g., for collation or number formatting), the underlying C code will hook into the system library and follow the rules defined there.

strcoll()

The strcoll() function, which works in a similar way to strcmp(), is able to interpret bytes via the system's locale setting. The default_locale can be set in PHP config (and we've covered PHP configuration in an earlier chapter), but here we're going to use setlocale(), which gets and sets the desired system locale at runtime. Here's a quick example: we have four lovely Turkish friends – Şimal, Çağari, Alek, and Maya – and we're going to put them in name order. We'll use the usort() function (details available in Chapter 5, "Array") in combination with strcmp() and strcoll() as the comparison callback functions.

```
$turkishFriends = ["\u{15e}imal", "\u{c7}a\u{11f}ari", "Alek", "Maya",];
usort($turkishFriends, 'strcmp');
print_r($turkishFriends);

setlocale(LC_COLLATE, 'tr_TR.UTF-8');
usort($turkishFriends, 'strcoll');
print_r($turkishFriends);
```

Output:
```
Array
(
    [0] => Alek
    [1] => Maya
    [2] => Çağari
    [3] => Şimal
)
Array
(
    [0] => Alek
    [1] => Çağari
    [2] => Maya
    [3] => Şimal
)
```

First, we create an array of strings, $turkishFriends, and use Unicode escapes for the names that have Turkish characters (and PHP's default encoding is UTF-8, so these will be multi-byte characters). The first sort – `usort($turkishFriends, 'strcmp');` – will sort the array using the no-frills binary comparison of `strcmp()`. Predictably enough, we end up with the wrong collation; the names beginning with Turkish characters have been sorted to the end of the array.

Next, we call `setlocale(LC_COLLATE, 'tr_TR.UTF-8');`, which tells PHP that when we perform collation, we wish to use the rules for the "tr_TR.UTF-8" locale. If that locale is installed on the system (which is the case for the Docker images for this book), then when we call `usort()` with `'strcoll'` specified as the comparison function, the order is correct. (If you are following along at home and using the Docker images that can be built from this book's GitHub repository, those images have the "tr_TR.UTF-8" locale installed and enabled already.)

`strcoll()` is a venerable old thing; it has been with us since the dark days of PHP 4, and it is also dependent on the underlying operating system to function correctly. A more modern approach to localized collation is the `Collator` class, which is part of PHP's `intl` module and is compiled against `libicu`. It is independent of the operating system and recommended over juggling `setlocale()` and `strcoll()`.

Similarity

Table 8-9. String similarity functions

`levenshtein()`	Calculate Levenshtein distance between two strings
`metaphone()`	Calculate the metaphone key
`similar_text()`	Count matching chars
`soundex()`	Calculate the soundex key

metaphone(), soundex()

Sometimes, when two strings are not precisely equal, it is useful to know the degree of similarity between them. There are two general forms of analysis available in PHP. One technique examines the phonetic properties of strings, for which there are two similar functions (implementing different algorithms): `metaphone()` and `soundex()`.

```
var_dump(metaphone("algorithm"));
var_dump(metaphone("algo-rhythm"));

var_dump(soundex("algorithm"));
var_dump(soundex("algo-rhythm"));

Output:
string(6) "ALKROM"
string(6) "ALKROM"
string(4) "A426"
string(4) "A426"
```

The output might look a little weird; those are the Metaphone (and Soundex) keys of the input strings. Both algorithms aim to encode (English) homophones in similar ways: the example above demonstrates that "rithm" and "rhythm" have identical pronunciation, and we can see from the output that the two strings give the same results. Soundex is the older of the two algorithms, first patented in 1918 by Robert C. Russell and Margaret King Odell; PHP's implementation follows that described in *The Art of Computer Programming, Volume 3* (Donald Knuth, 1973). Metaphone was developed from Soundex and first published in *Computer Language, Vol. 7, No. 12* (Lawrence Philips, Dec 1990). Both algorithms were created for English language strings and do not handle UTF-8 characters:

```
var_dump(soundex("L"));
var_dump(soundex("\u{141}"));
var_dump(metaphone("L"));
var_dump(metaphone("\u{141}"));

Output:
string(4) "L000"
string(4) "0000"
string(1) "L"
string(0) ""
```

A detailed description of these two algorithms isn't required here (you can read the original publications for that), but know that Soundex always returns a four-character string where "0000" means that no letters were detected, and if Metaphone returns an empty string, then it too did not find any letters.

levenshtein()

As an alternative to phonetic analysis, it is possible to express the lexicographic distance (the number of inserts, deletes, or substitutions) between two strings. The Levenshtein distance algorithm (from *Binary codes capable of correcting deletions, insertions, and reversals* – Vladimir Levenshtein, 1966) provides a method for such computation, implemented in PHP with the levenshtein() function:

```
var_dump(levenshtein('Hello world', 'Hello world'));
var_dump(levenshtein('Hello WORLD', 'Hello world'));
var_dump(levenshtein('status', 'stats'));
```

Output:
```
int(0)
int(5)
int(1)
```

Without going too deep into the linear algebra behind it all, the Levenshtein algorithm finds the minimum number of insertions, deletions, and substitutions required to transform one string into another. In the code above, we can see the first comparison is between identical strings, so the distance is *0*. Next, we substitute WORLD for world, so the distance is *5* (because the function is case-sensitive), and finally, the distance between 'status' and 'stats' is *1* (deletion). The levenshtein() function also accepts additional arguments to provide integer weighting for the different types of transformation:

```
$insertCost = 2;
$replaceCost = 2;
$deleteCost = 1;

var_dump(levenshtein('status', 'statu',
    $insertCost,
    $replaceCost,
    $deleteCost
));
var_dump(levenshtein('status', 'statue',
    $insertCost,
    $replaceCost,
    $deleteCost
));
```

Output:
```
int(1)
int(2)
```

In the code above, we add a cost of *2* for insertion and replacement and *1* for deletion, which moves "statue" further away from "status" than "statu". A user inputting "statu" to our program is (probably) more likely to have meant to type "status" than if they had typed "statue". This is one of the common uses of Levenshtein's algorithm; for example, the version control system git makes use of it to suggest close matches when sub-commands are incorrectly entered:

```
$ git statu
git: 'statu' is not a git command. See 'git --help'.

The most similar commands are
    status
    stage
    stash
```

Be aware that levenshtein() performs a byte-level comparison, not a character comparison, so multi-byte string comparison will yield larger values than expected, depending on encoding. It should not be considered multi-byte safe, but it is otherwise binary safe.

An alternative algorithm is available via the similar_text() function:

```
$percentRef = 0.0;
var_dump(similar_text(
    "Hello World",
    "hello world",
    $percentRef
));
print "Strings are {$percentRef}% similar". PHP_EOL;
```

Output:
```
int(9)
Strings are 81.818181818182% similar
```

CHAPTER 8   STRINGS

The function returns an integer value of the number of matching bytes between the strings (not characters; like levenstein(), this function is binary safe but not multi-byte safe). similar_text() also accepts an optional third argument, which is passed by reference and will have the percentage similarity assigned if it is present (which saves you the bother of calculating it yourself).

Testing for Sub-strings

Perhaps the most common use case, after testing or comparing entire string values, is to do the same for just a portion (or sub-string) of a string. PHP offers several functions for searching for a particular sequence of bytes (or characters, for the mb_* functions) or comparing a subset of bytes:

Table 8-10. *Sub-string test functions*

str_contains() str_starts_with() str_ends_with()	Test for sub-string at start, end, or anywhere in a string
strncmp()	Binary-safe comparison of first N bytes
strpos(), mb_strpos() stripos(), mb_stripos() strrpos(), mb_strrpos() strripos(), mb_strripos()	Return position of first occurrence of sub-string
strspn(), strcspn()	Length of string consisting of chars in (or not in) a set

All of the functions above are concerned with searching a buffer of bytes to see if there is a subset of them that matches a given sequence. The mb_* functions will do this on a character basis.

str_contains(), str_starts_with(), str_ends_with()

The functions str_contains(), str_starts_with(), and str_ends_with() are all related: they accept the full string to be searched (the "haystack") as the first argument and a sub-string (the "needle") as the second. All return a boolean value.

461

CHAPTER 8 STRINGS

```
$text = "The skiing in Turkey is very well-kept secret. \u{1F970} \u{1F3BF}
Kartalkaya \u{1F3BF} \u{1F970}";

var_dump(str_contains($text, "skiing in Turkey"));
var_dump(str_contains($text, "\u{1F3BF}"));
var_dump(str_starts_with($text, "The"));
var_dump(str_starts_with($text, "skiing"));
var_dump(str_ends_with($text, "\u{1F970}"));
```

Output:
bool(true)
bool(true)
bool(true)
bool(false)
bool(true)

Note that we have multi-byte characters in the example code (as Unicode escapes) to demonstrate that although the three functions are not character aware *per se*, they can be safely used with multi-byte data: the byte-level comparison either finds the sub-string or it does not. All three are also binary safe; the following demonstrates that str_contains() will read beyond a null byte:

```
$text = "Let's go \x00 skiing!";

var_dump(str_contains($text, "go \x00 skiing"));
var_dump(str_contains($text, "go \x00 snowboarding"));
```

Output:
bool(true)
bool(false)

strpos(), mb_strpos(), et al.

If it is necessary to know where in a string a given sub-string can be found, there are several related functions for finding the answer: strpos() (and related case-insensitive/reversed forms) and the multi-byte equivalent forms mb_strpos() et al.

```
$quote = 'We demand rigidly defined areas of doubt and uncertainty!';

var_dump(strpos($quote, 'We demand'));
var_dump(stripos($quote, 'wE dEmAnD'));
```

```
var_dump(strpos($quote, 'and'));
var_dump(strrpos($quote, 'and'));
var_dump(strripos($quote, 'AnD'));
var_dump(strpos($quote, 'so long and thanks for all the fish'));
```

Output:
int(0)
int(0)
int(6)
int(41)
int(41)
bool(false)

The code above demonstrates all of the variants of strpos() (stripos(), strrpos(), and strripos()). The sub-string 'We demand' exists at the very beginning of the $quote string; the call to strpos() on line three returns an integer position of 0. If we accessed using array syntax, $quote[0] has a value of W, $quote[1] is e, and so on. The next line calls the case-insensitive form stripos(). (Remember that this will only work for ASCII characters!) with the same result of 0. The next two lines call strpos() and strrpos(), searching for the sub-string 'and', which is found twice in the $quote string. strpos() returns 6 (the first time the sub-string is found), and strrpos() - which is searching backwards from the end of $quote returns 41 (what a shame it wasn't 42).

The call to strripos() on line seven demonstrates the case-insensitive form of strrpos(), and finally we have a call to strpos() looking for a sub-string that does not exist in $quote. Pay careful attention here: the return value is boolean false, not an integer, but the str*pos() functions can also return integer 0, which will evaluate to boolean false in a weakly-typed comparison. *Always* use a type-strict test with the results of str*pos(), the expression (strpos($str, $subStr) == false) - note the weakly-typed equivalence operator - will evaluate to true if $subStr isn't found, and also if it is found at the beginning of the string.

All str*pos() functions also accept an optional integer third parameter as an offset: the functions will skip the first (or last, in the case of the reversed forms) N bytes before beginning the search.

CHAPTER 8   STRINGS

```
var_dump(strpos($quote,'and', 10));
```

Output:
int(41)

Remember that the str*pos() functions are returning integer values indicating which byte in the buffer the sub-string starts at, which is fine for single-byte encoded ASCII text but less useful for multi-byte encodings where it is generally more intuitive to work with character positions. The mb_str*pos() functions work at the character level and with a range of multi-byte encoding formats (UTF-8 being the default for PHP and the most ubiquitous on today's internet). Here's a short demonstration; let's start with some multi-byte data:

```
$quote = "\u{15e}\u{fc}phe ve belirsizlik i\u{e7}ermeyen kat\u{131} kurallar talep ediyoruz!";
print $quote . PHP_EOL;
```

Output:
Şüphe ve belirsizlik içermeyen katı kurallar talep ediyoruz!

We've translated $quote to Turkish (many thanks to my good friend Esra for providing the translation); the non-ASCII characters are expressed as Unicode escapes, and the result is a string that is mostly single-byte ASCII with some multi-byte characters. If you are using the provided Docker image for the book, then the default encoding will be UTF-8, as we can see if we obtain the byte values for the first five characters.

```
var_dump(bin2hex("\u{15e}\u{fc}phe"));
```

Output:
string(14) "c59ec3bc706865"

The byte sequence is *0xC5 0x9E* (Latin Capital S with Cedilla – Ş), *0xC3 0xBC* (Latin Small U with Diaresis – ü), then *0x70 0x68 0x65* (Latin Small P, H, and E, all in the ASCII range). Let's compare strpos() with mb_strpos():

```
var_dump(strpos($quote, 'phe ve'));
var_dump(mb_strpos($quote, 'phe ve'));
```

Output:
int(4)
int(2)

As you might expect, strpos() returns 4, because phe ve is indeed four bytes from the start of $quote. mb_strpos() returns 2 because it is aware of UTF-8 character encoding and is able to evaluate the first four bytes as two distinct characters. The mb_str*pos() functions will accept an optional offset value as a third argument and are also able to work with other multi-byte encodings, which can be specified as an optional fourth argument, in case you need to work with something other than UTF-8.

strspn(), strcspn()

If you are interested in finding how many bytes at the start of a string match a set of values (or do not match, as the case may be), but are not concerned about an exact sub-string match, it is possible to define a collection of bytes, known as a mask, which the sub-string must contain, and use the strspn() and strcspn() functions.

```
$book = 'ISBN-978-1484267905 PHP 8 Objects, Patterns, and Practice';
var_dump(strspn($book, '.-BINSO123456789'));
```

Output:
int(19)

Here we define a mask that contains all of the (ASCII) characters in the sub-string ISBN-978-1484267905, and strspn() returns 19, which means the length of the sub-string containing only the bytes defined in the mask is nineteen.

To achieve the same outcome but with inverted logic, use strcspn():

```
var_dump(strcspn($book, ' '));
```

Output:
int(19)

Here we've determined that the first twenty bytes do not contain an ASCII space character. Note that both strspn() and strcspn() are binary safe...

```
$binaryStr = "ab\x00cdef";
var_dump(strspn($binaryStr, "a\x00bc"));
var_dump(strcspn($binaryStr, "def"));
```

Output:
int(4)
int(4)

...but not multi-byte safe:

```
$mbStr = "\u{1F920} kaboom!"; // a single emoji char, then a space,
                                then kaboom!
var_dump(bin2hex("\u{1F920}")); // bytes 0xf0 0x9f 0xa4 0xa0 in UTF-8
var_dump(strspn($mbStr, "\u{1F920}")); // returns 4 because of multi-
                                byte char
var_dump(strcspn($mbStr, " ")); // also returns 4
var_dump(strspn($mbStr, "\x9f\xa0\xf0\xa4")); // also returns 4 despite
                                scrambling the byte order
```

Output:
string(8) "f09fa4a0"
int(4)
int(4)
int(4)

These two functions simply analyze the input strings at the byte level; they'll handle a null byte, but there is no awareness of encoding. Although not shown here, the two functions also accept optional length and offset parameters, in case you need to restrict the search to a subset of the input string bytes.

Counting

Another common task is to find the length of a string or find the number of times a particular pattern occurs, for which PHP offers the following functions:

Table 8-11. String counting functions

count_chars()	count occurrences of byte values in a string
strlen(), mb_strlen()	return number of bytes in a string
substr_count(), mb_substr_count()	count occurrences of sub-string in a string

count_chars()

CHAPTER 8 STRINGS

For a byte-level analysis of string data, the count_chars() function will meet a number of use cases. It operates in five different modes and will return either an array or string depending on the mode parameter passed in when called. Its job is to simply report on byte values found or not found in the entire string being analyzed; it is not aware of character encodings and therefore will not provide information about multi-byte characters (it should probably have been called count_bytes(), but this function comes from a time and place where *byte* and *character* were synonymous).

```
var_dump(count_chars("abcd"));
```

Output:
```
Array
(
    [0] => 0
    ...
    [96] => 0
    [97] => 1
    [98] => 1
    [99] => 1
    [100] => 1
    [101] => 0
    ...
```

By default, count_chars() outputs a 256-element array of integers; each element position corresponds to a byte value count. The output above shows that bytes *97–100* (remember these are decimal values) each have a count of one. Every other byte has a count of zero. Our input string contained the ASCII letters "abcd", which correspond to those points in the ASCII codepage (the letter "a" is ASCII byte *0x61*, which has a decimal value of *97*, and so on). Remember that we can also pass an extra (integer) argument to the function to control its behavior:

```
print_r(count_chars("abcd", 1));
```

Output:
```
Array
(
    [97] => 1
    [98] => 1
```

CHAPTER 8   STRINGS

```
    [99] => 1
    [100] => 1
)
```

The default value for the mode argument is 0; if we explicitly pass 1, then the function only returns non-zero counts, as we see above. If we passed 2, it would return only zero-counted byte values. The final two modes will return strings containing only the bytes found or only the bytes not found:

```
var_dump(count_chars("hello world", 3));
var_dump(count_chars("abcd", 4));
```

Output:
```
string(8) " dehlorw"
string(252) "
!"#$%&'()*+,-./01234
```

Mode 3 returns each byte encountered (in order), and mode 4 gives us all of the bytes not encountered. This includes all of the non-printing control bytes in the *0x00–0x1F* range, which is why the output string looks that way: the first 32 bytes are control characters (including the "bell" character *0x07* – your terminal might make a noise when running the second line of the example), and the first display characters are the space at *0x20* and the exclamation mark at *0x21*.

strlen(), mb_strlen() + secret bonus

The simplest case is usually "How long is my string?" In other words, how many bytes are in this buffer? This is often a useful thing to know, perhaps for iterating over strings or for measuring how many bytes to tell a remote client to expect from your program (e.g., in a Content-Length: header). Good old strlen() has this use case covered.

```
$response = '<!DOCTYPE html><html><head></head><body>Lots of lovely content.</body></html>';

$contentLength = strlen($response);
var_dump($contentLength);
var_dump(strlen("abc\x00def"));
```

Output:
int(77)
int(7)

strlen() is very simple: you give it a string, and it tells you how many bytes are in there. It's binary safe, as the second strlen() call shows, and since its job is to count bytes, using it with multi-byte data won't break anything (provided you remember it is counting bytes, not characters).

```
$mbStr = "\u{1F920}";
var_dump(bin2hex($mbStr));
var_dump(strlen($mbStr));
```

Output:
string(8) "f09fa4a0"
int(4)

Unicode codepoint *0x1F920* ("Face with Cowboy Hat") is encoded with four bytes in UTF-8, which the output confirms. But what if we actually need a character count? The mbstring extension has us covered by providing the function mb_strlen():

```
var_dump(mb_strlen($mbStr));
```

Output:
int(1)

Marvelous. We have an accurate character count of a multi-byte string. And now, because I'm in one of my moods, allow me to present this:

```
$prideFlag = "\u{1F3F3}\u{FE0F}\u{200D}\u{1F308}";
print $prideFlag . PHP_EOL;
var_dump(mb_strlen($prideFlag));
```

Output:

🏳️‍🌈

int(4)

I've thrown you a curveball. This is the Unicode Rainbow Flag character, which is multi-codepoint – remember our Bald Man (Man + ZERO_WIDTH_JOINER + Bald) from earlier? This is the same thing; it's using multiple UTF-8 characters to represent a single emoji. Kind of a pain to count character length now, huh. Let me introduce you to a new concept: *graphemes*. Graphemes are simply symbols that represent the smallest unit of language in a writing system, and they can be single images or sequences of letters that represent a single sound. PHP's intl extension offers some grapheme-aware functions; here's a quick example (you'll need the intl PHP module installed, natch):

```
var_dump(bin2hex($prideFlag));
var_dump(grapheme_strlen($prideFlag));
```

Output:
```
string(28) "f09f8fb3efb88fe2808df09f8c88"
int(1)
```

We can see that our flag is represented by fourteen bytes, which constitute four UTF-8 characters (one for each codepoint we used): *0xF0 0x9F 0x8F 0xB3 + 0xEF 0xB8 0x8F + 0xE2 0x80 0x8D + 0xF0 0x9F 0x8C 0x88*. mb_strlen() is UTF-8 aware and dutifully reports *4* characters, but grapheme_strlen() is also aware of multi-codepoint encoding and returns *1*. Here's our bald man causing the same problems for us:

```
$baldMan = "\u{1F468}\u{200D}\u{1F9B2}";
var_dump(mb_strlen($baldMan));
var_dump(grapheme_strlen($baldMan));
```

Output:
```
int(3)
int(1)
```

substr_count(), mb_substr_count()

Moving on from basic counts of total length, how about counting occurrences of substrings? Here's a simple example using substr_count():

```
$sayHello = 'hello hello hello';
var_dump(substr_count($sayHello, 'hello'));
var_dump(substr_count($sayHello, 'll'));
var_dump(substr_count($sayHello, 'l'));
```

Output:
```
int(3)
int(3)
int(6)
```

Pretty straightforward stuff, 'hello' occurs three times, as does 'll', and there are six instances of l in $sayHello. substr_count() is also binary safe:

```
var_dump(substr_count("a\x00 a\x00 a\x00", "\x00"));
var_dump(substr_count("a\x00 a\x00 a\x00", 'a'));
```

Output:
int(3)
int(3)

You can also supply offset and length arguments to test sub-string of the first argument:

```
var_dump(substr_count($sayHello, "hello", 0, 11));
```

Output:
int(2)

When it comes to multi-byte safety, it really comes down to knowing what encoding you're dealing with. There is an mbstring function mb_substr_count(), which will analyze the encodings of both input strings (and internally convert them to UTF-8 if either is in a different format); otherwise, it functions identically to substr_count(). Take a look at the following:

```
$name = "\u{C7}a\u{11F}ari";
var_dump(substr_count($name, 'a'));
var_dump(substr_count($name, "\u{C7}"));
```

Output:
int(2)
int(1)

As we can see this is working correctly, because substr_count() is simply traversing the bytes of $name and looking for the same byte sequences in 'a' (the first call) or "\u{C7}" (the second call). The encoding (which should be UTF-8 if following coding standard PSR-1) used to create the string data for $name will match the encoding for the string literals, so the byte sequences will match, and we'll get a correct count. If we change the encoding of $name using the mb_convert_encoding() function to UTF-16, we get the following:

CHAPTER 8 STRINGS

```
$name = mb_convert_encoding("\u{C7}a\u{11F}ari", 'utf16');
var_dump(substr_count($name, 'a'));
var_dump(substr_count($name, "\u{C7}"));

var_dump(bin2hex($name));
var_dump(bin2hex('a'));
var_dump(bin2hex("\u{C7}"));
```

Output:
int(2)
int(0)
string(24) "00c70061011f006100720069"
string(2) "61"
string(4) "c387"

There are a few things to unpack here. First of all, we search for 'a' and get a count of 2. Secondly, we search for the Unicode character at codepoint U+00C7 (the Turkish letter Ç) and get a count of 0. Finally, we get a dump of byte values for the UTF-16 string $name, then for the sake of this explanation, the same dump for 'a' and "\u{C7}". Can you spot what's going on?

We found 'a' simply because the UTF-16 encoding is a two-byte sequence *0x00 0x61* (told you there were redundant bytes in fixed-width encodings), the ASCII (and therefore UTF-8) encoding for 'a' is *0x61*, and that byte value does indeed appear twice in the $name byte stream. We get lucky because UTF-16 doesn't deviate too much from the ASCII range character byte values, and substr_count() is completely agnostic of encoding. Things aren't so great when we move outside the ASCII range. U+00C7 is encoded quite differently between UTF-16 and UTF-8 (*0x00 0xC7* and *0xC3 0x87*, respectively), and we get a count of *0*. The problem works both ways:

```
$name = mb_convert_encoding("\u{C387}", 'UTF-16'); // U+C387 is a Korean
                                                   Hangul Syllable
var_dump(substr_count($name, "\u{C7}")); // U+00C7 is a Latin Capital C
                                            with Cedilla
```

Output:
int(1)

By mixing our encodings we get a false positive, because the UTF-16 encoding for U+C387 is *0xC3 0x87*, which matches the UTF-8 encoding for U+00C7. Now at this point, you might be thinking, "it's OK, we have mb_substr_count() and surely that can handle mixed encodings" and if that's the case, then sorry, but no. The C implementation of mb_substr_count() is essentially identical to substr_count(), with an added (faulty) attempt to normalize the encoding of both strings to UTF-8.

(For reference, the C source code for both functions can be found with the following links.)

https://github.com/php/php-src/blob/734f686ac4708abc1606a0661ce435d1a7851152/ext/mbstring/mbstring.c#L808

https://github.com/php/php-src/blob/f91dcad567379856d2883531fdf070ebaca0fd5f/ext/standard/string.c#L5685

```
$utf16Str = mb_convert_encoding("\u{C7}a\u{11F}ari", 'UTF-16');
$utf32Str = mb_convert_encoding("\u{C7}a\u{11F}ari", 'UTF-32');

var_dump(bin2hex($utf16Str));
var_dump(bin2hex($utf32Str));

var_dump(mb_substr_count($utf16Str, "\u{11F}ari"));
var_dump(mb_substr_count($utf32Str, "\u{11F}ari"));
```

Output:
```
string(24) "00c70061011f006100720069"
string(48) "000000c70000006100000011f0000006100000007200000069"
int(0)
int(0)
```

As we can see, the encoding conversion works just fine; we get UTF-16 and UTF-32 encoded strings (all those null bytes…), but mb_substr_count() does not normalize them to UTF-8: if it did, then we would have non-zero returns. mb_substr_count() does accept a third parameter, allowing you to specify the encoding, but this applies to *both* arguments, and we're left with the same problem:

```
var_dump(mb_substr_count($utf16Str, "\u{11F}ari", 'UTF-16'));
var_dump(mb_substr_count($utf32Str, "\u{11F}ari", 'UTF-32'));
```

Output:
int(0)
int(0)

The problem here, of course, is that the string literal "\u{11F}" is UTF-8 (assuming a default encoding of UTF-8). At this point we could choose to use mb_convert_encoding() so our strings are identically encoded...

```
var_dump(mb_substr_count(
    $utf32Str,
    mb_convert_encoding("\u{11F}ari", 'UTF-32')
));
```

Output:
int(1)

... but why bother? If we know (or can determine in code) the encoding of the strings, we might as well just use substr_count() after the necessary conversion(s). As long as both strings are encoded correctly, then all we need is the byte-level comparison of substr_count().

```
var_dump(substr_count(
    mb_convert_encoding($utf32Str, 'UTF-8', 'UTF-32'),
    "\u{11F}"
));
```

Output:
int(1)

Note that mb_substr_count() does not offer the length and offset parameters of substr_count(), so a solution like the one above actually offers *more* utility than its mbstring counterpart. The mbstring extension has a few gotchas like this, and some tools (of varying quality) for dealing with them. There are also alternative extensions for handling multi-byte data. We'll look at them in more detail later in the chapter.

Phew! That was quite a lot to take in, wasn't it? It's inevitable, I'm afraid. PHP exists to crunch text because that's what the internet did back in the day (it wasn't all funny pictures of cats and TikTok in the 90's). Well done for getting this far; treat yourself to a cup of tea, and we'll get on with the next category...

Conversion and Extraction

Here we're going to focus on the string functions that PHP offers for making new data from existing string data. These functions take two general forms: functions for creating (or populating existing) arrays containing sub-strings of the original and functions for extracting single sub-strings.

Creating Arrays or Variables

Table 8-12. *String parsing and conversion functions*

explode()	Create array of sub-strings from a string using a separator sequence
str_split(), mb_str_split()	Create an array of sub-strings with a fixed size
str_getcsv()	Parse delimited string data, create an array
sscanf()	Parse a string using a sprintf format, create variables
parse_str(), mb_parse_str()	Parse a string in HTTP query format, populates an array

Let's start with one of the most wonderfully named functions in the history of programming...

explode()

A very common use-case is the creation of an array containing the words (or some other text sub-unit) in a string, where each word is separated by a given character (usually a space or a newline).

```
$quote = 'We demand rigidly defined areas of doubt and uncertainty!';

print_r(explode(' ', $quote));
```

Output:
```
Array
(
    [0] => We
    [1] => demand
```

        [2] => rigidly
        [3] => defined
    ...

There we have it, a pretty simple function to understand. The original string has been chopped up into an array of sub-strings, the separator character being a space character. Note that the separator character is removed from the resulting sub-string, and it's also worth noting that the separator can be a sequence, not just a single byte value (yes, I'm still harping on about byte values; we could have used explode("\x20", $quote); to achieve the same results). Take a look at this:

```
print_r(explode("\x61\x6e", $quote));
```

Output:
```
Array
(
    [0] => We dem
    [1] => d rigidly defined areas of doubt
    [2] => d uncertainty!
)
```

The byte sequence "\x61\x6e" is simply the ASCII letters 'an', and we can see that the string has been split at every occurrence of that sequence (and those characters are not present in the resulting data). explode(), like most other string functions, is binary safe:

```
$weirdString = "So long, and thanks\x00for all the fish.";
```

```
print_r(explode("\x00", $weirdString));
```

Output:
```
Array
(
    [0] => So long, and thanks
    [1] => for all the fish.
)
```

str_split(), mb_str_split()

Similar to explode() is the str_split() function:

```
var_export(str_split("Thanks for all the fish."));
```

Output:
```
array (
  0 => 'T',
  1 => 'h',
  2 => 'a',
```

By default str_split() returns an array of single bytes but will accept a second integer argument to control the byte length of each element in the array:

```
var_export(str_split("Thanks for all the fish.", 12));
```

Output:
```
array (
  0 => 'Thanks for a',
  1 => 'll the fish.',
)
```

Naturally, this will present problems with multi-byte encodings:

```
$bytes = str_split("\u{5408}\u{6c23}\u{9053}"); // 合氣道 - will be UTF-8
                                                   encoded on *nix systems
foreach ($bytes as $byte) {
    print "0x" . bin2hex($byte) . " ";
}
```

Output:
```
0xe5 0x90 0x88 ...
```

The three Unicode escape sequences generate a UTF-8 encoded string, but str_split() is not encoding-aware and simply chops it into an array of single bytes. We can see the byte values in the output thanks to bin2hex(), and the first three are indeed the correct encoding for the 合 character. Not particularly useful, the original meaning of the text has been thoroughly mangled and would require careful reassembly to restore. Fortunately there is an mbstring equivalent function, mb_str_split(), which works on characters rather than bytes:

CHAPTER 8   STRINGS

```
$chars = mb_str_split("\u{5408}\u{6c23}\u{9053}"); // 合氣道 - will be
                                                   UTF-8 encoded on
                                                   *nix systems
foreach ($chars as $char) {
    print $char . PHP_EOL;
}
```

Output:
合
氣
道

Like str_split(), mb_str_split() also accepts an integer argument to control the character width of the returned array elements; it also accepts a third string argument to specify the encoding used in the input data.

```
$utf16str = "\x54\x08\x62\xc3\x90\x53"; // 合氣道 - raw byte values for
                                        UTF-16 encoding
$chars = mb_str_split($utf16str, 1, 'UTF-16');
foreach ($chars as $char) {
    print bin2hex($char) . PHP_EOL;
}
```

Output:
5408
62c3
9053

str_getcsv()

str_getcsv() is very similar to explode(): it takes a single string as input and returns an array of strings, and the input string is parsed according to the CSV (comma-separated values) format. Note the escape: named parameter on both str_getcsv() calls: This parameter (either named or positional form) is required from PHP 8.4 onwards (and will emit an E_DEPRECATED error if omitted):

```
$species = "Dentrassis,Dolphins,G'Gugvuntt,Vl'hurgs,Golgafrinchans";
print_r(str_getcsv($species, escape: '\\'));

$species = "Dentrassis|Dolphins|G'Gugvuntt|Vl'hurgs|Golgafrinchans";
```

478

CHAPTER 8   STRINGS

```
print_r(str_getcsv($species, separator: '|', escape: '\\'));
```

Output: (for both print_r() statements)
```
Array
(
    [0] => Dentrassis
    [1] => Dolphins
    [2] => G'Gugvuntt
    [3] => Vl'hurgs
    [4] => Golgafrinchans
)
```

CSV as a method of structured data interchange dates way back to the days of flared trousers, loud shirts, and IBM FORTRAN (the 1970s, in case you don't remember). As you can see from the example above, values are delimited by a comma by default but can be separated by any character (in the second case this is the pipe character; the ASCII horizontal tab character *0x09* is another common choice). This is quite a common method of structuring data, and it is by no means unusual to see it in use today. I would, however, advise that you take care when using str_getcsv() and exercise particular caution around what constitutes valid CSV data in your application. Let's take a look at more complex cases.

```
$csvRow1 = "Douglas Adams,"
    . "you may think it's a long way down the road to the chemist's, but
    that's just peanuts to space.";
$csvRow2 = "Iain M. Banks,"
    . '"I am not an animal brain, I am not even some attempt to produce an
    AI through software running on a computer"';

print_r(str_getcsv($csvRow1, escape: '\\'));
print_r(str_getcsv($csvRow2, escape: '\\'));
```

Output:
```
Array
(
    [0] => Douglas Adams
    [1] => you may think it's a long way down the road to the chemist's
    [2] =>  but that's just peanuts to space.
)
```

479

CHAPTER 8 STRINGS

```
Array
(
    [0] => Iain M. Banks
    [1] => I am not an animal brain, I am not even some attempt to produce
    an AI through software running on a computer
)
```

The code above illustrates an obvious problem with the CSV format: what happens when the delimiter character is also field data? Both quotes are full sentences with grammatically correct commas, but as we can see from parsing $csvRow1, we end up with three strings in the output array. $csvRow2 solves the problem using the field enclosure method described in RFC 4180 (and was in conventional use prior to the RFC's publication); here we enclose the field data with double-quote meta-characters. We can see from the output that this gives correct results: the second field is returned as a single string, and the comma survives intact. Oh? What's that I hear you say? Yes, absolutely correct. The next problem we now have is handling the enclosure character itself. Well spotted! The RFC and most tools that create CSV data (MS Excel, Google Docs...) make use of a second instance of the enclosure character as an escape sequence, as we can see here:

```
$csvRow3 = 'Iain M. Banks,';
$csvRow3 .= '"""Jernau Gurgeh,"" the machine said, making a sighing noise,
""a guilty system recognizes no innocents..."""';

print_r(str_getcsv($csvRow3, escape: '\\'));
```

Output:
```
Array
(
    [0] => Iain M. Banks
    [1] => "Jernau Gurgeh," the machine said, making a sighing noise, "a
        guilty system recognizes no innocents..."
)
```

It's ugly syntax, but it works. This is how the popular tools implement it, and it's how the RFC specifies it should work. Interestingly, the official documentation for str_getcsv() states that a backslash character can be used to escape the enclosure character, which does work to some extent. Let's throw some awful data at this function and see what happens.

```
$csvRow4 = 'binary' . "\x00" . 'safe_field'
    . ',we"ird"_fi"eld"_1'  // multiple enclosure chars mid-data,
                                not wrapped
    . ',"we"ird"_fi"eld"_2"'  // multiple enclosure chars wrapped between
                                RFC-compliant enclosures
    . ',"we\"ird\"_fi\"eld\"_3"'  // slash-escaped enclosures between RFC-
                                compliant enclosures
;
print_r(str_getcsv($csvRow4, escape: '\\'));

Output:
Array
(
    [0] => binarysafe_field
    [1] => we"ird"_fi"eld"_1
    [2] => weird"_fi"eld"_2"
    [3] => we\"ird\"_fi\"eld\"_3
)
```

From above, we can deduce a few things. First, str_getcsv() is binary safe, like most other core string functions: we get binarysafe_field as our first string despite the null byte in the middle. Second, the enclosure character can be used freely in a data field provided the field isn't enclosed but behaves strangely if the field is enclosed: we can see from weird_field_2 that one of the double-quotes has simply vanished, and we get an extra double-quote character at the end of the field data. Finally, if we use the slash escape mechanism, the double-quotes that are liberally spread around the field data are handled correctly, but we get the escape character as part of the output. I suppose the moral of this story is to always use the RFC enclosure and escape mechanisms and to thoroughly test your code and check the input data. str_getcsv() does accept additional arguments, allowing you to define your own enclosure and escape characters, but your mileage may vary: the standard/conventional ways are far more portable.

Another thing to bear in mind: str_getcsv() only deals with *single* lines. There are many posts and blogs out there on the theme of "PHP's str_getcsv() function is broken" that are often problems in file handling. The full RFC 4180 specification stipulates how to handle multi-line CSV data, which becomes important when field

CHAPTER 8 STRINGS

data might *also* contain line breaks. Simply wrapping str_getcsv() (to parse the fields) around explode() (to break multi-line data into an array of strings) can (and usually does) lead to broken data.

sscanf()

Now we come to quite a powerful function, sscanf(). It belongs to a family of functions (such as sprintf() et al., which we'll see more of in this section) with a rich history in computer programming. The BCPL language (first implemented in 1967) contained a function WRITEF() which took a specially formatted string expression and interpolated further argument data into a returned string, and the C language has had a scanf() function in <stdio.h> since the days of Version 7 Unix. PHP's sscanf() wraps the C equivalent and will extract portions of an input string according to a formatting expression. The function also accepts any number of additional variables, which will have the extracted data assigned to them (they are passed by reference by default); otherwise, an array of the extracted data is returned. This sounds complicated (and it can certainly get complicated), so let's start with a simple example:

```
$str = 'Gender: M, Height: 1.85m, Weight: 95kg';
var_dump(sscanf($str, 'Gender: %1s, Height: %fm, Weight: %dkg'));
```

Output:
```
array(3) {
  [0]=>
  string(1) "M"
  [1]=>
  float(1.85)
  [2]=>
  int(95)
}
```

The second argument to scscanf() is the formatting expression, and the parts of the expression triggering the extraction are %1s, %f, and %d. These are *conversion specifications*, which have the syntax % followed by certain meta-characters to describe width, precision, or to control other behavior, and then a *specifier* ("d" for decimal integer, "f" for float, "s" for string, and so on). In our expression above, %1s matches "a single string byte," %f matches "number with a decimal point," and %d matches an integer. The rest of the formatting expression is a literal match of all other characters, which have to match the input exactly, with the exception of spaces (including tabs): a single space in the formatting expression will match any amount of whitespace in the input.

Here's an example that uses reference variables as extra arguments (passed by reference) and a * modifier to suppress the assignment of the first conversion specification (the single "Gender:" character, which we're ignoring because who cares). Note that the input string $str has extra spaces and a tab character, which do not affect the outcome:

```
$str = "Gender:    M, Height:\t1.85m, Weight:    95kg";
sscanf($str, 'Gender: %*1s, Height: %fm, Weight: %dkg', $height, $weight);
var_dump($height, $weight);
```

Output:
```
float(1.85)
int(95)
```

sscanf() will also accept regular expressions as conversion specifications, though this is undocumented in the official PHP documentation:

```
$str = 'Gender: M, Height: 1.85m, Weight: 95kg';
var_dump(sscanf($str, 'Gender: %[^,], Height: %[0-9\.]m, Weight: %[0-9]kg'));
```

Output:
```
array(3) {
  [0]=>
  string(1) "M"
  [1]=>
  string(4) "1.85"
  [2]=>
  string(2) "95"
}
```

The example above substitutes regular expression character classes instead of specifiers. %[^,] matches "any characters that are not commas," %[0-9\.] means "any decimal digits or dot characters" (the backslash is necessary because dots are metacharacters in regular expressions), and of course %[0-9] matches "any decimal digits." Notice that all elements in the returned array have the string data type: by using regular expressions, sscanf() no longer has information about the required data types of the matched portions of the input.

I could go on and on about sscanf(). Its conversion specification syntax, combined with the ability to use regular expressions, makes it a complex and powerful beast. But the fact that it accepts regular expressions begs the question – why not just use a regular expression function? sscanf() offers no extra benefit over its counterpart preg_match() (which will happily extract data for you and assign the results elsewhere) other than that it is possible to have fine control over data types, and in any case, type casting after extraction with preg_match() is very straightforward. sscanf() has also historically been the source of buffer overflow exploits in PHP (and other languages based on the standard C implementation).

My advice is to stick to preg_match() (which is a far more conventional tool for this job), but be aware that you might encounter sscanf() on your travels through legacy codebases. preg_match() and its brethren are covered in the upcoming section on regular expressions. For reference, you can find the "full" documentation for sscanf() at https://www.php.net/manual/en/function.sscanf.php, and if you insist on using this function with regular expression specifiers, you'll need to trawl the usual places (Stack Overflow, etc.) for help and may God have mercy on you.

Extracting Sub-strings

Table 8-13. *Sub-string extraction functions*

strstr(), mb_strstr() stristr(), mb_stristr() strrchr(), mb_strrchr() mb_strrichr()	Extract up to (or from) first or last occurrence of sub-string
strpbrk()	Return portion of string beginning with any char of a set
strtok()	Extracts portion of string up to first occurrence of a token character
substr(), mb_substr()	Return specific amount of bytes starting at an offset
mb_str_cut()	Byte-level variant of mb_substr(), (but still multi-byte safe)

The functions in this sub-section are similar to functions we've already seen. `strpos()`, `str_contains()`, etc., can be used to test if sub-strings exist, but these functions differ in that they will return portions of the input string rather than positional values. These extraction functions use more memory than their search counterparts, so only use them if you care about the extracted data.

substr(), mb_substr(), mb_str_cut()

Let's start with `substr()`, which is a fine-grained tool for extracting a sub-string based on byte lengths. The function takes an input string as the first argument, an integer offset value as the second, and an optional integer length value as the third. If offset is negative, then bytes are counted from the end of the input string, and if it exceeds the length of the string, then an empty string is returned. If length is negative, then that many bytes are omitted from the end of the returned string, and if that means the offset is exceeded, then you get an empty string again. It is possible to specify a length of zero (resulting in an empty string return) or even null (which has the same effect as passing no length argument at all: the remainder of the string is returned).

```
$input = "An\x00Outside Context Problem was the sort of thing most civilisations encountered just once";

print substr($input, 3, 23) . PHP_EOL;
```

Output:
```
Outside Context Problem
```

And there we have it, fairly straightforward stuff. We told `substr()` to extract twenty-three bytes, starting with the byte at position three (remember we're counting from zero; think of it like a byte array). The fourth byte is "O", just after the null byte, and we start counting length from there. The null byte is included here to demonstrate binary safety. Do not use this function on multi-byte data, because you risk chopping through the middle of a valid multi-byte sequence:

```
$name = "Hello, \u{141}ukasz!"; // \u{141} = UTF-8 0xC5 0x81

print substr($name, -7) . PHP_EOL;
```

Output:
```
?ukasz!
```

CHAPTER 8   STRINGS

The exact output will depend on how your environment (assuming PHP is using its default UTF-8 encoding) handles the *0x81* byte value, but this demonstrates that we've truncated the $name string precisely in the middle of a multi-byte sequence. The following demonstrates exactly what has happened:

```
print bin2hex("\u{141}ukasz") . PHP_EOL;
print bin2hex(substr("\u{141}ukasz", 1)) . PHP_EOL;
```

Output:
c581756b61737a
81756b61737a

Fortunately, there are a couple of mbstring variants that solve this problem. mb_substr() operates on character offsets and lengths and is encoding-aware.

```
print mb_substr($name, -7) . PHP_EOL;
```

Output:
Łukasz!

mb_strcut() is halfway between substr() and its multi-byte equivalent in that it operates on byte values but is still encoding-aware and won't truncate multi-byte characters: If a cut would occur in the middle of a multi-byte sequence, then mb_strcut() will include all preceding bytes to the character boundary:

```
print bin2hex(mb_strcut("\u{141}ukasz", 1)) . PHP_EOL;
```

Output:
c581756b61737a

Despite asking mb_strcut() to discard byte zero, it has been included in output because it was part of the UTF-8 character *0xC5 0x81*.

strstr(), stristr(), strrchr()

strstr() (and its alias strchr()) will search a string and return the portion that matches the first occurrence; stristr() does the same but is case insensitive:

```
$ship = 'Registration: NCC-1701-D';
print strstr($ship, 'NCC') . PHP_EOL;
var_dump(strstr($ship, 'ncc'));
print stristr($ship, 'ncc') . PHP_EOL;
```

Output:
NCC-1701-D
bool(false)
NCC-1701-D

The code above demonstrates strstr() and stristr() in action, and it's straightforward. We search for the sub-string "NCC", which exists in input string $ship, so the return is the remaining portion of $ship, including the search pattern. Using strstr() to search for lowercase "ncc" returns boolean false, but stristr() is quite happy to map lowercase ASCII letters to uppercase, as we can see in the final line. As always, remember that this is simply a byte-level comparison with some extra mapping rules for the upper-to-lowercase logic of stristr(). The following demonstrates binary and multi-byte safety:

```
$ship = "Registration: \x00NCC-1701-D";
print strstr($ship, "\x00NCC") . PHP_EOL;

$name = "Name: \u{141}ukasz";
print strstr($name, "\u{141}") . PHP_EOL;

var_dump(stristr($name, "\u{142}"));
```

Output:
NCC-1701-D
Łukasz
bool(false)

First, we can see that strstr() will handle null bytes without any issues, like the vast majority of PHP's core string functions. stristr() is similarly binary-safe, although that is not shown here. Secondly, we can see that although strstr() is not multi-byte aware, a simple binary comparison of two UTF-8 strings yields correct results. However, the third example would require stristr() to be encoding-aware in order to map U+141 (uppercase Polish Ł) to U+142 (lowercase Polish ł) in order to succeed. stristr() is only aware of the ASCII English alphabet and therefore returns boolean false. We'll cover the multi-byte safe forms of these functions in a moment.

Finally, if you wish to return the portion of the input string up to (rather than from) the first occurrence of the search string, simply add a boolean true as the third argument. strstr($ship, 'NCC', true); would therefore return the string

"Registration: " – note that when operating in this way, strstr() does not return the search sub-string in the result.

The corollary to the functions we've just seen is strrchar(), which functions in all ways as strstr() does except that it searches for the last occurrence of a sub-string:

```
$ships = 'NCC-1701-B NCC-1701-C NCC-1701-D';
print strrchr($ships, 'NCC') . PHP_EOL;
print strrchr($ships, 'NCC', true) . PHP_EOL;
```

Output:
NCC-1701-D
NCC-1701-B NCC-1701-C

Remember when I told you that there were inconsistencies with the conventions of PHP core string functions? Here's one of them: there is no case-insensitive form of strrchr(). There is, however, a case-insensitive form of the mbstring equivalent, which you can use quite safely on ASCII-encoded data (though it comes with a slight performance overhead). Speaking of mbstring...

mb_strstr(), mb_stristr(), mb_strrchr(), mb_strrichr()

There are multi-byte safe equivalents for strstr(), stristr(), and strrchr(). There's even an mb_strrichr() function even though there's no "strrichr" equivalent (no, I have no idea why). All of them have the same function signature as their core counterparts but will take an additional string to specify the encoding (otherwise the default encoding will be used. Let's take another look at the problematic Polish UTF-8 character from an earlier example.

```
$name = "Name: \u{141}ukasz";
print mb_stristr($name, "\u{142}");
```

Output:
Łukasz

By replacing stristr() with mb_stristr(), the full Unicode mapping of upper-and-lowercase characters is made available, and we get the expected result. Here's the same thing again, but this time using raw byte values for UTF-16 encoding:

```
//           N       a       m      e       :       <SPC>
$utf16name = "\x00\x4e\x00\x61\x00\x6d\x00\x65\x00\x3a\x00\x20"
```

```
//    Ł    u    k    a    s    z
     . "\x01\x41\x00\x75\x00\x6b\x00\x61\x00\x73\x00\x7a";
//              ł
var_dump(mb_stristr($utf16name, "\x01\x42", false, 'UTF-16'));
```

Output:
```
string(12) "Aukasz"
```

Notice the output? It's what you'll see when running the code on a UTF-8-based system and shows what happens when UTF-16 is treated like it is UTF-8. *0x01* is an ASCII (and therefore UTF-8) non-printing control character, *0x41* is capital "A", then the rest of the return string alternates between *0x00* (null byte) and ASCII/UTF-8 letters "u", "k", "a", and so on. A nice demonstration of the point I'm trying to hammer home about how text really works!

It's also worth mentioning here that pretty much all `mbstring` functions work internally only with UTF-8 text. Using them with any other multi-byte encoding will (when the non-UTF-8 encoding is specified in the function arguments) trigger internal conversion to UTF-8, and any string data being returned is converted back to its original encoding for output. This makes the `mbstring` functions significantly slower (and consume more memory) than their core PHP counterparts, and therefore worth thinking about if handling large amounts of text. We'll revisit the internals – and resulting performance impact – of the `mbstring` module later in the chapter. For now, here's something to think about:

```
$res = mb_strstr($utf16name, "\x01\x41\x00\x75", false, 'UTF-16');
var_dump(bin2hex($res));

$res = mb_strstr($utf16name, "\x01\x41\x00\x75");
var_dump(bin2hex($res));

$res = strstr($utf16name, "\x01\x41\x00\x75");
var_dump(bin2hex($res));
```

Output:
```
string(24) "01410075006b00610073007a"
string(24) "01410075006b00610073007a"
string(24) "01410075006b00610073007a"
```

Using the same raw UTF-16 bytes of $utf16name as the previous example, the code above demonstrates that not only does mb_strstr() not require any information about the encoding of the input strings, but it also does not need to be called at all! Provided that both string arguments match encoding, a comparison of byte values is all that is required; neither strstr() nor mb_strstr() needs any awareness of encoding to do that. Even worse, in the first call to mb_strstr(), the encoding is specified as 'UTF-16', which will trigger conversion to (and from) UTF-16, costing us CPU usage and memory overheads. There are a few instances where mbstring functions offer little-to-no added value over core functions, which we'll cover in a bit.

strpbrk()

strpbrk() is very similar in operation to strstr() and will perform a case-sensitive search that returns the remainder of the input string from the first occurrence, the difference being that strpbrk() treats the search string as a set: only one of the searched-for bytes needs to match. For example:

```
$ship = 'Not Invented Here';

print strpbrk($ship, "der") . PHP_EOL;
print strpbrk($ship, "red") . PHP_EOL;
```

Output:
ented Here
ented Here

Hopefully the code above should illustrate how this function works. The first string argument is searched for the first occurrence of any byte in the second string. In both cases that byte is the ASCII letter "e", it does not matter how the bytes in the second string argument are arranged, and the returned sub-string begins with the first matched byte. strpbrk() is binary safe but (obviously) not multi-byte safe:

```
$ship = "Not Invented\x00 Here";

print strpbrk($ship, "d\x00er") . PHP_EOL;
print strpbrk("\u{142}ukasz, \u{141}ukasz", "\u{141}") . PHP_EOL;
```

Output:
ented Here
łukasz, Łukasz

As we can see, null bytes do not present any problems but check the output when we used `strpbrk()` with some multi-byte (UTF-8) characters. Although we specified U+141 (uppercase "Ł") for our search pattern, the function returns from the very beginning of the input (lowercase "ł"). Can you work out why? The reason is that both U+0141 and U+0142 are UTF-8 encoded as *0xC5 0x81* and *0xC5 0x82*, respectively. `strpbrk()` tests the very first byte of the `$ship` string against our search bytes (*0xC5* and *0x81*); it matches *0xC5*, and so we get the entire input string returned. There is no `mbstring` equivalent of this function, but the same results can be achieved with a multi-byte safe regular expression, as we shall see shortly.

strtok()

Our final sub-string extractor function is `strtok()`, which is quite specialized. `strtok()` is used to split strings into tokens and is not often used outside of the context it is designed for. If you have been programming for a while, you'll probably have at least encountered the term "tokenization"; it is one of the processes involved in compiling source code into something executable.

To a compiler or interpreter (compilers produce independently executable artifacts such as .exe files, interpreters compile *and* execute in one go – PHP binaries are interpreters), the source code of a program is initially just one long string of text. This string must first be parsed for correctness before it can be transformed into lower-level instructions that a machine can follow, and the first step in parsing is lexical analysis: the string must be broken into sub-units; we call these sub-units tokens. We briefly encountered these concepts earlier in the book.

PHP offers user-space constants for all of its internal token values (identifiers such as keywords or variable names are T_STRING, the object operator -> is T_OBJECT_OPERATOR, and so on), and I encourage you to familiarize yourself with them here: https://www.php.net/manual/en/tokens.php. However, demonstrating `strtok()` by parsing PHP itself is probably not where we should start, so let's go with something simpler.

```
$text = <<<EOT
    Hi there, and
    welcome to tokens!
    EOT;
$delimiters = " \n";
```

```
$token = strtok($text, $delimiters);

while ($token !== false) {
    print "token: {$token}" . PHP_EOL;
    $token = strtok($delimiters);
}
```

Output:
token: Hi
token: there,
token: and
token: welcome
token: to
token: tokens!

strtok() requires initialization with two arguments when first called; the first argument is the string to be tokenized, and the second defines the characters (remember: byte values) to be treated as delimiters. strtok() simply walks along the string until it hits a delimiter character (in our case above that's a space or a newline); it returns the characters it has found so far and waits for further instructions. As you can see above, we're required to make more calls to strtok() to obtain subsequent tokens (each time passing in the delimiters again), and strtok() will eventually return false when there are no more tokens found in the string. To summarize, call strtok() with two arguments to initialize (the string being analyzed is held in memory between calls) and call strtok() with a single argument to process the in-memory string. If at any point strtok() receives two arguments, this will reset the in-memory string, and the process starts again. The analysis is complete when strtok() returns false.

The ability to switch delimiters between calls allows for some flexibility in parsing; here is an example:

```
$query = 'foo=bar&cat=miaow&dog=bark';
$delims = ['=', '&'];
$index = 0;

$token = strtok($query, $delims[$index]);
```

```
while ($token !== false) {
    print "{$token}\n";
    $index = !$index % 2;
    $token = strtok($delims[$index]);
}
```
Output:
foo
bar
cat
miaow
dog
bark

Here we are alternating between two delimiters and parsing a URL query string (the evil-looking expression !$index % 2 simply flip-flops between 0 and 1 on each loop iteration). Why didn't we just use '=& as a single delimiter value? Here's why...

```
$query = 'foo=b=ar&ca&t=miaow&dog=bark';
// rest of code as before...
```

Output:
foo
b=ar
ca&t
miaow
dog
bark

If we simply defined the delimiters as '&=' on every call, the tokens would be foo, b, ar, ca, and so on. We can change our delimiters on each token fetch to suit whatever framework of rules we wish to tokenize with. With that said, this is *not* the way I recommend that query strings be parsed! There is the core function parse_str() for that task, which is featured in Chapter 11, "Programming for the Internet."

One final word of caution: strtok(), as you can probably guess, is not multi-byte safe. If you need to tokenize multi-byte strings, the safest way to do that in PHP is to use one of the regular expression functions, and we'll be meeting those later in the chapter.

Transformation and Formatting

Now we move onto the set of functions I have characterized as functions used for transformation tasks, including formatting. These functions all have a common application: they take an input string and output that string with some form of change (a few have alternative modes that process and return arrays of strings). They could be used for tasks like encoding or encryption but should not be; PHP has dedicated functions for those tasks, and they are treated separately in this text. The functions covered in this section are

Table 8-14. String transformation functions

chunk_split()	Insert a separator byte sequence every N bytes
lcfirst(), mb_lcfirst()	Make the first character lowercase
ltrim() rtrim() chop()	Strip whitespace from the beginning or end of a string
nl2br()	Inserts an HTML line break at every newline byte sequence
number_format()	Formats a numeric string with grouped thousands and an optional decimal separator
printf(), sprintf() fprintf() vprintf(), vfprintf()	Interpolate variables into a formatted string
str_shuffle()	Reorder bytes randomly (not for cryptography!)
str_repeat()	Generate a new string that is the original string repeated N times
str_pad(), mb_str_pad	Add specified byte sequence to the beginning or end of a string with a specified length
strtolower(), mb_strtolower() strtoupper(), mb_strtoupper()	Convert a limited set of ASCII printable chars to all upper- or lowercase

(continued)

Table 8-14. (*continued*)

strtr()	Replace single-byte characters with alternative byte values, or replace byte sequences with alternatives
substr_replace()	Replace specified bytes with a new byte sequence
str_replace()	Replace all occurrences of a sequence with a new sequence
strrev()	Reverse the byte order of a string
trim()	Strip specified bytes from the beginning or end of string
ucfirst(), mb_ucfirst() ucwords()	Make the first character of a string uppercase, or the first char of all words in a string
wordwrap()	Add a specified byte sequence every N bytes, with additional logic for long words
mb_convert_case()	Multi-byte safe case conversion: upper, lower, sentence, etc.
mb_strimwidth()	Truncate string to specified character width
mb_substitute_character	Get/set substitute character

Now, that's quite a number of functions to cover, and it will help if we categorize them further. I've grouped them into general functionalities: insertion, substitution, edge transformation (functions that affect the beginning or end of the string), and whole string transformation.

Insertion

These functions all share a common feature: they will add bytes to an existing string. A common reason for doing this is to prepare a long string of text for rendering in a fixed-width display. This might be a bash terminal or a web page (indeed, one of the functions will insert an HTML character sequence). Another scenario you're likely to encounter as a PHP developer is needing to render numeric strings in a regional format, which will require the insertion of spaces, commas, and so forth. We'll also look at the venerable printf() family of functions here, which is how string variable interpolation worked in the dark ages.

CHAPTER 8 STRINGS

Table 8-15. Transform by insertion functions

chunk_split()	Insert a separator byte sequence every N bytes
nl2br()	Inserts an HTML line break at every newline byte sequence
number_format()	Formats a numeric string with grouped thousands and an optional decimal separator
printf() sprintf() fprintf() vprintf() vfprintf()	Interpolate variables into a formatted string
wordwrap()	Add a specified byte sequence every N bytes, with additional logic for long words

chunk_split(), wordwrap()

chunk_split() is a simple function that simply inserts the ASCII "CRLF" bytes (*0x13* carriage-return and *0x10* line-feed) at set intervals as separator characters. By default, this is every seventy-six bytes; the example below specifies an interval of 4:

print chunk_split('A string of text', 4);

Output:
A st
ring
 of
text

If necessary, a third argument can be used to specify the byte sequence used for separation. Splitting strings like this is useful for conforming to internet standards for transmitting various messages (such as email). Note that this function operates at a binary level; it is not aware of character boundaries for multi-byte encoding and will cheerfully break any encoding that is not single-byte.

In a similar way, wordwrap() also inserts newlines but works a little differently. As you can see in the previous example, chunk_split() does not care about word boundaries and will simply insert the newline sequence in the middle of a word (in this case, "string" was transformed into "st\r\nring"). wordwrap() by default will keep "long" words (words that would otherwise have newlines inserted into them) intact:

```
print wordwrap('A string of text', 4);
```

Output:
A
string
of
text

And because wordwrap() is aware of word boundaries, it can handle UTF-8 data safely. The example below shows multi-byte (in fact, multi-codepoint) characters in a string processed with a width value of 1: Observe that the flag glyphs emerge unscathed. (Your mileage may vary with other encodings; be warned and test thoroughly!)

```
print wordwrap("\u{1F3F3}\u{FE0F}\u{200D}\u{1F308} \u{1F3F4}\u{200D}\
u{2620}\u{FE0F}", 1);
```

Output:
🏳️‍🌈

As before, the "bald man" caveat applies: if your system cannot parse/render multi-codepoint glyphs correctly, then your output will differ.

nl2br()

Another function with its roots in the early internet is nl2br(), which inserts the HTML <br> tag (or the XHTML <br /> tag) in front of every newline character in a string. Web browsers reduce all whitespace and newline characters to a single whitespace, and this trick makes newline sequences (CRLF, LFCR, LF, and CR) behave in the browser as they would in, say, a terminal window.

CHAPTER 8 STRINGS

```
$str = "Old skool markup.\r\nRocking it like\nit's 2004...\n";
print nl2br($str);
```

Output:
```
Old skool markup.<br />
Rocking it like<br />
it's 2004...<br />
```

In these more enlightened times, injecting tags into strings like this is generally not the done thing; text layout is usually controlled via better structured data, block-level elements, and CSS.

number_format()

This function has been discussed already in Chapter 7, "Numbers," and, although it takes a numeric type as input, it outputs a string and is considered a core string function in the official PHP documentation. Here's a short recap of number_format():

```
$decimalDigits = 2;
$decSep = '.';
$thousandsSep = '_';

print number_format(
    1000000000.888,
    $decimalDigits,
    $decSep,
    $thousandsSep
);
```

Output:
```
1_000_000_000.89
```

printf(), sprintf(), fprintf(), vprintf(), vfprintf()

This family of functions has a long history in computing, and we've already encountered the variant sscanf() earlier in the chapter. printf() et al. take a format string and then data to be interpolated into the initial string according to the format syntax. A summary of syntax rules for the format string has already been given when we saw sscanf(), so there is no need to repeat them here. The differences between the functions in this section are given in the table below.

Table 8-16. printf-based functions

fprintf($stream, $format, ...$values)	Variable number of value arguments, writes output to handle
printf($format, ...$values)	Variable values, sends output (e.g., terminal, or HTTP client)
sprintf($format, ...$values)	Variable values, returns output
vfprintf($stream, $format, $valuesArray)	Single array of values, writes to handle
vprintf($format, $valuesArray)	Single array, sends output
vsprintf($format, $valuesArray)	Single array, returns value

Substitution

These functions have the common mechanism of changing one byte value (or set of byte values) for another throughout the entire string.

Table 8-17. Transform by substitution functions

strtolower(), mb_strtolower() strtoupper(), mb_strtoupper()	Convert a limited set of ASCII printable chars to all upper or lower case
strtr()	Replace single-byte characters with alternative byte values, or replace byte sequences with alternatives
substr_replace()	Replace specified bytes with a new byte sequence
str_replace()	Replace all occurrences of a sequence with a new sequence
ucfirst(), mb_ucfirst() ucwords(), mb_ucwords()	Make the first (ASCII alphabet) char of a string uppercase, or the first char of all words in a string
mb_convert_case()	Multi-byte safe case conversion: upper, lower, sentence, etc.

strtolower(), mb_strtolower(), strtoupper(), mb_strtoupper()

To convert case between upper and lower, you can use strtolower() and its counterpart strtoupper(). These two functions only work on the ASCII range characters *0x41* to *0x5a*, like so:

```
print strtolower("IT DOES WHAT IT SAYS ON THE TIN.") . PHP_EOL;
print strtoupper("AnD nOt mUcH eLsE.") . PHP_EOL;
```

Output:
```
it does what it says on the tin.
AND NOT MUCH ELSE.
```

These two functions work with UTF-8 in that they will convert the case of ASCII range bytes in a UTF-8 string (as we've seen, UTF-8 cleverly avoids multi-byte characters being mistaken for ASCII), but that is all these two functions do: adding (or subtracting) decimal *32* for each byte value in the a–z/A–Z range. Extended ASCII and multi-byte character sets will not be transformed correctly. For true multi-byte safety there are mbstring equivalents:

```
$quote = "\u{15e}\u{fc}phe ve belirsizlik i\u{e7}ermeyen kat\u{131} kurallar talep ediyoruz!";
$lower = mb_strtolower($quote);
$upper = mb_strtoupper($quote);

print $quote . PHP_EOL;
print $lower . PHP_EOL;
print $upper . PHP_EOL;
```

Output:
```
Şüphe ve belirsizlik içermeyen katı kurallar talep ediyoruz!
şüphe ve belirsizlik içermeyen katı kurallar talep ediyoruz!
ŞÜPHE VE BELIRSIZLIK IÇERMEYEN KATI KURALLAR TALEP EDIYORUZ!
```

But we still have a problem. For those of you that don't speak Turkish, the example above highlights a potential issue with these two functions. mb_strtoupper() (and its counterpart) is not locale-aware: in the Turkish alphabet, the correct capitalization of i should be İ (içermeyen should have been transformed to İÇERMEYEN, and so on). This isn't a bug as such; it is simply following (one of) the Unicode specifications for

CHAPTER 8　STRINGS

case mapping – the rules for mapping characters when converting case. I promise this will make more sense when we examine the mb_convert_case() function (which is the underlying implementation for mb_strtoupper() and its counterpart) below.

ucfirst(), ucwords(), lcfirst()

A pair of simple functions, and like strtolower(), they only act on the ASCII alphabet (a–z, bytes *0x61* to *0x7a*). In the case of ucwords(), every word in the string is affected, where a word is considered to be any set of bytes that is not a separator byte. Default separators are *0x09* (horizontal tab), *0x0A* (new-line), *0x0B* (vertical-tab), *0x0C* (new-page), *0x0D* (carriage-return), and *0x20* (space) – but can be overridden by supplying a string of bytes as a second argument if required.

```
print ucfirst('only affects the very first letter. nothing else.');
print PHP_EOL;
print ucwords('every first letter of eVERY wORD.');
```

```
Output:
Only affects the very first letter. nothing else.
Every First Letter Of EVERY WORD.
```

The results of the function calls are self-explanatory. Although not shown here, the function lcfirst() exists and does the inverse of ucfirst(). I'm sure there's a use-case for it... In previous versions of PHP, these functions were more sophisticated and would vary their behavior with locale settings. Since PHP 8.2 they only work on the basic ASCII Latin alphabet. For more robust case conversion and multi-byte safety, we have a better option – mb_convert_case() – which we'll get to very shortly.

mb_ucfirst(), mb_lcfirst()

A new feature for PHP 8.4, mb_ucfirst() and mb_lcfirst() are the multi-byte safe equivalents to ucfirst() and lcfirst(). Whereas these core functions only process bytes in the ASCII range (and will cause havoc for non-UTF-8 multibyte data), the mbstring equivalents are both safe to use on any (supported) multibyte encoding and are Unicode-aware.

```
$lcname = "\u{142}ukasz";
$ucname = "\u{141}UKASZ";
```

501

```
print "{$lcname} > " . lcfirst($lcname) . PHP_EOL;
print "{$lcname} > " . mb_lcfirst($lcname) . PHP_EOL;
print "{$ucname} > " . mb_ucfirst($ucname);
```

Output:
łukasz > łukasz
łukasz > łukasz
ŁUKASZ > ŁUKASZ

The first line of output shows that the core function lcfirst() has no effect (because the first byte of character U+0142 is *0xC5*, outside the ASCII Latin-1 range). The next lines show the mbstring functions doing their thing, converting the UTF-8 Polish characters correctly. Bicameral character sets (having upper and lowercase forms) will convert correctly, but with a small caveat:

```
print mb_ucfirst("idil"); // Correct transform should be İdil - U+0130
```

Output:
Idil

This looks like we have a regional problem. For the Turkish character i, the correct uppercase form is İ, but mb_ucfirst() converts it to a standard Latin capital I. Unicode has a set of special rules for these localization issues, so perhaps we just need to change the locale before we make the function call?

```
setlocale(LC_ALL, 'tr_TR.UTF-8');
print mb_ucfirst("idil"); // Not working despite locale
```

Output:
Idil

It still doesn't work. The reason for this is that both mb_ucfirst() and mb_lcfirst() are internally calling another function, mb_convert_case(), and the "problem" (it's a deliberate design choice) lies there.

mb_convert_case()

strtoupper(), ucfirst(), and all the rest do what they do and are fine for straightforward use-cases. mb_convert_case(), on the other hand, offers all of the utility of the functions we've seen in this section by specifying different modes (via function argument) and, of course, offering multi-byte support. Many of the mbstring functions that have any kind of case conversion functionality are simply wrappers around internal calls to mb_convert_case(), with particular modes specified. Here are a few examples:

```
$str = 'wHo cAreS aBoUt ThE fIfTh eArl oF bAtHsDrOp aNd lAdY hIgGeNboTtOm';

print mb_convert_case($str, MB_CASE_UPPER) . PHP_EOL;
print mb_convert_case($str, MB_CASE_LOWER) . PHP_EOL;
print mb_convert_case($str, MB_CASE_TITLE) . PHP_EOL;
```

```
Output:
WHO CARES ABOUT THE FIFTH EARL OF BATHSDROP AND LADY HIGGENBOTTOM
who cares about the fifth earl of bathsdrop and lady higgenbottom
Who Cares About The Fifth Earl Of Bathsdrop And Lady Higgenbottom
```

The code above calls mb_convert_case() with three different modes, specified with the constants MB_CASE_UPPER, MB_CASE_LOWER, and MB_CASE_TITLE. And here's how those calls work with ASCII data: exactly the same as strtolower(), strtoupper(), and ucwords() - and I really do mean *exactly* the same. mb_convert_case(), as a performance enhancement, will pass any ASCII bytes into the same fast byte value manipulation that strtolower() et al. uses. Otherwise, a mapping operation is performed, which takes the Unicode codepoint ordinal of the source character and applies some rules for changing it to a new ordinal value (and then swapping the old byte values for the ones that match the new character). But how are these mapping rules defined? Well, remember the difficulties with Turkish I and İ characters. I mentioned that this wasn't a bug with mb_strtolower(), and it isn't: the function simply implements one of the Unicode standards for case mapping, and the problem lies there.

Case mapping simply means "one-to-one character mappings for bicameral alphabets" (e.g., bicameral alphabets have two characters for the same letter – A and a, B and b). Naturally, this mapping is simple for the basic Latin alphabet. Things start to become more challenging when trying to incorporate characters from, well, all of the alphabets, and the Unicode standard has a section entirely devoted to the various complications arising from locale, context, and the language conventions of particular character sets. You can read about them in section 5.18 of https://www.unicode.org/versions/Unicode15.1.0/ch05.pdf

In order to solve the edge cases of messy human language, Unicode defines "normal" and "special" mappings. The "normal" rules provide a base of one-to-one character mappings, with "special" rules dealing with complications arising from locale, context, and other quirks. The Unicode special mappings are conditional; they only apply under certain circumstances, such as system locale settings; otherwise, the standard specifies falling back to normal rules. When it comes to the locale-based problem of converting certain Turkish characters, mb_convert_case() (by design) ignores locale settings and only applies the normal mappings:

```
/*
 * https://www.unicode.org/Public/15.1.0/ucd/SpecialCasing.txt
 * Format: <code>; <lower>; <title>; <upper>; (<condition_list>;)? # <comment>
 * I > ı    0049; 0131; 0049; 0049; tr Not_Before_Dot; # LATIN CAPITAL LETTER I
 * i > İ    0069; 0069; 0130; 0130; tr; # LATIN SMALL LETTER I
 *
 * https://www.unicode.org/Public/15.1.0/ucd/UnicodeData.txt
 * Format:  <code>;<name>;2;3;4;5;6;7;8;9;10;11;<upper>;<lower>;<title>
 * I > i    0049;LATIN CAPITAL LETTER I;Lu;0;L;;;;;N;;;;0069;
 * i > I    0069;LATIN SMALL LETTER I;Ll;0;L;;;;;N;;;0049;;0049
 */

setlocale(LC_ALL, 'tr_TR.UTF-8'); // assumes system locale is installed

print "Test that i maps to \u{130}: "
    . mb_convert_case('i', MB_CASE_UPPER) . PHP_EOL;
print "Test that I maps to \u{131}: "
    . mb_convert_case("I", MB_CASE_LOWER);

Output:
Test that i maps to İ: I
Test that I maps to ı: i
```

The code above contains a comment block detailing the Unicode standard's normal and special rules as defined in some important files: the UnicodeData.txt and SpecialCasing.txt machine-readable mapping files are made publicly available via https://www.unicode.org and are intended for use in programming languages, system libraries, and so on. PHP's mbstring source code is compiled against these mapping files, and this is what controls mb_convert_case() behavior. We decode those rules as follows: The special rule when lowercasing I to ı is expressed as 0049; 0131; 0049;

0049; tr Not_Before_Dot;. In plain language, this means "U+0049 I maps to U+0131 ı when lower, U+0049 when title, U+0049 when upper, for the 'tr' region, and only where the source character is *not immediately before a dot*" (we'll come back to this last clause shortly; it's important).

Likewise, the special rule for uppercasing i to İ is 0069; 0069; 0130; 0130; tr;: "U+0069 i maps to U+0069 for lower. U+0130 İ for upper and title, for the 'tr' region." The eagle-eyed will have spotted something here: title case (as a character mapping, rather than a conversion pattern applied at word boundaries). The fun fact is that Unicode has three cases: upper, lower, and title. For most practical purposes, uppercase and title case character mappings are identical, and the distinction exists purely for a few edge cases involving combined characters. We'll limit the rest of this section on case conversion to upper and lower.

Continuing with our example code, after setting the locale to `'tr_TR.UTF-8'`, we then go on to call `mb_convert_case()` with two conversions that will reveal the underlying rules – i to upper and I to lower. Clearly the special rules are not enforced: i uppercased to I (U+0049) and I lowercased to i (U+0069), which are the normal Unicode rules for case mapping, despite explicitly setting our language locale to a UTF-8 variant of 'tr'. But the complications of case mapping are not limited to regional alphabets; there are some quirky rules that are restricted to character sets that are not related to the ASCII Latin range. Let's have a quick look at Greek, which has two variant lowercase letters for Sigma Σ...

```
/*
 * Special
 * 03A3; 03C2; 03A3; 03A3; Final_Sigma; # GREEK CAPITAL LETTER SIGMA
 * Σ > ς (03C2 if final letter)
 *
 * Normal
 * 03A3;GREEK CAPITAL LETTER SIGMA;Lu;0;L;;;;;N;;;;03C3;
 * Σ > σ (03C3)
 */

$finalSigmaTest = "FINAL\u{03A3} \u{03A3}NON-FINAL";
print $finalSigmaTest . PHP_EOL;
print mb_convert_case($finalSigmaTest, MB_CASE_LOWER);
```

Output:
FINALΣ ΣNON-FINAL
finalς σnon-final

Here the special rule is 03A3; 03C2; 03A3; 03A3; Final_Sigma; which means "U+03A3 Σ lowercases to U+03C2 ς, but only if it is the last letter of a word." Crucially, there is no locale ID in the condition. The normal rule is to simply always use the non-final, lowercase character U+03C3 σ as the lowercase form. As we can see from the output, the special rule is obeyed, and we get the two different lowercase characters depending on their position in the word. We're getting some of the special rules, but not all.

Now let's return to that final clause in the I to ı mapping rule: "Not_Before_Dot". What's that about? The format of `SpecialCasing.txt` specifies that "The casing context is always the context of the characters in the original string", in other words: the conditions apply to the original character not the result. 0049; 0131; 0049; 0049; tr Not_Before_Dot; means that the U+0049 character must not come before a dot? Which dot? In this case, it is the U+0307 "COMBINING DOT ABOVE" character, which combines with other codepoints to form a multi-codepoint character (which we're now familiar with thanks to flags and bald men). Our problem case of Turkish characters just got more interesting, because İ could be represented in two ways:

```
$singleCodepointChar = "\u{130}";
$multiCodepointChar = "\u{49}\u{307}";

print "Is it {$singleCodepointChar} or {$multiCodepointChar}?";
```

Output:
Is it İ or İ?

What happens if we feed these two strings into mb_convert_case()? Let's find out...

```
$convertedSingle = mb_convert_case($singleCodepointChar, MB_CASE_LOWER);
$convertedMulti = mb_convert_case($multiCodepointChar, MB_CASE_LOWER);

print bin2hex($convertedSingle) . PHP_EOL;
print bin2hex($convertedMulti);
```

Output:
69cc87
69cc87

Quite interesting, we've got an ASCII lowercase i *0x69*, followed by a (UTF-8) combining dot *0xCC 0x87*. Looks weird in code, might possibly look weird rendered too (hopefully the font chosen by your OS or web browser has the dots of the two combined glyphs perfectly aligned). In case you might be wondering, the `UnicodeData.txt` case conversion rules are being followed here: "\u{49}\u{307}" maps to \u{69}\u{307} (and vice versa), and "\u{130}" has a one-way mapping to \u{69}\u{307}. The 'tr' region-specific special rule for lowercasing "\u{49}\u{307}" would result in just single *0x69* byte.

This equivalence of single- and multi-codepoint characters raises another question: how can we evaluate that equivalence programmatically? Case-mapping is good for changing text and respecting the rules and expectations of a human audience, but...

```
print bin2hex($singleCodepointChar) . PHP_EOL;
print bin2hex($multiCodepointChar);
```

Output:
c4b0
49cc87

... clearly a dumb machine will look at the byte values and decide they're not the same thing. If only there was a special case conversion that was able to put the needs of machines over the needs of humans. Well, we could do what we just did above and lowercase the two versions of İ, but that would actually fail if `mb_convert_case()` implemented the 'tr' special regional rules. The conversion types of `MB_CASE_UPPER` and `MB_CASE_LOWER` are not intended to produce canonical results across all possible locales, character sets, and other complicating factors. There are also many other special rules; uppercase conversion might work for some, lowercase might work for others, and neither will work for all. The good news is that Unicode does make provision for precisely this scenario, with a related rule set called *case folding*, which is intended to produce consistent results that are independent of regional or other issues.

```
$singleCodepointChar = "\u{130}";
$multiCodepointChar = "\u{49}\u{307}";

var_dump(
    mb_convert_case($singleCodepointChar, MB_CASE_FOLD) ===
    mb_convert_case($multiCodepointChar, MB_CASE_FOLD)
);
```

Output:
bool(true)

Of course, in the case of İ, a conversion to lower case would also work, but that's purely circumstantial. mb_convert_case() doesn't pay attention to locale, and the normal rules just happen to produce identical results for that one character. Case-folding is the tool to use if you want to test equivalence between characters that look identical to human eyes, but be warned that the product of the conversion isn't intended for rendering. Canonical equivalence for machines isn't always going to result in case conversions that look correct to the human eye.

We've spent rather a lot of time looking at what is ostensibly a single function and mainly one weird regional mapping edge case, and we haven't even exhaustively covered everything mb_convert_case() does – though the internal workings of the function have been explained, and I'm sure you can figure the rest out for yourself! The point of the last few pages is really to drive home the following point: Unicode is hard. You can't always just throw mbstring at a problem and arrive at the correct solution (though multi-byte safety is a very good start). Test. Your. Code. With. Good. Data. Sets.

Edge

After that reasonably deep dive into Unicode's internals, you're probably ready for something a little lighter. The next of the functions are much simpler and only affect the beginning or end portion of an input string.

Table 8-18. Edge transform functions

ltrim(), mb_ltrim() rtrim(), mb_rtrim()	Strip whitespace from the beginning or end of a string
trim(), mb_strim()	Strip specified bytes from both ends of a string
str_pad(), mb_str_pad	Add a specified byte sequence to the beginning or end of a string with a specified length
mb_strimwidth()	Truncate string to specified character width

ltrim(), rtrim(), trim()

These three functions are self-explanatory: ltrim() removes bytes from the beginning of a string, rtrim() does the same but from the end, and trim() does both ends at once (which saves having to call rtrim(ltrim($string));). The default byte values that will be removed are the usual suspects: form-feed, horizontal tab, vertical tab, line-feed, carriage-return, and also the null byte *0x00*.

```
$padLeft = "\t\r\n\v text";
$padRight = "text\x00\t\r\n\v ";

print ltrim($padLeft) . PHP_EOL;
print strlen(rtrim($padRight));
```

Output:
text
4

Pretty straightforward stuff. The functions can also be used to strip any other bytes (ASCII characters or hexadecimal escapes, as you prefer):

```
print (ltrim('aaabbbcccThe text we care about', 'abc')) . PHP_EOL;
print (rtrim('Also the text we care aboutzzzzzzxxxy', 'xyz')) . PHP_EOL;
print (trim('aabbcczzAnd this text tooxxxyyzzzaaa', 'abcxyz'));
```

Output:
The text we care about
Also the text we care about
And this text too

Unsophisticated but surprisingly handy and used just about everywhere. Be aware that rtrim() also has an alias, chop(), which might be found in the wild from time to time. These three functions are safe to use on UTF-8 data but will break any other Unicode transfer format due to the null byte stripping.

mb_ltrim(), mb_rtrim(), mb_trim()

A new addition for PHP 8.4, this trio of functions works just like their core counterparts (with the added benefit of multibyte safety, of course). They also greatly extend the range of default characters that will be stripped from the edges. In addition to "\f\n\r\t\v", these functions will strip:

CHAPTER 8 STRINGS

- U+0085 (Next Line - NEL)
- U+00A0 (No-Break Space)
- U+1680 (Ogham Space Mark)
- U+180E (Mongolian Vowel Separator)
- U+2000–U+200A (first ten chars of "General Punctuation")
- U+2028 (General Punctuation - Line Separator)
- U+2029 (General Punctuation - Paragraph Separator)
- U+202F (General Punctuation - Narrow No-Break Space)
- U+205F (General Punctuation - Medium Mathematical Space)
- U+3000 (Ideographic Space)

```
// null, space, \t \n \v \f default strip chars
$defaultASCII = "\x00 \t\n\v\f\r";
$higherChars = "\u{85}\u{A0}\u{1680}\u{180E}";
$genPunct = "\u{2000}\u{2001}\u{2002}\u{2003}\u{2004}\u{2005}\
u{2006}\u{2007}"
    . "\u{2008}\u{2009}\u{200A}\u{2028}\u{2029}\u{202F}\u{205F}";
    $ideoSpace = "\u{3000}";

$stripped = mb_ltrim(
    $defaultASCII
    . $higherChars
    . $genPunct
    . $ideoSpace
    . "That's a lot of stripping."
);

print $stripped . PHP_EOL;
print bin2hex($stripped);

Output:
That's a lot of stripping.
5468...
```

Being encoding-aware, these functions are safe to use on strings that would otherwise break...

```
// raw byte data for UTF-16BE string " utf-16"
$utf16 = "\x00\x20\x00\x75\x00\x74\x00\x66\x00\x2d\x00\x31\x00\x36";
print bin2hex($utf16) . PHP_EOL;
print bin2hex(ltrim($utf16)) . PHP_EOL;
print bin2hex(mb_ltrim($utf16, encoding: 'UTF-16BE'));
```

Output:
0020007500740066002d00310036
7500740066002d00310036
007500740066002d00310036

Notice that the output of ltrim() has removed half of the UTF-16 encoding for the letter u: *0x00 0x75* has been truncated to *0x75*.

str_pad(), mb_strpad

The corollary to trimming strings is padding them: adding characters to either or both ends. str_pad() - in the grand tradition of consistency among PHP's core strings functions - does not have a left or right form. Directionality is controlled by the function argument.

```
$str1 = "First";
$str2 = "Second";
print str_pad($str1, 6) . $str2 . PHP_EOL;
```

Output:
First Second

Here we've asked str_pad() to pad the input $str1 so it is six bytes (ASCII characters) wide. The default padding direction is right (onto the end of the string), and the default byte is *0x20* (a single space). The input string is five bytes/characters wide, so just a single padding character is added, as we can see in the output. Additional arguments allow control of direction and padding bytes:

```
print str_pad($str1, 11, ',..,', STR_PAD_BOTH) . $str2 . PHP_EOL;
```

Output:
,..,First,..,Second

We can see the entire padding sequence is used (note that it gets truncated if the padded string would exceed the desired length), and the padding is in both directions (STR_PAD_LEFT and STR_PAD_RIGHT are the other constants available).

For multi-byte data, character length (as Unicode codepoints) is of more importance than byte length. A brand new addition in PHP 8.3, mb_str_pad() has an almost identical signature to str_pad(), but it treats the second argument as the desired number of codepoints in the resulting string, rather than the number of bytes. This has an impact on Unicode multi-codepoint characters: for example, flags are composed of four codepoints:

```
$paddingChars = "\u{1F3F3}\u{FE0F}\u{200D}\u{1F308} \u{1F3F4}\u{200D}\
u{2620}\u{FE0F}";
$text = 'Text';

print $paddingChars . PHP_EOL;
print mb_str_pad($text, 13, $paddingChars, STR_PAD_LEFT);
```

Output:
🏳️‍🌈 🏴‍☠️
🏳️‍🌈 🏴‍☠️Text

We have two flag symbols in our padding string, but they're constructed from four codepoints each (plus an ASCII space for another codepoint), so we need a target length of *original string length* + 9. Look what happens if we accidentally truncate the padding string:

```
print mb_str_pad($text, 5, $paddingChars, STR_PAD_LEFT);
```

Output:
🏳️
Text

We get a white flag as our padding character, because only the first codepoint made it into our padding: U+1F3F3 ("Waving White Flag"). Keep an eye on things when using the more exotic symbols like emojis. As before, this is a "bald man" multi-codepoint example; an ancient GUI terminal might garble the output.

mb_strimwidth()

Our final "working at the edges" function is mb_strimwidth(). This function removes characters from the end of the string to achieve a target length and will also remove characters from the beginning if desired. The following should make this clear:

```
$str = 'The quick brown fox';

print mb_strimwidth($str, 0, 6) . PHP_EOL;
print mb_strimwidth($str, 1, 6) . PHP_EOL;
print mb_strimwidth($str, 2, 6) . PHP_EOL;
print mb_strimwidth($str, 3, 6);
```

Output:
The qu
he qui
e quic
quick

It is also possible to append characters to the truncated string; the target length (argument three) will include these characters in its count:

```
print mb_strimwidth($str, 0, 6, '...') . PHP_EOL;
print mb_strimwidth($str, 0, 9, '...');
```

Output:
The...
The qu...

Like mb_str_pad(), there's a small but important qualifier for the concept of *width* when it comes to the output. mb_str_pad() counts codepoints, but mb_strimwidth() counts a rather confusing pair of properties called *halfwidth* and *fullwidth*. These are two terms that actually refer to typographic properties of characters, specifically those in East Asian text, although there are fullwidth forms of Latin text too. To make matters worse, there are half and full versions of many East Asian ideograms:

```
$halfSu = "\u{FF7D}"; // ス
$fullSu = "\u{30B9}"; // ス

print mb_strimwidth("Text", 0, 3, $halfSu) . PHP_EOL;
print mb_strimwidth("Text", 0, 3, $fullSu);
```

Output:
Teλ
Tス

As always, test your code!

Whole String

Our final set of formatting and transformation functions act on the entire input and return a string that is at least the same size. They are:

Table 8-19. Whole string transform functions

str_shuffle()	Reorder bytes randomly (not for cryptography!)
str_repeat()	Generate a new string that is the original string repeated N times
strrev()	Reverse the byte order of a string

str_shuffle()

This function simply randomly reorders all the bytes of the input string, pure and simple.

```
print str_shuffle("\x00randomise me");
```

Output:
deiem mrsona

The output will of course vary every time, but the function is byte-safe, and the output will always be the same length as the input. The function is definitely *not* multi-byte safe and will completely destroy such strings. Useful for inducing confusion, but the function is not intended for cryptography. We'll see better functions for those tasks shortly.

str_repeat()

Another simple function, it will simply output the input string, repeated a specified number of times:

```
print 'Bacon strips ' . str_repeat('& bacon strips ', 3);
```

Output:
```
Bacon strips & bacon strips & bacon strips & bacon strips
```

Voilà, a foolproof method for improving any recipe. Given the simple nature (and byte-safety) of the function, it is safe to use with multi-byte encodings.

strrev()

As you might expect from its name, `strrev()` reverses the order of bytes in a string:

```
print strrev("Uno\x00 reverse!");
```

Output:
```
!esrever onU
```

Byte-safe, as we can see, but like `str_shuffle()`, there is no awareness of multi-byte encoding, and such data will be transformed to garbage.

Encoding and Escaping

Moving on from formatting and transforming, we come to the functions intended for encoding or escaping data. When string data is intended for use in another context – where it might accidentally trigger problems if it contains meta-characters for that context – it is necessary to format the string so that the results function correctly. Likewise, incoming data might contain escape sequences or encoding that prevents a program from operating correctly and would require the process to be reversed.

A character "escape" is simply a special sequence starting with a backslash \ character that maps to another character; for example, \n conventionally maps to *0x0A* (line feed), and we've seen these previously in PHP double-quoted strings. Conversely, it is necessary to sometimes indicate that meta-characters should not be interpreted as such, for example, when a PHP double-quoted string contains a double-quote character, which would otherwise terminate the string early and create a syntax error.

```
$str = "I've heard of this "programming" thing..."; // syntax error
$str = "I've heard of this \"programming\" thing..."; // correctly escaped
```

CHAPTER 8 STRINGS

Encoding is essentially the same thing, but meta-characters are completely replaced with an alternative sequence. For example, the < and > characters used to form HTML tags can be encoded: <script> (which a browser would interpret as the opening tag of a JavaScript program) can be encoded as <script> (which a browser would convert back to the string <script> and simply render as text).

Encoding and escape functions are commonly used for the purposes of rendering or transmission across binary-unsafe transport layers. Raw HTML will need to be encoded to another form if it is intended for rendering in a web browser; similarly, some data transfer mechanisms are not 8-bit safe, and binary data needs to be encoded in a specific way to survive a journey (e.g., through email systems). The functions that are specific to these tasks are as follows:

Table 8-20. Escaping and encoding functions

addslashes() stripslashes() addcslashes() stripcslashes()	Add/remove backslash char for certain byte values
base64_encode() base64_decode()	Performs the MIME base64 encode for transport safety
convert_uuencode() convert_uudecode()	Binary safe conversion of bytes to printable chars (for transmission)
html_entity_decode() htmlentities()	Convert all applicable chars to/from HTML entities
htmspecialchars_decode() htmlspecialchars()	Convert a limit set of chars to/from HTML entities
strip_tags()	Remove HTML (and PHP) tags from a string
str_rot13()	Shift (ASCII) letters by 13 places (aka the rot13 transform)
quoted_printable_encode() quoted_printable_decode()	Convert string to/from RFC 2045 (Section 6.7) encoding
quotemeta()	Add backslash to .\+*?[]()^$ chars
mb_decode_numericentity() mb_encode_numericentity()	Multi-byte converts chars to/from HTML numeric entities

I've further categorized these functions according to their utility in rendering, transport safety, special interpolation (for handling strings in syntactic context), and (in one case only) fun factor. The functions for rendering and transport safety are not examined here. They can be found in Chapter 11, "Programming for the Internet" – where it makes more sense to explain those functions in their proper context. That leaves us with a handful of specialized oddities, which we'll look at briefly.

Special Interpolation

These functions are fairly limited in their utility. They are intended for escaping specific meta-characters when the source string is intended for interpolation into another string containing meta-characters. Historically they have been abused as sanitizing functions for creating database queries (looking at you, addslashes()); if you encounter them in legacy codebases, be *very* certain about their intended use.

addslashes(), stripslashes()

These functions will add (or remove) a backslash character in front of the ASCII characters ', ", \, and the null byte *0x00*. This can be useful when the string is intended for use in another context, but not, I repeat, *NOT* for use in writing something like a MySQL query (there are better and safer techniques for that, which we briefly looked at in the "Databases" section in Chapter 1, "Getting Started").

```
$str = "Some data for use 'elsewhere'\x00";
$str = addslashes($str);

print $str . PHP_EOL;
print stripslashes($str);

Output:
Some data for use \\'elsewhere\\'\\0
Some data for use 'elsewhere'
```

These functions are binary-safe and will work just fine on UTF-8 data (with an ASCII collision-avoidance mechanism). Other Unicode encodings will be utterly destroyed by the null-byte escaping.

addcslashes(), stripcslashes()

These two functions are similar in effect to the previous two, but the desired escape characters must be specified using a second argument. Useful when preparing strings for use in weird and arbitrary formats, which is a fairly niche use-case. The list of characters can simply be all the bytes requiring escape or a range (specified by a special .. sequence with the lowest value character going first).

```
$ship = 'What Are the Civilian Applications?';
print addcslashes($ship, 'Celrtu') . PHP_EOL;
print addcslashes($ship, 'e..r');
```

Output:
Wha\t A\r\e \th\e \Civi\lian App\lica\tions?
W\hat A\r\e t\h\e C\iv\i\l\ia\n A\p\p\l\icat\i\o\ns?

Although not shown here, it is possible for the second argument to hold multiple ranges, such as "\x00..\x1F\x41..\x5A" (which would put backslashes in front of every ASCII control character and every capital ASCII letter, not that I can think of a good reason to do so).

quotemeta()

Like the previous escape functions, quotemeta() will prepend a certain set of ASCII bytes with a backslash. This time, it's the regular expression meta-characters, which are . \ + * ? [^] ($). We're going to dive headfirst into regular expressions (you'll either love them or hate them!) later in the chapter, so let's not waste time here dissecting what each of those symbols means. Here's a quick example anyway, even though it's likely you'll never need to use this function (there's a better alternative).

```
$pattern = 'What Are the Civilian Applications?';
$regex = '/^' . quotemeta($pattern) . '$/';
print $regex;
```

Output:
/^What Are the Civilian Applications\?$/

Note that the question mark character in $ship is now escaped (because ? has special effects in these expressions, you'll see).

Just for Fun

And finally, in our short detour into the dustier corners of PHP string functions, we have... this... thing. A common exercise for computer science students (or software engineers undergoing tech tests in interviews) is to implement something called the "Caeser cipher" algorithm. This is a classic of cryptography dating from about a million years ago and is the simplest form of *substitution cipher*. We'll be learning more about those in an upcoming section. str_rot13() applies the ROT13 (rotate by thirteen places) transformation: each letter is moved forward in the alphabet by thirteen places, preserving case. Which means str_rot13() will be its own inverse for the Latin alphabet (this is an ASCII-only function).

```
print str_rot13("abcdef") . PHP_EOL;
print str_rot13("ABCdef") . PHP_EOL;
print str_rot13(str_rot13("I am not secure!"));
```

Output:
nopqrs
NOPqrs
I am not secure!

Handy if you need to make text slightly harder to read at a glance (maybe hiding spoilers on forum posts?). But that's about it. If true encryption is required, PHP has tools for that, and we'll see them soon.

Hashing and Error Checking

Adjacent to the topic of encoding is hashing. A hash is simply a string of fixed size that is calculated from another string (of arbitrary size). Unlike encoding, hash functions are not reversible, which means it is impossible to compute the original input data from the output data.

Hashes are useful for verifying the integrity of messages (a message is transmitted, a hash value is transmitted separately, and the two can be compared to ensure the message was not altered in transit), generating signatures (I sign a message with a shared secret key; other owners of the key are then able to verify both that the contents were not tampered with *and* the authenticity of the sender), and storing sensitive strings such as passwords (which should be stored as hashes – credentials are passed through an identical hashing scheme and compared to the stored hash).

PHP has a wide variety of functions and modules for hashing. We'll have a quick look here at the following core functions.

Table 8-21. Hash/error check functions

crc32()	Calculate the crc32 value of a string (used for error checking)
md5()	Calculate md5 hash value of a string
sha1()	Calculate sha1 hash value of a string

crc32()

Cyclic redundancy check (or checksum) is a space-efficient method of generating a value that can be used to verify binary data. The output is an integer, and two identical strings always generate the same value. It is, of course, possible for two different strings to give the same value, because the number of possible outputs of crc32() is limited to the range of possible integer values for the system on which it runs, which is finite (see Chapter 7, "Numbers," for more information on integer limits). This function is best deployed only for error checking (which is the main application of the algorithm – verifying network data packets).

```
print crc32('b5a7b602ab754d7ab30fb42c4fb28d82') . PHP_EOL;
print crc32('d19f2e9e82d14b96be4fa12b8a27ee9f');
```

Output:
2575120314
2575120314

The code above demonstrates a crc32() collision.

md5(), md5_file()

An alternative to integer-based crc32 is md5(). Based on the MD5 Message-Digest Algorithm, md5() is a fast hashing function that produces a wider range of potential (fixed width) string values than the integers of crc32(), so the collision probability is a lot lower (128 bits of output, 2^{128} possible values, small but still non-zero). Collisions are a problem because it is possible for two different values to appear to be identical, files such as SSL certificates, for example. md5() accepts a string argument and outputs the calculated MD5 value for it; md5_file() takes a string, which is evaluated to a file path, which is read into memory and processed in the same way (assuming the file exists and is readable for the PHP process).

The main reason md5() is not appropriate these days for cryptography is because of its speed: it's very quick on modern hardware. We'll cover what hash rate means for cryptography in an upcoming section in this chapter; just know that a single mid-tier GPU such as the RTX 3060 can calculate at a rate in the order of 10^4 MH/s. (That's tens of thousands of mega-hashes per second – $10^4 * 10^6 = 10^{10}$ hash values *per second*). Those md5 "encrypted" user passwords in your databases aren't looking so safe anymore....

PHP's md5() function returns a 32-character string by default, which is a hexadecimal representation of the 16-byte binary value that the algorithm produces. Alternatively, you can get the raw binary directly:

```
print md5('some data') . PHP_EOL;
print bin2hex(md5('some data', true)); // returns binary value
```

Output:
1e50210a0202497fb79bc38b6ade6c34
1e50210a0202497fb79bc38b6ade6c34

sha1(), sha_file()

Very similar in operation to the MD5 functions above, sha1() and sha1_file() also subject string (or file) data to a hashing algorithm; this time it is the US Secure Hashing Algorithm 1. And much like MD5, it is no longer considered useful for cryptography due to its speed.

```
print sha1('some data') . PHP_EOL;
print bin2hex(sha1('some data', true)); // returns binary value
```

Output:
baf34551fecb48acc3da868eb85e1b6dac9de356
baf34551fecb48acc3da868eb85e1b6dac9de356

As you can see, sha1 returns a longer hash value than md5(), which means that collision probability is lowered accordingly. We'll revisit hashing later in the chapter, in the section on cryptography.

Well Done!

Phew. That was a lot to take in; kudos for making it this far! The string functions of PHP are numerous and varied, have several conventions (not always intuitive), and have clearly evolved over many years and major versions. You'll most likely use just a handful of them on a daily basis if you choose PHP programming as part of your career or set of hobbies. There is *no* shame in not having memorized this lot (and beware any person or organization that expects you to have done so, frankly). The full documentation is available here: `https://www.php.net/manual/en/ref.strings.php`. It is far more important that you learn the underlying principles of what text data really is. I hope this chapter (and other relevant sections of the book) is helping you in that regard.

The `mbstring` Extension

Hopefully by now the differences in encoding systems are well embedded, and you'll have some familiarity with Unicode and its transfer formats, particularly UTF-8. The previous section focused on the core string functions of PHP, how they behave at a binary level, and how they cope with multi-byte data. It also featured functions from the `mbstring` extension where they exist as equivalents to core functions. There are several more functions provided by `mbstring` that don't have core equivalents and will be discussed here, but first let's have a very quick look at `mbstring` as a language extension.

Like other PHP extensions (aka modules), `mbstring` is typically included in most prepackaged PHP installers and prebuilt Docker images. To check that `mbstring` is available in your PHP installation, simply run the following command in a Linux environment:

```
$ php -m
[PHP Modules]
...
mbstring
```

You can also check the output of `phpinfo()` if running under a web server SAPI. If `mbstring` is not listed, general guidance for module installation is covered in Chapter 1, "Getting Started."

The purpose of mbstring, as you have no doubt figured out from the preceding section, is to provide a set of tools for safely handling multi-byte string data. It does this by providing a collection of global functions and constants. There are other extensions (which we will also be looking at shortly) designed for internationalization issues (of which encoding is just one) that provide OOP interfaces; mbstring opts for a purely functional style. (Yes, that was a deliberate pun). We've already seen the multi-byte equivalents of the core string functions, but that's only a small set of what mbstring offers. There are also functions provided for working with HTML/HTTP, regular expressions, examining string data, converting encoding, and managing program-wide settings. The functions for doing web-like things (such as MIME, HTTP, and so on) will be showcased in Chapter 11, "Programming for the Internet," and the regular-expression-specific functions are presented in the corresponding section of this chapter. (Something to look forward to!)

Configuration

The mbstring extension has a number of internal settings, each of which can be controlled through various functions or as ini file directives (each is prepended with mbstring, e.g., mbstring.detect_order):

- detect_order
- encoding_translation
- http_output_conv_mimetypes
- internal_encoding
- language
- regex_retry_limit
- regex_stack_limit
- substitute_character
- strict_detection

All of these strings exist as .ini config file entries (e.g., mb_string.language = neutral) and are also exposed via some of the functions. And the advice from me is… to leave them be, except in a few limited cases. The mbstring module on the surface looks like it offers robust internationalization but it does not. It was created primarily (by

Japanese engineers) with Japanese language support in mind (hence the esoteric mb_
convert_kana()), and it functions best when left as language-agnostic. (No disrespect
to the authors of mbstring; it's still fantastically useful!) The settings you're most likely to
ever need to care about are detailed below.

internal_encoding

mbstring processes text using an internal character encoding. Any incoming data
that is in a different format will be transformed to the internal encoding before processing
(any return data will be transformed back to match the input). Note that using mbstring.
internal_encoding in an .ini file is deprecated; you should use PHP's core default_
charset setting instead. Can be set at runtime with mb_internal_encoding().

detect_order

Many mbstring functions contain internal logic for automatically detecting
encoding. Various encoding systems will be tried; this setting defines in what order those
attempts are made. Values can be either auto (default order) or any available encoding
name. Multiple values are comma separated. Runtime configuration is available via
mb_detect_order().

substitute_character

If an invalid byte sequence is encountered by mbstring functions, or a decoded
codepoint does not exist in the output encoding, it is swapped with the substitution
character specified here. Values can be an integer ordinal Unicode codepoint or one
of "none", "long", or "entity". The runtime function is mb_substitute_character();
details follow further on in this section.

strict_detection

Controls the encoding detection behavior of mb_detect_encoding(). Detecting
encoding is usually an operation of last resort; it is far better to specify these things in
configuration, HTTP headers, and so forth. A non-strict detection will match the closest
from a list; strict requires that there's an exact match. We'll see this in action shortly
when we look at mb_detect_encoding().

Hopefully some of the above already makes sense, having seen many mbstring
functions at work in the previous section. Now, on with the show… Let's dive into more
functions!

(More) mbstring Functions

The following mbstring functions will be featured in this section:

Table 8-22. Featured mbstring functions

mb_check_encoding()	Validate encoding of a string
mb_convert_encoding()	Convert a string to a different encoding
mb_convert_kana()	Japanese-language-only alphabet conversion
mb_convert_variables()	Convert encoding of multiple strings in one call
mb_detect_encoding()	Attempt to detect probable encoding of a string
mb_detect_order()	Control the order in which to detect character encoding
mb_encoding_aliases()	Get aliases for encoding type (if known)
mb_get_info()	Returns internal configuration of mbstring module
mb_internal_encoding()	Get/set PHP's internal character encoding
mb_list_encodings()	Get list of all known encodings
mb_scrub()	Clean up a malformed string, replaces invalid sequences with a ? character
mb_substitute_character()	Get/set the substitution for invalid sequences

As in the previous section, these functions will be (roughly) grouped by functionality: info and settings, data inspection, and data conversion.

Info and Settings

mbstring offers utility functions for obtaining information about system encoding settings, information about the string data being processed, and for controlling encoding program-wide.

mb_get_info()

For a full and complete picture of how mbstring will behave, we have mb_get_info(), which returns all of the settings we looked at the start of the section.

```
print_r(mb_get_info());
```

Output:
```
Array
(
    [internal_encoding] => UTF-8
    [http_output] => UTF-8
    [http_output_conv_mimetypes] => ^(text/|application/xhtml\+xml)
    [mail_charset] => UTF-8
    [mail_header_encoding] => BASE64
    [mail_body_encoding] => BASE64
    [illegal_chars] => 0
    [encoding_translation] => Off
    [language] => neutral
    [detect_order] => Array
        (
            [0] => ASCII
            [1] => UTF-8
        )

    [substitute_character] => 63
    [strict_detection] => Off
)
```

By default, mb_get_info() returns an associative array of key/value pairs corresponding to all the internal parameters of mbstring. Some of the output (concerning web-related settings) has been omitted here and is dealt with in the relevant chapter. It is also possible to call mb_get_info() with a string argument corresponding to a parameter name:

```
print_r(mb_get_info('internal_encoding'));
print PHP_EOL;
print_r(mb_get_info('detect_order'));
```

Output:
```
UTF-8
Array
```

```
(
    [0] => ASCII
    [1] => UTF-8
)
```

There is one setting that has no .ini file equivalent nor a corresponding function: illegal_chars. There is no official documentation for this, and I had to delve into the C source code to figure out what it's used for. illegal_chars is initialized on program startup to an unsigned integer with a value of 0. It is used (very inconsistently) to keep a count of invalid byte sequences by just a handful of functions. The following code demonstrates how it can be used:

```
$invalid2Octet = "\xC3\x28";
$invalidSequenceId = "\xA0\xA1";

print mb_get_info('illegal_chars') . PHP_EOL;
$converted = mb_convert_encoding(
    "I am {$invalid2Octet}} broken {$invalidSequenceId}",
    'UTF-16BE',
    'UTF-8'
);
print $converted . PHP_EOL;
print bin2hex($converted) . PHP_EOL;
print mb_get_info('illegal_chars') . PHP_EOL;
```

Output:
```
0
I am ?( broken ??
004900200061...
3
```

The three invalid byte sequences (*0xC3*, *0xA0*, and *0xA1*-*0x28*, which is valid on its own as an opening-parenthesis (character) are substituted for the ASCII (decimal) ordinal value *63* (the sixty-third character: a question mark). The illegal_chars counter is incremented accordingly. The value will persist between calls; this way it is possible to keep track of how many illegal bytes are found as the program does its work. I can say with some certainty that mb_convert_encoding() and mb_output_handler() are the

CHAPTER 8 STRINGS

only two functions that will increment this internal counter. Be warned that this is not officially documented functionality; it could change without warning in the future.

mb_substitute_character()

The previous function swapped out invalid bytes for a question mark character, which has the (Unicode decimal) ordinal value 63 and corresponds to the substitute_character value obtained from mb_get_info(). A different Unicode ordinal can be set with mb_substitute_char(), which can be a pain to translate from the hexadecimal values we normally use when looking at Unicode codepoints, so remember we can just use a hexadecimal literal value:

```
$invalid2Octet = "\xC3\x28";
print mb_substitute_character() . PHP_EOL;
mb_substitute_character(0xFFFD);

$converted = mb_convert_encoding(
    "Te{$invalid2Octet}st",
    to_encoding: 'UTF-16BE',
    from_encoding: 'UTF-8',
);
print bin2hex($converted);
```

Output:
63
00540065fffd002800730074

The first call to mb_substitute_character() has no argument, so the function returns the current ordinal value that mbstring will use, which is the ASCII ? character. The next call passes the hexadecimal literal 0xFFFD, which means "use the Unicode U+FFFD character". U+FFFD is recommended by the Unicode standard; indeed, that particular character is named "Replacement Character" and intended for use as such. See https://www.unicode.org/reports/tr36/#Substituting_for_Ill_Formed_Subsequences for more detail. The UTF-8 string we pass to mb_convert_encoding() has an invalid two-byte sequence embedded in it, and the output contains the UTF-16 encoded substitute character (the UTF-16 encoding for U+FFFD is, of course, 0xFF 0xFD). You might have noticed that the output string also contains the sequence 0x00

0x28 immediately after the replacement character bytes: this is because *0x28* is a valid UTF-8 byte. mbstring has treated *0xC3* as the sole invalid byte, because *0x28* is a valid character.

Here's another example:

```
mb_substitute_character(0xFFFD);
$invalidSurrogatePair = "\xD8\x00\xD8\x00";
$validUtf16 = "\x00\x54\x00\x65\x00\x73\x00\x74";

$converted = mb_convert_encoding(
    $validUtf16 . $invalidSurrogatePair,
    to_encoding: 'UTF-8',
    from_encoding: 'UTF-16BE',
);
print $converted . PHP_EOL;
print bin2hex($converted);
```

Output:
Test��
54657374efbfbdefbfbd

This time we're creating some broken UTF-16BE by appending a broken surrogate pair onto the string "Test". Surrogate pairs in UTF-16 are the mechanism used to encode Unicode codepoints above U+FFFF, which require more than two bytes, just like we've seen several examples of multi-codepoint characters (such as bald men and flags). Without diving too deeply into UTF-16, just know that the sequence U+D800 U+D800 is invalid because U+D800 can only be followed by codepoints U+DC00 – U+DFFF. This time we get two substitute U+FFFD characters in the output, UTF-8 encoded as *0xEF 0xBF 0xBD*, because the invalid pair is treated as two distinct characters. You'll get wrinkles like this when characters are substituted due to invalid encoding; the main purpose of the mechanism isn't to make output strings look pretty but to make them safe. What's broken in one encoding might be perfectly valid in another, and indeed there have been exploits in the past that took advantage of this to sneak problem metacharacters (such as directory separators) past validation layers.

mb_list_encodings(), mb_encoding_aliases()

The encoding systems supported by mbstring are actually quite numerous: in addition to the most common encodings used today (UTF-8, UTF-16), mbstring provides support for obsolete encodings like UTF-7, a plethora of pre-Unicode multibyte systems of East Asian origin (e.g., ISO-2022-JP, Big5), and the extended ASCII systems ISO-8859-1, ISO-8859-2, and so on. There are also "encodings" such as Base64, which aren't character encodings (equivalent to ASCII or UTF-8) per se, but binary-to-text transforms to ensure safe transmission of data. To obtain the full list of all supported encodings:

```
print_r(mb_list_encodings());
```

Output:
```
Array
(
    [0] => BASE64
    ...
    [77] => CP50221
    [78] => CP50222
)
```

Each string can be used as input to the various mbstring functions that accept an encoding argument (which is most of them). Many encoding systems have more than one name, and mbstring is aware of most (all?) of them. To get the list of known aliases of a particular encoding name, use the following:

```
print_r(mb_encoding_aliases('ASCII'));
```

Output:
```
Array
(
    [0] => ANSI_X3.4-1968
    [1] => iso-ir-6
    ...
    [9] => cp367
    [10] => csASCII
)
```

As mentioned above, binary-to-text encodings are supported. However, these are flagged as deprecated in the latest mbstring source code https://github.com/php/php-src/blob/php-8.4.0beta4/ext/mbstring/mbstring.c#L256 and should not be used with general-purpose mbstring functions (some have specialized mbstring functions, which are fine to use). The table below lists the deprecations and alternative handlers.

Table 8-23. *Deprecated encoding aliases and alternatives*

Encoding	Alternative
Base64	base64_encode(), base64_decode()
QPrint	quoted_printable_encode, quoted_printable_decode()
HTML Entities	htmlspecialchars(), htmlentities() mb_encode_numericentity(), mb_decode_numericentity()
Uuencode	convert_uuencode(), convert_uudecode()

mb_internal_encoding()

To get or set the internal encoding of mbstring, use the function mb_internal_encoding(). You'll likely never need to use the function unless maintaining *seriously* old systems: UTF-8 is fairly ubiquitous these days (as it should be). Nevertheless, here's how to use it:

```
print mb_internal_encoding() . PHP_EOL;
var_dump(mb_internal_encoding('UTF-16BE')) . PHP_EOL;
print mb_internal_encoding();
```

Output:
UTF-8
bool(true)
UTF-16BE

This setting will affect how mbstring treats string data by default and impacts input and output. Here's a quick and simple demo of what I mean:

```
$rawUTF16BE = "\x00\x48\x00\x65\x00\x6C\x00\x6C\x00\x6F";

print mb_internal_encoding() . PHP_EOL;
print bin2hex(mb_convert_encoding($rawUTF16BE, to_encoding: 'UTF-8')) .
PHP_EOL;
```

CHAPTER 8 STRINGS

```
mb_internal_encoding("UTF-16BE");
print bin2hex(mb_convert_encoding($rawUTF16BE, to_encoding: 'UTF-8')) .
PHP_EOL;
```

Output:
UTF-8
00480065006c006c006f
48656c6c6f

With internal encoding set to UTF-8, the $rawUTF16BE string remains unchanged because the input is assumed to be UTF-8. When internal encoding is changed to UTF16-BE, mb_convert_encoding() now knows it should map the bytes to UTF-8 encoding, as shown in the final line of output.

mb_detect_order()

Some mbstring functions will examine input strings and attempt to guess the encoding. This is not the preferred method of managing encoding and transforms; the layers above and below your application should know how text data is encoded (and exercise control where possible). Nevertheless, it is sometimes necessary to guess, and there is also the use-case of verifying correct encoding for security purposes. mb_detect_order() will report the order in which encoding types are tested against input data and allow the order to be defined at runtime:

```
print_r(mb_detect_order()) . PHP_EOL;
print mb_detect_encoding("Single bytes") . PHP_EOL;
print mb_detect_encoding("\u{141}");
```

Output:
Array
(
    [0] => ASCII
    [1] => UTF-8
)
ASCII
UTF-8

Here we have two strings, both of which are valid UTF-8 (all ASCII remains valid when interpreted as UTF-8), but only one of which is also valid ASCII. With a detect order of ASCII > UTF-8, we can see which is which: The string containing the Unicode escape "\u{141}" will be encoded as *0xC5 0x81* (where `default_charset` is set to UTF-8). *0xC5* is outside the 7-bit range for ASCII but is a continuation byte in UTF-8. `mb_detect_encoding()` essentially counts "demerits" against encoding types when evaluating the input string: Invalid bytes and sequences score a demerit; the encoding with the fewest is the likeliest candidate (unless running in strict mode, as we'll see below). If we swap the order of encoding names, we get a different answer:

```
// could also be passed in as ['UTF-8', 'ASCII']
mb_detect_order('UTF-8,ASCII') . PHP_EOL;
print_r(mb_detect_order()) . PHP_EOL;
print mb_detect_encoding("Single bytes");
```

Output:
```
Array
(
    [0] => UTF-8
    [1] => ASCII
)
UTF-8
```

When evaluated as UTF-8, an ASCII string scores no "demerits," and because we asked for UTF-8 first, that's the answer returned by `mb_detect_encoding()`. Let's turn our attention to that function next.

Inspection

Checking that encoding is valid is quite important for some applications. There is the obvious problem of serving broken data back to clients; we don't want rogue question marks, squares, or random characters from different alphabets appearing in our application data. Another, rather more serious problem is one of security. Systems are normally tiered, or layered; a PHP application today usually relies on other systems for doing the heavy lifting with correctly directing network traffic. PHP prefers UTF-8 everywhere (it's even part of the PSR-1 standard), but there is a chance that other systems are using an alternative.

mb_detect_encoding()

CHAPTER 8   STRINGS

The effects of the last function we looked at, mb_detect_order(), were demonstrated with its complementary function, mb_detect_encoding(). By default, mb_detect_encoding() uses an internal scoring system to find the best match from the detect_order list. It is also possible to force strict matching (system-wide) with the mbstring.strict_detection config directive or control the function via an argument.

```
$invalidDoubleByte = "\xC2\x28";
$validUTF8 = "\u{141}ukasz";

print mb_get_info('strict_detection') . PHP_EOL;
var_dump(mb_detect_encoding(
    $validUTF8 . $invalidDoubleByte
));
print mb_get_info('illegal_chars') . PHP_EOL;

var_dump(mb_detect_encoding(
    $validUTF8 . $invalidDoubleByte,
    strict: true
));

Output:
Off
string(5) "UTF-8"
0
bool(false)
```

Here we take the invalid continuation sequence used in previous examples and append it to a perfectly legal UTF-8 string. PHP is configured for non-strict detection, and mb_detect_encoding() matches to UTF-8 because despite the invalid *0xC2* byte, it is still closer to UTF-8 than ASCII. Note that the internal illegal_chars counter has not been incremented: its use is inconsistent in the mbstring source code, and there's no sign of it in the C implementation of the function we're looking at (I checked). Visit https://github.com/php/php-src/blob/php-8.4.0beta4/ext/mbstring/mbstring.c#L3398 for the gory details. On the second call to mb_detect_encdoing(), we pass strict: true, and this time, the return is false, which means the input string was not an exact match for UTF-8. Far safer!

mb_check_encoding()

A very similar method to the above is to use mb_check_encoding():

```
$invalidDoubleByte = "\xC2\x28";
$validUTF8 = "\u{141}ukasz";

var_dump(ini_get('mbstring.strict_detection'));
var_dump(mb_check_encoding($validUTF8));
var_dump(mb_check_encoding($validUTF8 . $invalidDoubleByte));

mb_internal_encoding("UTF-16BE"); // previous int. enc. was default UTF-8
var_dump(mb_check_encoding($validUTF8));
```

Output:
```
string(1) "0"
bool(true)
bool(false)
bool(false)
```

Even without strict_detection (which is disabled - set to 0), the input string is strictly tested. It is possible to set the desired encoding to test against with an additional argument to mb_check_encoding(); we'll see that in a moment. Otherwise the internal_encoding setting is used. From the output of the example above, we can deduce the following: the input string is tested for correctness against internal_encoding (valid UTF-8 returns true initially, and false when internal encoding is changed to UTF-16BE), and the input string must not have any invalid sequences (adding a broken continuation sequence to the valid UTF-8 string results in a false return).

If an encoding type other than internal_encoding is required, pass the name as an argument:

```
$validSurrogatePair = "\xD8\x00\xDC\x01"; //LINEAR B SYLLABLE B038 E A

var_dump(mb_check_encoding($validSurrogatePair));
var_dump(mb_check_encoding($validSurrogatePair, 'UTF-16BE'));
```

Output:
```
bool(false)
bool(true)
```

CHAPTER 8 STRINGS

Although not shown here, mb_check_encoding() will also accept an array as the first argument and will check the encoding of every key and value. If all keys and values pass the strict check, it will return true.

Conversion

Finally, we come to conversion functions. These will transform strings from one encoding to another.

mb_convert_encoding()

When you simply need to transform a string from encoding type to another, mb_convert_encoding() does exactly what it says:

```
$name = "\u{141}ukasz";
print bin2hex($name) . PHP_EOL;
print bin2hex(mb_convert_encoding($name, to_encoding: 'UTF-16BE'));
```

Output:
c581756b61737a
01410075006b00610073007a

The input string will be converted to the target encoding, using internal_encoding as the source encoding by default. This might lead to unexpected results if the source encoding is valid in multiple types:

```
$utf16Name = "\x01\x41\x00\x75\x00\x6b\x00\x61\x00\x73\x00\x7a";
print bin2hex(mb_convert_encoding($utf16Name, to_encoding: 'UTF-8'));
```

Output:
01410075006b00610073007a

The reason why $utf16Name is unchanged is down to the fact that the original encoding is actually valid UTF-8 and can be interpreted as a sequence of Latin-1 ASCII characters separated by null bytes. We can change internal_encoding to get the desired result...

```
mb_internal_encoding("UTF-16BE");
print bin2hex(mb_convert_encoding($utf16Name, to_encoding: 'UTF-8'));
```

Output:
c581756b61737a

... or we can be more explicit about the source and target encoding types:

```
mb_internal_encoding("UTF-8");
print bin2hex(mb_convert_encoding(
    "\x01\x41\x00\x75\x00\x6b\x00\x61\x00\x73\x00\x7a",
    to_encoding: 'UTF-8',
    from_encoding: 'UTF-16BE'
));
```

Output:
c581756b61737a

mb_convert_encoding() will also accept an array of strings and will convert every element's encoding in the same way as demonstrated above.

mb_convert_variables()

If you find yourself in the unenviable position of needing to convert many strings in one call, mb_convert_variables() will take a variety of inputs and convert them for you.

```
$determinist = "\x00\x44\x00\x65\x00\x74\x00\x65\x00\x72\x00\x6d"
    . "\x00\x69\x00\x6e\x00\x69\x00\x73\x00\x74";
$revisionist = "\x00\x52\x00\x65\x00\x76\x00\x69\x00\x73\x00\x69"
    . "\x00\x6f\x00\x6e\x00\x69\x00\x73\x00\x74";

mb_convert_variables(
    'UTF-8',
    'UTF-16BE',
    $determinist,
    $revisionist
);

print bin2hex($determinist) . PHP_EOL;
print bin2hex($revisionist);
```

Output:
44657465726d696e697374
5265766973696f6e697374

CHAPTER 8   STRINGS

The first two arguments to mb_convert_variables() are the source and target encoding, respectively, every subsequent argument is passed by reference and will be passed through the encoding conversion algorithm. Just like mb_convert_encoding(), you can pass arrays into mb_convert_variables():

```
$data = [$determinist, $revisionist];
mb_convert_variables(
    'UTF-8',
    'UTF-16BE',
    $data
);
print bin2hex($data[0]) . PHP_EOL;
print bin2hex($data[1]);
```

The output will be identical to that of the previous example; note the array access in the bin2hex() call.

mb_scrub()

We've seen how character substitution works when converting encodings, but it is also possible to remove illegal byte sequences without performing an encoding transform. mb_scrub() will test the input string and substitute the sequence specified by the subtitution_character setting and retain the current encoding of the string. The input string is assumed to be in internal_encoding format.

```
// abc + broken surrogate pair
$brokenUtf16 = "\x00\x61\x00\x62\x00\x63\xD8\x00\xD8\x00";

mb_substitute_character(0xFFFD);
print bin2hex(mb_scrub($brokenUtf16)) . PHP_EOL;
print bin2hex(mb_scrub($brokenUtf16, 'UTF-16BE'));
```

Output:
006100620063efbfbd00efbfbd00
006100620063fffdfffd

The first call to mb_scrub() has no encoding argument. It is treated as UTF-8, which means that only the *0xD8* byte is treated as invalid (null bytes are fine). The UTF-8 encoding of U+FFFD is *0xEF 0xBF 0xBD*, and we can see that it is substituted into the string in place of the *0xD8* bytes. Conversely, under UTF-16 encoding, the sequence *0xD8 0x00* is a single invalid sequence and is substituted with the UTF-16 encoding of U+FFFD, which is (conveniently) *0xFF 0xFD*.

mb_convert_kana()

Finally, we have the Japanese language-specific mb_convert_kana(). It might seem odd that there isn't also, say, mb_convert_hebrew(), mb_convert_sanskrit(), or mb_convert_cuneiform(). I suspect that is because the authors of the mbstring extension are named Tsukada Takuya and Rui Hirokawa (https://github.com/php/php-src/blob/master/ext/mbstring/CREDITS), and that's fair enough, I suppose. Domo arigato gozaimashita for your hard work, both of you. This function takes an input string, a "mode" parameter, and an optional encoding type (otherwise the internal_encoding settings are used).

This function does have some utility, in that it converts between fullwidth and halfwidth characters. Should you need to mix and match East Asian and Latin symbols, it is possible to use this function:

```
print "関数があります。" . PHP_EOL;
print "abcdefg" . PHP_EOL;
print mb_convert_kana("abcdefg", 'A', 'UTF-8');
```

Output:
関数があります。
abcdefg
ａｂｃｄｅｆｇ

Cryptography

The desire for secrecy in communications is as old as, well, human communication. Transforming written language into a form that is indecipherable during transmission or storage and requiring special knowledge at the receiving end to decipher is a task that drove the development of modern computers as we know them. This section will not be an exhaustive analysis of cryptography (you might be glad to hear!) but will hopefully equip you with a basic understanding of the tools and some common use cases. Let's see what all the fuss is about.

It's difficult to keep data secret on a network, due to the underlying technologies. At the very bottom of the stack of hardware and software we have electronic signals that are easy to detect. A wired ethernet network has multiple participants all listening out for data: multiple machines will receive the same signal by design (and filter out their own traffic based on various address protocols). Likewise, Wi-Fi data is literally broadcast to all listeners. These days we web developers don't need to worry (too much) about encryption of the data traffic to and from our servers: protocols like HTTPS take care of the problem for us, as we'll see in Chapter 11, "Programming for the Internet." There is, however, one backend use-case for encryption that is very much our problem: password storage.

The Password Problem

In the (very, very) old days we stored and transmitted credentials (such as usernames and their corresponding passwords) in "the clear" (unencrypted plain text). With just a basic knowledge of IP networking, it was therefore trivial to extract these "secrets" when they were sent over the network or read them directly from storage (such as a filesystem or database) where possible. Today we have automatic encryption of (multiple layers of) network traffic, but we still need to store those secrets. Clearly, storing an encrypted form of a user's password is preferable: in such a system, every time the user supplies credentials, we can run the password through the same encryption process and compare the result to what we've stored. Such a process would need to be one-way; the results should not be reversible, and we've already explored hashing functions earlier in the chapter.

If we're storing hash values, then an attacker that gains access to them is still forced to perform some computation to figure out the original data. This is usually via some form of "brute-force" attack: test passwords are automatically generated, passed through the encryption algorithm, and then compared to the target hash. The following example illustrates this process by using sha1() to generate a target hash value for a password, then using a simple pair of foreach loops to build test passwords from a "dictionary" of words and computing the sha1() value each time. (Do not use sha1() for production-quality password hashing!)

```
$password = 'weaksauce';
$hash = sha1($password);
```

```php
$words = ['weak', 'strong', 'sauce', 'pickles', 'banana', 'infosec'];

foreach ($words as $word1) {
    testHash($word1, $hash);
    foreach ($words as $word2) {
        testHash($word1 . $word2, $hash);
    }
}

function testHash(string $word, string $hash): void {
    $ourHash = sha1($word);
    if ($ourHash == $hash) {
        exit("Password found! {$ourHash} / {$word}" . PHP_EOL);
    }
}
```

Output:
Password found! d31713bfca0fb0ca1d52ab365a5e70327d5a8942 / weaksauce

With a list of words and a trivial rule (the password is either one of the words or a concatenation of two words), we find the password. The code above is a very simplified form of *dictionary attack*, where common words are used to build test passwords, which are then passed through the hashing algorithm. Of course, we're encouraged to use substitute characters, punctuation, and so on when we create real passwords. This increase in complexity adds to the computational work an attacker needs to perform, but it's just a matter of time until the correct hash is found. To make matters worse, given what we've seen so far, we actually only need to generate a map of hash values to input strings once, after which we can simply reuse our pre-computed data. To add insult to injury, such pre-computed hash databases (known as *rainbow tables*) are available, saving an attacker the cost of initial computation. (Note: rainbow tables are a bit more sophisticated than simply a store of every potential password and hash value; they trade space for computation and are beyond the scope of this text. Just accept that their existence makes life difficult!)

So, what to do? Sure, we can add work to the hashing: the SHA1 is fast by modern standards, but there are other, more expensive algorithms available (the cost to us is irrelevant; we only need to make the calculation once per login), and we can add more work by insisting on punctuation characters, numbers, and so on (widening the pool of potential characters vastly increases the possible permutations). On the other hand, computers, especially modern systems with their focus on parallelism, are brilliant at crunching through data very quickly; a brute force dictionary attack will eventually succeed. What we need to do is find a way to defeat pre-computed hashes; we also need to make every hash in our password store unique even if there are common passwords in there (and in a real user database, there *will* be common passwords).

The Password (Storage) Solution

There is a very simple way to vastly increase the amount of work required to brute force all of your stored passwords and render rainbow tables ineffective. By adding a randomly generated string, known as a *salt*, to every password before performing the hash. The salt does not need to be secret, nor should it be; you're going to need it every time the user authenticates.

```
$password = 'weaksauce';

print sha1($password . random_bytes(8)) . PHP_EOL;
print sha1($password . random_bytes(8));
```

Output:
2fd158e2411ba5c5da51fe8341ffde81e887dc61
0572ef1520460768a0b9a551091055d1c614c31f

Even with two identical passwords, by adding some extra characters before hashing, we have generated two values that will not be easily found in a pre-computed table. Neither can passwords be correlated: the attacker is forced to compute for every password. Every single password in your database could be identical, but the addition of the salt means every hash value is different. Storing the salt alongside the password (e.g., in the same database table) does not present any additional security risk; it serves only to make life more difficult (expensive) for bad actors. Indeed, PHP offers a password hashing function that will return a string that includes the salt, as well as metadata concerning any relevant parameters used in the various algorithms. Using sha1() as we've seen so far is not the recommended approach, however, to securing your user's secrets: even with a salt the algorithm is still very fast by modern standards. We could, of course, roll our own password hashing, but PHP offers some dedicated functions that are more suited to the task.

password_hash(), password_verify()

The go-to password hashing function is password_hash(), which takes the source string and a constant parameter and outputs a formatted string. The output string contains all the information required to repeat the hash: algorithm type, cost, salt, and the hash value itself.

```
print password_hash('weaksauce', PASSWORD_DEFAULT);
```

Output:
$2y$10$a60.WN3IEZ1Bik1Zb7nbiuOjvuL/JCAMwhT45TIoAklR3yl9/nEF6

The example above breaks down as follows (note that parts of the output will be random every time because of the salt portion):

- $2y$ algorithm identifier (in this case, it's the default: Blowfish)
- 10$ cost/complexity
- a60.WN3IEZ1Bik1Zb7nbiu the salt (the Blowfish algorithm generates 22 characters, random every time)
- OjvuL/JCAMwhT45TIoAklR3yl9/nEF6 the hash (varies with salt)

To verify an incoming password that has been encrypted by password_hash(), there's no need to decompose the string like above (though it is entirely possible to do so). password_verify() will do the work for you; the first string argument is the user-supplied credential, and the second is a hash string generated by password_hash():

```
$hash = '$2y$10$a60.WN3IEZ1Bik1Zb7nbiuOjvuL/JCAMwhT45TIoAklR3yl9/nEF6';
var_dump(password_verify('weaksauce', $hash));
```

Output:
bool(true)

CHAPTER 8 STRINGS

The algorithm can also be varied by passing different constants to password_hash(), call password_algos() to see the available algorithms for your installation:

```
print_r(password_algos());
```

Output:
```
Array
(
    [0] => 2y
    [1] => argon2i
    [2] => argon2id
)
```

Most PHP installations will have the above by default, and PHP even defines core constants that map to those strings: PASSWORD_BCRYPT (which is also PASSWORD_DEFAULT), PASSWORD_ARGON2I, and PASSWORD_ARGON2ID map to 2y, argon2i, and argon2id, respectively. Remember that the hashes produced by password_hash() contain enough information about the algorithm used to verify a string, no extra arguments are required:

```
var_dump(password_verify(
    'weaksauce',
    password_hash("weaksauce", PASSWORD_DEFAULT)
));
var_dump(password_verify(
    'weaksauce',
    password_hash("weaksauce", PASSWORD_ARGON2I)
));
```

Output:
```
bool(true)
bool(true)
```

One other aspect of using password_verify() is that it takes a fixed length of time to execute. This is important because if the verifying code varies in the length of time it takes to reject a password, this opens up a vulnerability. By measuring variances in execution time, it would be possible to home in on the correct password (older versions of Windows had this problem). Exploits targeting such vulnerabilities – whereby an adjacent metric such as time, or variance in power consumption, can be used to gain useful information about encrypted data – are known as *side-channel* attacks.

Password Hashing Algorithms

What exactly are the differences between PASSWORD_BCRYPT, PASSWORD_ARGON2I etc? We've briefly touched on what these algorithms exist to do: provide a one-way method of generating unique, fixed-length identifiers for strings and generally make life difficult for bad actors to bulk-replicate these identifiers. Blowfish/bcrypt, argon2i, and argon2id are all hashing algorithms designed to maximize cost: they deliberately consume memory and CPU resources. In particular, the bcrypt algorithm takes a parameter to control the number of iterations (or cycles) to perform: the idea is that as computing power increases in capability (and reduces in cost), the hashing algorithm can become incrementally more expensive to match. To illustrate, here are a few examples (using both password_hash and another core function, crypt()), and a little extra code to demonstrate how long the calls take.

```
$password = 'weaksauce';

$start = microtime(true);
$hash1 = password_hash($password, PASSWORD_DEFAULT);
$end = microtime(true) - $start;
print "{$hash1} - took {$end} s" . PHP_EOL;
```

Output:
$2y$10$2alN7H818NP.8BZAoerYxebJIOTsNz4MItmDx1notHgXQwNGxsSCC - took 0.052612066268921 s

Here's the same code using crypt(), which is more versatile than password_hash() - indeed the PHP internal implementation of password_hash() is a simple wrapper around crypt(). The $2y$10$ portion of the output tells us that the bcrypt algorithm was used with a cost parameter of 10. Let's create a simple wrapper function that we can use to control the cost and measure its effect. We can run the password string and the salt (extracted from the output of password_hash()) to prove that crypt() is doing the same internal work:

```
function doHash(string $password, string $salt, int $cost = 10): void
{
    $start = microtime(true);
    $hash = crypt($password, "$2y\${$cost}\${$salt}");
    $end = microtime(true) - $start;
    print "{$hash} - took {$end} s" . PHP_EOL;
}
```

CHAPTER 8　STRINGS

```
$password = 'weaksauce';
$hash1 = '$2y$10$2alN7H818NP.8BZAoerYxebJIOTsNz4MItmDx1notHgXQwNGxsSCC';
$salt = substr($hash1, 7, 22);
doHash($password, $salt);
```

Output:
$2y$10$2alN7H818NP.8BZAoerYxebJIOTsNz4MItmDx1notHgXQwNGxsSCC - took 0.050182104110718 s

The precise measurement of time will vary between systems but should be approximately the same (in our case, *0.05* seconds). Finally, let's bump the cost parameter and see what happens:

```
doHash($password, $salt, 11);
doHash($password, $salt, 12);
doHash($password, $salt, 13);
doHash($password, $salt, 14);
```

Output:
$2y$11$2alN7H818NP.8BZAoerYxe3upXP1upofGTRoA1STfUjgKO8TWsDqu - took 0.099919080734253 s
$2y$12$2alN7H818NP.8BZAoerYxeeXK71J69fxDCEX/znx.Dwe9JJWkye06 - took 0.19856905937195 s
$2y$13$2alN7H818NP.8BZAoerYxeAF8CLsNd6oMOaetBD5lVOLX863ABuHK - took 0.39699101448059 s
$2y$14$2alN7H818NP.8BZAoerYxean/Pk/eNCocT9TKIN23.Jc2sMiHRMVC - took 0.79384803771973 s

Notice that as we increment the cost by one, the time taken doubles, and the hash portion of the string changes each time (because the hash is being recomputed on each cycle). The minimum value of cost for bcrypt is 04, the maximum is 31, and these are exponential values: a cost of 04 is 2^4, a cost of 31 is 2^{31} – it's possible to have this function run for a very long time indeed. A word of warning: remember rainbow tables, how I warned that they were more than just maps of hashes to strings? What we've just looked at in the example above is a *hash chain*, where the same hash algorithm is applied repeatedly. It is possible to pre-compute such chains, rainbow tables do just this and are therefore able to defeat the workload aspect of costly hash algorithms to a certain extent.

Verifying Integrity

If you remember when we first looked hashing functions in an earlier section (md5(), crc32(), etc.) I mentioned that hashing could also be used to verify data integrity and also sender identity. For these cases we do not need the complexity cost of a password hashing algorithm, because these types of application use shared secrets to "salt" the hash: by incorporating a shared secret key into the source string before hashing we ensure that the only way to reproduce the hash value at the receiving end is by possessing the same secret and original message. The name for this form of message integrity validation is *hash-based message authentication code* ("HMAC") and PHP's core hash extension provides some HMAC functions.

hash_hmac()

It's time to play spies. I have the secret key (the creation and distribution of such a shared secret is not shown here, but we can imagine it involves pieces of paper that have to be swallowed after reading), and a vital communication to send. By generating an HMAC hash I am able to verify my identity (or at least verify I know the key) and the message contents in one go. I can call hash_hmac() with three arguments: first the algorithm I wish to use, then the message, then the shared secret.

```
$secret = 'MySecretKey';
$message = 'The eagle flies at dawn.';
print hash_hmac("sha256", $message, $secret);
```

Output:
d41ecc4ad873d37f02e205f408f3d3d2275dc30eab0cee51ea7cb7b4764d9c33

The message would then be sent alongside the hash, the receiving end repeats the hash operation (the receiver has their own copy of the secret key, this must never be transmitted for obvious reasons), if the receiver's hash matches the transmitted hash then they know they can trust the message has not been changed and it was signed with the correct key. The message itself has not been encrypted in this scenario, what we're doing here is establishing trust in the sender and the validity of the data.

Like `password_hash()`, there are multiple HMAC algorithms available:

```
print_r(hash_hmac_algos());
```

Output:
```
Array
(
    [0] => md2
    [1] => md4
    [2] => md5
    [3] => sha1
    [4] => sha224
    ...
```

The full list will vary according to what's installed on your system, but there's likely going to be dozens. The relative merits and differences of hashing algorithms are a pretty specialized topic and not one we will explore here. If you have an interest, then there are ample resources to be found via your favorite search engine.

Encryption

Let's close out this section by looking at how to fully encrypt our data. Remember that hashing is one-way: it is impossible to compute the original data from which a hash is computed. We've seen how to use hashes to verify message (and sender) integrity, but how do we conceal the messages themselves such that if intercepted they are unreadable? This isn't much of a concern if your application is running over HTTPS, because the "S" portion is doing encryption for you: modern HTTPS systems have TLS – transport layer security – embedded, and this protocol ensures that sender and receiver have randomly generated session keys (shared secrets that are discarded after use, and never stored), which are used to encrypt and decrypt all the data flowing over the network while the two systems are connected. This is made possible by public/private key pairs: the client uses the server's public key to encrypt a random session key (generated by the client), and the server decrypts using its private key. Once the shared secret is established, it is used until the client disconnects. All of this happens far away from your PHP code; the HTTPS web server handles it for you, and HTTPS is fairly ubiquitous today, thanks to the efforts of the Electronic Frontier Foundation's `https://www.eff.org/https-everywhere` campaign. Thank you, EFF!

Of course, you might find yourself needing to encrypt data manually; not every PHP system out there is running via Apache or Nginx. It's also a fun exercise! So let's have a go and roll our own encryption code. PHP offers two modules we can use for this task: `openssl` and `sodium`. Most installations tend to offer both by default. Both extensions are very capable and offer tools for key/certificate management, hashing, side-channel attack prevention (preventing the inference of information from timing and memory use), encoding, and of course encryption. We'll use `sodium` here, but that's purely personal preference on my part, and two methods: using a shared secret and using a public/private key pair.

Shared Secret (Symmetric)

In time-honored tradition, we have two secret agents: Alice and Bob. Alice and Bob have a previously agreed-upon secret key, which they will both use to encrypt and decrypt messages to each other. We can use sodium's `sodium_crypto_secretbox()` function to encrypt messages, which takes three arguments: the message to be encrypted, a one-time use random byte sequence (called a *nonce*, which has an unfortunate meaning in modern British slang but is an old Middle English word for something temporary), and the shared secret. The shared secret has to be a certain number of bytes, and we can generate them with the `sodium_crypto_secretbox_keygen()` function:

```
$secret = sodium_crypto_secretbox_keygen();;
$message = 'WE RIDE AT DAWN.';

$nonce = random_bytes(SODIUM_CRYPTO_SECRETBOX_NONCEBYTES);
$encrypted_message = sodium_crypto_secretbox($message,
    $nonce,
    $secret
);

print bin2hex($message) . PHP_EOL;
print bin2hex($encrypted_message) . PHP_EOL;
```

Output:
57452052...
11e4274e...

The encrypted bytes are decrypted using the same nonce and key. Data encrypted in this way is normally Base64 encoded (for binary safety) before sending over a network, and the nonce is transmitted as part of the message (it exists simply to make the message unique and prevents malicious re-transmission by an attacker; it serves no additional purpose in obfuscating the message). Once the recipient has (if necessary) decoded and extracted the nonce, decryption is very straightforward:

```
$decrypted_message = sodium_crypto_secretbox_open(
    $encrypted_message,
    $nonce,
    $secret
);
print $decrypted_message;

Output:
WE RIDE AT DAWN.
```

Public Key

For a key-pair-based implementation, we use sodium's `sodium_crypto_box()` as our encryption function and create encryption key pairs by combining the private key of one party with the public key of the other. First, we'll create public/private keys (sodium generates ED25519-based keys, in case you're wondering):

```
$alicePair = sodium_crypto_box_keypair();
$pubAlice = sodium_crypto_box_publickey($alicePair);
$privAlice = sodium_crypto_box_secretkey($alicePair);

$bobPair = sodium_crypto_box_keypair();
$pubBob = sodium_crypto_box_publickey($bobPair);
$privBob = sodium_crypto_box_secretkey($bobPair);
```

`sodium_crypto_box_keypair()` creates both keys, unified into a single byte sequence. We then extract the public and private sections using `sodium_crypto_box_publickey()`, etc. Bob gets his own pair of keys using the same method. Next, we generate the encryption keys:

```
$aliceKey = sodium_crypto_box_keypair_from_secretkey_and_publickey(
    $privAlice,
    $pubBob
);
$bobKey = sodium_crypto_box_keypair_from_secretkey_and_publickey(
    $privBob,
    $pubAlice
);
```

Alice uses her private key and Bob's public key to create her encryption key pair. Bob does the same with his private key and Alice's public. At no point, do they need to share secrets: public keys are freely distributed; messages encrypted with a public key can only be decrypted by the matching private key (which is, of course, kept secret and never needs to be shared). Now we've set up our keys, we can use them to encrypt:

```
$message = 'The lamb lies down on Broadway.';
$nonce = random_bytes(SODIUM_CRYPTO_BOX_NONCEBYTES);
$encrypted_message = sodium_crypto_box($message, $nonce, $aliceKey);

print bin2hex($message) . PHP_EOL;
print bin2hex($encrypted_message) . PHP_EOL;

$decrypted_message = sodium_crypto_box_open(
    $encrypted_message,
    $nonce,
    $bobKey
);
print $decrypted_message;
```

Output:
546865206c...
0fe44c0f70...
The lamb lies down on Broadway.

And there we have it. `sodium_crypto_box()` scrambles our secret message with one key pair (and a random nonce value), `sodium_crypto_box_open()` unscrambles with the corresponding key pair, and the same single-use value.

CHAPTER 8 STRINGS

Regular Expressions

The time is finally upon us! I've been promising/threatening these for most of the chapter and decided to keep them for the end of our foray into all things text: saving the best until last. A regular expression (also known as *regex*, or *regexp*) is a sequence of characters and metacharacters used to define a pattern, which is then applied to text (often referred to as the *sample*): the regex engine will search for the pattern, and if found, it can then return portions of the text in or around the matching areas, or even replace the matching portions.

Regular expressions have their roots in the work of the mathematician Stephen Kleene, a student of Alonzo Church (see Chapter 3, "Functions"), who devised a notation system for describing (regular) events in neural networks in a 1951 Project RAND paper. (The * metacharacter – indicating zero or more repetitions and found in many guises of pattern matching systems in computing – is named the *Kleene star*.) Regular expressions as we would recognize them today were introduced by Ken Thompson (designer and implementer of technologies you might have heard of, such as Unix, C, Golang, UTF-8... quite an incredible list) in the late 1960s as text search functionality in the QED text editor. The syntax of regular expressions has varied over the decades but reached something of an apotheosis with the Perl programming language (of which I have many fond memories). PHP, like many other languages and systems, has adopted Perl's regular expression syntax (which is given the name PCRE, for "Perl-Compatible Regular Expressions"), and all of PHP's core PCRE functions are prefixed with `preg_` – such as `preg_match()`.

Before we get started, a word of caution. The study of regular expressions is an entire branch of programming and theory in its own right. This section is decidedly *not* a comprehensive dive; the intention is to just get you started. There are, happily, vast amounts of resources out there on the web and many excellent books devoted exclusively to the topic.

Basic Syntax

A Perl (and therefore PHP) regular expression is simply a string containing literal characters, and/or metacharacters, with a delimiter character (a forward slash / by convention) at the very beginning and end of the pattern. After the final delimiter there are some additional characters that can be used to modify behavior (such as case sensitivity). They "/look like this/", "/or (this)/i", or even "/like [Tt][Hh][Is][Ss]/".

Metacharacters control things like quantifying (e.g., the Kleene star), grouping, counting, and even capturing parts of the text being searched. Let's start with some simple examples.

```
$text = 'Highly irregular was the time I found a human foot in a
toaster oven';
$pattern = '/toaster/';
var_dump(preg_match($pattern, $text));
```

Output:
int(1)

Here we've used a core string function – `preg_match()` – to test that $pattern (as the first argument) can be successfully applied to $text (the second argument), and the function returns `int(1)` to indicate that the pattern exists (rather than, say, a boolean – by now you should have a feel for the inconsistencies in PHP string functions). The pattern itself – /toaster/ is very simple – characters in a regular expression represent themselves unless modified with a metacharacter – and that particular string does indeed exist in the search text. (Note that this is an inefficient way to match simple substrings, `strpos()` is much faster.)

There's a lot more to preg_match(), but we'll save the fine detail for when cover the various code and `mbstring` PCRE functions at the end of the section. Before then, let's go deep on the syntax and features of PCREs.

Delimiters

The patterns supplied to all the `preg_*` functions must be enclosed in matching delimiter characters. The convention is to use /, but other characters are available. Specifically, these are any non-alphanumeric, non-backslash, non-whitespace ASCII character. Hash symbols # and percentage signs % are common alternatives; the recommendation is to stick with forward slash unless it appears as a common character in the pattern (because it will make for a more difficult pattern to read, as you'll see in a moment).

```
var_dump(preg_match(' #toaster#', $text));
var_dump(preg_match('+toaster+', $text));
var_dump(preg_match('&toaster&', $text));
```

Output:
int(1)
int(1)
int(1)

The first valid delimiter character encountered in the pattern (ignoring any leading whitespace) becomes that pattern's delimiter and must be used to finish the pattern, and it must also be escaped (with a backslash character) if used as a literal character. Here's what I meant about switching delimiters if the delimiter itself is a common character in the pattern:

```
$text = 'http://www.iloveregex.com/';
var_dump(preg_match('/http:\/\/www/', $text));
var_dump(preg_match('#http://www#', $text));
```

Output:
int(1)
int(1)

Modifiers

Characters placed after the final delimiter of a pattern are evaluated as modifiers and control the behavior of the regex engine. The available modifiers are

Table 8-24. PCRE regex modifiers

Modifier	Effect
i	Case-insensitive match
m	Multiline match
s	Control behaviour of the . metacharacter
u	Enable Unicode property matching
x	Whitespace in pattern has no significance
A	Pattern is "anchored" to start of sample text
D	Control behaviour of the $ metacharacter
U	Control "greediness" of quantifiers

Multiple modifiers can be added to an expression, for example, /pattern/Aix would set the pattern matching to be anchored, case insensitive, and multiline. We'll look at a few of the modifiers now, and the rest when they become relevant as we work through this section. First of all, here's i and x modifiers in action:

```
var_dump(preg_match('/ToAsT/i', 'toaster'));
var_dump(preg_match('/To A sT/ix', 'toaster'));
```

Output:
int(1)
int(1)

The effects are fairly self-explanatory: our search pattern contains an assortment of uppercase and lowercase ASCII letters, but with the i modifier we still get a positive result from preg_match(). By adding x as a second modifier, all of the spaces in the pattern are ignored (otherwise they would have been treated as literal space characters and resulted in no match). To apply a regex pattern from the start of the sample, you can use the A modifier:

```
var_dump(preg_match_all('/toast/', 'toaster toaster'));
var_dump(preg_match_all('/toast/A', 'toaster toaster'));
```

Output:
int(2)
int(1)

By "anchoring" the pattern to the very beginning of the sample, we can only match the pattern once, even though it occurs multiple times in the sample. Note the use of preg_match_all() here; this is where PHP's implementation of PCRE differs slightly from Perl and other PRCE engines: other languages offer a g modifier for "global" matching where the pattern is applied throughout the entire string (otherwise it only has to match once). PHP does away with this modifier and enables it automatically, except for preg_match(). Now that we know how to anchor the pattern, we need to look at another modifier which controls how this anchoring is applied to complex sample text.

The multiline modifier – m – has subtle but profound effect on the PCRE engine. Without the m modifier, the entire sample string is simply one byte stream to which the pattern is applied across the entire length. If m is specified, the sample is treated as multiple strings, delimited by the *0x0A* newline character. The following example should make this clear; we'll also have a sneak peak at some more metacharacters:

CHAPTER 8 STRINGS

```
$text = <<<EOS
Highly irregular...
Highly irregular...
Highly irregular...
EOS;

var_dump(preg_match_all('/^Highly/', $text));
var_dump(preg_match_all('/^Highly/m', $text));
```

Output:
int(1)
int(3)

Our sample contains three lines of text, the line separations will be encoded either as *0x0A* (for Linux-based or similar systems), or as *0x0D 0x0A* (CRLF of Windows systems). The pattern /^Highly/ contains the ^ metacharacter at the very start, this instructs the PCRE engine to anchor the pattern to the beginning of the sample (like the A modifier). Without a multiline modifier the pattern can only match once, at the very start of the sample, but it we add it via /^Highly/m then the pattern is applied at the beginning of sequence immediately after the *0x0A* byte (the beginning of each new line), which is why we have a count of 1 in the first preg_match_all() call, but 3 in the second. The reason why I've chosen to use the ^ metacharater to demonstrate this is because using the A modifier with preg_match_all() has the (undocumented) side effect of disabling global matching:

```
var_dump(preg_match_all('/Highly/Am', $text));
```

Output:
int(1)

Since we're in the neighborhood, here's how to anchor a pattern to the end of the sample by placing the $ metacharacter at the end of the pattern...

```
var_dump(preg_match_all('/\.\.\.$/', $text));
var_dump(preg_match_all('/\.\.\.$/m', $text));
```

Output:
int(1)
int(3)

...and if you're wondering what those backslashes are doing in the pattern: they're escaping another metacharacter: . which (without the escape) matches any character except a newline. Let's look at escaping next.

Escape Sequences

We've just met the escape character, backslash, which we used to escape the delimiter metacharacter because we wanted to match a literal forward slash (two of them, in fact). Every other metacharacter (we'll get to those in a moment) that you wish to interpret as a literal character needs to be escaped in the same way. There are other uses for backslash, or in other words, there are different forms of escapes. There are escapes for representing non-printing ASCII characters (newline, tab, control characters) or for using byte values, more or less identically to the way we've used these in strings previously. There are also escape sequences for representing character types such as digits, words (formed from letters), and spaces (with and without directionality). Finally, there are sequences that are used to make simple assertions in the pattern, such as matching a pattern from the very start of the subject text or disabling metacharacters. That's a lot to take in, so let's work up a few examples to demonstrate.

"Non-printing" Characters

Something of a misnomer, "non-printing" characters often have effects on the text in which they're embedded but present a challenge to represent syntactically. You are free to use ASCII byte values with the \x sequence (\x20 is space, \x0A is newline, etc.) but the usual convenience escapes (\n, \r, \t, etc.) are available:

```
$text = <<<EOS
hello
world
EOS;
var_dump(preg_match_all('/o\nw/', $text));

Output:
int(1)
```

CHAPTER 8　STRINGS

The full list of these "non-printing" escapes is as follows:

Table 8-25. *PCRE non-printing regex escape sequences*

Escape sequence	ASCII character
\a	Alarm (BEL *0x07*)
\cx	Control character (allows representation of first 26 ASCII bytes)
\e	Escape (ESC *0x1B*)
\f	Formfeed (FF *0x0C*)
\n	Newline (NL *0x0A*)
\p{xx}	Character with Unicode property
\P{xx}	Character without Unicode property
\r	Carriage return (CR *0x0D*)
\R	Represent multiple forms of line break (\n, \r, \r\n)
\t	Horizontal tab (TAB *0x09*)
\xhh	Hexadecimal byte value, e.g., \x0A = n
\ddd	Octal escape up to three digits, e.g., \012 = \n

Some of these forms require explanation (or warnings). The control character escape \cx, where x is any ASCII alphabet character, produces a value that maps to one of the ASCII characters *0x01* to *0x1A* (in other words, 1–26). Brace yourself: it does this by calculating the ordinal value of the letter (in the ASCII codepage) modulo 32. If we take the letter J, for example, its ASCII ordinal value is *74*, *74 % 32* is *10*, and the tenth ASCII character is the newline character *0x0A*. Furthermore, there is no difference between upper and lower case, because each ASCII Latin upper/lowercase mapping is exactly *32* codepoints in distance – A ordinal position is *65*, a is *97*, B/b is *66/98*, etc. The output of the following code is int(1) for both (\cj and \cJ are equivalent):

```
var_dump(preg_match_all('/o\cjw/', $text));
var_dump(preg_match_all('/o\cJw/', $text));
```

Output:
int(1)
int(1)

Personally, I'd use hex escapes, but you need to be aware this exists. Octal escape syntax comes with a warning: always use the full three digits, \001 instead of \1, because there is some overlap with another regex feature called backreferencing. We'll get to backreferences in due course, but be aware that single-digit octal escapes can have unintended effects.

Unicode Properties

Unicode property escapes take the form \p{xx} (to assert the property exists for a character) and \P{xx} (to assert a property does not exist). The Unicode Standard assigns a variety of properties to characters as metadata attached to the codepoints defined in the Unicode data files that were mentioned earlier in this chapter. For example, the following line is taken from https://www.unicode.org/Public/15.1.0/ucd/UnicodeData.txt (Unicode compliant software is compiled against files such as this one)...

0020;SPACE;Zs;0;WS;;;;;N;;;;;

This is the Unicode definition for code point U+0020, which is the SPACE character (mapped to the spacebar on keyboards). The third field – ;Zs; – is a "General Category" code describing the character, in this case Zs stands for "Separator, space". It is these codes that are combined with the Unicode property escape to describe a class of characters in the pattern:

```
$text = 'Highly irregular was the time I found a human foot in a
toaster oven';
$pattern = '/\p{Zs}/';
var_dump(preg_match_all($pattern, $text));
```

Output:
int(13)

The sample data in $text contains thirteen spaces, the pattern /\p{Zs}/ therefore matches thirteen times, as we can see from the output. In addition to individual character properties, sets of codepoints are flagged as belonging to scripts (or "alphabets" if you prefer, though the term is contentious for certain writing systems). Here's an example:

CHAPTER 8   STRINGS

```
$cyrillic = "\u{421}\u{421}\u{421}\u{420}";
$pattern = '/\p{Cyrillic}/u'; // note the 'u' modifier
print $cyrillic . PHP_EOL;
var_dump(preg_match_all($pattern, $cyrillic));
```

Output:
СССР
int(4)

It's important to note the use of the u modifier here: this tells the PCRE engine to evaluate the sample as UTF-8 encoded text. The short-form Unicode properties will work without it, but it's a good idea to be explicit. PHP supports a wide variety of script names that can be used in conjunction with the \p and \P modifiers; Arabic, Braille, Cuneiform... all the way to Vai (not Steve!) and Yi. Some more useful property codes are given in the table below but be aware this is not exhaustive. The full list of Unicode property escapes in PHP is available at https://www.php.net/manual/en/regexp.reference.unicode.php

Table 8-26. *Unicode property codes*

L	Letter: includes all Ll, Lu, Lt etc.
Ll	Letter: lowercase
Lo	Letter, other: e.g., CJK Unified Ideographs
Lt	Letter: title case
Lu	Letter: uppercase
N	Number
Nd	Number, decimal
Nl	Number, letter: e.g., runic, Roman numerals
P	Punctuation
Sc	Currency symbol: e.g., $, £, €
Z	Separator: e.g., newline, space

Character Types

In a similar way to Unicode properties, there is a class of escapes that will match with ASCII characters that have common properties, such as decimal digits, Latin alphabet characters, and spaces (both horizontal and vertical). The full list is given below.

Table 8-27. PCRE character-type escape sequences

\d	Decimal digit
\D	Not a decimal digit
\h	Horizontal whitespace
\H	Not horizontal whitespace
\s	Any whitespace
\S	Not any whitespace
\v	Vertical whitespace
\V	Not vertical whitespace
\w	Contiguous "word" (alphanumeric) characters
\W	Not a "word" (space, punctuation, control, etc.)

Assertions

Finally, we have the assertion escapes. These escapes differ from the rest in one important aspect: *consumption* of characters in the sample string. Now, you might be wondering what exactly the word "consumption" means in this context. It means simply that when a character in the sample string matches with part of the pattern (be it a one-for-one character match, meta-character, escape, or so on), the PRCE engine moves along to the next byte (or byte sequence) in the sample (and the next sequence in the expression). Assertions, however, do not do this; they instead define conditions to be met at specific parts of the sample without any change in the particular sample byte or bytes under consideration. This style of (sub)pattern matching is sometimes called *zero width*.

The assertion escapes are as follows:

Table 8-28. PCRE assertion escape sequences

\b	Word boundary
\B	Not a word boundary
\A	The very start of the sample (not multiline)
\Z	The very end of the sample (not multiline)
\z	End of subject
\G	First matching position of subject

On first glance most of these probably seem straightforward, but there's some subtle logic at play. Here are some examples to illustrate, and we're going to use an additional feature of preg_match_all() by passing in an array as the third argument. This array is passed by reference by default and will have each matching part of the sample added to it, enabling a detailed inspection of the results.

```
$text = '... I found a human foot ...';
preg_match_all('/\w/', $text, $matches);
var_dump($matches[0]);
```

Output:
```
Array
(
    [0] => I
    [1] => f
    [2] => o
    [3] => u
    [4] => n
...
```

So far so good, \w matches with all sixteen alphanumeric characters in the sample. We can see each element of the $matches array contains the non-punctuation, non-space portions of $text: I, f, o, u, etc. The non-consumption/zero-width matching is irrelevant here, the PCRE engine moves on after each match regardless. The next example should make this point clearer:

```
function dumpMatches(array $arr): void {
    foreach ($arr[0] as $match) {
        print bin2hex($match) . PHP_EOL;
    }
    print PHP_EOL;
}
preg_match_all('/\w\b/', $text, $matches);
dumpMatches($matches);
```

Output:
49
64
61
6e
74

The function dumpMatches() is a simple loop that prints the hexadecimal byte values of each matched sub-string, and we can see that the pattern /\w\b/ matches just the word bytes without capturing the word boundary bytes. The pattern /\w / will perform a very similar search (the only word boundary character in $text is ASCII space *0x20*) but gives slightly different results:

```
preg_match_all('/\w /', $text, $matches);
dumpMatches($matches);
```

Output:
4920
6420
6120
6e20
7420

This time the word boundary character is included in the match, because the literal space in the pattern is not a zero-width assertion.

Metacharacters

PCRE metacharacters are special cases; they are not interpreted literally but instead have certain effects like quantifying, defining alternate sub-expressions, breaking the pattern into sub-patterns, anchoring a pattern to the start and/or the end of the sample (or each line if in multiline mode), and so on. Some metacharacters have multiple uses and change their effects depending on their context. Here's the full list of PCRE metacharacters supported by PHP:

Table 8-29. PCRE metacharacters

\	Escape (see above)
^	Anchor to start of sample or newline
$	Anchor to end of sample or newline
.	Match anything except newline
[	Begin character class
]	End character class
|	Alternate separator
(	Sub-pattern start
)	Sub-pattern end
?	Modify sub-pattern behavior; quantify "zero or one", modify quantifier behavior
*	"Zero or more" quantifier (The Keene Star)
+	"One or more" quantifier
{	Begin min/max quantifier
}	End min/max quantifier

Some of these have been introduced already: escapes, anchors, the * quantifier. We don't need to cover escapes again, and the anchor metacharacters ^ and $ have already been demonstrated. Otherwise, in no particular order, here's what the rest do.

Quantifiers

Specifying the number of times part of a pattern appears can be very useful. There are many cases where string data contains well-defined structure, which might be of interest in a program. Think along the lines of product serial numbers, ISBN's, for example. There is a general-purpose quantifier syntax, which is an open brace {, followed by a decimal integer (between *0* and *65535*), followed by a closing brace }. To define a range, add a comma after the first number, then an optional second integer (which must be larger than the first), and finally a closing brace }. For convenience, there are also some single character quantifiers: ? is "zero or one", + is "one or more", * is "zero or more". Put that all together and you have something like this:

Table 8-30. PCRE quantifiers

{5,}	At least five
{0,1}, ?	Zero or one
{1,}, +	One or more
{0,}, *	Zero or more
{42}	Exactly forty-two

Quantifiers, be they single characters or in the general form, are placed immediately after the part of the expression to be quantified. For example:

Table 8-31. PCRE quantifier examples

\d*	Any number of digits, including none
\w{7}\b	Exactly seven "word" characters immediately followed by boundary
\d{1,3}\.\d{1,3}\.\d{1,3}\.\d{1,3}	Four groups of up to three digits, separated by a literal dot: an IPv4 address.

Now, just to confuse things a little, the ? metacharacter has a double purpose for quantifying. If placed immediately after the closing brace of a general-purpose expression, it changes the *greediness* of the match (matches are greedy by default; the ? modifier flips this to non-greedy). A non-greedy match simply means the PCRE engine switches to matching the minimum portion of the sample to satisfy the pattern. The following examples demonstrate this:

```
preg_match_all('/\d+/', '12345', $matches);
print_r($matches[0]);
```

Output:
```
Array
(
    [0] => 12345
)
```

The pattern /\d+/ is a simple expression meaning "one or more digits." The sample is '12345', the match is greedy, so it consumes all five digits. If we switch to non-greedy...

```
preg_match_all('/\d+?/', '12345', $matches);
print_r($matches[0]);
```

Output:
```
Array
(
    [0] => 1
    [1] => 2
    [2] => 3
    [3] => 4
    [4] => 5
)
```

... we get the bare minimum that satisfies the "one or more digits" condition, which gives us five matches of one digit each.

Character Classes

Some escape sequences, such as \w, \d, and \s, define multiple characters. \d matches any of 0123456789, for example. These are character type escapes, sets of characters with common properties (Unicode properties are functionally the same thing too). It is possible to define custom character sets too, using the [and] metacharacters to form a *character class*. Within a character class definition, there are some differences in behavior with certain metacharacters, and in addition, the dash symbol – becomes a metacharacter used to define ranges, using ASCII collation rules. It is also possible to use the character type escape sequences within a character class. Here are some examples:

Table 8-32. PCRE character classes

[^dgAF]	Any character except d, g, A, F
[0-9]	The full range of decimal digits, equivalent to \d
[a-zA-Z]	All upper and lowercase Latin alphabet characters.
[\dABCDEF] [\dA-F] [0-9A-F]	Will match a hexadecimal digit
[\.\-,!]	Match any of .-,! punctuation chars

The caret character also takes a new role in character classes by negating them. Thus, [^0-9] means "any character that is not a decimal digit," [^a-f] is "any character that is not lowercase abcdef," and so on. Here's a demonstration:

```
$text = 'Highly Irregular Was The Time';
preg_match_all('/[^A-Z]+/', $text, $matches);
print_r($matches[0]);
```

Output:
```
Array
(
    [0] => ighly
    [1] => rregular
    [2] => as
    [3] => he
    [4] => ime
)
```

The pattern /[^A-Z]+/ defines a character class of "anything that isn't an ASCII uppercase letter," greedily matched one or more times; the resulting matches should be self-explanatory.

Alternates

In a similar way to character classes, the pipe character | can be used with grouping to define alternative byte sequences for matching.

CHAPTER 8 STRINGS

```
$text = 'brown bread, green apples, orange er... oranges';
preg_match_all('/brown|green|orange/', $text, $matches);
print_r($matches[0]);
```

Output:
```
Array
(
    [0] => brown
    [1] => green
    [2] => orange
    [3] => orange
)
```

By using three different patterns, separated by |, we're able to match in three different ways, and we can extract matches for the three colors in the pattern. "Orange" occurs twice in the matches array because why not name a fruit after a color? (Or is it the other way around?) Alternate patterns are applied to the sample in the order they're defined, left-to-right. They become more useful when combined with the following feature…

Sub-patterns

By adding parentheses - ( ) to an expression, it is possible achieve two outcomes: localizing a set of alternatives and capturing matching parts of the sample. These parenthesized expression components are called *sub-patterns* or sometimes *groups*. Captured sub-patterns/groups are made available to the caller (i.e., through the $matches pass-by-reference array we've been using in recent examples); they can also be used later in the pattern via an escape sequence, which we'll be looking at very shortly.

```
preg_match_all('/(brown|green|orange) apples/', $text, $matches);
print_r($matches);
```

Output:
```
Array
(
    [0] => Array
```

```
            (
                [0] => green apples
            )
        [1] => Array
            (
                [0] => green
            )
)
```

Hopefully this should make sense: by localizing the alternates, we are able to match any part of the sample $text, which is a color followed by 'apples'. This pattern would match 'brown apples' or (should they exist) 'orange apples'. The sub-pattern is in "capture mode," so the $matches array now has two elements: first the section(s) of the sample that match the entire expression, and a new section that contains just the section(s) matching the sub-pattern. If we add another sub-pattern, the $matches array will contain three sub-arrays:

```
preg_match_all('/(brown|green) (bread|apples)/', $text, $matches);
print_r($matches);
```

Output:
```
Array
(
    [0] => Array
        (
            [0] => brown bread
            [1] => green apples
        )
    [1] => Array
        (
            [0] => brown
            [1] => green
        )
```

CHAPTER 8 STRINGS

```
    [2] => Array
        (
            [0] => bread
            [1] => apples
        )

)
```

In a similar way to character classes, sub-patterns also have a few specific metacharacters (or metacharacters that behave differently in a sub-pattern context, if you prefer) that control the way they behave. Beginning a sub-pattern with (?: disables capturing, and modifiers (that would normally go after the closing pattern delimiter) can be inserted to enforce the modified behavior within the sub-pattern, for example, (?i: would force a sub-pattern match to be case insensitive. If modified behavior is required in a capturing sub-pattern, the beginning syntax is ((?i), and here's an example to demonstrate:

```
$text = 'bRoWn BrEaD, gReEn aPpLeS, oRanGe eR... OrAnGeS';
preg_match_all('/(?i:brown|green) ((?i)bread|apples)/', $text, $matches);
print_r($matches);
```

Output:
```
Array
(
    [0] => Array
        (
            [0] => bRoWn BrEaD
            [1] => gReEn aPpLeS
        )

    [1] => Array
        (
            [0] => BrEaD
            [1] => aPpLeS
        )

)
```

The difference between the two sub-patterns (?i:brown|green) and ((?i)bread|apples) should be apparent in the output: both are case insensitive (in an otherwise case-sensitive pattern, because there is no i modifier after the closing delimiter), but only the second sub-pattern will capture. It is also possible to give symbolic names to sub-patterns, which will work alongside the automatic numeric indexing. The syntax has three forms: (?P<name>), (?<name>), and (?'name'). The $matches array will now have array keys corresponding to the names chosen:

```
$text = 'brown bread, green apples, orange er... oranges';
preg_match_all("/(?'colour'brown|green) (?<type>bread|apples)/", $text, $matches);
print_r($matches);
```

Output:
```
Array
(
    [0] => Array ...
    [colour] => Array
        (
            [0] => brown
            [1] => green
        )
    [1] => Array ...
    [type] => Array
        (
            [0] => bread
            [1] => apples
        )
    ...
```

The output has been truncated somewhat to only show the interesting parts (the array keys matching the symbolic names in the sub-patterns).

Back-References

When capturing sub-patterns are defined, they will automatically create (when matching) something called a *back-reference*. These are made available for use in the rest of the pattern using an escape sequence (though of course they are only available *after* the sub-pattern is closed). If you remember from earlier, I recommended that octal escapes used all three digits – \001 instead of \1 – and promised you an explanation to come. Well, here we are because the syntax for using back-references in an expression is simply the ordinal number of the sub-pattern prefixed with an escaping backslash. \1 in a pattern would mean "octal value of 1" unless a sub-pattern is used, in which case it means "whatever was captured just now with the sub-pattern". Confused? Regexes can certainly get that way. Here's an example:

```
$text = 'hello hello world world';
preg_match_all('/(\w+)\s+\1/', $text, $matches);
print_r($matches);
```

Output:
```
Array
(
    [0] => Array
        (
            [0] => hello hello
            [1] => world world
        )
    [1] => Array
        (
            [0] => hello
            [1] => world
        )
)
```

The code above shows a common use case for back-references: finding repeating words. Let's break the pattern down. The sub-pattern (\w+) matches and captures one or more word characters (and the match is greedy so that entire words are captured), \s+ matches one or more space characters, and finally \1 to match whatever was captured in the sub-pattern. Thus, we have matches of 'hello hello' and 'world world', in the first sub array element of $matches, then each sub-pattern captured in the second ('hello', then 'world'). Note that the contents of the back-reference are overwritten on each match: \1 contains 'hello' until the PCRE engine reaches and matches the byte sequence of 'world', whereupon the former is overwritten with the latter.

There are alternative syntaxes for back-references, and it is also possible to use symbolic names (in conjunction with named sub-patterns). The escape sequence \g can be combined with an integer to create absolute and relative back-references:

```
preg_match_all('/(\w+) \g1/', $text, $matches);
preg_match_all('/(\w+) \g{1}/', $text, $matches);
preg_match_all('/(\w+) \g{-1}/', $text, $matches);
```

All of the patterns above will produce the same output (in $matches) as the first back-reference example. \g1, \g{1} both match the absolute ordinal value of 1 (the first sub-pattern), \g{-1} is a relative back-reference to the nearest sub-pattern to the left. (\g{-2} would match the second nearest to the left, and so on.) To reference a named sub-pattern, the following sequences all achieve the same (?P=name), \g<name>, \g{name}, \g'name', and the \g forms also accept \k as an alternative (\k<name> and so on).

```
preg_match_all('/(?<thing>\w+) \g<thing>/', $text, $matches);
print_r($matches);
```

Output:
```
Array
(
    [0] => Array ...
    [thing] => Array
        (
            [0] => hello
            [1] => world
        )
    ...
```

Once-Only

One of the principles that the PCRE engine works on is *backtracking*, especially when quantifiers are used. Consider an expression with a greedy matching character class – such as [^\d]+\s, which matches one or more non-digits followed by a single space – the engine would match as many non-digit characters as possible before moving to the next byte in the sample. If the next byte does not match, then the engine back-tracks and tries a sub-set of the sample before trying again, and again, and again. Let's say the sample contains 'abcdef123', the engine would match on abcdef, fail to match on the 1, and backtracks to bcdef, then cdef. Eventually it will give up, but not before consuming CPU resources in the process.

It is possible to instruct the PCRE engine to give up on non-matches in such expressions after a single greedy match. We know that 'abcdef123' will never match [^\d]+\s, but PCRE needs to backtrack multiple times before it knows for sure it can give up. Such things can give rise to serious performance issues for complex expressions or large samples, but by enclosing the quantified character class in a special sub-pattern syntax, the PCRE engine will change its behavior. The *once-only* sub-pattern syntax is (?>...). The modified form of our expression is now (?>[^\d]+)\s, and this modified form prevents the backtracking that would otherwise occur. PHP doesn't have any native way to capture performance statistics from the PCRE engine; there's no PHP I can produce that measures the difference in the number of internal backtracking calls that would be made.

There is, however, an abundance of regex tools on the internet. Regular expressions constitute an entire branch of programming expertise in their own right, after all. Here are two screenshots from https://regex101.com, which demonstrate the difference in "cycles" when a once-only sub-pattern is used (fewer cycles means fewer backtracking calls were made).

Figure 8-3. *Interactive regex editor before...*

Figure 8-4. *Interactive regex editor after...*

Lookahead, Lookbehind

Let's return to the idea of consuming characters when matching. The normal operation of the PCRE engine is to move along the sample string as it matches according to the expression. If we have a simple pattern like /abc(\w+)/ and a sample of 'abcdef', then the engine moves along the string one character at a time, matching first a, b, and c, then the remaining word characters of def (and in this case creating the \1 capture group, which contains def). In some cases, it is desirable to match without consuming, and for this we have *lookahead* and *lookbehind* assertions (collectively known as *lookaround*). A lookaround will check that the sample matches a sub-pattern without changing positions in the sample; they're another form of zero-width assertion.

The idea of looking ahead (or behind) but not consuming any part of the sample is subtle one, which can be explained with the following example. Imagine that you wanted to assert that one letter was not followed by another in a particular word; this would perhaps seem straightforward at first glance. We know how to use character type escapes

CHAPTER 8 STRINGS

such as \w for words, \D for non-digits, and character classes like [a-z] for lowercase ASCII Latin and [^c] for any character that isn't lowercase ASCII 'c'. Let's say we wanted to assert that in a word constructed of Latin alphabet characters, 'k' does not follow 'c'. We use a pattern such as /[a-zA-Z]+c[^k]/ but this actually means "One or more Latin alphabet characters, followed by c, followed by any character that isn't k", not "c without a following k" – a subtle but important difference, as the following demonstrates:

```
preg_match_all('/[a-zA-Z]+c[^k]/', 'Disc Dock', $matches);
print_r($matches);
```

Output:
```
    [0] => Array
        (
            [0] => Disc
        )
```

On first glance this looks fine; the string 'Disc' doesn't end in 'ck', and there's no match on 'Dock'. But let's look closer:

```
print bin2hex($matches[0][0]);
```

Output:
4469736320

We actually have five bytes in the match; the end byte is *0x20*, which is ASCII space: we've captured the space after 'Disc' because of the character class at the end of the pattern. Things are even more problematic if we do this:

```
preg_match_all('/[a-zA-Z]+c[^k]/', 'Dock Disc', $matches);
print_r($matches);
```

Output:
```
    [0] => Array
        (
        )
```

By moving 'Disc' to the end the string, we fail to match anything because there are no characters at all after the final 'c'. The PRCE engine cannot move beyond the 'c' to discover if the next character is "not a k". For our purposes we need to use a (negative) lookahead assertion, which checks the bytes ahead of the current match without moving to them. The syntax for doing so is (?!...) and here's what happens when we add it to the example above:

```
preg_match_all('/[a-zA-Z]+c(?!k)/', 'Dock Disc', $matches);
print_r($matches);
```

Output:
```
    [0] => Array
        (
            [0] => Disc
        )
```

This is the correct way to assert that 'c' is not followed by 'k', because it includes the case where nothing at all follows. Additionally, the assertion is zero-width, so there is no inclusion of the sample beyond the previous part of the pattern:

```
preg_match_all('/[a-zA-Z]+c(?!k)/', 'Disc Dock', $matches);
print bin2hex($matches[0][0]);
```

Output:
44697363

Here are all of the lookaround sub-pattern syntaxes available:

Table 8-33. PCRE lookaround sub-patterns

(?=...)	Positive lookahead
(?!...)	Negative lookahead
(?<=...)	Positive lookbehind
(?<!...)	Negative lookbehind

Conditional

PCRE, and PHP's implementation of PCRE, allow for an admittedly little-used but quite powerful feature: *conditional* sub-patterns. With this syntax it is possible to specify certain conditions that – if met (or not) – dictate a subsequent match. The test part of the sub-pattern works in one of two ways: either checking if numbered/named/relative

CHAPTER 8 STRINGS

capture groups are set, or if a lookaround was a success. After the conditional part of the pattern, if the condition is met (in other words, evaluates to true) then another expression is then tested against the sample for a match. Optionally, an alternative expression can be applied if the condition is not met. The general form of the syntax is (?(IF)THEN|ELSE). As ever, here's an example to demonstrate:

```
preg_match_all('/(USD)?\s(?(1)(\d+))/', 'USD 150', $matches);
print_r($matches);
```

Output:
```
    [0] => Array
        (
            [0] => USD 150
        )

    [1] => Array
        (
            [0] => USD
        )

    [2] => Array
        (
            [0] => 150
        )
```

Let's look at the regex itself – /(USD)?\s(?(1)(\d+))/ – and break it down. The portion before the conditional sub-pattern is (USD)?\s which matches the literal string 'USD' inside a capture group, with a following \s space character type. The quantifier ? means "zero or one times," and its position is very important. If it was inside the capture group, then this would have the effect of always setting the back-reference (either containing the 'USD' string, or nothing), but by placing it outside the capture, it can happen zero times, which means the back-reference is only created on a match with 'USD'. This is crucial for the next part of the pattern: (?(1)(\d+)), which tests for the existence of the back-reference with (1); if it exists, then the next part of the sub-pattern is applied, which is (\d+), and captures all digit characters after the space. The output shows the full pattern match (the entire sample string in this case), the first capture group contents 'USD', and the second capture group contents, which are the digits '150'.

Conditional sub-patterns also allow named and relative capture groups, as well as lookaround assertions. The various syntaxes are given below:

Table 8-34. *PCRE conditional sub-patterns*

(?(name)THEN|ELSE) (?(<name>)THEN|ELSE) (?('name')THEN|ELSE)	Named capture groups
(?(-1)THEN|ELSE)	Relative capture groups
(?(?=PATTERN)THEN|ELSE)	Positive lookahead
(?(?!PATTERN)THEN|ELSE)	Negative lookahead
(?(?<=PATTERN)THEN|ELSE)	Positive lookbehind
(?(?<!PATTERN)THEN|ELSE)	Negative lookbehind

Recursive

Recursive sub-patterns (not universally supported by all regex engines, but PHP will handle them) have the special syntax (?R) that simply means "repeat the expression so far." Here comes the tricky part though: the pattern is repeated up to the recursion marker as many times as the engine can match; each time this happens we add a level of recursion that, if we allow the recursion to match zero times with a ? quantifier, is then unwound – matching the remainder of the expression recursively. This should make more sense with an example:

```
$text = 'aaabbb';
preg_match_all('/a(?R)?b/', $text, $matches);
print_r($matches[0]);
```

Output:
```
Array
(
    [0] => aaabbb
)
```

You should have noticed that the pattern used contains no quantifiers for the literal characters (though the recursion is quantified with ?), yet we're able to match the full string 'aaabbb'. If the pattern had simply been /ab/ our match would have been just the two middle characters from the sample, by adding (?R)? we're asking the PCRE engine to keep matching a recursively, zero or one times and the zero is important because it allows the recursion to exit. Once the recursion is done, the rest of the pattern (a single 'b' character) is matched recursively. We have three 'a' characters, which means three levels of recursion, so there need to be three 'b' characters since they will be matched recursively too. The pattern /a(?R)?b/ will match any string that has any amount of 'a' followed by an equal number of 'b'.

PRCE Functions

Now we'll turn our attention to the functions that PHP provides for using regular expressions. The full list of core regex string functions is as follows:

Table 8-35. PREG functions

preg_filter()	Search sample with regex and replace matching portions
preg_grep()	Search array of strings and return matching elements
preg_last_error()	Get error code from the most recent PCRE call
preg_last_error_message()	Get error message from the most recent PCRE call
preg_match()	Search sample, return on first match
preg_match_all()	As preg_match(), but with implicit global modifier – returns all matches
preg_quote()	Escape all PCRE meta-characters in a string with backslash
preg_replace()	Search and replace matches with supplied string
preg_replace_callback()	As preg_replace() but using callable for replacement
preg_replace_callback_array()	As preg_replace_callback(), mapping patterns to callables
preg_split()	Split a single string into array of sub-strings, using a pattern

preg_grep()

This is a straightforward function that accepts a single regex pattern, an array of sample strings, and an optional flag parameter to control behavior. Each sample string in the array is checked for a match against the pattern and added to a new array, which is then returned.

```
$text = [
    'Iron Maiden - Somewhere in Time',
    'Iron Maiden - Powerslave',
    'Metallica - Master of Puppets'
];
print_r(preg_grep('/Iron Maiden/', $text));
```

Output:
```
Array
(
    [0] => Iron Maiden - Somewhere in Time
    [1] => Iron Maiden - Powerslave
)
```

The logic can be inverted to return non-matching strings by passing the constant PREG_GREP_INVERT:

```
print_r(preg_grep('/Iron Maiden/', $text, PREG_GREP_INVERT));
```

Output:
```
Array
(
    [2] => Metallica - Master of Puppets
)
```

Notice that the array keys are retained in the results.

preg_match(), preg_match_all()

We've seen these functions used throughout this section, so you already know that preg_match() returns only the first match, and preg_match_all() will return all matches (an implicit 'global' modifier). There's some additional functionality to be aware of, though; there are two optional parameters at the end of the function signature: one is a flag that adds more information to the $matches array, and the other is an offset value that starts the matching process at a specified byte in the sample string.

```
$text = 'Cowboy bebop';
preg_match('/\w*bo\w*/', $text, $matches, PREG_OFFSET_CAPTURE, 5);
print_r($matches);
```

Output:
```
    [0] => Array
        (
            [0] => bebop
            [1] => 7
        )
```

The PREG_OFFSET_CAPTURE flag adds the byte offset value for the match, and the integer 5 as the final argument tells PCRE to only start matching from the fifth byte in the sample. Thus our matching starts at the 'o' in Cowboy, so we get 'bebop' as our match and the value 7 as an extra element in the results array because that word begins at the seventh byte in the sample. The other flag supported by preg_match() is PREG_UNMATCHED_AS_NULL, which sets unmatched capture groups to null rather than an empty string:

```
preg_match('/\w*bo\w*(\d)?/', $text, $matches, PREG_UNMATCHED_AS_NULL);
var_dump($matches);
```

Output:
```
array(2) {
  [0]=>
  string(6) "Cowboy"
  [1]=>
  NULL
}
```

Notice that only 'Cowboy' is matched, even though 'bebop' is also a match for the pattern. We know by now that if we want global matching behavior, we should call preg_match_all(), and this function accepts the same offset and flags as preg_match(). It also has additional flags for controlling behavior.

```
preg_match_all('/(\w*)bo\w*/', $text, $matches, PREG_PATTERN_ORDER);
print_r($matches);
```

Output:
```
    [0] => Array
        (
            [0] => Cowboy
            [1] => bebop
        )

    [1] => Array
        (
            [0] => Cow
            [1] => be
        )
```

PREG_PATTERN_ORDER puts the full matches into one sub-array and the captured substrings into another. The alternative is to group matches and related captures together with PREG_SET_ORDER:

```
preg_match_all('/(\w*)bo\w*/', $text, $matches, PREG_SET_ORDER);
print_r($matches);
```

Output:
```
    [0] => Array
        (
            [0] => Cowboy
            [1] => Cow
        )

    [1] => Array
        (
            [0] => bebop
            [1] => be
        )
```

preg_quote()

This somewhat confusingly named function will transform a string that contains regex meta-characters with backslash escapes (not quotes). It accepts two arguments: the sample string and an optional string that defines a delimiter character:

```
print preg_quote("/(\d+)-[^a-Z].*/");
print PHP_EOL;
print preg_quote("/(\d+)-[^a-Z].*/", '/');
```

Output:
/\(\\d\+\)\-\[\^a\-Z\]\.*/
\/\(\\d\+\)\-\[\^a\-Z\]\.*\/

Note that delimiters are only escaped if the delimiter character is specified.

preg_filter()

This function accepts a pattern or an array of patterns, a replacement string or array of strings, and a sample string (or array thereof). There is also an optional parameter for setting limits on the number of replacements performed and a by-reference parameter for reporting on the number of replacements.

```
$text = 'I like bananas, oranges, and apples.';
print preg_filter('/(bananas|oranges|apples)/', 'fruit', $text);
```

Output:
I like fruit, fruit, and fruit.

Pretty straightforward stuff, and for simple replacements like above, it is advisable to use str_replace(), which will be faster. Things get more interesting (and useful) when you make use of back-references and arrays:

```
$text = 'The tortoise overtook the hare.';
$patterns = [
    '/(tortoise)/',
    '/(hare)/'
];
$replacements = [
    'slow ${1}',
    'quick ${1}',
];
```

```
print preg_filter($patterns, $replacements, $text);
```

Output:
```
The slow tortoise overtook the quick hare.
```

This is where preg_filter() shows that it has a lot more to offer than the simple byte comparison and swapping of str_replace(). The $patterns array contains expressions that are applied in the order they are defined in the array (not key order!), and the corresponding array elements of $replacements are used upon a successful match. The replacement strings are also expressions. In this case we're using the ${n} form, which is preferred over the \n syntax; be aware that named and relative capture groups are not supported. The sequential application of the matching and substitution means we can pull tricks like this:

```
$text = 'The goldfish overtook the shark.';
$patterns = [
    '/(goldfish)/',
    '/(nimble)/'
];
$replacements = [
    'nimble ${1}',
    '${1}, quick',
];
print preg_filter($patterns, $replacements, $text);
```

Output:
```
The nimble, quick goldfish overtook the shark.
```

The first pass applies the /(goldfish)/ pattern to the sample. There's a match, so the sample immediately becomes 'The nimble goldfish overtook the shark.'. The second pass uses the expression /(nimble)/, which the sample string now contains, so the second replacement is triggered, as we see in the final output. If there are more elements in $patterns than in $replacements, then those patterns that match in the sample but don't have a corresponding replacement will instead be replaced by an empty string. Here's what happens when we remove the second replacement from the example above:

CHAPTER 8 STRINGS

```
$replacements = ['nimble ${1}'];
print preg_filter($patterns, $replacements, $text);
```

Output:
The goldfish overtook the shark.

The first argument to the function can also be an array of strings, in which case all of them will be transformed in turn, equivalent to calling preg_filter() multiple times:

```
$text = [
    'The goldfish swam away from the shark.',
    'The shark ate the goldfish.'
];
$patterns = [
    '/(goldfish)/',
    '/(shark)/'
];
$replacements = [
    'sneaky ${1}',
    'naughty ${1}'
];
print_r(preg_filter($patterns, $replacements, $text));
```

Output:
```
Array
(
    [0] => The sneaky goldfish swam away from the naughty shark.
    [1] => The naughty shark ate the sneaky goldfish.
)
```

Note that the return value is now an array of transformed strings.

preg_replace(), preg_replace_callback(), preg_replace_callback_array()

preg_replace() is almost identical to preg_filter(): it has exactly the same parameters, and the only difference between the two is that preg_replace() will return the unchanged sample string(s) if no match is made:

```
$text = 'I contain no digits.';
print 'Filter: ' . preg_filter('/\d+/', '!', $text);
print PHP_EOL;
print 'Replace: ' . preg_replace('/\d+/', '!', $text);
```

Output:
Filter:
Replace: I contain no digits.

As an alternative to the simple string replacement in preg_filter() and preg_replace(), it is possible to use a callback function and preg_replace_callback(). Using this function, each time a match is made, the callback is invoked with an array argument that contains the matched portion of the sample string (and any capture groups if specified); the callback should return the desired replacement string. preg_replace_callback() is otherwise very similar to preg_replace(), and its other parameters are identical – it will accept strings or arrays of strings in the $pattern and $text positions and has support for offset, count, limit, and flag parameters. Here's a quick demonstration:

```
$text = 'The cat chased the bird, the dog chased the cat.';
$pattern = '/dog|cat|bird/';
print preg_replace_callback($pattern, function (array $matches): string {
    print 'callback invoked' . PHP_EOL;
    return match ($matches[0]) {
        'dog' => 'black dog',
        'cat' => 'white cat',
        'bird' => 'blue bird',
    };
}, $text);
```

Output:
callback invoked
callback invoked
callback invoked
callback invoked
The white cat chased the blue bird, the black dog chased the white cat.

The example above uses an anonymous function, but it is perfectly fine to use named functions or variables that reference a function. The other callback-based regex replacement function is preg_replace_callback_array(), which works a bit differently: an array is passed, which uses the keys as regex patterns, and the elements are the callback functions.

```
$callbacks = [
    '/\d+/' => function (array $matches): string {
        return number_format($matches[0], thousands_separator: ',');
    },
    '/\w+/' => function (array $matches): string {
        return strtoupper($matches[0]);
    },
];
print preg_replace_callback_array($callbacks, 'PoWeR LeVeL: 9001');
```

Output:
POWER LEVEL: 9,001

preg_split()

Like explode(), preg_split() takes a single input string and divides it into an array of sub-strings according to a pattern. If the pattern is very simple, it is recommended to use explode() for better performance; otherwise preg_split() can save you from needing a lot of tortuous string-handling logic:

```
$text = 'We just, want.the - words...from-this??string.';
print_r(preg_split("/[^a-zA-Z]+/", $text));
```

Output:
```
Array
(
    [0] => We
    [1] => just
    [2] => want
    [3] => the
    ...
    [8] =>
)
```

Notice the empty element at the end of the array? That's caused by the full-stop character at the end of the string, and empty matches can be suppressed by adding a PREG_* constant as a flags: parameter to the call: preg_split("/[^a-zA-Z]+/", $text, flags: PREG_SPLIT_NO_EMPTY).

preg_last_error(), preg_last_error_message()

Finally, we have the two error-handling preg_* functions. preg_last_error() returns an integer value indicating the error status of the last PCRE function call made, which is mapped by the following PCRE constants:

Table 8-36. PREG constants

PREG_NO_ERROR	No errors
PREG_INTERNAL_ERROR	PCRE error state not covered by any of the other conditions
PREG_BACKTRACK_LIMIT_ERROR	Backtrack limit exceeded
PREG_RECURSION_LIMIT_ERROR	Recursion limit exceeded
PREG_BAD_UTF8_ERROR	Malformed UTF-8 detected (when running in UTF-8 mode)
PREG_BAD_UTF8_OFFSET_ERROR	Function is called with an offset resulting in malformed UTF-8
PREG_JIT_STACKLIMIT_ERROR	If JIT pattern compilation is enabled and the stack size exceeded

JIT compilation, backtracking, and recursion limits are all configurable via the usual means. I encourage you to consult the official PHP documentation for the full list of PCRE constants and configuration parameters. The typical use case for preg_last_error() is to test for PREG_NO_ERROR and handle accordingly. The following example is adapted from the PHP official documentation:

```
$text = 'foobar foobar foobar';
preg_match('/(?:\D+|<\d+>)*[!?]/', $text);
if (preg_last_error() !== PREG_NO_ERROR) {
    print preg_last_error_msg();
}

Output:
Backtrack limit exhausted
```

Multi-byte Regex Functions

The `mbstring` module also provides a set of functions for handling regular expressions, with support for multi-byte encodings (as you might expect). The core `preg_*` functions we've just been looking at will support UTF-8 data – provided a u modifier is added after the closing delimiter of the pattern – but are otherwise not multi-byte aware and certainly do not support encodings such as UTF-16, etc. – for non-UTF-8 encodings, there are the `mb_ereg_*` functions.

Internally, the `mbstring` regex functions use the open source Oniguruma regular expression library https://github.com/kkos/oniguruma, which supports a wide variety of character encodings and expression syntaxes. Detailed documentation for the Oniguruma regex syntax can be found here: https://github.com/kkos/oniguruma/blob/master/doc/RE, though it is very similar to PCRE, everything demonstrated so far in this section should work just fine. One important practical difference, though, is that `mb_ereg_*` functions have a slightly different pattern syntax – they do not use delimiters.

```
$squid = "\u{1F991}";
var_dump(mb_ereg('.', $squid, $matches));
print_r($matches);
```

Output:
```
bool(true)
Array
(
    [0] => 🦑
)
```

Our pattern is a simple dot (note the lack of delimiters), which matches any single character, so `mb_ereg()` returns true. The UTF-8 encoding for U+1f991 (Squid) is *0xF0 0x9F 0xA6 0x91*, and it's clear that the function is correctly decoding the bytes to a single codepoint, as we can see in the `$matches` array. Now if we try the same string and pattern with `preg_match()`, the outcome depends on the modifiers used:

```
preg_match('/./', $squid, $matches);
print_r($matches);
```

Output:
```
Array
(
    [0] => ?
)
```

Without enabling UTF-8 mode, preg_match() matches the first byte *0xF0*, which has no printing character in the ASCII codepage. If we enabled UTF-8 mode, though, we would get the same result as mb_ereg():

```
preg_match('/./u', $squid, $matches);
print_r($matches);
```

Output:
```
Array
(
    [0] => 🦑
)
```

Like preg_match(), mb_ereg() does not do global matching, nor is there any way to add modifiers to the expression.

```
$text = 'Cowboy bebop';
mb_ereg('(\w*)bo\w*', $text, $matches);
print_r($matches);
```

Output:
```
Array
(
    [0] => Cowboy
    [1] => Cow
)
```

The full list of mb_ereg* functions is as follows:

Table 8-37. mbstring regex functions

mb_ereg() mb_eregi()	Non-global pattern match, with/without case sensitivity, optional results array
mb_ereg_match()	Anchored pattern match with various options, does not support a results array
mb_ereg_replace() mb_eregi_replace()	Similar to preg_replace, but no support for input arrays
mb_ereg_replace_callback()	Callback variant of mb_ereg_replace(), etc.
mb_ereg_search()	Performs search on string set by mb_ereg_search_init()
mb_ereg_search_getpos()	Used with mb_ereg_search() to get byte position for next match
mb_ereg_search_getregs()	Get result of last match from mb_ereg_search()
mb_ereg_search_init()	Initialise sample string for mb_ereg_search()
mb_ereg_search_pos()	Get position and length of last match from mb_ereg_search()
mb_ereg_search_regs()	Get matched part of expression for mb_ereg_search()
mb_ereg_search_setpos()	Set starting byte for mb_ereg_search()
mb_regex_encoding()	Set internal encoding scheme for mb_ereg*() functions
mb_regex_set_options()	Control behavior of mb_ereg*

mb_ereg_match(), mb_ereg_replace(), mb_eregi_replace(), mb_ereg_replace_callback()

This quartet of functions is more or less identical to their preg_* equivalents. mb_ereg_match() behaves just like preg_match() but does not support the $matches by-reference parameter, and the pattern is always implicitly anchored to the start of the sample. It does, however, allow the passing of options and has multiple syntax modes (so it is not limited to PCRE, although PCRE is expressive enough to get just about any job done that I've ever come across in the wild). We'll examine those options and modes in a moment when we get to mb_ereg_set_options(). It also returns bool(true) on a successful match, rather than the int(1) of preg_match().

mb_ereg_replace() - and the case-insensitive form mb_eregi_replace() - are pretty much the same as preg_replace() but do not handle arrays of sample strings, replacements, or patterns. They only deal with single strings but do accept a string of behavior modifiers and a mode (see mb_regex_set_options() below).

```
$text = "\u{142}ukasz";
print $text . PHP_EOL;
print mb_ereg_replace('\x{142}', "\u{141}", $text);
```

Output:
łukasz
Łukasz

Note the difference between Unicode escapes in strings and regex patterns: \u{nnn} for strings and \x{nnn} for the pattern. Case sensitivity is based on the Unicode data files, so no matter which character set is used, you should get correct regional equivalence:

```
print mb_eregi_replace('(\x{141}\w+)', 'My buddy \1', $text);
```

Output:
My buddy łukasz

Here we're searching for an uppercase 'Ł' (U+0141) in the pattern but running in case-insensitive mode. The Unicode data files that are used to compile mbstring map U+0141 and U+0142 as case equivalents, so the pattern matches even though it actually contains a U+0142 character. Also note that the backreference \1 is enclosed in a single-quoted string (it becomes another kind of escape if double quotes are used).

mb_ereg_replace_callback() is the counterpart to preg_replace_callback(). Again, it does not support arrays of patterns or sample strings but does accept modifiers and mode parameters.

```
$text = "\u{c7}a\u{11f}ari";
print $text . PHP_EOL;
print mb_ereg_replace_callback(
    "\w+",
    function ($matches) {
        return mb_strtoupper($matches[0]);
    },
```

```
    $text
);
```

Output:
Çağari
ÇAĞARI

`mb_ereg_search_init()`, `mb_ereg_search()` et. al.

Now we come to a group of related functions, which are the core of the `mbstring` regex functions. A sample string is initialized with a pattern like so:

```
$text = <<<EOS
Demelza: V\u{1EB1}n th\u{1EAF}n, H\u{1EE7} ti\u{1EBF}u
Paul: C\u{01A1}m chi\u{00EA}n D\u{01B0}\u{01A1}ng Ch\u{00E2}u
EOS;
print $text . PHP_EOL;

mb_ereg_search_init($text);
```

Output:
Demelza: Văn thắn
Paul: Cơm chiên Dương Châu

As we can see, Paul and Demelza are off to eat some delicious Vietnamese food. We can break the complete string into whatever pieces we like using different patterns at different points. `mb_ereg_search($pattern)` will apply a regex to the string that was initialized with `mb_ereg_search_init()`, and the results can be obtained by calling `mb_ereg_search_getregs()`:

```
// $text = ...; mb_ereg_search_init($text);
mb_ereg_search('^\w+:\s');
print_r(mb_ereg_search_getregs());
```

Output:
```
Array
(
    [0] => Demelza:
)
```

At this point, the PCRE engine has consumed part of the sample matching ^\w+:\s which is the sub-string 'Demelza: '. The next call we make will start at 'Vằn thắn...'. We can then perform another search with a different pattern. We can also perform the search and obtain the results in a single call with mb_ereg_search_regs(), so let's do that. The following code executes immediately after the previous example (it is now the second mb_ereg_search_regs() in the chain):

```
print_r(mb_ereg_search_regs('[^,\r\n]+'));
```

Output:
```
Array
(
    [0] => Vằn thắn
)
```

Now we're asking for a match on any character that isn't a comma, newline, or carriage return by using the negated character class [^,\r\n]+. We're using both \r and \n because different operating systems use slightly different line endings. Every call to mb_ereg_search() and mb_ereg_search_regs() will consume any matching parts of the sample string, so the next thing we'll do is gobble up the newlines. Then we can grab some more text that we care about, as the third mb_ereg_search() call:

```
mb_ereg_search('[\r\n]+');

print_r(mb_ereg_search_regs('\w+:\s'));
print_r(mb_ereg_search_regs('[^,\r\n]+'));
```

Output:
```
Array
(
    [0] => Paul:
)
Array
(
    [0] => Cơm chiên Dương Châu
)
```

CHAPTER 8 STRINGS

The functions mb_ereg_search_pos() and mb_ereg_search_setpos() allow you to evaluate and manipulate the position of matching. Be warned: this pair of functions counts bytes, not characters, which is admittedly counter-intuitive considering the other mb_ereg* functions operate on a multi-byte character basis. Anyway, mb_ereg_search_pos() will perform a pattern match, consuming the matching part of the sample in the process, and report back on the position and length of the match. Start again with a newly initialized search:

```
// $text = <<<EOS ...
// Reinitialise
mb_ereg_search_init($text);
// Match and consume 'Demelza: '
mb_ereg_search('^\w+:\s');
// Matches and consumes 'Vằn thắn'
print_r(mb_ereg_search_pos('[^,\r\n]+'));
print_r(mb_ereg_search_getregs());
```

Output:
```
Array
(
    [0] => 9
    [1] => 12
)
Array
(
    [0] => Vằn thắn
)
```

The output of mb_ereg_search_pos() is an array; the first element is the position (in bytes, *not* characters) of the match, and the second is the length of the match (also in bytes: we captured eight characters, two of them are multi-byte UTF-8, for a total of twelve bytes). mb_ereg_search_setpos() takes a single integer argument: the offset from the start of the sample you would like to move the focus to (or from the end of the sample if a negative integer is supplied). If we expand the example above, the position of the sample currently under scrutiny from the regex engine is the newline character(s) after 'Vằn thắn'.

```
// $text = <<<EOS ...
// Reinitialise
mb_ereg_search_init($text);

mb_ereg_search('^\w+:\s');

mb_ereg_search_pos('[^,\r\n]+');
mb_ereg_search_getregs();

print_r(mb_ereg_search_pos('[\r\n]+'));
mb_ereg_search_setpos(0);
print_r(mb_ereg_search_pos('^\w+:\s'));
```

Output:
```
Array
(
    [0] => 21
    [1] => 1
)
Array
(
    [0] => 0
    [1] => 9
)
```

The pattern [\r\n]+ matches one byte at offset twenty-one; at this point, we're about halfway through the sample. By calling mb_ereg_search_setpos(0), we begin matching from the very start of the sample again, and we're able to get a nine-byte match from ^\w+:\s (note the ^ anchoring character).

mb_regex_set_options()

As previously stated, it is possible with all of the mb_ereg* functions to supply a string of options or even change the dialect of regex in use (you never know, you might need to). Here's a quick example of how we can change the behavior of mb_ereg_match() by supplying an option parameter:

```
var_dump(mb_ereg_match('\x{141}\w+', "\u{142}ukasz"));
var_dump(mb_ereg_match('\x{141}\w+', "\u{142}ukasz", 'i'));
```

Output:
bool(false)
bool(true)

The i parameter puts the engine into case-insensitive mode for the duration of that one call. If an option needs to be persisted for several calls, we can do this:

```
mb_regex_set_options('i');
var_dump(mb_ereg_match('\x{141}\w+', "\u{142}ukasz"));
```

Output:
bool(true)

It is also possible to supply multiple options by combining them into a single string (we'll get to all the available options in a moment). The following shows the regex engine being set to both case-insensitive and *extended* modes (extended mode means that whitespace in the pattern is ignored unless escaped or used in a character class):

```
mb_regex_set_options('ix');
var_dump(mb_ereg_match('\w+ \s \w+ \s \x{141}\w+', "My buddy \u{142} ukasz"));
```

Output:
bool(true)

The full set of options is given below:

Table 8-38. *mbstring regex options*

i	Ignore case (Unicode aware)
x	Extended mode (ignore whitespace)
m	. matches newlines
s	Enable anchor escape sequences \A \Z
p	Same as m and s
l	Longest match (see below)
n	Ignore empty (see below)

Find Longest

Ordinarily the matching engine will find the shortest match for sub-pattern, but the l option inverts this:

```
mb_ereg_search_init('apples and pears and apples and pears');
print mb_ereg_search_regs('(?:apples|pears|and )+?')[0] . PHP_EOL;
mb_ereg_search_setpos(0);
print mb_ereg_search_regs('(?:apples|pears|and )+?', 'l')[0];
```

Output:
apples
 and apples and pears

Note the leading space with the second match (and although it's difficult to see, there will be a trailing space too).

Ignore Empty

We saw the effect that the PREG_SPLIT_NO_EMPTY flag had on preg_split() earlier in this section. The n option has a similar effect, demonstrated below:

```
mb_ereg_search_init('@@@ abc');
print_r(mb_ereg_search_pos('[abc]*'));
print_r(mb_ereg_search_pos('[abc]*', 'n'));
```

Output:
Array
(
    [0] => 0
    [1] => 0
)
Array
(
    [0] => 4
    [1] => 3
)

The pattern [abc]* isn't particularly clever because of the * quantifier and would match empty sequences several times in the sample string we've used.

Finally, mb_regex_set_options() also permits different syntax modes, if you have a burning desire to not use Perl-flavored expressions (may the creator have mercy on your soul). This must be the final character in the options string, and of course, only a single mode is supported.

Table 8-39. mbstring syntax modes

j	Java
u	GNU
g	grep
c	Emacs
r	Ruby
z	Perl
b	POSIX Basic
d	POSIX Extended

And that concludes our journey into regular expressions. As mentioned, there is a wealth of material to be found online for learning about and testing your expressions. I can recommend the following:

- https://regex101.com/ Build and test expressions with clear analysis of your patterns
- https://www.rexegg.com/ Egg-cellent tutorials with clear examples

Happy pattern building!

Other Language Extensions

Before we close out this chapter, I just want to highlight some other potentially useful PHP extensions for string handling. There are two modules that you'll most likely encounter in your journey as a PHP developer: iconv and intl.

The iconv module is a wrapper around the system libiconv library and is used for encoding conversion and encoding-aware equivalents of core functions like strpos() and substr(), but using character width rather than byte width. As such, there are equivalents in the mbstring module (and more besides).

The intl module is far more comprehensive: it wraps the ICU (International Components for Unicode) library and offers a large variety of tools for all your internationalization needs.

iconv

This module offers a small selection of functions, given below:

Table 8-40. iconv extensions functions

iconv()	Convert string encoding
iconv_get_encoding()	Get internal config of input, output, internal, or all
iconv_mime_decode()	Decode a single MIME header
iconv_mime_decode_headers()	Decode multiple MIME headers
iconv_mime_encode()	Generate a MIME header with encoding
iconv_set_encoding	Set input, output, and internal encoding
iconv_strlen()	Get character count of string according to encoding
iconv_strpos()	As strpos() but using character width, encoding aware
iconv_strrpos()	As strrpos() but using character width, encoding aware
iconv_substr()	As substr() but using character width, encoding aware
ob_iconv_handler()	Convert encoding, using output buffer handler

There's little here that isn't already covered by the mbstring functions; the official documentation can be found here: https://www.php.net/manual/en/book.iconv.php

intl

The intl extension consists of several APIs that provide functionality for various tasks such as collation, number formatting, and date and time formatting. All of the APIs offer both functional and object-oriented interfaces, and all input must be in UTF-8 (all output will also be UTF-8 encoded). Here are a couple of examples:

```
$formatter = new NumberFormatter('fr_FR', NumberFormatter::DECIMAL);
print $formatter->format(1000000000.01);
Output:
1 000 000 000,01
```

Earlier on in this chapter, we looked at collation; here's a recap:

```
$collator = new Collator('pl_PL.UTF-8');

$polishNames = [
    "Łukasz",
    "Marcin",
    "Tomasz",
];

$collator->sort($polishNames);
print_r($polishNames);
Output:
Array
(
    [0] => Łukasz
    [1] => Marcin
    [2] => Tomasz
)
```

The following APIs are offered by the `intl` module (most are OOP, with a few that simply offer functions); the list is not exhaustive:

Table 8-41. `intl` OOP APIs

Collator	Sorting functionality
NumberFormatter	Format numbers, including currency values
Locale	Manage regional settings (system dependent)
Normalizer	Transform characters for sorting and searching
MessageFormatter	Generate messages from fragments with localized structure
IntlCalendar	Manipulate and localize dates and time
IntlGregorianCalendar	Date and time localization, using the Gregorian system
IntlTimeZone	Manage regional time
IntlDateFormatter	Create dates regionally formatted for display
ResourceBundle	Create simple or complex regional data objects
Transliterator	Create conversion rules for case transformation, character-set transforms, etc.
IntlBreakIterator	Locate word boundaries in text
IntlRuleBasedIterator	Sub-class of `IntlBreakIterator` with custom rules
UConverter	Converts between character sets
grapheme functions	Set of functions that handles strings based on grapheme width (e.g., multi-codepoint glyphs)
IDN functions	Convert domain names to IDNA (ASCII or UTF-8)
IntlChar	Utilities for obtaining metadata for Unicode characters
IntlIterator	Multi-byte character-aware iteration
intl functions	Set of error-handling functions for the `intl` extension

A full analysis of the `intl` extension would cover at least a chapter in its own right, and we've already covered enough ground that it would be repeating a lot of what has already been shown. I highly recommend taking a look at the official documentation though; there are a lot of useful tools that will save you from having to roll your own code: https://www.php.net/manual/en/book.intl.php

Summary

The handling of text is essentially the core of what we do as web developers. I hope that this chapter has made it abundantly clear that strings are not magically meaningful to the machines that are processing them; what is ultimately rendered in the end-user's console or web browser is the culmination of layers of rules and your own understanding. Making the mental leap from byte streams to human language is an essential skill for any software engineer that takes their job seriously.

The vast majority of systems on the web today store and transmit strings as UTF-8, and indeed the PSR standards demand that PHP source code be stored in that encoding. Nevertheless, other layers might well opt for UTF-16 (hello JavaScript and older versions of Windows), and it's not unusual for older systems to opt for one of the extended ASCII formats. Hopefully there has been enough material and guidance in this chapter to help you navigate the pitfalls of legacy code. I wish you happy text-crunching!

CHAPTER 9

Dates and Times

Let's get one thing out of the way before we go any further: time is an absolute mess. Some physicists aren't even sure it's real; Einstein theorized – and it was later proved – that time (and space) distort with gravity and velocity; Douglas Adams proposed it was actually entirely bent. For crying out loud, we don't even measure it in Base 10! (Thanks, ancient Babylon.) Except that actually we do sometimes measure it in Base 10 because of science and computing. To give an extreme example of the difficulty of measuring time accurately in computer systems: the GPS (Global Positioning System) actually corrects for relativistic effects – a GPS satellite's internal clocks are tuned to be slightly slower on Earth so that when they're traveling at speed (Special Relativity), and in orbit (slightly weaker gravitational field, so General Relativity), they run at exactly the same speed relative to their counterparts on the ground. Without these corrections the GPS system would be less accurate.

Humans have been measuring time for thousands of years, mostly by observing the Sun. When the sun is at the highest point in the sky, we call it midday, but of course this is highly localized. Solar midday in London happens later than in, say, Berlin. Even within a single country, there can be a variance of several minutes between relatively nearby cities. This played havoc with early train timetables in the United Kingdom, but in 1884, we standardized on GMT (Greenwich Mean Time): we picked a point on the map and used that to set the time for the entire country. Indeed, GMT was an international standard until 1972. This idea of having a standard by which to reckon time across the world lives on in UTC (Coordinated Universal Time) and is the basis for how all computer systems measure and record time today. I'm sure anyone reading this book has at least heard of time zones, which are simply offsets from UTC time that are used in different regions of the world: CET (Central European Time) is UTC + 1 hour, PST (Pacific Standard Time) is UTC − 8 hours, and so on. We'll be having some fun with time zones in due course. Plus or minus an hour or so...

CHAPTER 9 DATES AND TIMES

By now we've seen all the data types (and pseudo-types) supported by PHP. Notice anything conspicuously absent? There is no native data type (pseudo or otherwise) for representing time (unlike, say, MySQL). Instead, we have an entire core extension (the date module, which will be installed by default) devoted to managing dates and times. This module provides a number of functions and an OOP API, and it's the de facto standard way of handling time in PHP code.

The Unix Epoch

Measuring time is one problem: knowing how much time has elapsed since you last looked is simple if you have a clock, which all computer systems do. Knowing the date and time, knowing *when* you are, is another problem, and a critical one. As systems became more integrated and distributed, the need to synchronize events, keep accurate logs, and so on grew. It's the train timetable problem, but this time with silicon. To solve the problem, an *epoch* date and time is chosen, and time is measured as the integer number of seconds elapsing since that epoch. There are a number of computing epochs (Windows and the C# programming language use 1 *CE* or 1601 *CE* depending on version), but the most widely used is the Unix Epoch, which is UTC midnight, January 1, 1970 – or 01-JAN-1970 00:00:00 or 1970-01-01 00:00:00, or... ah, look at that. There are so many ways to express a date and time. Who knew?! In fact, why don't we have a little preview of what's to come? We'll use the date module's OOP API, which provides the core DateTime class:

```
$epoch = new DateTime('1970-01-01 00:00:00');
var_dump($epoch->format(DateTime::ATOM));
var_dump($epoch->format(DateTime::COOKIE));
var_dump($epoch->format(DateTime::RFC7231));
var_dump($epoch->format(DateTime::W3C));
```

Output:
```
string(25) "1970-01-01T00:00:00+00:00"
string(34) "Thursday, 01-Jan-1970 00:00:00 UTC"
string(29) "Thu, 01 Jan 1970 00:00:00 GMT"
string(25) "1970-01-01T00:00:00+00:00"
```

And here's one more snippet, just to demonstrate that the integer count of seconds since the *exact moment* of the epoch is truly zero:

```
var_dump($epoch->getTimestamp());
```

Output:
int(0)

Keeping Time

The need for accurate timekeeping arose from the growing industrial and financial sectors in the eighteenth and nineteenth centuries: usually an industrious person would set a clock or watch from a reference device (e.g., the clock at the Greenwich Observatory) and then spend the day visiting customers (clock and watch makers, or banks in particular). The story of the Belville family (and Ruth Belville in particular) is an interesting one; I encourage you to search for "The woman who sold time" in your preferred search engine. This method of time synchronization is not particularly conceptually different from how modern computer systems solve the problem today.

Generally speaking, all computers will track the number of seconds elapsing since an epoch. Even when powered off, a personal computer has a battery-backed chip that's counting all the time. This is great, but not all clocks are created equal: eventually they will drift out of sync with true UTC time (unless your system is equipped with something staggeringly expensive involving radioisotopes). Which brings us to...

Network Time Protocol (NTP/ntpd)

Just like the banks of old relied on someone to bring the correct time to them, today we have a network protocol (NTP) that allows a system to ask for the correct time from a service that is backed by something staggeringly expensive and usually involving radioisotopes. On a MacOS system you can use the `sntp` cli utility to get detailed info about how time is synchronized on your system:

```
$ cat /etc/ntp.conf
server time.euro.apple.com
```

```
$ sntp -d time.euro.apple.com
...
sntp_exchange {
        result: 0 (Success)
        header: 24 (li:0 vn:4 mode:4)
       stratum: 01 (1)
          poll: 06 (64)
     precision: FFFFFFEB (4.768372e-07)
...
```

You should see multiple sets of debug output like the above. There's no need to go too deeply into how all this works; at the moment, it's enough for you to know that these tools and services exist and there's plenty of information and support for NTP out there on the web when you're ready to know more, or in the sticky predicament of *needing* to know more!

The tz Database

Another problematic aspect to timekeeping in computing is knowing *where* you are. You might have servers located in different geographical regions; they might even be nicely synchronized to UTC, but ask them what the time is and you'll get two different answers, because of course they are in different time zones. Naturally, there are systems and standards to manage time zones.

The `tz database` (a.k.a. `tzdata`, `zoneinfo`, or the `IANA time zone db`, occasionally known as the `Olson database` after its founder Arthur Olson) is fairly ubiquitous and is the basis for how PHP parses time zone information. Time zones in the `tz database` are canonically identified with strings such as `Europe/London` or `America/New York`, or their abbreviated forms such as `PST` and `GMT`. Note that the canonical regional names will aggregate to abbreviated names. For example, the regions `Europe/Paris` and `Europe/Amsterdam` are both in the `CET` time zone. More comprehensive information can be found at the following locations:

- https://www.php.net/manual/en/timezones.php
- https://en.wikipedia.org/wiki/Tz_database
- https://en.wikipedia.org/wiki/List_of_time_zone_abbreviations

Right then, it's time to get our hands dirty with... ahem... time.

OOP Interface

PHP 5.2 introduced a set of classes (and interfaces) for interacting with dates and times that are pretty much the standard way of doing these things in PHP. If you're not sure what a class or interface is, go read Chapter 6, "Object Fundamentals," which covers everything you'll need to make sense of this next section. Let's start by listing all of the components in the API, then looking at them in detail:

Table 9-1. DateTime classes

DateTime	The main class for representing dates and times
DateTimeImmutable	Very similar to DateTime but does not allow any changes to its timestamp
DateTimeInterface	The interface to the classes above, defines many useful constants too
DateTimeZone	Class representing time zones
DateInterval	Class for representing differences between two times
DatePeriod	Implements IteratorAggregate; this class allows iteration over sets of dates/times, covering a set period

DateTimeInterface

This interface is implemented by DateTime and DateTimeImmutable, which are the two main classes you'll be using whenever your programming involves dates/times – or perhaps you might be using a library such as Carbon – https://carbon.nesbot.com/ – which will be a wrapper around these core classes. DateTimeInterface offers around a dozen or so constants for formatting time: DateTime and DateTimeImmutable store a Unix timestamp integer value internally and offer a format() method that allows the timestamp to be expressed as a string in a multitude of ways; these constants are a way of maintaining consistency and offer compliance with various standard formats. We'll take a look at those formatting constants when we take the two implementing classes for a spin. The following public methods are also defined on DateTimeInterface and examined in detail in the implementing classes:

CHAPTER 9   DATES AND TIMES

Table 9-2. DateTimeInterface methods

diff($dateTime, $abs)	Returns a DateInterval instance based on the input DateTimeInterface object; $abs controls the behavior of the returned DateInterval
format($str)	Outputs a formatted date/time string for display, DB storage, and so on.
getOffset()	Returns UTC offset based on the current time zone
getTimestamp()	Return the Unix timestamp
getTimezone()	Returns the current time zone set for the object
__wakeup()	A "magic" method for handling serialization: see **Programming with Objects**

DateTime, DateTimeImmutable

The two core classes that see the most use in PHP tend to be DateTime and DateTimeImmutable. Both have the same interface as noted above and differ only in one respect: DateTime can have its value changed, but DateTimeImmutable cannot. The following code illustrates this point:

```
$dt = new DateTime();
var_dump($dt->getTimestamp());
$dt->modify('+1 day');
var_dump($dt->getTimestamp());

$dti = new DateTimeImmutable();
var_dump($dti->getTimestamp());
$dti->modify('+1 day');
var_dump($dti->getTimestamp());
```

Output:
int(1731947784)
int(1732034184)
int(1731947784)
int(1731947784)

610

The two objects are created without arguments, which means they both have an initial internal value of the current system timestamp, which is easily accessed via the ->getTimestamp() method. Remember that in the previous section we constructed a DateTime instance with a value -$epoch = new DateTime('1970-01-01 00:00:00'); – here we've omitted the string. More to come on this in a moment. The DateTime::modify() method accepts a string argument (usually in the form '(+|-) n (days|hours|minutes)') that adjusts its timestamp value. In this case, we've added one day (which means the timestamp increments by the exact number of seconds in a day, which is *86400*). DateTime simply adjusts its timestamp value; DateTimeImmutable, however, does not, but it will return a new instance with the adjusted value:

```
$dti = new DateTimeImmutable();
var_dump(spl_object_id($dti));
$dti2 = $dti->modify('+1 day');
var_dump(spl_object_id($dti2));
```

Output:
int(1)
int(2)

spl_object_id() is part of the SPL (Standard PHP Library) module and shows us that $dti and $dti2 are references to different objects. SPL offers many object utility functions and OOP APIs; we used spl_autoload_register() in Chapter 6, "Object Fundamentals." The ->modify() method, when called on a DateTime instance, returns a reference to the same object, rather than a new instance. Throughout the rest of this section, wherever the DateTime class is used, you can also substitute for DateTimeImmutable. They have exactly the same interface and behavior, with the caveat demonstrated above.

Building DateTime Objects

We've seen DateTime (and its immutable counterpart) constructed with and without arguments. The following demonstrates how flexible the constructor argument can be, any validly formatted date/time string can be used to instantiate a DateTime object, when we come to the DateTime::format() method, you'll see just how many ways there are to express dates and times. For now, here's a quick taster:

611

```
var_dump(
    (new DateTime('01-SEP-2024'))->format('Y-m-d H:i:s')
);
var_dump(
    (new DateTime('3rd September 2024 05:00'))->format('Y-m-d H:i:s')
);
```

Output:
```
string(19) "2024-09-01 00:00:00"
string(19) "2024-09-03 00:05:00"
```

I hope the Deep Space 9 fans out there immediately recognize those dates, and hopefully you also noticed that if no time component is given in the string, then the default will be the very start of the day: midnight (*00:00:00*). In addition to formatted absolute dates, it is also possible to use relative words like "now" (which is the default parameter value for the DateTime constructor) or "today":

```
var_dump(
    (new DateTime('now'))->format('Y-m-d H:i:s')
);
var_dump(
    (new DateTime('today'))->format('Y-m-d H:i:s')
);
```

Output:
```
string(19) "2024-11-18 17:25:06"
string(19) "2024-11-18 00:00:00"
```

Note that 'now' really does mean "right this second," while 'today' begins at midnight on the current date. For other relative values, use "today" or "now" with a valid DateTime::modify() string like so:

```
var_dump(
    (new DateTime('today + 1 day'))->format('Y-m-d H:i:s')
);
var_dump(
    (new DateTime('today - 12 hours'))->format('Y-m-d H:i:s')
);
```

Output:
string(19) "2024-11-19 00:00:00"
string(19) "2024-11-17 12:00:00"

It is also possible to instantiate `DateTime` with a timestamp integer value, using a special string format:

```
$dt = new DateTime('@1725148800');
print $dt->format('Y-m-d H:i:s');
```

Output:
2024-09-01 00:00:00

Formatting Output

By now you've probably realized that `DateTime::format()` is the go-to method for building strings intended for human-readable output. The year, month, day, hour, minute, second, and even milli- and microseconds have multiple ways that they can be expressed, and not all elements of the date and time need to be output. In addition, the time zone name, or UTC offset, can also be included in the output. Here are a few examples for dates:

```
$dt = new DateTime('01-SEP-2024');
// year
print $dt->format('Y y') . PHP_EOL;
// month
print $dt->format('F M m n') . PHP_EOL;
// day
print $dt->format('l D d j jS');
```

Output:
2024 24
September Sep 09 9
Sunday Sun 01 1 1st

CHAPTER 9 DATES AND TIMES

Here are some time formatting strings:

```
$dt = new DateTime('3rd September 2024 18:11:17');
// hour
print $dt->format('H h g hA ga') . PHP_EOL;
// minutes and seconds
print $dt->format('i s') . PHP_EOL;
//timezone and UTC offset - will vary with system settings if not explicitly
//specified at construction.
print $dt->format('T O');
```

Output:
```
18 06 6 06PM 6pm
11 17
UTC +0000
```

Characters in the formatting string that don't have any special meaning will simply be rendered as-is; it's common to use punctuation such as colons, dashes, or commas:

```
print $dt->format('l, F jS, Y') . PHP_EOL;
print $dt->format('i:s i,s');
```

Output:
```
Tuesday, September 3rd, 2024
11:17 11,17
```

There are also a number of predefined global date constants providing some standardized formatting strings, which are also exposed by the DateTimeInterface. I recommend using them at least to make your code easier to understand and maintain. A few examples are given below:

Table 9-3. `DateTimeInterface` / *date global constants*

Constant	Example
DateTime::COOKIE DATE_COOKIE	Sunday, 01-Sep-2024 08:00:00 UTC
DateTime::ISO8601 DATE_ISO8601	2024-09-01T08:00:00+0000
DateTime::RFC7231 DATE_RFC7231	Sun, 01 Sep 2024 08:00:00 GMT

All of the date module constants are also exposed as class constants of `DateTime`: `DATE_COOKIE` is `DateTime::COOKIE`, and so on. The full details for formatting dates are available at https://www.php.net/manual/en/datetime.format.php and https://www.php.net/manual/en/datetime.constants.php

DateTime and DateTimeZone

Unix timestamps are always in UTC time, but their expression as date and time strings depends on where in the world you happen to be, in other words, which time zone you are in. A `DateTime` object is at heart simply a UTC timestamp; its expression as a particular time and date depends on the timezone, and these are represented in PHP as `DateTimeZone` objects. When constructing `DateTime` objects with strings, you can include time zone information in various ways as part of the string:

```
$dt = new DateTime('Tuesday, 03-Sep-2024 05:00:00 PDT');
print $dt->format('Y-m-d H:i:s T') . PHP_EOL;
print $dt->format('Y-m-d H:i:s O') . PHP_EOL;
```

Output:
```
2024-09-03 05:00:00 PDT
2024-09-03 05:00:00 -0700
```

By adding the Pacific Daylight Time abbreviation of PDT to the formatted string, the time zone of the resulting `DateTime` object is now set (without it the time zone would be set to whatever the system settings are where PHP is running). `DateTime` instances will report their time zone settings as `DateTimeZone` class via the `DateTime::getTimezone()` method...

```
var_dump($dt->getTimezone());
```

Output:
```
object(DateTimeZone)#2 (2) {
  ["timezone_type"]=>
  int(2)
  ["timezone"]=>
  string(3) "PDT"
}
```

... alternatively `DateTimeZone` instances can be supplied as a constructor argument to `new DateTime()`, or set after construction via `DateTime::setTimezone()`. `DateTimeZone` objects themselves accept a string argument, which is either a UTC time offset, a time zone abbreviation such as "GMT," or a canonical `tzdata` name. We could use PDT or America/Los_Angeles to build a time zone object with the same internal value; let's go with the canonical `tz` database name:

```
$tz = new DateTimeZone('America/Los_Angeles');
$dt = new DateTime('Tuesday, 03-Sep-2024 05:00:00', $tz);
print $dt->format('Y-m-d H:i:s T');
```

Output:
```
2024-09-03 05:00:00 PDT
```

Note that `DateTime` objects can have a `DateTimeZone` instance as a second argument only if the first argument is not a Unix timestamp or contains any time zone information:

```
$dt = new DateTime('@1725148800', $tz);
print $dt->format('Y-m-d H:i:s T') . PHP_EOL;

$dt = new DateTime('Tuesday, 03-Sep-2024 05:00:00 CET', $tz);
print $dt->format('Y-m-d H:i:s T');
```

Output:
```
2024-09-01 00:00:00 GMT+0000
2024-09-03 05:00:00 CET
```

In both cases above, the time zone argument is ignored. The system time zone (which happens to be GMT on the system I ran this code on) is used in the first example (a Unix timestamp), and the time zone specified in the input string (CET) is used in the second. Things get a little tricky here: PHP will have a default timezone set via the date.timezone .ini config directive, and when DateTime objects are created with a date/time but no time zone, they will either use the default or a fixed zone, depending on whether the constructor argument is a timestamp or a formatted date/time string. Here's what I mean:

```
var_dump(date_default_timezone_get());
$dt = new DateTime('@1725148800');
print $dt->format('T') . PHP_EOL;

$dt = new DateTime('2024-09-01');
print $dt->format('T');
```

Output:
```
string(3) "UTC"
GMT+0000
UTC
```

The code above demonstrates a few things. Firstly, the date.timezone (default PHP time zone) is UTC, which we see from the output of date_default_timezone_get(). Next we instantiate a DateTime object with a Unix timestamp, which ignores the default timezone (as it should, because Unix timestamps are always UTC) and will always set the object's zone to GMT+0000. Finally, objects created with a formatted string will get PHP's default (UTC in our case). We've just had our first glimpse of one of the functions provided by the date module; we'll be seeing more of those in the next section.

Modifying DateTime

We've already seen DateTime::modify(), but there are other methods available for modifying data. In all cases a DateTime instance will be modified and return a reference to itself, and a DateTimeImmutable will return a new object of the same class. The methods are as follows:

CHAPTER 9   DATES AND TIMES

Table 9-4. *DateTime modification methods*

DateTime::add()	Accepts a DateInterval object and adjusts object time accordingly
DateTime::setDate()	Change the year, month, and day using integers
DateTime::setISODate()	Change the year, week number, and day number (ISO 8601 standard)
DateTime::setTime()	Change the hours, minutes, seconds, and microseconds of current time
DateTime::setTimestamp()	Change date/time using a Unix timestamp integer
DateTime::setTimezone()	Accepts a DateTimeZone object and changes time zone

Let's see some of those in action:

```
$dti = new DateTimeImmutable('@1725148800');
print $dti->format(DateTime::COOKIE) . PHP_EOL;

print $dti->setDate(2024, 9, 3)
    ->format(DateTime::COOKIE) . PHP_EOL;

print $dti->setTimeZone(new DateTimeZone('PST'))
    ->setISODate(2024, 36, 2)
    ->setTime(5, 0)
    ->format(DateTime::COOKIE) . PHP_EOL;

print $dti->setTimestamp(1725368400)
    ->setTimezone(new DateTimeZone('PST'))
    ->format(DateTime::COOKIE);
```

Output:
Sunday, 01-Sep-2024 00:00:00 GMT+0000
Tuesday, 03-Sep-2024 00:00:00 GMT+0000
Tuesday, 03-Sep-2024 05:00:00 PST
Tuesday, 03-Sep-2024 05:00:00 PST

We're using DateTimeImmutable to give us the same date and time for each demonstration. Each of the calls to setDate(), setTime(), etc., returns a DateTime reference or a new DateTimeImmutable instance, which means we can take advantage of a technique called *method chaining* and make multiple calls one after the other. Each example should be self-explanatory: setDate() (to the third day of the ninth month) and setISODate() (to the second day of the thirty-sixth week). Change the date accordingly (keeping the same time and time zone), setTime() (fifth hour, zeroth minute). Adjust only the time; setTimezone() requires a DateTimeZone instance and does exactly what it says, as does setTimestamp().

Bear in mind that setTimestamp() is always UTC (GMT+00:00), and also be aware that the order in which setTimezone() is called relative to setTime() et al. will affect the final outcome:

```
$dti = new DateTimeImmutable('@1725148800');
$new1 = $dti->setTimeZone(new DateTimeZone('PST'))
    ->setISODate(2024, 36, 2)
    ->setTime(5, 0);

$new2 = $dti->setISODate(2024, 36, 2)
    ->setTime(5, 0)
    ->setTimeZone(new DateTimeZone('PST'));

print $new1->format(DateTime::COOKIE) . PHP_EOL;
print $new2->format(DateTime::COOKIE);
```

Output:
```
Tuesday, 03-Sep-2024 05:00:00 PST
Monday, 02-Sep-2024 21:00:00 PST
```

We'll look at DateTime::add() next, together with its required argument type: DateInterval.

DateInterval, DatePeriod

The final two classes in the date extension are used for measuring and iterating time periods. A DateInterval object represents the amount of time between one DateTime and another. DatePeriod allows you to iterate in fixed time periods from a starting time. DateInterval objects are constructed using a string that is a formatted amount of time: these strings must start with the letter P (for period) followed by integers and the following designator letters:

CHAPTER 9   DATES AND TIMES

Table 9-5. DateInterval/DatePeriod period strings

Y	Years
M	Months
D	Days
W	Weeks

You can combine designators; the largest units must always be to the left.

```
$dt = new DateTimeImmutable('@1725148800');
print $dt->format(DateTime::COOKIE) . PHP_EOL;

print $dt->add(new DateInterval("P1D"))
    ->format(DateTime::COOKIE) . PHP_EOL;

print $dt->add(new DateInterval("P1Y1D"))
    ->format(DateTime::COOKIE);
```

Output:
```
Sunday, 01-Sep-2024 00:00:00 GMT+0000
Monday, 02-Sep-2024 00:00:00 GMT+0000
Tuesday, 02-Sep-2025 00:00:00 GMT+0000
```

Any interval period shorter than a day must be preceded by the letter T and the following designators:

Table 9-6. DateInterval/DatePeriod time strings

H	Hours
M	Minutes
S	Seconds

Here's how to use them:

```
print $dt->add(new DateInterval("PT5H10M20S"))
```

```
    ->format(DateTime::COOKIE) . PHP_EOL;

print $dt->add(new DateInterval("P3DT5H"))
    ->format(DateTime::COOKIE);
```

Output:
Sunday, 01-Sep-2024 05:10:20 GMT+0000
Wednesday, 04-Sep-2024 05:00:00 GMT+0000

DateInterval instances are also returned from the DateTime::diff() function when evaluating two different date/time values. The following example demonstrates both the use of diff() and an alternative way of creating DateTime instances:

```
$bellRiots = DateTime::createFromFormat(
    'Y-m-d H:i:s O',
    '2024-09-01 00:00:00 PST'
);
print $bellRiots->format(DateTime::COOKIE) . PHP_EOL;

$retakeSanctuary = DateTime::createFromFormat(
    'Y-m-d H:i:s O',
    '2024-09-03 05:00:00 PST'
);
print $retakeSanctuary->format(DateTime::COOKIE) . PHP_EOL;

$dti = $bellRiots->diff($retakeSanctuary);
print "Diff is {$dti->d} days, {$dti->h} hours";
```

Output:
Sunday, 01-Sep-2024 00:00:00 PST
Tuesday, 03-Sep-2024 05:00:00 PST
Diff is 2 days, 5 hours

Notice that we can access the public properties $dti->d and $dit->h. The interval object exposes the properties y, m, d, h, i, s, and f, which correspond to years, months, days, hours, seconds, and microseconds (as the float type, expressing fractions of a second). The public properties invert (1 if the interval is negative, 0 if positive), days (total number of full days in the interval, *only* if the object was created by

DateTime::diff()), and from_string (true if the interval was created with DateInterval::createFromString()) are also available. DateInterval::format() will return a formatted string in the same way as DateTimeInterface::format() but with a slight difference – DateInterval::format() requires that each format designator requires a % symbol in front of it (a little like a printf() formatting string).

```
print $dti->format("Y-m-d H:i:s") . PHP_EOL;
print $dti->format("%Y-%m-%d %H:%i:%s");
```

Output:
Y-m-d H:i:s
00-0-2 05:0:0

The DatePeriod class is in the same ballpark as DateInterval, but its purpose is slightly different. DatePeriod is intended for use in iterative code: it defines an interval of time that needs to elapse per repetition, a start time, and an end time. Between the start and end, every time an interval has elapsed, it triggers an iteration. DatePeriod implements the IteratorAggregte interface, which allows it to be used as an array in control structures like foreach.

```
$period = new DatePeriod(
    $bellRiots,
    new DateInterval('PT12H'),
    $retakeSanctuary
);
foreach ($period as $date) {
    echo $date->format(DateTimeImmutable::COOKIE) . PHP_EOL;
}
```

Output:
Sunday, 01-Sep-2024 00:00:00 PST
Sunday, 01-Sep-2024 12:00:00 PST
Monday, 02-Sep-2024 00:00:00 PST
Monday, 02-Sep-2024 12:00:00 PST
Tuesday, 03-Sep-2024 00:00:00 PST

As an alternative to specifying an end point DateTime, you can simply provide the number of required iterations. The following code produces identical output to the example above:

```
$period = new DatePeriod(
    $bellRiots,
    new DateInterval('PT12H'),
    4
);
```

Note that the start point is automatically included, and the end point is not. This behavior can be controlled with a pair of constants – DatePeriod::EXCLUDE_START_DATE and DatePeriod::INCLUDE_END_DATE – supplied as a fourth argument.

Functional Interface

The date module also provides a functional API. Certain parts of the functional API predate the OOP (PHP 4 vs. the object API introduction in PHP 5.2), and most of the date functions are wrappers around the OOP stuff. Quite a few of them will return some form of object instance. The functions that are OOP wrappers are given below:

Table 9-7. date extension functions (OOP wrappers)

Function	OOP Alias
date()	new DateTime($timestampString)->format()
date_add	DateTime::add()
date_create	new DateTime()
date_create_from_format()	DateTime::createFromFormat()
date_create_immutable	new DateTimeImmutable()
date_create_immutable_from_format()	DateTimeImmutable::createFromFormat()
date_date_set()	DateTime::setDate()
date_diff()	DateTime::diff()

(continued)

Table 9-7. (*continued*)

Function	OOP Alias
date_format()	DateTime::format()
date_get_last_errors()	DateTime::getLastErrors()
date_interval_create_from_date_string()	DateInterval::createFromDateString()
date_interval_format()	DateInterval::format()
date_isodate_set()	DateTime::setISODate()
date_modify()	DateTime::modify()
date_offset_get()	DateTime::getOffset()
date_sub()	DateTime::sub()
date_time_set()	DateTime::setTime()
date_timestamp_get()	DateTime::getTimestamp()
date_timestamp_set()	DateTime::setTimestamp()
date_timezone_get()	DateTime::getTimezone()
date_timezone_set()	DateTime::setTimezone()
gmdate()	new DateTime($formattedString)->format() but TZ defaults to GMT
time()	new DateTime('now')->getTimestamp()
timezone_abbreviations_list()	DateTimeZone::listAbbreviations()
timezone_identifiers_list()	DateTimeZone::listIdentifiers()
timezone_location_get()	DateTimeZone::getLocation()
timezone_name_get()	DateTimeZone::getName()
timezone_offset_get()	DateTimeZone::getOffset()
timezone_open()	new DateTimeZone()
timezone_transitions_get()	DateTimeZone::getTransitions()

Full documentation for the functional API can be found at https://www.php.net/manual/en/ref.datetime.php, and most of the OOP methods above were covered in the previous section, so I won't go into exhaustive detail here. We will, however, be looking at the date module functions that don't have OOP equivalents, which are:

Table 9-8. *date extension function (non-OOP wrappers)*

checkdate()	Validates a month/day/year combination (Gregorian)
date_default_timezone_get()	Gets the current default TZ
date_default_timezone_set()	Sets the current default TZ
date_parse()	Return array of information from formatted string input
date_parse_from_format()	Same as date_format() but takes a second string specifying format
date_sun_info()	Takes a Unix timestamp, latitude, and longitude, returns sunset/sunrise/twilight information
getdate()	Returns array of date information from input timestamp, or current system timestamp
gettimeofday()	Wraps the gettimeofday system call, returns an array
gmmktime()	Returns Unix timestamp for a set of integers interpreted as a GMT date
idate()	Like date() but the format string is single character
localtime()	Wraps the localtime system call, returns an array
microtime()	Return current timestamp with microsecond precision
mktime()	Like gmmktime() but uses default timezone
strtotime()	Parses input string, returns Unix timestamp

Without further ado, let's dive in.

checkdate()

This simple function takes exactly three integer arguments representing month, day, and year (following the US convention of month before day), returning true if the (Gregorian) date is valid, otherwise false:

```
var_dump(checkdate(1, 29, 2021));
var_dump(checkdate(
```

```
    month: 13,
    day: 32,
    year: 2021
));
```

Output:
bool(true)
bool(false)

date_default_timezone_get(), date_default_timezone_set()

We've seen this function already in the previous section, when comparing `DateTime` objects built with timestamps vs. formatted strings. The get form will report the configured (via the `date.timezone` .ini directive) default time zone. The set form, when called with a valid string containing a canonical time zone name, will change it. (There is some support for aliases, but it is recommended that valid canonical `tzdata` names are always used.)

All `DateTime` objects created with formatted date strings and without time zone data will have their time zone set to default:

```
date_default_timezone_set('America/Los_Angeles');
$dt = new DateTime('2024-09-01');
print $dt->format('Y-m-d H:i:s T') . PHP_EOL;

date_default_timezone_set('Europe/London');
$dt = new DateTime('2024-09-01');
print $dt->format('Y-m-d H:i:s T');
```

Output:
2024-09-01 00:00:00 PDT
2024-09-01 00:00:00 BST

date_parse(), date_parse_from_format()

These two functions take a date-formatted string (and in the case of `date_parse_from_format()`, another string defining the format) and return an array of useful information such as the date and time components (year, day, hour, etc.), time zone information if present, and even warnings and errors if there was a problem with the input:

```
print_r(date_parse('2024-09-01'));
```

Output:

```
Array
(
    [year] => 2024
    [month] => 9
    [day] => 1
    [hour] =>
    [minute] =>
    ...
```

As we can see from the output, if there was no information in the input about time, there is no default (unlike a new DateTime object that would default to 00:00:00). Next, we'll use date_parse_from_format() and include some more data:

```
print_r(date_parse_from_format(
    'Y-m-d H:i:s T',
    '2024-09-01 01:02:03 PDT'
));
```

Output:

```
    [year] => 2024
    [month] => 9
    [day] => 1
    [hour] => 1
    [minute] => 2
    [second] => 3
    ...
    [zone_type] => 2
    [zone] => -28800
    [is_dst] => 1
    [tz_abbr] => PDT
    ...
```

This time we have hours, minutes, and seconds; we also get some information about the time zone, such as its abbreviation (PDT) and *28800* seconds (*8* hours) behind GMT. Notice the is_dst element: we'll be covering things like daylight savings and leap years in the next section of the chapter. Finally, let's make a deliberate mistake:

CHAPTER 9 DATES AND TIMES

```
print_r(date_parse_from_format(
    'Y-m-d',
    '2024-09-01 01:02:03 PDT'
));
```

Output:

```
    [year] => 2024
    [month] => 9
    [day] => 1
    [hour] =>
    [minute] =>
    ...
    [error_count] => 1
    [errors] => Array
        (
            [10] => Trailing data
            ...
```

The error_count and errors elements can obviously form the basis for some error handling.

date_sun_info()

This function takes a Unix timestamp and geoposition data and returns an array of information about daylight hours (sunrise, sunset, twilight hours, and so on). Let's go with one of my favorite landmarks, San Francisco's Coit Tower, which is located at lat. *37.80257289230897*, long. *-122.40579001693803*:

```
print_r(date_sun_info(
    timestamp: 1725364800,
    latitude: 37.80257289230897,
    longitude: -122.40579001693803
));
```

Output:
```
Array
(
    [sunrise] => 1725370847
```

```
    [sunset] => 1725417397
    [transit] => 1725394122
    [civil_twilight_begin] => 1725369325
    [civil_twilight_end] => 1725418919
    ...
```

As you can see, all time-related data in and out of this function is a Unix timestamp. There are two functions – date_sunrise(), and date_sunset() – which are deprecated in PHP 8 (and will generate an error if called) but work in the same way as date_sun_info().

getdate(), gettimeofday(), localtime()

getdate() works in two ways depending on how it is called (either with no arguments or an integer Unix timestamp) and returns an array of data, which are the date/time component values:

```
print_r(getdate(1725148800));
```

Output:
```
Array
(
    ...
    [mon] => 9
    [year] => 2024
    [yday] => 244
    [weekday] => Sunday
    [month] => September
    [0] => 1725148800
)
```

```
print_r(getdate());
```

Output:
```
    [seconds] => 42
    [minutes] => 18
    [hours] => 14
```

CHAPTER 9   DATES AND TIMES

```
[mday] => 14
[wday] => 6
...
```

Most of the array keys are self-explanatory; mday is the numeric day of the month, and wday is the numeric day of the week (*0* is Sunday, *1* is Monday, and so on).

mktime(), gmmktime()

We've seen how to use DateTime::getTimestamp() to obtain a Unix timestamp, which of course requires instantiating a new DateTime object before you can invoke the method. An alternative approach is to use the mktime() or gmmktime() functions. These functions accept multiple integer arguments for hour, minute, second, month, day, and year, in that order (note the slightly odd ordering of day and month). The default values for any omitted argument are simply whatever is current for the system, as the following demonstrates:

```
$format = 'Y-m-d H:i:s';

$tstamp1 = mktime(0);
$tstamp2 = mktime(0, 0);
$tstamp3 = mktime(0, 0, 0);

print date($format, $tstamp1) . PHP_EOL;
print date($format, $tstamp2) . PHP_EOL;
print date($format, $tstamp3);
```

Output:
```
2025-01-03 00:47:28
2025-01-03 00:00:28
2025-01-03 00:00:00
```

mktime() *must* have at least one argument (hours) - we've used zero - since PHP 8.0. Prior versions of PHP allow for no arguments, and mktime() would behave like the time() function. PHP 8.0+ still allows the other mktime() arguments to be null, and in such cases the system's current time and date values are used:

```
// assuming current system date/time is 2025-01-03 15:47:25
$tstamp = mktime(
    hour: 0,         // overrides 15
```

```
    minute: null,    // defaults to 47
    second: 0,       // overrides 25
    month: null,     // defaults to 01
    day: null,       // defaults to 03
    year: 2001       // overrides 2025
);

print date($format, $tstamp);
```

Output:
2001-01-03 00:47:00

mktime() will happily handle out-of-range values and negative values too, which makes it quite versatile when combining dates and times with arithmetic. Negative values count backwards from the previous next-largest unit; for example, an hour value of -1 will be calculated as 23:00 hours of the previous day...

```
$tstamp = mktime(
    hour: -1,
    day: 10,
);
print date('d H', $tstamp);
```

Output:
09 23

... a minute value of -10 will be calculated as the fiftieth minute of the previous hour:

```
$tstamp = mktime(
    hour: 12,
    minute: -10,
);
print date('H:i', $tstamp);
```

Output:
11:50

Likewise, positive values that exceed the maximum for the field will increment the next highest unit:

CHAPTER 9   DATES AND TIMES

```
$tstamp = mktime(
    hour: 25,
    day: 10,
);
print date('d H', $tstamp) . PHP_EOL;

$tstamp = mktime(
    hour: 12,
    minute: 61,
);
print date('H:i', $tstamp);
```

Output:
```
11 01
13:01
```

A handy trick with mktime() is the ability to express the final day of any month as the zeroth day of the next:

```
print "Final day of Feb 2024: " . date('d',
    mktime(hour:0, month: 3, day: 0, year: 2024)
) . PHP_EOL;

print "Final day of Feb 2025: " . date('d',
    mktime(hour:0, month: 3, day: 0, year: 2025)
);
```

Output:
```
Final day of Feb 2024: 29
Final day of Feb 2025: 28
```

Note that mktime() uses the currently configured timezone for its calculations, as the following demonstrates:

```
date_default_timezone_set('UTC');
$tstamp = mktime(
    hour: 5,
    minute: 0,
    second: 0,
    month: 9,
```

```
    day: 3,
    year: 2024,
);
var_dump($tstamp);

date_default_timezone_set('America/Los_Angeles');
$tstamp = mktime(
    hour: 5,
    minute: 0,
    second: 0,
    month: 9,
    day: 3,
    year: 2024,
);
var_dump($tstamp);

Output:
int(1725339600)
int(1725364800)
```

PHP provides the gmmktime() function as a convenient way to ensure the timezone is set to UTC and is otherwise a wrapper around mktime():

```
date_default_timezone_set('America/Los_Angeles');
$tstamp = gmmktime(
    hour: 5,
    minute: 0,
    second: 0,
    month: 9,
    day: 3,
    year: 2024,
);
var_dump($tstamp);

Output:
int(1725339600)
```

Compare this output to the previous example's `mktime()` call with an explicit timezone of UTC.

idate()

The `idate()` function is essentially identical to the `date()` function (which behaves exactly like `new DateTime('@{$timestamp}')->format($format)`) but with the following differences: `idate()` accepts a format string consisting of a single character (be aware that the valid characters for `idate()` are a subset of those supported by the `format` method of `DateTimeInterface`) and an optional integer timestamp and only returns a single integer value (it is not possible to specify multiple units in the formatting string).

```
$tstamp = 1725339600;
var_dump(idate('d', $tstamp));
var_dump(idate('m', $tstamp));
var_dump(idate('y', $tstamp));
var_dump(idate('Y', $tstamp));
```

Output:
```
int(3)
int(9)
int(24)
int(2024)
```

microtime(), hrtime()

The final functions we'll look at in this section are used for high-precision time measurement. `microtime()`, which is fairly ubiquitous in any PHP code concerned with performance, returns the number of microseconds elapsed since the Unix Epoch. `hrtime()` offers nanosecond precision (but from an arbitrary point in time) and was added to the core functions in PHP 7.4 (prior to that it was part of the HRTime high-resolution timing extension). The most common use-case for `microtime()` overlaps that of `hrtime()` – namely, for measuring elapsed time between calls – and nanosecond precision is a highly unusual requirement for web applications, so you are far less likely to encounter `hrtime()` in your day-to-day. We'll focus on `microtime()` here, and just be aware that `hrtime()` exists and can be used in similar ways. First let's look at how to call `microtime()`:

```
var_dump(microtime());
var_dump(microtime(true));
```

Output:
```
string(21) "0.84775700 1738869451"
float(1738869451.847781)
```

microtime() accepts a single boolean argument (which defaults to false) and returns either a string containing milliseconds and seconds since the Epoch or the number of seconds elapsed as a float (the decimal portion providing enough precision for millisecond resolution). By far the most common use of microtime() is for diagnosing performance problems: a common technique is to wrap potentially time-costly calls with microtime() like so:

```
$start = microtime(true);
sleep(2);
$end = microtime(true);
print "Time elapsed : " . $end - $start . "s";
```

Output:
```
Time elapsed : 2.0040378570557s
```

In an environment where entire requests might need to meet SLAs measured in fractions of seconds, microtime() can be a very handy quick-and-dirty way to narrow down where to focus optimization effort.

Summary

Hopefully you now have an appreciation of the challenges presented by dealing with time in your PHP code and the tools available to address them. These problems are often exacerbated by the nature of PHP's typical environment: web applications. PHP code often has to interact with remote systems: the timezone of your web server may not exactly match that of a third-party API hosted in another country, and HTTP clients could be anywhere in the world (and one day maybe not even limited to Earth: there are already calls in the scientific community for a lunar timezone). There is also the tricky problem of managing daylight savings: those times and dates where clocks are changed to "better" suit a particular day/night cycle.

CHAPTER 9   DATES AND TIMES

It's not uncommon to see time data incoming from a browser request ultimately recorded in a database as an adjacent day. JavaScript's native Date class has its own quirks and pitfalls, which we won't delve into here, but suffice it to say that you should pay close attention to incoming date strings. The JS Date API does not support the setting of timezones and will simply use the client's system settings. A user might set a date in a form control as "today," which will be represented with a time of 00:00 hours in the browser's timezone (JS Date objects use Unix timestamps as their internal representation of time).

A sensible approach for handling time data in web apps is to use Unix timestamps in as many places as possible and treat the rendering of dates and times as a localization problem, to be solved only once you know as much as possible about the user's location and preferences. Most of the technology related to PHP will offer some API or function call to obtain a timestamp. JavaScript Date objects are implicit timestamps, and MySQL offers the TIMESTAMP data type and a UNIX_TIMESTAMP() function, which is equivalent to PHP's time(). MySQL also offers DATE and DATETIME types, which are simply formatted strings much like those produced by PHP's DateTime::format() method, but with the important difference that there is *no* timezone support for these types. Tread carefully around storing time with MySQL and its brethren (such as MariaDB).

The handling of daylight saving time (DST) presents challenges when performing arithmetic, and so too do leap years. Take a look at the following:

```
date_default_timezone_set('Europe/London');

$winterIsComing = new DateTime('26-OCT-2025');
print $winterIsComing->format(DateTime::COOKIE) . PHP_EOL;

$winterIsComing->add(new DateInterval('PT3H'));
print $winterIsComing->format(DateTime::COOKIE);
```

Output:
Sunday, 26-Oct-2025 00:00:00 BST
Sunday, 26-Oct-2025 02:00:00 GMT

The interval format PT3H specifies an addition of three hours, but the difference in time appears to be only two hours if we just look at the date and time. Of course, we've switched timezone due to DST – British Summer Time to GMT – thanks to it being the last Sunday in October (when the UK "falls back"). Daylight savings changes like these are handled pretty well by PHP; here's an inversion of the example above...

```
$midnight = new DateTime('26-Oct-2025 00:00:00 BST');
$threeHoursLater = new DateTime('26-Oct-2025 02:00:00 GMT');
print $midnight->diff($threeHoursLater)->format('%h hours');
```

Output:

3 hours

... demonstrating that DateTime and DateInterval are able to take DST changes into account in their calculations. Your own code might not be DST-aware, however, so take care when iterating date periods or adding/subtracting units of time.

CHAPTER 10

Programming with Objects

Object-oriented programming (OOP) as a paradigm first appeared in the 1960s. Two early pioneers were Ole-Johan Dahl and Kristen Nygaard, who created the Simula language. Simula introduced concepts such as classes, inheritance, and abstract methods (virtual procedures) and was a major influence on another very well-known OOP language: Smalltalk (Xerox PARC). Smalltalk went on to influence the OOP languages in use today, including PHP. Key features that were introduced in the Simula language are still predominant in OOP today; these were

- Objects and classes
- Inheritance and sub-typing
- Abstract methods (virtual procedures)

Modern PHP is by design an object-oriented language. From version 3 onwards the set of OOP features has continued to grow and be refined, and in this chapter, we will learn how best to deploy these features (collectively known as the "object model"). We've already looked at many of the fundamentals of OOP; this chapter assumes you have read and absorbed Chapter 6, "Object Fundamentals." To recap, this chapter assumes that you understand the following concepts:

- Object instantiation
- Properties and methods
- Accessing static and non-static members
- Object context vs. class context
- Classes, anonymous classes, and their members

- Overloading and late static binding
- Interfaces, abstract classes, the `final` keyword
- Inheritance and interfaces
- Traits

As OOP evolved over time, so too did the ideas on how best to use it. Objects on their own did not make software cheaper to produce or less error-prone. A milestone paper on the subject of object-oriented design (OOD) was published in 1982, the appropriately titled *Object-Oriented Analysis and Design* by Grady Booch (and was quite possibly the first publication to use the phrase). Booch proposed a design methodology that "controls the complexity of the problem solution" by "decomposing a system into modules."

Booch's methodology began with defining the problem, then the objects and attributes pertinent to that problem, followed by operations on the objects and the interfaces required. Only after this has been done is any implementation considered. We've covered a great deal of the implementation details of PHP's object model. Here is where we will learn how to make the best use of it.

As stated, this chapter expands on the foundational ideas introduced in Chapter 6, "Object Fundamentals." Here we will focus less on what the PHP object model is and more on why it has the features that it does. That chapter was all about explaining how objects in PHP work and the language tools that exist to facilitate OOP. This chapter is concerned with how to write good (or at least pain-free) OOP code, and we're going to focus on object-oriented analysis, designing classes, some fundamental principles of good OOP, and design patterns.

Analysis and Design

Before writing a single line of code, it is necessary to know what the software needs to do, and for that, one must first understand the problem that needs to be solved. We don't create software for its own sake. It is always intended to be used to address the needs of the people that it will end up serving. A little forethought before diving in is always a good idea. Like the saying goes, weeks of programming can save you days of planning! (In other words, time devoted to planning is time saved.)

Problems and Solutions

The set of information that defines the problem and any constraints on the solution is the *problem domain* (or sometimes, the *problem space*). The problem domain is a description of the real-world entities, processes, constraints, etc. that the software must model. These could include people (often with different roles to perform), commercial goods and services, resources (e.g., meeting rooms, physical documents), statutory time limits (perhaps the software manages legal casework, and certain documents have to be filed on time), and so on.

By considering the problem domain in terms of the entities in the system (together with their actions, their relationship to each other, and especially the outcomes that need to be achieved), the requirements for the solution – the software system we are creating – will emerge. When all the requirements are met, we have our solution, and the environment in which the solution exists is known as the *solution space*. The solution space is an abstraction that encompasses the process of developing the solution, the environment where it is built (the code we write, the server it runs on), and most importantly, its design.

The processes and techniques involved in analyzing businesses and arriving at a useful set of functional requirements for a software engineer to act upon are beyond the scope of this book (and there are many books out there on the topic), but we can certainly look at how to apply OOD to requirements.

Modeling

OOP software is organized into classes that represent real entities, the actions performed upon them, the services required for the software to function in its environment, and so on. From analyzing the problem domain, we learn which abstractions we will need. For example, suppose we had to create software to manage a chain of bookshops that also provided online retail services. Clearly, we will need to represent shops and books for starters. We will likely also need to represent customers, employees, warehouses, and so on.

Let's invent some formal requirements.

- We sell books.

- Multiple bricks-and-mortar shops with local inventory.

- Each shop has a manager and multiple employees.

- Employees need to be organized into shifts.
- Customers may browse and order from a website.
- Central warehouse supplies shop inventory.
- Central warehouse also fulfills online orders.

From these requirements, we can identify some entities (real things that need to be represented somehow in our system) ...

- Book
- Shop
- Customer
- Employee
- Manager
- Warehouse
- Inventory

... and some actions (with their related entities) ...

- Schedule shifts (employee, manager, shop)
- Order new inventory (manager, shop, warehouse)
- Make shop sales (book, inventory, shop, potentially customer too)
- Make online sales (book, customer, inventory, warehouse), etc.

This is an example of *modular decomposition*. We have taken the problem domain information and created a set of objects and interactions to represent it.

Without even considering the constraints on the solution space, we're already looking at hundreds (perhaps thousands) of lines of code across many classes. We could dive in and begin creating code at this point, but just using code and written requirements to manage our design would be quite a challenge.

It would be far better at this point to spend some time considering the classes we need, how they're structured, and how they interact. Finding problems at the design stage is less of a headache than during implementation. Wading through source code to build an overview of how our system functions is a difficult proposition. Visually designing classes (and their interactions) makes much more sense.

The UML

Grady Booch, as part of his work on OOD in the 1980s, also devised a visual object modeling language. This "Booch method" notation, together with other similar methods, was standardized in the 1990s as the Unified Modeling Language (the UML). Today, the UML is an ISO standard (ISO/IEC 19505). It consists of a set of notation standards covering behavior, interaction, and structure. First, we'll focus on structure.

Classes and Interfaces

The following figure is a UML diagram of how a Book class could be built.

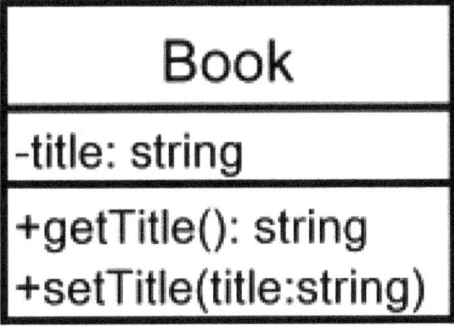

Figure 10-1. *A UML class*

A quick explanation: classes are represented by boxes, which can be sub-divided into up to three sections. The name of the class is always at the top. The section below contains the class "attributes" (a.k.a. properties); data types are optionally shown after the attribute name (names and types are separated by a colon). The final section contains the "operations" (methods). Operations always have parentheses after their names and may show parameters inside the parentheses and return types.

The figure above, therefore, shows that the Book class has one private string property called title and two public getter/setter methods. getTitle() returns a string, and setTitle() accepts a string parameter. Members (properties/attributes and methods/operations) have a symbol suffix to denote their visibility:

CHAPTER 10 PROGRAMMING WITH OBJECTS

Table 10-1. UML visibility suffixes

+	Public
#	Protected
-	Private

Interfaces are represented in the UML in a very similar manner. The following figure shows how inventory can be controlled in both shops and warehouses (both of which need to keep track of which books are available, and there's no need at this stage for either class to do things differently).

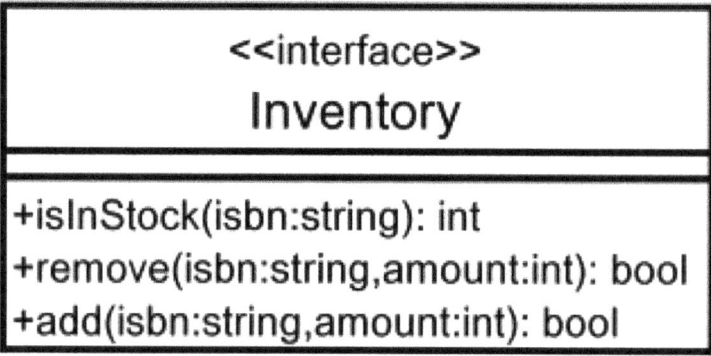

Figure 10-2. A UML interface

As we can see, interfaces look very much like classes. The notable difference is the stereotype (a UML extension) of "interface" in italics above the name.

This is a PHP interface, so there are no attributes (hence the middle section is empty), and all the operations are public. Our Inventory interface offers three members: isInStock() checks if a book is available (using the International Standard Book Number), and the other two methods allow us to control the flow of books in and out of inventory.

Inheritance and Interface Implementation

Relationships between parent and child classes, and between classes and interfaces, are represented with arrows. Solid lines with empty arrowheads are inheritance, and dotted lines with empty arrows are interface implementations.

CHAPTER 10   PROGRAMMING WITH OBJECTS

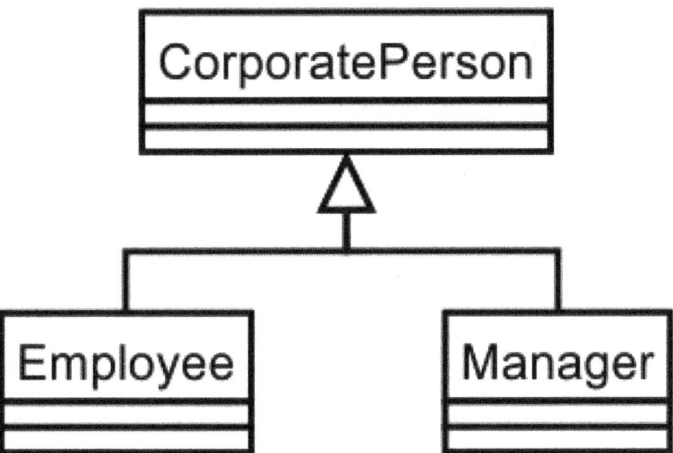

Figure 10-3. *UML inheritance relationships*

Here we have two child classes, Employee and Manager, that are derived from a parent, CorporatePerson (because managers are employees too). Between the start of this section and creating the diagram, we were hit with extra requirements from HR, and we had to refine our design.

Going back to the concept of Warehouse and Shop, both needing to keep track of inventory, let's assume that warehouses and shops differ in how they control stock (one deals with single volumes, one with pallets perhaps) but share a common interface. We can model the relationship like this:

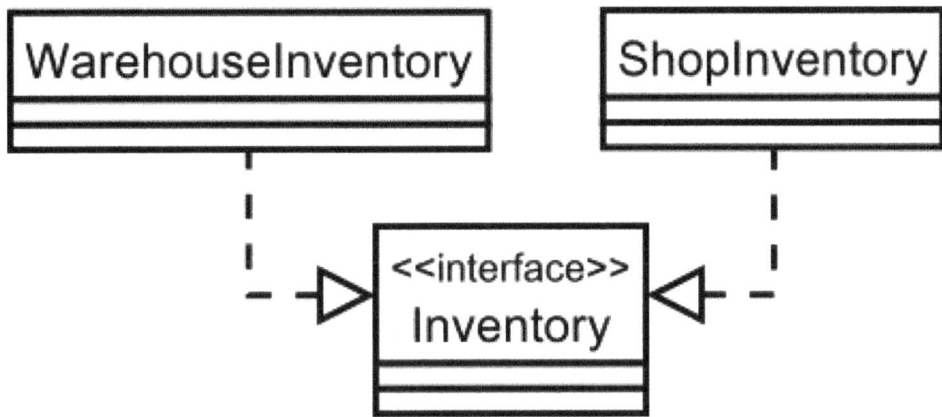

Figure 10-4. *UML interface implementation*

645

Traits

If you remember from Chapter 6, "Object Fundamentals," traits offered a way to mitigate PHP's single inheritance model. There is no specific representation of traits in the UML, but it could be approximated with a stereotyped parent class.

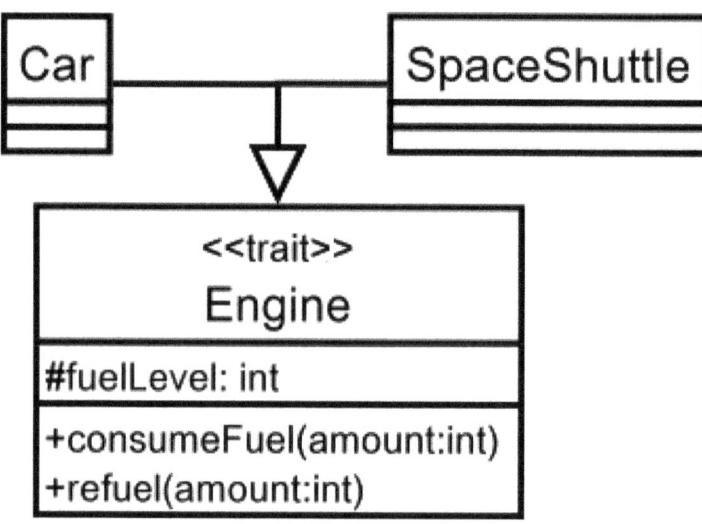

Figure 10-5. *A way to represent traits in UML*

Association

So far, we've seen how to describe inheritance and implementation with the UML, but this is only one way in which objects in a system can be related. Another form of relationship is *association*. An association arises when a class property is used to refer to instances of other classes.

It's safe to assume that an instance of Shop will need some way to communicate with an Inventory object; the simplest way would be to store a reference to Inventory, and so we have our first association type.

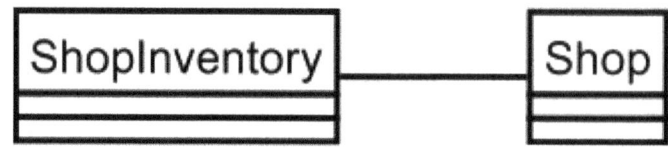

Figure 10-6. *Shop associated with Inventory*

Figure 10-6 shows the simplest form of association. A solid line simply declares that two entities are related somehow. It is possible to add more information, however.

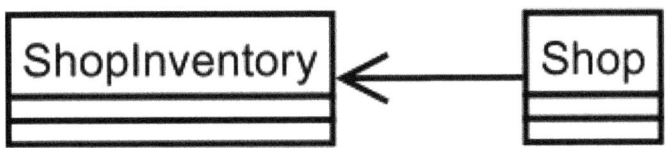

Figure 10-7. *Shop references Inventory*

By adding an open arrow, we've added a direction to the association; in this case, we're stating that Shop will have a reference to ShopInventory, but ShopInventory does not have a reference to Shop. This is *unidirectional*. If both classes held references to each other, then we would have arrowheads on both sides, showing a bi-directional relationship.

Of course, a class property might contain an array of references to another (to represent a collection), and it is possible to quantify associations by putting numbers (or an asterisk for any number) next to each class in the diagram. ShopInventory probably has more than one book in it, and we could show the association between ShopInventory and Book like this:

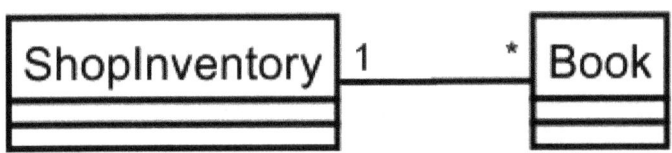

Figure 10-8. *One ShopInventory, many Books*

The figure above shows that our model now contains a single ShopInventory instance that refers to zero or more Book instances. It is also possible to show ranges in this form, if ShopInventory has a maximum capacity of 1000 books, we could replace the asterisk next to Book with 0..1000.

Aggregation

A UML aggregation is essentially a strong association. Like associations, an *aggregation* represents a class containing references to other classes. The key difference is that with an aggregation the referring class is only fully functional when it contains referred instances. Without the aggregation, there is no real need for the referring class to exist.

For example, imagine that our bookshops are now holding author signing events. We add an Event class to our model and associate Customer instances with it. The Event class has one main purpose: to organize the customers in the hopes that they will attend. To represent the aggregation of Customer instances into an Event, we use a line with an unfilled diamond like this:

Figure 10-9. *Customer and Event aggregation*

In this form of relationship, Customer instances can be associated with multiple Event instances. Cancelling an event and deleting its Event object in the system will not mean deleting any aggregated Customer objects.

If, however, a class is only ever associated with its containing class and cannot be referred to by any other, then the aggregation becomes *composition*.

Composition

Composition relationships are represented with a solid line and a filled diamond symbol. They indicate that the referred class can only be accessed via its container, and deleting a container instance will also delete its contents (because no more references to them will exist).

Our Event class could perhaps have its scheduling data encapsulated in, say, an EventSchedule object. EventSchedule might contain information like date and time, venue, and so on. The EventSchedule is so specific to an Event that its continued existence in the system should an Event be deleted would make no sense.

CHAPTER 10 PROGRAMMING WITH OBJECTS

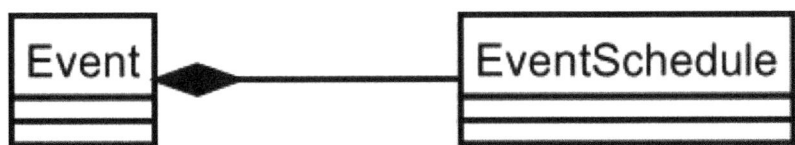

Figure 10-10. EventSchedule composition

Using Classes

Relationships also exist between classes where there is no related structure: no common parent or shared interface. It is quite common for objects to be passed around a system without needing to store references to them everywhere (in fact, it's better not to). These are modeled as *dependencies* in the UML (and frequently referred to as such when discussing OO software), and they occur when class methods require other classes as parameters or return other classes.

Dependency relationships are indicated with a dotted line and open arrowhead. Perhaps our bookshop data model now includes a module that makes queries on ShopInventory instances to prepare stock reports. StockTaker does not need to store a reference to ShopInventory to do this; it just needs an Inventory interface implementation to work with.

Figure 10-11 shows the relationship between the three classes, StockTaker, ShopInventory, and WarehouseInventory, and the Inventory interface. The inventory classes implement the Inventory interface (dotted line with unfilled solid arrow), and StockTaker has a dependency on Inventory (dotted line, open arrow).

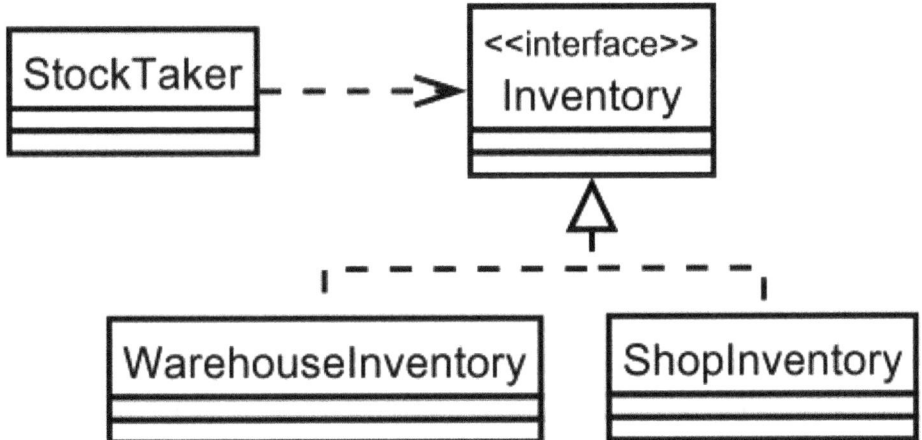

Figure 10-11. StockTaker dependency on Inventory

This diagram also serves another purpose. Remember in Chapter 6, "Object Fundamentals," when we looked at interfaces for the first time? I mentioned dependency inversion. The relationship between `StockTaker` and `WarehouseInventory` is another example. Rather than have `StockTaker` dependent on the two inventory classes, we instead insert an abstraction: the `Inventory` interface. In this way the relationship between each inventory class and the `StockTaker` is "inverted" (the arrows point away from the classes and toward the interface). `StockTaker` only ever needs to check that an incoming object implements the interface; its type is irrelevant.

This is the second time we've encountered one of the SOLID principles, so let's move onto that next.

The SOLID Principles

SOLID is a set of five principles intended to aid the design of OOP software. They were introduced by Robert C. Martin, one in a 1996 paper ("The Single Responsibility Principle") and the other four in a 2000 paper ("Design Principles and Design Patterns"). The SOLID acronym was coined by Michael Feathers, and it stands for the following.

- **S**ingle Responsibility
- **O**pen Closed
- **L**iskov Substitution
- **I**nterface Segregation
- **D**ependency Inversion

Let's explore each of those principles in turn.

Single Responsibility Principle (SRP)

A class should do one thing and therefore (from Martin's 1996 paper) "should have only one reason to change." There is some ambiguity around the phrase "reason to change," and Robert Martin clarified in later writing that his intention was to point out the "coupling between the term 'responsibility' and 'reason to change'" and that responsibility was a question of to whom rather than to what. This principle concerns the relationship between actors (people or groups of people) and the system they use.

It is people that require software to change, not the software itself, which I touched upon in the previous section when describing problem domains.

Consider the final example from the previous section: the StockTaker. This hypothetical class existed to query shop and warehouse inventories to calculate the remaining amounts of books. Likely its output will be used by other classes, perhaps to generate reports or financial forecasts. The reporting and forecasting functionality could be written directly into StockTaker, with a design like this:

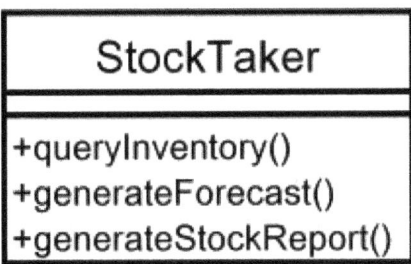

Figure 10-12. StockTaker class design

Now think about the stakeholders for this class, all of the people within the business that have an interest in what it does and, crucially, might one day need it to change. Finance wants the forecast, warehouse managers want the stock report, and so on. To say nothing of the rest of the code in the system that has a dependency on StockTaker. In order to isolate interested actors, we need to change the design.

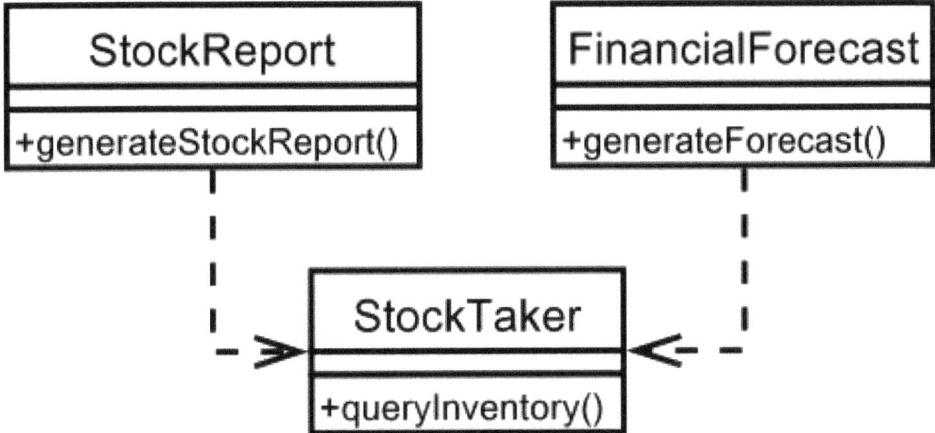

Figure 10-13. Isolating stakeholders by design

Now our design is in much better shape. By splitting the functionality across more specialized classes, we have reduced the impact of any change requests. Finance and warehouse management can both ask for change (concurrently, even), and it is easier to manage. This is because – with the new design – different components are servicing the needs of different groups of stakeholders, and the scope of each change becomes smaller: there's less code to modify (always a good thing).

Open-Closed Principle (OCP)

The term "open-closed principle" is credited to Bertrand Meyer, from his 1988 book *Object-Oriented Software Construction*. OCP states that modules should be open for extension but closed for modification. A well-designed class should not need to be modified if extra functionality is required; instead, the extra functionality should be provided by extending the class or by composing objects (building the functionality of a run-time object by adding other objects that define its behavior – we'll see this in action when we look at design patterns later on).

Let's see how inheritance-based OCP solves problems. A common "code-smell" (a sign that the design can be improved) is the use of logic to determine what an object represents in the problem domain. This can happen if a class is too generalized to accurately represent any particular problem domain entity.

```
class Vehicle
{
    public function __construct(private string $type)
    {
    }

    public function getMaxPassengers(): int
    {
        switch ($this->type) {
            case 'car':
                return 4;
                break;
            case 'bus':
                return 30;
                break;
```

```
            default:
                throw new Exception('unsupported vehicle type');
        }
    }
}
```

Clearly the problem domain contains vehicles that are cars and buses, but the solution space currently only contains a Vehicle class, and the differences in behavior between cars and buses are determined in a switch/case statement. If the problem domain grows and we need to support, say, motorbikes, then we'll have to modify the code of Vehicle.

The Vehicle is not closed to modification. On the contrary, with this design our solution space *requires* Vehicle to be modified every time we introduce new vehicle types. Additionally, Vehicle is not open for extension; there's no way for a child class to impact the number of passengers it needs to represent. This code is difficult to maintain and not particularly robust (note the use of Exception in the default case). However, we can fix this by applying OCP to the design.

```
class Vehicle
{
    protected int $maxPassengers = 0;

    public function getMaxPassengers(): int
    {
        return $this->maxPassengers;
    }
}
class Car extends Vehicle
{
    protected int $maxPassengers = 4;
}
class Motorbike extends Vehicle
{
    protected int $maxPassengers = 2;
}
```

```
$car = new Car();
$bike = new Motorbike();

print "A car can carry {$car->getMaxPassengers()} people" . PHP_EOL;
print "A motorbike can carry {$bike->getMaxPassengers()} people" . PHP_EOL;
```

Output:
car can carry 4 people
motorbike can carry 2 people

Now we have a `Vehicle` class that contains the common method of `getMaxPassengers()` which all children of `Vehicle` inherit, and all client code makes use of. The problem domain data that was previously controlled inside the `switch/case` block has now become an extendable class property: `protected int $maxPassengers`. Now when we need to add new vehicle types to the solution space, we simply extend `Vehicle` and set the `maxPassengers` property as required.

In this way we have closed `Vehicle` to modification and opened it to extension, and OCP is satisfied (and in doing so our code becomes more robust and easier to maintain). This is OCP by inheritance, which was the original method proposed by Meyer in 1988. Subsequent development of the idea by others (such as Robert Martin in his 1996 paper *The Open-Closed Principle*) introduced a refinement: abstractions (either abstract classes or interfaces) should be used to close the interface to modifications but allow different implementations in the derived classes.

Let's implement OCP for our vehicle problem domain using an `interface` abstraction.

```
interface Vehicle
{
    public function getMaxPassengers(): int;
}

class Train implements Vehicle
{
    public function __construct(private int $carriages)
    {
    }

    public function getMaxPassengers(): int
```

```
    {
        return $this->carriages * 30;
    }
}

$train = new Train(6);
print "This train can carry {$train->getMaxPassengers()} people" . PHP_EOL;

Output:
This train can carry 180 people
```

Here we have a Train class, which now implements a Vehicle interface. Vehicle specifies that a derived class must implement getMaxPassangers(), and the method must return an integer. Imagine that our previously derived vehicles implement a fixed value (cars still carry five people and so on), but trains are a special case: their carrying capacity is variable according to the number of carriages they have (determined when the object is constructed in this case).

With inheritance-based OCP, we'd have a problem: using a parent class of Vehicle wouldn't meet the needs of Train objects. We either have to add logic to the parent implementation or overload the parent, and not every derived class needs a carriages property. By only closing the interface, we are free to work with different implementations for different derived classes. This does, of course, raise the possible issue of violating the Don't Repeat Yourself (DRY) principle, but common implementations can be composed from a trait or the use of a Strategy pattern (where the required functionality is injected via another object), which we will look at later on in the chapter.

Liskov Substitution Principle (LSP)

Barbara Liskov presented a paper – *Data Abstraction and Hierarchy* – at a keynote address of the OOPSLA (Object-Oriented Programming Systems, Languages and Applications) conference in 1987. Her work, together with Jeannette Wing, concerned the data relationships between parent and child types and focused on their substitutability. The LSP concerns *strong behavioral subtyping*: namely that any child class should satisfy the expectations of clients that are written to use a parent class. Furthermore, the child class substitution should not just be safe (in that it causes no syntax errors, i.e., all parent members are found in the child), but it should behave correctly too.

If we take the inheritance-based OCP example from above, we can write a function designed to use the Vehicle type like this:

```
function useVehicle(Vehicle $vehicle): void
{
    print "This vehicle can carry {$vehicle->getMaxPassengers()} people" .
    PHP_EOL;
}

useVehicle(new Vehicle());
useVehicle(new Car());
```

Output:
This vehicle can carry 0 people
This vehicle can carry 4 people

As you can see, useVehicle() functions perfectly correctly even when an instance of Car is passed into it, because Car is a subclass of Vehicle. When overloading parent members, it is vital that the overloaded members behave in the same way. The internal implementation can, of course, change, but input and output data types should remain identical.

There are in fact some mechanisms in the PHP object model to prevent violations of the LSP. For example, if we attempt to change the visibility of getMaxPassengers() to private (which would change the interface of the class), we get an error.

```
class Car extends Vehicle
{
    protected int $maxPassengers = 4;
    private function getMaxPassengers(): int
    {
        return $this->maxPassengers;
    }
}
```

Output:
Fatal error: Access level to Car::getMaxPassengers() must be public (as in class Vehicle)

Likewise, we cannot change the return type.

```
class Car extends Vehicle
{
    public function getMaxPassengers(): string
    {
        // NumberFormatter requires the intl extension
        $formatter = new NumberFormatter('en', NumberFormatter::SPELLOUT);
        return $formatter->format($this->maxPassengers);
    }
}
```

Output:
Fatal error: Declaration of Car::getMaxPassengers(): string must be compatible with Vehicle::getMaxPassengers(): int

Score another point for declaring return types: if none had been specified in the parent declaration, we would be free to change the return type in the child and introduce potential bugs in client code. Finally, we cannot add or remove arguments to overloaded methods.

```
// new declaration for Vehicle::getMaxPassengers()
public function getMaxPassengers() {}

// Car::getMaxPassengers() with an argument...
public function getMaxPassengers($behaviour)
```

Output:
Fatal error: Declaration of Car::getMaxPassengers($behaviour) must be compatible with Vehicle::getMaxPassengers()

For older or less strict code, there is the option of declaring class members as `final`. Only methods, constants, or the class itself may be declared as final, and pre-PHP 8.1 private methods could not be declared in this way. `final` method and constants cannot be overloaded, and `final` classes cannot be extended (though of course that isn't relevant to the LSP).

```
// new declaration for Vehicle::getMaxPassengers()
final public function getMaxPassengers() {}

// Car::getMaxPassengers()
```

```
    public function getMaxPassengers()
```
Output:
Fatal error: Cannot override final method Vehicle::getMaxPassengers()

It's a bit of a brute-force technique for ensuring child classes adhere to the LSP and naturally introduces other issues: we risk violating OCP because the parent class has now become less open for extension.

Interface Segregation Principle (ISP)

This is another principle from the mind of Robert C. Martin, first published in 1996. The ISP advocates that interfaces should not be any larger than needed: that is to say that no client or subclass should be forced to depend on members it does not make use of or implement. Martin discussed "fat interfaces" and warned of classes that service the needs of different sets of clients, and such classes should be "broken up into groups of member functions."

I've mentioned design patterns already, and we'll get around to those in due course. There also exist "anti-patterns" that is patterns in OOD that are considered bad practice, and one of the worst offenders is "the blob." A blob is typically where the bulk of the system process lives, and dependent classes are usually small, contain little or no logic, and only exist to hold data. Clients of the blob are faced with a huge interface containing several (or several dozen!) methods that are of zero interest to them; subclasses of a blob now hold dozens of members that are of zero relevance to them. The source code for blob classes usually runs into thousands of lines.

Interface segregation eschews general-purpose interfaces for client-specific interfaces. Let's revisit our book empire for some examples. Shop and Warehouse both need to have orders fulfilled. Shops deal with customer orders (handling customer details in the process), and warehouses deal with wholesale orders (which require purchase orders). A component is created in our system to deal with order fulfillment and provides wholesaleOrder() and customerOrder() members in its interface. We can model the dependency between Warehouse, Shop, and OrderFulfillment like this:

CHAPTER 10 PROGRAMMING WITH OBJECTS

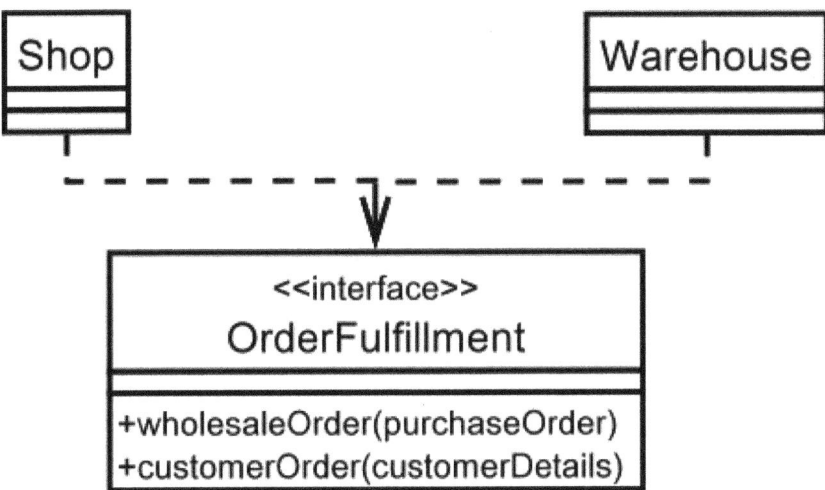

Figure 10-14. OrderFulfillment offers more than any one of its clients needs

On first glance, this might look OK. After all, OrderFulfillment looks nicely specialized to its job of placing orders. However, we now have a component that is offering Shop clients unnecessary wholesale order functionality, and likewise Warehouse clients are dealing with a component that allows customer order functionality, which Warehouse will never use.

There's also another problem. Remember single responsibility? If we consider the problem domain, we have two different sets of actors potentially driving change on OrderFulfillment – shop customers and warehouse managers. By ignoring the ISP, we have now violated the SRP.

The SOLID principles do not exist in isolation from each other. They are very much interrelated. Here's another example of how ISP relates to another SOLID principle.

```
class OrderFulfillment
{
    public function wholesaleOrder()
    {
        // wholesale stuff
    }
    public function customerOrder()
    {
        // customer stuff
    }
```

659

```
}

class OnlineShopOrder extends OrderFulfillment
{
    public function wholesaleOrder()
    {
        throw new Exception('wholesaleOrders not supported');
    }

    public function customerOrder()
    {
        // online customer stuff
    }
}
```

Here we've decided to create a new `OnlineShopOrder` class, using `OrderFulfillment` as its parent. `OnlineShopOrder` is obliged to implement `wholesaleOrder()` but has no use for it, so it replaces the parent implementation with an exception (it could, of course, silently fail or some other error state). What it does not do is behave at all in the same way as `OrderFulfillment::wholesaleOrder()` would be expected to (by adjusting inventory levels, sending messages, and so on), and we've violated the Liskov Substitution Principle. Exceptions being thrown on non-implemented methods is a classic code smell. Should you ever encounter them in the wild, it is a clear indication that application of the ISP is sorely needed somewhere in your codebase!

The examples above are contrived ISP violations writ small. It should not be too much of a cognitive leap to imagine the problem on a larger scale, where blob classes are offering interfaces that are difficult to document or understand (and use) or forcing subclasses to overload dozens of unnecessary public functions. One solution to our `OrderFulfillment` problem is, of course, to split it into specialized interfaces: one for shops and one for warehouses. An even better solution would be to simplify the interface to a single method and have `OrderFulfillment` composed with the correct components to service its client at run-time. We'll see some patterns for doing this later.

Dependency Inversion Principle (DIP)

Finally, there's dependency inversion. We've already met this principle at the end of the previous section. If you remember, we had a class called `StockTaker` with a dependency on inventory classes. Let's see what it looks like when we don't use dependency inversion.

CHAPTER 10 PROGRAMMING WITH OBJECTS

Figure 10-15 shows the dependency relationship between StockTaker and two inventory classes. Any StockTaker methods that work with an inventory object will need to be typed with each class, for example:

```
class StockTaker
{
    public function doInventoryWork(WarehouseInventory|ShopInventory
    $inventory)
```

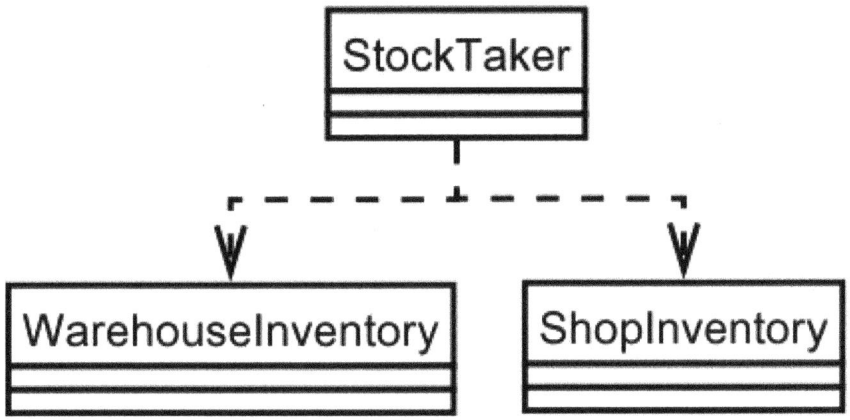

Figure 10-15. *StockTaker depends on multiple classes*

You might also remember that the UML diagram (Figure 10-11 in the previous section) showed an interface, Inventory, which was implemented by WarehouseInventory and ShopInventory, and StockTaker was instead made dependent on the interface. By making StockTaker dependent on an abstraction (for the purposes of this principle, an abstract base class and an interface are equivalent), we can simplify method declarations to use a single interface, for example:

```
class StockTaker
{
    public function doInventoryWork(Inventory $inventory)
```

If the problem domain expands and our software finds itself needing, say, KioskInventory, there's no need to modify the StockTaker class (provided that KioskInventory implements the Inventory interface).

661

Dependency inversion is the process of taking a single direction class-to-class dependency and inserting an abstraction between them. The dependent class now points to the interface, while on the other side the target class is now pointing (with an implementation arrow) to the interface. To sum up, the DIP turns a design like this...

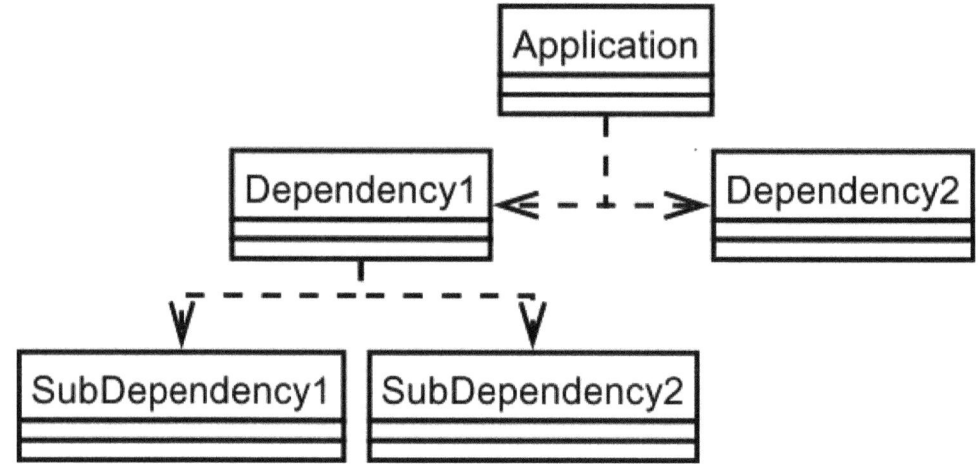

Figure 10-16. *Each layer points toward a lower layer*

...into a model like this...

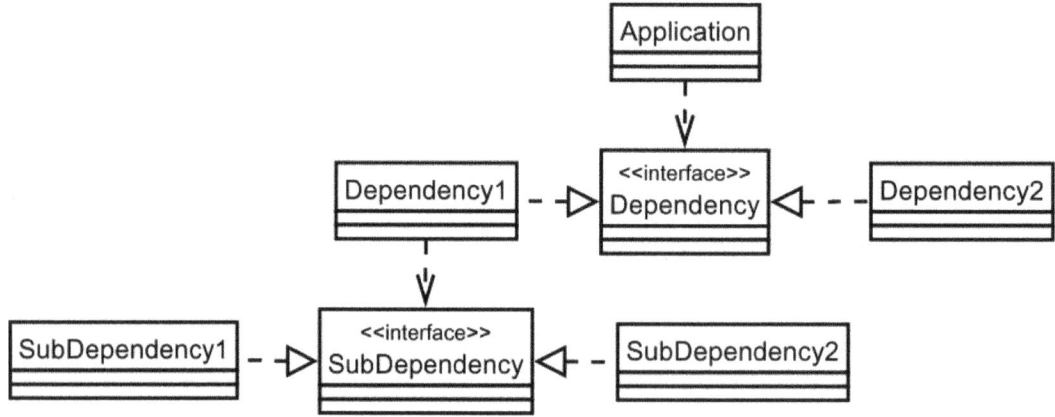

Figure 10-17. *Each layer points toward an abstraction*

...and the result is code that is much easier to manage. Client classes use the abstraction (interface or abstract class) in their arguments; dependency classes implement the interface. We are now free to add as many new implementing classes as we like, and we don't have to modify the client class each time we do.

In Conclusion

I hope that you have now grasped the underlying reasons for the SOLID principles. They exist to make change (which is inevitable) less impactful and easier to manage. By decoupling components from each other and shifting dependencies from classes to interfaces (or abstract classes), we reduce the impact that change requests have throughout the system. If we continuously evaluate classes in terms of the human actors that make use of them, we can anticipate change before it happens and ensure that any particular change request impacts the smallest amount of code possible.

You should now be aware that large interfaces are to be viewed with (extreme) suspicion, and likewise any instances of subclass members being overloaded with error handling code (or even no code at all) is a clear indicator of underlying design problems. By considering the open-closed principle and Liskov substitution, new classes that you design should be more robust and cause fewer maintenance headaches down the line. It is good practice to always consider the engineers that will work on your code in the future and try to make their lives as easy as possible – remember that you might be one of them!

Design Patterns

The SOLID principles are an excellent first step to designing better object-oriented software; classes that are designed with those principles in mind will generally be easier to understand, integrate with each other, and maintain throughout the life of the code. Building on these ideas of integration and reuse, we come to *design patterns*. It is rare to encounter genuinely novel problems in software engineering; most of the time the code that you write professionally will be treading well-worn paths: authenticating requests, sending emails, transforming raw data into something browsers can use... and so on. The generally agreed landmark work in the software design patterns space is *Design Patterns: Elements of Reusable Object-Oriented Software*, written by Erich Gamma, Richard Helm, Ralph Johnson, and John Vlissides (the so-called "Gang of Four" – often abbreviated to *GoF*), first published in 1994. Another notable text is *Patterns of Enterprise Application Architecture*, by Martin Fowler and first published in 2022.

Design patterns are reusable templates for class design, intended to solve common problem cases. Using patterns can speed up the development process: rather than needing to create novel solutions, one can simply choose an appropriate pattern, which has already received scrutiny from the engineering community and is a proven solution. The key to using patterns well is to thoroughly understand the problem space: a well-defined problem contains the seeds of its own solution, which is why time spent on planning and analysis is vital to creating good software.

This section is not intended as an exhaustive resource for all things concerning design patterns but should serve as a high-level introduction to the topic. Recommended further reading includes the two books already mentioned, and for PHP in particular there is *PHP 8 Objects, Patterns, and Practice* by my friend (and technical editor of this book!) Matt Zandstra, available from Apress Media. Now, without further ado, let us dive in.

Object-oriented design patterns are usually documented as UML class diagrams, which we have already seen earlier in the chapter, together with a description of the problems and solutions that the pattern is intended to address. The pattern might be a single class or a collection of classes related by inheritance or (especially) by interface dependencies and can be broadly sorted into the following types:

- Creational patterns
- Structural patterns
- Behavioral patterns

Creational Patterns

The process of creating new objects is straightforward; PHP's new keyword combined with a class name and parentheses will instantiate and return a reference to the new object, as described in Chapter 6, "Object Fundamentals." However, peppering your code with new objects can quickly lead to problems at runtime, and it is generally advisable to wrap object creation in code that is dedicated to managing the process. One venerable pattern intended to contain the (sometimes messy) business of making decisions around what to create (and how to create it) is the *Factory Method*. The idea behind the Factory Method is that as an application grows, classes often diversify into specialized sub-classes, and code that creates generalized objects representing products such as, say, physical books, might in the future need to create more specialized products, such as magazines or comics. As the new requirements pour in, your code can become a mess of conditional statements creating new Book(), or new Magazine(), and so on.

CHAPTER 10 PROGRAMMING WITH OBJECTS

A Factory Method implementation still creates products (and in the case of PHP will still use the new keyword), but the act of creation is delegated to a single class method. Client code that was previously directly instantiating new objects directly now instead calls a creator to do the work for it. By doing this we are able to define a single interface that we are free to implement as we see fit as new products enter the design. Here is a class diagram showing how to implement the pattern:

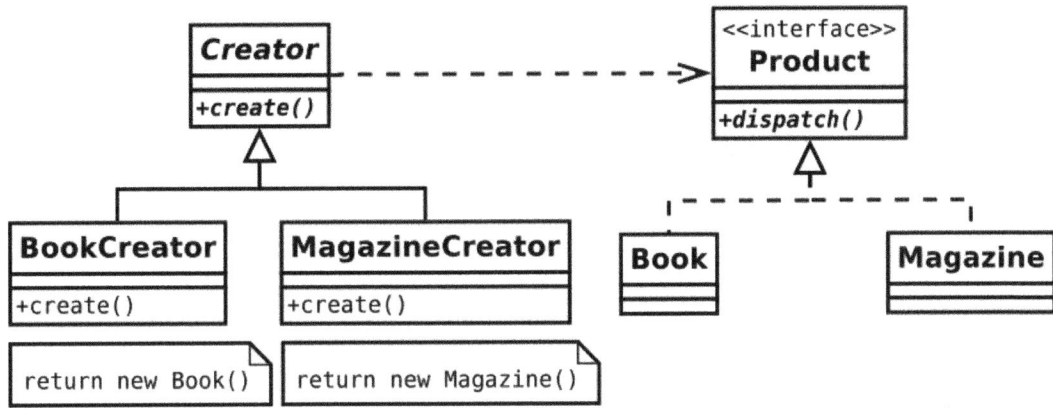

Figure 10-18. *Factory Method pattern*

The eagle-eyed among you might have spotted something familiar: the use of interfaces (Product) and abstract base classes (Creator) looks very much like the dependency inversion diagram in the previous section. This is of course exactly what is going on here, and you will encounter SOLID principles throughout design patterns. Depending on the specifics of your use-case, the Creator abstract class might not need to be a class at all: if the only reason for it to exist is to force inheriting subclasses to implement the create() method, it is probably better off being an interface too. A good pattern should offer some flexibility in the fine details and will serve as a framework for the overall design of your solution.

Moving on from Factory Method, a more complex problem space might introduce the need to create families of related objects. Our hypothetical print media retailer might branch out in the future and start selling, say, digital versions of the same media. We still need to represent Book, Magazine, and so on, but now we have an additional axis to model, resulting in DigitalBook, PrintBook, and DigitalMagazine. A more complex creational pattern exists for handling exactly this kind of complexity: the *Abstract Factory*. This pattern incorporates Factory Method but exchanges a single create() method for product-specific methods like createBook(), createMagazine(), and concrete factory classes are now specialized to the product family rather than the products:

665

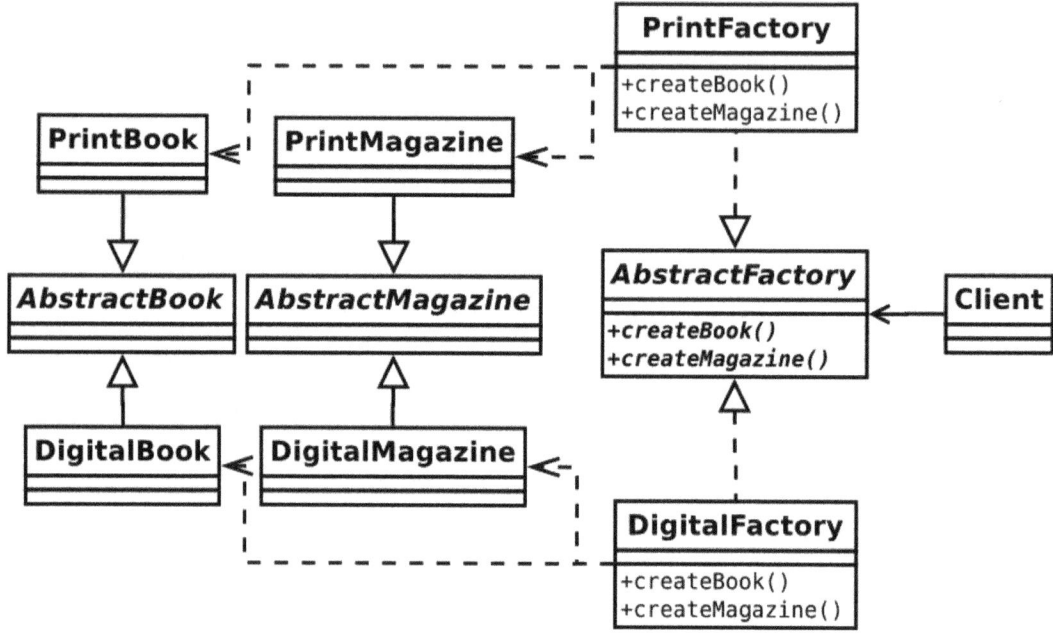

Figure 10-19. Abstract Factory pattern

Things get even more complex when dealing with objects that are composed of other objects (e.g., the structural pattern known as *Composite*, which is discussed below) or needing to control the number of instances of a class. Naturally there are creational patterns to suit those cases: the other main types are

- Builder (creates composite objects)
- Singleton (ensures only a single instance of an object exists globally)
- Prototype (creates copies of objects without introducing additional dependencies)

We won't look at these in detail here; detailed information is readily available online or in the aforementioned books. Also worth mentioning at this point are some patterns that are adjacent to object creation. By now you should be comfortable with the concept of dependency: objects and functions often rely on other objects/functions/data for their correct operation. There are patterns for managing that too, and they are collectively known as *Dependency Injection*. Two common patterns are:

- Service Locator (objects and/or functions are centrally registered for runtime access)
- Service Container (manages dependencies in multiple ways)

Both are covered in detail in *PHP Objects, Patterns, and Practice*; I highly recommend obtaining a copy. (Other resources are available, though.)

Structural Patterns

Class design can quickly get out of hand as the complexity of the problem space grows (or perhaps your understanding of the problem space grows). Classes that were once streamlined and focused can begin to accumulate new properties and methods, and elegant interfaces grow into something ugly and difficult to manage. Breaking large classes into smaller, related ones is a good way to tackle interface bloat but introduces new problems around how to manage closely related objects at run time. This is where the structural patterns come in: they provide efficient ways to assemble individual objects into larger structures and ensure the results play nicely with the rest of your code. As before, we'll look at a quick example, and I'll list some other common patterns that you can investigate in your own time.

Let's take the first class of problem mentioned in the preceding paragraph: adding functionality to existing classes in an elegant way. It is not uncommon for classes that model business processes to accumulate extra methods or become split into subclasses as businesses grow and diversify. Imagine we start a pop-up food stall, and it sells one thing: the best pizza you ever tasted. There is only one product: the Pizza, made the same way every time. Business is good, and the software is simple: we represent a unit of pizza (in the app we made for people to place their orders) as a single class: Pizza. Over time we expand our offering: blue cheese is very popular, and so too are truffle shavings. Now we sell pizza, with or without blue cheese, and with or without truffle. We could model the various pizzas in our app as the classes OriginalPizza, BlueCheesePizza, TrufflePizza, and TruffleAndBlueCheesePizza – if we weren't thinking very hard. Later on, we add more ingredients, creating more permutations of pizza… Very quickly we could end up with dozens of classes, all identical in their interfaces – or worse, differing in their interfaces! – increasing cognitive load on engineers and raising maintenance costs. All for the sake of some extra toppings.

Fortunately, there is a fix for just this scenario, called the *Decorator Pattern*. This pattern defines a single class to represent the top level of the hierarchy (pizza, in our case) and another class to add functionality, called the decorator (or *wrapper*) class.

CHAPTER 10 PROGRAMMING WITH OBJECTS

The beauty of this pattern lies in the fact that an arbitrary number of decorators can be used to wrap the main component, which allows you to fine-tune the functionality of the component without resorting to adding subclasses for each permutation. The component and the decorator share a common interface; the decorator is constructed with an instance of that interface, and this allows decorators to wrap other decorators. Decorators delegate their implementations of the interface methods to their wrapped objects while adding their own additions. First, let's look at a class diagram that shows how the component, interface, and decorator(s) are related:

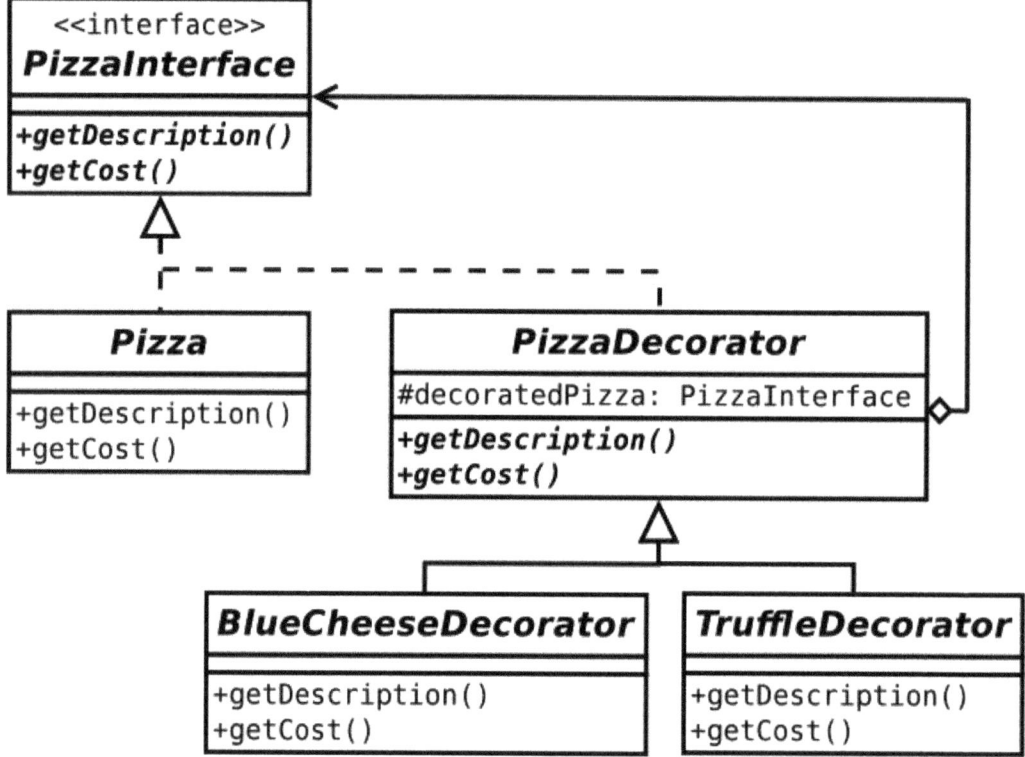

Figure 10-20. Decorator pattern

The following code shows simple implementations for a Pizza component class, an abstract base decorator (which really only exists here to save having to define the same constructor in each subclass), and two concrete decorator classes:

```
// PizzaInterface defines two public methods: getCost() and
getDescription()
```

```php
class Pizza implements PizzaInterface
{
    public function getDescription(): string
    {
        return 'Our famous pizza';
    }

    public function getCost(): float
    {
        return 10.99;
    }
}

abstract class PizzaDecorator implements PizzaInterface
{
    public function __construct(
        protected PizzaInterface $decoratedPizza
    ) {
    }

    abstract public function getDescription(): string;
    abstract public function getCost(): float;
}

class BlueCheeseDecorator extends PizzaDecorator
{
    public function getDescription(): string
    {
        return $this->decoratedPizza->getDescription() . ', with blue
        cheese';
    }

    public function getCost(): float
    {
        return $this->decoratedPizza->getCost() + 2.50;
    }
}
```

```
class TruffleDecorator extends PizzaDecorator
{
    public function getDescription(): string
    {
        return $this->decoratedPizza->getDescription() . ', with truffle
        shavings';
    }
    public function getCost(): float
    {
        return $this->decoratedPizza->getCost() + 3.50;
    }
}
```

All we need to do now is order some pizza!

```
$orderOne = new BlueCheeseDecorator(new Pizza());
$orderTwo = new TruffleDecorator(new BlueCheeseDecorator(new Pizza()));

print $orderOne->getDescription() . '. Costs ' . $orderOne->getCost() .
PHP_EOL;
print $orderTwo->getDescription() . '. Costs ' . $orderTwo->getCost() .
PHP_EOL;
```

Output:
Our famous pizza, with blue cheese. Costs 13.49
Our famous pizza, with blue cheese, with truffle shavings. Costs 16.99

As you can see, the description and costs are obtained from the outermost decorator objects, assembled as they delegate to their wrapped object(s). Note that we've instantiated all the required objects in one statement; a real application is, of course, free to add decorators at any point, no doubt using some other (creational) design pattern: good patterns will play nicely with other patterns.

This is just a taster (sorry) of structural patterns; there are others:

- Adapter (allows collaboration between objects with incompatible interfaces)

- Bridge (splits large sets of components into separate hierarchies)

- Composite (builds a tree structure of related objects that behaves as a single object)

- Facade (wraps a complex interface in a simplified version)

- Flyweight (minimize memory use by allowing objects to share common data)

- Proxy (provides a substitute object, allowing additional functionality before or after calling the target)

Behavioral Patterns

We've seen *how* to build objects, we've considered *what* objects to build, and now we'll look at patterns for controlling how our objects behave as they do their work. Behavioral patterns provide a set of templates that are primarily concerned with how objects communicate with each other and also how they can alter their behavior as your program executes.

One idea that repeatedly crops up in OOP (and to be fair, programming in general) is the idea of *coupling*. Coupling is the degree to which one component is aware of (and thus dependent on) another. In particular, *loose coupling* is the ideal: where components are weakly associated (so that changes in one will have the most reduced effect on another), and there is little to no special knowledge of one component in another. Components that are loosely coupled are easily altered or replaced, which means maintaining code is less expensive (both in monetary cost and engineer well-being). The behavioral patterns are all designed with this goal in mind, so let's look at an example.

The problem case we'll consider is one where a range of possible behaviors (or algorithms) exists, only one of which is required and can only be determined at runtime. This is a very common problem, and the naive solution is to wrap each code block that defines the behavior in a construct such as a `switch` block or a set of `if` statements (we've seen these in Chapter 4, "Logic and Control"). To give an example scenario: you might have an application that serves up data to a web client in a variety of file formats, maybe as delimited values (such as CSV, PSV, etc.) or a full-blown spreadsheet. The application retrieves data from a database and converts it to the relevant format based on information contained in the HTTP request. The algorithm (build a comma-separated file, pipe-separated, tab-separated, or build something in a spreadsheet format) needs to be selected after the application has begun to execute, and the selection code might look something like this:

```
// request URL contains query string '?format=$FILE_FORMAT'
$format = $_GET['format'];

switch ($format) {
    case 'csv':
        $csvFormatter->buildOutput($data);
        break;
    case 'psv':
        $psvFormatter->buildOutput($data);
        break;
    case 'tsv':
        $tsvFormatter->buildOutput($data);
        break;
    case 'xls':
        $xlsFormatter->buildOutput($data);
        break;
}
```

Such code is fine as it goes but can become unwieldy as new behaviors (in our case, supported file formats) are introduced. Also, notice that the client code holds references to all the possible output formatting objects, despite only ever needing one of them. It is exactly this scenario that the *Strategy Pattern* is designed for. With this pattern, each algorithm is wrapped in a class that conforms to a common Strategy interface. At run time, another object – called a Context – is used to wrap the chosen strategy, and the client code is given a reference to the context. For our hypothetical problem the class diagram would look like this:

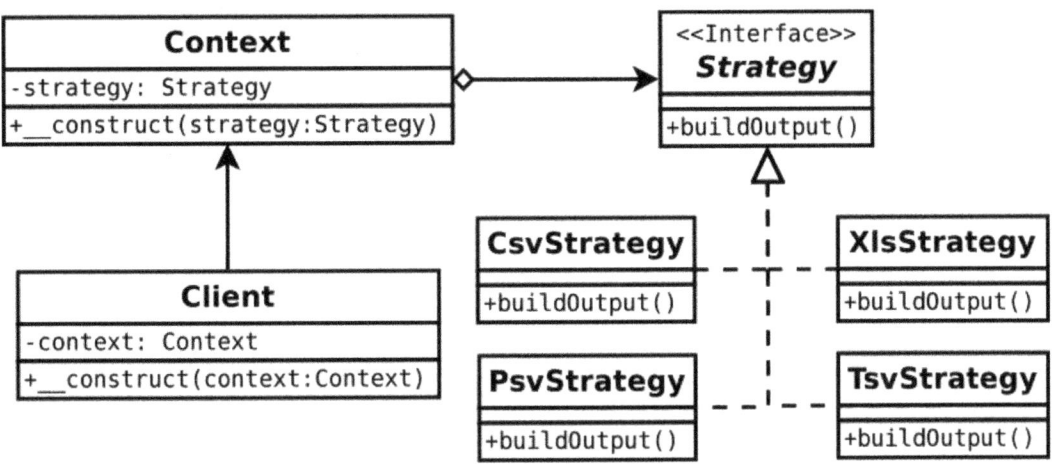

Figure 10-21. Each layer points toward an abstraction

The Client instance is given a Context instance via constructor injection (it's perfectly fine for client code to make its own Context or have it set after instantiation, but constructor injection is all the rage these days); in turn, the Context instance is created with a concrete implementation of a Strategy interface. How this is done is up for grabs, and naturally a creational pattern of some kind can handle the work for you (good patterns always integrate well with each other). It's likely that *somewhere* there's a logical construct working on the incoming format query parameter, but the key point is that it is not the Client instance doing it. Concerns have been separated as they should be. The Strategy Pattern is quite a common thing to see in modern PHP. Runtime algorithm selection is a ubiquitous problem, and this pattern is Tried and Tested™.

As before, here is a list of well-known behavioral patterns for you to read up on at your own convenience:

- Chain of Responsibility (notify handler objects in a chain, each one deciding whether to process or pass to the next)
- Command (package an event/request a stand-alone object containing all necessary information for processing)
- Iterator (traverse a collection without exposing the underlying structure, e.g., list, tree, etc.)
- Mediator (reduce dependency between closely related components by delegating interactions to a single component)

- Memento (save/restore an object's state without revealing implementation details)
- Observer (mechanism for multiple objects to receive notifications about events)
- State (allows an object to change behavior based on internal state)
- Template Method (partially define an algorithm in a superclass; subclasses can override arbitrary steps)
- Visitor (traverse an object structure with a set of algorithms held in a special class)

We'll end our quick journey into design patterns here. The scope of this section is after all to simply introduce the topic and encourage further reading. Hopefully you'll also have spotted that there are strong elements of the SOLID principles to be found in design patterns. For example, the Strategy Pattern demonstrates dependency inversion (by using an interface for the `Strategy` classes), and single responsibility (by moving each strategy into a dedicated class). The Visitor Pattern, although not shown in detail here, is a good example of the open-closed principle: by placing new behavior in the special visitor object, we ensure that the visited object structure remains closed to modification.

As for further reading, there's a wealth of material available online, and a certain PHP-specific text (edited by yours truly) has been mentioned multiple times already. I encourage you to explore!

Summary

Object-orientation by itself is not going to ensure your code is amazing. Like any set of programming language features, it needs to be used correctly. In Chapter 6, "Object Fundamentals," we learned how PHP makes objects work. This chapter was more concerned with how to actually use them well. For that we need to think beyond programming and dip our toes into the world of analysis and design.

Hopefully, by giving you a basic introduction to the concept of the problem and solution spaces and modular decomposition, I've whetted your appetites for more study. I promise this will pay dividends if you intend to pursue programming as (at the very least) a meaningful pastime. The more thought you give to why your software needs to exist, who is going to use it, and for what, the better your code will be. In particular, a well-designed class hierarchy will make for an easier time as you build out functionality. A messily implemented method can be rewritten with impunity provided there's no change to the public interface (that's the beauty of OOP), but a badly designed set of classes is going to cause headaches (and likely be thrown away and rewritten down the road). As the saying goes, weeks of coding can save you days of planning.

We also looked at the SOLID principles, which in turn underpin design patterns. You will find these principles and patterns used everywhere in enterprise-grade PHP software. The most popular frameworks and tools are chock full of strategy-this and mediator-that (often given other names, but if you know the patterns, you'll start spotting them everywhere). If the classes you create adhere to SOLID, then they will stand up to reuse and integrate easily with other code.

CHAPTER 11

Programming for the Internet

Finally, we come to what can probably be appropriately described as the crux of the entire book. It is also the final chapter of the book; everything that has come before has been leading up to this. PHP was originally created by Rasmus Lerdorf for processing hypertext (HTML) on web servers (aka "the backend"). It was only natural that PHP's feature set grew to include tools for dealing with HTML-adjacent tasks, such as interacting with the protocols for transferring hypertext (HTTP), connecting to databases, transferring files (FTP), or sending email (SMTP). In the very first chapter – "Getting Started" – we saw how PHP can be run via various server APIs (SAPIs) the majority of which involve some form of web server. PHP even has a limited server built in, though it exists purely for development purposes and is not to be used in any other context. PHP – standing first for *Personal HomePage*, then later *PHP Hypertext Preprocessor* – and the internet have grown together over the last twenty-plus years, and certainly the PHP of today (version 8.4) is a far cry from anything that came before version 5.

The vast majority of code examples in this book have been deliberately created to be agnostic of the SAPI, you should have had equal success typing them into an interactive PHP shell (via `php -a`), running them from files (via `php file.php`), or via the slightly more convoluted web-server SAPIs. The intent was to demonstrate the language features free from context: numbers, strings, arrays, objects... these will all do the same things whether the SAPI is `cli`, `php-fpm`, `cli-server`, and so on. However, there are certain aspects of the language (e.g., some of the string handling functions) that I've kept back until now because they exist to solve common problems when your code executes within the context of an HTTP request. With that in mind, every code example in this chapter is intended to be run via some form of PHP web SAPI: please revisit Chapter 1, "Getting Started", for information on how to get PHP running via a web server if you aren't sure how to do this.

In order to understand those PHP features that are specific to web use cases it's a good idea to look at the fundamentals underpinning the internet itself. Therefore, we'll be looking at the basics of internet application protocols (HTTP, FTP, SMTP), and HTML (Hypertext Markup Language). From there we'll examine common security issues that can arise when dealing with user input (which is never *ever* to be trusted), and in particular when that data has to be passed to other systems (such as databases or passed back to web clients). We'll then close out the chapter by looking at some of the great tools that are out there in Open-Source land that will enable you to build robust, secure, and scalable applications for today's internet. The topics covered in this chapter are

- Internet protocols
- Lifecycle of an HTTP request in PHP
- HTML
- The DOM
- Traversing and modifying the DOM
- Templating
- Input validation and sanitizing

Hypertext Transfer Protocol (HTTP)

Unless you've been living under a rock for the last twenty-five years, you'll have heard of this thing called "the Internet," and likely be more than familiar with its use. You've probably used an application called a web browser (Chrome, Firefox, Edge, Opera… maybe even Internet Explorer if you are of sufficient vintage!) on a device such as a laptop, smartphone, or perhaps even a TV or games console, which magically (or not so magically, depending on the depth of your knowledge) receives beautifully constructed pages of information and functionality from a (usually) remote computer elsewhere in the world. In this scenario, your device is the *client*, and the machine sending you your page is the (web) *server*. This shouldn't be particularly revelatory, especially if you have read Chapter 1, "Getting Started", where we looked at multiple ways of running a web server together with PHP (or indeed, using PHP as a limited-functionality web server). The client and server might even be running on the same machine, which is often the case in a development environment (and also very likely if you're following along at home with the examples in this chapter).

Web clients and servers have to follow a set of rules and procedures in order to successfully and correctly exchange data. These rules are more accurately known as *protocols*, which operate at various layers of your system (from network hardware up to the web application itself), and there are dozens of them involved in the process of requesting and interacting with web pages. For the internet, these rules are defined in a set of standards documents known as RFCs (Requests for Comments) by an organization called the IETF (Internet Engineering Task Force). RFCs describe in fine detail how systems should interoperate and, for the most part, boil down to when and what messages (usually in the form of strings of English text) should be sent over the network connection. For example, RFC 1945 – which can be found at `https://www.ietf.org/rfc/rfc1945.txt` – is the original standards document for HTTP (dating from 1996 and since obsoleted several times by more current standards). It's never a terrible idea to read RFCs, but it's rare that you'll need to know about any particular protocol in that level of detail – you'll be glad to know no such knowledge is assumed or required for this chapter. In this section, we'll examine in detail the protocol that you will encounter most when using PHP to build web applications.

The Hypertext Transfer Protocol is an application layer set of rules that enable the exchange of hypertext documents (and other related resource types) between systems via a lower-level (network) protocol (such as TCP/IP). HTTPS is simply HTTP with transport layer security (TLS) baked in to provide encryption to all the data exchanged between client and server; there is little functional difference as far as PHP is concerned. With HTTP, a *client* initiates a connection and then sends a *request message*. This message is then handled by another system acting as the *server*, which sends data back to the client in a *response message*. We won't go deep into the network side of things (you'll need another book for that); just know that after a bit of low-level negotiation between the client and server, a network connection is established between the two (by convention on TCP port 80 for HTTP and TCP 443 for HTTPS). Both request and response messages are simply a byte stream of ASCII text sequences that adhere to the protocol specification.

Please bear in mind that this section won't be an exhaustive reference for HTTP – we're just going to focus on the aspects commonly seen when processing web requests in PHP (e.g., you'll likely never need to worry about handling a CONNECT request in PHP; these are intended for controlling proxy servers). For the full details on HTTP (and other related technologies), I highly recommend looking at the Mozilla Foundation's excellent developer reference documents; the HTTP reference guide can be found at `https://developer.mozilla.org/en-US/docs/Web/HTTP`.

CHAPTER 11   PROGRAMMING FOR THE INTERNET

URLs

HTTP is driven by URLs (Uniform Resource Locators), which are specially formed strings that contain enough information for a client to make the right request, for the right resource, at the right location. The client making the request will parse the URL and use the encoded information to drive the HTTP request. URLs are formed from up to five "components"...

- Scheme (usually the desired protocol)
- Authority (domain name, port number)
- Path
- Query (sometimes called "parameters")
- Fragment (sometimes called "anchor")

...and take the form `scheme:<//authority>path<?query><#fragment>`. For our purposes here, `<scheme>` will be `http` or `https`. The following examples illustrate this syntax; each URL conforms to the pattern of scheme, authority, path, and so on, though not all components are required for a URL to be valid.

- `http://some.server.com/insecure.php`
- `http://some.server.com/index.html#magic_id`
- `https://pault:notsosecret@my.domain.com:4430/chapters?name=How_the_internet_works`
- `file:///Users/pault/Documents/local_file.php`

First, we have `http://some.server.com/insecure.php`, which instructs an HTTP client to connect to the server at `some.server.com` on TCP 80 (the default port) and ask for the resource found at `/insecure.php` – all very straightforward (and unencrypted).

Next is a similar URL but with a fragment (or anchor) component, which acts like a "bookmark" within the resource: in the case of HTTP URLs, the browser will use this fragment data to scroll to wherever in the document a matching element identifier can be found. It's worth noting that the fragment data is never sent to the server; it is only used by the client.

The next URL is more complex: its authority component contains both a "userinfo" subcomponent (which is a username and password combination delimited from the rest of the component by the @ character) and a TCP port number (delimited by the : character). An HTTP client using this URL is going to connect to TCP 4430 (not the standard HTTPS port of TCP 443). There is also the query component (delimited by ?) which would assign a value of "How_the_internet_works" to a "name" parameter (which is exposed via a superglobal). What about that userinfo subcomponent of pault:notsosecret? Well, there was a time when that data would end up in an HTTP header and be used for basic authorization, but browser support has long since been withdrawn (and rightly so). Userinfo data is not made available anywhere in PHP.

Finally, purely for illustration and comparison, the URL file:///Users/... uses the "file" scheme and has no authority component at all, which is fine. A URL component without characters is considered to be empty, and the only component that cannot be empty is the scheme. So, in this case, the local system is assumed to be the recipient of the request, the path is /Users/pault/Documents/local_file.php, and a URL like this, if used with a web browser, would simply have it open the file. All that's going to happen here though is the contents of local_file.php will be rendered as text (web browsers don't execute PHP, nor should they).

Those of you vaguely familiar with how URLs work might be wondering about query strings at this point. Query strings are another data-passing method that operate via the path portion of the URL string and are appended with a ? separator character – https://some.domain.com/index.html?foo=bar is a URL with a query string foo=bar. Query strings are not part of the HTTP specification as such: provision was made for them in URL syntax in the original RFC, but they were otherwise dealt with in a separate document (RFC 3986). Even then no formal standard defines their operation (although the standards do assert what they *shouldn't* do), and they operate purely on well-established conventions. We'll get to those in a moment when we look at resource paths in more detail; meanwhile, let's examine what happens when an HTTP request is made.

HTTP(S) Requests

From the perspective of PHP, the main components of an HTTP(S) request message are *method*, *resource path*, *headers*, and *body*. In addition, a special header-based mechanism exists (as an extension to the HTTP specification) known as *cookies* (you've probably heard of them). The client and server communicate using the HTTP protocol, and eventually PHP is invoked (via Common Gateway Interface, or as an embedded Apache module) with the request data made available via superglobal variables or built-in functions. According to the protocol specification, once the TCP connection is established, an HTTP client should start by sending a request line constructed like so:

- Request method (case sensitive) followed by a single space
- Resource path (commonly known as the URI) and another space
- Protocol version
- ASCII CR\LF bytes (carriage-return, line-feed)

These are the very first bytes the web server should receive after the connection is established. Here's an example request line: `GET /index.html HTTP/1.1`, which uses the `GET` method (more on this in a moment) to fetch the resource located via the path `/index.html` (which could be a simple file containing HTML text or something more complex that generates HTML output), using version 1.1 of the HTTP protocol. That's really all there is to the HTTP protocol: roughly human-readable strings of text. I should note here that HTTP/2 onwards uses something called a *binary framing layer*, which encapsulates the request line and headers and turns them into something more machine-optimized for performance reasons, but the heart of the protocol is still the HTTP/1.1 text we're covering here. Note that there is one HTTP method (`CONNECT`) that does not require a resource path.

After the request line come the request header fields, which hold a wide variety of metadata for the request. Headers are used to communicate additional information about the request, such as the client's capabilities and preferences. Some headers are also specific to the response and give detail about encoding, compression, instructions for caching, and so on. A header line is structured in the following way:

- Header name
- Colon character followed by an optional space
- The header's value
- Another optional space

Each header is separated by a `CR\LF` sequence. HTTP 1.1 requires at least the "Host" header (prior to 1.1 there are no request header requirements); here's an example header: `Host: www.example.com`, and the value is, of course, taken from the hostname portion of the URL. As noted earlier, the `Cookie:` header is special: you'll likely have heard of these, and thanks to recent regulation, you will have needed to give permission for their use on just about all websites based in an EU country. HTTP cookies are a client-side data storage mechanism, with a persistence mechanism operating via the client filesystem (cookies are not "the files" per se; some only ever live in memory) and important enough to have dedicated PHP functions and their own honorable mention later in this section.

Finally, after the request line and headers are sent, the request may then contain an optional body. The request body is simply arbitrary data that the server generally requires to successfully complete the request. This data might be an encoded set of fields and values, a web form submission, or a stream of JSON (JavaScript Object Notation) formatted text. It could even be binary data, which presents some challenges, which we'll be looking at in the *Transport Safety* section. Now, with the three main components of the *request message* in mind, let's look in more detail at these components.

Request Methods

The current HTTP standard (RFC 9110) allows the following tokens for the request method (sometimes called the "verb"); the following table is taken from the RFC document.

Table 11-1. HTML request methods

Token	Description
GET	Transfer a current representation of the target resource.
HEAD	Same as GET, but do not transfer the response content.
POST	Perform resource-specific processing on the request content.
PUT	Replace all current representations of the target resource with the request content.
DELETE	Remove all current representations of the target resource.
CONNECT	Establish a tunnel to the server identified by the target resource.
OPTIONS	Describe the communication options for the target resource.
TRACE	Perform a message loop-back test along the path to the target resource.

CHAPTER 11   PROGRAMMING FOR THE INTERNET

These methods are intended to control the behavior of the web server, forming an overarching agreement between the client and server about what effects on the target resource the request will have. Some methods – such as GET or HEAD – do not change the resource: these are read-only methods used only to fetch data. Other methods are intended to cause some change to the resource: PUT creates the resource, POST is intended to trigger some processing or partial change, and of course DELETE is for removing the resource. There is also an HTTP extension method, PATCH, which is not part of the RFC 9110 standard (it is instead proposed in RFC 5789) but is supported by cli-server. PATCH is intended for "partial updates," and such a request would only contain the data required for the partial update. It is quite common to see POST requests doing the job of PATCH.

It's about time we saw some of this working within the context of PHP, so let's launch a web server and make a request so we can see how to interact with request data. PHP's cli-server SAPI is a good choice here; after all, its intended use is for quick-and-dirty debugging and development. Way back in Chapter 1, "Getting Started", we saw how to run a Dockerized PHP web server, but here's a quick recap. Open two command line terminals, and make sure the current directory is the same for both (you can check with the $ pwd command on just about any *nix-like system). In the first one, run the following command:

```
$ docker run -it --rm \
  -p 8080:8080 \
  -v "$PWD":/usr/src/myapp \
  -w /usr/src/myapp \
  php:8.4-cli \
  php -S 0.0.0.0:8080
```

After the docker output (potentially fetching the php:8.4-cli image if it isn't found on your system), you should see the following line...

```
PHP 8.4.6 Development Server (http://0.0.0.0:8080) started
```

... which means the PHP cli binary is bound to TCP 8080 and ready to accept requests from any IP address. Leave this terminal window running, and in another, create a file called index.php. This file needs to exist where the PHP web server was run (as per the -v "$PWD":/usr/src/myapp command line option). The contents of the file should be...

CHAPTER 11   PROGRAMMING FOR THE INTERNET

```
<?php

$method = $_SERVER['REQUEST_METHOD'];
print "HTTP request method: {$method}" . PHP_EOL;
```

… and we're now ready to make an HTTP request to fetch it. We'll use a common *nix CLI utility called curl for this…

```
$ curl http://localhost:8080/index.php
HTTP request method: GET
```

… but you could also use a web browser if you prefer. Remember to enter the full http://localhost:8080/index.php URL into the browser address bar: Most browsers will default to the https scheme, and PHP's cli-server will not handle HTTPS requests. You should see the following response:

Figure 11-1. *Successful response page*

In either case, you will have HTTP request method: GET in the output, and if you check the terminal running the PHP cli-server process, you'll see some log data too:

```
[...] 172.17.0.1:50752 [200]: GET /index.php
[...] 172.17.0.1:50752 Closing
```

Notice the line that contains the method GET and resource path /index.php – the [200] part indicates the HTTP *response code* (which, in this case, is 200 OK, shorthand for "the request completed successfully," more to come on these messages soon). We can also use curl with an option to easily change the request method:

```
$ curl -X 'POST' http://localhost:8080/index.php
HTTP request method: POST
$ curl -X 'PUT' http://localhost:8080/index.php
HTTP request method: PUT
```

Now, if you remember the table from earlier, POST and PUT are methods that are intended to change the state of the resource on the server. If you check the contents of index.php, you will note that they haven't changed. Nor do we have any data source backing the PHP code, which might have changed. The HTTP method is fundamentally just a string with a particular meaning in terms of the protocol specification: the web server isn't obliged to change state just because it received a POST request, just as it isn't obliged to prevent state change on a GET request. It's up to the web server's implementation to honor the contract made by accepting the request: you, dear programmer, need to make sure each PUT, PATCH, POST et al. behaves correctly. If our simple code inside index.php isn't capable of correctly handling anything other than a GET request, we should probably update it...

```
$method = $_SERVER['REQUEST_METHOD'];
if ($method !== 'GET') {
    print "HTTP request method not allowed: {$method}" . PHP_EOL;
} else {
    print "HTTP request method: {$method}" . PHP_EOL;
}
```

... and now we should get a different response body depending on the method we use:

```
$ curl -X 'PUT' http://localhost:8080/index.php
HTTP request method not allowed: PUT
```

We could even get a little ahead of ourselves and turn our attention to the response message side of the protocol. The `curl` command above should have generated a line like this in the `cli-server` terminal:

```
[...] 172.17.0.1:54154 [200]: PUT /index.php
[...] 172.17.0.1:54154 Closing
```

Notice the 200 response code, which means "OK" in the context of a GET request. But is this really OK? Imagine if index.php was supposed to return the homepage of your shiny website? What if there's a response code for this situation, where the server is telling us off for not using the correct method token? In fact there is – 405 Method Not Allowed – so let's add that in too...

```
$method = $_SERVER['REQUEST_METHOD'];

if ($method !== 'GET') {
    http_response_code(405);
    print "HTTP request method not allowed: {$method}" . PHP_EOL;
} else {
    http_response_code(200);
    print "HTTP request method: {$method}" . PHP_EOL;
}
```

... and now when we run curl -X 'PUT' http://localhost:8080/index.php and check the cli-server log, we see this:

```
[...] 172.17.0.1:60330 [405]: PUT /index.php
```

By using PHP's built-in http_response_code() function, we can set the status of the response message: 405 Method Not Allowed if the method isn't GET; otherwise, 200 OK. And, importantly, we as engineers are a step closer to being responsible citizens of the internet. Users often don't get to see HTTP statuses, but machines always do. Anyone using your web application to power their own will thank you for taking the time to properly indicate what went on inside your systems or will at least complain if you don't!

The vast majority of the time you'll be dealing with GET, POST, PUT, PATCH, and DELETE. Choosing which method(s) to implement for a particular resource should be a matter of what happens to the resource in the event of a successful request, and getting that choice right means you'll have an HTTP interface that is logical and easy to use elsewhere. To aid in the choosing, it is necessary to give some thought to a key feature of HTTP methods: *idempotence*.

Idempotence

Have you ever experienced a social media platform (or an online forum, if you're as old as me) creating two comments or posts despite only ever hitting the save button once? A common scenario is that the server was able to create the new resource but did not respond with a success message (or did not respond in time). At this point, the request might automatically retry or report an error and have you retry manually, depending on the logic implemented in the client... And now you have two copies of your message on the server. This happens because the different HTTP methods for changing resources (POST, PUT, DELETE, and PATCH) vary in their idempotence: an idempotent operation is simply one that can be repeated many times without any subsequent change in state beyond the initial change. POST requests are not idempotent and should therefore result in a change in state every time they are made regardless of the data, and this is where we get the multiple comments/forum posts from when web apps have slight hiccups.

As noted earlier, PUT requests will contain all the data necessary to create a new resource or fully replace an existing one. Therefore, making the same PUT request repeatedly should have the same effect as making it (successfully) once, and such a request is said to be idempotent. GET, HEAD, OPTIONS, and TRACE are all technically idempotent too (and indeed these four methods are also said to be "safe" because they should never result in any data changing on the server). DELETE requests are idempotent because you can only delete a specific resource once. On the other hand, POST and PATCH requests are not idempotent, because they do not replace entire resources.

When considering if the request your application handles should be POST, PUT, etc., consider what would happen if the request was replayed with identical data. If the second request should result in a different state for, say, entities in your database, then the request is not idempotent, and you should go with POST (or PATCH).

Resource Paths and Routing

Now, I appreciate that the idea of idempotent methods and choosing the most correct HTTP method for the operation might not make much sense right now. So far we've been considering resource paths in terms of them mapping directly to different files that can be read by the web server: GET /index.php causes the web server (PHP's built-in cli-server in the case of this chapter so far) to search for a file called index.php in some part of the server's filesystem, read (or perhaps execute via CGI binary) the contents, and shove the results into the request body. POST /subdir/entity.php has the server traversing the filesystem to the subdir sub-directory and looking for the file entity.php... and so on.

This one-to-one mapping of resource paths in requests to files on a disk is fine for small projects, but web servers today are capable of far more complexity, and it is more common these days to logically decouple the URI from the file where all the magic begins. Typically, you will configure the server to first check if the resource exists on disk, and if not, then fall back to a single file (by convention, this file is usually index.php). What benefits could this bring? Consider a more complex resource path, one that might include a more meaningful filename and a query string with metadata used to locate a record in a database, such as /article.php?id=12345. Without needing to worry about what code lives inside article.php, we can guess that it is targeting a specific article entity indicated by the id query parameter. To differentiate between CRUD (Create, Read, Update, Delete) operations, you might put the relevant functionality into differently named PHP files: read_article.php, delete_article.php, and so forth. The trouble here is that we're accumulating URLs, and they're not particularly pretty. What if we could replace this...

- /read_article?id=123
- /create_article
- /delete_article?id=123
- /update_article?id=123

... with this:

- GET /article/123
- POST /article
- PUT /article/123
- DELETE /article/123
- PATCH /article/123

Hopefully we can all agree that the second URL scheme is far tidier; it's also more SEO-friendly, which will make any members of your team with the word "product" in their job title much happier! The key innovation is that we've removed the ?id=x query parameter and replaced it with a path component. For this to work we need to move the logic of mapping the HTTP resource path out of the web server and into our application, where we have far more freedom. To achieve this, you'll need to configure the web server to fall back to a single file when it can't map the path in the request to a filepath on the server.

Going back to our nginx web server (for which we're using the same resources found in the "Web Server Integration" section of Chapter 1, "Getting Started"), we're now going to update the main nginx config file (`default.conf`). Here's that file with a few alterations:

```
server {
    listen 0.0.0.0:80;
    root /var/www/html;
    location / {
        try_files $uri /index.php$is_args$args;
    }
    location ~ ^/index\.php($/|$) {
        include fastcgi_params;
        fastcgi_pass php-fpm:9000;
        fastcgi_index index.php;
        fastcgi_param SCRIPT_FILENAME $document_root/$fastcgi_script_name;
    }
}
```

The main difference is the `location /` block, which used to contain `index index.php index.html;` – this simply told the server that requests for the root path should be mapped to index.php or index.html. Now we have a `try_files` directive set up to fall back to index.php if it cannot find a file that maps to the requested resource. We'll use a slightly tweaked `docker-compose.yaml` file here to force Docker to build us a new image:

```
version: "3"
services:
  nginx:
    build:
      context: .
      dockerfile: ./Dockerfile
    image: paultregoing/nginx:http_routing
    ports:
      - "8080:80"
    networks:
      - internal
    volumes:
      - ./:/var/www/html
```

```
  php-fpm:
    image: php:8.4-fpm
    networks:
      - internal
    volumes:
      - ./:/var/www/html
networks:
  internal:
    driver: bridge
```

The Dockerfile that this depends on is as follows:

```
FROM nginx:1.25
ADD default.conf /etc/nginx/conf.d
```

The only thing left to do is run `docker compose`, which should leave us with a containerized nginx server. This nginx instance is configured to serve a default `index.php` script if the URL doesn't specify a particular resource. Stop any other running containers, such as the PHP `cli-server` from earlier, using `docker ps` and `docker container stop`, then get building:

```
$ docker compose up
...
 ✓ Container nginx-php-fpm-1   Created        0.1s
 ✓ Container nginx-nginx-1     Created        0.1s
Attaching to nginx-nginx-1, nginx-php-fpm-1
...
nginx-php-fpm-1  | [28-Aug-2025 15:56:51] NOTICE: fpm is running, pid 1
nginx-php-fpm-1  | [28-Aug-2025 15:56:51] NOTICE: ready to handle
connections
```

The last two lines in the log output ("fpm is running" and "ready to handle connections") let us know that the nginx container is now running in the foreground and logging to STDOUT/STDERR. Make sure the following code is placed in `index.php`, which must reside in the same directory where you ran `docker compose up`:

```
$routes = [
    'new.article' => [
        'method' => 'POST',
```

CHAPTER 11   PROGRAMMING FOR THE INTERNET

```
            'pattern' => '/^\/article$/',
        ],
        'read.article' => [
            'method' => 'GET',
            'pattern' => '/^\/article\/\d*$/',
        ]
    ];

    $uri = $_SERVER['REQUEST_URI'];
    $method = $_SERVER['REQUEST_METHOD'];
    $matchedRoute = match_route($routes, $uri, $method);

    print "HTTP Method: '{$method}'" . PHP_EOL;
    print "Requested resource path is '{$uri}'" . PHP_EOL;
    print "Matched resource path and method to route '{$matchedRoute}'" .
    PHP_EOL;

    function match_route(array $routes, string $uri, string $method): ?string
    {
        foreach ($routes as $route => $meta) {
            if (
                $meta['method'] === $method &&
                preg_match($meta['pattern'], $uri)
            ) {
                return $route;
            }
        }
        return null;
    }
```

Before we look in detail at how this code works, let's see what it does:

```
$ curl -X 'POST' http://localhost:8080/article
HTTP Method: 'POST'
Requested resource path is '/article'
Matched resource path and method to route 'new.article'
```

```
$ curl -X 'GET' http://localhost:8080/article/123
HTTP Method: 'GET'
Requested resource path is '/article/123'
Matched resource path and method to route 'read.article'
```

What we have created here is a rudimentary URL *router*. This is a very common concept, which you will encounter in many mainstream PHP frameworks, such as Symfony. The code in `index.php` simply examines the HTTP method and applies a regular expression to the contents of the `$_SERVER['REQUEST_URI']` superglobal. It's common convention for router libraries to consider both the request method and path when matching routes. In our case, the method and URI pattern are mapped to a route name (which we've implemented as a simple check on the keys of the `$routes` array). If the HTTP method and URI pattern match, then we could go on to call the function or object method intended to handle that particular request. In a production-quality framework, routing is usually config-driven (either in standalone config or, more commonly, by adding annotations or PHP attributes to classes and methods designed to interact with HTTP requests). I encourage you to investigate further, and the Symfony Routing component is an excellent place to start. https://symfony.com/doc/current/routing.html

Request Headers

An important aspect of HTTP requests to be aware of is the *headers*. These are implemented in the protocol simply as lines of text containing the header field name, a colon character, and the value of the header. They are, however, used for some fairly serious things, such as controlling server (or proxy) behavior, precisely describing the size and nature of request data, or the capabilities of the client… which makes them quite powerful little lines of text!

In terms of the protocol, headers come after the initial request line, and each `field: value` pair is separated by a new line. Header fields are standardized in the IANA HTTP Field Name Registry and are fully documented at https://www.iana.org/assignments/http-fields/http-fields.xhtml, which will make excellent bedtime reading if you are having trouble sleeping. Header fields can be grouped by their context; for example, the `Content-Length:` header field might describe the size (in bytes) of the response data or the payload data in the request. You might encounter the concept of "request headers" in terms of those fields only used for controlling a request (in other words, "request-only" headers such as `User-Agent:`, `Accept:`, or `Referrer:`), but for our purposes, here we're simply interested in all of the headers set by the client when the request is made.

The most reliable way to get the request headers is via the $_SERVER superglobal. Put the following code into a file index.php and serve with the container of your choice. You could carry on with the nginx container we just built or take it down and run another cli-server. It's up to you.

```
// index.php
var_dump($_SERVER);
```

Assuming you're running your server on TCP 8080, try the following curl command:

```
$ curl http://localhost:8080/index.php
array(19) {
  ["DOCUMENT_ROOT"]=>
  string(14) "/usr/src/myapp"
  ["REMOTE_ADDR"]=>
  string(10) "172.17.0.1"
  ...
  ["HTTP_HOST"]=>
  string(14) "localhost:8080"
  ["HTTP_USER_AGENT"]=>
  string(10) "curl/8.7.1"
  ["HTTP_ACCEPT"]=>
  string(3) "*/*"
  ...
```

Pay attention to all of the array keys starting with HTTP_ ... These are the header fields sent in the request. Each field name is capitalized, prepended with HTTP_, and any dashes in the field names are replaced with underscores (thus User-Agent: becomes HTTP_USER_AGENT, and so on). The value of the field is mapped to the key in $_SERVER. We can test this by injecting our own headers with a -H 'Header: value' option in the curl request:

```
$ curl -H 'X-Custom-Header: some value' http://localhost:8080/index.php
  ...
  ["HTTP_X_CUSTOM_HEADER"]=>
  string(10) "some value"
  ...
```

CHAPTER 11 PROGRAMMING FOR THE INTERNET

Note that the convention of adding X- to "custom" headers is officially deprecated, but you will see it used in abundance even today. If you are running the cli-server SAPI or any flavor of the Apache SAPI, PHP provides the getallheaders() convenience function for obtaining request headers:

```
// index.php
var_dump(getallheaders());
$ curl -H 'X-Custom-Header: some value' http://localhost:8080/index.php
array(4) {
  ["Host"]=>
  string(14) "localhost:8080"
  ["User-Agent"]=>
  string(10) "curl/8.7.1"
  ["Accept"]=>
  string(3) "*/*"
  ["X-Custom-Header"]=>
  string(10) "some value"
}
```

One thing to note: the HTTP specification allows for multiple instances of a field in the headers. We can demonstrate this by writing another PHP script to request the one we've been using up to now, and it also serves as a handy demo for writing your own socket-level HTTP requests in PHP code:

```
$opts = ['http' => [
    'method' => 'GET',
    'header' => [
        'User-Agent: PHP',
        'X-Foo: foo',
        'X-Foo: bar',
    ],
]];

$res = file_get_contents(
    filename: 'http://localhost:8080/index.php',
    context: stream_context_create($opts)
);
```

```
var_dump($res);
```

Output:

```
...
["HTTP_USER_AGENT"]=>
string(3) "PHP"
["HTTP_X_FOO"]=>
string(8) "foo, bar"
...
```

You'll need to run this via a CLI PHP binary that isn't containerized so it is able to access port 8080 of the host, or make sure your CLI container is able to communicate with your server container (a fun exercise for the reader). Notice that the HTTP_X_FOO value is assigned foo, bar, which is the semantics for a value list in the HTTP RFC. If you find yourself doing any heavy lifting with making HTTP requests in PHP, I highly recommend the Guzzle library (which has a fairly painless interface for making promise-based asynchronous requests to speed things up), which you can find at https://github.com/guzzle/guzzle.

Cookies

Closely related to headers are cookies. These are the things that recent EU law required websites to warn us about on the first visit, generally with annoying pop-ups. You'll probably know that they're little snippets of data that usually wind up clogging up some corner of your browser profile data (e.g., Chrome implements persistent cookies as an on-disk SQLite database). Cookies are simple at heart; they're just text-based key/value pairs. They are passed to the server via the Cookie: request header (and can be set by the server in the Set-Cookie: response header); each cookie pair in the header is separated by a semicolon. When cookies are set, it is usually with some metadata to bind them to a domain (or sub-domain) and path with an expiry timestamp (any cookies set without an expiry will be treated as "session-only" and vanish once the browser is closed). On each request the browser will check its cookie storage and find all those that match the domain and path URL components and haven't expired yet.

CHAPTER 11 PROGRAMMING FOR THE INTERNET

PHP makes request cookies available via the $_COOKIE superglobal (make sure the variables_order ini directive contains a "C" in its value). Let's have a quick demo:

```
// index.php
var_dump($_COOKIE);
```

The curl binary allows us to send multiple cookie pairs with the -b switch:

```
$ curl -b cat=miaow -b dog=woof http://localhost:8080/index.php
array(2) {
  ["cat"]=>
  string(5) "miaow"
  ["dog"]=>
  string(4) "woof"
}
```

Here's another way to do it, using the Cookie: header:

```
$ curl -H 'Cookie: cat=miaow; dog=woof' http://localhost:8080/index.php
```

To set cookies in the response, use the setcookie() and setrawcookie() functions:

```
// index.php
setcookie(
    name: 'flavour',
    value: 'choc chip obvs'
);
print "Thanks for visiting!\n";
```

To see the effect of setting a cookie, we need to see the response headers, which requires running curl in verbose mode with -v:

```
$ curl -v http://localhost:8080/index.php
* Host localhost:8080 was resolved.
* IPv6: ::1
* IPv4: 127.0.0.1
*   Trying [::1]:8080...
* Connected to localhost (::1) port 8080
> GET /index.php HTTP/1.1
> Host: localhost:8080
```

```
> User-Agent: curl/8.7.1
> Accept: */*
>
* Request completely sent off
< HTTP/1.1 200 OK
< Host: localhost:8080
< Date: Tue, 08 Jul 2025 15:32:00 GMT
< Connection: close
< X-Powered-By: PHP/8.4.6
< Set-Cookie: flavour=choc%20chip%20obvs
< Content-type: text/html; charset=UTF-8
<
Thanks for visiting!
* Closing connection
```

Don't be alarmed if the formatting of your output varies slightly from that given above; different versions of cURL, different platforms... such is the nature of open-source software. The important details will still line up: the header names and values should be identical. Note that the Set-Cookie: header has been encoded, with spaces transformed to the character sequence %20. This specific encoding format is known as "url encoding," which turns certain illegal characters in URLs into numeric sequences prepended with a % symbol. We'll be looking at common encoding methods in a later section of this chapter when we examine security concerns.

The original cookie specification from Netscape (shout out to anyone old enough to remember Navigator) stated that space, comma, and semicolon were illegal characters, and although most modern systems will handle spaces in cookie data, it's a good idea to encode them. Should you need it, PHP's setrawcookie() does away with the encoding. Remember that cookies are set by headers and therefore cannot be sent if even a single byte of the response body has been sent. In the example above we created a very simple key/value cookie with no other information, and we can see in the Set-Cookie: header there is no expiry timestamp, so this cookie is session-only. If we add an integer timestamp to the setcookie() call, then we can add a UTC timestamp, which will have the effect of persisting the cookie:

```
// index.php
setcookie(
    name: 'flavour',
```

```
    value: 'choc chip obvs',
    expires_or_options: time() + 3600,
);
print "Thanks for visiting!\n";

$ curl -v http://localhost:8080/index.php
...
< Set-Cookie: flavour=choc%20chip%20obvs; expires=Wed, 09 Jul 2025 10:42:08
GMT; Max-Age=3600
```

To delete a cookie, simply set the `expires_or_options` parameter to a timestamp in the past, which will instruct the client to remove the cookie from its store.

```
setcookie(
    name: 'flavour',
    value: '',
    expires_or_options: time() - 3600,
)
```

One more thing to note, it is possible to create structured cookie data by using array notation like this...

```
// index.php
setcookie(
    name: 'flavour[best]',
    value: 'choc chip obvs'
);
setcookie(
    name: 'flavour[worst]',
    value: 'there is no worst'
);
```

... which would result in two `Set-Cookie:` response headers:

```
...
< Set-Cookie: flavour[best]=choc%20chip%20obvs
< Set-Cookie: flavour[worst]=there%20is%20no%20worst
```

The subsequent Cookie: request header would then appear as Cookie: flavour[best]=choc%20chip%20obvs; flavour[worst]=there%20is%20no%20worst and would result in the following data appearing in $_COOKIE:

```
array(1) {
  ["flavour"]=>
  array(2) {
    ["best"]=>
    string(14) "choc chip obvs"
    ["worst"]=>
    string(17) "there is no worst"
  }
}
```

That said, it is not unusual to see structured cookie data encoded as JSON. There is some haziness surrounding the support for structured data in the specification – RFC6265, sections 4 and 5 https://datatracker.ietf.org/doc/html/rfc6265 – and using a JSON string neatly steps around the problem.

Query String Data

If URL routing and headers don't meet your needs for data passing, we have some additional mechanisms to look at. We've already touched upon query strings above, which allow arbitrary data to be sent from client to server during requests. The request data (aka "payload") itself has some handy utility wrappers; PHP exposes request data in a couple of easy-to-use ways.

Query strings operate on a key=value basis and are placed after the resource path in the URL (delimited by a ? character), with each key/value pair delimited by a & character. PHP has a number of helper functions for parsing and constructing these URL components; we'll focus on the parsing here. Create a new index.php and serve as before; the contents simply need to be as follows:

```
// index.php
var_dump($_GET);

$ curl 'http://localhost:8080/index.php?foo=bar&cow=moo'
array(2) {
  ["foo"]=>
```

```
    string(3) "bar"
    ["cow"]=>
    string(3) "moo"
}
```

You'll see that $_GET contains our query data, all neatly parsed into an associative array (please note the URL argument to the `curl` command is enclosed in quotes because most shells will treat the & as a special character). It is also possible to give structure to query string data, using familiar-looking array syntax:

```
$ curl 'http://localhost:8080/index.php?animals[]=cat&animals[]=dog'
array(1) {
  ["animals"]=>
  array(2) {
    [0]=>
    string(3) "cat"
    [1]=>
    string(3) "dog"
  }
}
```

... and even associative arrays (make sure to add -g to the curl command to avoid a parsing error by the curl binary):

```
$ curl -g 'http://localhost:8080/index.php?animals[feline]=cat&animals[canine]=dog'
array(1) {
  ["animals"]=>
  array(2) {
    ["feline"]=>
    string(3) "cat"
    ["canine"]=>
    string(3) "dog"
  }
}
```

CHAPTER 11   PROGRAMMING FOR THE INTERNET

You can also parse raw query strings in PHP (available via $_SERVER['QUERY_STRING']). Using the parse_str() built-in function, the resulting associative array is identical to the one created for $_GET, but you must pass in a variable as a second argument to capture it (I've no idea why it can't just return an array; the older parts of PHP are just like that sometimes):

```
parse_str('animals[]=cat&animals[]=dog', $queryData); // second param
                                                      is by-ref
var_dump($queryData);
```

```
Output:
array(1) {
  ["animals"]=>
  array(2) {
    [0]=>
    string(3) "cat"
    [1]=>
    string(3) "dog"
  }
}
```

Request (Body) Data

All of the query string examples above were made as GET requests (the curl command's default HTTP method if not passing a -X option). Query strings will also work just as well with POST and PUT. The following commands...

```
$ curl -X 'POST' http://localhost:8080/index.php?foo=bar
$ curl -X 'PUT' http://localhost:8080/index.php?foo=bar
```

  ... will produce the same output:

```
array(1) {
  ["foo"]=>
  string(3) "bar"
}
```

It's possibly a little counterintuitive that query string data will always be exposed via $_GET regardless of the request method. Think of it like this: GET requests only really have one option to pass data to the server (the query string). POST and PUT have another mechanism available: the request body. PHP has some helpful automagical convenience features for this too. Create the following index.php...

```
// index.php
var_dump($_SERVER['HTTP_CONTENT_TYPE']);
print PHP_EOL;
var_dump(file_get_contents('php://input'));
print PHP_EOL;
var_dump($_POST);
```

... and make the following curl request:

```
$ curl -X 'POST' -d 'human=anna&cat=jess' http://localhost:8080/index.php
string(33) "application/x-www-form-urlencoded"

string(19) "human=anna&cat=jess"

array(2) {
  ["human"]=>
  string(4) "anna"
  ["cat"]=>
  string(4) "jess"
}
```

There are a few things to pay attention to here. We've changed the request method to POST, and we're supplying string data via the -d option, which tells curl that we want the 'human=anna&cat=jess' string to be transmitted to the server as the request body (so it'll be sent after the initial request line and subsequent request headers). You'll notice that the format is identical to the query strings we've been using previously.

The output above also shows the Content-Type: header, which curl has automatically set to application/x-www-form-urlencoded. Content-Type: is a very important header, and the values allowed are controlled by IANA and known as "media types" (and by their old name: "MIME types"). More details can be found at https://www.iana.org/assignments/media-types/media-types.xhtml. In our case, the application/x-www-form-urlencoded value of this header triggers some behavior on

PHP's part: it will decode the request body, build the corresponding array structure, and expose it via the $_POST superglobal. Here's some slightly more complex form-encoded data:

```
$ curl -X 'POST' -d 'animals[cat]=jess&humans[]=anna&humans[]=paul' \
  'http://localhost:8080/index.php'
...
array(2) {
  ["animals"]=>
  array(1) {
    ["cat"]=>
    string(4) "jess"
  }
  ["humans"]=>
  array(2) {
    [0]=>
    string(4) "anna"
    [1]=>
    string(4) "paul"
  }
}
```

As you can see, the syntax of x-www-form-urlencoded request data works just like the previous query string examples. This way of passing data in POST (and PUT) requests is baked into HTML as the <form> element, which will submit data via a POST request with minimal setup https://developer.mozilla.org/en-US/docs/Web/HTML/Reference/Elements/form. As mentioned above, the automatic decoding of the request data and population of the $_POST superglobal depends on the Content-Type: HTTP header, which must be set to application/x-www-form-urlencoded or multipart/form-data. x-www-form-urlencoded is used for simple form-based data exchange (key/value pairs) as demonstrated here; multipart/form-data is for more complex scenarios including the transmission of binary data (such as files). We'll be looking at this in more detail very shortly.

Another very common approach for sending data to servers is to use JSON, especially when making calls that don't rely on user input (and therefore wouldn't have an HTML form in the loop). As a reminder, here's the code for index.php...

```php
// index.php
var_dump($_SERVER['HTTP_CONTENT_TYPE']);
print PHP_EOL;
var_dump(file_get_contents('php://input'));
print PHP_EOL;
var_dump($_POST);
```

... and here's how we can POST some JSON data with curl:

```
$ curl -X 'POST' -H 'Content-Type: application/json' \
  -d '{"animals":[{"cat":"jess"}],"humans":["anna","paul"]}' \
  'http://localhost:8080/index.php'
string(16) "application/json"

string(44) "{"animals":[{"cat":"jess"}],"humans":["anna","paul"]}"

array(0) {
}
```

Notice that the $_POST superglobal is now just an empty array because we've set the Content-Type: header to application/json, and the request data is now the JSON equivalent of the previous form-encoded string. The request body is still available via a file_get_contents('php://input') call, but we'll have to manually intervene to turn that string into something we can use in our PHP code. Let's tweak index.php a little. We'll make use of PHP's built-in json_decode() function...

```php
// index.php
$json = file_get_contents('php://input');
$requestData = json_decode($json, true);
var_dump($requestData);
```

... and make our curl request again:

```
$ curl -X 'POST' -H 'Content-Type: application/json' \
  -d '{"animals":[{"cat":"jess"}],"humans":["anna","paul"]}' \
  'http://localhost:8080/index.php'
array(2) {
  ["animals"]=>
  array(1) {
    [0]=>
```

```
    array(1) {
      ["cat"]=>
      string(4) "jess"
    }
  }
  ["humans"]=>
  array(2) {
    [0]=>
    string(4) "anna"
    [1]=>
    string(4) "paul"
  }
}
```

json_decode() will return either an associative array or a structure composed of stdClass objects, depending on the second boolean argument: we've opted for an associative array here. JSON is widely used these days for sending structured data in a POST or PUT and is generally preferred because it is very easy to work with in browsers (which run JavaScript). You might also encounter XML in your travels, particularly in older corners of the internet. Let's rejig the example accordingly, using PHP's SimpleXML module, which should be installed by default...

```
// index.php
$requestBody = file_get_contents('php://input');
$xml = new SimpleXMLElement($requestBody);
var_dump($xml->children());
```

... and tweak our curl command by changing Content-Type: to application/xml and reformatting the request data as valid XML:

```
$ curl -X 'POST' -H 'Content-Type: application/xml' \
  -d '<?xml version="1.0" encoding="utf-8"?>
  <data>
  <animals>
    <cat><jess/></cat>
  </animals>
  <humans>
```

```
      <anna/>
      <paul/>
   </humans>
   </data>' \
   'http://localhost:8080/index.php'
object(SimpleXMLElement)#2 (2) {
  ["animals"]=>
  object(SimpleXMLElement)#3 (1) {
    ["cat"]=>
    object(SimpleXMLElement)#5 (1) {
      ["jess"]=>
      object(SimpleXMLElement)#6 (0) {
      }
    }
  }
  ["humans"]=>
  object(SimpleXMLElement)#4 (2) {
    ["anna"]=>
    object(SimpleXMLElement)#5 (0) {
    }
    ["paul"]=>
    object(SimpleXMLElement)#6 (0) {
    }
  }
}
```

There will be more to come on handling HTML and XML data in PHP later in the chapter.

Uploading Complex (and Binary) Data

As mentioned previously in this section, the `multipart/form-data` request media type (as specified via the `Content-Type:` header) should be used for transmitting complex and/or binary request data to a server. In fact, this particular media type will also allow you to mix different data types into a single request: you can upload an image, send JSON or other text, and so on. The default behavior of a web browser using an HTML form to upload file data is to create this type of request, so this is what we'll look at here. (We'll be examining the other side of this equation when we take a look at HTML in the next section.)

A client that is capable of multipart requests (any web browser, or even the curl binary) will split the request into multiple parts separated by a *boundary string*; each part has its own headers and body data. This will make more sense if we look at some practical examples, so let's upload a file first. The behavior around POST uploaded files is controlled by a number of .ini settings, detailed in the following table.

Table 11-2. PHP ini directives for uploads

Directive	Default	
file_uploads	"1"	Allow (or not) file uploads via POST and PUT
upload_max_filesize	"2M"	Maximum size of an uploaded file must be larger than post_max_size
upload_temp_dir	null	Location for temporary uploads (PHP will use system default if null)
post_max_size		Maximum size (Content-Length) of POST data
max_input_time	"-1"	Maximum time allowed to parse request data

To get started, let's just have a very simple look at the $_FILES superglobal that PHP creates when handling file uploads. Create yet another index.php file like this:

// index.php

var_dump($_FILES);

Then use the following curl command, which assumes that a ./random.jpg file is available in the current working directory (otherwise curl will exit with an error message about failing to "open/read local data"). Any old data will do; it just needs to exist in the correct place on your local filesystem. All being well, you'll see the following output from the PHP handler:

```
$ curl -v -F 'file=@./random.jpg' http://localhost:8080/index.php
* Host localhost:8080 was resolved.
...
> Content-Length: 612379
```

```
> Content-Type: multipart/form-data; boundary=------NqepV8M1YXB3iLRd1yjoC0p
* upload completely sent off: 612379 bytes
< HTTP/1.1 200 OK
...
array(1) {
  ["file"]=>
  array(6) {
    ["name"]=>
    string(10) "random.jpg"
    ["full_path"]=>
    string(10) "random.jpg"
    ["type"]=>
    string(10) "image/jpeg"
    ["tmp_name"]=>
    string(27) "/tmp/phptlpptkkrp5rf0azkKKY"
    ["error"]=>
    int(0)
    ["size"]=>
    int(612179)
  }
}
```

Note the Content-Type: header is set to multipart/form-data with an additional component: boundary=------------------qepV8M1YXB3iLRd1yjoC0p. This is the boundary string separating the parts of the request data, but you won't need to worry about that; by the time PHP passes control to your code, it will have processed the request body into POST data structure(s) and file data. This is controlled by Content-Disposition: and Content-Type: sub-headers in the multipart body, the raw request data from the above would look like this:

```
POST /index.php HTTP/1.1
Content-Type: multipart/form-data; boundary=--------------------
qepV8M1YXB3iLRd1yjoC0p
--------------------qepV8M1YXB3iLRd1yjoC0p
Content-Disposition: form-data; name="file"; filename="random.jpg"
Content-Type: image/jpeg

<BINARY_DATA>
```

Those two sub-headers instruct PHP to take all the bytes it finds up to the next occurrence of the boundary string (multipart request bodies are always terminated by a final instance of the boundary string) and treat them as a single file. The resulting bytes are then written to the `tmp_name` filepath as detailed in the `$_FILES` data.

Now, before you go digging around the `/tmp` directory of your cli-server container for the uploaded file, bear in mind that it's a temporary file and PHP will remove it once the request is processed and the script terminates. Occasionally these files aren't removed if a script terminates unexpectedly, but in our case we're just looking at a superglobal data structure; there really isn't much to go wrong. We'll need to do a little more work to persist the upload to the local filesystem. There are two functions that interact with file uploads: `is_uploaded_file()` is a simple function that tests if a file was uploaded via POST; `move_uploaded_file()` will move an uploaded file (and will also perform the same verification). It is recommended to use these functions to interact with file uploads – rather than alternative PHP filesystem functions – because they will ensure the target file is a genuine POST upload. As before, create a new index.php file with the following code...

```
// index.php

$tmpFile = $_FILES['file']['tmp_name'];
var_dump(is_uploaded_file($tmpFile));
var_dump(is_uploaded_file('/etc/passwd'));
var_dump(move_uploaded_file($tmpFile, __DIR__ . '/uploaded.jpg'));
var_dump(is_uploaded_file($tmpFile));
```

... and run the following curl command, which assumes that you are working in the same directory from which you launched your cli-server container, and there is a `./random.jpg` image file available:

```
$ curl -F 'file=@./random.jpg' http://localhost:8080/index.php
bool(true)
bool(false)
bool(true)
bool(false)
```

The code in index.php calls `is_uploaded_file()` first to verify that `$_FILES['file']['tmp_name']` is a genuine POST upload (which returns `true`, so it is), then a quick demonstration that a critical system file `/etc/passwd` is not (this time the return is `false` because /etc/passwd was most definitely NOT uploaded during this request, and you should probably leave it alone!). Next we call `move_uploaded_file()` with a second argument to specify where we'd like to move the upload to – remember the `__DIR__` constant maps to the directory of the current source code file – which has the effect of moving the upload from /tmp/ to the same directory as our `index.php` file and renames it to `uploaded.jpg` in the process. Finally, another call to `is_uploaded_file()` confirms the file move; it now returns `false` because the temporary file no longer exists. We can confirm with a quick check of the filesystem:

```
$ ls
index.php    uploaded.jpg
```

In a production system you will of course have far more secure settings in place; it is unlikely the owning account of the PHP process will have write access to the source code directory, nor should your code (or indeed the web server) be able to access somewhere like /etc. Also, bear in mind that POST requests are not idempotent, and multiple identical requests should create a new file every time (no matter if it's the same file each time). Our simple script above behaves more like a PUT upload (which we'll look at in a moment) because the result is the same `uploaded.jpg` file every time. In a real-world situation, you would probably want to include some unique identifier in the filename.

One more thing to look at for multipart POST data: as you might recall, I said it is possible to mix different content types with a `multipart/form-data` POST request; indeed, this is what this media type is designed for. Remember that each content section (delimited by the boundary string) can have its own `Content-Type:` and `Content-Disposition:` headers, so you can upload a mix of file data and more conventional POST encoded data, or even multiple files in one request. Let's have a quick look at how that works from PHP's perspective. The code we'll need in our `index.php` is as follows...

```
// index.php
var_dump($_FILES);
var_dump($_POST);
```

... and our curl command is:

```
$ curl -F 'file=@./random.jpg' \
  -F 'animals[cat]=jess&humans[]=anna&humans[]=paul' \
  http://localhost:8080/index.php
```

```
array(1) {
  ["file"]=>
  array(6) {
    ["name"]=>
    string(10) "random.jpg"
...
array(1) {
  ["animals"]=>
  array(1) {
    ["cat"]=>
    string(32) "jess&humans[]=anna&humans[]=paul"
  }
}
```

As you can see, we have two distinct sets of POST data, as dictated by the multipart Content-Type: and Content-Disposition: sub-headers. You might think this would result in a $_POST array that matches previous examples above where we sent the POST data using curl's -d option, but as you can see, the $_POST data hasn't actually decoded in the same way. This isn't a PHP problem per se; it's down to how we've used curl. The raw request data created from the above curl command would look something like this:

```
POST /index.php HTTP/1.1
Content-Type: multipart/form-data; boundary=---------DtcO7DDvZ3jzJIDOEPsbxK
-------------------DtcO7DDvZ3jzJIDOEPsbxK
Content-Disposition: form-data; name="file"; filename="random.jpg"
Content-Type: image/jpeg
<BINARY_DATA>
-------------------DtcO7DDvZ3jzJIDOEPsbxK
Content-Disposition: form-data; name="cat";
jess&humans[]=anna&humans[]=paul
```

When creating multipart form requests with curl, it is necessary to provide each POST variable in a separate -F string, like this...

```
$ curl -F 'file=@./random.jpg' \
  -F 'animals[cat]=jess' \
  -F 'humans[]=anna' \
```

```
  -F 'humans[]=paul' \
  http://localhost:8080/index.php
array(1) {
  ["file"]=>
  array(6) {
...
array(2) {
  ["animals"]=>
  array(1) {
    ["cat"]=>
    string(4) "jess"
  }
  ["humans"]=>
  array(2) {
    [0]=>
    string(4) "anna"
    [1]=>
    string(4) "paul"
  }
}
```

... and now our $_POST array makes a lot more sense! Generally speaking, when making multipart requests with curl, you should break up POST data strings wherever you encounter an & character in the `form-urlencoded` string.

It is also possible to upload files using the PUT request method, and, in some respects, it is a much simpler way of doing things. A raw PUT request will usually look something like this...

```
PUT /index.php HTTP/1.1
User-Agent: <user agent>
Accept: <accepted response media types>
Content-Length: <length of file in bytes>
<binary data>
```

... there might be a Content-Type: header, perhaps others too, but it's still far simpler than a multipart/form-data request. Let's see how PHP behaves; create the following index.php:

```
// index.php

var_dump($_FILES);
var_dump($_POST);
var_dump(file_get_contents('php://input'));
```

Adding the --upload-file option to a curl command will trigger a PUT request without a Content-Type: header. Create a file meow.txt in your working directory and add a line of text to it, ideally something feline in nature. Now run the following curl command:

```
$ curl -v --upload-file meow.txt 'http://localhost:8080/index.php'
> PUT /index.php HTTP/1.1
> Host: localhost:8080
> User-Agent: curl/8.7.1
> Accept: */*
> Content-Length: 47
...
array(0) {
}
array(0) {
}
string(47) "Jess is pretending she hasn't been fed. Again.
"
* Closing connection
```

Here we can see that both $_FILES and $_POST are empty. PHP takes no special action with the request data of a PUT. We have to go to STDIN (via the file_get_contents('php://input') call) to access the request body. You can imagine the rest for yourself: read from php://input, write to a file handle obtained from fopen(), and so on.

It is perfectly fine (from HTTP's perspective) to make a multipart/form-data PUT request; we can get curl to do this by using a -F option to trigger the desired Content-Type: and -X 'PUT' to override the default HTTP method:

```
$ curl -v -X 'PUT' -F 'file=@./meow.txt' 'http://localhost:8080/index.php'
> PUT /index.php HTTP/1.1
> Host: localhost:8080
> User-Agent: curl/8.7.1
> Accept: */*
> Content-Length: 210
> Content-Type: multipart/form-data; boundary=-------Tb2Qb7aQRVJTEcBlTehHvR
...
string(245) "--------------------Tb2Qb7aQRVJTEcBlTehHvR
Content-Disposition: form-data; name="file"; filename="meow.txt"
Content-Type: text/plain

Jess is pretending she hasn't been fed. Again.
----------------------------------Tb2Qb7aQRVJTEcBlTehHvR--
"
* Closing connection
```

In this case, we can see the raw sub-headers in our request body, because PHP isn't doing anything magical with the request data (remember PHP will only populate $_FILES and $_POST if the request method is POST). You'll need to do a little extra work with these types of requests to make sure the sub-headers, extra newlines, and boundary strings are stripped from the file data.

Building and Parsing URLs

Before we move on to looking at HTTP responses, let's look again at URLs. At the start of this section we learned that URLs are specially formatted strings that can be divided into five components (scheme, authority, path, and so on). When we looked at headers I gave a quick example of using PHP's sockets API (file_get_contents() and stream_context_create()) to make a request but simply used a string literal for the URL (supplied as the filename: argument to file_get_contents()). In reality you will likely need a lot more control over URL construction, and fortunately PHP provides some useful functions for doing just that.

CHAPTER 11   PROGRAMMING FOR THE INTERNET

PHP has a built-in function parse_url(), which will generate an associative array of URL components:

```
$url = 'https://www.cats.com:8080/nutters/jess?status=hungry#meow';
var_dump(parse_url($url));
```

Output:
```
array(6) {
  ["scheme"]=>
  string(5) "https"
  ["host"]=>
  string(12) "www.cats.com"
  ["port"]=>
  int(8080)
  ["path"]=>
  string(13) "/nutters/jess"
  ["query"]=>
  string(13) "status=hungry"
  ["fragment"]=>
  string(4) "meow"
}
```

You can also tell parse_url() to only return a specific component by adding a constant (such as PHP_URL_QUERY, PHP_URL_HOST, and so on) as a second argument:

```
var_dump(parse_url($url, PHP_URL_QUERY));
```

Output:
```
string(13) "status=hungry"
```

Constructing a URL from data like this is pretty straightforward:

```
$url = 'https://www.cats.com:8080/nutters/jess?status=hungry#meow';
$components = parse_url($url);
print $components['scheme'] . '://'
    . $components['host'] . ':'
    . $components['port']
    . $components['path'] . '?'
```

```
        . $components['query'] . '#'
        . $components['fragment']
;
```

Output:
https://www.cats.com:8080/nutters/jess?status=hungry#meow

Be aware that parse_url() does *not* validate the string as a URL, and passing a malformed URL into the function can result in complete nonsense being returned! We will look at data validation later in the chapter.

Things get a little more complicated when manipulating query data. You might be tempted to simply have at it with regular expressions or other string manipulation functions, but I don't recommend it. I've fixed numerous bugs over the years where edge cases in such code have broken URL creation in PHP code. Far better to work with structured data and generate your own, and for this we have the built-in parse_str() and http_build_query():

```
$url = 'https://localhost/whatever?complex[]=data&complex[]=here';
parse_str(parse_url($url, PHP_URL_QUERY), $query);
var_dump($query);
```

Output:
```
array(1) {
  ["complex"]=>
  array(2) {
    [0]=>
    string(4) "data"
    [1]=>
    string(4) "here"
  }
}
```

Notice the $query variable: this is passed by reference, and if present, it will receive the associative array of parsed data; otherwise, PHP will create a set of variables (with names matching those in the query data) in the current scope, which is generally not a great idea. Use http_build_query() to assemble a string from structured data:

CHAPTER 11   PROGRAMMING FOR THE INTERNET

```php
$data = [
    'cats' => ['Jess'],
    'humans' => ['Anna', 'Paul']
];

print http_build_query($data) . PHP_EOL;
```

Output:
cats%5B0%5D=Jess&humans%5B0%5D=Anna&humans%5B1%5D=Paul

The output above might look a little strange; this is because PHP has encoded the query string using a scheme known as "percent encoding" or "url encoding" (you'll hopefully recognize this name from the application/x-www-form-urlencoded media type we encountered earlier in the chapter). This is absolutely fine; it's just a safety mechanism, which we'll get to in a moment. The unencoded data looks like this:

```php
// $data = [...
print urldecode(http_build_query($data));
```

Output:
cats[0]=Jess&humans[0]=Anna&humans[1]=Paul

The use of explicit numbered array indices is just how PHP rolls; "cats[0]=Jess&humans[0]=Anna&humans[1]=Paul" and "cats[]=Jess&humans[]=Anna&humans[]=Paul" will result in exactly the same structured data when parsed.

So, what was all that %5B %5D stuff about? Chances are that you've encountered these weird-looking sequences in URLs before. URLs (or more precisely, URIs) require that certain reserved characters be encoded into sequences starting with a % character. These are characters with a "reserved purpose" in the URI specification, for example, the & character separates key/value pairs in a query string. The problem is this: what if the values of the query parameters contain reserved characters? Just writing them into a query string verbatim will screw up the syntax and create havoc with the resulting parsed data. Let's start with the obvious: the & character delimits key/value pairs in the query, so if the values themselves contain that character, we'd need to deal with it somehow:

```php
$data = [
    'var1' => '&val1',
    'var2' => '&val2',
];
```

```
print http_build_query($data);
```

Output:
```
var1=%26val1&var2=%26val2
```

Notice how the values &val1 and &val2 have been encoded to %26val1 and %26val2? If this wasn't done, we'd break the syntax of the query string. Let's see what happens if those %26 sequences were just literal & characters:

```
parse_str('var1=&val1&var2=&val2', $mess);
var_dump($mess);
```

Output:
```
array(4) {
  ["var1"]=>
  string(0) ""
  ["val1"]=>
  string(0) ""
  ["var2"]=>
  string(0) ""
  ["val2"]=>
  string(0) ""
}
```

Ugh. What a mess. We end up with four parameters and no values. The parser reads var1=&, which is interpreted as "the var1 parameter has no value," next it reads val1&, and despite the lack of an = symbol, this is also treated as a parameter with no value. And so on. A similar problem exists if we encoded all the & characters:

```
parse_str('var1=%26val1%26var2=%26val2', $mess);
var_dump($mess);
```

Output:
```
array(1) {
  ["var1"]=>
  string(16) "&val1&var2=&val2"
}
```

CHAPTER 11 PROGRAMMING FOR THE INTERNET

With no delimiting metacharacters, the parser would assign everything after the first = assignment to a single var1 parameter. Tread carefully and only encode the values, not the entire query string – the best way is to use http_build_query().

Hopefully you'll now know how to transform a query string into structured data and vice versa, and you'll understand what percent encoding (url encoding) is for. The above example should serve as a simple demonstration that URI reserved characters are reserved for a reason! Hopefully you will also appreciate that http_build_query() can be used to construct POST data strings, because the formatting rules are identical (remember that POST data strings have a media type of application/x-www-form-urlencoded and so should always be percent encoded).

PHP also offers some functions for doing your "manual" percent encoding: urlencode()/urldecode() and rawurlencode()/rawurldecode(). The difference between urlencode() and rawurlencode() is simply how spaces are handled:

```
print urlencode('cat=jess the cat') . PHP_EOL;
print rawurlencode('cat=jess the cat');
```

Output:
cat%3Djess+the+cat
cat%3Djess%20the%20cat

By default, http_build_query() will encode spaces as +, but it can switch to the other method via its encoding_type parameter:

```
print http_build_query(
    data: [
        'cat' => 'Jess the cat',
        'human' => 'Anna the human'
    ],
    arg_separator: '&',
    encoding_type: PHP_QUERY_RFC3986
);
```

Output:
cat=Jess%20the%20cat&human=Anna%20the%20human

HTTP(S) Responses

By now you've already had some exposure to the response side of HTTP. Many examples in this section have had curl running in verbose mode (thanks to the -v option), which will show both request and response headers. Let's just take another look at that output. Assuming you still have your cli-server container running, we'll do a simple fetch of index.php (the contents don't matter for our purposes here):

```
$ curl -v http://localhost:8080/index.php
...
* Request completely sent off
< HTTP/1.1 200 OK
< Host: localhost:8080
< Date: Mon, 14 Jul 2025 16:12:53 GMT
< Connection: close
< X-Powered-By: PHP/8.4.6
< Content-type: text/html; charset=UTF-8
...
* Closing connection
```

Everything after the "* Request completely sent off" line is the response. You'll notice the first line – "HTTP/1.1 200 OK" – looks a little like the first line of a request; this is the *status line*. A status line consists of the protocol version, a space, a *status code*, another space, then a "reason phrase" (which can be empty), terminated by a CRLF sequence. In this case our status code is 200, and the reason phrase is OK; this tells the client that we didn't have any issues on our end and the content of the response should be considered correct (whether that's true or not is now a problem for the client and/or the end user). Status codes control fundamental behavior of the client; they might tell the client that they should visit a new location, or that their request wasn't made correctly, or even just that the server caught fire and died.

Following the status line, we have the response headers (one per line), and yes, they look pretty much the same as request headers. The header name and header value are delimited by a colon character, and each pair terminates with CRLF. You'll recognize Content-Type: with its IANA-approved media name ("text/html"). You should also note the use of an X-Powered-By: PHP/8.4.6 "custom" header (despite such X- prefixing behavior being officially deprecated), which you'll see if using the PHP cli-server

SAPI. Advertising your server-side technology stack is just asking for trouble, and we'll see how we can modify that behavior in a moment. First, let's break down the status line and headers in more detail.

Response Status

Much like HTTP request methods, HTTP status codes are governed by a set of RFCs and maintained in an official registry by the IANA. The full registry of status codes can be found at https://www.iana.org/assignments/http-status-codes/http-status-codes.xhtml. The codes themselves are three-digit numbers where the first digit indicates the class of response.

Table 11-3. HTML status code groups

1xx	Informational (request received but not processed)
2xx	Success (request was understood and accepted, usually with a response)
3xx	Redirection (details in the `Location:` header)
4xx	Client error (you did something wrong)
5xx	Server error (we did something wrong)

You won't need to worry about a lot of these codes, because PHP is only going to get to work once the request is fully received and ready for processing. Anything involving, say, switching protocols (`101 Switching Protocols`, usually to tell a client to move from HTTP to HTTPS) or proxy issues (`502 Bad Gateway`) is going to be dealt with by the web server before control passes to your program. As a PHP developer, you'll mostly be dealing with setting 4xx and 5xx to communicate error states, perhaps 3xx if redirection is handled in your application logic (rather than server config). By default, PHP will set the status code to 200 when running in a web server SAPI, and the function `http_response_code()` can be used to get the current status or set a new one:

```
// index.php
$oldCode = http_response_code();
http_response_code(403);

print "HTTP Status Code was {$oldCode}\n";
print "But I don't like you so you are forbidden.\n";
```

```
$ curl -v http://localhost:8080/index.php
...
< HTTP/1.1 403 Forbidden
< Host: localhost:8080
< Date: Mon, 14 Jul 2025 17:00:54 GMT
< Connection: close
< X-Powered-By: PHP/8.4.6
< Content-type: text/html; charset=UTF-8
<
HTTP Status Code was: 200
But I don't like you so you are forbidden.
```

Notice that the status code was set with http_response_code(403) *before* any output was printed. There's a reason for this. When running in a web server SAPI, PHP will send a status line and response headers as soon as a single byte of output is generated. Once the status line and headers are sent, they cannot be modified. Any attempt to set headers or a different status code after the response has begun will emit an error; this is what happens if we try to set a status code once we've begun to emit output bytes:

```
...
print "But I don't like you so you are forbidden.\n";

http_response_code(403);
$ curl -v http://localhost:8080/index.php
< HTTP/1.1 200 OK
< Host: localhost:8080
< Date: Mon, 14 Jul 2025 17:12:16 GMT
< Connection: close
< X-Powered-By: PHP/8.4.6
< Content-type: text/html; charset=UTF-8
<
HTTP Status Code was 200
But I don't like you so you are forbidden.
<br />
<b>Warning</b>:  http_response_code(): Cannot set response code - headers
already sent...
```

You can see that we did not set our status code to 403, and we get an error. In this case the error message – "Warning: http_response_code(): Cannot set response code - headers already sent..." – is appended to the response body as formatted HTML, which is what the official php:8.4-cli docker image is configured to do. Depending on your setup, you might need to take a look in the error logs. This is logical; the status code and headers were already sent to the client when we started to create output from our program. There's no way for us to change them and not break the HTTP protocol. There is a way round this, which we will be examining at the end of this section.

Response Headers

Hopefully by now you'll be quite comfortable with HTTP headers and what they do. Some common and important HTTP/1.1 headers typically seen in responses are:

Table 11-4. Common response headers

Cache-Control:	Fine control of browser caching
Connection	Keep network connection after current response, deprecated in HTTP/2
Content-Type:	IANA media type, possible `charset` param indicates encoding
ETag:	Version control of resources, for browser cache and bandwidth efficiency
Expires:	Controls expiry of browser cached resources
Last-Modified:	Controls browser caching, crawler frequency
Location:	Controls client redirection in 3xx responses
Set-Cookie:	Sets a cookie key/value pair

To set a header in PHP, simply use the built-in header() function. You can also view the current response headers (before or after they are sent) with the apache_response_headers(), which (despite the name) is available in a variety of server SAPIs, including cli-server and php-fpm. Remember the problematic X-Powered-By: header from earlier? Let's get rid of that:

```
$headers = apache_response_headers();
header("X-Powered-By: none/of-your-business");
var_dump($headers);
print "Thanks for visiting!";
```

```
$ curl -v http://localhost:8080/index.php
< HTTP/1.1 200 OK
< Host: localhost:8080
< Date: Mon, 14 Jul 2025 17:47:03 GMT
< Connection: close
< X-Powered-By: none/of-your-business
< Content-type: text/html; charset=UTF-8
<
array(1) {
  ["X-Powered-By"]=>
  string(9) "PHP/8.4.6"
}
Thanks for visiting!
```

As you can see, we've changed the X-Powered-By: header to the new value, and we're no longer advertising the precise version of PHP powering our endpoint (and therefore no longer helping a malicious actor fine-tune an attack). Notice that we had to call header() before we dumped the stored output of apache_response_headers(). This could get quite tiresome and make for some tortuous logic if our code actually did real work...

Output Buffering

As demonstrated already, PHP will emit output immediately: any statement such as print or echo, or functions that can emit output such as var_dump() or print_r(), will trigger a status line and response headers when running under a web server SAPI. If you want the freedom to begin emitting output but make changes to HTTP status or headers, you will need to make use of PHP's output buffering mechanism. Let's recycle an earlier example of the problem. Remember that this code...

```
print "HTTP Status Code was " . http_response_code() . "\n";
print "But I don't like you so you are forbidden.\n";

http_response_code(403);
```

... caused PHP to emit a warning error message. We can get around this with the built-in output buffering functions. When output buffering is enabled (with the ob_start() function), bytes emitted by PHP as output will be stored in memory rather than passed to STDOUT or Apache. This way you can accumulate output without triggering any side effects such as response headers or status lines. Let's see what happens:

```
// index.php
```

```
ob_start();
print "HTTP Status Code was " . http_response_code() . "\n";
print "But I don't like you so you are forbidden.\n";
http_response_code(403);

print "While we're at it let's sort that X- header out.\n";
header('X-Powered-By: none/of-your-business');
```

```
$ curl -v http://localhost:8080/index.php
< HTTP/1.1 403 Forbidden
< Host: localhost:8080
< Date: Mon, 14 Jul 2025 18:00:53 GMT
< Connection: close
< X-Powered-By: none/of-your-business
< Content-type: text/html; charset=UTF-8
<
HTTP Status Code was 200
But I don't like you so you are forbidden.
While we're at it let's sort that X- header out.
```

Now we're able to emit as much output as we like; the output buffer is catching everything, and that allows us to make changes to the status code and headers freely. What we didn't do, though, was clean up after ourselves nicely. The output buffer continued to accumulate data until the script exited, which triggered a flush of the buffer as a side effect. It's better practice to do it yourself with an explicit call either to `flush()` (outputs the contents of the buffer but does not disable the buffer) or `ob_end_flush()` (flushes the buffer and stops any further buffering).

Output buffering in PHP can get quite complex; for example, you can pass a callable to `ob_start()`, which will be called on each flush event. The contents of the buffer are passed to the callback when the buffer is flushed:

```
ob_start(function ($buffer) {
    return str_replace('Jess', 'Naughty Jess', $buffer);
});

print "A cat called Jess is begging for food again.\n";
print "This is forbidden.\n";
http_response_code(403);

flush();

$ curl -v http://localhost:8080/index.php
...
< HTTP/1.1 403 Forbidden
< Host: localhost:8080
< Date: Mon, 14 Jul 2025 18:19:36 GMT
< Connection: close
< X-Powered-By: PHP/8.4.6
< Content-type: text/html; charset=UTF-8
<
A cat called Naughty Jess is begging for food again.
This is forbidden.
```

It is even possible to have nested levels of buffering, and there are many other functions for manipulating the buffering mechanism. If you are interested in finding out more, you can start with the official documentation at https://www.php.net/manual/en/book.outcontrol.php

Using a Library

We can pause here for a moment. We've covered quite a bit of ground with HTTP and how PHP interacts with it. My aim here was to teach the fundamentals of the protocol in addition to the behavior and tools that PHP offers. In a real-world application, I would *strongly* advise you to consider using a library rather than rolling your own code. When I introduced the concept of URL routing, I recommended the Symfony Routing component. There also exists the rather spiffy Symfony HttpFoundation component, which provides "an object-oriented layer for the HTTP specification." A word of warning: there is a PSR standard for representing HTTP messages (PSR-7 https://www.php-fig.org/psr/psr-7/), and Symfony HttpFoundation isn't strictly compliant with it. If this

CHAPTER 11 PROGRAMMING FOR THE INTERNET

is an issue for you, there exists the Symfony PSR-7 Bridge `https://symfony.com/doc/current/components/psr7.html` or you can use something ultra-lightweight, such as `https://github.com/Nyholm/psr7`.

By using `symfony/http-foundation` in your project, the entire request can be easily encapsulated with one line of code. It can be installed with Composer (which had a brief mention in the autoloading section of Chapter 6, "Object Fundamentals"). Visit `https://getcomposer.org` to get started. (Composer is also well covered in *PHP 8 Objects, Patterns, and Practice*.)

```
$ composer require symfony/http-foundation
```

The `Symfony\Component\HttpFoundation\Request` class instance then exposes all of the facets of the protocol through various properties and methods. Make sure your autoloading boilerplate is in place (Composer is a great help with this), then interacting with HTTP requests is as simple as doing things like this:

```
use Symfony\Component\HttpFoundation\Request;

$request = Request::createFromGlobals();

$request->cookies; // access cookies
$request->query; // access query params
$request->getMethod(); // HTTP request method
// etc.
```

HttpFoundation also provides a nice OOP API for building responses...

```
use Symfony\Component\HttpFoundation\Response;

$response = new Response(
    $responseBody,
    Response::HTTP_OK,
    ['Content-Type:', 'text/html']
);
$response->send();
```

... and even different response classes for common cases such as returning JSON-encoded data...

```
use Symfony\Component\HttpFoundation\JsonResponse;

// automatically JSON encode assoc. array, set correct media-type header
$response = new JsonResponse(
    ['data' => 'will be encoded automatically']
);
```

... or redirecting the client:

```
use Symfony\Component\HttpFoundation\RedirectResponse;

// respond with 302 Found status code and Location: header
$response = new RedirectResponse('http://example.com/');
```

Full documentation can be found at https://symfony.com/doc/current/components/http_foundation.html

Sessions

HTTP is "stateless" by design, which means that every request must independently contain enough information to fulfill that request, and there is no mechanism within the protocol itself to retain any information about the state of a particular connection between one request and another. On the other hand, a web application will likely want to store information about its users, for at least as long as the browser window (or tab) contains the site. The concept of a user making a sequence of related requests to the same web server within a timeframe has a name: *session*. Although the HTTP protocol itself does not assume any persistence of state, there is no barrier to doing this within the web application itself. Web browsers have various options for persisting data, such as the localStorage and sessionStorage APIs - see https://developer.mozilla.org/en-US/docs/Web/API/Window/localStorage and https://developer.mozilla.org/en-US/docs/Web/API/Window/sessionStorage for more information. And of course, there's the very first solution to the problem, which is the Cookie API.

We've already looked at cookies, which were invented to allow the persistence of arbitrary data (based on domain and resource paths) between HTTP requests, but they have their limits. In particular, there are usually limits on the size of a single header - remember that cookies are passed in a single Cookie: header - and that limit is not enormous; in fact, it's pretty tiny by modern standards. The HTTP specification itself does not place an upper limit on header sizes, but web servers tend to. For example, Apache is normally configured at 8 KB – that's approximately 8100 ASCII characters, which isn't much, especially when you consider that this limit applies to the entire set of headers plus the request line. The other data-passing mechanisms of HTTP do not fare any better. There are size limits on URLs and POST data… and imagine the mess you'd create constructing and managing URLs with thousands of characters in their query strings… Ugh.

So, we have a problem to solve if we want to accumulate user data to improve our application. Sending data from the client side has some tight restrictions in terms of how much of it can be sent in a single HTTP request. In today's world an 8KB budget for header data is quickly eroded, and this could in fact be a lot lower when factoring in, say, an nginx proxy configured for only 4KB of headers. Storing data server-side therefore offers some obvious advantages, and there are multiple ways to approach this, but the one we're going to focus on in this section is PHP's built-in session support.

A Basic PHP Session

Put simply, PHP sessions are data that is stored between requests and exposed in the $_SESSION superglobal. Users are assigned a unique ID, which is usually stored in a PHPSESSID cookie (it can also be inserted into the URL if required), and PHP uses it to store and retrieve data. The cookie name is configurable with the `session.name` ini directive, so if you prefer another name, simply set `session.name = MYSESSIONID` in your ini file. The storage mechanism is the filesystem by default, though other storage "modules" are available: A database is an obvious alternative, and two popular in-memory solutions are

- Redis `https://github.com/phpredis/phpredis?tab=readme-ov-file#php-session-handler`
- Memcached `https://www.php.net/manual/en/memcached.sessions.php`

We will focus on filesystem-based sessions in this section. To start a session, you call the built-in `session_start()` function (PHP can also be configured to always activate a session with the `session.auto_start = 1` ini directive). The official PHP documentation states that "a record of a session is not created" until data is added to the $_SESSION superglobal, but certainly with PHP 8.4 this does not seem to be the case:

```
// index.php

session_start();
```
```
$ curl -v http://localhost:8080/index.php
...
< Set-Cookie: PHPSESSID=3fe1329aa9a3575373814ebf8aa59857; path=/
```

Simply calling `session_start()` is enough to get PHP to generate a PHPSESSID cookie, and a file will be written to the configured filesystem path. The location of PHP session files is set with the `session.save_path` ini directive. If you are using the official PHP cli image to follow the examples at home, this location will be /tmp inside the container. Launch a shell inside your container with `docker run`, and you can see for yourself (use `docker ps` to obtain the container ID for your local environment; it will be different from the one given below in the text):

```
$ docker ps
CONTAINER ID    IMAGE...
0d72be74121b    php:8.4-cli...

$ docker exec -it 0d72be74121b bash
root@0d72be74121b:/usr/src/myapp# php --ini
Configuration File (php.ini) Path: /usr/local/etc/php
...

root@0d72be74121b:/usr/src/myapp# grep -rn "session.save_path" /usr/local/etc/php
...
/usr/local/etc/php/php.ini-development:1292:;session.save_path = "/tmp"

root@0d72be74121b:/usr/src/myapp# ls /tmp
sess_3fe1329aa9a3575373814ebf8aa59857

root@0d72be74121b:/usr/src/myapp# cat /tmp/sess_3fe1329aa9a3575373814ebf8aa59857
root@0d72be74121b:/usr/src/myapp#
```

Session data is automatically serialized (encoded into a string) when a request finishes and a script terminates, and the inverse happens when a script starts a session (usually as one of the first actions taken, or automatically on script start depending on configuration). In our case above, $_SESSION has no data, and when we output the contents with the cat command, we get zero bytes. Let's see what happens when we start putting data into $_SESSION:

```
// index.php
session_start();

// if no 'visits' key in session, initialise at 0
$_SESSION['visits'] = $_SESSION['visits'] ?? 0;
$_SESSION['visits']++;

var_dump($_SESSION);
```

Now if we make a request that includes our PHPSESSID cookie, we can see how our simple $_SESSION['visits'] counter can be used to store a count of requests:

```
$ curl -v --cookie 'PHPSESSID=3fe1329aa9a3575373814ebf8aa59857' \
  http://localhost:8080/index.php
...
> GET /index.php HTTP/1.1
> Cookie: PHPSESSID=3fe1329aa9a3575373814ebf8aa59857
...
array(1) {
  ["visits"]=>
  int(1)
}
$ curl --cookie 'PHPSESSID=3fe1329aa9a3575373814ebf8aa59857' \
  http://localhost:8080/index.php
array(1) {
  ["visits"]=>
  int(2)
}
```

It was possible in earlier versions of PHP to send PHPSESSID as a query string (GET) or POST parameter if the session.use_only_cookies = 1 ini directive was not set. Setting a session ID via a URL like

http://localhost:8080/index.php?PHPSESSID=3fe1329aa9a3575373814ebf8aa59857

introduces some security issues, which we'll get to later in this section. You should be aware that this mechanism is deprecated in PHP 8.4 and is set to disappear completely in PHP 9 (I wasn't kidding about the security risks). Returning to the cli-server container, we can see how PHP has serialized data in the session file:

```
root@0d72be74121b:/usr/src/myapp# cat /tmp/sess_3fe1329aa9a3575373814e
bf8aa59857
visits|i:2;
```

Session Cookie Management

The eagle-eyed amongst you hopefully spotted something in the first example of this section: the PHPSESSID cookie that was set when we initialized the session with session_start() (and did not pass a PHPSESSID cookie with the request) had no expiry metadata, which means it will persist only until the client session terminates (when you close the browser). Session cookie parameters are configurable with the following ini directives:

Table 11-5. *PHP session ini directives*

Directive	Default	
session.cookie_lifetime	0	Expiration timestamp relative to server time
session.cookie_path	"/"	The path value of the cookie
session.cookie_domain	""	The domain
session.cookie_secure	0	If set to 1, only send cookie with HTTPS scheme
session.cookie_httponly	0	Only send with HTTP scheme
session.cookie_samesite	""	Set SameSite attribute

You can view the current parameters during script execution using the session_get_cookie_params() function, and you can set them on-the-fly with session_set_cookie_params() and pass an associative array of options and values – session_set_cookie_params(['lifetime' => 3600]); would trigger the addition of Max-Age and Expires parameters to the Set-Cookie: response header. Be sure to call session_set_cookie_params() *before* the session is started.

```
// index.php
session_set_cookie_params(['lifetime' => 3600]);
session_start();

$ curl -v http://localhost:8080/index.php
...
< Set-Cookie: PHPSESSID=<SESSION_ID>; expires=Thu, 17 Jul 2025 18:02:48
GMT; Max-Age=3600; path=/
...
```

Session Data

The way that PHP serializes session data is set with the `session.serialize_handler` ini directive, which is usually set as `session.serialize_handler = php` in most docker images/OS packages. This is very (very) similar to the serialization method that's used by PHP's `serialize()`/`unserialize()` functions. I'll use `serialize()` to demonstrate the principles, but bear in mind that the official PHP documentation states that the session default method is not identical. Obviously, you will not need to do your own serialization when using native PHP sessions because it's baked in. The following is presented purely for information and education purposes! With that in mind, place the following code in your `index.php` file…

```
// index.php
session_start();

$_SESSION['data'] = [
    'cat' => 'Jess',
    'humans' => [
        'Anna',
        'Paul'
    ]
];

var_dump(serialize($_SESSION['data']));
```

… we can compare the output of `serialize()`…

```
$ curl --cookie 'PHPSESSID=3fe1329aa9a3575373814ebf8aa59857' http://
localhost:8080/index.php
string(76) "a:2:{s:3:"cat";s:4:"Jess";s:6:"humans";a:2:{i:0;s:4:"Anna";i:1;
s:4:"Paul";}}"
```

... with the contents of the session file:

```
root@0d72be74121b:/usr/src/myapp# cat /tmp/sess_3fe1329aa9a3575373814e
bf8aa59857
datala:2:{s:3:"cat";s:4:"Jess";s:6:"humans";a:2:{i:0;s:4:"Anna";i:1;s:4:
"Paul";}}
```

Session data need not be associative arrays; session serialization (and the serialize() function) will handle just about any data type, including objects (but not resources). Objects are serialized as their property names and values, including protected or private properties. The following example runs without the need for a web server, and in this case is better for it because some versions of curl might complain about "binary output" – all those metacharacters! It demonstrates object serialization using serialize() and session_encode(), which returns a serialized string representing the current state of $_SESSION:

```
class Foo
{
    public string $name = 'foo';
    private string $typeString = 'Instance of Foo';
    protected array $family = [
        'cat' => 'Jess',
        'humans' => ['Anna', 'Paul']
    ];
}
session_start();
print serialize(new Foo()) . PHP_EOL;

$_SESSION['data'] = new Foo();
print session_encode();
```

Output:
O:3:"Foo":3:{s:4:"name";s:3:"foo";s:15:"FootypeString";s:15:"Instance of Foo";s:9:"*family";a:2:{s:3:"cat";s:4:"Jess";s:6:"humans";a:2:{i:0;s:4:"Anna";i:1;s:4:"Paul";}}}
data10:3:"Foo":3:{s:4:"name";s:3:"foo";s:15:"FootypeString";s:15:"Instance of Foo";s:9:"*family";a:2:{s:3:"cat";s:4:"Jess";s:6:"humans";a:2:{i:0;s:4:"Anna";i:1;s:4:"Paul";}}}

Be aware that only named classes or instances of stdClass are serializable. Anonymous classes cause serialize() to emit an error:

```
// index.php

session_start();

$_SESSION['data'] = new Class {
    private string $cat = 'Jess';
};

$ curl --cookie 'PHPSESSID=3fe1329aa9a3575373814ebf8aa59857' http://localhost:8080/index.php
...
Uncaught Exception: Serialization of 'class@anonymous' is not allowed
```

Other serialization handlers are available. The session.serialize_handler = php_binary ini directive switches to a binary format (which is faster and will save you some storage space), and session.serialize_handler = wddx will use the Web Distributed Data eXchange format, although you are unlikely to see this in installations of PHP beyond 7.4 (PHP 7.4 removed WDDX from core PHP and moved it instead to the PECL repository; the PECL package is currently not maintained). You can even write your own if you wish. Let's look at that next.

OOP API

PHP offers a (somewhat) object-oriented API in addition to the handful of session functions we've seen so far. The class that does the most work is SessionHandler, which is defined as follows:

```
class SessionHandler implements SessionHandlerInterface,
SessionIdInterface {
    /* Methods */
    public close(): bool
    public create_sid(): string
    public destroy(string $id): bool
    public gc(int $max_lifetime): int|false
    public open(string $path, string $name): bool
    public read(string $id): string|false
    public write(string $id, string $data): bool
}
```

I say "somewhat" because this class isn't intended to be used directly; you wouldn't instantiate it yourself and call the methods directly. Only the functional API is intended for consumption by developers. The SessionHandler class is still useful though, because an instance of this class is used internally by the session functions (e.g., calling session_start() will result in a call to SessionHandler::open()), and this internal object can be replaced. The session_set_save_handler() function can be passed a new instance of SessionHandler, which replaces the default handler with the new one. In this way you can inject your own implementation(s) by extending the SessionHandler class and overloading one or more of the handler methods:

```
class ModifiedSessionHandler extends SessionHandler
{
    public function read(string $id): string
    {
        $data = parent::read();
        // new code goes here...
        return $data;
    }
    // other overloaded methods as required...
}

// do this before session_start()!
session_set_save_handler(new ModifiedSessionHandler());
session_start();
```

The official PHP documentation contains an example of overriding the base SessionHandler class to implement encryption of session data (which, as you've seen, is human readable by default). If you're interested, you can take a look at https://www.php.net/manual/en/class.sessionhandler.php

Security Considerations

Session data can potentially contain sensitive data; it's up to you (and your team) to determine the trade-off between convenience and risk to the user. As a general rule, if PII (Personally Identifiable Information, that's everything from names and addresses to medical or bank records) would be exposed by a malicious actor gaining access to a user session, then you should consider that as a high level of risk. There will undoubtedly be legislative protections in place, such as the EU's General Data Protection Regulations (GDPR), which mandate that data-controlling organizations must implement appropriate technical measures to protect users' personal data. PHP sessions are only as secure as you make them, and there are unfortunately various techniques available to gain access to a user's session.

Session Fixation

PHP's session manager is adaptive by default, which means it will accept uninitialized session IDs. This means it's possible to pass PHP the session ID you'd like it to use, and it will create that session if it doesn't already exist. If we pass a PHPSESSID cookie that doesn't have a session created for it, we will get one created with that ID:

```
# Remove all session files inside the cli-server container
root@0d72be74121b:/usr/src/myapp# rm /tmp/*

// index.php
session_start();

# make a curl request into the cli-server container from host
$ curl --cookie 'PHPSESSID=abc123' http://localhost:8080/index.php

# check the session files, sid abc123 now exists
root@0d72be74121b:/usr/src/myapp# rm /tmp/*
sess_abc123
```

So why is this a bad thing? The idea is that a malicious actor tricks your unsuspecting user into creating a known (to the attacker) session ID. A server that is happy to make use of a user-supplied session ID is sometimes said to be "adopting" a session ID (and this form of fixation attack is known as *session adoption*). Admittedly this is more difficult to do with cookies, which is why `session.use_only_cookies = 1` is a good idea and is the default for PHP 8.4. It is far easier to achieve with URL-based session IDs and a little social engineering. PHP 8.4 deprecates the passing of session IDs in URLs (by defaulting the ini directive to 0 and making it a non-configurable value), and PHP 9 will remove the mechanism entirely. The `session.use_only_cookies = 0` directive, together with `session.use_strict_mode = 0`, would allow the client to control the session ID on older versions, and we can demonstrate with the following code (make sure to use a version of PHP older than 8.4 for this one):

```
session_id($_GET['PHPSESSID']);
session_start();
```

```
$ curl -v http://localhost:8080/index.php?PHPSESSID=abc123
...
< Set-Cookie: PHPSESSID=abc123; path=/
```

Now imagine that your user was tricked into clicking a malicious link ... the attacker now knows the session ID and can interact with it. To prevent fixation attacks, do not allow session IDs that are not created inside your application.

Disable Transparent SID Support

In the olden days of a decade or so ago, it was common to pass session IDs in URLs, and PHP would intervene with the processing of HTML elements that supported URLs (e.g., `<a href="...` `<frame src="..."`). Modern PHP still contains the remnants of support for these mechanisms, known as "transparent SID support" which automagically adds session ID parameters into URLs. Obviously, a terrible idea these days and the good news is it is being expunged from PHP 8.4 onwards. Be wary of `session.use_trans_sid`, `session.trans_sid_tags` and `session.trans_sid_hosts` ini directives on older installations.

PHP 8.4 entirely deprecates the changing of `session.use_only_cookies`, `session.use_trans_sid`, `session.trans_sid_tags`, `session.trans_sid_hosts`, and `session.referer_check` ini directives, and defaults to the most secure settings.

Session ID (Re-) Creation

It is a good idea to regenerate session IDs periodically, especially if the session contains sensitive data, and cycling IDs is a good way to invalidate stolen sessions. Storing expiry timestamps in the session itself allows you to detect when to expire a session ID and generate a new one. Storing an "obsolete" flag is another good idea – this way you can detect attempts to access an obsolete session in addition to knowing when to regenerate the session ID. Here's some code that will achieve that:

```
session_start();

$now = time();
$_SESSION['expire'] = $_SESSION['expire'] ?? $now + 30;

if ($now > $_SESSION['expire']) {
    $_SESSION['obsolete'] = true;
    session_regenerate_id();
    unset($_SESSION['obsolete']);
    $_SESSION['expire'] = $now + 30;
    print "Session expired! Regenerated with new ID: " . session_
    id() . "\n";
} else {
    print "Session still active with ID: " . session_id() . "\n";
}
```

This simple code will set a 30-second expiry timestamp inside the session if one does not already exist (i.e., when a user visits with no PHPSESSID cookie set). On each request, the $_SESSION['expiry'] value is tested against the current time; when the server time exceeds the expiry, we add a $_SESSION['obsolete'] boolean to the session data, then call session_regenerate_id() to retain the current session data but with a new ID. Obviously this is going to result in a cookie header, so it must be called before output begins (remember to use output buffering if this causes problems for script logic). Since we're now dealing with a "new" session, we unset the obsolete flag and add a new expiry stamp. Let's put it to the test, using curl's cookie support (the -b and -c options specify a file to read and write cookie data):

```
$ curl -b ~/.curl_cookies -c ~/.curl_cookies http://localhost:8080/
index.php
Session still active with ID: 54a9a1f51c7842c0a58d0b971cb463d1
```

```
$ curl -b ~/.curl_cookies -c ~/.curl_cookies http://localhost:8080/
index.php
Session still active with ID: 54a9a1f51c7842c0a58d0b971cb463d1

# 30 seconds later...

$ $ curl -b ~/.curl_cookies -c ~/.curl_cookies http://localhost:8080/
index.php
Session expired! Regenerated with new ID: e59d41cd5d48fd347ce5ece6e6a944e2
```

If you feel inclined, you can check the contents of the session save path (defaults to /tmp) inside your cli-server container; you'll notice obsolete|b:1 appears in expired files. An attempt to access an expired session ID should be viewed with suspicion (after all, the client should now be using the new ID), but bear in mind that there could be benign reasons for a legitimate user to make a request with an old session ID (e.g., switching devices). Note that session_regenerate_id() accepts a boolean argument: session_regenerate_id(true); would trigger the immediate removal of the old session ID, but this can cause problems for legitimate users. Typically, you would preserve the old session data and rely on PHP's session garbage collection mechanism to clean up old session data, which we'll look at in a moment.

Careful with That Cookie

There are other ways for bad actors to control your users' session IDs. If the attacker can't trick your users into asking for specific IDs via a URL, they can still utilize other methods. Cookies can be set via JavaScript's document.cookie object and HTML's <meta http-equiv="Set-Cookie"> tag. Both of these methods will require some form of injection vulnerability, which would have to be within the domain under attack (i.e., it's "your" injection vulnerability). If a request has a session ID cookie set and that session does not exist, it should probably be treated as a potential attack. Depending on the session module in use (files, memcached, Redis), you could have a dig around in the data store and validate that the session is known, which means searching a filesystem or some other equivalent API call.

Alternatively, PHP's session management will do the work for you. As mentioned already, the session.use_strict_mode = 1 ini directive will ensure that an unknown session ID will be discarded. Even better, you can enforce strictness at the moment the session starts by passing some information to session_start():

```
// index.php

session_start(['use_strict_mode' => true]);
print "sessionId: " . session_id() . "\n";

# Simulate cookie previously set by malicious injection attack...
$ curl -v --cookie "PHPSESSID=abcdef123456789abcdef123456789ab" \
  http://localhost:8080/index.php
...
> Cookie: PHPSESSID=abcdef123456789abcdef123456789ab
< Set-Cookie: PHPSESSID=b91b04c21ca8e270aaab9e9b1d0db7c8; path=/
...
sessionId: b91b04c21ca8e270aaab9e9b1d0db7c8
```

Given that PHP did not manage to find any existing session data, we lose nothing by discarding the supplied PHPSESSID value. `session_start()` would normally (with a default config of `session.use_strict_mode = 0`) use the value supplied in the cookie. By using strict session IDs, we negate any possible cookie-based session adoption, and our user data is safe. An additional tactic sometimes seen is to capture the IP address (usually at login) of the client when the session ID is generated, which is exposed via `$_SERVER['REMOTE_ADDR']` – if you start seeing requests with that session ID but from a different address, then it can be flagged as possibly malicious (you might at least require the user to authenticate again).

Tidying Up

Session data is not intended to live forever, or at least a session ID is not (I've discussed why it's a good idea to frequently generate new session IDs). To prevent your filesystem (or memcached/Redis/SQLite, or whatever storage mechanism is persisting your sessions) from filling up over time, there is a *garbage collection* mechanism built into PHP. This mechanism does have some idiosyncrasies, however.

When a session is started (by any user request), PHP performs a calculation based on the ini directives `session.gc_probability` and `session.gc_divisor`. Default values for these directives are 1 (probability) and 100 (divisor), which works out to a 1 in 100 chance for a script that calls `session_start()` to trigger automatic garbage collection.

If it is triggered, the session garbage collection will check the last access time of all sessions, and if they exceed the value of session.gc_maxlifetime (default value is 1440 seconds to 24 minutes), then those sessions are purged (the files are deleted, or the Redis keys are removed, and so on).

For large and/or very high traffic sites you'll probably want to either change gc_probability and gc_divisor or move the session clean-up away from requests entirely and use your operating system's scheduler to do the work. This could take the form of a simple bash script, called via cron on a Linux-based system, that checks file timestamps (or the memcache/Redis equivalent), or even better, you could run a PHP CLI script that uses session_start() in conjunction with session_gc(). If doing this, make sure you configure session.gc_probability to 0 (so it will never trigger during a user request).

You can test this in your cli-server container; just run php -a to run PHP in interactive shell mode:

```
root@cacfcef67c60:/usr/src/myapp# ls /tmp
sess_54a9a1f51c7842c0a58d0b971cb463d1  sess_963229a0f8fe5dd892a14ecf645b4c43
sess_71315a640a6f21e2f55773b24cef24bf  sess_b91b04c21ca8e270aaab9e9b1d0db7c8

root@0d72be74121b:/usr/src/myapp# php -a
php > session_start();
php > session_gc();
php > ^C

root@cacfcef67c60:/usr/src/myapp# ls /tmp
sess_20fb90fe176daa80df6614c839c2f213
```

In the example above, all of the files in /tmp were over 24 minutes old. After running session_start()/session_gc(), only the new session file (created by the session started interactively) remains.

Functions

Table 11-6 presents a partial list of commonly used PHP session functions with a brief description of functionality.

Table 11-6. *PHP session handling functions*

session_abort()	Discard all changes made this request to $_SESSION and end the session.
session_cache_expire()	Controls Expires: and max-age directive of Cache-Control: headers
session_cache_limiter()	Controls caching behavior of client and/or proxies
session_commit()	Alias of session_write_close()
session_create_id()	Create a new (collision free) session ID string
session_gc()	Trigger session garbage collection
session_id()	Get/set the current session ID
session_module_name()	Get/set the session module – file/Redis/memcached, etc.
session_regenerate_id()	Generate a new ID for current session, optionally delete old session
session_set_cookie_params()	Control cookie parameters (expiry, max-age, same-site, etc.)
session_set_save_handler()	Replace default instance of SessionHandler with a modified instance
session_start()	Begin/resume a session
session_unset()	Equivalent to $_SESSION = [];
session_write_close()	Write $_SESSION to storage and end the current session

Full information for all session functions can be found at https://www.php.net/manual/en/ref.session.php and all ini directives are documented at https://www.php.net/manual/en/session.configuration.php

Modifying HTML (and XML)

Without further ado, it's time for the main event, the reason why PHP was invented! The acronym PHP originally stood for "Personal Home Page," then revised/retconned to the recursive "PHP Hypertext Preprocessor." Either way, the message is clear: PHP exists to process HTML. It is certainly my favorite back-end language for the task. Just as PHP has a large assortment of tools for handling HTTP requests, it is also loaded with functions and APIs for manipulating the content of responses to those requests, which is usually in HTML, XML, or JSON format. As always, we'll start with first principles and build from there. This section will provide you with an explanation of what HTML is, how to parse and modify it with PHP, and signposts where to find more information.

You might wonder why we are first learning how to manipulate existing HTML first, rather than jumping straight into building our own? The reason I chose this approach is that outputting your own web content comes with a number of implicit problems to solve beyond simply understanding how to write good markup. I want the creation of HTML to focus on things like security and good practice; those messages are important and might be diluted if you also have to wrap your head around what HTML actually is. To that end, in this section we'll learn how to take existing markup and turn it into data that can be processed in concise and efficient ways in PHP so that, when we get to the sticky business of outputting your own, you'll already have a secure foundation to build on.

Readers that are already fluent in HTML (perhaps you're coming to PHP from a front-end engineering background) and know their DOM manipulation from their complex CSS selectors can probably skim this section for the PHP specifics. Though it never hurts to review the fundamentals at any stage in your journey...

What Is HTML?

HyperText (or Hyper Text) Markup Language defines the structure (and with HTML5, the meaning) of web documents. The "Hyper" portion of the name refers to the links embedded in those documents that clients can follow to other parts of the same document or to new documents entirely. "Markup Language" means that annotations (in the form of meta-character enclosed tags) are added to the text of the document to define structure, formatting, and meaning. The tags themselves are not rendered by a client but instead instruct the client on how the document is structured and therefore how it should be rendered. The tags also impart semantic information: clients are informed about document elements such as images, tables, headers, and footers and can treat them appropriately. There are adjacent technologies to HTML to further control document appearance and behavior. Cascading Style Sheets (CSS) allows the control of things like positioning, size, fonts, and even animation of elements. JavaScript is ubiquitous as the event-driven programming language interface in web browsers to control the behavior of a document.

Markup languages in general are a family of programming languages, all of which use annotations or tags to wrap content (intended for human consumption) in order to assign machine-readable meaning to that content. The other markup language we'll look at in this section is XML (eXtensible Markup Language), which is very similar to HTML but differs in one crucial aspect: XML allows you to define any tags you like, but HTML uses predefined tags (you can't just make new ones up). Most HTML tags are used in opening/closing pairs to form *elements*. Elements can contain text for display and other elements to form a tree structure. Other elements do not require a closing tag because they are not intended to contain text or other elements (and are said to be "self-closing"). For example:

```
<a href="...">I am a hyperlink</a>
<img src="..." />
```

Above are two HTML elements represented as `<a></a>` (anchor) and `<img />` (image) tags. All of the text between the opening and closing chevron characters is treated as metadata for that element, and these are known as *attributes*. In the example above, the anchor tag has an `href` attribute, and the `<img>` tag has a `src` attribute.

Anchors are the fundamental "currency" of HTML; these form the links in documents that you can click on (when using a web browser) to go elsewhere. The text content inside the `<a></a>` tags is the part that is rendered by the client, usually with some visual cues to show that it is a link. The `href` attribute of `<a>` tags tells the client where to go if the link is followed; for example, `<a href="https://www.yahoo.com">...` would take the user to https://www.yahoo.com if clicked.

Images are, of course, the pretty pictures that make your content engaging. Note the closing meta-characters of the image tag – `/>` – this is the "self-closing" syntax I mentioned (images don't contain any other text or HTML content, so they don't require the closing-tag syntax). Image tags have `src` attributes, which tell the client where to load the image from, which can be from the same site or another one entirely. `<img src="/images/cat.jpg"` is a *relative URL*, which would attempt to load the image from the current domain, starting at the root. If you want to load a resource relative to the current resource path, omit the leading slash: `<img src="images/cat.jpg"` would append to the current resource path, `../images/cat.jpg` would attempt to load from one level up from the current path. Exactly like a filepath in fact. If the request to fetch the image resource results in a valid image file response it would then be rendered in place in the document.

HTML Standards

There are, of course, dozens of other HTML tags, and there are also some rules about how they should be structured. HTML that conforms to these rules is said to be *valid*, and it's generally a good idea to make sure your PHP is producing valid HTML. Malformed HTML (missing closing tags, broken hierarchy, etc.) is *invalid* and can cause issues for clients (web browsers can cope with invalid HTML to an extent but might behave unpredictably). As we discussed earlier, HTTP (and a plethora of other internet technologies) is defined by IETF standards documents (RFCs). HTML is, of course, also governed by standards, which have evolved greatly since its beginnings in the 1990s. Modern HTML should follow the HTML5 standard, which is maintained by the Web Hypertext Application Technology Working Group (WHATWG). The HTML5 "Living Standard" can be found at https://html.spec.whatwg.org/dev/ and is quite a read, so let's ease you in gently...

All minimally valid HTML documents have the following basic structure:

```
<!DOCTYPE html>
<html>
  <head>
    <title>My page.</title>
  </head>
  <body></body>
</html>
```

The first line of the example above is the *doctype declaration* and is "required preamble" according to the HTML5 specification. This line gives fundamental instructions to the client about the required rendering mode. It is case-insensitive but is conventionally given in the form shown, with capitalized DOCTYPE, one or more whitespaces, and lowercase html. The doctype line does not form part of the HTML document itself: that begins with the first start (opening) tag.

Our first start tag is <html>; it is the root-level element in our document (also known as "document element" because its parent is the document itself). It is possible to omit this tag and the corresponding </html> closing tag if there are no comments (an HTML comment has the syntax <!-- a comment -->) before the next start tag (<head> in our case) or after the final closing tag. The following is also considered valid HTML5…

```
<!DOCTYPE html>
<head>
  <title>My page.</title>
</head>
<body></body>
```

... but it is better practice to explicitly include the opening/closing `<html>`...`</html>` tags. Where the tags are omitted, the root `html` element is implicit: the data structure that the client builds from this HTML will include a root `html` element. In addition, an `html` element must include `head` and `body` child elements, and the `head` element must have a non-empty `title` child element, which will control the title of the page and is usually shown in the web browser as the name of the tab containing the page. A `head` element will typically also contain many other elements that are treated as document metadata. The `body` element can be empty and still be valid, though the client is going to render a fairly pointless empty page. The `body` element contains all the content that you wish to be displayed to the user.

Some History…

The HTML doctype declaration is a blunt instrument; it simply tells the client, "this is HTML." In the really, really olden days (when I was still a young person), HTML documents were typically written in a couple of ways, one version for Netscape Navigator (RIP) and one for MS Internet Explorer (aka Exploder, also RIP). Then along came the W3C (World Wide Web Consortium) standards, which were great but introduced a problem: they broke most sites on the internet at the time. The two browsers in question began to offer different rendering modes, one that adhered to the new standards ("standards mode") and one that did not ("quirks mode"), and the doctype declaration was used to switch between the two.

In "quirks mode," browsers behaved like Navigator 4 and Internet Explorer 5… told you this was ancient history! `<!DOCTYPE html>` is simply an instruction to the browser to render in modern "standards mode," and I'm fairly certain you will never have to worry about quirks because you are reading this in 2025 (or later). Also consigned to the bin of history is XHTML (which is HTML written to conform to XML syntax rules). XHTML was an attempt to enforce some (arguably unnecessary) rigor to HTML but in practice it made generating pages much more difficult. An XHTML document has the `Content-Type: application/xhtml+xml` header, which browsers will use to go automatically into standards mode, and you'll very rarely encounter one of these days, much less need to maintain one yourself. (If you're ever asked to, the correct response is "tell me why HTML5 doesn't meet your use case").

HTML Document Metadata

Anyway, back to our modern standards. The head element does not contain any data intended for display (apart from the title element). The valid elements allowed as children of head are:

Table 11-7. HTML <head> content elements

<title>	Contains only text, controls the page title, cannot be omitted or empty
<base>	Sets a base URL for all relative URLs in the document, optional
<link>	Link to external resource, commonly used to link CSS files
<style>	Contains CSS for the page, external stylesheets are preferred
<meta>	Metadata that cannot be represented by other elements
<script>	Contains executable code/data, or refers to external resource
<noscript>	Inserts HTML if scripting is unsupported
<template>	Holds HTML fragments for use by a script

As back-end engineers we're most concerned with <meta> because there's a whole lot of fundamental stuff you can communicate to the client with these tags. Specifically, you can achieve the following:

- Provide document-wide metadata with <meta name="..." content="..." />
- Simulate HTTP headers with <meta http-eqiv="..." content="..." />
- Set character encoding with <meta charset="..." />
- Set arbitrary metadata with <meta itemprop="..." />

Note that the `http-equiv` and `name` attributes also require an additional `content` attribute. At a bare minimum, you should be using `<meta>` to tell the browser you are using UTF-8 encoding (and of course you've read Chapter 8, "Strings", and know how and why to use UTF-8 everywhere). A lot of HTML5 validators will tell you off for not declaring encoding in the document, so make sure to always include it. Some commonly used examples are given below:

```html
<!DOCTYPE html>
<html>
  <head>
    <!-- tell a new browser we're in UTF-8 -->
    <meta charset="utf-8" />
    <!-- tell an older browser the same -->
    <meta http-equiv="Content-Type" content="text/html; charset=utf-8" />
    <meta name="description" content="SEO optimised stuff goes here" />
    <meta name="keywords" content="HTML, programming, PHP" />
    <title>My page.</title>
  </head>
  <body></body>
</html>
```

You can even use `<meta>` to perform a redirect (where, perhaps, the more conventional HTTP 302 / `Location:` header mechanism won't work for you), which `<meta http-equiv="refresh" content="2;url=https://www.yahoo.com" />` will force the browser to redirect to http://www.yahoo.com after two seconds.

Full information about the HTML head element can be found at https://developer.mozilla.org/en-US/docs/Web/HTML/Reference/Elements/head

HTML Body Content

Per the HTML5 specification, the body element represents the (user-facing) contents of the document. Valid HTML contains only one body element as an immediate child of the root `html` document element. In here you will find everything intended to be consumed by the user making the request. At this point, I could probably write another book's worth of material, but really you are (hopefully) here for the PHP side of things. That said, we'll take a look at some useful basics and go from there.

CHAPTER 11   PROGRAMMING FOR THE INTERNET

The simplest job HTML does is to structure text. This is achieved by wrapping the text you want your users to see in certain tags to form *block-level* elements. "Block-level" means that the content inside the element starts on a new line in the browser and occupies the full available width of the parent element, pushing subsequent content onto a new line. Examples of block-level elements:

Table 11-8. *Some HTML block-level elements*

<div>	Division (generic) container
<p>	Paragraph
<h1> to <h6>	Heading text (six levels)
<ul>, <ol>, <li>	Unordered and Ordered lists, and their list elements
<form>	HTML form
<header>, <footer>, <nav> <article>, <aside>, <main>	HTML5 semantic elements
<main>, <section>	HTML5 main content, and (grouped) related content

Let's see some in action. Launch a `cli-server` PHP server (see the "HTTP" section earlier in the chapter for full details)…

```
$ docker run -it --rm -p 8080:8080 \
  -v "$PWD":/usr/src/myapp \
  -w /usr/src/myapp php:8.4-cli \
  php -S 0.0.0.0:8080
PHP 8.4.6 Development Server (http://0.0.0.0:8080) started
```

… and create the following HTML document (save it as something like block_level.html):

```
<!DOCTYPE html>
<html>
  <head>
    <meta charset="utf-8" />
    <title>Block level element demo</title>
  </head>
```

```
<body>
  <main>
    <h1>Top-level heading</h1>
    <p>A simple demo of block level elements</p>
    <div>
      &#60;hgroup&#62; elements were deprecated in the HTML5 spec
    </div>
  </main>
</body>
</html>
```

In a local web browser, request the file (via `http://localhost:8080/block_level.html`):

Figure 11-2. Block-level elements demo

Hopefully that should make sense, with each block-level element rendering on its own line. Note the use of < and >, which are rendered as chevron characters by the browser. As you might have guessed, this is an encoding scheme (HTML numeric entity encoding to be precise), which is necessary to avoid adding an unclosed <hgroup> tag to our content (more on this to come later). The corollary to the block-level is the *inline element*, which does not trigger new lines or take up any more width than necessary. Examples include:

Table 11-9. Some HTML inline elements

`<span>`	Generic inline container for grouping/styling
`<a>`	Anchor: defines hyperlinks
`<img>`	Embed an image
`<input>`, `<label>`	Inputs and associated labels inside `<form>`
`<button>`	Creates a clickable button

I could go on... for chapters and chapters, but that is not the point of this book. If you've found your appetite whetted for front-end development, then you could do a lot worse than starting with the Mozilla Developer Network's introductory tutorials on the subject, found at https://developer.mozilla.org/en-US/docs/Learn_web_development/Getting_started

The Document Object Model

This section so far constitutes the bare minimum of HTML knowledge you'll need for the remaining PHP-focused material, but there's one concept we should look at because it transfers over to PHP, and that's the *Document Object Model* (aka DOM). The DOM is an in-memory data structure used by the browser to represent the HTML document and to connect pages to their scripts. JavaScript can make changes to the DOM, which are then reflected by updates to the rendered page. In addition to the structure of the page, the browser DOM also exposes a number of APIs for interacting with the document, elements of the document, events, and even the browser itself (with certain secure limits).

At the risk of being accused of putting the cart before the horse, I'm going to first show how to manipulate existing HTML (and XML) in PHP (e.g., your code is consuming markup from an external API or website). Then with these lessons firmly secure in your mind, we can dive into techniques for generating your own markup from scratch, safe in the knowledge that you'll have a very clear idea of what well-formed markup should look like. DOM manipulation is also a very common requirement when writing client-side JavaScript, and most PHP developers (including me) will usually have to get their hands dirty with front-end code at some point. The concepts presented here transfer quite readily to code written for execution in a web browser context, I promise!

PHP dom Module

JavaScript (in a browser) has the DOM baked-in; PHP has an equivalent API provided by the dom extension, which offers a number of built-in classes for DOM representation. The (new for PHP 8.4) Dom\HTMLDocument class will parse HTML5 and create a data structure representation of our markup, which the following code demonstrates. You can run all of the code in this section from the command line; there is no need to serve via cli-server or equivalent. I'll give you a clear warning when we return to needing a web server SAPI, for example, to work properly.

```
$validHtml = <<<EOS
// ... HTML as per last example
EOS;

$dom = Dom\HTMLDocument::createFromString($validHtml);
var_dump($dom->doctype->name);
var_dump($dom->charset);
```

Output:
```
string(4) "html"
string(5) "UTF-8"
```

For versions of PHP prior to 8.4, the DOMDocument class does a similar job but is not aware of HTML5 and parses HTML as version 4, which means the semantic elements introduced by HTML5 will cause Warning errors to be emitted (more on this later). The createFromString() method (and the other factory method createFromFile()) will emit a Warning error if the HTML is malformed (say, a missing closing tag) but does not fully validate the HTML, and even invalid HTML will still result in a DOM structure. Dom\HTMLDocument extends Dom\Document, which is the "modern, spec-compliant equivalent of DOMDocument"; however, the DOMDocument::validate() method is not present on the new class. This is a brand-new feature for PHP 8.4, and hopefully the missing functionality will be added in the future. For now, you'll need to use an external library or service for HTML5 validation.

The Dom\HTMLDocument class exposes the body and head elements as simple read-only properties (remember that head and body are required attributes for valid HTML):

```
// ... $validHtml and $dom as before
var_dump($dom->head->innerHTML);
```

Output:
```
string(74) "
    <meta charset="utf-8">
    <title>Block level element demo</title>
  "
```

```php
// ... $validHtml and $dom as before
var_dump($dom->body->innerHTML);
```

Output:
```
string(202) "
    <main>
      <h1>Top-level heading</h1>
      <p>A simple demo of block level elements</p>
      <div>
        &lt;hgroup&gt; elements were deprecated in the HTML5 spec
      </div>
    </main>
```

The body and head properties are instances of Dom\HTMLElement, which are PHP class representations of HTML elements. They possess properties to represent tag names, attributes, and the special case attributes of class and id, which we'll look at in a moment.

Elements and Nodes

The DOM data structure is essentially a tree of *nodes*; all elements are nodes (Dom\Node instances) in addition to being types of data (such as Dom\HTMLElement, which is a subclass of Dom\Node), and this tree can be naturally navigated programmatically. $dom->body is an instance of Dom\HMTLElement, which has a childNodes property...

```php
// ... $validHtml and $dom as before
var_dump($dom->body->childNodes);
```

Output:
```
object(Dom\NodeList)#3 (1) {
  ["length"]=>
  int(3)
}
```

... which is a Dom\NodeList object. Node lists function like arrays (they are iterable and countable), so let's iterate over them:

```
// ... $validHtml and $dom as before
foreach ($dom->body->childNodes as $child) {
    print "child is an instance of " . get_class($child) . PHP_EOL;
    var_dump($child->nodeType);
}
```

```
Output:
child is an instance of Dom\Text
int(3)
child is an instance of Dom\HTMLElement
int(1)
child is an instance of Dom\Text
int(3)
```

Ah… only one of the children in childNodes is actually a Dom\HTMLElement instance. Also notice the values of $child->nodeType: these correspond to some built-in XML constants, which we'll look at in a moment. The first and last child nodes in the list are instances of Dom\Text, so what gives? This might make more sense if we tweak the input HTML a little:

```
$validHtml = <<<EOS
...
  <body>
    Before main element
    <main>
    ...
    </main>
    After main element
  </body>
...
EOS;
```

All we've done here is add some text above and below the <main> tags (inside the body element). Let's iterate over Dom\HTMLDocument::body again…

```
foreach ($dom->body->childNodes as $child) {
    if ($child->nodeType === XML_TEXT_NODE) {
        var_dump($child->data);
    }

    if ($child->nodeType === XML_ELEMENT_NODE) {
        var_dump($child->tagName);
    }
}
Output:
string(29) "
    Before main element
    "
string(4) "MAIN"
string(27) "
    After main element
```

... and hopefully it now makes sense that the text content of an element itself is treated as a node in the DOM. The full list of dom constants can be found at https://www.php.net/manual/en/dom.constants.php – most of them are nodeType integers and can be used to identify the type of node a DOM object represents. Some examples are given below:

Table 11-10. PHP dom extension constants

XML_ELEMENT_NODE	An HTML element
XML_ATTRIBUTE_NODE	An element attribute
XML_TEXT_NODE	Plain text contained within an element
XML_HTML_DOCUMENT_NODE	The full HTML document (node is a Dom\HTMLDocument instance)

By matching the nodeType property to XML_ELEMENT_NODE in our example above, we know that the child element can be treated as an HTML element and that it will have a tagName (which is the qualified HTML name of the element – main in this case – uppercased).

Attributes

We've not dived too deeply into HTML attributes yet, but you have already seen them. `<meta charset="utf-8" />` is a meta element with a `charset` attribute. All HTML attributes follow the form `name="value"` and are placed inside the tag, after the tag name, separated by at least one whitespace/tab/new line character. An HTML element can have any number of attributes, many of which are predefined and have special meaning. There are many predefined attributes, some of which are "global" (can apply to any element), such as the important `class` (which is used to drive CSS styling and JavaScript) and `id` (a unique ID string given to just one element in the entire DOM, again to drive styling and behavior). Some predefined attributes are specific to a tag; for example, the `http-equiv` attribute only has meaning inside a `meta` element. "Custom" attributes – that have no special predetermined effect on rendering or behavior by default – are often used to drive front-end libraries and frameworks (the Angular.io TypeScript framework, for example, uses HTML attributes prefixed with `ng-`).

Attributes are exposed by the dom API in much the same way as nodes: via public property. We can access the attributes of the `meta` element in our example HTML like so:

```
$metaNodes = $dom->getElementsByTagName('meta');

foreach ($metaNodes as $metaNode) {
    if ($metaNode->nodeType === XML_ELEMENT_NODE) {
        foreach ($metaNode->attributes as $attr) {
            var_dump(get_class($attr));
            var_dump($attr->name);
            var_dump($attr->value);
        }
    }
}
```

Output:
```
string(8) "Dom\Attr"
string(7) "charset"
string(5) "utf-8"
```

Here we make use of the method `Dom\HTMLDocument::getElementsByTagName()`, which will traverse the entire DOM tree and return an array of all matching element nodes. This method is also inherited by any class in the dom API that extends `Dom\Element`.

We iterate over the returned node list, and for all matching nodes with a type matching XML_ELEMENT_NODE, we then iterate over those element's attributes property (which is itself another node list). Hopefully by now you're starting to get a feel for this: nodes represent nearly *everything* in the DOM (from the entire document down to a single element's attributes), and consequently Dom\Node and Dom\NodeList are the basic unit of currency.

class and id

As mentioned above, class and id attributes are special. They provide mechanisms for identifying elements individually and for grouping elements together that might otherwise be in very different places in the DOM. Both JavaScript and CSS are heavily dependent on these attributes: the former for hooking behavior to the DOM, the latter for applying rendering rules. When classes and ids are applied to elements, they become much easier to find, and the dom extension offers a powerful tool for doing just that. Let's tweak our sample HTML a little to demonstrate:

```
$validHtml = <<<EOS
<!DOCTYPE html>
<html>
  <head>
    <meta charset="utf-8" />
    <title>Block level element demo</title>
  </head>
  <body>
    <main>
      <h1>Top-level heading</h1>
      <p id="first_para">A simple demo of block level elements</p>
      <div>
        &#60;hgroup&#62; elements were deprecated in the HTML5 spec
      </div>
      <p class="another_para">...continuing demo...</p>
      <p class="another_para">End of the demo</p>
    </main>
  </body>
</html>
EOS;
```

```
$dom = Dom\HTMLDocument::createFromString($validHtml);
$xpath = new Dom\XPath($dom);

$queryOne = $xpath->query('//*[@id="first_para"]');
$queryTwo = $xpath->query('//*[@class="another_para"]');

print "Query returns instances of " . get_class($queryOne) . PHP_EOL;
print "... which contains instances of " . get_class($queryOne[0]) .
PHP_EOL;
```

Output:
```
Query returns instances of Dom\NodeList
... which contains instances of Dom\HTMLElement
```

The Dom\XPath class implements the *XML Path Language*, which we will get to in a moment. For now, just accept that Dom\XPath::query('//*[id="first_para"]'); translates to "start at the root element of the document and return all elements that have an id attribute of 'first_para'". The query() method returns (surprise!) a Dom\NodeList, which contains DOM\HTMLElement objects representing each matching element in the DOM. class and id values can be accessed on these objects directly (no need to go through the entire attributes list):

```
var_dump($queryOne[0]->id);
var_dump($queryTwo[0]->className);
var_dump($queryTwo[1]->className);
```

Output:
```
string(10) "first_para"
string(12) "another_para"
string(12) "another_para"
```

XPath

The last example showed the basics of using the Dom\XPath class, which allows you to use the powerful XPath expression syntax to quickly find elements in an XML document (and therefore an HTML document). For quick traversal of the DOM, it is your go-to tool; it will enable you to access nodes deep within a DOM hierarchy with a tiny handful of code. Quick, concise DOM navigation will make for far more maintainable code when you have to process HTML, which is really the entire point of this section. I'm showing you the correct way to work on existing HTML by using a DOM parser, which will allow you to search and ultimately modify a DOM. We will get to the modification and output functionality of Dom\HTMLDocument in due course.

As we saw, the Dom\XPath::query() method takes an XPath expression string as an argument, which it uses to find and return matching nodes in the DOM. XPath expressions work a little like filesystem paths: you address a location in the filesystem by specifying a path such as ./documents/git/my_project (which is an instruction to navigate from the current directory, descend to documents, from there to git, and so on) with XPath you address the tree structure of the document. Given an XML document like this...

```
<root>
  <documents>
    <git>
      <my_project>
      </my_project>
    </git>
  </documents>
</root>
```

... the XPath expression to address the <my_project> node is simply /root/documents/git/my_project. Notice how the / character acts just like a directory separator in a file path. In XPath syntax this is a path separator between localization steps: in plain language the tokens on the right of the / are node names that are subordinate to (descendent from) those on the right, which are superordinate (ancestors of). Thus our root node is the immediate superordinate/ancestor of documents, which in turn is the immediate superordinate/ancestor of git... and so on and so on.

The expression /root/documents localizes the path to the documents node; each node-name expression is a *localization step*, with / being the *path separator*. Localization steps themselves have three parts:

- *Axis*: required, determines navigation direction
- *Node test*: required, filters the node set of the current axis by name or type
- *Predicates*: optional, additional filtering of the node set

Axes (Not the Chopping Kind)

So far so completely clear and understandable, huh? Don't worry, this will soon make sense with some examples. First of all, let's look at axes ("ax-ees" – the plural of axis). There are thirteen possible axes in the XPath specification (don't panic at `namespace::`, we'll be covering XML/HTML namespaces in due course):

Table 11-11. XPath axes

`child::`	All immediate subordinate (one level down) nodes
`descendant::`	All subordinate nodes (at any depth)
`descendant-or-self::`	All descendant nodes and the current node
`parent::`	All immediate superordinate (one level up) nodes
`ancestor::`	All superordinate nodes (at any depth)
`ancestor-or-self::`	All ancestor nodes and the current node
`attribute::`	The attributes of nodes matching the current path
`following::`	All subsequent nodes except descendants
`following-sibling::`	All subsequent nodes from current (with the same parent)
`preceding::`	All preceding nodes except ancestors
`preceding-sibling::`	All preceding nodes from current (with the same parent)
`self::`	The current node (useful in certain contexts)
`namespace::`	All nodes in the given namespace

The axis component of the localization step can be written in the long form, with a `::` character sequence to delimit it from the node test. Some of you might be wondering at this stage why the XPath expression that we used – `'//*[@id="..."]'` – doesn't have any `::` in it. The reason is *abbreviations*.

Abbreviations

Common axis names have some handy shortcuts in order to make the expression syntax more concise. The default axis is `child::`; you can omit the axis name entirely, and the XPath engine will assume you mean the child (which makes sense; if you're used to thinking in filesystem paths, then parent/child comes quite naturally). In the same way, parent:: becomes .. again, just like a filesystem path. The full list of axis abbreviations is as follows:

Table 11-12. XPath axis abbreviations

Long form	Abbreviation	
child::	blank	/child::div/child::p/ becomes /div/p
attribute::	@	node/attribute::id becomes node/@id
descendant-or-self::	//	/descendant-or-self::node()/child::thing becomes //thing
parent::	..	//parent::main becomes //main/..
self::	.	[self::node()//*contains(...)] becomes [.//*contains(...)]

The last example is a sneak peek of predicate syntax. (A note to the cautious: the last item [.//*contains()] does not return the same set as [//*contains()], and you should always rigorously test your expressions – if stuff looks weird, try adding a self:: axis).

Node Tests

A node test is usually very simple: a match on the node (tag) name. No special syntax is required: you can use a localization path of axis::node_name, and the XPath engine knows that you meant "find me all the nodes of this name on this axis from the current context." I also mentioned that the node test component can be against node type, and for this, you need a function (yes, XPath has functions, 25 of them, in fact, in the XPath 1.0 spec):

CHAPTER 11   PROGRAMMING FOR THE INTERNET

Table 11-13. *XPath node test functions*

node()	Select all nodes
text()	Select all text nodes (remember the XML_TEXT_NODE test earlier!)
comment()	Select all comment nodes
processing-instruction()	Select processing instructions, e.g., <?xml-stylesheet ...>

You won't normally need to worry about processing-instruction() because they're not supported in HTML documents. Now let's put it together. We'll use some simple XML with the Dom\XMLDocument class, but know that the lessons taught here will transfer to HTML and Dom\HTMLDocument (after all, HTML is, roughly speaking, just a specialized form of XML):

```
$xml = <<<EOS
<?xml version="1.0" encoding="UTF-8"?>
<!-- A document comment -->
<data>
  <!-- An element comment -->
  <documents>
    <git>
      <project name="javascript">Lovely JS</project>
      <project name="php">Lovely PHP</project>
      <project name="VB6" status="abandoned">Nasty VB6</project>
      <project>EMPTY</project>
    </git>
  </documents>
</data>
EOS;

$dom = Dom\XMLDocument::createFromString($xml);
$xpath = new Dom\XPath($dom);

$results = $xpath->query('/child::data');
print "Found {$results->length} data node(s)" . PHP_EOL;
var_dump($results[0]->tagName);
```

```
$results = $xpath->query('/child::comment()');
print "Found {$results->length} comment node(s)" . PHP_EOL;
var_dump($results[0]->textContent);

$results = $xpath->query('/child::data/child::comment()');
print "Found {$results->length} comment node(s)" . PHP_EOL;
var_dump($results[0]->textContent);
```

Output:
```
Found 1 data node(s)
string(4) "data"
Found 1 comment node(s)
string(20) " A document comment "
Found 1 comment node(s)
string(20) " An element comment "
```

The heart of this example consists of three XPath queries, which serve to illustrate an important concept: the *document element*. The first query is /child::data, which returns a node list with a single node, which we can see from the tagName property is our data node, the root element of our XML data structure. But we used a child axis in our localization step. How come? Well, our data element has a parent: the document itself. This is further demonstrated when our /child::comment() localization returns the comment that lies outside data, just below the <?xml version ...> declaration; the textContent property of the returned node is "A document comment". Logically enough, when we localize with /child::data/child::comment(), we're asking XPath to first localize to "nodes named data that are children of the document node context," then another step of "all comment nodes found in this context" (the context being data at this point). Remember that comment() is a function that selects nodes that have the type of comment. The only comment node found inside the data element contains the text "An element comment", which is seen in the final output.

Now let's get a bit more crafty. We can make use of the attribute axis to select all the attributes of all nodes in a context like this:

```
// ... $xml, $dom, and $xpath init as before
$results = $xpath->query(
    '/child::data/descendant::git/child::project/attribute::*'
);
var_dump($results);
```

Output:
```
object(Dom\NodeList)#7 (1) {
  ["length"]=>
  int(4)
}
```

Our expression is /child::data/descendant::git/child::project/attribute::*, which means "from the document node, localize to the immediate child node data, then localize to child node(s) git at any depth, then to immediate child nodes project, then finally to the entire set of attributes for occurrences of the project nodes." If we were interested only in a particular attribute name, we would swap the wildcard * for the name, /attribute::class, for example, would return all the class attributes of all nodes in the context. In our case the result of ...attribute::* is a node list of length four. Now, our git node contains four child project elements...

```
...
    <git>
      <project name="javascript">Lovely JS</project>
      <project name="php">Lovely PHP</project>
      <project name="VB6" status="abandoned">Nasty VB6</project>
      <project>EMPTY</project>
    </git>
...
```

... but what exactly did we get back from our query? Did we get four project elements? Let's dig into those results:

```
foreach ($results as $node) {
    print get_class($node) . " has value: {$node->value}" . PHP_EOL;
}
```

Output:
```
Dom\Attr has value: javascript
Dom\Attr has value: php
Dom\Attr has value: VB6
Dom\Attr has value: abandoned
```

What we actually got was four attribute nodes, one for each attribute set on all of the project children. They are inserted into the node list results in the order they are encountered. Just to prove the point, and to demonstrate that (rather handily) Dom\XPath::query() returns *references* to node objects inside our Dom\XMLDocument object; we can traverse the DOM from the nodes in the list we got back from query():

```
foreach ($results as $node) {
    print "Parent contains : {$node->parentNode->textContent}" . PHP_EOL;
}
Output:
Parent contains : Lovely JS
Parent contains : Lovely PHP
Parent contains : Nasty VB6
Parent contains : Nasty VB6
```

Hopefully you can see that we're actually dealing with three project elements, and the "Nasty VB6" appears twice because that element has two attributes. This isn't necessarily tremendously useful, but it lays the groundwork for something that is very useful indeed – *predicates*.

Predicates

The third component of a localization step is zero or more predicates, which are sub-expressions that allow you to further filter the nodes in the context. Here we can see some real power. Remember that class and id are plastered liberally around most HTML elements because those special attributes are used to drive CSS and JavaScript. We can also make use of them in XPath. Rather than fumbling around the DOM with loops or recursive functions, or needing lots of prior knowledge about a document, you can instead make use of class and id to write very concise expressions to get right where you need to be.

The fundamental mechanism of CSS is the *selector* expression, which allows styling directives to be applied to elements that match the selector pattern. PHP 8.4 does offer support for DOM traversal using selector expressions, which we will get to after we're done with XPath, but in the meantime, here are a couple of quick examples: .large div { /*declaration*/ } would match all div elements that are descendants of any element that has class="large", p.small { /*declaration*/ } matches all <p class="small"> elements, div > p { /*declaration*/ } would match all <p> that

767

are immediate children of a `<div>`... you get the idea. I'm hoping that you might see some parallels between CSS selectors and XPath (it's quite common to see XPath "cheat sheets" online that show equivalent CSS selectors; a lot of developers are more used to thinking in CSS rather than XPath).

The node test portion of localization we've just looked at allows for a basic level of filtering (by element name, by type), but for precision filtering, we need to add a predicate to our localization step. Predicates are sub-expressions contained in [ ] bracket characters and can be formulated with path expressions, functions, operations, strings, and numbers. XPath predicates can even be nested, used as list indexes, chained, and used as arguments to functions called in other predicates! These features allow for some mightily powerful effects: all CSS selector expressions have XPath equivalents, but the inverse is not true. When a localization step contains a predicate, the nodes that have been selected by the current axis and node test are then tested against the predicate expression, which returns true or false for each node; those that evaluate to true are included in the final list of results.

Let's see how we can use a predicate to filter our XML by attribute:

```
// ... $xml, $dom, and $xpath init as before
$results = $xpath->query(
    '/descendant::project[attribute::name="php"]'
);
print "Found {$results->length} matching node(s)" . PHP_EOL;
var_dump(get_class($results[0]));
var_Dump($results[0]->tagName);
var_Dump($results[0]->textContent);
```

Output:
```
Found 1 matching node(s)
string(11) "Dom\Element"
string(7) "project"
string(10) "Lovely PHP"
```

Perfect! We asked XPath to fetch all `project` nodes that are descendants of the document node and to filter them based on the name attribute, specifying that `attribute::name` had to match a value of the string "php". As we can see from the output, we get a single node in the list of results – a Dom\Element instance – and the tagName and textContent confirm it's the correct element from our original XML document.

For selection by class, simply use [attribute::class="..."], and for id use [attribute::id="..."]. Alternatively, there's an abbreviated form of attribute::, which is the @ character. We can therefore shorten [attribute::class="..."] to [@class="..."]. And now you understand the very first XPath expression I showed: '//*[@id="first_para"]' is the abbreviated form of /descendant-or-self::*[attribute::id="first_para"]. Before we go diving into the abbreviations of XPath, let's check out some more predicate features.

A word of warning about class: real-world HTML elements can and frequently do have multiple classes, which are assigned as a space-delimited list: <div class="large green"> means that the div element has the classes large and green. If we use = to test for either of these classes, the result is empty:

```
// modify our original XML
$xml = <<<EOS
...
  <documents>
    <git>
      <project class="javascript code">Lovely JS</project>
...
```

Here we've given one of our project elements a class="javascript code" attribute and removed its name attribute. Now if we try to search for one of those class values...

```
// ... $xml, $dom, and $xpath init as before
$results = $xpath->query('//project[@class="code"]');
print "Found {$results->length} matching node(s)" . PHP_EOL;
```

Output:
Found 0 matching node(s)

... we get an empty set. This is straightforward enough: there's no special logic in XPath that recognizes that class="javascript code" represents two values. XPath will simply see the entire attribute value of "javascript code", whereas the CSS engine has logic to treat class attributes as a space-delimited list. For XPath to do the same, we need to use a function:

```
// ... $xml, $dom, and $xpath init as before
$results = $xpath->query(
    '//project[contains(@class, "code")]'
);
print "Found {$results->length} matching node(s)" . PHP_EOL;
var_dump($results[0]->textContent);

Output:
Found 1 matching node(s)
string(9) "Lovely JS"
```

You won't (normally) need to do this with `id` because well-formed HTML does not have multiple elements with the same `id` value.

Predicate Operators and Functions

We've seen one operator in action already, `[@class="first_para"]` using the `=` relational operator to compare an attribute value to a string. There are other relational operators, arithmetic, and logical operators too. They mostly align with the same operators in PHP, so you should hopefully recognize them (Tables 11-14, 11-16, and 11-15).

Table 11-14. XPath relational operators

Operator	Meaning
=	Equals
!=	Not equals
<	Less than
>	Greater than
<=	Less than or equal
>=	Greater than or equal

Table 11-15. XPath mathematical operators

Operator	Meaning
+	Addition
-	Subtraction
*	Multiplication
div	Division
mod	Modulo

Table 11-16. XPath logical operators

Operator	Meaning
and	Logical AND
or	Logical OR

There is also a variety of functions available for use in predicates; for example, `//button[contains(text(), "Submit")]` would match `<button>Submit this form </button>` by using the `contains()` function to test that the `button` element text contents (returned by the `text()` function) contains "Submit" as a sub-string. There are quite a few functions in XPath, but the ones most likely to see use in the context of parsing HTML are:

Table 11-17. Some XPath functions

`name()`	Fetch qualified name of a node or first node in a set
`text()`	Fetch the text inside an element
`contains(haystack, needle)`	True if string `haystack` contains sub-string `needle`
`starts-with(haystack, needle)` `ends-with(haystack, needle)`	True if `haystack` starts/ends with `needle`
`normalize-space(string)`	Remove leading/trailing space from `string`, reduce all space sequences to a single space
`not(EXPR)`	True if expression EXPR evaluates to false
`count()`	Get size of node set
`position()`	Index of current node
`last()`	Matches last node

The following examples demonstrate some ways to combine indexes, paths, operations, and functions in just about any combination you're likely to need...

Table 11-18. *XPath expression examples*

[*]	Has children (is not a leaf node)
[1]	First node
[last()]	Last node
[not(last())]	All nodes except the last
[position()>1]	All nodes except the first
[position()=2] [2]	Second node
[@class="foo"][1]	First node with *only* a foo class
[contains(@class, "foo")][1]	First node that has class foo (and any number of others)
[.//div[@id="foo"]]	Return node only if it contains `<div id='foo'>` descendant
ul[count(li) > 2]	Return ul elements with two or more li children
ul[count(li[contains (@class, "hide")]) > 0]	Return ul elements containing at least one `<li class="hide">`
[contains(@class, "foo") and position() = 2]	Return nodes in the second position that also have a foo class

... and yep, there's wacky-looking stuff in there. Let's take a minute to look at some of these at work on a real DOM, for which we'll build a more complex XML document, build a Dom\XMLDocument object, and throw it at Dom\XPath (again, XML is standing in for HTML here, but all the concepts transfer, and this is a deliberate choice on my part... you'll see why):

```
$xml = <<<EOS
<?xml version="1.0" encoding="UTF-8"?>
<data>
  <projects>
    <project class="software javascript">
      <codebase name="frontend" status="live">
        React with 10k dependencies
```

```
      </codebase>
      <codebase name="microservice" status="live">
        node.js with 10k dependencies
      </codebase>
      <codebase name="concept" status="wip">WIP CONCEPT</codebase>
    </project>
    <project class="software php">
      <codebase name="website" status="live">
        It's honest work
      </codebase>
    </project>
    <project class="software vb6">
      <codebase name="legacy_horror" status="eol">
        I was there... 3000 years ago
      </codebase>
    </project>
    <project class="book">
      <book title="Exploring PHP8" status="unfinished">
        Deadlines make a whistling noise as they fly past
      </book>
    </project>
  </projects>
</data>
EOS;

$dom = Dom\XMLDocument::createFromString($xml);
$xpath = new Dom\XPath($dom);
```

Ok, we're all set. Let's play with positional predicates first and show something important:

```
$results = $xpath->query('/data/projects/project[position()=0]');
print "Found {$results->length} matching node(s)" . PHP_EOL;

$results = $xpath->query('/data/projects/project[position()=1]');
print "Found {$results->length} matching node(s)" . PHP_EOL;
var_dump($results[0]->tagName);
var_dump($results[0]->getAttribute('class'));
```

Output:
Found 0 matching node(s)
Found 1 matching node(s)
string(7) "project"
string(19) "software javascript"

The principle lesson here is that node position is always counted from 1, not 0, so be aware of that if you were to generate XPath expressions from looping structures. Otherwise, the XPaths above should be pretty straightforward: we navigate to `child::data` from the (implicit/virtual) document node, then `child::projects`. In that context, we then test the `position()` value of each `project` node; none are at position 0, and one is present at position 1. We confirm it is the first `project` element in our XML by writing out its `class` attribute. We could (and should) shorten this expression to /data/projects/project[1] - the `position()` function is best deployed when excluding nodes; for example, `[position() > 1]` would return all but the first node in a list.

Now for something more common: finding nodes based on class. Let's find all the `project` nodes that have a `software` class. Remember we'll need to call `contains()` rather than using an equality test because we're mimicking HTML class behavior (assigning multiple classes):

```
// ... $xml, $dom, and $xpath init as before
$results = $xpath->query('//project[contains(@class, "software")]');
print "Found {$results->length} matching node(s)" . PHP_EOL;
```

Output:
Found 3 matching node(s)

Great, we found the three `project` elements in our document that have "software" somewhere in their `class` attribute. Now let's pretend that we did that because we're actually more interested in the `codebase` child elements. Sure, we could use the `project` elements in the node list that we got back from our first query and iterate over their children, but there's a much neater way to do it by tweaking the XPath query:

```
// ... $xml, $dom, and $xpath init as before
$results = $xpath->query('//project[contains(@class, "software")]/codebase');
```

```
foreach ($results as $node) {
    var_dump(trim($node->textContent));
}
```

Output:
```
string(27) "React with 10k dependencies"
string(29) "node.js with 10k dependencies"
string(11) "WIP CONCEPT"
string(16) "It's honest work"
string(29) "I was there... 3000 years ago"
```

Remember that the predicate is applied only to the localization step between the / separators, and you're perfectly fine to tack another step on afterwards. Don't forget you can use logical operations within predicates; here's how you can find all the child nodes of projects that have either "php" or "book" as one of their classes:

```
// ... $xml, $dom, and $xpath init as before
$results = $xpath->query(
    '//project[contains(@class, "php") or contains(@class, "book")]/*'
);
print "Found {$results->length} matching node(s)" . PHP_EOL;
foreach ($results as $node) {
    var_dump(trim($node->textContent));
}
```

Output:
```
Found 2 matching node(s)
string(16) "It's honest work"
string(49) "Deadlines make a whistling noise as they fly past"
```

Neat huh? One final curveball to throw at you: there's one special token in the XPath syntax that defies categorization because it belongs neither in axis, node test, nor predicate. It is possible to use multiple expressions with a union operator (which will combine the node list results of both expressions into a single set). The following examples return the same output as the previous...

```
// ... $xml, $dom, and $xpath init as before
$results = $xpath->query(
    '//project[contains(@class, "php")] | //project[contains(@class,
                                                "book")]'
);
print "Found {$results->length} matching node(s)" . PHP_EOL;
foreach ($results as $node) {
    var_dump(trim($node->textContent));
}
```

... but do bear in mind performance issues for large DOMs or complex queries (the union requires two passes of the DOM, the predicate with an or requires one).

But I'm Not Running PHP 8.4 :(

We're pretty much done with looking at creating and navigating the DOM; the next logical step is making modifications. Before we do that, though, I promised to explain why our XPath examples were all using XML and not HTML. The reason for this is HTML5 and PHP's support for it. Prior to version 8.4, PHP didn't have a proper HTML5-compliant parser, which is a little mind-boggling considering what PHP is designed to do, not to mention the fact that HTML5 is knocking on for sixteen years old now... but here we are. Native HTML parsing before 8.4 was achieved with DOMDocument (which still exists in PHP 8.4), and the underlying XML implementation for DOMDocument (libxml2) only supports HTML up to version 4.01. One of the big differences between HTML versions 5 and <= 4.01 is the DOCTYPE declaration: HTML 4 and earlier DOCTYPE contained extra information called a DTD (Document Type Declaration), which is a schema document: a declaration of all the elements and their attributes that are valid in the document. Prior to HTML5, a DOCTYPE line would look something like this: `<!DOCTYPE HTML PUBLIC "-//W3C//DTD HTML 4.01//EN" "http://www.w3.org/TR/html4/strict.dtd">`, where http://www.w3.org/TR/html4/strict.dtd is used as the schema (the rules that define how valid documents should be structured), you can feed that URL into a browser and have a look for yourself if you feel inclined!

HTML5 did away with dtd's in the DOCTYPE. The end result is that DOMDocument has no DTD to work with when parsing an HTML5 `<!DOCTYPE ...>` statement, so it falls back to a default (HTML 4), and this is what happens if DOMDocument is given some HTML5 elements to parse:

```
$html5 = <<<EOS
<!DOCTYPE html>
<html>
  <head>
    <meta charset="utf-8" />
    <title>HTML5 is lovely</title>
  </head>
  <body>
    <header>Page header</header>
    <main>Main content</main>
    <footer>Page footer</footer>
  </body>
</html>
EOS;

$dom = new DOMDocument();
$dom->loadHTML($html5);

Output:
PHP Warning:  DOMDocument::loadHTML(): Tag header invalid...
PHP Warning:  DOMDocument::loadHTML(): Tag main invalid...
PHP Warning:  DOMDocument::loadHTML(): Tag footer...
```

The header, main, and footer semantic elements were introduced in HTML5. They don't exist in http://www.w3.org/TR/html4/strict.dtd, and PHP duly spits out some warnings. But! We still get a DOM tree to play with, because DOMDocument (and Dom\HTMLDocument) are pretty forgiving, which is definitely in the spirit of Getting Things Done On The Web...

```
$nodes = $dom->getElementsByTagName('header');
print "Found {$nodes->length} matching node(s)" . PHP_EOL;
var_dump($nodes[0]->textContent);

Output:
Found 1 matching node(s)
string(11) "Page header"
```

... and we can even use the old DOMXPath utility class (which behaves exactly the same as Dom\XPath):

```
$xpath = new DOMXPath($dom);
$results = $xpath->query('//footer');
print "Found {$results->length} matching node(s)" . PHP_EOL;
var_dump($results[0]->textContent);
```

Output:
Found 1 matching node(s)
string(11) "Page footer"

So, all is not lost if you're stuck on PHP 8.3 (or earlier). It would be nice if we could get rid of those initialization errors though, especially if our HTML is chock-full of new elements. Luckily there are a couple of ways to do it:

```
// ... $html5 heredoc as before
libxml_use_internal_errors(true);
$dom = new DOMDocument();
$dom->loadHTML($html5);
print "Document loaded." . PHP_EOL;
var_dump(libxml_get_errors());
```

Output:
```
Document loaded.
array(3) {
  [0]=>
  object(LibXMLError)#2 (6) {
    ["level"]=>
    ...
    ["message"]=>
    string(19) "Tag header invalid
    ...
```

libxml_use_internal_errors(true) will suppress error emission and instead store them in an internal array, which can be accessed with libxml_get_errors(). Re-enable normal error behavior by calling libxml_use_internal_errors(false). Alternatively, you can suppress errors completely when loading the document...

```
// ... $html5 heredoc as before
$dom->loadHTML($html5, LIBXML_NOERROR);
print "Document loaded." . PHP_EOL;
var_dump(libxml_get_errors());

Output:
Document loaded.
array(0) {
}
```

... but as you can see, you will then lose a lot of possibly important information. Parsing HTML5 with `DOMDocument` comes with a fairly hefty disclaimer: if the HTML is not well-formed, you will likely get a different DOM structure compared to the same markup parsed with `Dom\HTMLDocument`. The rules for handling things like missing closing tags differ between HTML4 and 5.

Namespaces (Again!)

I still haven't fully addressed my decision to demonstrate `Dom\XPath`, and the answer to that lies with `Dom\HTMLDocument` and namespaces. Now, you'll recognize the word "namespace" because PHP namespaces were introduced in Chapter 3, "Functions," and were also explored in **Object Fundamentals**. Namespaces also exist in XML (and therefore HTML). They exist as a mechanism to allow elements with different contents and meaning to coexist in the same document (and avoid things like conflicts when combining XML fragments from different sources, just like we would use them to avoid naming conflicts when using classes from different libraries that share a name). They work by prepending element names (tags in the document) with a namespace name. A book `<project>` could become `<b:project>`, a coding project could become `<c:project>`, and so on. XML namespaces must be defined, which can be done with an `xmlns:<PREFIX>="URI"` attribute in the start tag of the first namespaced element:

```
<data>
  <c:project xmlns:c="http://some.domain/code_project">
    <c:codebase></c:codebase>
  </c:project>
```

```
  <b:project xmlns:b="http://some.domain/book_project">
    <b:book></b:book>
  </b:project>
</data>
```

The URI of the namespace is not that important; it doesn't need to be a valid URL, it just needs to be unique, though they are often used to point to pages containing information about the namespace. Another way to introduce namespaces into XML documents is to put them all in the root element like this...

```
<data xmlns:c="http://some.domain/code_project"
xmlns:b="http://some.domain/book_project">
  <c:project>
    <c:codebase></c:codebase>
  </c:project>
  <b:project>
    <b:book></b:book>
  </b:project>
</data>
```

... and yet another way to do it is to define a *default namespace* for the parent element and skip having to shove those prefixes in all the child elements:

```
<project xmlns="http://some.domain/code_project">
  <codebase></codebase>
</project>
```

It is this default namespace mechanism that contributed to my decision to demonstrate XPath with Dom\XMLDocument, because Dom\HTMLDocument automatically puts HTML that it parses into the default namespace of "http://www.w3.org/1999/xhtml" (note that DOMDocument does not exhibit this behavior). This is entirely correct behavior, but it would have meant dumping namespaces on you before you had a chance to get comfortable with the basics of HTML, XML, and DOM. A quick demo will show you what I'm talking about:

```
// ... $html5 heredoc as before
$dom = Dom\HTMLDocument::createFromString($html5);
$xpath = new Dom\XPath($dom);
```

```
$results = $xpath->query('//footer');
print "Found {$results->length} matching node(s)";
```

Output:
Found 0 matching node(s)

What gives? We just used the //footer XPath localization step with DOMXpath::query(), and it worked just fine. The problem here is that without any information about the default namespace, Dom\XPath doesn't know where to search for the footer element. The entire document, from its html root downwards, is sat inside the "http://www.w3.org/1999/xhtml" namespace. Fortunately, we can grab that namespace from the (slightly magical) document element and tell Dom\XPath about it:

```
$xpath->registerNamespace(
    'ns',
    $dom->documentElement->namespaceURI
);

$results = $xpath->query('//ns:footer');
print "Found {$results->length} matching node(s)" . PHP_EOL;
var_dump($results[0]->textContent);
```

Output:
Found 1 matching node(s)
string(11) "Page footer"

Here we grab the document element's namespace, which will always have the same value because it is standardized (it's up to you if you want to access it from the document element or just use your own constant string) and register it (with a prefix) on Dom\Xpath. Once the XPath object is aware of the namespace, we are able to correctly address the footer element. Think of it like XPath trying to find a PHP class called Footer in the root namespace, but it was actually declared in the Ns namespace, and its correct name is Ns\Footer. Registering the default HTML namespace, a bit long-winded, and if you prefer, you can prevent Dom\HTMLDocument from default namespacing entirely by passing in the \Dom\HTML_NO_DEFAULT_NS constant as an option...

```
// ... $html5 heredoc as before
$dom = Dom\HTMLDocument::createFromString(
    $html5,
    \Dom\HTML_NO_DEFAULT_NS
);
$xpath = new Dom\XPath($dom);
$results = $xpath->query('//header');
print "Found {$results->length} matching node(s)" . PHP_EOL;
var_dump($results[0]->textContent);

Output:
Found 1 matching node(s)
string(11) "Page footer"
```

... but be warned that this will mean that your DOM now deviates from the HTML5 specification. The official PHP documentation warns that some methods of classes in the \Dom (PHP) namespace depend on the HTML namespace. Not having the default namespace set will also impact any HTML that is output from your DOM, because the HTML5 schema is not applied (little problems like self-closing tags suddenly picking up closing tags will start to creep in). We'll cover that at the appropriate point.

As you might have already guessed, the pre-8.4 DOMXPath class does not have this quirk, because DOMDocument does not do any automatic namespacing. Some things to note on parsing differences between HTML5 (Dom\HTMLDocument) and earlier (DOMDocument): the HTML5 spec allows custom elements, which some JavaScript frameworks (like React) make liberal use of. Nothing to be alarmed about, DOMDocument will emit an error (which you've just seen how to handle) but still generate a DOM tree.

One More Thing…

There's a final nifty trick I'd like to show you with Dom\XPath (and DOMXPath) – you can register any PHP function as an XPath function, or even write your own, and use them in expressions. The Dom\XPath::registerPhpFunctions() method accepts a string that matches a function name, an array of function name strings, or an associative array of callable objects (where the keys are used as the function names). You can even call it without arguments to add *every* PHP function if you wish. However, you must first register the php namespace, because all of the function imports will be bound to that namespace.

```
$dom = Dom\HTMLDocument::createFromString($html5);
$xpath = new Dom\XPath($dom);
$xpath->registerNamespace('ns', $dom->documentElement->namespaceURI);
$xpath->registerNamespace('php', 'http://php.net/xpath');
```

With all that set up, you can now start registering your own PHP functions for use in an XPath query. Here we'll pass a `callable` as an anonymous function, for extra cool points (and avoid polluting global scope with an extra function name):

```
$xpath->registerPhpFunctions(['containsLovely' => function
(array|string $arg) {
    print "calling containsLovely() ..." . PHP_EOL;
    if (is_string($arg)) {
        print "testing a string ..." . PHP_EOL;
        return str_contains($arg, 'lovely');
    }

    foreach ($arg as $node) {
        if ($node->nodeType == XML_ELEMENT_NODE) {
            print "testing a Dom\Element ..." . PHP_EOL;
            return str_contains($node->textContent, 'lovely');
        }
    }

    return false;
}]);
```

This function doesn't do anything particularly amazing; at heart, it's just a `str_contains()` call with some parameter handling. We could have just registered `str_contains()` like this: `Dom\XPath::registerPhpFunctions('str_contains');` but then we'd need to put extra logic into the XPath expression itself. This way we're keeping our expression concise (always a good idea) as well as creating a learning opportunity, which you'll see in a moment. To call the function mapped to the `containsLovely` string, we use the syntax `php:function(<NAME>, <ARG>)` where `<ARG>` is an XPath localization step:

```
$result = $xpath->query(
  '//ns:head[php:function("containsLovely", ns:title)]'
);
print "Found {$result->length} matching node(s)" . PHP_EOL;
```

Output:
calling containsLovely() ...
testing a Dom\Element ...
Found 1 matching node(s)

We can see from the output that Dom\XPath::query() called our anonymous function and passed an array containing a single Dom\Element instance (actually a sub-child Dom\HTMLElement instance) – a Dom\NodeList might have been more appropriate in my humble opinion, but you can't have everything. This element's text content contains the sub-string "lovely", so we return true, which means the predicate in our XPath expression is true and we get our match on the title child of head. Please note the namespacing of the HTML elements as well as the PHP function string.

You might at this point be wondering why our anonymous function has a union data type (array|string) for its single parameter. I'm glad you asked, because it allows us to do this…

```
$result = $xpath->query(
    '//ns:head/ns:title[php:functionString("containsLovely", .)]'
);
print "Found {$result->length} matching node(s)" . PHP_EOL;
```

Output:
calling containsLovely() ...
testing a string ...
Found 1 matching node(s)

… which demonstrates a handy shortcut, php:functionString(), which will extract the text content of all the nodes in the current context, rather than passing the array of nodes and making you do it yourself. Notice also that I've tweaked the rest of the expression by moving the ns:title localization step out of the php:functionString() call and replacing it with an abbreviated self:: step. It's functionally identical to the previous form and just a matter of preference (keeping predicate sub-expressions as clean as possible).

If, for some reason, you'd prefer your registered function to exist in a namespace other than php, then you can use Dom\XPath::registerPhpFunctionNS() to do something like this:

```
$xpath->registerNamespace('foo', 'urn:foo.ns');
$xpath->registerPhpFunctionNS(
    'urn:foo.ns',
    'someFunction',
    function (array $nodes) {
        // do something with $nodes here...
    }
);
$xpath->query('//ns:body[foo:someFunction(.)]');
```

querySelector() (Because XPath Looks Hard)

I've gone (fairly) deep on XPath because I'm opinionated, and my principle reason was that XPath gives you more tools for DOM traversal than CSS selectors; there are tricks you can pull with XPath that just don't exist with CSS selectors. With that said, though, I would be doing you a disservice if I didn't also show a couple of alternatives. I mentioned earlier in this section that PHP 8.4 introduces support for using selector expressions for DOM traversal. Specifically, this is via Dom\HTMLDocument and DOM\HTMLElement - the HTML5-compliant replacements for DOMDocument and DOMElement. These new classes provide a couple of methods that have been "borrowed" from JavaScript's own DOM API, named querySelector() and querySelectorAll(). (These new methods exist on the Dom\Document and Dom\Element parent classes, so you can use them with HTML or XML).

CSS (Cascading Style Sheets) is a declarative language used to describe how an HTML document should be presented (rendered) by a client. The most fundamental unit of CSS is the ruleset, which is formed from selector expressions followed by declaration blocks. The declarations in each block are applied to the elements that match the selector; the general syntax is as follows:

```
<selector_expression> {
    <declaration>;
    <declaration>;
}
```

For example, you might want to have bold text for h1 elements that have a main ancestor:

```
main h1 {
    font-weight: bold;
}
```

Popularizing the idea of using CSS selector syntax as a means to quickly fly around a DOM structure can be credited to the venerable jQuery library (inspired by the earlier cssLibrary), which made JavaScript a far nicer place to work – especially for back-end duffers like me – way back in the mists of time (2006, to be precise). Of particular note was its core traversal mechanism, where you simply called the global jQuery object as a function with a CSS selector string as an argument. This returned one or more references to matching DOM elements that could then be messed about with to your heart's content. The idea was so popular that it eventually made its way into JavaScript standards as the Selectors API (around 2013). An exhaustive list of jQuery functionality that has found its way into modern JavaScript can be found here: https://youmightnotneedjquery.com/

PHP has for a while had third-party libraries that implement the same feature – Symfony's DomCrawler component is a good example https://symfony.com/doc/current/components/dom_crawler.html – and now PHP 8.4 gives us native support. Time for a quick demo.

```
$html5 = <<<EOS
<!DOCTYPE html>
<html>
  <head>
    <meta charset="utf-8" />
    <title>HTML5 is lovely</title>
  </head>
  <body>
    <header>Page header</header>
    <main class="main-content">
      <p class="large">Para One</p>
      <p class="small">Para Two</p>
      <p class="small">Para Three</p>
    </main>
    <footer>Page footer</footer>
```

```
    </body>
</html>
EOS;

$dom = Dom\HTMLDocument::createFromString($html5);
var_dump($dom->querySelectorAll('body p'));
var_dump($dom->querySelector('body p'));
var_dump($dom->querySelector('body p')->textContent);

Output:
object(Dom\NodeList)#5 (1) {
  ["length"]=>
  int(3)
}
object(Dom\HTMLElement)#5 (29) {
  ["namespaceURI"]=>
  string(28) "http://www.w3.org/1999/xhtml"
  ...
}
string(8) "Para One"
```

The above shows the main difference between querySelector(), which always returns a single node, and querySelectorAll(), which always returns a node list. This example also shows that querySelector() returns the first match, as we can deduce when accessing the returned node's textContent property. The list returned by querySelectorAll() is said to be "static" (which matches the behavior of JavaScript's equivalent document.querySelectorAll()), static node lists do not update if there are changes to the DOM structure after selection. If we obtained a list of p element children of main and then added another p element, we would not see the new element in the list (the query would have to run again to obtain a new list). A querySelectorAll() node list contains references to the matching DOM nodes, so any changes to those nodes' attributes, contents, or child elements would be accessible without needing to query again.

Selector Syntax

Earlier I gave some examples of CSS selectors and showed how `div > p` would match all `p` elements that are direct children of any `div` element: `div > p` is equivalent to XPath `/descendant-or-self::div/child::p` (abbreviates to `//div/p`). CSS selector expressions are roughly equivalent to XPath's, you can think of them as localization steps, where the leftmost step is closest to the root of the document (the document element) and, as we progress to the right of the expression, we descend the DOM tree. The precise syntax rules of CSS selectors are different from XPath. Sufficiently so that it's worth defining them before we do any deep comparison.

Selector Structure

The basic structure of a CSS selector is this: "simple" selectors can be combined into "compound" selectors to act on single elements. These simple/compound sequences are (fairly) equivalent to XPath localization steps. Simple/compound selectors can be further joined with *combinators* to form a "complex" selector sequence, just as XPath localization steps are joined together to form an XPath expression.

A simple CSS selector is a single instance of one of four basic selectors: `basic`, `attribute`, `pseudo-class`, and `pseudo-element`.

Table 11-19. CSS selector basic types

Simple type	Detail	Example
basic	Asterisk (aka "universal"), element name (aka "type"), class, id	`* div .class #id`
attribute	Any attribute (including `class` and `id` if you wish)	`[id] [href~="php"]`
pseudo-class	Matches state of an element	`:visited :paused` `:checked :has`
pseudo-element	Matches a part of an element	`::first-letter` `::selection`

Some of these simple selectors don't make much sense in the context of PHP's DOM ..., for example, many of the pseudo-class selectors rely on things like UI events or browser history, none of which exist in your PHP script. In fact, the querySelector() and querySelectorAll() DOM methods in PHP don't have full support for the full spectrum of CSS selectors exactly for this reason. The pseudo-class most likely to be relevant to you is :has, which is a nifty hack that allows for (in a roundabout way) the selection of parents or ancestors, but others aren't supported and will trigger a fatal error. For example, :visited isn't supported…

```
$visitedLinks = $dom->querySelectorAll('main a:visited');
```

Output:
PHP Fatal error: Uncaught DOMException: Invalid selector (Selectors. Not supported: visited)

… because it requires a browser with history. This is the case for many other pseudo-classes, so test your selector expressions with care.

You can combine simple selectors to form compound selectors, which are just a sequence of simple selectors without a combinator (a single space character is one of the combinators in CSS, so compound selectors do not contain spaces). If a compound selector contains a type (element name) or universal (asterisk) selector, it must come first and must be the only instance. Here are some examples:

Table 11-20. CSS compound selectors

.green	Any element with a green class
*.green	Equivalent to .green
div.green	Any div element with a green class
p[id]	Any p element possessing an id attribute
p#special.green.large	A p element with id "special" with both green AND large classes

And finally, complex selectors use combinators to join simple and compound selectors together. You can think of combinators as functioning like the axes of XPath: a space in CSS is descendant::, a > is child::, and so on. The CSS combinators are:

Table 11-21. CSS combinators

Combinator	Detail	Example
" "	Descendant at any depth	`main div p h1.large #special a`
>	Immediate child	`div > p`
~	Subsequent siblings: A ~ B matches *all* B preceded by A where both share a parent	`h1 ~ div`
+	Next sibling: A + B matches *first* B preceded by A	`h1 + p`

Descendant and immediate child have obvious parallels in the XPath `child::` and `descendant::` axes. Subsequent ~ behaves like `following-sibling::` and next sibling + behaves like `following-sibling::node[1]`. There also exists the "column combinator" `||` (which is misnamed) and the "namespace separator/combinator" `|` (it is also not a combinator) neither of which you are likely to need to worry about.

Hopefully the above has given some insight into how powerful and flexible CSS selector expressions can be, and I think it's time we saw some practical PHP examples that will give XPath a run for its money:

```
// ... $html5 heredoc as before
$dom = Dom\HTMLDocument::createFromString($html5);
$parasAfterLarge = $dom->querySelectorAll('main > p.large ~ p');
print "Selected paragraphs:" . PHP_EOL;
foreach ($parasAfterLarge as $node) {
    print $node->textContent . PHP_EOL;
}

$firstParaAfterLarge = $dom->querySelectorAll('main > p.large + p');
print "Selected paragraphs:" . PHP_EOL;
foreach ($firstParaAfterLarge as $node) {
    print $node->textContent . PHP_EOL;
}

Output:
Selected paragraphs:
Para Two
```

Para Three
Selected paragraphs:
Para Two

The two selector expressions driving the example above demonstrate complex expressions composed of two combinators, child > with ~ subsequent sibling, and child > with + first sibling. You can build expressions as complex as you like, with any (or at least an arbitrarily large) number of simple/compound selectors.

I mentioned earlier that the :has pseudo-class is supported by PHP 8.4 and will probably prove the most useful and relevant. The main reason is that this is how CSS provides equivalent functionality to the XPath axes ancestor:: and parent::. *:has(p) is equivalent to XPath p/ancestor::* and *:has(> div) is the same as /div/parent:: ... you get the idea. As always, here are some examples:

```
// ... $html5 heredoc as before
$dom = Dom\HTMLDocument::createFromString($html5);
$ancestor = $dom->querySelectorAll('*:has(p)');
print "Ancestors:" . PHP_EOL;
foreach ($ancestor as $node) {
    print $node->localName . PHP_EOL;
}
```

Output:
Ancestors:
html
body
main

If we changed the inner selector of :has() to use the child combinator > and feed it through the same foreach loop we get just the parent node:

```
// ... $html5 heredoc as before
$dom = Dom\HTMLDocument::createFromString($html5);
$parent = $dom->querySelectorAll('*:has(> p)');
print "Parent:" . PHP_EOL;
foreach ($parent as $node) {
    print $node->localName . PHP_EOL;
}
```

Output:
Parent:
main

Other useful (to us, in PHP world) positional pseudo-classes are:

Table 11-22. *CSS pseudo-classes*

Pseudo-class	XPath Equivalent
:first-child	/*[1]
:last-child	/*[last()]
:nth-child(n)	/*[n]
:first-of-type	/node[1] or *[1][name() = "node"]
:last-of-type	/node[last()] or *[last()][name() = "node"]
:nth-of-type(n)	/node[n] or *[n][name() = "node"]
:only-child or :first-child:last-child	[count() = 1]

That will do to get you started with CSS selectors, and like before, I highly recommend the MDN CSS learning guides, starting with https://developer.mozilla.org/en-US/docs/Web/CSS/CSS_selectors/Selector_structure. For the rest of this section I'll use Dom\XPath and Dom\HTMLDocument::querySelectorAll() interchangeably so you can get used to seeing both.

DOM Modification and Output

Let's take a moment and review what we've learned. HTML is a markup language (a specialized form of XML, in fact) that allows you to create a document that mixes literal text with metadata (in the form of tags such as <head>, <body>, <div>, and so on) to form a data structure called a DOM. The structure is a tree, with html as its root element, which must have both head and body child elements. The head element contains at least a title element and usually other children like meta and link. These head elements allow you to do things like define document metadata like character encoding and inclusion of external resources like scripts and style sheets. The body element is the user-facing content, and the bulk of the structure in there is intended for rendering (you can also put script and other non-rendering elements if you like). We've seen how to parse an HTML string with Dom\HTMLDocument (or DOMDocument for older PHP installations) to create a tree of DOM objects, and we've learned how to navigate our way around this tree with XPath.

You now have a nice set of tools for interacting with HTML programmatically, without having to resort to searching for sub-strings or, worse (so much worse), regular expressions. (Never ever ever parse HTML with regular expressions. Ever.) The next logical step is modifying the DOM and generating new HTML. We've seen that the classes in the PHP 8.4 Dom namespace (and the root namespace classes provided by the dom extension for previous versions) expose a lot of information via public properties. Naturally, this makes it straightforward to change those properties.

Moving Elements

The base Dom\Node class (and its DOMNode predecessor) also provides a number of utility methods for adding, removing, and moving elements. Remember that just about all PHP classes in the Dom namespace (and the predecessors in the root namespace) are sub-classed from these, so you can call ::appendChild() on an XMLElement, HTMLElement, or even HTMLDocument. The functions are detailed below:

Table 11-23. PHP Dom\Node methods for child node manipulation

::appendChild($node, $child)	Add new node at end of children
::removeChild($child)	Remove child node
::replaceChild($node, $child)	Remove child, add new node at same position
::insertBefore($node, $child)	Add new node before child, or move existing node to new position
::cloneNode()	Create a copy of an existing node object

Let's start with moving existing things around: we're going to change the order of those p children around in our main element of $html5, which means we'll need to grab references to the nodes we want to work with. I'll include the HTML string we've

CHAPTER 11 PROGRAMMING FOR THE INTERNET

been working with so far as a reminder of the document structure, and we're going to make use of a constant in the Dom namespace (the reasons why will become apparent further down):

```
use const Dom\HTML_NO_DEFAULT_NS;

$html5 = <<<EOS
<!DOCTYPE html>
<html>
  <head>
    <meta charset="utf-8" />
    <title>HTML5 is lovely</title>
  </head>
  <body>
    <header>Page header</header>
    <main class="main-content">
      <p class="large">Para One</p>
      <p class="small">Para Two</p>
      <p class="small">Para Three</p>
    </main>
    <img src="./foo.jpg" />
    <footer>Page footer</footer>
  </body>
</html>
EOS;

$dom = Dom\HTMLDocument::createFromString(
    $html5,
    HTML_NO_DEFAULT_NS
);
$xpath = new Dom\XPath($dom);
$main = $xpath->query('//main')[0];

$firstPara = $dom->querySelector('main > p:first-child');
$lastPara = $dom->querySelector('main > p:last-child');
```

... which we've done with a mix of XPath::query() and HTMLDocument::query Selector(). Note the ::query()[0] syntax is equivalent to ::querySelector() – we're grabbing the first matched element in the returned arrays, so we're working with Dom\Node instances (or some sub-class). Next we'll use Node::insertBefore() to put a "new" node in front of an existing – this method is smart enough to realize when the "new" node is actually an existing node in the DOM, in which case the end result is the node repositioned relative to the child...

```
// $lastPara is inserted before $firstPara
$main->insertBefore($lastPara, $firstPara);
```

... after this call is made, the $lastParam node will have been moved to the first-child position, and $firstPara will now be the second child of main, which we can prove by writing out the new markup using HTMLDocument::saveHTML($node):

```
print $dom->saveHTML($main);
```

Output:
```
<main class="main-content">
    <p class="small">Para Three</p><p class="large">Para One</p>
    <p class="small">Para Two</p>
</main>
```

Don't worry about the lack of newline character between the closing and opening tags of the first p children of main; it's still a perfectly well-formed HTML fragment. Speaking of which, what we have generated here isn't a full document, which should be obvious from the lack of a <!DOCTYPE declaration and missing head, title, and body elements. HTMLDocument::saveHTML() takes a DOM node object argument and will generate the HTML from that point of the tree. Handy if you just need to generate a fragment for use elsewhere. If you want to save the entire document, call it without arguments:

```
print $dom->saveHTML();
```
Output:
```
<!DOCTYPE html><html><head>
  <meta charset="utf-8"></meta>
  <title>HTML5 is lovely</title>
  ...
```

Ah, but wait! What's up with that meta tag? HTML meta tags are self-closing (because they never contain child elements), so why did we pick one up? If you look back to when the DOM was created via $dom = Dom\HTMLDocument::createFromString(...); you'll notice the HTML_NO_DEFAULT_NS constant was supplied as an argument. This made our XPath code slightly easier (no need to register the default namespace, etc.), but it introduces an issue. Hopefully you'll recall me saying that a lack of correct namespace introduces issues to HTMLDocument; this is one of them. Without the HTML5 schema, the rules for writing the markup, the parser isn't aware that meta, img et al. don't need closing tags and "helpfully" puts one in for you. If you intend to generate HTML5 markup from your DOM, it will need the correct default namespace:

```
$dom = Dom\HTMLDocument::createFromString($html5);
print $dom->saveHTML();
```

Output:
```
<!DOCTYPE html><html><head>
  <meta charset="utf-8">
```

Don't be concerned about the lack of forward slash on the closing chevron of meta; the HTML5 spec doesn't require them, and the Lexbor library that powers all of this is sticking to the standards.

Manipulating class

Going back to our newly rearranged DOM, now that we've juggled the order of the p elements, we might want to adjust the classes – a fairly common job when processing a DOM. With PHP 8.4, the dom extension provides some useful utilities for interacting with an element's class attribute. The Dom\Element::classList property is an instance of Dom\TokenList...

```
var_dump($lastPara->classList);
Output:
object(Dom\TokenList)#6 (2) {
  ["length"]=>
  int(2)
  ["value"]=>
  string(12) "small  blah "
}
```

... which offers ::add() and ::remove() methods to make manipulating classes much easier:

```
$lastPara->classList->remove('small');
$lastPara->classList->add('large');
$firstPara->classList->remove('large');
$firstPara->classList->add('small');
```

```
print $dom->saveHTML();
```

Output:

```
...
<main class="main-content">
  <p class="large">Para Three</p><p class="small">Para One</p>
```

Dom\TokenList::remove() will accept a variable number of string arguments to allow the removal of multiple classes in one call. If an element had class="small green bold article" classes, then classList->remove('small', 'green', 'bold'); would result in the element retaining just class="article". The TokenList class also offers ::contains(token) to search the list for a given token and ::replace(token, newToken) to swap one token for another in a single call. The previous example could have also been written as:

```
$lastPara->classList->replace('small', 'large');
$firstPara->classList->replace('large', 'small');
```

Unfortunately, PHP <= 8.3 does not offer an equivalent interface for class manipulation; there is no DOMTokenList class I'm afraid. You'll be forced to jump through string handling hoops to make changes, but DOMElement does expose the classes in a className string property.

Manipulating Other Attributes

Of course, other attributes will need attention too. The public Dom\Element::id string property can be directly read/written to control any element's id property (no need for fancy lists and utility methods; the id attribute is only ever a single value – just make sure they're unique throughout the DOM). All other attributes can be accessed via the Dom\Node::attributes property...

CHAPTER 11   PROGRAMMING FOR THE INTERNET

```php
// ... $html5 heredoc as before
$dom = Dom\HTMLDocument::createFromString($html5);
$meta = $dom->querySelector('head meta:first-child');
var_dump($meta->attributes);
foreach ($meta->attributes as $attr) {
    var_dump($attr);
}
```

Output:
```
object(Dom\NamedNodeMap)#3 (1) {
  ["length"]=>
  int(1)
}
object(Dom\Attr)#5 (21) {
  ...
  ["name"]=>
  string(7) "charset"
  ["value"]=>
  string(5) "utf-8"
  ...
```

... which returns a Dom\NamedNodeMap which can be iterated like an array as above, or you can grab a Dom\Attr from the collection by the attribute name, like this:

```php
var_dump($meta->attributes->getNamedItem('charset'));
```

Attributes are easily removed via their names and added as name/value pairs:

```php
$meta->removeAttribute('charset');
$meta->setAttribute('http-equiv', 'Content-Type');
$meta->setAttribute('content', 'text/html; charset=utf-8');
print $dom->saveHTML($dom);
```

Output:
```
<!DOCTYPE html><html><head>
  <meta http-equiv="Content-Type" content="text/html; charset=utf-8">
  ...
```

Naturally, the value of an existing attribute can be changed via the `setAttribute()` method too. You'll be glad to know that `DOMNamedNodeMap` and `DOMAttr` classes exist in the pre-8.4 world (and it's these classes you'll likely make use of if handling element `class` attributes).

Removing Elements

To delete a DOM node, we use the `Dom\Node::removeChild()` method (which is inherited by `Dom\Element`, `Dom\Document`, and their respective sub-classes). You'll need a reference to the node to be removed and its parent. Luckily all node instances have a `::parentNode` property that references the parent...

```
$footer = $dom->querySelector('body footer');
$footer->parentNode->removeChild($footer);
print $dom->saveHTML();
```

Output:
```
...
    <p class="small">Para Three</p>
  </main>
</body></html>
```

... and voilà, the `footer` is gone from the DOM. You still have the `Dom\Element` object available in your code though – `::removeChild()` always returns a reference to the (now orphaned) node object – in case you want to put it back.

Creating and Adding New Elements

Finally, let's make a new element from scratch and insert it. To do this you'll need to first make a brand-new `Dom\Element`, set its properties, then attach it to the DOM in the correct place. First, we call `Dom\Document::createElement()` to create the element (we'll go with `img` because web pages should have pictures of cats) and set the relevant attributes (`src` for the image URL and `alt` to set alternative text for any visually impaired users):

```
$img = $dom->createElement('img');
$img->setAttribute('src', './jess.jpg');
$img->setAttribute('alt', 'A picture of Jess the cat');
```

Next, we'll find somewhere to put it. We've already seen that Dom\Node offers an ::insertBefore() method, as well as ::appendChild(). Dom\Element provides some extra insertion/removal methods that offer a lot more flexibility and power:

Table 11-24. *PHP Dom\Element manipulation methods*

Element::append(...nodes)	Add one or more nodes after last child of Element
Element::insertAdjacentElement (where, node)	Insert node relative to Element controlled by where
Element::insertAdjacentText(where, text)	Insert a text node relative to Element controlled by where
Element::prepend(...nodes)	Add one or more nodes before first child of Element
Element::remove()	Remove Element from the DOM
Element::replaceChildren(... nodes)	Replace current children of Element with new nodes
Element::replaceWith(...nodes)	Replace Element with nodes

Now let's put our newly created img into our DOM, using insertAdjacentElement(), so we can also look at what exactly the where parameter does. The first parameter of Dom\ Element::insertAdjacentElement() is taken from the Dom\AdjacentPosition enum, which has four values, which are the strings that the old DOMElement::insertAdjacentP osition() method accepted:

Table 11-25. *PHP Dom\AdjacentPosition / DOMElement equivalence*

Enum	DOMElement string	Detail
AdjacentPosition::BeforeBegin	"beforebegin"	Insert before target element
AdjacentPosition::AfterBegin	"afterbegin"	Insert as first child of target
AdjacentPosition::BeforeEnd	"beforeend"	Insert after last child of target
AdjacentPosition::AfterEnd	"afterend"	Insert after target

As you can see, you insert the new element on either side of a target or as a child (first or last) of the target. Let's use `AdjacentPosition::BeforeBegin`...

```
$target = $dom->querySelector('main p:nth-child(2)');
var_dump($target->textContent);
$target->insertAdjacentElement(Dom\AdjacentPosition::BeforeBegin, $img);
print $dom->saveHTML();
```

Output:
```
string(8) "Para Two"
...
    <main class="main-content">
      <p class="large">Para One</p>
      <img src="./jess.jpg" alt="A picture of Jess the cat">
      <p class="small  ">Para Two</p>
      <p class="small">Para Three</p>
    </main>
...
```

... and as we can see the img element we created with `Dom\Document::createElement()` has been inserted before the p target we specified with our `main p:nth-child(2)` selector.

Time for Coffee

This concludes our deep dive into the DOM. You should now have a good feel for what HTML really is – a serialized XML string that represents a tree data structure of element nodes that follows a specification (the HTML schema). We covered the types of elements you'll encounter and where they should live in the schema (e.g., `meta` elements only live in `head`), and that elements have special metadata called attributes – particularly, the important `class` and `id` attributes.

We saw how to create a DOM structure with `Dom\HTMLDocument` (or `DOMDocument`) and how to traverse it with XPath queries or the new CSS-driven `Dom\Document::querySelector*()` methods, which included a crash course in XPath and CSS syntax. We also saw how to manipulate the DOM by moving elements around, changing their attributes, and removing and adding new elements in the DOM. That's a fair bit to digest, so please feel free to relax with a beverage of your choice before we move onto the next section, where we'll build HTML from scratch.

Generating HTML

With markup and DOM now firmly secured in our mind, we can turn our attention to the art of creating it from scratch. The vast majority of PHP exists to create HTML; it's what the language was created to do, and PHP is chock-full of HTML functionality. In addition to PHP's built-in tools, there is also a rich ecosystem of libraries and frameworks, as you might expect for a language that has quietly been getting on with the business of making web pages for over two decades. Of particular interest to us here are third-party tools for *templating*, which is a method of combining HTML fragments and data to assemble a whole document, and I'll be making a strong case for why you should incorporate a templating library into any decently sized project. First, let's look at the fundamentals of producing HTML from PHP.

Printing a String

The previous section had many examples of storing a full valid HTML5 document as a complete string, which we used to power Dom\HTMLDocument but could also just be sent directly to the client. When a web server SAPI (cli-server, apache, fpm-fcgi, et al.) PHP program emits data (e.g., with a print or echo statement), the emitted bytes are dispatched to the client as the response body. All you need to do is ensure that the emitted data is HTML (well-formed and valid, always!). And hey presto you have a web page. Launch a cli-server container to function as our web server...

```
$ docker run -it --rm \
  -p 8080:8080 \
  -v "$PWD":/usr/src/myapp \
  -w /usr/src/myapp \
  php:8.4-cli \
  php -S 0.0.0.0:8080
```

... and let's build the easiest web page you'll ever create:

```
// index.php
print <<< EOS
<!DOCTYPE html>
<html>
  <head>
```

```
    <meta charset="utf-8" />
    <title>The easiest page you'll ever create</title>
  </head>
  <body>
      <h1>Lorem ipsum dolor sit amet</h1>
      <p>consectetur adipiscing elit</p>
  </body>
</html>
EOS;
```

You can check the results in a web browser if you like, via http://localhost:8080/index.php

Figure 11-3. *A simple page*

Getting response body data to the client is super easy, but this code isn't particularly useful. You don't need PHP to just echo out a static document; a static HTML file would be faster and less effort. Real applications will be full of logic and data interpolation, building the final content dynamically. Now let's add some string interpolation to our example:

```
$mainPara = '<p>consectetur adipiscing elit</p>';
print <<< EOS
<!DOCTYPE html>
```

```
<html>
  <head>
    <meta charset="utf-8" />
    <title>The easiest page you'll ever create</title>
  </head>
  <body>
      <h1>Lorem ipsum dolor sit amet</h1>
      {$mainPara}
  </body>
</html>
EOS;
```

The code above will render the same page as before, but now we're building the HTML dynamically by injecting one HTML fragment into another to form a complete document. It's a *very* simplified example, but this is essentially how you'll be constructing your pages from scratch.

The Old-Fashioned Way

An alternative method exists to the string handling demonstrated above, which is not recommended (by me) in modern PHP but nevertheless still exists out there in the wild lands of Legacy Code. All PHP is wrapped in special tags, which we covered way back in Chapter 1, "Getting Started," and every source code file you create must have a valid opening tag even if it contains nothing but PHP code. The opening tags are `<?php`, a short form `<?` (this "short opening tag" is not recommended and is prohibited by the PSR-1 standard because it can be disabled by ini directive), and `<?=` (the "short echo tag" is equivalent to `<?php echo`), and the closing tag is `?>` (which can and should be omitted in pure PHP files to avoid accidental echoing of newline characters triggering headers). Looks a little bit like markup, right? This is because PHP was originally intended to be interspersed with HTML: the PHP interpreter will treat anything not wrapped in PHP tags as text to be emitted immediately (though you can of course switch on output buffering before any text characters are encountered), and only the text wrapped in PHP tags is parsed as code. This allows you to pepper your HTML with PHP, like this:

```php
<?php ob_start(); ?>
<!DOCTYPE html>
<?php $mainPara = '<p>consectetur adipiscing elit</p>' ?>
<?php header('Content-type: text/html; charset=utf-8'); ?>
<html>
  <head>
    <meta charset="utf-8" />
    <title>The easiest page you'll ever create</title>
  </head>
<body>
  <h1>Lorem ipsum dolor sit amet</h1>
  <?= $mainPara ?>
</body>
</html>
```

Now, that is actually a pretty neat trick; you can just write your markup and only have logic and variable data injected where it's needed. This is what templating is: text with placeholders that have their values filled dynamically to create the final output. PHP has multiple (excellent) HTML templating libraries available, but it is in fact also its own templating language. So why am I recommending that you don't use native PHP templating? The answer lies in something we touched on in Chapter 10, "Programming With Objects": *separation of concerns.*

The Problem

The power of having access to the entire range of functions and features of PHP while also assembling markup for output introduces a potential problem: you can do literally *anything*. Need a quick database fetch? No problem, just shove `<?php $pdoConnection->query('SELECT ...'); ?>` where it's needed. The trouble is that you now have to keep track of potentially time-consuming calls *and* assemble a response. With a complex page, you might choose to break your markup into multiple files and only fetch the ones you need with a `require()` or `include()` statement. Now imagine that one of those included files has a DB read call in there, and it's being included in a loop structure... all of a sudden, you're making multiple DB reads when only one was sufficient.

Such code is also, frankly, a pain to understand and maintain. Arbitrarily flicking between data fetching, application logic, and markup generation adds cognitive load to what is already a pretty difficult task. Nobody wants to deal with a pile of unstructured spaghetti code. Just as it's good OOP design to ensure that classes don't do too much (c.f. "blob" or "god object" anti-pattern https://en.wikipedia.org/wiki/God_object), and we have design patterns that give us good class hierarchies for certain problem spaces, we also have architectural patterns describing over-arching system design to help us avoid creating unmaintainable messes.

A Solution

A tried-and-tested architectural pattern for web applications is Model-View-Controller – MVC. This separates out three fundamental web application design aspects – processing the HTTP request itself (in a controller), fetching data and applying logic (the model), and rendering the resulting model back to the client (the view). Separating out the chief concerns of an application means that, amongst other benefits, different teams can work concurrently on the components without impacting each other's work. Other positive outcomes of MVC are increased testability (components can be tested in isolation) and better organization and maintainability of source code.

A good way to enforce that the view components of your application only contain logic concerned with final rendering output is to use a templating library. Although it's a bad idea to pepper your views with reams of code, you will still benefit from some programming tools as you form the output: iterating over arrays to write out `li` elements, varying layout depending on the presence of flags… or whatever it might be. Clearly your application will benefit from making use of at least *some* of PHP's features, and this is where a templating library comes in. This section will be using the popular Twig library (which is the default rendering component of the Symfony framework). Others are available, such as Blade (as used in the Laravel framework), but a lot of the concepts you'll learn here with Twig will transfer to others.

The Philosophy of Twig (and MVC)

Twig is a *Domain Specific Language* (DSL), which means that its features and syntax are restricted to a narrow problem space: templating. DSLs are implemented in a general-purpose language: in our case this is PHP (which started life as a limited set of CGI binaries written in C for handling specific web-related tasks... PHP was also originally a DSL of sorts). DSLs are characterized by restricted syntax and a narrow focus: they are not intended to solve problems outside of their specific domain but will make working on in-scope problems much easier. Think of Twig as a way of restricting access to the full spectrum of PHP functionality, focusing only on the parts that assist the creation of (hyper) text and wrapping those parts in a markup-like syntax that plays nicely inside HTML documents (or any other type of template; you can generate anything you like with Twig).

If you run into difficulties when trying to achieve something with Twig that would otherwise be trivial to accomplish in PHP, there's likely a very good reason: you are no longer solving a view problem, and you probably need to look elsewhere in the MVC architecture. Earlier I gave the example of database access inside a template: Twig offers precisely no functions for this (out of the box, anyway), because data processing is a concern of the model, not the view. Ditto messing about with HTTP requests: that's a controller's job, not something you should have to do when rendering a view. It is possible to extend Twig and define your own functions for use in templates, but you should be *very* wary of doing so!

Getting Started with Twig

Use composer to install Twig in the directory of your choice, make sure that the subdirectories views and cache exist, and create the following composer.json file:

```
{
    "name": "exphp8/generate-with-twig",
    "description": "Exploring PHP8 - Twig rendering examples",
    "type": "project",
    "minimum-stability": "dev",
    "require": {
        "twig/twig": "4.x-dev",
        "twig/html-extra": "4.x-dev"
    }
}
```

Next, we need to have Composer parse that file and follow its instructions. Because we love Docker (and because you might be on an older system with an older version of Composer, if at all), we'll run `composer` from a container. This will be much like we've been doing things with PHP, where we mount the current directory into the container so that, when the work is done, the results remain on the host disk.

```
$ alias dcomposer='docker run --rm --interactive --tty --volume $PWD:/app composer:2.8'
$ dcomposer install
...
  - Installing twig/twig (4.x-dev c649c16): Extracting archive
  - Locking twig/html-extra (4.x-dev a1b1158)
```

This installs Twig core and its `HtmlExtension` (which is not installed by default for some reason). Some examples in this section require that `Twig\Extra\Html\HtmlExtension` are available. Now create an `index.php` file, where we'll pull in the composer-generated `autoload.php` file (this was created when `composer install` executed) and some boilerplate to get Twig ready:

```
// index.php
require_once __DIR__ . '/vendor/autoload.php';
$loader = new \Twig\Loader\FilesystemLoader(__DIR__ . '/views');
$twig = new \Twig\Environment($loader, [
    'cache' => __DIR__ . '/cache',
]);
```

The chunk of code above is important: it's the minimum boilerplate required to get `Twig\Environment` bootstrapped and ready for work. For the rest of this section, wherever a code example contains a `$twig` variable, assume the three lines above are present unless specified otherwise!

The heart of Twig is a `Twig\Environment` object, which stores configuration and loads templates via a loader – here we've used the built-in `FilesystemLoader`, which will search for template files on the path given to it at instantiation (you can configure multiple paths by instantiating with an array of paths or adding them with `FilesystemLoader::addPath()`). The `Environment` object constructor also accepts an associative array of config options – we've set the `cache` option here to configure where Twig will cache compiled templates. All that's left to do now is to create our first Twig template and render it.

Template Syntax

A Twig template is just a regular text file, and the contents will be output exactly as they are written. The magic happens when Twig encounters tags written in the Twig syntax, which are delimited with {% %} and {{ }} characters. Twig also supports its own comment syntax {# #}, and these tags (and their contents) will be omitted from the final output. Here's a simple template that demonstrates the three types...

```
<!DOCTYPE html>
<html>
  <head>
    <title>{{ title }}</title>
  </head>
  <body>
    {% if content %}
      {{ content }}
    {% else %}
      {# Default content #}
      <p>PLACEHOLDER CONTENT</p>
    {% endif %}
  </body>
</html>
```

... save this file exactly as shown in views/my-first.html.twig (templates can have any name you like, but the convention is to usually end the name with .content-type.twig). This template contains the variables {{ title }} and {{ content }} – if those exist when the template renders, then their values are substituted for the {{ variable }} portion of the template. It also contains the expression {% if %}...{% else %}... {% endif %}, which functions exactly like PHP's if and else control structures – in this case, we're testing if the content variable exists; if it does, we'll print out value; otherwise, we have alternative default content.

All we need to do now is render it; simply add the following code to index.php:

```
print $twig->render('my-first.html.twig', [
    'title' => 'RENDERED WITH TWIG'
]);
```

This instructs Twig to load index.html.twig template - which will be delegated to the FilesystemLoader we instantiated with the search path "./views" - read in the contents and compile. The second argument to ::render() is an associative array. The keys of this array become the variable names made available to the template when it compiles. This means that the {{ title }} variable should be replaced with a RENDERED WITH TWIG string when our template compiles.

With a cli-server container launched from the directory, you placed the index.php and views/index.html.twig files (and with Twig installed into vendor/twig, composer autoloader in vendor/autoload.php, etc.), make the request to http://localhost:8080/index.php, the result should be:

```
$ curl http://localhost:8080/index.php
...
  <head>
    <title>RENDERED WITH TWIG</title>
  </head>
  <body>
    <p>PLACEHOLDER CONTENT</p>
  </body>
...
```

Great success! You can see that we have the correct title metadata and that our template rendered the default body content because we didn't set a content variable when we called the ::render() method. You can also obtain a template object with the Twig\Environment::load() method and call render() on that. The example above could also have been written as:

```
$template = $twig->load('my-first.html.twig');
print $template->render([
    'title' => 'RENDERED WITH TWIG'
]);
```

Twig offers so much more than the simple variable interpolation and control structures demonstrated here, but the basic grammar of a template won't change beyond those three tags. Your own output might vary slightly on spacing and indenting from the above, but this doesn't impact the structure of the HTML. Slight variations are bound to creep in; a nicely indented template doesn't necessarily produce a perfectly indented HTML document. Clients will not be affected; well-formedness is all that matters. Your HTML could exist on a single line like `<!DOCTYPE html><html><head>...</body></html>` and all would be well.

All Twig output given in this section will have normalized spacing and indentation for the sake of not driving the typesetters crazy, and you shouldn't be concerned if your own code produces a p tag that is indented twice here or there, or there are extra newline characters. You can always check the validity of your output with an online HTML5 validator tool if you feel inclined, and most of those tools also implement a "pretty print" function to adjust spacing, etc.

Twig Variables

We've established that Twig is a DSL, abstracting the implementing language PHP. This begins at the data type level, with Twig offering a simplified form of the types provided by PHP. The Twig scalar types are string, number (integer or float), boolean, and null. The compound types are iterable (PHP arrays and iterable objects that implement Countable Iterable interfaces) and object (non-iterable objects). The data type of the underlying PHP variable determines the Twig type, and Twig is pretty fast and loose with typing: there's no explicit type casting or composite types here; PHP's type declaration system (nullable, union, disjunctive normal form, etc.) is entirely absent from Twig's template syntax.

There's no special syntax for distinguishing variable names from any other keyword in Twig, so it's a good idea to check that your variable names don't collide with existing Twig symbols. If you happened to do this, then Twig is intelligent enough to distinguish variables from other keywords and will evaluate the context of the symbol (I'll demonstrate in a minute). In most cases you will be setting up the data that your templates use before making the render call, but Twig does offer some variable manipulation allowing you to create new variables and perform operations. Use the following PHP code...

```
// index.php
require_once __DIR__ . '/vendor/autoload.php';

$loader = new \Twig\Loader\FilesystemLoader(__DIR__ . '/views');
$twig = new \Twig\Environment($loader);
```

Now that Twig is ready to do things, let's have it generate some markup for us:

```
print $twig->render('variables.html.twig', [
    'cat' => 'Jess',
    'set' => 'This is not a good idea.'
]);
```

... note we are not setting a cache config value when we create the Twig environment object, avoiding activating Twig's caching features for now. Unless otherwise stated, all remaining Twig examples in this section do not use caching and assume you're using the same autoloader and Twig instantiation boilerplate. With that done, add the following variables.html.twig template to your views directory:

```
{# views/variables.html.twig #}
{% set displayCat = cat ~ ' the Cat' %}
<p>{{ displayCat }} says "meow".</p>
<p>{{ set }}</p>
```

Now you can either run the new index.php file directly from the command line or request it from a cli-server instance with curl:

```
$ curl http://localhost:8080/index.php
<p>Jess the Cat says "meow".</p>
<p>This is not a good idea.</p>
```

The `{% set %}` tag allows us to create a new variable displayCat, which can then be used in output tags as `{{ displayCat }}` - if displayCat was already defined, then Twig simply overwrites it with the new value. Here we've used a string concatenation operator ~ to build a new string, and we'll be looking in detail at this and many others later in this section. You'll notice I created a set variable in the render() call, but the Twig engine is clever enough to know that `{% set ... %}` is meant to be a variable setting call, and `{{ set }}` should write out the data assigned to the template when we called render(). It's a good feature to save yourself from blowing up your templates, but it's better to avoid the problem in the first place. If you find you just can't avoid colliding with an existing word in the Twig language (such as if, for, cache, block... there are quite a few), use the following trick, which also serves as a neat demo for accessing structured data:

```
// index.php
$dataObj = new stdClass();
$dataObj->name = "A basic object.";

print $twig->render('structured-data.html.twig', [
    'array_data' => [
        'cat' => 'Jess',
        'humans' => ['Anna', 'Paul'],
    ],
    'object' => $dataObj,
]);
```

```
{# views/structured-data.html.twig #}
<div>{{ array_data.cat }}</div>
<div>{{ array_data.humans.0 }}, {{ array_data.humans.1 }}</div>
<div>{{ object.name }}</div>
```

We've introduced two new Twig concepts here: *sequences* and *mappings*. These are the Twig abstractions representing arrays and associative arrays or objects, respectively. Twig dot operator is used to access the attributes of iterables and objects, where attributes are PHP array keys and indices ($array['humans'][0] translates to array.humans.0, etc.) or object properties ($object->name translates to object.name). Twig also allows attribute/property access with square bracket notation, for example, {{ myMapping['foo'] }}, {{ mySequence[0] }}. The template above renders the following output:

```
$ curl http://localhost:8080/index.php
<div>Jess</div>
<div>Anna, Paul</div>
<div>A basic object.</div>
```

Twig Escaping

Part of the reason why we looked at DOM manipulation first is because I wanted you to get to this section of the book already having a firm grasp of the essentials of HTML. This way the focus can be on templating without being cluttered with HTML-101 lessons. Another supremely important takeaway from this section will be escaping any HTML in the data that you use for rendering. We actually touched on this briefly during our examination of all things HTTP when discussing URL encoding (remember we needed to URL encode POST data to change meta-characters that would otherwise change the structure of the decoded data). The problem we have here is very similar: when generating HTML from a template, what if the data we're injecting into the template also contains HTML? Why could it be a problem?

Let's start with a simple example. Imagine that we're handling a form POST request, and somewhere in that form data is some markup; we'll simulate that with the hard-coded $postData array. This exercise intentionally does not use Twig in order to demonstrate one of the reasons why Twig (or something like it) is a Jolly Good Idea. Make a new index.php file and put this as the first code:

```php
// index.php
$postData = [
    'title' => 'Lulzsec',
    'name' => 'Mr Trustworthy',
    'age' => 49,
    'occupation' => '<script>window.alert("I control the browser now.")</script>',
];
```

With our data in place, we'll create a naive string-interpolating "template" similar to the my-first.html.twig template from earlier. Add the following lines below the $postData statement:

```php
print <<<EOS
<!DOCTYPE html>
<html>
  <head>
    <title>{$postData['title']}</title>
  </head>
  <body>
    <h1>{$postData['name']}</h1>
    <p>Age: {$postData['age']}</p>
    <p>Occupation: {$postData['occupation']}</p>
  </body>
</html>
EOS;
```

CHAPTER 11 PROGRAMMING FOR THE INTERNET

What will happen here is that the <script>...</script> text defined in the "template" data is written into the p child of the body and becomes a valid script element, which means the browser parses it as JavaScript. We're all done, and you can go ahead and request that. Use a web browser rather than curl to get the full effect:

Figure 11-4. Oops...

Oh dear. What we have here is a classic Cross-Site Scripting (XSS) vulnerability. These happen when someone else is able to inject (usually malicious) code into your HTML, and there are a number of methods to achieve this, either in the client or via server. Naturally we're focusing on the server-side here, and one thing you really must do is NEVER TRUST DATA. I cannot stress this enough: if there is data flowing into your application from anywhere, either in the request itself or fetched from a database or API call, it must be treated with suspicion, *even if you (or your organization) own the data source*. Malicious employees exist; malicious users certainly exist. You must *filter* any data that is sent to the client.

Twig will (unless told otherwise) automatically escape HTML in any interpolated data, converting HTML meta-characters to named entities (and numeric entities where there are no named equivalents). It's worth noting that other PHP templating libraries do similar things too, which is another good reason for choosing one over vanilla PHP for outputting markup. Let's repeat the above example, but this time using a Twig template. Add the Twig autoloader/boilerplate and replace the entire print/heredoc statement with the following...

```
// ... $postData as before
require_once __DIR__ . '/vendor/autoload.php';

$loader = new \Twig\Loader\FilesystemLoader(__DIR__ . '/views');
```

CHAPTER 11   PROGRAMMING FOR THE INTERNET

```
$twig = new \Twig\Environment($loader);
// $postData as before

print $twig->render('auto-filter.html.twig', [
    'postData' => $postData
]);
```

... and put the following into a views/auto-filter.html.twig template:

```
{# views/auto-filter.html.twig #}
<!DOCTYPE html>
<html>
<head>
    <title>{{ postData.title }}</title>
</head>
<body>
  <h1>{{ postData.name }}</h1>
  <p>Age: {{ postData.age }}</p>
  <p>Occupation: {{ postData.occupation }}</p>
</body>
</html>
```

Now when we request the page, we see this...

Mr Trustworthy

Age: 49

Occupation: <script>window.alert("I control the browser now.")</script>

Figure 11-5. Slightly safer...

... because by default Twig will filter any data that is placed into your template with the {{ }} syntax. The script element has been encoded so that the browser won't parse the script tags; you can view the page source to see how:

```
<p>Occupation: &lt;script&gt;window.alert(&quot;I control the browser now.&quot;)&lt;/script&gt;</p>
```

This particular type of encoding is *html entity encoding*, which itself comes in two flavors: character (or name) encoding and numeric encoding. They exist because you might want to render text like `<script>` in a page (and not have the contents parsed as JavaScript), and some exist from the olden days when it was easier to rely on encoding for certain characters than trust the myriad of ISO extended ASCII character encodings. The following table gives examples of some common ones (notice that the punctuation meta-character numeric entity values correspond to their ASCII code page decimal values):

Table 11-26. HTML entity encoding

Meta-character	Name encoding	Numeric encoding
<	&lt;	&#60;
>	&gt;	&#62;
&	&amp;	&#38;
"	&quot	&#34;
™	&trade;	&#8482;

We'll come back to the nuts and bolts of entity encoding for later, once we're done with Twig.

Controlling Escaping

The default escaping strategy for Twig is to treat everything as HTML, and it is enabled by default. To turn this feature off, use the `autoescape` config key when the `Twig\Environment` object is instantiated. Change the previous example so that the `Twig\Environment` boilerplate has an array as its second constructor argument. The array needs to contain an `autoescape` key, like this:

```
// index.php
$twig = new \Twig\Environment($loader, [
    'autoescape' => false,
]);
```

Now if you request the page, you'll see that the template now renders unsafely:

```
$ curl http://localhost:8080/index.php
...
  <p>Occupation: <script>window.alert("I control the browser now.")
  </script></p>
...
```

If Twig is running in this mode, data can be manually escaped by appending |escape or the short-form |e to the variable:

```
<p>Occupation: {{ postData.occupation|e }}</p>
```

Conversely, you can skip autoescaping when it is enabled by appending |raw but your reasons had better be good. Twig offers several escape contexts, and these can be supplied as arguments when escaping with |e(). Use the modified Twig\Environment boilerplate (turning off autoescaping) as before with the following code:

```
// index.php
print $twig->render('escape.css.twig', [
    'selector' => 'body > main .link',
]);

print PHP_EOL;

print $twig->render('html-attr-escape.html.twig', [
    'srcAttr' => 'x" onerror"=alert(\'script injection\')"'
]);
```

Here we're rendering two different templates, escape.css.twig...

```
{# views/escape.css.twig #}
{{ selector|e('css') }} {
    font-weight: bold;
}
```

… and html-attr-escape.html.twig:

```
{# views/html-attr-escape.html.twig #}

<img src="{{ srcAttr|e('html_attr') }}"/>
$ curl http://localhost:8080/index.php
body\20 \3E \20 main\20 \2E link {
    font-weight: bold;
}
<img src="x&quot;&#x20;onerror&quot;&#x3D;alert&#x28;&#x27;script&#x20;
injection&#x27;&#x29;&quot;"/>
```

The full list of Twig escape contexts are:

Table 11-27. Twig escape contexts

html	Entity encoding
js	Backslash escaping, making data safe for use in JS or JSON output
css	CSS hexadecimal escape syntax
url	URL encoding, e.g., for use with query parameters
html_attr	Treats string as a single attribute value

You can also control escaping at a template block level by using the {% autoescape %} {% endautoescape %} tags; all content between these tags will be subjected to autoescaping regardless of any global setting. You can use these tags to switch strategies: for example, {% autoescape 'js' %} will apply the js escape context, {% autoescape false %} will disable autoescaping, and so on. Twig is also intelligent enough to only apply escaping once; an {% autoescape %} block inside a template already rendering with escaping enabled will not trigger a second pass (which would result in "double escaping" and mangled output).

Twig Filtering

Similar to escaping data, filters can be applied in Twig data expressions in a similar way using the | operator followed by the filter name (|escape is just a very specialized filter). Filters allow a degree of data processing in order to do things like transform data to strings or apply regional formatting for dates and numbers. For example, {{ "Hello\

nworld"|nl2br }} will convert newline characters to HTML br tags and render as Hello
world. Some filters take arguments: {{ myArray|join(', ') }} will convert an array to a string, with each element delimited by the ', ' sequence. There are quite a few filters available, for example:

Table 11-28. Twig filters

|striptags	Completely remove all HTML tags from a string
|capitalize	Equivalent to mb_ucfirst() function
|upper	Wrapper for mb_strtoupper() function
|lower	Wrapper for mb_strtolower() function
|first	Output first element of array, or character of a string
|last	Last element, or character
|number_format	Wrapper for number_format() functions
|join	Concatenate a sequence of elements, with optional separator and final separator characters
|format_time |format_date |format_datetime	Formatting for a valid PHP datetime string
|format_number	Regional formatting for numbers
|reverse	Reorder elements in a sequence
|shuffle	
|sort	
|default	Sets a default string for potentially empty values

The filters that play with things like case conversion tend to be multi-byte safe (essentially wrappers for the mbstring equivalent functions). You can also apply filters to entire blocks of template content. Use the apply tag with the filter name like this: {% apply upper %} {% endapply %}. All text between those tags, whether it is literal template text or interpolated from variables, will be filtered accordingly. You can also chain filters together {{ myVar|striptags|upper }} would first remove HTML tags, then convert the remaining text to uppercase (using the mb_strtoupper() function internally). The full list of Twig filters, and their documentation, can be found at https://twig.symfony.com/doc/filters/index.html

Twig Control Structures

PHP's control structures are abstracted by the following tags:

Table 11-29. *Twig control structures*

| {% if %} {% endif %} | Test a logical expression, and render the block if true |
| {% for %} {% endfor %} | Iterate a sequence, rendering the block each time |

The following PHP and template code demonstrates some simple use cases:

```
// index.php
print $twig->render('control-structures.html.twig', [
    'renderA' => true,
    'renderB' => false,
    'family' => ['Jess', 'Anna', 'Paul'],
]);

{# views/control-structures.html.twig #}
{% if renderA %}
  <ul>
    {% for member in family %}
      <li>{{ member }}</li>
    {% endfor %}
  </ul>
{% endif %}
{% if renderB %}
  <p>Hello from B</p>
{% endif %}

$ curl http://localhost:8080/index.php
  <ul>
    <li>Jess</li>
    <li>Anna</li>
```

```
<li>Paul</li>
</ul>
```

Twig Operators and Expressions

The example above uses very plain expressions to demonstrate the {% if %} and {% for %} tags, but Twig supports expressions in {% %} tags and {{ }} output. As you might expect, these are broadly equivalent to PHP expressions but with a layer of abstraction/simplification applied. You can perform all the usual mathematical, logical, and comparison operations, and Twig (in the more recent releases) even supports new PHP functionality such as ?? null-coalesce, and ... spread. You can even make use of => arrow function notation (tread carefully). We're now going to look at the building blocks of Twig expressions, which start out as more or less directly equivalent to PHP's underlying implementations, with some complex (but common) operations abstracted to simple word-based statements rather than falling back to having to write out small functions or blocks of code.

Literals

Table 11-30. Twig literal value syntax

`"abc" '123'`	Any character(s) wrapped in quotes is a string
`"string #{EXPR} interpolation"`	#{} interpolates EXPR into double-quote strings only
`123 -123.4 1_234_567`	Integers, floats, underscores permitted for readability
`\" \'`	Backslash escape for strings containing quote characters
`\r \n \t` etc.	ASCII backslash escapes ()
`\0 - \377`	Octal ASCII escape values
`['foo', 'bar']`	Array (or "sequence")
`{'cat': 'Jess'} {humans: ['Anna', 'Paul']}`	Associative array (or "mapping"), quoting keys is optional
`true false`	Booleans
`null`	null

CHAPTER 11 PROGRAMMING FOR THE INTERNET

The usual PHP type-casting rules apply. If you were to attempt to interpolate $object into a string with "blah #{object} blah" then that object would need to implement the Stringable interface (possess a __toString() method).

Mathematics

The Twig mathematical operators are identical to their PHP counterparts, with a tiny sprinkle of syntactic sugar in one case:

Table 11-31. Twig mathematical operators

+	Addition
-	Subtraction
/	Divide
*	Multiply
%	Modulus
//	Floored integer result of a division (like calling round(x / y))
**	Exponentiation (x ** y raises x to the power y)

Again, PHP type coercion is at work here; see Chapter 7, "Numbers," for the rules and pitfalls.

Logical

Here, Twig opts for words rather than symbols such as && or ||...

Table 11-32. Twig logical operators

and	true if both operands are true
or	true if at least one operand is true
xor	true if only one operand is true
not	Negates an expression
()	Groups an expression
b-and	Bitwise AND, OR, and XOR
b-or	
b-xor	

Comparison

Comparison operations are where things start to get abstract. The usual shorthand characters are present, but some operations use a syntax formed from full words:

Table 11-33. Twig comparison operators

==	Equals
!=	Does not equal
<	Less than
<=	Less than or equal
>	Greater than
>=	Greater than or equal
<=>	PHP "spaceship" operator - returns -1, 0 or 1 when comparing operands
same as	Equivalent to PHP ===

Tests

The `is` keyword (which can be negated to `is not`) is used to form an expression with a value as the left operand and a sub-expression as the right. The right-hand sub-expression is usually formed using one of the following words:

Table 11-34. Twig test sub-expressions

defined	Variable is defined
divisible by N	Variable divides by N (equivalent to var % N == 0)
empty	Equivalent to PHP's empty() (with all the attendant type coercion problems)
even	Variable is an even number
iterable	Variable is a sequence or mapping
null	Variable is null
odd	Variable is an odd number

For example, to render template section if `myVar` is not an empty string, empty sequence/mapping, `false`, or `null` use `{% if myVar is not empty %}`.

String Tests

Table 11-35. Twig string tests

starts with	true if lefthand string begins with characters of righthand string
ends with	true if string ends with specified characters
matches	Test a string with a regular expression

The following template snippet demonstrates the last five items in the table, all of the expressions shown below evaluate to `true`:

```
{# views/comparison-expressions.txt.twig #}
{{ 'Jess the cat' matches '/^[Jj]ess/' }}
{{ 'abcdef' starts with 'abc' }}
{{ 'abcdef' ends with 'def' }}
```

Output:
1
1
1

Iterable Tests

Sequence (arrays) and mappings (associative arrays) have specialized tests:

> in | true if lefthand value is found in a sequence or mapping |
>
> has some CLOSURE | Test that at least one element returns true from CLOSURE |
>
> has every CLOSURE | Test that all elements return true from CLOSURE |

The following examples all evaluate to true (note the type coercion in the first expression):

```
{# views/iterable-tests.txt.twig #}
{{ '1' in [1, 2 ,3] }}
{{ [2,3,4] has every v => v > 1 }}
{{ ['Jess', 'Anna', 'Paul'] has some v => v == 'Jess' }}
```

Miscellaneous Operators

The remaining operators are given below:

Table 11-36. Twig miscellaneous operators

|	Filter - `seq|join(', ')`
..	Range - `{% for i in 1..10 %}`
~	Concatenate string with explicit type cast - `cat ~ ' the cat.'`
. []	Access element in a mapping/sequence - `user.name`, `collection[1]`
?:	Ternary - `value ? var : 'default'`
??	Null coalesce - `value ?? 'default'` creates and assigns `value` if undefined
...	Spread operator, same as PHP
=>	Arrow function, same as PHP (see below)

Twig Functions

A number of functions are provided by Twig for use in template expressions; the syntax for calling them is exactly the same as PHP. A full list of functions plus documentation links can be found at `https://twig.symfony.com/doc/functions/index.html`, and some commonly used functions are given below:

Table 11-37. Twig functions

`constant()`	Access a PHP global or class constant
`date()`	Creates a `DateTime` object from a PHP date format compatible string
`dump()`	Output debug info for a var, (`Twig\Extension\DebugExtension` loaded, debug option set)
`html_classes()`	With `Twig\Extra\Html\HtmlExtension` loaded, generates an attribute string
`min()` `max()`	Get min/max values in a sequence or mapping
`random()`	Return random element from sequence, character from string, or number from range

Calling Functions

We can take a moment here to look at the mechanics of using Twig functions in expressions. Let's use html_classes() because it's pretty neat, and some of the other features of Twig while we're at it. Here's a reminder of the Twig boilerplate, including a call to load HtmlExtension...

```php
// index.php
require_once __DIR__ . '/vendor/autoload.php';

use Twig\Extra\Html\HtmlExtension;

$loader = new \Twig\Loader\FilesystemLoader(__DIR__ . '/views');
$twig = new \Twig\Environment($loader);
$twig->addExtension(new HtmlExtension());

$state = new stdClass();
$state->errors = false;
$state->focused = true;

print $twig->render('html-classes.html.twig', [
    'classList' => [
        'flex', 'centered',
    ],
    'state' => $state,
]);
```

... our template looks like this...

```twig
{# views/html-classes.html.twig #}
<div class="{{ html_classes({
    'errors': state.errors,
    'focused': state.focused
}, ...classList) }}">
    Some content goes here.
</div>
```

... notice that we do the ...classList array unpacking in the html_classes() call after normal arguments, just like regular PHP. html_classes() takes any number of string arguments and glues them together into a single attribute string; it will also accept a mapping where key names will be included as HTML classes if their values are true. The final result is as follows:

```
curl http://localhost:8080/index.php
<div class="focused flex centered">
    Some content goes here.
</div>
```

Defining Functions

Twig also provides limited support for defining your own functions. The => arrow function operator behaves like its PHP counterpart: you are permitted a single (Twig) statement, which is automatically evaluated and returned. This deliberately limits what you can achieve with them, for example, you can't put Twig tags into an arrow function.

Using the {% set %} tag, you can assign the arrow function to a template variable. If the arrow function has more than one parameters; make sure to wrap them in parentheses. With that done, the template variable is then used with the |invoke filter; any arguments are passed in parentheses. Be warned that the output of an invoked arrow function will be subject to autoescaping (as it can be the recipient of non-template string data), even if that markup exists in a string literal...

```
{# views/arrow-func.html.twig #}
{% set myFunc = (arg1, arg2) => "<li>cat: #{arg1}</li>\n<li>human: #{arg2}</li>" %}
<ul>
    {{ myFunc|invoke(cat, human) }}
</ul>
<ul>
    {{ myFunc|invoke(cat, human)|raw }}
</ul>
```

... it will be subject to encoding. Notice the difference between the first `myFunc` output and the output filtered with `|raw` (which also serves as a nice demonstration of chaining filters together). Let's render this template with some data:

```
// index.php
print $twig->render('arrow-func.html.twig', [
    'cat' => 'Jess',
    'human' => 'Anna',
]);
$ curl http://localhost:8080/index.php
<ul>
  &lt;li&gt;cat: Jess&lt;/li&gt;
  &lt;li&gt;human: Anna&lt;/li&gt;
</ul>
<ul>
  <li>cat: Jess</li>
  <li>human: Anna</li>
</ul>
```

Using a template-defined function to insert snippets of markup is not recommended, and the previous example merely serves as a demonstration for `|invoke` and arrow functions. The `{% if %}` and `{% for %}` tags provide a good degree of control over iterative rendering, but as your page grows in complexity, it will become necessary to break your templates into related or reusable units (or lose your sanity trying to maintain one enormous template file... your choice).

Twig `include()`

Twig has a very simple mechanism for stitching templates together: the `include()` function. This works like PHP's `include` language construct: at the point it is encountered, the target file is parsed and rendered before control passes back to the calling template. `include()` accepts a variable number of arguments; in order, these are the relative filepath of the target file (required, relative to the path(s) defined for `FilesystemLoader`), an optional mapping of variables and values for use in the target template, and the remainder are named boolean parameters:

Table 11-38. Twig include options

Option	Default	Effect
ignore_missing	false	Render empty string instead of emitting error if target not found
sandboxed	false	Requires SandboxExtension, used to restrict functionality in untrusted templates
with_context	true	Control exposure of calling template's context (variables)

Time for a quick demo:

```
// index.php
print $twig->render('include-demo.html.twig');
```

This time we'll need two templates, the one that TwigEnvironemnt::render() will parse first...

```
{# views/include-demo.html.twig #}
<!DOCTYPE html>
<html>
    {% set pageTitle = 'Twig include() demo.' %}
    {{ include(
        'inc/head.html.twig',
        {title: pageTitle},
        with_context: false,
        ignore_missing: true
    ) }}
  <body></body>
</html>
```

... and the one that the first template includes, which needs to be saved in a views/inc sub-directory (remember that we're initializing an instance of Twig\Loader\FilesystemLoader with a __DIR__ . 'views' argument, so the full path to this sub-template will be views/inc/head.html.twig relative to your project root):

```
{# views/inc/head.html.twig #}
<head>
  <title>{{ title }}</title>
</head>
```

All being well, you should see the following output:

```
$ curl http://localhost:8080/index.php
<!DOCTYPE html>
<html>
  <head>
  <title>Twig include() demo.</title>
</head>
...
```

The call to Twig's `include()` show in the example demonstrates the argument order. Remember, the file path is always required as the first argument, followed by an optional mapping – the keys of this map become context variables in the sub-template. Finally, the three named parameters follow in any order, all of which are optional. In our case, we specified `with_context: false`, which means the only context data `head.html.twig` has to work with is the explicitly supplied `title` variable.

Twig's template inclusion mechanism is a great way to specialize parts of your page, allowing you to define different versions of the same content that can be easily switched in and out with a little logic and some flags set in the data passed to the `::render()` call. It doesn't particularly lend itself to repeatable units of content... well actually you *could* abuse `include()` to, say, render an array of web cards or suchlike; `include()` will get the job done. But there is a better way…

Twig Macros

It is possible to define reusable units of HTML in regular templates and insert them as many times as needed using a function-like syntax. Twig calls this feature *macros*, and they work like this:

```
// index.php
print $twig->render('macro-demo.html.twig');

{# views/macro-demo1.html.twig #}
{% macro listItem(text) %}
  <li>{{ text }}</li>
{% endmacro %}
```

```
<ul>
  {% for item in ['Jess', 'Anna', 'Paul'] %}
    {{ _self.listItem(item) }}
  {% endfor %}
</ul>
```

The text between the `{% macro %}` and `{% endmacro %}` tags will now be inserted wherever it is referenced in the rest of the template. Macros are called in a function-like way, via the magic `_self` variable, and they behave like functions in that they have scoping rules: they don't have access to the rest of the template's data, and any variables defined inside the macro with `{% set %}` are unavailable outside. Data has to be explicitly passed using parameters/arguments and can even have default values defined – e.g., `{% macro listItem(text = 'not set') %}`.

Importing Macros

Macros are always local to the template in which they are defined; they are not available in included templates (or child templates, which we'll get to next). It would be an enormous pain to have to define the same macro in every template it is used in, but fortunately the `{% import %}` tag means you only have to define the macro once:

```
{# views/inc/macro.html.twig #}
{% macro listItem(text) %}
    <li>{{ text }}</li>
{% endmacro %}

{# views/macro-demo2.html.twig #}
{% import 'inc/macro.html.twig' as macros %}
<ul>
    {% for item in ['Jess', 'Anna', 'Paul'] %}
        {{ macros.listItem(item) }}
    {% endfor %}
</ul>
```

Twig Inheritance

Twig also features an inheritance mechanism, whereby a common base template can have units called *blocks* defined, which the inheriting child templates will override. Blocks can be empty or have default content placed inside them. The {% extends %} tag tells the templating engine that the current template is a child; the parent is then fetched and rendered, with child blocks overriding the parent blocks.

Extending a Template

Let's define a very simple parent template…

```
{# views/parent.html.twig #}
<!DOCTYPE html>
<html>
  <head>
    {% block titleEle %}
      <title>BASE</title>
    {% endblock %}
  </head>
  <body>
    {% block bodyContent %}{% endblock %}
  </body>
</html>
```

… and a child template that extends it:

```
{# views/child.html.twig #}
{% extends 'parent.html.twig' %}

{% block titleEle %}
  <title>CHILD</title>
{% endblock %}

{% block bodyContent %}
  <div>CHILD CONTENT HERE...</div>
{% endblock %}
```

It's important to note here that any template containing an {% extends %} tag – which should be the first tag in the template for the sake of sanity – is only permitted to contain content that is wrapped in {% block %} tags (otherwise Twig won't know what to do with it and duly throw an exception). Now, to render the entire thing, we actually tell Twig to render the child...

```
// index.php
print $twig->render('child.html.twig');
```

... because the {% extends %} tag contains the information Twig requires to fetch the parent. The resulting output should be:

```
$ curl -v http://localhost:8080/index.php
<!DOCTYPE html>
<html>
  <head>
    <title>CHILD</title>
  </head>
  <body>
    <div>CHILD CONTENT HERE...</div>
  </body>
</html>
```

You'll have hopefully noticed that not every {% block %} tag in parent.html.twig contained content. This is perfectly fine; if the child doesn't provide an override, then the result is just an empty string at that position. It is also possible to access the parent block content from the child via the parent() function, which will output the entire parent block content at the position it is called.

Using Other Templates

Twig's inheritance model, like PHP, is single. A child can extend exactly one parent. However, the block mechanism is pretty useful, and you can make use of it via the {% use %} tag, which is sort of like (if you squint a little) multiple inheritance (more accurately, it is horizontal reuse). {% use %} with block tags is a little like {% import %} with macros: the blocks defined in the "used" template become part of the "using" template. The following example should clarify:

```
// index.php
print $twig->render('block-use.html.twig', [
    'parent' => 'parent.html.twig'
]);

{# views/block-use.html.twig #}
{% extends parent %}
{% use 'inc/blocks.html.twig' %}
{% block titleEle %}
  <title>{{ '{%' }} use {{ '%}' }} DEMO</title>
{% endblock %}

{# views/inc/blocks.html.twig #}
{% block bodyContent %}
  <p>Content from blocks.html.twig</p>
{% endblock %}
```

When we put this all together, we get the following content rendered:

```
$ curl -v http://localhost:8080/index.php
<!DOCTYPE html>
<html>
  <head>
    <title>{% use %} DEMO</title>
  </head>
  <body>
    <p>Content from blocks.html.twig</p>
  </body>
</html>
```

The `{% use 'inc/blocks.html.twig' %}` tag tells Twig to read in the specified template and treat all `block` tags as if they exist in the calling template. This opens up even more strategies for organizing your templates into reusable units. I've also taken the opportunity to demo a couple of other features: the `{% extends %}` tag in `block-use.html.twig` is using a variable rather than a string literal (and will take any other Twig expression), and the `titleEle` block in that template is using `{{ '{%' }}` string literals to escape Twig syntax (which is the recommended method).

There are a few more tricks you can pull with blocks, such as nesting and a conditional form of {% extend %} (which accepts Twig expressions, not just string literal file paths). You can read about them at https://twig.symfony.com/doc/tags/extends.html and https://twig.symfony.com/doc/tags/use.html

Extending Twig in PHP

What if you just cannot achieve what you want using Twig's syntax and features? Well, there's always the nuclear option! It is possible to extend the Twig templating language in PHP: you can add your own global variables, filters, and functions with ease. Whether you should do so is another question; the logic or functionality you want to introduce into the view might be better off elsewhere in the MVC architecture (perhaps as a service or logic in a controller). Generally speaking, you should have everything in order (data fetched, decisions made, environment configured, etc.) before passing control to the view. Ducking out to fetch more data or apply more business logic when you're halfway through assembling your content is a bad idea. Nevertheless, there are occasionally cases where adding extra functionality to your templating engine is appropriate.

The basic principle for either is straightforward: for filters and functions, Twig provides Twig\TwigFilter and Twig\TwigFunction classes, which can be constructed with a name string and some way to call through to the underlying PHP implementation (anonymous function, static class method, and so on). An optional third argument is an array of options to control behavior (such as HTML escaping). These objects are then registered with the Twig\Environment object that will be doing the rendering. Adding a "global" is even easier: any data you like can be exposed to all the templates visited by ::render() by simply binding a context name to it:

```
$twig->addGlobal('amazingHelper', $object);
```

The code above exposes all of the public properties and methods of $object via amazingHelper, and they are accessed in the usual way: {{ amazingHelper.property }}, {% amazingHelper.method() %} anywhere in the chain of extends, use, or include calls.

Adding a Filter

For reasons that are utterly opaque, we'd like certain strings to contain a cat, so we'll add an |addcat filter to achieve this. First, let's build the filter object:

```php
// index.php
require_once __DIR__ . '/vendor/autoload.php';

$loader = new \Twig\Loader\FilesystemLoader(__DIR__ . '/views');
$twig = new \Twig\Environment($loader);

$filter = new \Twig\TwigFilter('addcat', function ($string) {
    return $string . "... and Jess the cat. Meow.";
});
```

Next, we register that filter object with Twig before rendering…

```php
$twig->addFilter($filter);
print $twig->render('add-cat.html.twig');
```

… now we can make use of the |addcat filter in the rendered template (and of course any other template that is extended, used, or included; the filter is available globally in that Twig environment):

```twig
{# views/add-cat.html.twig #}
<div>
    {{ 'Anna, Paul'|addcat }}
</div>
$ curl -v http://localhost:8080/index.php
<div>
    Anna, Paul... and Jess the cat. Meow.
</div>
```

We've chosen to work with string data here, but a filter could also be applied to an object, depending on the Twig expression and underlying PHP data type. For example, a context variable that is bound to a DateTime instance would pass the object to the filter callable when used. In the filter expression, everything on the left-hand side of the | pipe character expression is evaluated and passed as an argument to the anonymous function we used to construct the Twig\TwigFilter object. The data arriving at the callback can be any PHP type. Alternative methods of creating a Twig filter object callable are:

Table 11-39. TwigFilter class instantiation techniques

new TwigFilter('filter_name', 'func_name')	Registers the PHP named function
new TwigFilter('filter_name', 'Class::method')	Registers static method defined in Class
new TwigFilter('filter_name', ['Class', 'method'])	Registers static method defined in Class
new TwigFilter('filter_name', [$this, 'method'])	Registers method defined of object $this

Controlling Behavior

Given the nature of filters, there is some flexibility around escaping and safety. By default, your filter extension's output is subject to autoescaping just like the built-in ones, which might not be ideal if your filter is already handling escaping. Conversely, you might require that input is already escaped before your own code gets to work on it, rather than working with raw input. Twig also provides mechanisms for injecting the template context (the set of variables accessible from that template) and even the entire Twig\TwigEnvironment instance, should it be required. These options are controlled by passing an associative array of booleans as the third argument constructor and result in extra parameters for the filter callable:

```
// index.php
$filter = new \Twig\TwigFilter('addcat', function (array $context,
$string) {
    return $string . "... and Jess the cat. {$context['catNoise']}.";
}, ['needs_context' => true]);
$twig->addFilter($filter);

print $twig->render('add-cat.html.twig', [
    'catNoise' => 'Purr purr'
]);
```

```
$ curl -v http://localhost:8080/index.php
<div>
    Anna, Paul... and Jess the cat. Purr purr.
</div>
```

Here the `addcat` filter is modified so that the template context is available when the callable executes; you can see the differences in the filter object construction. The `needs_context` option tells the `TwigFilter` object to pass the context array when the filter is used in a template and the underlying callable is invoked, demonstrated by creating a simple context variable when we make the `::render()` call. Table 11-40 contains a synopsis of useful options and their corresponding effects:

Table 11-40. TwigFilter class constructor options

Option	Effect
`'needs_charset' => true`	Passes (string $charset, $input) to callable
`'needs_context' => true`	Passes (array $context, $input)
`'needs_environment' => true`	Passes (\Twig\TwigEnvironment $twig, $input)
`'pre_escape' => 'html'`	Applies html escaping (or any of the others) to input
`'is_safe' => 'html'`	Suppresses html autoescaping (or any of the others) of output

In cases where multiple options are required that would result in callable parameter changes, the arguments are supplied in the order the options are defined: `['needs_context' => true, 'needs_charset' => true]` would result in callable parameters `(array $context, string $charset, $input)`.

Adding a Function

Adding a function to templates is a very similar process; the main difference is their use inside templates, and that function extensions don't support `pre_escape` and `preserves_safety` options.

```
// index.php
require_once __DIR__ . '/vendor/autoload.php';
```

```
$loader = new \Twig\Loader\FilesystemLoader(__DIR__ . '/views');
$twig = new \Twig\Environment($loader);

$func = new \Twig\TwigFunction('add_humans', function ($string) {
    return $string . " is in charge. Anna and Paul are her slaves.";
});
$twig->addFunction($func);

print $twig->render('add-humans.html.twig', [
    'cat' => 'Jess'
]);

{# views/add-humans.html.twig #}
<div>
  {% if cat == 'Jess' %}
    {% set cat = add_humans(cat) %}
  {% endif %}
  <p>{{ cat }}</p>
</div>

$ curl http://localhost:8080/index.php
<div>
  <p>Jess is in charge. Anna and Paul are her slaves.</p>
</div
```

The example above is self-explanatory and is not a particularly good use of a function: it would be better implemented as a filter. Tread carefully when introducing functions (or any other extension to Twig); the more logic and data fetching/transformation that is involved, the more you are probably straying from the path of MVC and setting up potential problems in the future. Twig, or any other modern templating library, is not frictionless – far from it – but remember that the friction is there for a reason: to segregate content generation from other tasks that are better implemented elsewhere.

Making Safe HTML (Native PHP)

Making data safe is not the sole remit of a view, and it would be remiss of me to skip over how to safely work with untrusted data outside of a templating system. Incoming form data might well be dispatched to another system or stored in a database not everything is going to end up inside HTML content. PHP offers a range of built-in functions to detect and/or remove potentially malicious data before it can do any harm inside a web browser.

String Manipulation

Code injection is almost always a matter of injecting one string into another, so it makes sense that PHP has a number of string-handling functions designed to mitigate those risks. I deliberately omitted these functions from Chapter 8, "Strings" (which was already quite huge!), because they would make more sense explained here in the context of all things HTML and HTTP. As we're all nice and fresh from the previous section on all things Twig and templating, these functions should look familiar in their effects. For good reason, too: Twig utilizes some of these functions in its internal implementation (see the \Twig\Runtime\EscaperRuntime class). The PHP string functions that deal with markup safety do one of two things: encode meta-characters or remove markup.

Table 11-41. PHP markup safety functions

htmlentities()	Convert the maximum range of potential characters to HTML entities
html_entity_decode()	Reverse of htmlentities()
htmlspecialchars()	Convert a minimal range of characters
htmlspecialchars_decode()	Reverse of htmlspecialchars()
get_html_translation_table()	Returns array of mappings for htmlentities() or htmlspecialchars()
strip_tags()	Returns string with HTML and PHP tags removed

Encoding Meta-Characters

The two functions you'll see used the most are `htmlspecialchars()` and `htmlentities()` (and their decoding counterparts). They function in the same way, and the former will encode a smaller set of characters. The following example sums things up:

```
$str = '"&\'<>£¥©®';

print htmlspecialchars($str) . PHP_EOL;
print htmlentities($str);

Output:
&quot;&&#039;&lt;&gt;£¥©®
&quot;&&#039;&lt;&gt;&pound;&yen;&copy;&reg;
```

`htmlspecialchars()` will encode precisely five meta-characters: " ' & < > which should be enough to render most markup-containing strings safe for use. To see the full translation table, call `get_html_translation_table(HTML_ENTITIES)`, which will dump an array of characters to entities – call without the HTML_ENTITIES constant to see the limited map for `htmlspecialchars()`. Be aware that these functions are aware of the `default_charset` ini setting and if an invalid byte sequence is detected in the input, an empty string is returned. You can specify the encoding of the input with an encoding: parameter, for example, `htmlspecialchars($data, encoding: 'cp1252');` would mean the function treats the data as CP1252 encoded (Windows-1252 Western-European).

Removing Tags

For those hopefully extremely limited cases where markup is *supposed* to be injected (you'll encounter this in ancient, cobbled-together content management systems), `strip_tags()` can be used to remove potentially harmful tags, such as <script>. Obviously, a situation like this is less than ideal, and you should vigorously resist implementing such a feature from scratch. Keep your HTML structure in templates, not a database. But this is PHP, some of which has been around for decades; it isn't unheard of to allow people maintaining content to add some structural elements (such as lists or paragraphs) around their text. The problem is that `strip_tags()` isn't very clever and does not pay attention to element attributes. A malicious content editor could, for example, inject JavaScript via one of an allowed tag's event attributes, such as onmouseover(). Treat the presence of strip_tags() in your codebase as a warning flag and tread very carefully around it.

Nevertheless, let's see what strip_tags() can do. By default it will remove *anything* that looks like either an HTML tag or a PHP tag:

```
$str = <<<EOS
<!-- a comment -->
<p>
  Hi, I am a disgruntled employee.
  This is my leaving gift to the company.
  <script src="http://haxx.exploit/pwn_user.js"></script>
  <img src=x onmouseover="horribleJsGoesHere();andHere();">
</p>
For good measure:
<?php /* malicious server-side code goes here */ ?>
Ok, I'm done.
EOS;
print strip_tags($str);
```

Output:
```
  Hi, I am a disgruntled employee.
  This is my leaving gift to the company.

For good measure:

Ok, I'm done.
```

We can also pass a list of tags to strip_tags(), which it will use as a whitelist:

```
print strip_tags($str, ['p', 'img']);
```
Output:
```
<p>
  Hi, I am a disgruntled employee.
  This is my leaving gift to the company.
  <img src=x onmouseover="horribleJsGoesHere();andHere();">
</p>
...
```

You'll notice that the `img` element can serve as an XSS vector here, using a malformed `src` attribute attack. `strip_tags()` is a bit of a blunt instrument and does not care about well-formedness or validation. Nor is this function an HTML parser, and malformed markup will likely result in more text being removed than desired. Speaking of HTML parsers, I highly recommend using one to validate and sanitize any markup injection you are permitting, rather than this function.

But Couldn't I Just Use a Regular Expression?

No. **Thou shalt not parse (X)HTML with a regex.** HTML is not a regular language. HTML is a context-free grammar. It is not possible to express the grammar of HTML using regular expressions, which is the path of madness. Do not be tempted to hunt for chevron characters and tag names; you will uncover things that are *best left undisturbed*. Follow this link for a detailed explanation: https://stackoverflow.com/a/1732454

Filter Functions

PHP – since way back in the days of 5.2 – also has an entire module devoted to finding and cleaning data: the `filter` extension will be installed by default. It comprises a handful of functions and a slew of constants to control behavior.

Table 11-42. PHP `filter_*` functions

`filter_input()` `filter_input_array()`	Return filtered data direct from original input (not $_GET, $_POST, etc.)
`filter_var()` `filter_var_array()`	Filter data supplied as argument
`filter_list()`	Returns array of supported filter names
`filter_has_var()`	Test if variable exists in original input data
`filter_id()`	Get numerical value of filter by name

Some of these functions are a bit quirky and interact with the input data supplied to the script. And I don't mean the $_GET or $_POST superglobals; I mean the data from which the superglobals are constructed. For example, `filter_has_var(INPUT_POST, $varName)` would check if $varName existed in the original POST data, not $_POST.

Your best bet is to avoid these and just use `filter_var()` / `filter_var_array()`, which are the two we'll focus on here.

FILTER_VALIDATE_*

The `filter_var*()` functions don't do anything without being passed at least one constant in addition to the data under scrutiny. There's a plethora of FILTER_VALIDATE_* and FILTER_SANITIZE_* constants, which control the functions' basic behavior, which can often be fine-tuned with additional FILTER_FLAG_* arguments (warning: some flag constants deviate from this naming convention). In this way the `filter` module avoids accumulating dozens of functions, unlike, say, the core string functions.

Table 11-43. PHP FILTER_VALIDATE constants

Validation Constants	Logic
FILTER_VALIDATE_INT	Is integer or valid string representation
FILTER_VALIDATE_FLOAT	Is float or valid string
FILTER_VALIDATE_BOOL	See below!
FILTER_VALIDATE_URL	Validate string per RFC 2396 (obsolete)
FILTER_VALIDATE_EMAIL	Per RFC 822 (also obsolete)
FILTER_VALIDATE_IP	Is IP address (v4 and v6 supported)
FILTER_VALIDATE_MAC	Is MAC address
FILTER_VALIDATE_REGEXP	Validate using regex

So, we have two general types of behavior: validating and sanitizing. Presumably validating operations return a boolean to indicate if the supplied data met some criteria or other, and sanitizing will return transformed input data so that it meets a certain set of criteria? Well, let's see some of this in action:

```
var_dump(filter_var(1234, FILTER_VALIDATE_INT));
var_dump(filter_var('1234', FILTER_VALIDATE_INT));
var_dump(filter_var('123.4', FILTER_VALIDATE_INT));
var_dump(filter_var('123.4', FILTER_VALIDATE_FLOAT));
```

Output:
int(1234)
int(1234)
bool(false)
float(123.4)

Ah. Straight away, we can already see that things are... quirky. In fact, the entire filter module is – how can I put it – a little janky. Validating numbers returns either boolean false or... a type-cast value. Which isn't the end of the world; you can base a test on the result of the type: FILTER_VALIDATE_INT will always return an integer on success; FILTER_VALIDATE_FLOAT will always return a float. Perhaps FILTER_VALIDATE_BOOL will be better behaved:

```
var_dump(filter_var(true, FILTER_VALIDATE_BOOL));
var_dump(filter_var('1', FILTER_VALIDATE_BOOL));
var_dump(filter_var('true', FILTER_VALIDATE_BOOL));
var_dump(filter_var('yes', FILTER_VALIDATE_BOOL));
```

Output:
bool(true)...

All of the above evaluate to boolean true, whether the input data is a strictly typed true or some string that's roughly equivalent, such as... "yes"(!). But not "ja", or "はい", only "yes". Baffling, but there you go. Speaking of baffling...

```
var_dump(filter_var(1.0, FILTER_VALIDATE_BOOL));
var_dump(filter_var('1.0', FILTER_VALIDATE_BOOL));
```

Output:
bool(true)
bool(false)

The float 1.0 is apparently considered a boolean, but the string '1.0' is not. That's barmy. Speaking of barmy, check this out:

```
var_dump(filter_var(false, FILTER_VALIDATE_BOOL));
var_dump(filter_var('false', FILTER_VALIDATE_BOOL));
var_dump(filter_var('0', FILTER_VALIDATE_BOOL));
var_dump(filter_var('no', FILTER_VALIDATE_BOOL));
var_dump(filter_var('unsigned 2003 Toyota Yaris', FILTER_VALIDATE_BOOL));
```

Output:
bool(false)...

Somewhat counter-intuitively, FILTER_VALIDATE_BOOL will return false even if the input data is an actual honest-to-goodness boolean false, as well as when the data is clearly not a boolean at all. Thankfully there is a mitigation for this madness; the flag FILTER_NULL_ON_FAILURE will ensure that genuinely non-booleans return null instead of false:

```
var_dump(filter_var(
    'unsigned 2003 Toyota Yaris',
    FILTER_VALIDATE_BOOL,
    FILTER_NULL_ON_FAILURE
));
```

Output:
NULL

There are other gotchas in the validation behavior of filter_var*(), and we could spend another ten pages going through them all. Most notable is probably FILTER_VALIDATE_URL, which implements RFC 2396 to check if a string is a valid URL. That's very nice, but the RFC was obsoleted by 3986. FILTER_VALIDATE_URL will return false for perfectly valid URLs if they happen to contain non-Latin Unicode characters, which for today's internet is frankly ridiculous.

FILTER_SANITIZE_*

Let's turn our attention to sanitizing. The full list of FILTER_SANITIZE_* constants in PHP >= 8.1 is:

Table 11-44. PHP FILTER_SANITIZE constants

Sanitize constant	Logic
FILTER_SANITIZE_ENCODED	URL encode a string
FILTER_SANITIZE_SPECIAL_CHARS	Like htmlspecialchars()
FILTER_SANITIZE_FULL_SPECIAL_CHARS	Like htmlentities()
FILTER_SANITIZE_EMAIL	Removes non-Latin characters and digits, plus some meta-characters. Unfit for purpose.
FILTER_SANITIZE_URL	Similar to email sanitisation. Also unfit for purpose in 2025.
FILTER_SANITIZE_NUMBER_INT	Remove non digit characters and +/- symbols
FILTER_SANITIZE_NUMBER_FLOAT	Similar to integer, can be flagged to allow decimals
FILTER_SANITIZE_ADD_SLASHES	Like addslashes()

You might encounter FILTER_SANITIZE_STRING or FILTER_SANITIZE_STRIPPED on your travels, which stripped tags and encoded quote characters. These filters were deprecated in PHP 8.1.0. FILTER_SANITIZE_MAGIC_QUOTES used to be an alias of FILTER_SANITIZE_ADD_SLASHES but was deprecated in PHP 7.1.0.

It probably won't surprise you to find out that this too has oddities and weirdness.

```
var_dump(filter_var('1234abc', FILTER_SANITIZE_NUMBER_INT));
var_dump(filter_var('123.4abc', FILTER_SANITIZE_NUMBER_FLOAT));

Output:
string(4) "1234"
string(4) "1234"
```

FILTER_SANITIZE_NUMBER_INT is comparatively sane: it will extract the integer portion of a string. FILTER_SANITIZE_NUMBER_FLOAT however, appears to be unaware of decimal numbers, which is a shame given its name. In this case the filter has given us a number that is ten times the value of the one contained in the input string, which is less than useful. Again, we can mitigate with a flag...

```
var_dump(filter_var(
    '123.4',
    FILTER_SANITIZE_NUMBER_FLOAT,
    FILTER_FLAG_ALLOW_FRACTION
));
```

Output:
```
string(5) "123.4"
```

... but why this isn't the default behavior is beyond me.

`FILTER_SANITIZE_SPECIAL_CHARS` and `FILTER_SANITIZE_FULL_SPECIAL_CHARS` function like `htmlspecialchars()` and `htmlentities()`, respectively, and it is recommended that you just call those functions rather than going round the houses with `filter_var()`. Nevertheless, here they are at work:

```
$str = '"&\'<>£¥©®';

var_dump(filter_var($str, FILTER_SANITIZE_SPECIAL_CHARS));
var_dump(filter_var($str, FILTER_SANITIZE_FULL_SPECIAL_CHARS));
```

Output:
```
string(33) "&#34;&#38;&#39;&#60;&#62;£¥©®"
string(48) "&quot;&&#039;&lt;&gt;&pound;&yen;&copy;&reg;"
```

I do not recommend touching `FILTER_SANITIZE_EMAIL` or `FILTER_SANITIZE_URL` at all. Both will destroy any non-Latin UTF-8 characters, which are used increasingly in URLs in this brave new modern era. Accented characters have been permitted in the email address specification for a while now and are quite common even in English-speaking regions. You don't want to annoy any colleagues or customers with Irish or Scottish heritage now, do you?

We can wrap up this quick delve into the `filter` extension here. I think I've made it clear that for all its utility, it does have a lot of pitfalls, so tread carefully when using it. I realize that "don't use the URL or email functionality" isn't particularly helpful if validating/sanitizing those patterns is a problem you need to solve, so in the spirit of being helpful: emails can be validated by an RFC 6532 compliant pattern or library such as `https://github.com/egulias/EmailValidator`, and URLs need to be validated with support for IDN (Internationalized Domain Name), punycode (ASCII representation of Unicode), and IPv6 addresses – `https://github.com/Fleshgrinder/php-url-validator` is one such library.

Remember: *trust no one*.

Summary

In this, the final chapter of the book, we have delved into the very reason for PHP's existence: to create web content. We covered the fundamentals of how web clients and servers communicate with each other with the HTTP protocol by examining in detail the special messages that are exchanged between them. HTTP requests are composed of a request line, which tells the server what the request method is, the resource the client would like to access, and the version of the protocol to use. Header lines provide more detail concerning what the client's capabilities are, as well as those all-important cookies. We then looked at sessions, which are used to manage state in what is otherwise a stateless protocol.

With the nuts and bolts of HTTP in place, we moved onto the main event: HTML. Beginning with the fundamentals of HTML structure and syntax, we covered the parsing of HTML into a Document Object Model (DOM) data structure and navigating/modifying it with `Dom\HTMLDocument` et al. before progressing to generating markup. My approach to HTML generation was to delegate the task to a library – the popular Twig templating library, to be precise. Other PHP books might prefer to focus on using PHP itself as the templating language, for that is how PHP started life. However, given the enormous increase in the scope of the language, I feel that today's PHP offers too much in the context of generating web content (a "view" in MVC terminology). Twig or similar alternatives are de facto standard tools in modern PHP development, and knowing how to use templates will serve you better than knowing how to do it "the old-fashioned way."

Moving on from Twig, we looked under the bonnet at something Twig does by default: filtering data. The reasons for why this is necessary were repeating themes throughout the chapter: trust nobody on the internet. All incoming data is to be viewed as a potential source of malicious effects, even if you or your organization own the source. Rounding out the section on `htmlentities()`, etc., was a relatively light-hearted look at PHP's `filter` extension: useful within its limits but with some interesting foibles.

CHAPTER 11 PROGRAMMING FOR THE INTERNET

There is much more I could have written, but there is only so much space in the book. By going fairly deep on a limited set of core concepts (and the ones you'll most likely need to know about when working with a system powered by PHP), I hope I've shown you how to do the same with related topics. Omitted here were details on interacting with SMTP, FTP, DNS... but do not be alarmed. These protocols have their own RFCs and work in similar ways. If you understand the fundamentals of HTTP, you can easily learn the fundamentals of FTP and the rest. I hope I have ignited within you a desire to know and learn more, and everything you need is out there in the public domain. All of this technology is open, and nothing is stopping you from teaching yourself, just as I have been teaching myself all these years. Thank you for reading!

Appendix A

Chapter 1, "Getting Started," introduced the PSR-12 PHP coding standard and mentioned two tools for enforcing standards and fixing any issues that might be found, and these were PHPCodeSniffer's `phpcs` and `phpcbf` utilities. This appendix concerns their installation and use. CodeSniffer can be installed by downloading the `.phar` single-file archive: a PHAR – PHP Archive – is a self-contained distribution of PHP code and other assets, and a bootstrap file that instructs your system to run the PHAR contents using your PHP CLI binary.

```
$ curl -OL https://squizlabs.github.io/PHP_CodeSniffer/phpcs.phar
$ sudo mv ./phpcs.phar /usr/local/bin/phpcs
$ sudo chmod +x /usr/local/bin/phpcs
$ which phpcs
/usr/local/bin/phpcs
```

Doing it this way means that you will likely also need to install some additional PHP system packages, because `phpcs` needs the `tokenizer`, `xmlwriter`, and `SimpleXML` PHP extensions to function. If running `phpcs` reports an error along the lines of "Please enable xmlwriter and SimpleXML," then you'll need to install those extensions (`apt-get install -y php-tokenizer php-xml` or equivalent).

In addition, `phpcs` can usually be installed via your system's package manager:

Debian

```
$ apt-cache search phpcs
php-codesniffer - PHP, CSS and JavaScript coding standard analyzer
and checker

$ sudo apt-get install -y php-codesniffer
Reading package lists... Done
...
```

APPENDIX A

```
$ which phpcs
/usr/bin/phpcs
```

Your mileage might vary with this depending on the version of Debian in use.

Fedora

```
$ dnf search php-codesniffer
php-pear-PHP-CodeSniffer.noarch : PHP coding standards enforcement tool

$ sudo dnf install -y php-pear-PHP-CodeSniffer.noarch
...
Installing:
 php-pear-PHP-CodeSniffer    noarch    3.7.2-1.fc38.remi    remi    818 k
...
Complete!

$ which phpcs
/usr/bin/phpcs
```

MacOS

```
$ brew search php-codesniffer
==> Formulae
php-code-sniffer

$ brew install php-code-sniffer
==> Downloading https://ghcr.io/v2/homebrew/core/php-code-sniffer/manifests/3.7.2
==> Fetching php-code-sniffer
...

$ which phpcs
/usr/local/bin/phpcs
```

Perhaps you're wondering if we could do this with a Docker container... of course, we can! We can build our own image from the official PHP 8.4 image with the following Dockerfile...

Docker

```
FROM php:8.4-cli

RUN pear update-channels \
    && pear install PHP_CodeSniffer

ENTRYPOINT ["phpcs"]
CMD ["--version"]
```

This Dockerfile is making use of a feature called ENTRYPOINT and overwriting the CMD of the base php:8.4-cli image. The ENTRYPOINT instruction simply sets the container's primary process. In our case, we want the container environment of php:8.4-cli to provide everything we need (including the PHP binary itself!) to support the phpcs process. Essentially, running docker run -it ... with this image ENTRYPOINT turns the docker run ... command (on the host) into a direct invocation of phpcs (inside the container). Now build the image (run this command, making sure the current directory contains the Dockerfile above):

```
$ docker build -t local/php-codesniffer:8.4 .
```

Using Codesniffer

Next, let's create some code that violates some PSR standards. Save the following as phpcs_broken.php

```
$num = 1+ 1 ;

class badClassName
{
    function BadMethodName ( $arg1 , $arg2 ) {}
}
```

APPENDIX A

Finally, use the image we built to run a containerized phpcs command:

```
$ alias docker-phpcs='docker run -it --rm -v "$PWD":/usr/src/myapp -w /usr/src/myapp local/php-codesniffer:8.4'

$ docker-phpcs
PHP_CodeSniffer version 3.7.2 (stable) by Squiz (http://www.squiz.net)

$ docker-phpcs --standard=PSR12 ./phpcs_broken.php

FILE: /usr/src/myapp/phpcs_broken.php
--------------------------------------------------------------------------------
FOUND 12 ERRORS AND 1 WARNING AFFECTING 4 LINES
--------------------------------------------------------------------------------
 1 | WARNING | [ ] A file should declare new symbols (classes, functions,
   |         |     constants, etc.) and cause no other side effects, or it
   |         |     should execute logic with side effects, but should not
   |         |     do both. The first symbol is defined on line 5 and the
   |         |     first side effect is on line 3.
 3 | ERROR   | [x] Expected at least 1 space before "+"; 0 found
 5 | ERROR   | [ ] Each class must be in a namespace of at least one level
   |         |     (a top-level vendor name)
 5 | ERROR   | [ ] Class name "badClassName" is not in PascalCase format
 7 | ERROR   | [ ] Method name "badClassName::BadMethodName" is not in
   |         |     camel caps format
 7 | ERROR   | [ ] Visibility must be declared on method "BadMethodName"
 7 | ERROR   | [ ] Expected "function abc(...)"; found "function abc (...)"
 7 | ERROR   | [x] Expected 0 spaces after opening parenthesis; 1 found
 7 | ERROR   | [x] Expected 0 spaces before opening parenthesis; 2 found
 7 | ERROR   | [x] Expected 0 spaces between argument "$arg1" and comma; 1
   |         |     found
 7 | ERROR   | [x] Expected 0 spaces before closing parenthesis; 1 found
 7 | ERROR   | [x] Opening brace should be on a new line
 7 | ERROR   | [x] Closing brace must be on a line by itself
--------------------------------------------------------------------------------
PHPCBF CAN FIX THE 7 MARKED SNIFF VIOLATIONS AUTOMATICALLY
--------------------------------------------------------------------------------
```

APPENDIX A

And there we have it; `phpcs` has parsed the file and found all of the PSR-12 violations it contains. CodeSniffer will also check multiple files in a single run when invoked with a directory path rather than a specific file. It is also highly configurable and customizable, with an XML-based config system that allows you to define your own rules (or use another project's rules). The full documentation can be found on the project's GitHub page: https://github.com/squizlabs/PHP_CodeSniffer/wiki.

Fixing Things

Note that toward the bottom of the output is a message about PHPCBF (PHP Code Beautifier and Fixer), another tool bundled with `phpcs` that allows for automatic fixing of standards violations. When we built the image and installed PHP_CodeSniffer via pear, it bundled the phpcbf PHAR as well. We can therefore repurpose our `phpcs` Docker image and have it run phpcbf by simply changing the container ENTRYPOINT, which can be done either with a new Dockerfile or with a simple command line option when running the container:

```
$ alias docker-phpcbf='docker run -it --rm -v "$PWD":/usr/src/myapp -w /usr/src/myapp --entrypoint phpcbf local/php-codesniffer:8.4'

$ docker-phpcbf --standard=PSR12 ./phpcs_broken.php
PHPCBF RESULT SUMMARY
----------------------------------------------------------------------
FILE                                             FIXED   REMAINING
----------------------------------------------------------------------
/usr/src/myapp/phpcs_broken.php                    7        5
----------------------------------------------------------------------
A TOTAL OF 7 ERRORS WERE FIXED IN 1 FILE
----------------------------------------------------------------------
```

The contents of phpcs_broken.php should now be as follows:

```
$num = 1 + 1 ;

class badClassName
{
    function BadMethodName($arg1, $arg2)
```

APPENDIX A

```
        {
        }
}
```

As the output of phpcs stated, phpcbf will not fix all errors, just the ones concerning layout and spacing. Changing the names of classes and methods will impact any other code relying on them; changing them automatically would be potentially unsafe. If we run docker-phpcs again on the file, we can see the remaining issues that need to be addressed:

```
$ dphpcs --standard=PSR12 phpcs_broken.php

FILE: /usr/src/myapp/phpcs_broken.php
--------------------------------------------------------------------------
FOUND 4 ERRORS AND 1 WARNING AFFECTING 3 LINES
--------------------------------------------------------------------------
 1 | WARNING | A file should declare new symbols (classes, functions,
   |         | constants, etc.) and cause no other side effects, or it
   |         | should execute logic with side effects, but should not do
   |         | both. The first symbol is defined on line 5 and the first
   |         | side effect is on line 3.
 5 | ERROR   | Each class must be in a namespace of at least one level (a
   |         | top-level vendor name)
 5 | ERROR   | Class name "badClassName" is not in PascalCase format
 7 | ERROR   | Method name "badClassName::BadMethodName" is not in camel
   |         | caps format
 7 | ERROR   | Visibility must be declared on method "BadMethodName"
--------------------------------------------------------------------------
```

Again, I encourage you to read the PSR-1 and PSR-12 standards in full and make good use of tools like phpcs. It's quite common for large PHP projects in professional environments to automatically check standards on changes and prevent any violations from making their way into production code (and usually sending team members pithy emails in the process).

Bibliography

Books

Fowler, Martin. *Patterns of Enterprise Application Architecture* Addison-Wesley, 2002

Gamma, Erich, Richard Helm, Ralph Johnson, and John Vlissides. *Design Patterns: Elements of Reusable Object-Oriented Software* Addison-Wesley, 1994

Hunt, Andy and Dave Thomas. *The Pragmatic Programmer: From Journeyman to Master* Addison-Wesley, 1999

Knuth, Donald E. *The Art of Computer Programming (vol. II)* Addison-Wesley Longman Inc., 1998

Knuth, Donald. *The Art of Computer Programming, vol. 3: Sorting and Searching* Addison-Wesley, 1973, pp. 391-392

Meyer, Bertrand. *Object-Oriented Software Construction* Prentice Hall, 1988

Articles

Booch, Grady. *Object-Oriented Analysis and Design* ACM SIGAda Ada Letters, vol. 1, issue 3, 1982

Davis, Mark and Michel Suignard. *UNICODE SECURITY CONSIDERATIONS* Unicode Technical Report #36, 19 Sep 2014

Holmevik, Jan Rune. *Compiling Simula: A historical study of technological genesis* IEEE Annals of the History of Computing vol. 16, issue 4, 1994

Kleene, Stephen. *Representation of Events in Nerve Nets and Finite Automata* U.S. Air Force Project RAND Research Memorandum, 15 Dec 1951

Levenshtein, Vladimir I. *"Binary codes capable of correcting deletions, insertions, and reversals."* Soviet Physics Doklady, Feb 1966, pp. 707-710

Liskov, Barbara. *Data Abstraction and Heirarchy* OOPSLA Keynote Address, 1987

Liskov, Barbara H and Jeannette M Wing. *A Behavioral Notion of Subtyping* ACM Transactions on Programming Languages and Systems, vol. 16, issue 6, 1994

Martin, Robert C. *Design Principles and Design Patterns,* https://objectmentor.com/resources/articles/Principles_and_Patterns.pdf, 2000

Martin, Robert C. *The Interface Segregation Principle* The C++ Report, vol. 8, 1996

Martin, Robert C. *The Open-Closed Principle* C++ Report, vol. 8, Jan 1996

Martin, Robert C. *The Single Responsibility Principle,* https://objectmentor.com/resources/articles/srp.pdf, 1996

Martin, Robert C. *The Single Responsibility Principle,* https://blog.cleancoder.com/uncle-bob/2014/05/08/SingleReponsibilityPrinciple.html, 2014

Philips, Lawrence. *Hanging on the Metaphone.* Computer Language, vol. 7, issue 12, Dec 1990

Russell, R. C. *US patent 1261167.* Issued 1918-04-02

IEEE 754-2019/IEEE Standard for Floating-Point Arithmetic IEEE 754_WG – Working Group for Floating-Point Arithmetic, 2019

Sites

Carbon https://carbon.nesbot.com
Composer https://getcomposer.org/
Docker Hub https://hub.docker.com
Debian https://www.debian.org
Electronic Frontier Foundation https://www.eff.org
Fedora https://www.fedoraproject.com
Fleshgrinder/php-url-validator https://github.com/Fleshgrinder/php-url-validator
GNU https://gnu.org
Guzzle https://github.com/guzzle/guzzle
HTML: The Living Standard https://html.spec.whatwg.org/dev/
Homebrew https://brew.sh
IANA https://www.iana.org
IETF https://www.ietf.org
Nyholm/psr7 https://github.com/Nyholm/psr7
PHP https://www.php.net
PHP-FIG https://php-fig.org
PHP Mess Detector https://phpmd.org
PHPRedis https://github.com/phpredis/phpredis
Regex 101 https://regex101.com
Rexegg https://www.rexegg.com

Stack Overflow https://stackoverflow.com
The Symfony Project https://symfony.com
The Mozilla Foundation – HTTP Reference https://developer.mozilla.org/en-US/docs/Web/HTTP
The Unicode Foundation https://www.unicode.org
Twig https://twig.symfony.com
W3C https://www.w3.org
Wikipedia https://wikipedia.org
youmightnotneedjquery https://youmightnotneedjquery.com

Index

A

Abstract classes, 321–323
Abstract factory, 665, 666
Abstraction, 425, 650, 654, 662, 673
addcslashes(), 518
addslashes(), 517
Aggregation, 648
American National Standards Institute (ANSI), 422
American Standard Code for Information Interchange (ASCII), 71, 78, 422, 423, 429, 435, 437, 455, 472, 533
Anchoring, 555
Anonymous classes, 302, 303
Anonymous functions
    arrow functions, 150, 151
    closure, 146
    declaration, 146, 147
    defined, 146
    passing functions, 147–149
    and scope, 149, 150
    testing, 152–153
ANSI, *see* American National Standards Institute (ANSI)
Anti-patterns, 658
Apache, 30
apache_response_headers(), 724
Arguments, 102
Arithmetic operators, 377, 378
array_chunk(), 221
array_count_values(), 281
array_intersect(), 254

ArrayObject, 213–215
Arrays, 49
    array_merge(), 239, 240
    array_replace(), 243, 244
    associative, 211, 212, 242, 243
    callbacks, 251–257
    comparing keys and values, 248–250
    comparison functions, 252
    comparison operators, 244–246
    elements, 209–211
    extraction
        array_slice(), 236, 237
        extract(), 232–236
        list(), 231
        list() with keys, 231, 232
    finding common elements, 247, 248
    finding uncommon elements, 246, 247
    functional processing, 274–284
    iteration
        assignment, 228–230
        counting elements, 223, 224
        foreach, 222, 223
        for statement, 224, 225
        loop expressions, 225, 226
        skipping, 226, 227
        terminating early, 227
        traversing multidimensional arrays, 227, 228
    keys, 209
    manipulation
        appending elements, 216
        arbitrary positions, 217, 218

Arrays (*cont.*)
    changing element values, 215
    prepending elements, 216
    reindexing elements, 219, 220
    removing elements, 218, 219
    splitting, 220, 221
  multidimensional, 212–215
  normalizing keys, 250, 251
  operands, 237
  properties, 207
  searching
    callback, 261, 262
    finding key value, 260
    minimum and maximum values, 260
    test key exists, 258, 259
    test value exists, 258
  sorting
    callback, 269, 270
    by key, 264, 265
    natural, 271, 272
    preserving keys, 265
    randomizing, 272, 273
    by size, 267, 268
    modifying sort() behavior, 266, 267
    by value, 263, 264
  splat operator, 238, 239
  splicing, 240–242
  syntax, 208
  very large, 283, 284
array_splice(), 217, 220, 241
array_uintersect(), 254, 269
Array unpacking, 127
array_values(), 220
Arrow functions, 150, 151
ASCII, *see* American Standard Code for Information Interchange (ASCII)
ASCII63, 422, 423

Assertions, 561–563
Association, 646, 647
Associative arrays, 211, 212, 242, 243
Associativity, 181, 182
Attributes, 643, 746
  defined, 364
  example, 364
  making, 366–369
  predefined, 365
  syntax, 364
Autoloading, 44, 345–349

B

Back-references, 572, 573
Backtracking, 574
Base types, 110, 111
BCMath functions, 401–403
Big-endian *vs.* little-endian, 72
Binary framing layer, 682
Binary safety, 440, 441
Binary strings, 420, 421
Bitwise operators, 186, 187, 379–383
Block-level elements, 751, 752
Blocks, 834
Booch's methodology, 640, 643
Boundary string, 708–710
Bracktracing, 201
Brute-force attack, 540
Brute-force technique, 658
Buffers, 434
Bug reports, 100
Byte values, 71, 72, 78

C

Caeser cipher algorithm, 519
Callback function, 146, 251–257, 261, 262, 269, 270

INDEX

Cascading style sheets (CSS), 745
    combinators, 789, 790
    pseudo-classes, 792
    ruleset, 785
    selectors
        compound, 789
        expression, 767
        structure, 788–792
        syntax, 786, 788
        types, 788
Case folding, 507, 508
Case mapping, 503
cast() method, 339
Central European Time (CET), 605
CET, *see* Central European Time (CET)
Character class, 566, 567
Character encoding, 420, 421, 424, 817
Character mapping, 505
Character ordinal values, 72
checkdate(), 625
chunk_split(), 496, 497
C language, 73
Classes
    anonymous, 302, 303
    constants, 307, 308
    constructors, 297–299
    defining, 291–294
    destructors, 299, 300
    finding and loading, 344–349
    magic methods, 300, 301
    property
        getters and setters, 294, 295
        hooks, 296, 297
    types, 110
Codepages, 71, 422
Codepoints, 422
Codesniffer, 45, 853, 855, 857
Code space, 422

Cognitive load, 277, 445
Collation, 455–457
Command line arguments, 49–51
Comma-separated values (CSV), 478, 480
Common gateway interface (CGI), 1, 2, 682
Comparison operators, 178, 179, 244–246, 379, 436, 439
Composite, 666
Composite types, 110, 113
Composition, 331, 648, 649
Compound types, 85, 86, 105
Constants
    defined, 88–90
    magic, 91
    predefined, 90
Constructor property promotion, 298
Constructors, 193, 297–299
contains() function, 771
Content-Disposition header, 709, 711
Content-Type header, 703, 709, 711
Continuation bytes, 428
Control functions, 176
Control structures
    constructs, 175
    decision-making, 165–169
    defined, 164
    miscellaneous, 174, 175
    repetition
        nesting, break, continue, 172, 174
        for, foreach, 169, 170
        while, do-while, 170–172
Cookies, 681, 696–700, 741, 742
Coordinated Universal Time (UTC), 605
Copy-on-write, 107
count_bytes(), 467
count_chars(), 467, 468
Counting, 466–474

INDEX

Coupling, 671
crc32(), 520
createFromString() method, 754
Create, Read, Update, Delete (CRUD) operations, 689
Cross-site scripting (XSS), 815
Cryptography
    analysis, 539
    encryption, 548, 549
    password hashing algorithms, 545–546
    password problem, 540-542
    password (storage) solution, 542–544
    public key, 550, 551
    shared secret (symmetric), 549, 550
    verifying integrity, 547
CSS, *see* Cascading style sheets (CSS)
CSV, *see* Comma-separated values (CSV)
curl command, 685, 686, 694, 706, 708, 714
Cyclic redundancy check, 520

D

Databases
    connecting PDO extension, 64–66
    definition, 63
    executing statements, 66, 67
    launching, 63, 64
    mongodb, 63
    prepared statements, 68, 69
    programming, 63
    selecting results, 67, 68
Date extension functions
    non-OOP wrappers, 625
    OOP wrappers, 623, 624
Data hiding, 291, 295
Data source name (DSN), 65
Data types
    automatic conversion, 79–81
    callable data, 75
    coercion, 77
    compound/composite, 74
    defined, 73
    operations and calls, 75, 76
    resource, 75
    types, 74
    unsigned, 76
date_default_timezone_get(), 626
date_default_timezone_set(), 626
DateInterval, 619, 620
date_parse(), 626, 627
date_parse_from_format(), 626, 627
DatePeriod, 619, 620, 622
date_sun_info(), 628
DateTime
    building objects, 611, 613
    classes, 609
    constants, 615
    formatting output, 613–617
    modification, 617–623
DateTimeImmutable, 609–611, 619
DateTimeInterface, 609, 610, 615
DateTimeZone, 615, 616
Daylight saving time (DST), 636
Debian, 853
Debian-based systems, 3, 34
debug_backtrace(), 203, 204
debug_print_backtrace(), 203, 204
dechex() function, 77
Decision-making, 118, 165–169
Decorator pattern, 667, 668
Decorator (wrapper) class, 667
Default arguments, 125
Default namespace mechanism, 780
Delimiters, 553
Dependency injection, 666
Dependency inversion, 314, 662, 665

Dependency inversion principle
  (DIP), 660–662
Destructors, 299, 300
detect_order, 524
Deterministic algorithms, 399
Disjunctive normal form (DNF), 117, 118
DivisionByZeroError exceptions, 196, 197
Docker, 855
  cleaning up, 21
  containers, 12, 13
  daemon processes, 13
  defined, 12
  images and containers, 15–17
  installations
    Debian/Apt, 13
    Fedora/DNF, 14
    MacOS/Homebrew, 14
    Windows, 14
  Linux, 15
  MacOS, 15
  multiple versions, 22
  PHP, 18–21
  verify server, 14, 15
Document element, 747, 765
Document object model (DOM), 777
  attributes, 797, 799
  child node manipulation, 793
  classes, 796, 797
  creating and adding elements, 799–801
  defined, 753
  elements, 793–796
  manipulation, 753
  modification and output, 792, 793
  removing elements, 799
  structure, 801
Document type declaration (DTD), 776
DOM, *see* Document object model (DOM)
Domain modeling, 62

Domain specific language (DSL), 806
Don't Repeat Yourself (DRY), 99, 318
Double-quoted strings, 412–414
do-while structure, 172
DRY, *see* Don't Repeat Yourself (DRY)
DSL, *see* Domain specific language (DSL)
DSN, *see* Data source name (DSN)
DTD, *see* Document type
  declaration (DTD)
dumpMatches(), 563

E

Edge transform functions, 508–514
Electromechanical systems, 372
Electronic signals, 540
Electronic systems, 372
Embedded Apache module, 682
Encapsulation, 286, 291
Encoding
  aliases and alternatives, 531
  ASCII, 422, 423, 429
  defined, 422
  and escaping, 515–517
  extended ASCII, 423
  FSS-UTF, 429
  PHP, 430, 432–434
  schemes, 422
  transformation formats, 426–428
  Unicode, 424–426
  UTF-1, 428
  UTF-8, 430, 432–434
  variable-width, 428
Encryption, 548, 549
Enums
  backed, 337, 338
  basic/pure, 336, 337
  classes, 338–341

INDEX

Enums (cont.)
    constants, 334
    drawback, 336
    implementation, 334
    strings, 334
Environment variables, 33
    error_reporting()
        function, 189
Errors
    checking, 519–521
    control, 189–191
    handling, 191–192
    ini config directives, 191
    levels, 188, 189
    PHP 7, 195
Exceptions
    catching, 194–197
    concepts, 193
    DIY, 198
    finally…, 198, 199
    handling, 199, 200
    stack traces, 201–206
    throwing, 193, 194
explode(), 475, 476
Extended ASCII, 423
Extensible markup language (XML)
    defined, 746

F

Factory method, 664, 665
FastCGI, 2, 23
FastCGI Process Manager (FPM), 23, 27
fclose(), 54
Fedora, 854
fgets(), 54
file_get_contents(), 715
File handling, 61

File System Safe UCS Transformation
    Format (FSS-UTF), 429
Filter functions, 845–851
FILTER_SANITIZE_* constants, 848–851
Filter_var*() functions, 846–848
First-class functions, 160
Floating-point numbers, 390–393
Floating-point precision, 394–398
fopen(), 54, 56, 57, 714
Formula, 8
form-urlencoded string, 713
FP, see Functional programming (FP)
fprintf(), 498
FSS-UTF, see File System Safe UCS
    Transformation Format (FSS-UTF)
Fullwidth, 513
Functional array processing
    array_map(), 277–278
    array_reduce(), 279–280
    array_walk(), 274–277
Functional programming (FP), 148, 159, 160
Functions
    arguments and parameters, 102
    bool value, 176
    concepts, 99
    declarations, 109
    empty(), 177
    hoisting, 101
    logical expressions, 176
    named, declaring and calling, 100, 101
    returning, 103, 104
    scalar type coercion, 104, 106
    strict types, 106

G

Garbage collection, 299, 742
GB 2312-1980 encoding standard, 424

GDPR, *see* General Data Protection Regulations (GDPR)
General Data Protection Regulations (GDPR), 738
Generator, 283, 284
getallheaders() function, 695
getCallbackWithArg(), 150
get_called_class(), 355
get_class_methods(), 357
get_class_vars(), 357
getCounter(), 109
getdate(), 629
get_declared_classes(), 353
get_declared_interfaces(), 353
get_declared_traits(), 353
getInstance() method, 310
get_mangled_object_vars(), 359
get_object_vars(), 357
getQuote(), 292, 313
gettimeofday(), 629
Global namespace, 155, 347
Global positioning system (GPS), 605
Global *vs.* local scope, 135–137
gmmktime(), 630–633
GMP, *see* GNU multiple precision (GMP)
GMT, *see* Greenwich Mean Time (GMT)
GNU multiple precision (GMP), 404, 405
Graphemes, 470
Greenwich Mean Time (GMT), 605

H

Halfwidth, 513
Hash-based message authentication code (HMAC), 547
Hash chain, 546
hash_hmac(), 547, 548
Hashing algorithm, 406, 519–521, 541

header() function, 724
HEREDOC, 38, 66
Heredoc syntax, 417, 419
Hexadecimal values, 71
Hex edit, 431, 432
Higher-order function, 160
HMAC, *see* Hash-based message authentication code (HMAC)
hrtime(), 634, 635
HTML, *see* Hypertext markup language (HTML)
HTTP, *see* Hypertext transfer protocol (HTTP)
http_build_query(), 717, 720
http_response_code(), 722
Hypertext markup language (HTML)
    anonymous function, 784
    attributes, 758–760
    body content, 750–753
    callable objects, 782
    concept, 744, 745
    CSS (*see* Cascading style sheets (CSS))
    defined, 745–746
    document metadata, 749, 750
    PHP dom extension constants, 757
    PHP dom module, 754, 755
    DOM (*see* Document object model (DOM))
    elements and nodes, 755–757
    entity encoding, 817
    history, 748, 749
    inline elements, 753
    <head> content elements, 749
    namespaces, 779–782
    parsing, 776
    printing string, 802–804
    registered function, 784
    request methods, 683

INDEX

Hypertext markup language
    (HTML) (*cont.*)
  standards, 747, 748
  status code groups, 722
  templating, 802, 805
  versions, 776
  XPath, 760, 761 (*see also* XPath)
Hypertext preprocessor (PHP)
  accessing environment data, 52
  accessing files, 53–56
  built-in mathematics functions, 371
  coding standards, 43–45
  command line arguments, 49–51
  configuration
    directives, 30
    directive syntax, 31, 32
    overriding ini settings, 33, 34
    ini files, 30
    logging errors, 30
    modes, 31
    module (extension), 34, 35
    system search paths, 32, 33
  enforcing standards, 45
  ini directives, 708
  installation
    Apt, 3–5
    DNF, 5–8
    extensions, 11, 12
    Homebrew, 8–10
    package management system, 3
    Windows, 10
  interpreter, 1, 42
  markup safety functions, 842
  misc filesystem functions, 55, 56
  opening tags, 804
  output buffer, 48, 49
  outputting data, 47, 48
  output mechanisms, 47

  problem, 805, 806
  read functions, 54
  remote files and streams, 56–61
  removing tags, 843, 845
  shell command, 1
  SimpleXML module, 706
  socket-level HTTP requests, 695
  solution, 806
  structure and syntax
    embedded, 36–38
    expressions, 40
    header statements, 40
    line of code, 40
    operations, 40
    pure files, 38, 39
    rules, 39
    source code files, 35, 36
    tokens, 42
  UTF-8, 430, 432–434
  web SAPI, 677
  wrapper I/O streams, 59
  write functions, 55
Hypertext transfer protocol (HTTP)
  complex and binary data, 707–715
  cookies, 696–700
  idempotence, 687, 688
  using library, 727–729
  lower-level (network) protocol, 679
  output buffering, 725–727
  query string data, 700–702
  request (body) data, 702–707
  request headers, 693–696
  request message, 679, 681–683
  request method, 683–687
  resource paths and routing, 688–693
  response headers, 724, 725
  response message, 679
  response page, 685

response status, 722-724
RFCs, 679
status line, 721
URLs, 680-681, 715-720
web browser, 678
web clients and servers, 679

I

iconv functions, 601
idate() function, 634
IDE, *see* Integrated development environment (IDE)
Idempotence, 687, 688
illegal_chars, 527
Imperative programming, 36, 163
Indexed arrays, 212
Inheritance, 196, 316, 644, 645, 834
  accessing parent members, 323-325
  defined, 318
  DRY principle, 318
  final classes, 328, 329
  late static binding, 325, 326
  parent and child classes, 319, 320
  readonly, 326-328
  subclasses, 318
ini_set() function, 30
Injection attacks, 68
Injection vulnerability, 741
Integer keys, 209
Integer overflow, 388, 389
Integers, 387-390
Integrated development environment (IDE), 96, 130
Interfaces
  concepts, 311
  constants, 317
  declaration, 312-314

extending, 316
multiple, 314, 316
SimpleXMLElement object, 311, 312
Interface segregation principle (ISP), 658-660
Internal character encoding, 524
internal_encoding, 524
Internal error conditions, 187
Internet, 678
Internet application protocols, 678
Internet Engineering Task Force (IETF), 429, 679
Interoperability, 424
Intersection types, 116, 117
intl functions, 601-603
Introspection, 352
is_numeric() function, 81
ISO-8859, 423, 433
ISO-10646, 426, 428
ISP, *see* Interface segregation principle (ISP)
is_uploaded_file() function, 710
IteratorAggregte interface, 622

J, K

Japanese Industrial Standard (JIS), 424
JavaScript Object Notation (JSON), 683, 704, 706
JIS, *see* Japanese Industrial Standard (JIS)
jQuery object, 786
JSON, *see* JavaScript Object Notation (JSON)
json_decode() function, 705, 706
json_encode() function, 314

L

Lambda Calculus, 99
Language extensions, 600-603

INDEX

Late static binding, 325, 326
lcfirst(), 501
Legacy code, 804
levenshtein(), 459, 461
Levenshtein distance algorithm, 459
Lexical analysis, 491
Lexical scope, 134
Limits, 387
Liskov substitution principle
    (LSP), 655–658
Literal types, 118, 119
Literal values, 41
localtime(), 629
Local *vs.* global scope, 158
Logical errors, 81
Logical expressions, 42, 164, 178–187, 453
Logical operators, 179, 180
logMessage(), 152, 153
Loose coupling, 671
LSP, *see* Liskov substitution
    principle (LSP)
ltrim(), 509

M

MacOS, 854, 855
Macros, 832, 833
Magic constants, 349–352
Magic methods, 300, 301
match(), 168
Mathematical constants, 383, 384
Mathematical functions, 384–386
mb_check_encoding(), 535, 536
mb_convert_case(), 502–508
mb_convert_encoding(), 536, 537
mb_convert_kana(), 539
mb_convert_variables(), 537, 538
mb_detect_encoding(), 534

mb_detect_order(), 532, 533
mb_encoding_aliases(), 530, 531
mb_eregi_replace(), 592, 593
mb_ereg_match(), 592, 593
mb_ereg_replace(), 592, 593
mb_ereg_replace_callback(), 592, 593
mb_ereg_search(), 594–597
mb_ereg_search_init(), 594–597
mb_get_info(), 525–527
mb_internal_encoding(), 531, 532
mb_lcfirst(), 501, 502
mb_list_encodings(), 530, 531
mb_ltrim(), 509, 511
mb_regex_set_options(), 597, 598
mb_rtrim(), 509, 511
mb_scrub(), 538, 539
mb_str_cut(), 485, 486
mb_strimwidth(), 513, 514
mbstring extension
    commands, 522
    concepts, 522
    configuration, 523, 524
    features, 525
    info and settings, 525–533
    purpose, 523
    syntax modes, 600
mb_stristr(), 488–490
mb_strlen(), 468–470
mb_str_pad(), 511, 512
mb_strpos(), 462–465
mb_strrchr(), 488–490
mb_strrichr(), 488–490
mb_str_split(), 477, 478
mb_strstr(), 488–490
mb_strtolower(), 500, 501
mb_strtoupper(), 500, 501
mb_substitute_character(), 528, 529
mb_substr(), 485, 486

mb_substr_count(), 470–474
mb_trim(), 509, 511
mb_ucfirst(), 501, 502
md5(), 520, 521
md5_file(), 520, 521
Media types, 703
Members, 287
Metacharacters, 564, 570, 843
metaphone(), 457
microtime(), 634, 635
MIME types, *see* Media types
Mixed (super) type, 119, 120
Mixing call styles, 132–134
mktime(), 630–633
Model-view-controller (MVC), 806, 837
Modular decomposition, 642
Modularity, 286
move_uploaded_file() function, 710, 711
Multi-byte encodings, 477
Multi-byte safety, 441–444, 450
Multidimensional arrays, 212–215, 227, 228, 253, 280–282
MVC, *see* Model-view-controller (MVC)

N

Named function, 100, 101, 138
Named parameters, 129–132
Namespaced functions
    calling functions, 155, 156
    collision(), 154
    example, 154
    global, 155
    multiple statements, 155
    qualified calls, 156, 157
    scope, 158, 159
    usage, 157

Namespacing, 13, 198, 341–343, 779–782
networks.internal node, 24
Network time protocol (NTP), 607, 608
Nginx, 23–27
nl2br(), 497, 498
Non-boolean values, 164
Nowdoc syntax, 419
NTP, *see* Network time protocol (NTP)
Nullable types, 113
Null coalescing operator, 184, 185
Null safe operator, 185, 186
number_format(), 498
Number systems
    bases, 372
    built-in functionality, 372
    converting bases, 374, 375
    defined, 372
    formatting, 375, 376
    non-decimal integer
        literals, 372, 373
    scientific notation, 374
Number types, 80
Numerical strings, 405–408
Numeric encoding, 817

O

Object functions, 352
Object instance, 354
Object model, 639
Object-oriented design
    (OOD), 321, 640
Object-oriented exception model, 187
Object-oriented programming (OOP),
    159, 736, 738
    advantages, 286
    classes, 290–303
    cloned objects, 289, 290

INDEX

Object-oriented programming
(OOP) (cont.)
concepts, 639
design patterns
behavioral patterns, 671–674
creational patterns, 664–667
development process, 663
ideas, 663
structural patterns, 667–671
types, 664
features, 285
functional API, 623
modeling, 641, 642
new objects, 287–289
problems and solutions, 641
Simula language, 639
SOLID principles, 650–663
UML (see Unified modeling
language (UML))
Object-Oriented Programming Systems,
Languages and Applications
(OOPSLA), 655
OCP, see Open-closed
principle (OCP)
Olson database, 608
OOD, see Object-oriented design (OOD)
OOP, see Object-oriented
programming (OOP)
OOPSLA, see Object-Oriented
Programming Systems, Languages
and Applications (OOPSLA)
Open-closed principle (OCP),
329, 652–655
Operator overloading, 129
Operator precedence, 179, 181, 182
ord() function, 78
Output buffering mechanism, 725–727
Overriding, 320

P

Pacific Standard Time (PST), 605
Parameters, 102
parse_str(), 717
parse_url(), 716, 717
PascalCase, 291
Pass-by-reference, 123
Passing in data, 104
password_hash(), 543, 544
password_verify(), 543, 544
Pattern matching, 552
PCRE, see Perl-Compatible Regular
Expressions (PCRE)
Percent encoding, 718, 720
Perl-Compatible Regular Expressions
(PCRE), 552
Personally identifiable information
(PII), 738
PCRE, see Perl-Compatible Regular
Expressions (PCRE)
PHP, see Hypertext
preprocessor (PHP)
PHPCBF, see PHP Code Beautifier and
Fixer (PHPCBF)
PHP Code Beautifier and Fixer
(PHPCBF), 857
PHP Framework Interop Group
(PHP-FIG), 44
PHP-FIG, see PHP Framework Interop
Group (PHP-FIG)
PHP Standards Recommendations
(PSR), 44
PHPUnit, 360
PII, see Personally identifiable
information (PII)
prayerOfHealing() method, 360
Precision, 387

Precision filtering, 768
preg_filter(), 584–586
preg_grep(), 581
preg_last_error(), 589
preg_last_error_message(), 589
preg_match(), 581–583
preg_match_all(), 581–583
preg_quote(), 584
preg_replace(), 586, 588
preg_replace_callback(), 586, 588
preg_replace_callback_array(), 586, 588
preg_split(), 588
Primitive types, 74
printf(), 498, 499
Private constructors, 308–311
Problem domain, 641
Procedures, 99
Property hooks, 296, 297, 317, 318
Prosigns, 422
Protocols, 679
    specification, 686
Pseudorandom, 399
Pseudo-types, 109
PSR, *see* PHP Standards Recommendations (PSR)
PSR-1 standard, 44, 159
PSR-4 standard, 343
PSR-12 standard, 45, 166, 342, 364
PST, *see* Pacific Standard Time (PST)
Pure functions, 160

Q

Quantifiers, 565, 566
querySelector(), 785–787
querySelectorAll(), 785, 787
Query strings, 681, 700–702, 720
Quicksort algorithm, 270, 273

Quoted strings, 412
quotemeta(), 518

R

Rainbow tables, 541
Random number generation (RNG), 399
Random numbers, 398–400
RDBMS, *see* Relational database management system (RDBMS)
Reason phrase, 721
recursive_array_count(), 282
Recursive functions, 280–282
Redhat-based systems, 5
Reference vs. value, 107–109
Referencing, 93–95
Reflection methods, 360–364
Reflective programming, 360
Regular expression, 430
    alternatives, 567, 568
    assertions, 561–563
    back-references, 572, 573
    character classes, 566, 567
    character types, 561
    conditional sub-patterns, 577–579
    defined, 552
    delimiters, 553
    escape sequences, 557
    finding longest, 599
    ignore empty, 599, 600
    lookahead and lookbehind assertions, 575–577
    mbstring functions, 592
    metacharacters, 564
    modifiers, 554–557
    multi-byte functions, 590–598
    non-printing characters, 557–559
    notation system, 552

INDEX

Regular expression (*cont.*)
    once-only sub-pattern, 574
    PREG functions, 580–589
    quantifiers, 565, 566
    recursive sub-patterns, 579
    sub-patterns, 568–571
    syntax, 552, 553
    Unicode properties, 559, 560
Relational database management system (RDBMS), 63
Replacement character, 528
Requests for comments (RFCs), 679
Resource paths, 688–693
Return-only types, 110, 120–123
Return type declarations, 111, 112
Return types, 123–124
Reusability, 286
RFCs, *see* Requests for comments (RFCs)
RNG, *see* Random number generation (RNG)
Rounding strategies, 395
Routines, 99
Routing, 688–693
rtrim(), 509
Runtime errors, 188

S

Salt, 542, 547
SAPIs, *see* Server APIs (SAPIs)
Scalar types, 74, 80, 84, 85, 104, 106
Scope
    anonymous functions, 149, 150
    defined, 134
    function arguments, 138, 139
    global *vs.* local, 135–137
    multiple files, 141, 142
    named functions, 138

    namespaces, 158, 159
    outer() and inner(), 143
    rules, 143
    static variables, 139, 141
Scope resolution operator, 304, 308, 325
Selector expressions, 767
Self-calling function, 147
Self-invoking function, 147
Self-synchronization, 430
serialize(), 734
Server APIs (SAPIs), 2, 22, 29, 46, 47, 677
services.nginx node, 25
session_encode(), 735
session_get_cookie_params() function, 733
Sessions
    adoption, 739
    cat command, 732
    concept, 729
    cookie management, 733
    cookies, 741, 742
    data, 734–736
    data-passing mechanisms, 730
    filesystem, 730
    fixation, 738, 739
    functions, 743, 744
    ID creation, 740, 741
    ini directives, 733
    in-memory solutions, 730
    localStorage and sessionStorage APIs, 729
    OOP API, 736, 738
    security, 733, 738
    tidying up, 742, 743
    transparent SID support, 739
session_set_cookie_params() function, 733

INDEX

session_set_save_handler() function, 737
session_start(), 730, 742
setcookie() function, 697, 698
set_exception_handler() function, 200
setQuoteStash(), 295
setrawcookie() function, 697, 698
setTimestamp(), 619
setTimezone(), 619
sha1(), 521
sha_file(), 521
Shell variable, 52
ShinyLogs, 152
Short-circuiting, 180
Single inheritance, 329
Single responsibility principle
    (SRP), 650–652
Singleton, 311
Slash escape mechanism, 481
Smalltalk, 639
sodium_crypto_secretbox() function, 549
Solution space, 641
SORT_NUMERIC, 267
SORT_REGULAR, 267
SORT_STRING, 267
soundex(), 457
Special (resource) type, 86
Splat operator, 127, 238, 239, 295
spl_autoload_register() function, 345
sprintf(), 498
SRP, *see* Single responsibility
    principle (SRP)
sscanf(), 482–484
Stack traces, 201–206
Stakeholders, 651, 652
Standalone pseudo-types, 110, 118
Startup/compile time error, 189
Static members
    class context, 306, 307

context resolution operator, 304
    getCount() function, 305
    object instance, 303
    syntax and rules, 303
Static variable, 108, 139–141
Status code, 721
Status line, 721
StockTaker class design, 651
Strategy pattern, 672, 674
strcasecmp(), 448, 449, 451
strcmp(), 448, 450–452
strcoll(), 456, 457
str_contains(), 461, 462
strcspn(), 465, 466
stream_context_create(), 715
Stream functions, 61–62
str_ends_with(), 461, 462
str_getcsv(), 478–482
strict_detection, 524
Strict types, 106
Strings
    analysis, 446, 447
    binary, 420, 421
    categories, 445
    comparison, 446–449
    concatenation, 435
    conversion, 536–539
    counting, 466–474
    creating arrays/variables, 475–484
    data type, 434–438
    extensions, 445
    formatting, 494, 495
    goals, 445
    heredoc and nowdoc, 417–420
    insertion, 495–498
    inspection, 533–536
    letter escape sequences, 414
    manipulation, 842

INDEX

Strings (*cont.*)
    numeric escape sequences, 416
    operations, 77, 78, 163
    operators and type coercion, 439, 440
    parsing and conversion functions, 475
    problem domains, 444
    quoted, 412
    safety, 440–444
    similarity functions, 457–461
    special character escapes, 414–415
    special interpolation, 517–518
    symbol escape sequences, 415
    transformation, 494, 495
    unicode escape sequences, 417
    variable interpolation
        (substitution), 412–414
stripcslashes(), 518
stripslashes(), 517
strip_tags(), 843, 844
stristr(), 486–488
strlen(), 468–470
strnatcasecmp(), 448, 449, 451
strnatcmp(), 448, 449, 451
strncasecmp(), 452, 453
strncmp(), 452, 453
str_pad(), 511, 512
strpbrk(), 490, 491
strpos(), 462–465
strrchr(), 486–488
str_repeat(), 514
strrev(), 515
str_shuffle(), 514
str_split(), 477, 478
strspn(), 465, 466
str_starts_with(), 461, 462
strstr(), 486–488
strtok(), 491–493
strtolower(), 500, 501

strtoupper(), 500, 501
StudlyCaps, 291
Sub-patterns, 568–571
Sub-routines, 99
substitute_character, 524
Substitution, 499–508
Substitution cipher, 519
substr(), 485, 486
substr_compare(), 453–455
substr_count(), 470–474
Sub-string extraction functions, 484–493
Sub-string test functions, 461–466
Superglobals, 91–93, 236
surpriseBoom() function, 197
Switches, 50
Symfony, 693

T

Ternary chaining, 184
Ternary expressions, 183, 184
Ternary logical operator, 183
testGlobalVars(), 137
testScope(), 135
The Blob, 658
Timekeeping, 607
TLS, *see* Transport layer security (TLS)
Tokenization, 491
Traits
    composition, 331
    declaration, 329, 330
    extension and constants, 332, 333
    properties/methods, 331
Transparent SID support, 739
Transport layer security (TLS), 548, 679
Transport safety, 683
trim() function, 105, 509
Twig

adding filter, 838
adding function, 840, 841
calling functions, 828, 829
comparison operations, 824
composer.json file, 807
controlling behavior, 839, 840
controlling escaping, 817–819
control structures, 821, 822
defining your own functions, 829, 830
DSLs, 806
escape contexts, 819
escaping, 813–817
examples, 808
extending PHP, 837
extending template, 834, 835
filtering, 819–821
functions, 827
include(), 830–832
inheritance, 834
instantiation, 808
iterable tests, 826
literals, 822
logical operators, 823, 824
macros, 832, 833
mathematical operators, 823
miscellaneous operators, 826, 827
operators and expressions, 822
PHP functionality, 807
reasons, 807
sequences and mappings, 813
string tests, 825
template, 809–811, 835–837
test sub-expressions, 825
variables, 811–813
TwigFilter class constructor, 840
TwigFilter class instantiation techniques, 839
Type casting, 87

Type checking, 123
Type coercion, 76, 86, 104, 164, 211, 266, 379, 439, 440
    comparison, 408, 409
    numeric string, 405–408
Type juggling, 76
Type system *vs.* type declaration, 110
tz database, 608

U

ucfirst(), 501
UCS, *see* Universal Coded Character Set (UCS)
ucwords(), 501
UML, *see* Unified modeling language (UML)
Unicode, 424–426, 559
    codepoint escape syntax, 425
    escape sequence, 427
Unified modeling language (UML)
    aggregation, 648
    association, 646, 647
    classes, 643, 644, 649, 650
    composition, 648, 649
    defined, 643
    inheritance and interface implementation, 644, 645
    interfaces, 643, 644
    traits, 646
    visibility suffixes, 644
Uniform resource locators (URLs)
    authority, 681
    building and parsing, 715–720
    components, 680
    defined, 680
    encoding, 698, 718, 814
    fopen(), 57

Uniform resource locators (URLs) (*cont.*)
    fragment/anchor, 680
    path, 681
    query, 681
    resource path, 700
    router, 693
    routing, 727
    scheme, 680
    schemes, 58
Union types, 114–116
Universal Coded Character Set (UCS), 426
Unix domain socket, 66
Unix epoch, 606, 607
Unpacked arguments, 132
unserialize(), 734
unset() function, 83
URLs, *see* Uniform resource locators (URLs)
useQuoteBot() function, 314
User-defined types, 110
useVehicle() functions, 656
UTC, *see* Coordinated Universal Time (UTC)
UTF-1, 428
UTF-8, 430, 432–434, 436
UTF-16, 427, 428, 472
UTF-32, 427
Utility functions, 384, 386, 443

V

Variables
    echo keyword, 82
    functions, 144–146
    initialization, 87
    legal names, 83, 84
    string literal, 82
    symbolic name, 82

Variable variables, 95, 96
Variadic function, 125–129
Variadic parameters, 127
vfprintf(), 498
Virtual machine, 12
Visitor pattern, 674
vprintf(), 498

W

W3C, *see* World Wide Web Consortium (W3C)
Web browser, 678
Web development, 371, 427
Web Hypertext Application Technology Working Group (WHATWG), 747
Web server integration, 690
    Apache module, 30
    built-in functionality, 23
    built-in web-server, 27–29
    Nginx, 23–27
WHATWG, *see* Web Hypertext Application Technology Working Group (WHATWG)
Whole string, 514, 515
Wi-Fi data, 540
Windows Subsystem for Linux (WSL), 11
wordwrap(), 496, 497
World Wide Web Consortium (W3C), 748
wrongFunc(), 146
WSL, *see* Windows Subsystem for Linux (WSL)

X, Y

XCode command line tools, 8
XPath

abbreviations, 762, 763
axes, 762, 789
cheat sheets, 768
DOM navigation, 760
examples, 775, 790
expression, 761, 772, 774
functions, 771
localization, 761, 783
logical operators, 770, 771
node tests, 763–767
predicates, 767–770
query, 774
querySelector(), 785–787
relational operators, 770, 771
XSS, *see* Cross-site scripting (XSS)

Z

Zero width, 561
Zval, 94

GPSR Compliance

The European Union's (EU) General Product Safety Regulation (GPSR) is a set of rules that requires consumer products to be safe and our obligations to ensure this.

If you have any concerns about our products, you can contact us on

ProductSafety@springernature.com

In case Publisher is established outside the EU, the EU authorized representative is:

Springer Nature Customer Service Center GmbH
Europaplatz 3
69115 Heidelberg, Germany